NOTES

ON THE

New Testament

EXPLANATORY AND PRACTICAL

BY

ALBERT BARNES

Enlarged Type Edition

EDITED BY
ROBERT FREW, D.D.

JAMES, PETER, JOHN, AND JUDE

BAKER BOOK HOUSE
Grand Rapids, Michigan

Library of Congress Catalog Card Number: 50-7190

ISBN: 0-8010-0531-0

First Printing, October 1949
Second Printing, December 1950
Third Printing, December 1953
Fourth Printing, April 1957
Fifth Printing, February 1959
Sixth Printing, January 1961
Seventh Printing, December 1962
Eighth Printing, November 1964
Ninth Printing, February 1967
Tenth Printing, April 1969
Eleventh Printing, December 1969
Twelfth Printing, April 1971
Thirteenth Printing, September 1972

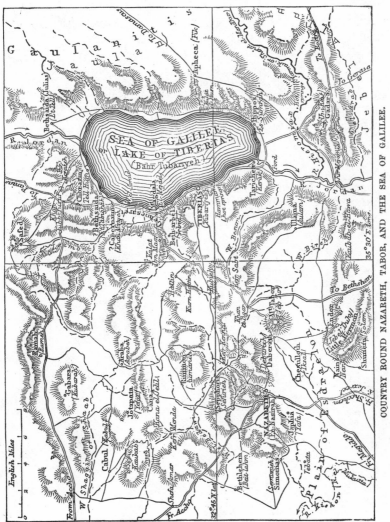

COUNTRY ROUND NAZARETH, TABOR, AND THE SEA OF GALILEE.

GENERAL INTRODUCTION

SEVEN CATHOLIC EPISTLES.

----

§ 1. *The Antiquity and Reason of the term* GENERAL *or* CATHOLIC, *applied to these Epistles.*

THE seven Epistles embraced in the New Testament between the Epistle to the Hebrews and the book of Revelation, are denoted by the term *General* or *Catholic* (καθολικαι). This word does not occur in the New Testament, except in the inscriptions to these epistles ; and these inscriptions are no part of the inspired writings, and are of no authority, as it is evident that the writers themselves would not affix the title to them. Indeed, the term is not applied with strict propriety to the second and third Epistles of John ; but those Epistles are ranked under the general appellation, because they were usually annexed to his first Epistle in transcribing, partly because they were the work of the same author, and partly because they were so small, that there might otherwise be danger of their being lost.—*Michaelis.* The Greek word *catholic* (καθολικαι) applied to these Epistles, means *general, universal;* and it was given to them because they were not addressed to particular churches or individuals, but to Christians at large. Even the Epistles of Peter, however, as well as the second and third of John, had originally a definite direction, and were designed for certain specified churches and Christians, as really as the Epistle to the Romans or Corinthians ; see 1 Pet. i. 1. There is, therefore, no good reason for retaining the title now, and it is omitted in the editions of Tittman and Hahn. It was, however, early applied to the Epistles, and is found in most of the editions and versions of the New Testament. Thus Eusebius, having given an account of James, called the Just, and our Lord's brother, says, " Thus far concerning this James, who is said to be the author of the first of the Epistles called *catholic.*" In another place he says, " That, in his Institutions, Clement of Alexandria had given short explications of all the canonical Scriptures, not omitting those which are contradicted—I mean the Epistle of Jude, and the other *catholic* Epistles." John's first Epistle is several times called catholic by Origen. So Athanasius, Epiphanius, and other Greek writers, mention the seven Epistles under the term *catholic.*—Lardner, Works, vi. 158. Ed. Lond., 1829. Comp. Hug's Intro., ch. iii., § 151. " The didactic writings of the apostles were separated into two collections ; the one comprising the Epistles of Paul, and bearing generally the title ἀπόστολος (*apostle*); the other containing the Epistles of the rest of the apostles, with the title καθολικαὶ ἐπιστολαί (*catholic epistles*), or καθολικαὶ ἐπιστολαί τῶν ἀποστόλων (*catholic epistles of the apostles*)."—*Hug*. Hug supposes that the appellation was given to them to designate them as a class of biblical writings, comprising the writings of *all* the apostles, except those of Paul. The Gospels and the Acts, he supposes, comprised one class by themselves; the Epistles of Paul a second; and these seven Epistles, under the title of *general* or *catholic*, a third, embracing the writings of all the apostles, Paul excepted. In the course of time, however, the signification of the term became changed, and they were called catholic, because they were not addressed to any church in particular.—Intro., pp. 605, 606. Ed. And., 1836. At all events, this last is the sense in which the word is used by Theodoret, and by subsequent commentators. On this point, see also Koppe, New Tes., vol. ix. 1, seq., and Noesselt, In conjecturis ad historiam catholicæ Jacobi epistolæ. Opusc. Fasc., ii., p. 303, seq., and Bertholdt, Historisch-kritische Einleitung in sammtliche kanonische und apokryphische Scriften des A. und N. T., i. p. 216, seq.

It may be added, that the term ' canonical' was given to these Epistles, about the middle of the sixth century, by Cassiodorius, and by the writer of the prologue to these Epistles, ascribed to Jerome, though not his. The reason why this appellation was given is not known.—Lardner, Works, vi. 160.

§ 2. *The canonical Authority of these Epistles.*

" Before the fourth century," says Hug, Intro., p. 606, " in which, for the first time, undeviating unanimity in all the churches, in respect to the canon, was effected, Christian writers with perfect freedom advocated or denied the authenticity of certain writings of the New Testament. Individual Fathers admitted or rejected certain books, according as their judgment dictated. Besides the Epistle to the Hebrews and the Apocalypse, this was the case, as is well known, in regard to several of the catholic Epistles, viz., that of James, the second and third of John, the second of Peter, and that of Jude." It is of some importance here to inquire what bearing this fact should have on the question of the canonical authority of these Epistles, or the question whether they are to be regarded as constituting a part of the inspired writings. Some general remarks only will be made here; a more particular examination will be proper in considering the evidences of the genuineness of the several Epistles. See the Introduction to James, to second Peter, to second and third John, and to Jude.

The *facts* in the case, in regard to these disputed Epistles, were these:—

(1.) They were always circulated under the names of the respective authors whose names they bear, and, by established custom, were subjoined to the other biblical books, though they had not universally the estimation which was given to the others.

(2.) In most of the churches, these Epistles were made use of, as Eusebius testifies, equally with the other Scriptures.

(3.) There was supposed by many to be a want of *positive* historical testimony in their favour; at least of the evidence which existed in favour of the other books of the New Testament.

(4.) It was not supposed that there was any positive testimony *against* the genuineness of these writings. The sole ground of doubt with *any* of the Fathers was, that there were not the same historical vouchers for their genuineness which there were for the other books.

(5.) They were never regarded as books that were certainly to be rejected. Those who entertained doubts in regard to them did not argue *against* their genuineness, but only expressed *doubts* in respect to their canonical authority.

(6.) Even these doubts were in time removed, and after the fourth century these Epistles were everywhere received as a part of the genuine inspired writings. The progress of investigation removed *all* doubt from the mind, and they were allowed a place among the undisputed writings of the apostles, as a part of the word of God.

In regard, therefore, to the influence which this fact should have on the estimate which we form of their genuineness and canonical authority, we may observe,

(1.) That the settled and established voice of antiquity is in their favour. That opinion became at length harmonious, and was all the more valuable, from the fact that there ever had been any doubts. The general judgment of the church now in their favour is the result of long and careful inquiry; and an opinion is always more valuable when it is known to have been the result of long and careful investigation.

(2.) The facts in regard to these epistles showed that there was great *caution* in the early Christian church about admitting books into the canon. None were received without examination; none where the evidence was not supposed to be clear. The honest doubts of the early Christian Fathers were stated and canvassed, and passed for what they were worth; and the highest care was taken to remove the doubts, when any existed. No books were admitted into the canon by a mere *vote* of a synod or council, or by any ecclesiastical body. The books which were admitted were received because there was *evidence* that they were genuine, which satisfied the church at large, and they were recognised as canonical by common consent.

(3.) It has been observed above, that there never was any *positive* evidence against the authority and genuineness of the disputed books. But, as Hug has remarked (p. 607), even the *negative* argument loses much of its force when its character is considered. Such is their brevity, that it was less easy to establish their authority, or to demonstrate their authorship by any *internal* evidence, than in regard to the longer Epistles. It happened, also, from the brevity of the Epistles, that they were less frequently quoted by the early Fathers than the longer ones were, and hence it was more difficult to demonstrate that they were early received. But it is clear that this arose, not from any thing *in* the Epistles which was calculated to excite suspicion as to their origin, but from the nature of the case. On the supposition that they are genuine, and were early regarded as genuine, this difficulty would be as great as on the supposition that they are not. But if so, the difficulty is manifestly of no force. On this whole subject, the reader may find all that is necessary to be said in the Prolegomena of Koppe in Epistolas Catholicas. See also Hug's Intro.. § 151, 152.

EPISTLE OF JAMES.

INTRODUCTION.

§ 1. *The Question who was the Author of this Epistle.*

THERE have been more difficult questions raised in regard to the Epistle of James than perhaps any other portion of the New Testament. Those questions it is of importance to examine as fully as is consistent with the design of these Notes ; that is, so far as to enable a candid inquirer to see what is the *real* difficulty in the case, and what is, so far as can be ascertained, the truth.

The first question is, Who was the author? It has been attributed to one of three persons :—to James 'the elder,' the son of Zebedee, and brother of John ; to James 'the less,' son of Alpheus or Cleophas ; and to a James of whom nothing more is known. Some have supposed, also, that the James who is mentioned as the 'Lord's brother,' (Gal. i. 19,) was a different person from James the son of Alpheus.

There are no methods of determining this point from the Epistle itself. All that can be established from the Epistle is, (1.) That the name of the author was *James*, ch. i. 1; (2.) That he professed to be a "servant of God," ch. i. 1; (3.) That he had been probably a Jew, and sustained such a relation to those to whom he wrote, as to make it proper for him to address them with authority ; and, (4.) That he was a follower of the Lord Jesus Christ, ch. ii. 1; v. 8.

There are two persons, if not three, of the name of *James*, mentioned in the New Testament. The one is James, the son of Zebedee, Matt. iv. 21; Mark iii. 17; Luke vi. 14; Acts i. 13, *et al.* He is usually mentioned in connection with him ; Matt. iv. 21; xvii. 1; Mark v. 37; xiii. 3, *et al.* The name of their mother was Salome. Comp. Matt. xxvii. 56, with Mark xv. 40. He was put to death by Herod Agrippa, about A.D. 41. Acts xii. 2 He was called the major, or the elder—to distinguish him from the other James, the younger, or the *less*, Mark xv. 40; called also, in ancient history, James the Just.

The other James was a son of Alpheus or Cleophas ; Matt. x. 3; Mark iii. 18; Acts i. 13; Luke xxiv. 18. That Alpheus and Cleophas was the same person is evident from the fact that both the words are derived from the Hebrew חלפי— *hhalphi.* The name of the mother of this James was Mary, (Mark xv. 40;) and James, and Joses, and Simon, and Judas, are mentioned as brethren ; Matt. xiii. 55. There is also a James mentioned in Matt. xiii. 55; Mark vi. 3; and Gal. i. 19, as a "brother of our Lord." On the meaning of this expression, see Notes on Gal. i. 19.

It has been a question which has been agitated from the earliest times, whether the James who is mentioned as the son of Alpheus, and the James who is mentioned as the "Lord's brother," were the same or different persons. It is not necessary for the purposes of these Notes to go into an examination of this question. Those who are disposed to see it pursued, may consult Hug's Intro., § 158, and the works there referred to; Neander's History of the Planting and Training of the Christian Church, vol. ii. p. 2, seq., Edin. Ed.; and Michaelis' Intro., vol. iv. 271, seq. The question, says Neander, is one of the most difficult in the apostolic history. Hug supposes that James the son of Alpheus, and James the brother of the Lord, were the same. Neander supposes that the James mentioned by the title of the "Lord's brother" was a son of Joseph, either by a former marriage, or by Mary, and consequently a "brother" in the stricter sense.

It is remarked by Michaelis, that James may have been called "the Lord's brother," or mentioned as one of his brethren, in one of the following senses :— (1.) That the persons accounted as the "brethren of the Lord" (Matt. xiii. 55, et al.) were the sons of Joseph, not by Mary the mother of Jesus, but by a former wife. This, says he, was the most ancient opinion, and there is in it nothing improbable. If so, they were older than Jesus. (2.) It may mean that they were the sons of Joseph by Mary, the mother of Jesus. Comp. Notes on Matt. xiii. 55. If so, James was an own brother of Jesus, but younger than he. There is nothing in this opinion inconsistent with any statement in the Bible ; for the notion of the perpetual virginity of Mary is not founded on the authority of the Scriptures. If either of these suppositions were true, however, and James and Judas, the authors of the Epistles which bear their names, were literally the brothers of Christ, it would follow that they were not apostles ; for the elder apostle James was the son of Zebedee, and James the younger was the son of Alpheus. (3.) A third opinion in relation to James, and Joses, and Simon, and Judas, is, that they were the sons of Joseph by the widow of a brother who had died without children, and to whom, therefore, Joseph, by the Mosaic laws, was obliged to raise up issue. This opinion, however, is entirely unsupported, and is wholly improbable ; for (a) the law which obliged the Jews to take their brothers' widows applied only to those who were single (Michaelis) ; and (b) if this had been an instance of that kind, all the requirement of the law in the case would have been satisfied when one heir was born. (4.) It might be maintained that, according to the preceding opinion, the brother of Joseph was Alpheus, and then they would be reckoned as his sons ; and in this case, the James and Judas who are called the brothers of Jesus, would have been the same as the apostles of that name. But, in that case, Alpheus would not have been the same as Cleopas, for Cleopas had a wife—the sister of Joseph's wife. (5.) A fifth opinion, and one which was advanced by Jerome, and which has been extensively maintained, is, that the persons referred to were called 'brethren' of the Lord Jesus only in a somewhat lax sense, as denoting his near kinsmen. See Notes on Gal. i. 19. According to this, they would have been cousins of the Lord Jesus, and the relationship was of this kind :—James and Judas, sons of Alpheus, were the apostles, and consequently Alpheus was the father of Simon and Joses. Farther, Alpheus is the same as Cleopas, who married Mary, the sister of the mother of Jesus (John xix. 25), and consequently the sons of Cleopas were cousins of the Saviour.

Which of these opinions is the correct one, it is impossible now to determine. The latter is the common opinion, and perhaps, on the whole, best sustained ; and if so, then there were but two Jameses referred to, both apostles, and the one who wrote this Epistle was a cousin of the Lord Jesus. Neander, however, supposes that there were two Jameses besides James the brother of John, the son of Zebedee, and that the one who wrote this Epistle was not the apostle, the son of Alpheus, but was, in the stricter sense, the 'brother' of our Lord, and was trained up with him. Hist. of the Planting of Christianity, ii., p. 3, seq.

It is a circumstance of some importance, in showing that there was but one James besides James the brother of John, and that this was the apostle, the son of Alpheus, that after the death of the elder James (Acts xii. 1,) no mention is made of more than one of that name. If there had been, it is hardly possible, says Hug, that there should not have been some allusion to him. This, however, is not conclusive; for there is no mention of Simon, or Bartholomew, or Thomas after that time.

There is but one serious objection, perhaps, to this theory, which is, that it is said (John vii. 5) that "his brethren did not believe on him." It is possible, however, that the word 'brethren' in that place may not have included *all* his kinsmen, but may have had particular reference to the larger portion of them (ver. 3,) who were not believers, though it might have been that some of them *were* believers.

On the whole, it seems probable that the James who was the author of this Epistle was one of the apostles of that name, the son of Alpheus, and that he was a cousin of our Lord. Entire certainty on that point, however, cannot be hoped for.

If the author of this Epistle was a different person from the one who resided at Jerusalem, and who is often mentioned in the Acts of the Apostles, then nothing more is known of him. That James was evidently an apostle (Gal. i. 19,) and perhaps, from his relationship to the Lord Jesus, would have a special influence and authority there.

Of this James, little more is certainly known than what is mentioned in the Acts of the Apostles. Hegesippus, as quoted by Neander, says, that from childhood he led the life of a Nazarene. He is described by Josephus (Archæol. xx. 9,) as well as by Hegesippus and Eusebius, as a man eminent for his integrity of life, and as well meriting the appellation or surname which he bore among the Jews, of צדיק, δικαιος, *the Just.* He is mentioned as one who set himself against the corruptions of the age, and who was thence termed the bulwark of the people —עפל עם—περιοχη του λαου. His manner of life is represented as strict and holy, and such as to command in an eminent degree the confidence of his countrymen, the Jews. Hegesippus says that he frequently prostrated himself on his knees in the Temple, calling on God to forgive the sins of his people, praying that the divine judgments on the unbelievers might be averted, and that they might be led to repentance and faith, and thus to a participation of the kingdom of the glorified Messiah. Neander, as quoted before, p. 10.

In the New Testament, James appears as a prominent and leading man in the church at Jerusalem. In later times he is mentioned by the ecclesiastical writers as 'Bishop of Jerusalem;' but this title is not given to him in the New Testament, nor is there any reason to suppose that he filled the office which is now usually denoted by the word *bishop.* He appears, however, from some cause, to have had his home permanently in Jerusalem, and, for a considerable portion of his life, to have been the only apostle residing there. As well, as well as from his near relationship to the Lord Jesus, and his own personal worth, he was entitled to, and received, marked respect. His prominence, and the respect which was shown to him at Jerusalem, appear in the following circumstances : (1.) In the council that was held respecting the rules that were to be imposed on the converts from the Gentiles, and the manner in which they were to be regarded and treated (Acts xv.), after the other apostles had fully delivered their sentiments, the views of James were expressed, and his counsel was followed. Acts xv. 13–29. (2.) When Peter was released from prison, in answer to the prayers of the assembled church, he directed those whom he first saw to 'go and show these things to *James,* and to the brethren.' Acts xii. 17. (3.) When Paul visited Jerusalem after his conversion, James is twice mentioned by him as occupying a prominent position there. First, Paul says that when he went there on the first occasion, he saw none of the apostles but Peter, and 'James the Lord's brother.' Gal. i. 18, 19. He is here mentioned as one of the apostles, and as sustaining a near relation to the Lord Jesus. On the second occasion, when Paul went up there fourteen years after, he is mentioned, in enumerating those who gave to him the right hand of fellowship, as one of the 'pillars' of the church; and among those who recognised him as an apostle, he is mentioned first. "And when James, Cephas, and John, who seemed to be pillars, perceived the grace that was given unto me, they gave me and Barnabas the right hand of fellowship." Gal. ii. 9. (4.) When Paul went up to Jerusalem after his visit to Asia

Minor and to Greece, the whole matter pertaining to his visit was laid before James, and his counsel was followed by Paul. Acts xxi. 18—24.

The leading points in the character of James seem to have been these:—(1.) Incorruptible integrity; integrity such as to secure the confidence of all men, and to deserve the appellation of 'the Just.' (2.) An exalted regard for the rites and ceremonies of the ancient religion, and a desire that they should be respected everywhere and honoured. He was more slow in coming to the conclusion that they were to be superseded by Christianity than Paul or Peter was (comp. Acts xxi. 18; Gal. ii. 12), though he admitted that they were not to be *imposed* on the Gentile converts as absolutely binding. Acts xv. 19–21, 24–29. Repeated intimations of his great respect for the laws of Moses are found in the Epistle before us, thus furnishing an internal proof of its genuineness. If he was educated as a Nazarene, and if he always resided with the Jews, in the very vicinity of the Temple, this is not difficult to be accounted for, and this might be expected to tinge his writings. (3.) The point from which he contemplated religion particularly was, *conformity to the law.* He looked at it as it was intended, to regulate the life, and to produce holiness of deportment, in opposition to all lax views of morals and low conceptions of holiness. He lived in a corrupt age, and among corrupt people; among those who sought to be justified before God by the mere fact that they were Jews, that they had the true religion, and that they were the chosen people of God, and who, in consequence, were lax in their morals, and comparatively regardless of the obligations to personal holiness. He therefore contemplated religion, not so much in respect to the question how man may be justified, as to the question to what kind of *life* it will lead us; and his great object was to show that *personal holiness* is necessary to salvation. Paul, on the other hand, was led to contemplate it mainly with reference to another question—how man may be justified; and it became necessary for him to show that men cannot be justified by their own works, but that it must be by faith in the Redeemer. The error which Paul particularly combats, is an error on the subject of justification; the error which James particularly opposes, is a practical error on the influence of religion on the life. It was because religion was contemplated by these two writers from these different points of view, and not from any real contradiction, that the apparent discrepancy arose between the Epistle of James and the writings of Paul. The peculiarity in the character and circumstances of James will account for the views which he took of religion; and, keeping this in mind, it will be easy to show that there is no real contradiction between these writers. It was of great importance to guard against each of the errors referred to; and the views expressed by both of the apostles are necessary to understand the nature and to see the full developement of religion.

How long James lived, and when and how he died, is not certainly known. It is agreed by all that he spent his last days in Jerusalem, and that he probably died there. On the subject of his death there is a remarkable passage in Josephus, which, though its genuineness has been disputed, is worth transcribing, as, if genuine, it shows the respect in which James was held, and contains an interesting account of his death. It is as follows:—" The emperor [Roman] being informed of the death of Festus, sent Albinus to be prefect of Judea. But the younger Ananus, who, as we said before, was made high priest, was haughty in his behaviour, and was very ambitious. And, moreover, he was of the sect of the Sadducees, who, as we have also observed before, are, above all other Jews, severe in their judicial sentences. This, then, being the temper of Ananus, he, thinking he had a fit opportunity, because Festus was dead, and Albinus was yet on the road, calls a council. And, bringing before them James, the brother of him who is called Christ, and some others, he accused them as transgressors of the laws, and had them stoned to death. But the most moderate men of the city, who were also reckoned most skilful in the laws, were offended at this proceeding. They therefore sent privately to the king [Agrippa the younger], entreating him to send orders to Ananus no more to attempt any such things."—

Aut., B. xx. A long account of the manner of his death, by Hegesippus, is preserved in Eusebius, going much more into detail, and evidently introducing much that is fabulous.   The *amount* of all that can now be known in regard to his decease would seem to be, that he was put to death by violence in Jerusalem, a short time before the destruction of the Temple.   From the well-known character of the Jews, this account is by no means improbable.   On the subject of his life and death, the reader may find all that is known in Lardner's Works, vol. vi. pp. 162–195; Bacon's Lives of the Apostles, pp. 411–433; and Neander, Hist. of the Planting of the Christian Church, ii., pp. 1–23, Edin. Ed.

The belief that it was this James, the son of Alpheus, who resided so long at Jerusalem, who was the author of this Epistle, has been the common, though not the unanimous opinion of the Christian church, and seems to be supported by satisfactory arguments.   It must evidently have been written either by him or by James the elder, the son of Zebedee, or by some other James, the supposed literal brother of our Lord.

In regard to these opinions, we may observe,

I. That the supposition that it was written by some third one of that name, 'wholly unknown to fame,' is mere hypothesis.   It has no evidence whatever in its support.

II. There are strong reasons for supposing that it was not written by James the elder, the son of Zebedee, and brother of John.   It has been indeed ascribed to him.   In the old Syriac version, in the earlier editions, it is expressly attributed to him.   But against this opinion the following objections may be urged, which seem to be conclusive.   (1.) James the elder was beheaded about the year 43, or 44, and if this epistle was written by him, it is the oldest of the writings of the New Testament.   It is possible, indeed, that the epistle may have been written at as early a period as that, but the considerations which remain to be stated, will show that this epistle has sufficient internal marks to prove that it was of later origin.   (2.) Before the death of James the elder, the preaching of the gospel was chiefly confined within the limits of Palestine; but this epistle was written to Christians 'of the dispersion,' that is, to those who resided out of Palestine.   It is hardly credible that in so short a time after the ascension of our Lord, there were so many Christians scattered abroad as to make it probable that a letter would be sent to them.   (3.) This epistle is occupied very much with a consideration of a false and perverted view of the doctrine of justification by faith.   It is evident that false views on that subject prevailed, and that a considerable corruption of morals was the consequence.   But this supposes that the doctrine of justification by faith had been extensively preached; consequently that considerable time had elapsed from the time when the doctrine had been first promulgated.   The perversion of a doctrine, so as to produce injurious effects, seldom occurs until some time after the doctrine was first preached, and it can hardly be supposed that this would have occurred before the death of James, the son of Zebedee.   See these reasons stated more at length in *Benson.*

III. There are strong probabilities, from the epistle itself, to show that it was written by James the Less.   (1.) His position at Jerusalem, and his eminence among the apostles, as well as his established character, made it proper that he should address such an epistle to those who were scattered abroad.   There was no one among the apostles who would command greater respect from those abroad who were of Jewish origin than James.   If he had his residence at Jerusalem; if he was in any manner regarded as the head of the church there; if he sustained a near relation to the Lord Jesus; and if his character was such as has been commonly represented, there was no one among the apostles whose opinions would be treated with greater respect, or who would be considered as having a clearer right to address those who were scattered abroad.   (2.) The character of the epistle accords with the well-known character of James the Less.   His strong regard for the law; his zeal for incorruptible integrity; his opposition to lax notions of morals; his opposition to all reliance on faith that was not productive of good works, all appear in this epistle. The necessity of conformity to the law of God, and of a holy life, is everywhere apparent, and the views expressed in the epistle agree with all that is stated of the early education and the established character of James. While there is no real contradiction between this epistle and the writings of Paul, yet it is much more easy to show that this is a production of James than it would be to prove that it was written by Paul. Comp. *Hug*, Intro., § 159.

§ 2. *To whom was the Epistle written ?*

The epistle purports to have been written to 'the twelve tribes scattered abroad' —or the 'twelve tribes *of the dispersion*'—ἐν τῇ διασπορᾷ ; ch. i. 1. See Notes on 1 Pet. i. 1, and Notes on ch. i. 1 of this epistle. No mention of the *place* where they resided is made ; nor can it be determined to what portion of the world it was first sent, or whether more than one copy was sent. All that can be conclusively determined in regard to the persons to whom it was addressed, is, (1.) That they were of Jewish descent—as is implied in the phrase 'to the twelve tribes' (ch. i. 1), and as is manifest in all the reasonings of the epistle ; and, (2.) That they were Christian converts, ch. ii. 1. But by whose labours they were converted, is wholly unknown. The Jewish people who were 'scattered abroad' had two central points of union, the dispersion in the East, of which Babylon was the head, and the dispersion in the West, of which Alexandria was the head, Hug. § 156. Peter wrote his epistles to the latter (1 Pet. i. 1), though he was at Babylon when he wrote them (1 Pet. v. 13), and it would seem probable that this epistle was addressed to the former. Beza supposed that this epistle was sent to the believing Jews, dispersed all over the world ; Grotius, that it was written to all the Jews living out of Judea ; Lardner, that it was written to all Jews, descendants of Jacob, of every denomination, in Judea, and out of it. It seems plain, however, from the epistle itself, that it was not addressed to the Jews *as such*, or without respect to their being already Christians, for (*a*) if it had been, it is hardly conceivable that there should have been no arguments to prove that Jesus was the Messiah, and no extended statements of the nature of the Christian system ; and (*b*) it bears on the face of it evidence of having been addressed to those who were regarded as Christians ; ch. ii. 1 ; v. 7, 11, 14. It may be difficult to account for the fact, on any principles, that there are no more definite allusions to the nature of the Christian doctrines in the epistle, but it is morally certain that if it had been written to Jews *as such*, by a Christian apostle, there would have been a more formal defence and statement of the Christian religion. Compare the arguments of the apostles with the Jews in the Acts, *passim.* I regard the epistle, therefore, as having been sent to those who were of Jewish origin, but who had embraced the Christian faith, by one who had been himself a Jew, and who, though now a Christian apostle, retained much of his early habits of thinking and reasoning in addressing his own countrymen.

§ 3. *Where and when was the Epistle written ?*

There are no certain indications by which it can be determined *where* this epistle was written, but if the considerations above suggested are well founded, there can be little doubt that it was at Jerusalem. There are indeed certain internal marks, as Hug has observed (Intro. § 155), pertaining to the *country* with which the writer was familiar, and to certain features of natural scenery incidentally alluded to in the epistle. Thus, his native land was situated not far from the sea (ch. i. 6; iii. 4) ; it was blessed with valuable productions, as figs, oil, and wine (ch. iii. 12) ; there were springs of saline and fresh water with which he was familiar (ch. iii. 11) ; the land was much exposed to drought, and there were frequently reasons to apprehend famine from the want of rain (ch. v. 17, 28) ;

there were sad devastations produced, and to be dreaded, from a consuming, burning wind (ch. i. 11); and it was a land in which the phenomena known as 'early and latter rains' were familiarly understood ; ch. v. 7. All these allusions apply well to Palestine, and were such as would be employed by one who resided in that country, and they may be regarded as an incidental proof that the epistle was written in that land.

There is no way of determining with certainty *when* the epistle was written. Hug supposes that it was after the epistle to the Hebrews, and not before the beginning of the tenth year of Nero, nor after the accession of Albinus ; *i. e.* the close of the same year. Mill and Fabricius suppose it was before the destruction of Jerusalem, and about a year and a half before the death of James. Lardner supposes that James was put to death about the year 62, and that this epistle was written about a year before. He supposes also that his death was hastened by the strong language of reprehension employed in the epistle. It is probable that the year in which it was written was not far from A.D. 58 or 60, some ten or twelve years before the destruction of Jerusalem.

§ 4. *The canonical Authority of the Epistle.*

On the question generally respecting the canonical authority of the disputed epistles, see the Intro. to the Catholic Epistles, § 2. The particular proof of the canonical authority of this epistle is contained in the evidence that it was written by one of the apostles. If it was written, as suggested above (§ 1), by James the Less, or if it be supposed that it was written by James the elder, both of whom were apostles, its canonical authority will be admitted. As there is no evidence that it was written by any other James, the point seems to be clear.

But there are additional considerations, derived from its reception in the church, which may furnish some degree of confirmation of its authority. These are, (*a*) It was included in the old Syriac version, the Peshita, made either in the first century or in the early part of the second, thus showing that it was recognised in the country to which it was probably sent ; (*b*) Ephrem the Syrian, in his Greek works, made use of it in many places, and attributed it to James, the brother of our Lord (*Hug*); (*c*) It is quoted as of authority by several of the Fathers ; by Clement of Rome, who does not indeed mention the *name* of the writer, but quotes the words of the epistle (James iii. 13; iv. 6, 11; ii. 21, 23); by Hermas; and by Jerome. See Lardner, vol. vi. pp. 195–199, and Hug, § 161.

§ 5. *The evidence that the writer was acquainted with the writings of Paul; the alleged contradiction between them; and the question how they can be reconciled.*

It has been frequently supposed, and sometimes affirmed, that this epistle is directly contradictory to Paul on the great doctrine of justification, and that it was written to counteract the tendency of his writings on that subject. Thus Hug strangely says, " In this epistle, Paul is (if I may be allowed to use so harsh an expression for a while) contradicted so flatly, that it would seem to have been written in opposition to some of his doctrines and opinions." § 157. It is of importance, therefore, to inquire into the foundation of this charge, for if it be so, it is clear that either this epistle or those of Paul would not be entitled to a place in the sacred canon. In order to this investigation, it is necessary to inquire to what extent the author was acquainted with the writings of Paul, and then to ask whether the statements of James are susceptible of any explanation which will reconcile them with those of Paul.

(1.) There is undoubted evidence that the author was acquainted with the writings of Paul. This evidence is found in the *similarity* of the. expressions occurring in the epistles of Paul and James ; a similarity such as would occur not merely from the fact that two men were writing on the same subject, but such as occurs only where one is acquainted with the writings of the other. Between two persons writing on the same subject, and resting their opinions on the same general reasons, there might be indeed a general resemblance, and possibly there might be expressions used which would be precisely the same. But it might happen that the resemblance would be so minute and particular, and on points where there could be naturally no such similarity, as to demonstrate that one of the writers was familiar with the productions of the other. For example, a man writing on a religious subject, if he had never heard of the Bible, *might* use expressions coincident with some that are found there; but it is clear also that he might in so many cases use the same expressions which occur there, and on points where the statements in the Bible are so peculiar, as to show conclusively that he was familiar with that book. So also a man might show that he was familiar with the Rambler or the Spectator, with Shakspeare or Milton. Such, it is supposed, are the allusions in the epistle of James, showing that he was acquainted with the writings of Paul. Among these passages are the following :—

JAMES.	PAUL.
i. 3. Knowing this, that the trying of your faith worketh patience.	Rom. v. 3. Knowing that tribulation worketh patience.
i. 2. Count it all joy when ye fall into divers temptations.	Rom. v. 3. We glory in tribulations also.
i. 4. Wanting nothing.	1 Cor. i. 7. Ye come behind in no gift.
i. 6. He that wavereth is like a wave of the sea, driven with the wind and tossed.	Eph. iv. 14. Tossed to and fro, carried about with every wind of doctrine.
i. 12. When he is tried, he shall receive the crown of life.	2 Tim. iv. 8. There is laid up for me a crown of righteousness.
i. 15. When lust hath conceived, it bringeth forth sin; and sin, when it is finished, bringeth forth death.	Rom. vii. 7, 8. I had not known lust, except the law had said, Thou shalt not covet. But sin, taking occasion by the commandment, wrought in me all manner of concupiscence.
i. 18. That we should be a kind of first-fruits of his creatures.	Rom. viii. 23 Ourselves also which have the first-fruits of the Spirit.
i. 21. Lay apart all filthiness and superfluity of naughtiness, &c.	Col. iv. 8. But now ye also put off all these; anger, wrath, malice, blasphemy, filthy communications out of your mouth.
i. 22. But be ye doers of the word, and not hearers only, &c.	Rom. ii. 13. For not the hearers of the law are just before God, but the doers of the law.
ii. 5. Hath not God chosen the poor of this world, rich in faith, &c.	1 Cor. i. 27. But God hath chosen the foolish things of the world, to confound the wise, &c.

Compare also, on this subject, the passage in James v. 14–26, with Romans iii. 20, seq.; the examples of Abraham and Rahab, referred to in ch. ii. 21, 25, with the reference to Abraham in Rom. iv.; and James iv. 12, with Rom. ii. 1, and xiv. 4.

These passages will show that James had an acquaintance with the writings of Paul, and that he was familiar with his usual method of expressing his thoughts. These allusions are not such as two men would be likely to make who were total strangers to each other's mode of speaking and of writing.

It may be added here, also, that some critics have supposed that there is another kind of evidence that James was acquainted with the writings of Paul, than that which arises from mere similarity of expression, and that he *meant* to refer to him, with a view to correct the influence of some of his views. Thus, Hug. in the passage already referred to (§ 157), says, " In this Epistle, the apostle Paul is (if I may be allowed to use so harsh an expression for a while) contradicted so flatly, that it would seem to have been written in opposition to some of his doctrines and opinions. All that Paul has taught respecting faith, its efficacy in justification, and the inutility of works, is here directly contravened." After citing examples from the Epistle to the Romans, and the Epistle of James, in support of this, Hug adds, " The Epistle was therefore written of set purpose against Paul, against the doctrine that faith procures man justification and the divine favour." The contradiction between James and Paul appeared so palpable to Luther, and the difficulty of reconciling them seemed to him to be so great, that for a long time he rejected the Epistle of James altogether. He subsequently, however, became satisfied that it was a part of the inspired canon of Scripture.

(2.) It has been, therefore, an object of much solicitude to know how the views of Paul and James, apparently so contradictory, can be reconciled ; and many attempts have been made to do it. Those who wish to pursue this inquiry to greater length than is consistent with the design of these Notes, may consult Neander's History of the Planting of the Christian Church, vol. ii., pp. 1–23, 228–239, and Dr. Dwight's Theology, serm. lxviii. The particular consideration of this pertains more appropriately to the exposition of the Epistle (see the remarks at the close of ch. iii.) ; but a few general principles may be laid down here, which may aid those who are disposed to make the comparison between the two, and which may show that there is no *designed*, and no *real* contradiction.

(*a*) The view which is taken of any object depends much on the point of vision from which it is beheld—the *stand-point*, as the Germans say ; and in order to estimate the truthfulness or value of a description or a picture, it is necessary for us to place ourselves in the same position with him who has given the description, or who has made the picture. Two men, painting or describing a mountain, a valley, a waterfall, or an edifice, might take such different positions in regard to it, that the descriptions which they give would seem to be quite contradictory and irreconcilable, unless this were taken into the account. A landscape, sketched from the top of a high tower or on a level plain ; a view of Niagara Falls, taken above or below the falls—on the American or Canada side ; a view of St. Paul's, taken from one side or another, from the dome or when on the ground, might be very different ; and two such views might present features which it would be scarcely possible to reconcile with each other. So it is of moral subjects. Much depends on the point from which they are viewed, and from the bearings and tendencies of the doctrine which is the particular subject of contemplation. The subject of *temperance*, for example, may be contemplated with reference, on the one hand, to the dangers arising from too lax a view of the matter, or, on the other, to the danger of pressing the principle too far ; and in order to know a man's views, and not to do injustice to him, it is proper to understand the particular aspect in which he looked at it, and the particular object which he had in view.

(*b*) The *object* of Paul—the 'stand-point' from which he viewed the subject of justification—on which point alone it has been supposed that he and James differ—was to show that there is no justification before God, except by faith ; that the meritorious cause of justification is the atonement ; that good works do not enter into the question of justification as a matter of merit, or as the ground of acceptance ; that if it were not for faith in Christ, it would not be possible for man to be justified. The point which he *opposes* is, that men can be justified by good works, by conformity to the law, by dependence on rites and ceremonies, by birth or blood. The aim of Paul is not to demonstrate that good works are not necessary or desirable in religion, but that they are not the ground of justification. The point of view in which he contemplates man, is *before* he is converted, and with reference to the question *on what ground* he can be justified :

and he affirms that it is only by faith. and that good works come in for no share in justification, as a ground of merit.

(c) The object of James—the 'stand-point' from which he viewed the subject —was, to show that a man cannot have evidence that he is justified, or that his faith is genuine, unless he is characterized by good works, or by holy living. His aim is to show, not that faith is not essential to justification, and not that the real ground of dependence is not the merit of the Saviour, but that conformity to the law of God is indispensable to true religion. The point of view in which he contemplates the subject, is *after* a man professes to be justified, and with reference to the question whether his faith is *genuine;* and he affirms that no faith is of value in justification but that which is productive of good works. By his own character, by education, by the habits of his whole life, he was accustomed to look on religion as obedience to the will of God; and every thing in his character led him to oppose all that was lax in principle, and loose in tendency, in religion. The point which he *opposed*, therefore, was, that mere *faith* in religion, as a revelation from God; a mere assent to certain doctrines, without a corresponding life, could be a ground of justification before God. This was the prevalent error of his countrymen; and while the Jews held to the belief of divine revelation as a matter of speculative faith, the most lax views of morals prevailed, and they freely indulged in practices entirely inconsistent with true piety, and subversive of all proper views of religion. It was not improper, therefore, as Paul had given prominence to one aspect of the doctrine of justification, showing that a man could not be saved by dependence on the works of the law, but that it must be by the work of Christ, that James should give due prominence to the other form of the doctrine, by showing that the essential and necessary tendency of the true doctrine of justification was to lead to a holy life; and that a man whose life was not conformed to the law of God, *could* not depend on any mere assent to the truth of religion, or any speculative faith whatever. Both these statements are necessary to a full exposition of the doctrine of justification; both are opposed to dangerous errors; and both, therefore, are essential in order to a full understanding of that important subject.

(d) Both these statements are true. (1.) That of Paul is true, that there can be no justification before God on the ground of our own works, but that the real ground of justification is faith in the great sacrifice made for sin. (2) That of James is no less true, that there can be no genuine faith which is not productive of good works, and that good works furnish the evidence that we have true religion, and are just before God. A mere faith; a naked assent to dogmas, accompanied with lax views of morals, can furnish no evidence of true piety. It is as true, that where there is not a holy life there is no religion, as it is in cases where there is no faith.

It may be added, therefore, that the Epistle of James occupies an important place in the New Testament, and that it could not be withdrawn without materially marring the proportions of the scheme of religion which is there revealed. Instead, therefore, of being regarded as contradictory to any part of the New Testament, it should rather be deemed indispensable to the concinnity and beauty of the whole.

Keeping in view, therefore, the general design of the Epistle, and the point of view from which James contemplated the subject of religion; the general corruptions of the age in which he lived, in regard to morals; the tendency of the Jews to suppose that mere assent to the truths of religion was enough to save them; the liability which there was to abuse the doctrine of Paul on the subject of justification,—it will not be difficult to understand the general drift of this Epistle, or to appreciate its value. A summary of its contents, and a more particular view of its design, will be found in the Analyses prefixed to the several chapters.

THE GENERAL

EPISTLE OF JAMES.

CHAPTER I.

JAMES, a servant *a* of God and of the Lord Jesus Christ, to the twelve *b* tribes which are scat- tered *c* abroad, greeting.

a Jude 1.   *b* Ac.26.7.   *c* Ac.8.1.

CHAPTER I.

ANALYSIS OF THE CHAPTER.

This chapter seems to comprise two general classes of subjects; the statement in regard to the first of which is complete, but the second is only commenced in this chapter, and is continued in the second. The first is the general subject of temptation and trial (vs. 1–15); the second is the nature of true religion:— the statement that all true religion has its origin in God, the source of purity and truth, and that it requires us to be docile and meek; to be doers of the word; to bridle the tongue, and to be the friends of the fatherless and the widow, vs. 16–27.

I. The general subject of temptation or trial, vs. 1–15. It is evident that those to whom the epistle was directed were, at that time, suffering in some form, or that they were called to pass through temptations, and that they needed counsel and support. They were in danger of sinking in despondency; of murmuring and complaining, and of charging God as the author of temptation and of sin. This part of the chapter comprises the following topics:

1. The salutation, ver. 1.

2. The subject of temptations or trials. They were to regard it, not as a subject of sorrow, but of gladness and joy, that they were called to pass through trials; for, if borne in a proper manner, they would produce the grace of patience, and this was to be regarded as an object worth being secured, even by much suffering, vs. 2–4.

3. If in their trials they felt that they had lacked the wisdom which they needed to enable them to bear them in a proper manner, they had the privilege of looking to God, and seeking it at his hand. This was a privilege conceded to all, and if it were asked in faith, without any wavering, it would certainly be granted, vs. 5–7.

4. The importance and value of stability, especially in trials; of being firm in principle, and of having one single great aim in life. A man who wavered in his faith would waver in every thing, ver. 8.

5. An encouragement to those who, in the trials which they experienced, passed through rapid changes of circumstances. Whatever those changes were, they were to rejoice in them as ordered by the Lord. They were to remember the essential instability of all earthly things. The rich especially, who were most disposed to murmur and complain when their circumstances were changed, were to remember how the burning heat blasts the beauty of the flower, and that in like manner all worldly splendour must fade away, vs. 9–11.

6. Every man is blessed who endures trials in a proper manner, for such an endurance of trial will be connected with a rich reward—the crown of life, ver. 12.

7. In their trials, however, in the allurements to sin which might be set before them; in the temptations to apostatize, or to do any thing wrong, which might be connected with their suffering condition, they were to be careful never to charge *temptation as such on God.* They were never to allow their minds to feel for a moment that

he allured them to sin, or placed an inducement of any kind before them to do wrong. Every thing of that kind, every disposition to commit sin, originated in their own hearts, and they should never allow themselves to charge it on God, vs. 13–15.

II. The nature of true religion, vs. 16–27.

1. It has its origin in God, the source of every good gift, the Father of lights, who has of his own will begotten us again, that he might raise us to an exalted rank among his creatures. God, therefore, should be regarded not as the author of sin, but as the source of all the good that is in us, vs. 16–18.

2. Religion requires us to be meek and docile; to lay aside all disposition to dictate or prescribe, all irritability against the truth, and all corruption of heart, and to receive meekly the ingrafted word, vs. 19–21.

3. Religion requires us to be doers of the word, and not hearers only, vs. 23, 24, 25.

4. Religion requires us to bridle the tongue, to set a special guard on our words, ver. 26.

5. Religion requires us to be the friends of the fatherless and the widow, and to keep ourselves unspotted from the world, ver. 27.

1. *James, a servant of God.* On the meaning of the word *servant* in this connexion, see Note on Rom. i. 1. Comp. Note on Philem. 16. It is remarkable that James does not call himself *an apostle;* but this does not prove that the writer of the epistle was not an apostle, for the same omission occurs in the epistle of John, and in the epistle of Paul to the Philippians, the Thessalonians, and to Philemon. It is remarkable, also, considering the relation which James is supposed to have borne to the Lord Jesus as his ' brother' (Gal. i. 19; Intro. § 1). that he did not refer to that as constituting a ground of claim to his right to address others; but this is only one instance out of many, in the New Testament, in which it is regarded as a higher honour to be the ' servant of God,' and to belong to his family, than to sustain *any* relations of blood or kindred. Comp. Matth. xi. 50. It may be ob-

served also (Comp. the Intro. § 1), that this term is one which was peculiarly appropriate to James, as a man eminent for his integrity. His claim to respect and deference was not primarily founded on any relationship which he sustained; any honour of birth or blood; or even any external office, but on the fact that he was a ' *servant of God.*' ¶ *And of the Lord Jesus Christ.* The ' servant of the Lord Jesus,' is an appellation which is often given to Christians, and particularly to the ministers of religion. They are his servants, not in the sense that they are *slaves,* but in the sense that they voluntarily obey his will, and labour for him, and not for themselves. ¶ *To the twelve tribes which are scattered abroad.* Gr. ' The twelve tribes which are *in the dispersion,*' or of the dispersion (ἐν τῇ διασπορᾷ). This word occurs only here and in 1 Pet. i. 1, and John vii. 35. It refers properly to those who lived out of Palestine, or who were scattered among the Gentiles. There were *two* great ' dispersions;' the Eastern and the Western. The first had its origin about the time when the ten tribes were carried away to Assyria, and in the time of the Babylonian captivity. In consequence of these events, and of the fact that large numbers of the Jews went to Babylon, and other Eastern countries, for purposes of travel, commerce, &c., there were many Jews in the East in the times of the apostles. The other was the Western ' dispersion,' which commenced about the time of Alexander the Great, and which was promoted by various causes, until there were large numbers of Jews in Egypt and along Northern Africa, in Asia Minor, in Greece proper, and even in Rome. To which of these classes this epistle was directed is not known ; but most probably the writer had particular reference to those in the East. See the Intro. § 2. The phrase ' the twelve tribes,' was the common term by which the Jewish people were designated, and was in use long after the ten tribes were carried away, leaving, in fact, but two of the twelve in Palestine. Comp. Notes on Acts xxvi. 7. Many have supposed that James here addressed them *as* Jews, and that the epistle was sent

2 My brethren, count it all joy *a* when ye fall into divers temptations;

a Matt.5.12.   1 Pet.4.13-16.

3 Knowing *this*, that the trying of your faith worketh *b* patience.

4 But let patience *c* have *her*

b Ro.5.3.   c Lu. 8.15; 21.19.

to them *as* such. But this opinion has no probability; for (1) had this been the case, he would not have been likely to begin his epistle by saying that he was 'a servant of Jesus Christ,' a name so odious to the Jews ; and (2) if he *had* spoken of himself as a Christian, and had addressed his countrymen as himself a believer in Jesus as the Messiah, though regarding them *as Jews*, it is incredible that he did not make a more distinct reference to the principles of the Christian religion ; that he used no arguments to convince them that Jesus was the Messiah ; that he did not attempt to convert them to the Christian faith. It should be added, that at first most converts were made from those who had been trained in the Jewish faith, and it is not improbable that one in Jerusalem, addressing those who were Christians out of Palestine, would naturally think of them as of Jewish origin, and would be likely to address them as appertaining to the 'twelve tribes.' The phrase 'the twelve tribes' became also a sort of technical expression to denote the people of God—the church. ¶ *Greeting.* A customary form of salutation, meaning, in Greek, *to joy, to rejoice;* and implying that he wished their welfare. Comp. Acts xv. 23.

2. *My brethren.* Not brethren *as Jews*, but *as Christians.* Comp. ch. ii. 1. ¶ *Count it all joy.* Regard it as a thing to rejoice in ; a matter which should afford you happiness. You are not to consider it as a punishment, a curse, or a calamity, but as a fit subject of felicitation. Comp. Notes Matt. v. 12. ¶ *When ye fall into divers temptations.* On the meaning of the word *temptations,* see Notes on Matt. iv. 1. It is now commonly used in the sense of placing allurements before others to induce them to sin, and in this sense the word seems to be used in vs. 13, 14 of this chapter. Here, however, the word is used in the sense of *trials,* to wit, by persecution, poverty, calamity of any kind. These cannot be said to be direct inducements or allurements to sin, but

VOL

they try the faith, and they show whether he who is tried is disposed to adhere to his faith in God, or whether he will apostatise. They so far *coincide* with temptations, properly so called, as to *test* the religion of men. They *differ* from temptations, properly so called, in that they are not brought before the mind *for the express purpose* of inducing men to sin. In this sense it is true that God never *tempts* men, vs. 13, 14. On the sentiment in the passage before us, see Notes on 1 Pet. i. 6, 7. The word *divers* here refers to the various kinds of trials which they might experience—sickness, poverty, bereavement, persecution, &c. They were to count it a matter of joy that their religion was subjected to any thing that tried it. It is well for us to have the reality of our religion tested, in whatever way it may be done.

3. *Knowing this, that the trying of your faith worketh patience.* Patience is one of the fruits of such a trial, and the grace of patience is *worth* the trial which it may cost to procure it. This is one of the passages which show that James was acquainted with the writings of Paul. See the Intro. § 5. The sentiment expressed here is found in Rom. v. 3. See Notes on that verse. Paul has carried the sentiment out farther, and shows that tribulation produces other effects than patience. James only asks that patience may have its perfect work, supposing that every Christian grace is implied in this.

4. *But let patience have* her *perfect work.* Let it be fairly developed ; let it produce its appropriate effects without being hindered. Let it not be obstructed in its fair influence on the soul by murmurings, complaining, or rebellion. Patience under trials is fitted to produce important effects on the soul, and we are not to hinder them in any manner by a perverse spirit, or by opposition to the will of God. Every one who is afflicted should desire that the *fair* effects of affliction should be produced on his mind, or that there should be pro-

B

perfect work, that ye may be per- him ask of God, that *a* giveth to all
fect and entire, wanting nothing.   *men* liberally, and upbraideth not;
5 If any of you lack wisdom, let   and *b* it shall be given him.

a Pr.2.3-6.   *b* Je.29.12.

duced in his soul precisely the results
which his trials are adapted to accomplish. ¶ *That ye may be perfect and
entire.* The meaning of this is explained
in the following phrase—'wanting nothing ;' that is, that there may be nothing lacking to complete your character. There may be the elements of a
good character ; there may be sound
principles, but those principles may not
be fully carried out so as to show what
they are. Afflictions, perhaps more than
any thing else, will do this, and we
should therefore allow them to do all
that they are adapted to do in developing
what is good in us. The idea here is,
that it is desirable not only to have the
elements or *principles* of piety in the
soul, but to have them fairly carried
out, so as to show what is their real
tendency and value. Comp. Notes on 1
Pet. i. 7. On the word *perfect*, as used
in the Scriptures, see Notes on Job i. 1.
The word rendered *entire* (ὁλόκληροι)
means, *whole in every part.* Comp.
Notes on 1 Thess. v. 23. The word
occurs only in these two places. The
corresponding noun (ὁλοκληρία) occurs in
Acts iii. 16, rendered *perfect soundness.*
¶ *Wanting nothing.* ' Being left in
nothing ;' that is, every thing being
complete, or fully carried out.
   5. *If any of you lack wisdom.* Probably this refers particularly to the
kind of wisdom which they would need
in their trials, to enable them to bear
them in a proper manner, for there is
nothing in which Christians more feel
the need of heavenly wisdom than in regard to the manner in which they should
bear trials, and what they should *do* in
the perplexities, and disappointments,
and bereavements that come upon them ;
but the language employed is so general,
that what is here said may be applied to
the need of wisdom in all respects. The
particular kind of wisdom which we need
in trials is to enable. us to understand
their design and tendency ; to perform
our duty under them, or the new duties which may grow out of them ; to
learn the lessons which God designs

to teach, for he always designs to teach
us *some* valuable lessons by affliction ;
and to cultivate such views and feelings
as are appropriate under the peculiar
forms of trial which are brought upon
us ; to find out the sins for which we
have been afflicted, and to learn how
we may avoid them in time to come.
We are in great danger of going wrong
when we are afflicted ; of complaining
and murmuring ; of evincing a spirit of
insubmission, and of losing the benefits
which we *might* have obtained if we had
submitted to the trial in a proper manner. So in all things we ' lack wisdom.'
We are short-sighted ; we have hearts
prone to sin ; and there are great and
important matters pertaining to duty
and salvation on which we cannot but
feel that we need heavenly guidance.
¶ *Let him ask of God.* That is, for the
specific wisdom which he needs ; the
very wisdom which is necessary for him
in the particular case. It is proper to
bear the very case before God ; to make
mention of the specific want ; to ask of
God to guide us in the very matter
where we feel so much embarrassment.
It is one of the privileges of Christians,
that they may not only go to God and
ask him for that *general* wisdom which
is needful for them in life, but that
whenever a particular emergency arises,
a case of perplexity and difficulty in
regard to duty, they may bring that
particular thing before his throne, with
the assurance that he will guide them.
Comp. Ps. xxv. 9 ; Isa. xxxvii. 14 ; Joel
ii. 17. ¶ *That giveth to all* men *liberally.* The word *men* here is supplied
by the translators, but not improperly,
though the promise should be regarded
as restricted to those who *ask.* The
object of the writer was to encourage
those who felt their need of wisdom, to
go and ask it of God ; and it would not
contribute any thing to furnish such a
specific encouragement to say of God
that he gives to all men liberally *whether
they ask or not.* In the Scriptures, the
promise of divine aid is always limited
to the desire. No blessing is promised

6 But ^a let him ask in faith, nothing wavering. For he that

wavereth, is like a wave of the sea, driven with the wind and tossed.

to man that is not sought; no man can feel that he has a right to hope for the favour of God, who does not value it enough to pray for it; no one *ought* to obtain it, who does *not* prize it enough to ask for it. Comp. Matt. vii. 7, 8. The word rendered *liberally* (ἁπλῶς) means, properly, *simply;* that is, in simplicity, sincerity, reality. It occurs nowhere else in the New Testament, though the corresponding *noun* occurs in Rom. xii. 8; 2 Cor. i. 12; xi. 3, rendered *simplicity;* in 2 Cor. viii. 2; ix. 13, rendered *liberality*, and *liberal;* 2 Cor. ix. 11, rendered *bountifulness;* and Eph. vi. 5; Col. iii. 22, rendered *singleness*, scil., of the heart. The idea seems to be that of openness, frankness, generosity; the absence of all that is sordid and contracted; where there is the manifestation of generous feeling, and liberal conduct. In a higher sense than in the case of any man, all that is excellent in these things is to be found in God; and we may therefore come to him feeling that in his heart there is more that is noble and generous in bestowing favours than in any other being. There is nothing that is stinted and close; there is no partiality; there is no withholding of his favour because we are poor, and unlettered, and unknown. ¶ *And upbraideth not.* Does not reproach, rebuke, or treat harshly. He does not coldly repel us, if we come and ask what we need, though we do it often and with importunity. Comp. Luke xviii. 1–7. The proper meaning of the Greek word is to rail at, reproach, revile, chide; and the object here is probably to place the manner in which God bestows his favours in contrast with what sometimes occurs among men. He does not reproach or chide us for our past conduct; for our foolishness; for our importunity in asking. He permits us to come in the most free manner, and meets us with a spirit of entire kindness, and with promptness in granting our requests. We are not always sure, when we ask a favour of a man, that we shall not encounter something that will be repulsive, or that will

mortify us; we are certain, however, when we ask a favour of God, that we shall never be reproached in an unfeeling manner, or meet with a harsh response. ¶ *And it shall be given him.* Comp. Jer. xxix. 12, 13, "Then shall ye call upon me, and go and pray unto me, and I will hearken unto you. And ye shall seek me, and find me, when ye shall search for me with your whole heart." See also Matt. vii. 7, 8; xxi. 22; Mark xi. 24; 1 John iii. 22; v. 14. This promise in regard to the *wisdom* that may be necessary for us, is absolute; and we may be sure that if it be asked in a proper manner it will be granted us. There can be no doubt that it is one of the things which God is able to impart; which will be for our own good; and which, therefore, he is ever ready to bestow. About many things there might be doubt whether, if they were granted, they would be for our real welfare, and therefore there may be a doubt whether it would be consistent for God to bestow them; but there can be no such doubt about *wisdom.* That is always for our good; and we may be sure, therefore, that we shall obtain that, if the request be made with a right spirit. If it be asked in what way we may expect he will bestow it on us, it may be replied, (1.) That it is through his word—by enabling us to see clearly the meaning of the sacred volume, and to understand the directions which he has there given to guide us; (2.) By the secret influences of his Spirit (*a*) *suggesting* to us the way in which we should go, and (*b*) *inclining* us to do that which is prudent and wise; and (3.) By the events of his Providence making plain to us the path of duty, and removing the obstructions which may be in our path. It is easy for God to guide his people; and they who 'watch daily at the gates, and wait at the posts of the doors' of wisdom (Prov. viii. 34), will not be in danger of going astray. Ps. xxv. 9.

6. *But let him ask in faith.* See the passages referred to in ver. 5. Comp. Notes on Matt. vii. 7, and on Heb. xi

7 For let not that man think that he shall receive any thing of the Lord.

8 A double-minded man is unstable in all his ways.

6. We cannot hope to obtain any favour from God if there is not faith; and where, as in regard to the *wisdom* necessary to guide us, we are sure that it is in accordance with his will to grant it to us, we may come to him with the utmost confidence, the most entire assurance, that it will be granted. In this case, we should come to God without a doubt that, if we ask with a proper spirit, the very thing that we ask will be bestowed on us. We cannot in all other cases be so sure that what we ask will be for our good, or that it will be in accordance with his will to bestow it; and hence we cannot in such cases come with the same kind of faith. We can then only come with unwavering confidence in God, that he will do what is right and best; and that if he sees that what we ask will be for our good, he will bestow it upon us. Here, however, nothing prevents our coming with the assurance that *the very thing* which we ask will be conferred on us. ¶ *Nothing wavering.* (μηδὲν διακρινόμενος.) 'Doubting or hesitating as to nothing, or in no respect.' See Acts xx. 20; xi. 12. In regard to the matter under consideration, there is to be no hesitancy, no doubting, no vacillation of the mind. We are to come to God with the utmost confidence and assurance. ¶ *For he that wavereth, is like a wave of the sea,* &c. The propriety and beauty of this comparison will be seen at once. The wave of the sea has no stability. It is at the mercy of every wind, and seems to be driven and tossed every way. So he that comes to God with unsettled convictions and hopes, is liable to be driven about by every new feeling that may spring up in the mind. At one moment, hope and faith impel him to come to God; then the mind is at once filled with uncertainty and doubt, and the soul is agitated and restless as the ocean. Comp. Isa. lvii. 20. Hope on the one hand, and the fear of not obtaining the favour which is desired on the other, keep the mind restless and discomposed.

7. *For let not that man think that he shall receive any thing of the Lord.* Comp. Heb. xi. 6. A man can hope for favour from God only as he puts confidence in him. He sees the heart; and if he sees that there is no belief in his existence, or his perfections—no real trust in him—no reliance on his promises, his wisdom, his grace—it cannot be proper that he should grant an answer to our petitions. That will account sufficiently for the fact that there are so many prayers unanswered; that we so frequently go to the throne of grace, and are sent empty away. A man that goes to God in such a state of mind, should not *expect* to receive any favour.

8. *A double-minded man.* The word here used, δίψυχος occurs only here and in ch. iv. 8. It means, properly, one who has two souls; then one who is wavering or inconstant. It is applicable to a man who has no settled principles; who is controlled by passion; who is influenced by popular feeling; who is now inclined to one opinion or course of conduct, and now to another. ¶ *Is unstable in all his ways.* That is, not merely in regard to prayer, the point particularly under discussion, but in respect to every thing. From the instability which the wavering must evince in regard to *prayer*, the apostle takes occasion to make the general remark concerning such a man, that stability and firmness could be expected on no subject. The hesitancy which he manifested on that one subject would extend to all; and we might expect to find such a man irresolute and undetermined in all things. This is always true. If we find a man who takes hold of the promises of God with firmness; who feels the deepest assurance when he prays that God will hear prayer; who always goes to him without hesitation in his perplexities and trials, never wavering, we shall find one who is firm in his principles, steady in his integrity, settled in his determinations, and steadfast in his plans of life—a man whose character we shall feel that we understand, and in

9 Let the brother of low degree ¹ rejoice in that he is exalted:

1 Or, *glory*.

whom we can confide. Such a man eminently was Luther; and the spirit which is thus evinced by taking firmly hold of the promises of God is the best kind of religion.

9. *Let the brother of low degree.* This verse seems to introduce a new topic, which has no other connection with what precedes than that the apostle is discussing the general subject of trials. Comp. ver. 2. Turning from the consideration of trials in general, he passes to the consideration of a particular kind of trials, that which results from a change of circumstances in life, from poverty to affluence, and from affluence to poverty. The idea which seems to have been in the mind of the apostle is, that there is a great and important *trial of faith* in *any* reverse of circumstances; a trial in being elevated from poverty to riches, or in being depressed from a state of affluence to want. Wherever *change* occurs in the external circumstances of life, there a man's religion is put to the test, and there he should feel that God is trying the reality of his faith. The phrase ' of low degree ' (ταπεινὸς) means one in humble circumstances; one of lowly rank or employment; one in a condition of dependence or poverty. It stands here particularly opposed to one who is *rich;* and the apostle doubtless had his eye, in the use of this word, on those who had been poor. ¶ *Rejoice*, marg. *glory.* Not because, being made rich, he has the means of sensual gratification and indulgence ; not because he will now be regarded as a rich man, and will feel that he is above want ; not even because he will have the means of doing good to others. Neither of these was the idea in the mind of the apostle ; but it was, that the poor man that is made rich should rejoice *because his faith and the reality of his religion are now tried;* because a *test* is furnished which will show, in the new circumstances in which he is placed, whether his piety is genuine. In fact, there is almost no trial of religion which is more certain and decisive than that furnished by a sudden transition from poverty to affluence,

from adversity to prosperity, from sickness to health. There is much religion in the world that will bear the ills of poverty, sickness, and persecution, or that will bear the temptations arising from prosperity, and even affluence, which will not bear the transition from one to the other; as there is many a human frame that could become accustomed to bear either the steady heat of the equator, or the intense cold of the north, that could not bear a rapid transition from the one to the other. See this thought illustrated in the Notes on Phil. iv. 12. ¶ *In that he is exalted.* A good man *might* rejoice in such a transition, because it would furnish him the means of being more extensively useful ; most persons *would* rejoice because such a condition is that for which men commonly aim, and because it would furnish them the means of display, of sensual gratification, or of ease ; but neither of these is the idea of the apostle. The thing in which we are to rejoice in the transitions of life is, that a test is furnished of our piety ; that a trial is applied to it which enables us to determine whether it is genuine. The most important thing conceivable for us is to know whether we are true Christians, and we should rejoice in every thing that will enable us to settle this point.

[Yet it seems not at all likely that an Apostle would exhort a poor man to *rejoice* in his exaltation to wealth. An exhortation to fear and trembling appears more suitable. Wealth brings along with it so many dangerous temptations, that a man must have greater confidence in his faith and stability than he ought to have, who can rejoice in its acquisition, simply as furnishing occasion to *try* him: the same may be said of poverty, or of the transition from riches to poverty. The spirit of Agar is more suitable to the humility of piety, " Give me neither poverty nor riches ; feed me with food convenient for me, lest I be full and deny thee, and say, Who is the Lord ? or lest I be poor, and steal, and take the name of my God in vain," Prov. xxx. 8, 9. Besides, there is no necessity for resorting to this interpretation. The words will, without any straining, bear another sense, which is both excellent in itself, and suitable in its connection. The poor man, or man in humble life, may

10 But the rich, in that he is made low: because as the flower of the grass *a* he shall pass away.

11 For the sun is no sooner risen with a burning heat, but it wither-

eth the grass, and the flower thereof falleth, and the grace of the fashion of it perisheth: so also shall the rich man fade away in his ways.

a Is.40.6.

well rejoice "in that he is exalted" to the dignity of a child of God, and heir of glory. If he be depressed with his humble rank in this life, let him but think of his spiritual elevation, of his relation to God and Christ, and he shall have an antidote for his dejection. What is the world's dignity in comparison of his! The rich man, or the man of rank, on the other hand, has reason to rejoice "in that he is made low" through the possession of a meek and humble spirit which his affluence illustrates, but neither destroys nor impairs. It would be matter of *grief* were he otherwise minded; since all his adventitious splendour is as evanescent as the flower which, forming for a time the crown of the green stalk on which it hangs, perishes before it. This falls admirably in with the design of the Apostle, which was to fortify Christians against trial. Every condition in life had its own trials. The two great conditions of poverty and wealth had theirs; but Christianity guards against the danger, both of the one state and of the other. It elevates the poor under his depression, and humbles the rich in his elevation, and bids both rejoice in its power to shield and bless them. The passage in this view is conceived in the same spirit with one of Paul, in which he beautifully balances the respective conditions of slaves and freemen, by honouring the former with the appellation of the *Lord's freemen*, and imposing on the latter that of *Christ's servants*, 1 Cor. vii. 22.]

10. *But the rich, in that he is made low.* That is, because his property is taken away, and he is made poor. Such a transition is often the source of the deepest sorrow; but the apostle says that even in that a Christian may find occasion for thanksgiving. The *reasons* for rejoicing in this manner, which the apostle seems to have had in view, were these: (1) because it furnished a *test* of the reality of religion, by showing that it is adapted to sustain the soul in this great trial; that it cannot only bear prosperity, but that it can bear the rapid transition from that state to one of poverty; and (2) because it would furnish to the mind an impressive and salutary illustration of the fact that *all* earthly glory is soon to fade away. I may remark here, that the transition from affluence to poverty

is often borne by Christians with the manifestation of a most lovely spirit, and with an entire freedom from murmuring and complaining. Indeed, there are more Christians who could safely bear a transition from affluence to poverty, from prosperity to adversity, than there are who could bear a sudden transition from poverty to affluence. Some of the loveliest exhibitions of piety which I have ever witnessed have been in such transitions; nor have I seen occasion anywhere to love religion more than in the ease, and grace, and cheerfulness, with which it has enabled those accustomed long to more elevated walks, to descend to the comparatively humble lot where God places them. New grace is imparted for this new form of trial, and new traits of Christian character are developed in these rapid transitions, as some of the most beautiful exhibitions of the laws of matter are brought out in the rapid transitions in the laboratory of the chemist. ¶ *Because as the flower of the grass he shall pass away.* That is, since it is *a fact* that he will thus pass away, he should rejoice that he is reminded of it. He should, therefore, esteem it a favour that this lesson is brought impressively before his mind. To learn this effectually, though by the loss of property, is of more value to him than all his wealth would be if he were forgetful of it. The comparison of worldly splendour with the fading flower of the field, is one that is common in Scripture. It is probable that James had his eye on the passage in Isaiah xl. 6–8. See Notes on that passage. Comp. Notes on 1 Pet. i. 24, 25. See also Ps. ciii. 15; Matt. vi. 28–30.

11. *For the sun is no sooner risen with a burning heat.* Isaiah (xl. 7) employs the word *wind*, referring to a burning wind that dries up the flowers. It is probable that the apostle also refers not so much to the sun itself, as to the hot and fiery wind called the *simoom*, which often rises *with* the sun, and

12 Blessed *is* the man that endureth temptation: for when he is tried, he shall receive the crown *a* of life, which *b* the Lord hath promised to them that love him.

a 2 Ti.4.8. Re.2.10.   *b* Is.64.4.

which consumes the green herbage of the fields. So Rosenmüller and Bloomfield interpret it. ¶ *It withereth the grass.* Isa. xl. 7. It withereth the *stalk*, or that which, when dried, produces hay or fodder—the word here used being commonly employed in the latter sense. The meaning is, that the effect of the hot wind is to wither the stalk or spire which supports the flower, and when that is dried up, the flower itself falls. This idea will give increased beauty and appropriateness to the figure —that *man himself* is blasted and withered, and then that all the external splendour which encircled him falls to the ground, like a flower whose support is gone. ¶ *And the grace of the fashion of it perisheth.* Its beauty disappears. ¶ *So shall the rich man fade away in his ways.* That is, his splendour, and all on which he prideth himself, shall vanish. The phrase ' in his ways,' according to Rosenmüller, refers to his counsels, his plans, his purposes ; and the meaning is, that the rich man, with all by which he is known, shall vanish. A man's ' ways,' that is, his mode of life, or those things by which he appears before the world, may have somewhat the same relation to him which the flower has to the stalk on which it grows, and by which it is sustained. The idea of James seems to be, that as it was indisputable that the rich man *must* soon disappear, with all that he had of pomp and splendour in the view of the world, it was well for him to be reminded of it by every change of condition ; and that he should therefore rejoice in the providential dispensation by which his property would be taken away, and by which the reality of his religion would be tested. We should rejoice in *anything* by which it can be shown whether we are prepared for heaven or not.

12. *Blessed* is *the man that endureth temptation.* The apostle seems here to use the word *temptation* in the most general sense, as denoting *anything* that will try the reality of religion, whether affliction, or persecution, or a direct inducement to sin placed before the mind. The word *temptation* appears in this chapter to be used in two senses ; and the question may arise, why the apostle so employs it. Comp. vs. 2, 13. But, in fact, the word *temptation* is in itself of so general a character as to cover the whole usage, and to justify the manner in which it is employed. It denotes *anything* that will try or test the reality of our religion ; and it may be applied, therefore, either to afflictions or to direct solicitations to sin—the latter being the sense in which it is now commonly employed. In another respect, also, essentially the same idea enters into both the ways in which the word is employed. Affliction, persecution, sickness, &c., may be regarded as, in a certain sense, temptations to sin ; that is, the question comes before us whether we will adhere to the religion on account of which we are persecuted, or apostatize from it, and escape these sufferings ; whether in sickness and losses we will be patient and submissive to that God who lays his hand upon us, or revolt and murmur. In each and every case, whether by affliction, or by direct allurements to do wrong, the question comes before the mind whether we have religion enough to keep us, or whether we will yield to murmuring, to rebellion, and to sin. In these respects, in a general sense, *all* forms of trial may be regarded as *temptation.* Yet in the following verse (13) the apostle would guard this from abuse. So far as the form of trial involved an allurement or inducement *to sin,* he says that no man should regard it as from God. *That* cannot be his design. The *trial* is what he aims at, not the *sin.* In the verse before us he says, that whatever may be the form of the trial, a Christian should rejoice in it, for it will furnish an evidence that he is a child of God. ¶ *For when he is tried.* In any way—if he bears the trial. ¶ *He shall receive the crown of life.* See Notes on 2 Tim. iv. 8. It is *possible* that James had that passage in his eye.

13 Let no man say when he is tempted, I am tempted of God: for

1 Or, *evils*.

God cannot be tempted with ¹evil, neither tempteth he any man.

Comp. the Intro., § 5. ¶ *Which the Lord hath promised.* The sacred writers often speak of such a crown as promised, or as in reserve for the children of God. 2 Tim. iv. 8; 1 Pet. v. 4; Rev. ii. 10; iii. 11; iv. 4. ¶ *Them that love him.* A common expression to denote those who are truly pious, or who are his friends. It is sufficiently distinctive to characterize them, for the great mass of men do not love God. Comp. Rom. i. 30.

13. *Let no man say when he is tempted, I am tempted of God.* See the remarks on the previous verse. The apostle here seems to have had his eye on whatever there was in trial of any kind to induce us to commit *sin*—whether by complaining, by murmuring, by apostacy, or by yielding to sin. So far as *that* was concerned, he said that no one should charge it on God. He did nothing in any way with a view to *induce* men to do evil. That was only an incidental thing in the trial, and was no part of the divine purpose or design. The apostle felt evidently that there was great danger, from the general manner in which the word *temptation* was used, and from the perverse tendency of the heart, that it would be charged on God that he so arranged these trials, and so influenced the mind, as to present *inducements* to sin. Against this, it was proper that an inspired apostle should bear his solemn testimony; so to guard the whole subject as to show that whatever there was in *any* form of trial that could be regarded as an inducement or allurement to sin, is not the thing which he contemplated in the arrangement, and does not proceed from him. It has its origin in other causes; and if there was nothing *in the corrupt human mind itself* leading to sin, there would be nothing in the divine arrangement that would produce it. ¶ *For God cannot be tempted with evil.* Marg. *evils.* The sense is the same. The object seems to be to show that, in regard to the whole matter of temptation, it does not pertain to God. Nothing can be presented to *his* mind as an in-

ducement to do wrong, and as little can he present any thing to the mind of man to induce *him* to sin. Temptation is a subject which does not pertain to him. He stands aloof from it altogether. In regard to the *particular* statement here, that 'God cannot be tempted with evil,' or to do evil, there can be no doubt of its truth, and it furnishes the highest security for the welfare of the universe. There is nothing *in* him that has a tendency to wrong; there can be nothing presented from without to induce him to do wrong. (1.) There is no evil *passion* to be gratified, as there is in men; (2.) There is no want of *power*, so that an allurement could be presented to seek what he has not; (3.) There is no want of *wealth*, for he has infinite resources, and all that there is or can be is his (Ps. l. 10, 11); (4.) There is no want of *happiness*, that he should seek happiness in sources which are not now in his possession. Nothing, therefore, could be presented to the divine mind as an *inducement* to do evil. ¶ *Neither tempteth he any man.* That is, he places nothing before any human being with a view to induce him to do wrong. This is one of the most positive and unambiguous of all the declarations in the Bible, and one of the most important. It may be added, that it is one which stands in opposition to as many feelings of the human heart as perhaps any other one. We are perpetually thinking—the *heart* suggests it constantly—that God *does* place before us inducements to evil, with a view to lead us to sin. This is done in many ways: (*a*) Men take such views of his decrees as if the doctrine implied that he *meant* that we should sin, and that it could not be otherwise than that we should sin. (*b*) It is felt that all things are under his control, and that he has made his arrangements with a *design* that men should do as they actually do. (*c*) It is said that he has created us with just such dispositions as we actually have, and knowing that we would sin. (*d*) It is said that, by the **arrange-**

14 But every man is tempted,

a Hos.13.9.

when he is drawn away of his own *a* lust, and enticed.

---

ments of his Providence, he actually places inducements before us to sin, knowing that the effect will be that we will fall into sin, when we might easily have prevented it. (*e*) It is said that he suffers some to tempt others, when he might easily prevent it if he chose, and that this is the same as tempting them himself. Now, in regard to these things, there may be much which we cannot explain, and much which often troubles the heart even of the good; yet the passage before us is explicit on one point, and all these things *must* be held in consistency with that—that God does not place inducements before us *with a view* that we should sin, or *in order* to lead us into sin. None of his decrees, or his arrangements, or his desires, are based on that, but all have some other purpose and end. The real force of temptation is to be traced to some other source—to ourselves, and not to God. See the next verse.

14. *But every man is tempted, when he is drawn away of his own lust.* That is, the fountain or source of *all* temptation is in man himself. It is true that external inducements to sin may be placed before him, but they would have no force if there was not something in himself to which they corresponded, and over which they might have power. There must be some ' lust;' some desire; some inclination; something which is unsatisfied now, which is made the foundation of the temptation, and which gives it all its power. If there were no capacity for receiving food, or desire for it, objects placed before us appealing to the appetite could never be made a source of temptation; if there were nothing in the soul which could be regarded as the love of acquisition or possession, gold would furnish no temptation; if there were no sensual propensities, we should be in that quarter above the power of temptation. In each case, and in every form, the power of the temptation is laid in some propensity of our nature, some desire of that which we do not now possess. The word rendered ' *lust* ' in this place (ἐπι-θυμία), is not employed here in the

narrow sense in which it is now commonly used, as denoting libidinousness. It means *desire* in general; an earnest wish for any thing.   Notes, Eph. iv. 22 It seems here to be used with reference to the original propensities of our nature —the desires implanted in us, which are a stimulus to employment—as the desire of knowledge, of food, of power, of sensual gratifications; and the idea is, that a man may be *drawn along* by these *beyond* the prescribed limits of indulgence, and in the pursuit of objects that are forbidden. He does not stop at the point at which the law requires him to stop, and is therefore guilty of *transgression.* This is the source of all sin. The original propensity *may* not be wrong, but may be perfectly harmless—as in the case of the desire of food, &c. Nay, it may furnish a most desirable stimulus to action; for how could the human powers be called forth, if it were not for this? The error, the fault, the sin, is, not restraining the indulgence where we are *commanded* to do it, either in regard to the *objects* sought, or in regard to the *degree* of indulgence. ¶ *And enticed.* Entrapped, caught; that is, he is seized by this power, and held fast; or he is led along and beguiled, until he falls into sin, as in a snare that springs suddenly upon him.

[Ἐπιθυμία in the New Testament, is sometimes employed in a good sense, Luke xxii. 15; 1 Phil. i. 23; 1 Thess. ii. 17: often in a bad sense, as in Mark iv. 19; John viii. 44; Rom. i. 24; vi. 12; vii. 7; 1 John ii. 16; but there is no difficulty in making the distinction; the context easily determining the matter. And this passage in James seems at once to fix down on Ἐπιθυμία the sense of *evil* or *corrupt* desire. That it can mean a ' harmless propensity;' or that it is a propensity on whose *character* the apostle does not at all pronounce, is incredible. It is said to ' draw away a man and entice him;' to ' conceive and bring forth sin:' and a principle from which such fruit springs cannot be very *harmless*. Without doubt, the apostle traces the whole evil of temptation, which some falsely ascribed to God, to the *sinful* desires of the human heart; and, as our author remarks, he seems to take the common sense view without entertaining any thought of nice philosophical distinction. We cannot for a moment suppose the apostle to say

15 Then when lust hath [a] conceived, it bringeth forth sin: and

sin, when it is finished, bringeth
forth death.[b]

a Job 15.35.   b Ro.6.21-23.

—'the evil is not to be traced to God, but to a
harmless propensity.'

The whole passage, with *the words and figures
which are used,* show that the idea in the apostle's mind was that of an enticing harlot. The
επιθ. is personified. She persuades the understanding and will into her impure embrace.
The result of this fatal union is the 'conception' and ultimate 'bringing forth' of actual
sin, which again brings forth death. This is
the true genealogy of sin (M'Knight); and to
say that the *επιθ.*, or evil desire, of which the
apostle says that it is the *origo mali,* is harmless,
—is to contradict him, and Paul also, who in a
parallel passage says that he had not known the
επιθ., or inward desire after forbidden objects,
to be sinful, unless the law had enlightened him
and said 'thou shalt not covet.' Mr. Scott has
spoken in strong terms of the folly of some
parties who understand *επιθ.* here only of the
desire of sensual gross indulgence, to the exclu-
sion of other sinful desires; but the extreme of
interpreting it as meaning nothing sinful at all,
deserves equal reprehension. The reader, however, will notice that the author does not venture
on this assertion. He says "it *may* be so," and
otherwise modifies his view.]

15. *Then when lust hath conceived.*
Comp. Job xv. 35. The allusion here
is obvious. The meaning is, when the
desire which we have naturally is
quickened, or made to act, the result is
that sin is produced. As our desires
of good lie in the mind by nature, as
our propensities exist as they were created, they cannot be regarded as sin,
or treated as such; but when they are
indulged, when plans of gratification are
formed, when they are developed in
actual life, the effect is sin. In the mere
desire of good, of happiness, of food, of
raiment, there is no sin ; it becomes sin
when indulged in an improper manner,
and when it leads us to seek that which
is forbidden—to invade the rights of
others, or in any way to violate the laws
of God. The Rabbins have a metaphor
which strongly expresses the general
sense of this passage :—" Evil concupis-
cence is at the beginning like the thread
of a spider's web; afterwards it is like a
cart rope." *Sanhedrin,* fol. 99. ¶ *It
bringeth forth sin.* The result is sin—
open, actual sin. When that which is
conceived in the heart is matured, it is

seen to be sin. The *design* of all this
is to show that sin is not to be traced to
God, but to man himself ; and in order
to this, the apostle says that there is
enough in the heart of man to account
for all actual sin, without supposing
that it is caused by God. The solution
which he gives is, that there are certain
propensities in man which, when they
are suffered to act themselves out, will
account for all the sin in the world. In
regard to those native propensities themselves, he does not *say* whether he regards them as sinful and blameworthy
or not; and the probability is, that he
did not design to enter into a formal
examination, or to make a formal statement, of the nature of these propensities themselves. He looked at man as
he is—as a creature of God—as endowed with certain animal propensities
—as seen, in fact, to have strong passions
by nature ; and he showed that there
was enough in him to account for the
existence of sin, without bringing in the
agency of God, or charging it on him.
In reference to those propensities, it
may be observed that there are two
kinds, either of which may account for
the existence of sin, but which are frequently both combined. There are,
first, our natural propensities ; those
which we have as men, as endowed with
an animal nature, as having constitutional desires to be gratified, and wants
to be supplied. Such Adam had in in-
nocence ; such the Saviour had ; and
such are to be regarded as in no respect
in themselves sinful and wrong. Yet
they may, in our case, as they did in
Adam, lead us to sin, because, under
their strong influence, we may be led to
desire that which is forbidden, or which
belongs to another. But there are,
secondly, the propensities and inclinations which we have as the result of the
fall, and which are evil in their nature
and tendency; which as a matter of
course, and especially when combined
with the former, lead to open transg es-
sion. It is not always easy to separate
these, and in fact they are often com-

16 Do not err, my beloved brethren.

17 Every ^a good gift and every

perfect gift is from above, and cometh down from the Father of

<hr>

a Jno.3.27. 1 Co.4.7.

<hr>

bined in producing the actual guilt of the world. It often requires a close analysis of a man's own mind to detect these different ingredients in his conduct, and the one often gets the credit of the other. The apostle James seems to have looked at it as a simple matter of fact, with a common sense view, by saying that there were *desires* (ἐπιθυμίας) in a man's own mind which would *account* for all the actual sin in the world, without charging it on God. Of the truth of this, no one can entertain a doubt. —[See Supplementary Note above on v. 14.] ¶ *And sin, when it is finished, bringeth forth death.* The result of sin, when it is fully carried out, is death—death in all forms. The idea is, that death, in whatever form it exists, is to be traced to sin, and that sin will naturally and regularly produce it. There is a strong similarity between this declaration and that of the apostle Paul (Rom. vi. 21–23) ; and it is probable that James had that passage in his eye. See the sentiment illustrated in the Notes on that passage, and on Romans v. 12. Any one who indulges in a sinful thought or corrupt desire, should reflect that it *may* end in death—death temporal and eternal. Its natural tendency will be to produce such a death. *This* reflection should induce us to check an evil thought or desire at the beginning. Not for one moment should we indulge in it, for soon it may secure the mastery and be beyond our control ; and the end may be seen in the grave, and the awful world of woe.

16. *Do not err, my beloved brethren.* This is said as if there were great danger of error in the point under consideration. The *point* on which he would guard them, seems to have been in respect to the opinion that God was the author of sin, and that the evils in the world are to be traced to him. There was great danger that they would embrace that opinion, for experience has shown that it is a danger into which men are always prone to fall. Some of the sources of this danger have been already alluded to. Notes on ver. 13.

To meet the danger he says that, so far is it from being true that God is the source of evil, he is in fact the author of all that is good : every *good* gift, and every *perfect* gift (ver. 17), is from him, ver. 18

17. *Every good gift and every perfect gift.* The difference between *good* and *perfect* here, it is not easy to mark accurately. It may be that the former means that which is *benevolent* in its character and tendency ; the latter that which is *entire*, where there is nothing even apparently wanting to complete it ; where it can be regarded as good as a whole and in all its parts. The general sense is, that God is the author of all good. Every thing that is good on the earth we are to trace to him ; evil has another origin. Comp. Matt. xiii. 28. ¶ *Is from above.* From God, who is often represented as dwelling above—in heaven. ¶ *And cometh down from the Father of lights.* From God, the source and fountain of all light. Light, in the Scriptures, is the emblem of knowledge, purity, happiness; and God is often represented as *light*. Comp. 1 John i. 5. Notes 1 Tim. vi. 16. There is, doubtless, an allusion here to the heavenly bodies, among which the sun is the most brilliant. It appears to us to be the great original fountain of light, diffusing its radiance over all worlds. No cloud, no darkness seems to come from the sun, but it pours its rich effulgence on the farthest part of the universe. So it is with God. There is no darkness in him (1 John i. 5); and all the moral light and purity which there is in the universe is to be traced to him. The word *Father* here is used in a sense which is common in Hebrew (Comp. Notes Matt. i. 1) as denoting that which is the source of any thing, or that from which any thing proceeds. Comp. Notes on Isa. ix. 6. ¶ *With whom is no variableness, neither shadow of turning.* The design here is clearly to contrast God with the sun in a certain respect. As the source of light, there is a strong resemblance. But in the sun there are certain changes. It does not shine on all parts of the earth at the same time,

lights, with whom *a* is no variableness, neither shadow of turning.

a 1 Sa.15.29. Mal.3.6.   b Jno.1.13.
c Je.2.3. Ep.1.12. Re.14.4.

18 Of *b* his own will begat he us with the word of truth, that we should be a kind of first-fruits *c* of his creatures.

nor in the same manner all the year. It rises and sets; it crosses the line, and seems to go far to the south, and sends its rays obliquely on the earth; then it ascends to the north, recrosses the line, and sends its rays obliquely on southern regions. By its revolutions it produces the changes of the seasons, and makes a constant variety on the earth in the productions of different climes. In this respect God is *not* indeed like the sun. With him there is *no* variableness, not even the appearance of turning. He is always the same, at all seasons of the year, and in all ages; there is no change in his character, his mode of being, his purposes and plans. What he was millions of ages before the worlds were made, he is now; what he is now, he will be countless millions of ages hence. We may be sure that whatever changes there may be in human affairs; whatever reverses we may undergo; whatever oceans we may cross, or whatever mountains we may climb, or in whatever worlds we may hereafter take up our abode, *God* is the same.— The *word* which is here rendered *variableness* (παραλλαγή) occurs nowhere else in the New Testament. It means change, alteration, vicissitude, and would properly be applied to the changes observed in astronomy. See the examples quoted in Wetstein. The phrase rendered *shadow of turning* would properly refer to the different *shade* or *shadow* cast by the sun from an object, in its various revolutions, in rising and setting, and in its changes at the different seasons of the year. God, on the other hand, is as if the sun stood in the meridian at noon-day, and never cast *any* shadow.

18. *Of his own will*. Gr. *willing*. βουληθείς. The idea is, that the fact that we are 'begotten' to be his children is to be traced solely to his *will*. He purposed it, and it was done. The *antecedent* in the case on which all depended was the sovereign will of God. See this sentiment explained in the Notes on John i. 13. Comp. Notes on

Eph. i. 5. When it is said, however, that he has done this by his mere *will*, it is not to be inferred that there was no *reason* why it should be done, or that the exercise of his will was arbitrary, but only that his will determined the matter, and that is the cause of our conversion. It is not to be inferred that there are not in all cases good reasons why God wills as he does, though those reasons are not often stated to us, and perhaps we could not comprehend them if they were. The *object* of the statement here seems to be to direct the mind up to God as the source of *good* and not *evil;* and among the most eminent illustrations of his goodness is this, that by his mere *will*, without any external power to control him, and where there *could* be nothing but benevolence, he has adopted us into his family, and given us a most exalted condition, as renovated beings, among his creatures. ¶ *Begat he us.* The Greek word here is the same which in ver. 15 is rendered 'bringeth forth,'—'sin *bringeth forth* death.' The word is perhaps designedly used here in contrast with that, and the object is to refer to a different kind of production, or bringing forth, under the agency of *sin*, and the agency of *God.* The meaning here is, that we owe the beginning of our spiritual life to God. ¶ *With the word of truth.* By the instrumentality of *truth.* It was not a mere creative act, but it was by truth as the seed or germ. There is no effect produced in our minds in regeneration which the *truth* is not fitted to produce, and the agency of God in the case is to secure its fair and full influence on the soul. ¶ *That we should be a kind of first-fruits of his creatures.* Comp. Eph. i. 12. For the meaning of the word rendered *first-fruits*, see Note on Rom. viii. 23. Comp. Rom. xi. 6; xvi. 5; 1 Cor. xv. 20, 23; xvi. 15; Rev. xiv. 4. It does not elsewhere occur in the New Testament. It denotes, properly, that which is first taken from any thing; the portion which was usually offered to God. The phrase here does not primarily

19 Wherefore, my beloved bre-
a Ec.5.2.   b Pr.16.32.

thren, let every man be swift to hear,
slow *a* to speak, slow *b* to wrath :

denote eminence in honour or degree, but refers rather to *time*—the first in time ; and in a secondary sense it is then used to denote the honour attached to that circumstance. The meaning here is, either (1) that, under the gospel, those who were addressed by the apostles had the honour of being first called into his kingdom as a part of that glorious harvest which it was designed to gather in this world, and that the *goodness* of God was manifested in thus furnishing the first-fruits of a most glorious harvest ; or (2) the reference may be to the rank and dignity which all who are born again would have among the creatures of God in virtue of the new birth.

19. *Wherefore, my beloved brethren.* The connection is this : 'since God is the only source of good ; since he tempts no man ; and since by his mere sovereign goodness, without any claim on our part, we have had the high honour conferred on us of being made the first-fruits of his creatures, we ought to be ready to hear his voice, to subdue all our evil passions, and to bring our souls to entire practical obedience.' The necessity of *obedience*, or the doctrine that the gospel is not only to be *learned* but *practised*, is pursued at length in this and the following chapter. The particular statement here (vs. 19-21) is, that religion requires us to be meek and docile ; to lay aside all irritability against the truth, and all pride of opinion, and all corruption of heart, and to receive meekly the ingrafted word. See the analysis of the chapter. ¶ *Let every man be swift to hear, slow to speak.* That is, primarily, to listen to the instructions of that *truth* by which we have been begotten, and brought into so near relation to him. At the same time, though this is the primary sense of the phrase here, it may be regarded as inculcating the *general* doctrine that we are to be more ready to hear than to speak ; or that we are to be disposed to *learn* always, and from any source. Our appropriate condition is rather that of *learners* than *instructors;* and the attitude of mind which we should cultivate is that of a readiness to receive information from

any quarter. The ancients have some sayings on this subject which are well worthy of our attention. ' Men have two ears, and but one tongue, that they should hear more than they speak.' ' The ears are always open, ever ready to receive instruction ; but the tongue is surrounded with a double row of teeth, to hedge it in, and to keep it within proper bounds.' See *Benson.* So Valerius Maximus, vii. 2. ' How noble was the response of Xenocrates! When he met the reproaches of others with a profound silence, some one asked him why he alone was silent ? Because, says he, I have sometimes had occasion to regret that I have spoken, *never that I was silent.*' See Wetstein. So the son of Sirach, ' Be swift to hear, and with deep consideration (ἐν μακροθυμίᾳ) give answer,' ch. v. 11. So the Rabbins have some similar sentiments. ' Talk little and work much.' Pirkey Aboth. c. i. 15. ' The righteous speak little and do much ; the wicked speak much and do nothing.' Bava Metsia, fol. 87. A sentiment similar to that before us is found in Ecclesiastes v. 2. ' Be not rash with thy mouth, and let not thine heart be hasty to utter any thing before God.' So Prov. x. 19. ' In the multitude of words there wanteth not sin.' xiii. 3. ' He that keepeth his mouth keepeth his life.' xv. 2. ' The tongue of the wise useth knowledge aright, but the mouth of fools poureth out foolishness.' ¶ *Slow to wrath.* That is, we are to govern and restrain our temper ; we are not to give indulgence to excited and angry passions. Comp. Prov. xvi. 32, ' He that is slow to anger is greater than the mighty ; and he that ruleth his spirit than he that taketh a city.' See also on this subject, Job v. 2 ; Prov. xxxvii. 8 ; xi. 17 ; xiii. 10 ; xiv. 16 ; xv. 18 ; xix. 19 ; xxii. 24 ; xxv. 28 ; Eccl. vii. 9 ; Rom. xii. 17 ; 1 Thess. v. 14 ; 1 Pet. iii. 8. The particular point here is, however, not that we should be slow to wrath as a general habit of mind, which is indeed most true, but in reference particularly *to the reception of the truth.* We should lay aside all anger and wrath, and should

20 For the wrath of man worketh not the righteousness of God.

21 Wherefore lay apart *a* all filthiness and superfluity of naughtiness,

and receive with meekness the engrafted word, which is able to save your souls.

a Col.3.5-8. He.12.1. 1 Pe.2.1,2.

come to the investigation of truth with a calm mind, and an imperturbed spirit. A state of wrath or anger is always unfavourable to the investigation of truth. Such an investigation demands a calm spirit, and he whose mind is excited and enraged is not in a condition to see the value of truth, or to weigh the evidence for it.

20. *For the wrath of man worketh not the righteousness of God.* Does not produce in the life that righteousness which God requires. Its tendency is not to incline us to keep the law, but to break it; not to induce us to embrace the truth, but the opposite. The meaning of this passage is not that our wrath will make God either more or less righteous; but that its tendency is not to produce that upright course of life, and love of truth, which God requires. A man is never sure of doing right under the influence of excited feelings; he *may* do that which is in the highest sense wrong, and which he will regret all his life. The particular meaning of this passage is, that wrath in the mind of man will not have any tendency to make him righteous. It is only that candid state of mind which will lead him to embrace the truth which can be hoped to have such an effect.

21. *Wherefore.* In view of the fact that God has begotten us for his own service; in view of the fact that excited feeling tends only to wrong, let us lay aside *all* that is evil, and submit ourselves wholly to the influence of truth. ¶ *Lay apart all filthiness.* The word here rendered *filthiness*, occurs nowhere else in the New Testament. It means properly *filth;* and then is applied to evil conduct considered as *disgusting* or *offensive.* Sin may be contemplated as a *wrong* thing; as a violation of law; as evil in its nature and tendency, and *therefore* to be avoided; or it may be contemplated as *disgusting, offensive, loathsome.* To a pure mind, this is one of its most odious characteristics; for, to such a mind, sin in any form is more

loathsome than the most offensive object can be to any of the senses. ¶ *And superfluity of naughtiness.* Literally, 'abounding of evil.' It is rendered by Doddridge, 'overflowing of malignity;' by Tindal, 'superfluity of maliciousness;' by Benson, 'superfluity of malice;' by Bloomfield, 'petulance.' The phrase '*superfluity* of naughtiness,' or of evil, does not exactly express the sense, as if we were only to lay aside that which *abounded*, or which is *superfluous*, though we might retain that which does not come under this description; but the object of the apostle is to express his deep abhorrence of the thing referred to by strong and emphatic language. He had just spoken of sin in one aspect, as *filthy, loathsome, detestable;* here he designs to express his abhorrence of it by a still more emphatic description, and he speaks of it not merely as an *evil*, but as an evil *abounding, overflowing;* an evil in the highest degree. The thing referred to had the essence of *evil* in it (*κακία*); but it was not merely *evil*, it was evil that was aggravated, that was overflowing, that was eminent in degree (*περισσία*). The particular reference in these passages is to the reception of the truth; and the doctrine taught is, that a *corrupt* mind, a mind full of sensuality and wickedness, is not favourable to the reception of the truth. It is not fitted to see its beauty, to appreciate its value, to understand its just claims, or to welcome it to the soul. Purity of heart is the best preparation always for seeing the force of truth. ¶ *And receive with meekness.* That is, open the mind and heart to instruction, and to the fair influence of truth. Meekness, gentleness, docility, are everywhere required in receiving the instructions of religion, as they are in obtaining knowledge of any kind. See Notes on Matt. xviii. 2, 3. ¶ *The engrafted word.* The gospel is here represented under the image of that which is implanted or engrafted from another source; by a figure

22. But be ye doers *a* of the word, and not hearers only, deceiving your own selves.

23 For if any be a hearer of the word, and not a doer, he is like

a Mat.7.21.

unto a man beholding his natural face in a glass :

24 For he beholdeth himself, and goeth his way, and straightway forgetteth what manner of man he was.

---

that would be readily understood, for the art of *engrafting* is everywhere known. Sometimes the gospel is represented under the image of seed sown (Comp. Mark vi. 14, seq.); but here it is under the figure of *a shoot* implanted or engrafted, that produces fruit of its own, whatever may be the original character of the tree into which it is engrafted. Comp. Notes on Rom. xi. 17. The meaning here is, that we should allow the principles of the gospel to be thus *engrafted* on our nature; that however crabbed or perverse our nature may be, or however bitter and vile the fruits which it might bring forth of its own accord, it might, through the engrafted word, produce the fruits of righteousness. ¶ *Which is able to save your souls.* It is not, therefore, a weak and powerless thing, merely designed to show its own feebleness, and to give occasion for God to work *a miracle;* but it has *power,* and is *adapted* to save. Comp. Notes on Rom. i. 16; 1 Cor. i. 18; 2 Tim. iii. 15.

22. *But be ye doers of the word, and not hearers only.* Obey the gospel, and do not merely listen to it. Comp. Matt. vii. 21. ¶ *Deceiving your own selves.* It is implied here, that by merely *hearing* the word but not *doing* it, they would deceive their own souls. The nature of this deception was this, that they would imagine that that was all which was required, whereas the main thing was that they should be obedient. If a man supposes that by a mere punctual attendance on preaching, or a respectful attention to it, he has done all that is required of him, he is labouring under a most gross self-deception. And yet there are multitudes who seem to imagine that they have done all that is demanded of them when they have heard attentively the word preached. Of its influence on their lives, and its claims to obedience, they are utterly regardless.

23, 24. *For if any be,* &c. The ground of the comparison in these verses is obvious. The apostle refers to what all persons experience, the fact that we do not retain a distinct impression of ourselves after we have looked in a mirror. While actually looking in the mirror, we see all our features, and can trace them distinctly; when we turn away, the image and the impression both vanish. When looking in the mirror, we can see all the defects and blemishes of our person ; if there is a scar, a deformity, a feature of ugliness, it is distinctly before the mind ; but when we turn away, that is 'out of sight and out of mind.' When unseen it gives no uneasiness, and, even if capable of correction, we take no pains to remove it. So when we hear the word of God. It is like a mirror held up before us. In the perfect precepts of the law, and the perfect requirements of the gospel, we see our own short-comings and defects, and perhaps think that we will correct them. But we turn away immediately, and forget it all. If, however, we were ' *doers* of the word,' we should endeavour to remove all those defects and blemishes in our moral character, and to bring our whole souls into conformity with what the law and the gospel require. The phrase ' natural face,' (Gr. face of birth), means, the face or appearance which we have in virtue of our natural birth. The word *glass* here means *mirror.* Glass was not commonly used for mirrors among the ancients, but they were made of polished plates of metal. See Notes on Isa. iii. 24, and Job xxxvii. 18.

24. *For he beholdeth himself.* While he looks in the mirror he sees his true appearance. ¶ *And goeth his way, and straightway forgetteth.* As soon as he goes away, he forgets it. The apostle does not refer to any *intention* on his part, but to what is known to occur as a matter of fact. ¶ *What manner of*

25 But whoso looketh ^a into the perfect law of liberty, ^b and continueth *therein*, he being not a forgetful hearer, but a doer of the

a 2 Co.3.18.

work, this man ^c shall be blessed in his ¹ deed.

26 If any man among you seem to be religious, and bridleth not his

b Ps.119.45.   c Lu.6.47,&c.   1 Or, *doing.*

man he was. How he looked; and especially if there was any thing in his appearance that required correction.

25. *But whoso looketh* (παρακύψας). This word means, to stoop down near by any thing; to bend forward near, so as to look at any thing more closely. See the word explained in the Notes on 1 Pet. i. 12. The idea here is that of a close and attentive observation. The object is not to contrast the *manner* of looking in the glass, and in the law of liberty, implying that the former was a '*careless* beholding,' and the latter an attentive and careful looking, as Doddridge, Rosenmüller, Bloomfield, and others suppose; for the word used in the former case (κατενόησε) implies intense or accurate observation, as really as the word used here; but the object is to show that if a man would attentively look into, and *continue* in the law of liberty, and not do as one who went away and forgot how he looked, he would be blessed. The emphasis is not in the manner of *looking,* it is on the duty of *continuing* or persevering in the observance of the law. ¶ *The perfect law of liberty.* Referring to the law of God, or his will, however made known, as the correct standard of conduct. It is called the *perfect* law, as being wholly free from all defects; being just such as a law *ought* to be. Comp. Ps. xix. 7. It is called *the law of liberty,* or freedom, because it is a law producing freedom from the servitude of sinful passions and lusts. Comp. Ps. cxix. 45; Notes on Rom. vi. 16–18. ¶ *And continueth therein.* He must not merely *look* at the law, or see what he *is* by comparing himself with its requirements, but he must yield steady obedience to it. See Notes on John xiv. 21. ¶ *This man shall be blessed in his deed.* Marg. *doing.* The meaning is, that he shall be blessed in the very act of keeping the law. It will produce peace of conscience; it will impart happiness of a high order to his mind; it will exert a good influence over

his whole soul. Ps. xix. 11. 'In keeping of them there is great reward.'

26. *If any man among you seem to be religious.* Pious, or devout. That is, if he does not restrain his tongue, his other evidences of religion are worthless. A man may undoubtedly have many things in his character which *seem* to be evidences of the existence of religion in his heart, and yet there may be some one thing that shall show that all those evidences are false. Religion is designed to produce an effect on our whole conduct; and if there is any one thing in reference to which it does not bring us under its control, that one thing may show that *all* other appearances of piety are worthless. ¶ *And bridleth not his tongue.* Restrains or curbs it not, as a horse is restrained with a bridle. There may have been some reason why the apostle referred to this particular sin which is now unknown to us; or he may perhaps have intended to select this as a *specimen* to illustrate this idea, that if there is any one evil propensity which religion does not control, or if there is any one thing in respect to which its influence is not felt, whatever other evidences of piety there may be, this will demonstrate that all those appearances of religion are vain. For religion is designed to bring the whole man under control, and to subdue every faculty of the body and mind to its demands. If the tongue is not restrained, or if there is *any* unsubdued propensity to sin whatever, it proves that there is no true religion. ¶ *But deceiveth his own heart.* Implying that he *does* deceive his heart by supposing that any evidence can prove that he is under the influence of religion if his tongue is unrestrained. Whatever love, or zeal, or orthodoxy, he may have, this one evil propensity will neutralize it all, and show that there is no true religion at heart. ¶ *This man's religion* is *vain.* As all religion must be which does not control all the faculties of the

tongue, *a*but deceiveth his own heart, this man's religion *is* vain.

27 Pure religion, and undefiled before God and the Father, is this,

To visit *b* the fatherless and widows in their affliction, *and* to keep himself unspotted *c* from the world.

Ps.34.13. *b* Is.1.16,17; 58.6,7. *c* Ro.12.2.

---

body and the mind. The truths, then, which are taught in this verse are, (1.) That there may be evidences of piety which seem to be very plausible or clear, but which in themselves do not prove that there is any true religion. There may be much zeal, as in the case of the Pharisees; there may be much apparent love of Christians, or much outward benevolence; there may be an uncommon gift in prayer; there may be much self-denial, as among those who withdraw from the world in monasteries or nunneries; or there may have been deep conviction for sin, and much joy at the time of the supposed conversion, and still there be no true religion. Each and all of these things may exist in the heart where there is no true religion. (2.) A single unsubdued sinful propensity neutralizes all these things, and shows that there is no true religion. If the tongue is not subdued; if *any* sin is indulged, it will show that the *seat* of the evil has not been reached, and that the soul, *as such*, has never been brought into subjection to the law of God. For the very *essence* of all the sin that there was in the soul may have been concentrated on that one propensity. Every thing else which may be manifested may be accounted for on the supposition that there is no religion; this cannot be accounted for on the supposition that there is any.

27. *Pure religion.* On the word here rendered *religion* (θρησκεία), see Notes on Col. ii. 18. It is used here evidently in the sense of *piety*, or as we commonly employ the word *religion*. The object of the apostle is to describe what enters essentially into religion; what it will do when it is properly and fairly developed. The phrase 'pure religion' means that which is genuine and sincere, or which is free from any improper mixture. ¶ *And undefiled before God and the Father.* That which God sees to be pure and undefiled. Rosenmüller supposes that there is a metaphor here taken from pearls or gems, which should

be pure, or without stain. ¶ *Is this.* That is, this enters into it; or this *is* religion such as God approves. The apostle does not say that this is *the whole* of religion, or that there is nothing else essential to it; but his general design clearly is, to show that religion will lead to a holy life, and he mentions this as a specimen, or an instance of what it will lead us to do. The *things* which he specifies here are in fact two: (1.) That pure religion will lead to a life of practical benevolence; and (2.) That it will keep us unspotted from the world. If these things are found, they show that there is true piety. If they are not, there is none. ¶ *To visit the fatherless and widows in their affliction.* To go to see, to look after, to be ready to aid them. This is an instance or specimen of what true religion will do, showing that it will lead to a life of practical benevolence. It may be remarked in respect to this, (1.) That this has always been regarded as an essential thing in true religion; for (*a*) it is thus an imitation of God, who is 'a father of the fatherless, and a judge of the widows in his holy habitation,' (Ps. lxviii. 5); and who has always revealed himself as their friend, Deut. x. 18; xiv. 29; Ps. x. 14; lxxxii. 3; Isa. i. 17; Jer. vii. 7; xlix. 11; Hos. xiv. 3; (*b*) religion is represented as leading its friends to do this, or this is required everywhere of those who claim to be religious, Isa. i. 17; Deut. xxiv. 17; xiv. 29; Ex. xxii. 22; Job xxix. 11–13. (2.) Where this disposition to be the real friend of the widow and the orphan exists, there will also exist other corresponding things which go to make up the religious character. This will not stand alone. It will show what the heart is, and prove that it will ever be ready to do good. If a man, from proper motives, is the real friend of the widow and the fatherless, he will be the friend of every good word and work, and we may rely on him in any and every way in doing

CHAPTER II.

MY brethren, have not the faith of our Lord Jesus Christ, *the*

good. ¶ And *to keep himself unspotted from the world.* Comp. Notes Rom. xii. 2; James iv. 4; 1 John ii. 15–17. That is, religion will keep us from the maxims, vices, and corruptions which prevail in the world, and make us holy. These two things may, in fact, be said to constitute religion. If a man is truly benevolent, he bears the image of that God who is the fountain of benevolence; if he is pure and uncontaminated in his walk and deportment, he also resembles his Maker, for he is holy. If he has *not* these things, he cannot have any well-founded evidence that he is a Christian; for it is always the nature and tendency of religion to produce these things. It is, therefore, an easy matter for a man to determine whether he has any religion; and equally easy to see that religion is eminently desirable. Who can doubt that that is good which leads to compassion for the poor and the helpless, and which makes the heart and the life pure?

CHAPTER II.

ANALYSIS OF THE CHAPTER.

This chapter is evidently made up of three parts, or three subjects are discussed:—

I. The duty of impartiality in the treatment of others, vs. 1–9. There was to be no favouritism on account of rank, birth, wealth, or apparel. The *case* to which the apostle refers for an illustration of this, is that where two persons should come into an assembly of Christian worshippers, one elegantly dressed, and the other meanly clad, and they should show special favour to the former, and should assign to the latter a more humble place. The *reasons* which the apostle assigns why they should not do this are, (*a*) that God has chosen the poor for his own people, having selected *his* friends mainly from them; (*b*) because rich men in fact oppressed them, and showed that they were worthy of no special regard; (*c*) because they were often found among revilers, and in fact despised their reli-

Lord of glory, with respect *a* of persons.

2 For if there come unto your

α Pr.28.21; Jude 16.

gion; and (*d*) because the law required that they should love their neighbours as themselves, and if they did this, it was all that was demanded; that is, that the love of the *man* was not to be set aside by the love of splendid apparel.

II. The duty of yielding obedience to the *whole* law in order to have evidence of true religion, vs. 10–13. This subject seems to have been introduced in accordance with the general principles and aims of James (see the Intro.) that religion consists in obeying the law of God, and that there can be none when this is not done. It is not improbable that, among those to whom he wrote, there were some who denied this, or who had embraced some views of religion which led them to doubt it. He therefore enforces the duty by the following considerations: (1.) That if a man should obey every part of the law, and yet be guilty of offending in one point, he was in fact guilty of all; for he showed that he had no genuine principle of obedience, and was guilty of violating the law as a whole, ver. 10. (2.) Every part of the law rests on the same authority, and one part, therefore, is as binding as another. The same God that has forbidden murder, has also forbidden adultery; and he who does the one as really violates the law as he who does the other, ver. 11. (3.) The judgment is before us, and we shall be tried on impartial principles, not with reference to obeying one part of the law, but with reference to its whole claim; and we should so act as becomes those who expect to be judged by the whole law, or on the question whether we have conformed to every part of it, vs. 12, 13.

III. The subject of justification, showing that *works* are necessary in order that a man may be justified, or esteemed righteous before God, vs. 14–26. For a general view of the design of this part of the epistle, see Intro., § 5. The object here is to show that *in fact* no one can be regarded as truly righteous before God who does not lead

¹ assembly a man with a gold ring, | in goodly apparel; and there come

1 *synagogue.*

in also a poor man in vile raiment;

---

an upright life; and that if a man professes to have faith, and has not works, he cannot be justified; or that if he have *real* faith, it will be shown by his works. If it is *not* shown by works corresponding to its nature, it will be certain that there is *no* true religion, or that his professed faith is worth nothing. The 'stand-point' from which James views the subject, is not that faith is unnecessary or worthless, or that a man is not justified by faith rather than by his own works, in the sense of its being the ground of acceptance with God; or, in other words, the place where the apostle takes his position, and which is the point from which he views the subject, is not *before* a man is justified, to inquire in what way he *may be* accepted of God, but it is *after* the act of justification by faith, to show that if faith does not lead to good works it is 'dead,' or is of no value; and that in fact, therefore, the evidence of justification is to be found in good living, and that when this is not manifest, all a man's professed religion is worth nothing. In doing this, he (*a*) makes the general statement, by a pointed interrogatory, that faith cannot *profit*, that is, cannot *save* a man, unless there be also works, ver. 14. He then (*b*) appeals, for an illustration, to the case of one who is hungry or naked, and asks what mere *faith* could do in his case, if it were not accompanied with proper acts of benevolence, vs. 15–17. He then, (*c*) by a strong supposable case, says that real faith will be evinced *by* works, or that works are the proper evidence of its existence, ver. 18. He then (*d*) shows that there is a kind of faith which even the devils have on one of the most important doctrines of religion, and which can be of no value; showing that it cannot be by *mere* faith, irrespective of the question of what sort the faith is, that a man is to be saved, ver. 19. He then (*e*) appeals to the case of Abraham, showing that *in fact* works performed an important part in his acceptance with God; or that if it had not been for his works—that is, if there had been

no spirit of true obedience in his case, he could have had no evidence that he was justified, or that his works were the proper *carrying out* or *fulfilment* of his faith, vs. 20–24. He then (*f*) shows that the same thing was true of another case recorded in the Old Testament—that of Rahab (ver. 25); and then observes (ver. 26) that faith without works would have no more claim to being true religion than a dead body, without a soul, would be regarded as a living man.

1. *My brethren.* Perhaps meaning brethren in two respects—as Jews, and as Christians. In both respects the form of address would be proper. ¶ *Have not the faith of our Lord Jesus Christ.* *Faith* is the distinguishing thing in the Christian religion, for it is this by which man is justified, and hence it comes to be put for religion itself. Notes on 1 Tim. iii. 9. The meaning here is, 'do not hold such views of the religion of Christ, as to lead you to manifest partiality to others on account of their difference of rank or outward circumstances.' ¶ The Lord *of glory.* The glorious Lord; he who is glorious himself, and who is encompassed with glory. See Notes on 1 Cor. ii. 8. The *design* here seems to be to show that the religion of such a Lord should be in no way dishonoured. ¶ *With respect of persons.* That is, you are not to show respect of persons, or to evince partiality to others on account of their rank, wealth, apparel, &c. Comp. Prov. xxiv. 23; xxviii. 21; Lev. xix. 15; Deut. i. 17; x. 17; 2 Chron. xix. 7; Ps. xl. 4. See the subject explained in the Notes on Acts x. 34; Rom. ii. 11.

2. *For if there come into your assembly.* Marg., as in Gr., *synagogue.* It is remarkable that this is the only place in the New Testament where the word *synagogue* is applied to the Christian church. It is probably employed here because the apostle was writing to those who had been Jews; and it is to be presumed that the word *synagogue* would be naturally used by the early converts from Judaism to designate a Christian place of worship, or a Chris-

3 And ye have respect to him that weareth the gay clothing, and say unto him, Sit thou here [1] in a

1 or, *well;* or, *seemly.*

good place; and say to the poor, Stand thou there, or sit here under my footstool:

tian congregation, and it was probably so employed until it was superseded by a word which the Gentile converts would be more likely to employ, and which would, in fact, be better and more expressive—the word *church.* The word *synagogue* (συναγωγην) would properly refer to the whole congregation, considered *as assembled together,* without respect to the question whether all were truly pious or not; the word *church* (ἐκκλησία) would refer to the assembly convened for worship as *called out,* referring to the fact that they were called out from the world, and convened as worshippers of God, and would, therefore, be more applicable to a body of spiritual worshippers. It is probable that the Christian church was modelled, in its general arrangements, after the Jewish synagogue; but there would be obviously some disadvantages in retaining the name, as applicable to Christian worship. It would be difficult to avoid the associations connected with the *name,* and hence it was better to adopt some other name which would be free from this disadvantage, and on which might be engrafted all the ideas which it was necessary to connect with the notion of the Christian organization. Hence the word *church,* liable to no such objection as that of synagogue, was soon adopted, and ultimately prevailed, though the passage before us shows that the word *synagogue* would be in some places, and for a time, employed to designate a Christian congregation. We should express the idea here by saying, 'If a man of this description should come *into the church.*' ¶ *A man with a gold ring.* Indicative of rank or property. Rings were common ornaments of the rich; and probably then, as now, of those who desired to be *esteemed* to be rich. For proof that they were commonly worn, see the quotations in Wetstein, *in loc.* ¶ *In goodly apparel.* Rich and splendid dress. Comp. Luke xvi. 19. ¶ *A poor man in vile raiment.* The Greek here is, *filthy, foul;* the

meaning of the passage is, in sordid, shabby clothes. The reference here seems to be, not to those who commonly attended on public worship, or who were members of the church, but to those who might accidentally drop in to witness the services of Christians. See 1 Cor. xiv. 24.

3. *And ye have respect to him that weareth the gay clothing.* If you show him superior attention on account of his rich and gay apparel, giving him a seat by himself, and treating others with neglect or contempt. Religion does not forbid proper respect to rank, to office, to age, or to distinguished talents and services, though even in such cases it does not require that we should feel that such persons have any peculiar claims to salvation, or that they are not on a level with all others, as sinners before God; it does not forbid that a man who has the means of procuring for himself an eligible pew in a church should be permitted to do so; but it requires that men shall be regarded and treated according to their moral worth, and not according to their external adorning; that all shall be considered as in fact on a level before God, and entitled to the privileges which grow out of the worship of the Creator. A stranger coming into any place of worship, no matter what his rank, dress, or complexion, should be treated with respect, and every thing should be done that can be to win his heart to the service of God. ¶ *And say unto him, Sit thou here in a good place.* Marg., as in Gr., *well* or *seemly;* that is, in an honourable place near the pulpit; or in some elevated place where he would be conspicuous. The meaning is, you treat him with distinguished marks of respect on the first appearance, merely from the indications that he is a rich man, without knowing any thing about his character. ¶ *And say to the poor, Stand thou there.* Without even the civility of offering him a seat at all. This may be presumed not *often* to occur

4 Are ye not then partial in yourselves, and are become judges of
evil thoughts?

5 Hearken, my beloved brethren,
a Hath not God chosen the poor of
this world, rich *b* in faith, and heirs

of ¹ the kingdom *c* which he hath
promised to them that love him?

6 But ye have despised the poor.
Do not rich men oppress you, and

a 1 Co.1.26-28. *b* Re.2.9. 1 or, *that.* *c* Mat.5.3.
Lu.12.32; 22.29.

in a Christian church; yet it practically does sometimes, when no disposition is evinced to furnish a stranger
with a seat. ¶ *Or sit here under my
footstool.* Perhaps some seats in the
places of worship were raised, so that
even the footstool would be elevated
above a lower seat. The meaning is,
that he would be treated as if he were
not worth the least attention.

4. *Are ye not then partial in yourselves?* Among yourselves. Do you not
show that you are partial? ¶ *And are
become judges of evil thoughts.* There
has been considerable difference of
opinion respecting this passage, yet the
sense seems not to be difficult. There are
two ideas in it: one is, that they showed
by this conduct that they took it upon
themselves to be *judges,* to pronounce
on the character of men who were
strangers, and on their claims to respect
(Comp. Matt. vii. 1); the other is, that
in doing this, they were not guided by
just rules, but that they did it under
the influence of improper 'thoughts.'
They did it not from benevolence; not
from a desire to do justice to all according to their moral character; but from
that improper feeling which leads us to
show honour to men on account of their
external appearance, rather than their
real worth. The *wrong* in the case was
in their presuming to 'judge' these
strangers at all, as they practically did
by making this distinction, and then by
doing it under the influence of such an
unjust rule of judgment. The sense is,
that we have no right to form a decisive
judgment of men on their first appearance, as we do when we treat one with
respect and the other not; and that
when we make up our opinion in regard
to them, it should be by some other
means of judging than the question
whether they can wear gold rings, and
dress well, or not. Beza and Doddridge
render this, 'ye become judges who reason ill.'

5. *Hearken, my beloved brethren.* The
apostle now proceeds to show that the
rich, as such, had no special claim on
their favour, and that the poor in fact
might be made more entitled to esteem
than they were. For a view of the
arguments by which he does this, compare the analysis of the chapter. ¶ *Hath
not God chosen the poor of this world?*
Those who are poor so far as this world
is concerned, or those who have not
wealth. This is the first argument
which the apostle suggests why the
poor should not be treated with neglect.
It is, that God has had special reference
to them in choosing those who should
be his children. The meaning is not
that he is not as *willing* to save the rich
as the poor, for he has no partiality;
but that there are circumstances in the
condition of the poor which make it
more likely that they will embrace the
offers of the gospel than the rich; and
that in fact the great mass of believers
is taken from those who are in comparatively humble life. Comp. Notes on
1 Cor. i. 26-28. The fact that God
has chosen one to be an 'heir of the
kingdom' is as good a reason now why
he should not be treated with neglect,
as it was in the times of the apostles.
¶ *Rich in faith.* Though poor in this
world's goods, they are rich in a higher
and more important sense. They have
faith in God their Saviour; and in this
world of trial and of sin, that is a more
valuable possession than piles of hoarded
silver or gold. A man who has that is
sure that he will have all that is truly
needful for him in this world and the
next; a man who has it not, though he
may have the wealth of Crœsus, will be
utterly without resources in respect to
the great wants of his existence.

"Give what thou wilt, without thee we are poor;
And with thee rich, take what thou wilt away."

Faith in God the Saviour will answer
more purposes, and accomplish more
valuable ends for man, than the wealth

draw you before the judgment-seats?

7 Do they not blaspheme that ^a worthy name by the which ye are called?

8 If ye fulfil the royal law, according to the Scripture, ^b Thou shalt love thy neighbour as thyself, ye do well :

a Ps.111.9.   b Le.19.18.

of the Indies could: and this the poor may have as well as the rich. Comp. Rev. ii. 9. ¶ *And heirs of the kingdom*, &c. Marg. *that*. Comp. Notes on Matt. v. 3.

6. *But ye have despised the poor.* Koppe reads this as an interrogation: 'Do ye despise the poor?' Perhaps it might be understood somewhat ironically : ' You despise the poor, do you, and are disposed to honour the rich ! Look then, and see how the rich treat you, and see whether you have so much occasion to regard them with any peculiar respect.' The *object* of the apostle is to fix the attention on the impropriety of that partiality which many were disposed to show to the rich, by reminding them that the rich had never evinced towards them any such treatment as to lay the foundation of a claim to the honour which they were disposed to render them. ¶ *Do not rich men oppress you ?* Referring probably to something in their conduct which existed particularly then. The meaning is not that they oppressed the poor as such, but that they oppressed those whom James addressed. It is probable that then, as since, a considerable portion of those who were Christians were in fact poor, and that this would have all the force of a personal appeal ; but still the particular thought is, that it was a characteristic of the rich and the great, whom they were disposed peculiarly to honour, to oppress and crush the poor. The Greek here is very expressive : ' Do they not imperiously lord it over you?' The statement here will apply with too much force to the rich in every age. ¶ *And draw you before the judgment-seats.* That is, they are your persecutors rather than your friends. It was undoubtedly the case that many of the rich were engaged in persecuting Christians, and that on various pretences they dragged them before the judicial tribunals.

7. *Do they not blaspheme that worthy*

name ? This is another argument to show that the rich had no special claim to the honour which they were disposed to show them. The ' worthy name ' here referred to is, doubtless, the name of the Saviour. The thing here affirmed would, of course, accompany persecution. They who persecuted Christians, would revile the name which they bore. This has always occurred. But besides this, it is no improbable supposition that many of those who were *not* disposed to engage in open persecution, would revile the name of Christ, by speaking contemptuously of him and his religion. This has been sufficiently common in every age of the world, to make the description here not improper. And yet nothing has been more remarkable than the very thing adverted to here by James, that notwithstanding this, many who profess to be Christians have been more disposed to treat even such persons with respect and attention than they have their own brethren, if they were poor ; that they have cultivated the favour, sought the friendship, desired the smiles, aped the manners, and coveted the society of such persons, rather than the friendship and the favour of their poorer Christian brethren. Even though they are known to despise religion in their hearts, and not to be sparing of their words of reproach and scorn towards Christianity ; though they are known to be blasphemers, and to have the most thorough contempt for serious, spiritual religion, yet there is many a professing Christian who would prefer to be at a party given by such persons than at a prayer-meeting where their poorer brethren are assembled ; who would rather be known by the world to be the associates and friends of such persons, than of those humble believers who can make no boast of rank or wealth, and who are looked down upon with contempt by the great and the gay.

8. *If ye fulfil the royal law.* That is, the law which he immediately men-

9 But if ye have respect *a* to persons, ye commit sin, and are convinced of the law as transgressors.

a ver. 1.

10 For whosoever shall keep the whole law, and yet offend in one point, he *b* is guilty of all.

b De.27.26.

tions requiring us to love our neighbour as ourselves. It is called a 'royal law,' or *kingly* law, on account of its excellence or nobleness; not because it is ordained by God *as a king*, but because it has some such prominence and importance among other laws as a king has among other men; that is, it is majestic, noble, worthy of veneration. It is a law which ought to govern and direct us in all our intercourse with men —as a king rules his subjects. ¶ *According to the Scripture, Thou shalt love thy neighbour as thyself.* Lev. xix. 18. Comp. Matt xix. 19. See it explained by the Saviour, in the parable of the good Samaritan, Luke x. 25–37. In regard to its meaning, see Notes on Matt. xix. 19. ¶ *Ye do well.* That is, 'if you fairly comply with the spirit of this law, you do all that is required of you in regulating your intercourse with others. You are to regard all persons as your "neighbours," and are to treat them according to their real worth; you are not to be influenced in judging of them, or in your treatment of them, by their apparel, or their complexion, or the circumstances of their birth, but by the fact that they are fellow-beings.' This is another reason why they should not show partiality in their treatment of others, for if, in the true sense, they regarded all others as 'neighbours,' they would treat no one with neglect or contempt.

9. *But if ye have respect to persons, ye commit sin.* You transgress the plain law of God, and do wrong. See the references on ver. 1. ¶ *And are convinced of the law as transgressors.* Gr. '*By* the law.' The word *convinced* is now used in a somewhat different sense from what it was formerly. It now commonly refers to the impression made on a man's mind by showing him the truth of a thing which before was doubted, or in respect to which the evidence was not clear. A man who doubted the truth of a report or a proposition may be *convinced* or *satisfied*

of its truth; a man who has done wrong, though he supposed he was doing what was proper, may be *convinced* of his error. So a man may be *convinced* that he is a sinner, though before he had no belief of it, and no concern about it; and this may produce in his mind the feeling which is technically known as *conviction*, producing deep distress and anguish. See Notes on John xvi. 8. Here, however, the word does not refer so much to the effect produced on the mind itself, as to the fact that the law would hold such an one to be guilty; that is, the law pronounces what is done to be wrong. Whether they would be personally *convinced* of it, and troubled about it as convicted sinners, would be a different question, and one to which the apostle does not refer; for his object is not to show that they would be *troubled* about it, but to show that the law of God condemned this course, and would hold them to be guilty. The *argument* here is not from the *personal distress* which this course would produce in their own minds, but from the fact that the law of God *condemned* it.

10. *For whosoever shall keep the whole law.* All except the single point referred to. The apostle does not say that this in fact ever *did* occur, but he says that if it *should*, and yet a man should have failed in only one particular, he must be judged to be guilty. The case supposed seems to be that of one who *claimed* that he had kept the whole law. The apostle says that even if this should be admitted for the time to be true in all other respects, yet, if he had failed in any *one* particular—in showing respect to persons, or in anything else— he could not but be held to be a transgressor. The design of this is to show the importance of yielding *universal* obedience, and to impress upon the mind a sense of the enormity of sin from the fact that the violation of any one precept is in fact an offence against the whole law of God. The *whole law* here means all the law of God; all that he has re-

11 For ¹ he that said, ᵃ Do not commit adultery, said also, Do not kill. Now if thou commit no adul-tery, yet if thou kill, thou art be-come a transgressor of the law.

quired; all that he has given to regulate us in our lives. ¶ *And yet offend in one point.* In one respect ; or shall violate any one of the commands included in the general word *law.* The word *offend* here means, properly, to stumble, to fall ; then to err, or fail in duty. See Notes on Matt. v. 29; xxvi. 31. ¶ *He is guilty of all.* He is guilty of violating the law as a whole, or of violating the law of God as such ; he has rendered it impossible that he should be justified and saved *by* the law. This does not affirm that he is *as* guilty as if he had violated *every* law of God ; or that all sinners are of equal grade because all have violated some one or more of the laws of God ; but the meaning is, that he is guilty of violating the law of God *as such;* he shows that he has not the true spirit of obedience ; he has exposed himself to the penalty of the law, and made it impossible now to be saved *by* it. His acts of obedience in other respects, no matter how many, will not screen him from the charge of being a violator of the law, or from its penalty. He must be held and treated as a transgressor for *that* offence, however upright he may be in other respects, and must meet the penalty of the law as certainly as though he had violated every commandment. One portion of the law is as much binding as another, and if a man violates any one plain commandment, he sets at nought the authority of God. This is a simple principle which is everywhere recognised, and the apostle means no more by it than occurs every day. A man who has stolen a horse is held to be a violator of the law, no matter in how many other respects he has kept it, and the law condemns him for it. He cannot plead his obedience to the law in other things as a reason why he should not be punished for this sin; but however upright he may have been in general, even though it may have been through a long life, the law holds him to be a transgressor, and condemns him. He is as *really* condemned, and as much thrown from the protection of law, as though he had violated every command. So of murder, arson, treason, or any other crime. The law judges a man for what he has done *in this specific case,* and he cannot plead in justification of it that he has been obedient in other things. It follows, therefore, that if a man has been guilty of violating the law of God in any one instance, or is not perfectly holy, he cannot be justified and saved by it, though he should have obeyed it in every other respect, any more than a man who has been guilty of murder can be saved from the gallows *because* he has, in other respects, been a good citizen, a kind father, an honest neighbour, or has been compassionate to the poor and the needy. He cannot plead his act of truth in one case as an offset to the sin of falsehood in another; he cannot defend himself from the charge of dishonesty in one instance by the plea that he has been honest in another; he cannot urge the fact that he has done a good thing as a reason why he should not be punished for a bad one. He must answer for the specific charge against him, and none of these other things can be an *offset* against this one act of wrong. Let it be re-marked, also, in respect to our being justified by obedience to the law, that no man can plead before God that he has kept all his law *except* in one point. Who is there that has not, in spirit at least, broken each one of the ten com-mandments? The sentiment here ex-pressed by James was not new with him. It was often expressed by the Jewish writers, and seems to have been an ad-mitted principle among the Jews. See Wetstein, *in loc.*, for examples.

11. *For he that said, Do not commit adultery, said also, Do not kill.* That is, these are parts of the same law of God, and one is as obligatory as the other. If, therefore, you violate either of these precepts, you transgress the law of God *as such*, and must be held to be guilty of violating it as a whole. The penalty of the law will be incurred, what-ever precept you violate.

12 So speak ye, and so do, as they that shall be judged by the law *a* of liberty.

13 For he *b* shall have judgment without mercy, that hath showed no mercy, and mercy [1] rejoiceth *c* against judgment.

a James 1.25.   b Pr.21.13. Mat.6.15; 7.1,2.
1 Or, *glorieth.*   c Ps.85.10.

12. *So speak ye, and so do, as they that shall be judged by the law of liberty.* On the phrase, 'the law of liberty,' see Notes on ch. i. 25. Comp. Notes on ch. iv. 11. The meaning is, that in all our conduct we are to act under the constant impression of the truth that we are soon to be brought into judgment, and that the law by which we are to be judged is that by which it is contemplated that we shall be set free from the dominion of sin. In the rule which God has laid down in his word, called ' the law of liberty,' or the rule by which true *freedom* is to be secured, a system of religion is revealed by which it is designed that man shall be emancipated not only from *one* sin, but from *all.* Now, it is with reference to such a law that we are to be judged; that is, we shall not be able to plead on our trial that we were under a necessity of sinning, but we shall be judged under that law by which the arrangement was made that we might be free from sin. If we might be free from sin; if an arrangement was made by which we could have led holy lives, then it will be proper that we shall be judged and condemned if we are not righteous. The sense is, ' In all your conduct, whatever you do or say, remember that you *are to be judged,* or that you are to give an impartial account; and remember also that the *rule* by which you are to be judged is that by which provision is made for being delivered from the dominion of sin, and brought into the freedom of the gospel.' The argument here seems to be, that he who habitually feels that he is soon to be judged by a law under which it was contemplated that he *might* be, and *should* be, free from the bondage of sin, has one of the strongest of all inducements to lead a holy life.

13. *For he shall have judgment without mercy, that hath showed no mercy.* This is obviously an equitable principle, and is one which is everywhere found in the Bible. Prov. xxi. 13. ' Whoso stoppeth his ears at the cry of the poor, he also shall cry himself, but will not be heard.' 2 Sam. xxii. 26, 27, ' With the merciful thou wilt show thyself merciful, and with the froward thou wilt show thyself unsavoury.' Comp. Ps. xviii. 25, 26 ; Matt. vi. 15; vii. 1, 2. The idea which the apostle seems to design to convey here is, that there will certainly be a judgment, and that we must expect that it will be conducted on equitable principles ; that no mercy is to be shown when the character is not such that it will be proper that it should be; and that we should habitually feel in our conduct that God will be impartial, and should frame our lives accordingly. ¶ *And mercy rejoiceth against judgment.* Marg. *glorieth.* Gr. Boasts, glories, or exults. The idea is that of glorying over, as where one is superior to another, or has gained a victory over another. The reference all along here is to the judgment, the trial of the great day; and the apostle is stating the principles on which the trial at that day will be conducted—on which one class shall be condemned, and the other acquitted and saved. In reference to one class, the wicked, he says that where there has been no mercy shown to others—referring to this as *one* evidence of piety—that is, where there is no true piety, there will be judgment without mercy; in the other case there will be, as it were, a *triumph* of mercy, or mercy will appear to have gained a victory over judgment. Strict justice would indeed plead for their condemnation, but the attribute of mercy will triumph, and they will be acquitted. The attributes of mercy and justice would seem to come in conflict, but mercy would prevail. This is a true statement of the plan of salvation, and of what actually occurs in the redemption of a sinner. Justice *demands,* as what is her due, that the sinner should be condemned; mercy *pleads* that he may be saved—and mercy prevails. It is not uncommon that there

14 What *a doth it* profit, my brethren, though a man say he hath faith, and have not **works?** **Can** faith save him?

a Mat.7.26.

---

seems to be a conflict between the two. In the dispensations of justice before human tribunals, this often occurs. Strict justice *demands* the punishment of the offender ; and yet there are cases when mercy pleads, and when every man feels that it would be desirable that pardon should be extended to the guilty, and when we always rejoice if mercy triumphs. In such a case, for example, as that of Major André, this is strikingly seen. On the one hand, there was the undoubted proof that he was guilty; that he had been taken as a spy ; that by the laws of war he ought to be put to death ; that as what he had done had tended to the ruin of the American cause, and as such an act, if unpunished, would always expose an army to surprise and destruction, he ought, in accordance with the law of nations, to die. On the other hand, there were his youth, his high attainments, his honourable connections, his brilliant hopes, all pleading that he might live, and that he might be pardoned. In the bosom of Washington, the promptings of justice and mercy thus came into collision. Both could not be gratified, and there seemed to be but one course to be pursued. His sense of justice was shown in the act by which he signed the death-warrant ; his feelings of compassion in the fact that when he did it his eyes poured forth a flood of tears. How every generous feeling of our nature would have been gratified if mercy could have triumphed, and the youthful and accomplished officer could have been spared ! In the plan of salvation, this does occur. Respect is done to justice, but mercy triumphs. Justice indeed pleaded for the condemnation of the sinner, but mercy interposed, and he is saved. Justice is not disregarded, for the great Redeemer of mankind has done all that is needful to uphold it ; but there is the most free and full exercise of mercy, and, while the justice of God is maintained, every benevolent feeling in the breasts of all holy beings can be gratified in the salvation of countless thousands.

14. *What* doth it *profit, my brethren, though a man say he hath faith?* The apostle here returns to the subject adverted to in ch. i. 22–27, the importance of a practical attention to the duties of religion, and the assurance that men cannot be saved by a mere speculative opinion, or merely by holding correct sentiments. He doubtless had in his eye those who abused the doctrine of justification by faith, by holding that good works are unnecessary to salvation, provided they maintain an orthodox belief. As this abuse probably existed in the time of the apostles, and as the Holy Ghost saw that there would be danger that in later times the great and glorious doctrine of justification by faith would be thus abused, it was important that the error should be rebuked, and that the doctrine should be distinctly laid down that good works *are* necessary to salvation. The apostle, therefore, i⸳ the question before us, implicitly asserts that faith would not ' profit' at all unless accompanied with a holy life, and this doctrine he proceeds to illustrate in the following verses. See the analysis of this chapter ; and Intro. § 5, (2). In order to a proper interpretation of this passage, it should be observed that the *stand-point* from which the apostle views this subject is not *before* a man is converted, inquiring in what way he *may* be justified before God, or on what ground his sins may be forgiven; but it is *after* a man is converted, showing that that faith can have no value which is not followed by good works ; that is, that it is not *real* faith, and that good works are necessary if a man would have evidence that he is justified. Thus understood, all that James says is in entire accordance with what is taught elsewhere in the New Testament. ¶ *Can faith save him?* It is implied in this question that faith *cannot* save him, for very often the most emphatic way of making an affirmation is by asking a question. The meaning here is, that that faith which does *not* produce good works, or which would not produce

15 If a brother or sister be naked, and destitute of daily food,

16 And one of you say unto them, Depart in peace, be *ye* warmed and filled; notwithstanding ye give them not those things which are needful to the body; what *a doth it* profit?

17 Even so faith, if it hath not works, is dead, being ¹ alone.

a 1 Jno.3.18.   ¹ *by itself.*

holy living if fairly acted out, will save no man, for it is not genuine faith.

15, 16, 17. *If a brother or sister be naked,* &c. The comparison in these verses is very obvious and striking. The sense is, that faith in itself, without the acts that correspond to it, and to which it would prompt, is as cold, and heartless, and unmeaning, and useless, as it would be to say to one who was destitute of the necessaries of life, ' depart in peace.' In itself considered, it might seem to have something that was good; but it would answer none of the purposes of faith unless it should prompt to action. In the case of one who was hungry or naked, what he wanted was not good wishes or kind words merely, but the *acts* to which good wishes and kind words prompt. And so in religion, what is wanted is not merely the abstract state of mind which would be indicated by faith, but the life of goodness to which it ought to lead. Good wishes and kind words, in order to make them what they should be for the welfare of the world, should be accompanied with corresponding action. So it is with faith. It is not enough for salvation without the benevolent and holy acts to which it would prompt, any more than the good wishes and kind words of the benevolent are enough to satisfy the wants of the hungry, and to clothe the naked, without correspondent action. Faith is not and cannot be shown to be genuine, unless it is accompanied with corresponding acts; as our good wishes for the poor and needy can be shown to be genuine, when we have the means of aiding them, only by actually ministering to their necessities. In the one case, our wishes would be shown to be unmeaning and heartless; in the other, our faith would be equally so. In regard to this passage, therefore, it may be observed, (1), that in fact faith is of no more value, and has no more evidence of genuineness when it is unaccompanied with good works, than such empty wishes for the welfare of the poor would be when unaccompanied with the means of relieving their wants. Faith is designed to lead to good works. It is intended to produce a holy life; a life of activity in the service of the Saviour. This is its very essence; it is what it always produces when it is genuine. Religion is not designed to be a cold abstraction; it is to be a living and vivifying principle. (2) There is a great deal of that kindness and charity in the world which is expressed by mere good wishes. If we really have not the means of relieving the poor and the needy, then the expression of a kind wish may be in itself an alleviation to their sorrows, for even sympathy in such a case is of value, and it is much to us to know that others *feel* for us; but if we *have* the means, and the object is a worthy one, then such expressions are mere mockery, and aggravate rather than soothe the feelings of the sufferer. Such wishes will neither clothe nor feed them; and they will only make deeper the sorrows which we ought to heal. But how much of this is there in the world, when the sufferer cannot but feel that all these wishes, however kindly expressed, are hollow and false, and when he cannot but feel that relief would be easy! (3) In like manner there is much of this same kind of worthless *faith* in the world—faith that is dead; faith that produces no good works; faith that exerts no practical influence whatever on the life. The individual professes indeed to believe the truths of the gospel; he may be in the church of Christ; he would esteem it a gross calumny to be spoken of as an infidel; but as to any influence which his faith exerts over him, his life would be the same if he had never heard of the gospel. There is not one of the truths of religion which is bodied forth in his life; not a deed to which he is prompted by religion; not an act which could not be accounted for on the supposition that

18 Yea, a man may say, Thou hast faith, and I have works: show me thy faith ¹without thy works, and I ᵃ will show thee my faith by my works.

1 some copies read, *by*.　　　ᵃ James 3.13.

he has no true piety. In such a case, faith may with propriety be said to be dead. ¶ *Being alone.* Marg., *by itself.* The sense is, ' being by itself;' that is, destitute of any accompanying fruits or results, it shows that it is dead. That which is alive bodies itself forth, produces effects, makes itself visible; that which is dead produces no effect, and is as if it were not.

18. *Yea, a man may say,* &c. The word which is rendered '*yea*' (ἀλλὰ) would be better rendered by *but.* The apostle designs to introduce an objection, not to make an affirmation. The sense is, ' some one might say,' or, ' to this it might be urged in reply.' That is, it might perhaps be said that religion is not always manifested in the same way, or we should not suppose that, because it is not always exhibited in the same form, it does not exist. One man may manifest it in one way, and another in another, and still both have true piety. One may be distinguished for his faith, and another for his works, and both may have real religion. This objection would certainly have some plausibility, and it was important to meet it. It would *seem* that all religion was not to be manifested in the same way, as all virtue is not; and that it *might* occur that one man might be particularly eminent for one form of religion, and another for another; as one man may be distinguished for zeal, and another for meekness, and another for integrity, and another for truth, and another for his gifts in prayer, and another for his large-hearted benevolence. To this the apostle replies, that the two things referred to, faith and works, were not independent things, which could exist separately, without the one materially influencing another— as, for example, charity and chastity, zeal and meekness; but that the one was the *germ* or *source* of the other, and that the existence of the one was to be known only by its developing itself in the form of the other. A man could not show that he possessed the one un-

less it developed itself in the form of the other. In proof of this, he could boldly appeal to any one to show a case where faith existed without works. He was himself willing to submit to this just trial in regard to this point, and to demonstrate the existence of his own faith *by* his works. ¶ *Thou hast faith, and I have works.* You have one form or manifestation of religion in an eminent or prominent degree, and I have another. You are characterized particularly for one of the virtues of religion, and I am for another; as one man may be particularly eminent for meekness, and another for zeal, and another for benevolence, and each be a virtuous man. The expression here is equivalent to saying, ' One may have faith, and another works.' ¶ *Show me thy faith without thy works.* That is, you who maintain that faith is enough to prove the existence of religion; that a man may be justified and saved by that alone, or where it does not develope itself in holy living; or that all that is necessary in order to be saved is merely *to believe.* Let the reality of any *such* faith as that be shown, if it can be; let *any* real faith be shown to exist *without* a life of good works, and the point will be settled. *I,* says the apostle, will undertake to exhibit the evidence of *my* faith in a different way—in a way about which there can be no doubt, and which is the *appropriate* method. It is clear, if the common reading here is correct, that the apostle meant to *deny* that true faith could be evinced without appropriate works. It should be said, however, that there is a difference of reading here of considerable importance. Many manuscripts and printed editions of the New Testament, instead of *without* [works—χωρίς], read *from* or *by* (ἐκ), as in the other part of the verse, ' show me thy faith by thy works, and I will show thee my faith by my works.' This reading is found in Walton, Wetstein, Mill; and in the received text generally; the other [*without*] is found in many MSS., and in the Vulgate, Syriac,

19 Thou believest that there is one God; thou doest well: the devils *a* also believe, and tremble.

a Mar.1.24; 5.7

Coptic, English, and Armenian versions; and is adopted by Beza, Castalio, Grotius, Bengel, Hammond, Whitby, Drusius, Griesbach, Tittman, and Hahn, and is now commonly received as the correct reading. It may be added that this reading seems to be demanded by the similar reading in ver. 20, 'But wilt thou know that faith *without works* (χωρὶς τῶν ἔργων) is dead,' evidently implying that something had been said before about 'faith *without* works.' This reading also is so natural, and makes so good sense in the connection, that it would seem to be demanded. Doddridge felt the difficulty in the other reading, and has given a version of the passage which showed his great perplexity, and which is one of the most unhappy that he ever made. ¶ *And I will show thee my faith by my works.* I will furnish in this way the best and most certain proof of the existence of faith. It is implied here that true faith is adapted to lead to a holy life, and that such a life would be the appropriate evidence of the existence of faith. By their fruits the principles held by men are known. See Notes on Matt. vii. 16.

19. *Thou believest that there is one God.* One of the great and cardinal doctrines of religion is here selected as an illustration of all. The design of the apostle seems to have been to select one of the doctrines of religion, the belief of which would—if mere belief in *any* doctrine could—save the soul; and to show that even *this* might be held as an article of faith by those who could be supposed by no one to have any claim to the name of Christian. He selects, therefore, the great fundamental doctrine of all religion,—the doctrine of the existence of one Supreme Being,—and shows that if even this were held in such a way as it might be, and as it was held by devils, it could not save men. The apostle here is not to be supposed to be addressing such an one as *Paul*, who held to the doctrine that we are justified by faith; nor is he to be supposed to be *combating* the doctrine of Paul, as some have maintained, (see the

Intro.); but he is to be regarded as addressing one who held, in the broadest and most unqualified sense, that provided there was *faith*, a man would be saved. To this he replies, that even the devils might have faith of a certain sort, and faith that would produce sensible effects on them of a certain kind, and still it could not be supposed that they had true religion, or that they would be saved. Why might not the same thing occur in regard to man? ¶ *Thou doest well.* So far as this is concerned, or so far as it goes. It is a doctrine which *ought* to be held, for it is one of the great fundamental truths of religion. ¶ *The devils.* The *demons*,—(τὰ δαιμόνια.) There is, properly, but *one* being spoken of in the New Testament as *the devil*—ὁ διάβολος, and ὁ Σατᾶν—though *demons* are frequently spoken of in the plural number. They are represented as evil spirits, subject to Satan, or under his control, and engaged with him in carrying out his plans of wickedness. These spirits or demons were supposed to wander in desert and desolate places, (Math. xii. 43), or to dwell in the atmosphere, (Notes, Eph. ii. 2); they were thought to have the power of working miracles, but not for good, (Rev. xvi. 14; comp. John x. 21); to be hostile to mankind, (John viii. 44); to utter the heathen oracles, (Acts xvi. 17); to lurk in the idols of the heathen, (1 Cor. x. 20); and to take up their abodes in the bodies of men, afflicting them with various kinds of diseases, Matt. vii. 22; ix. 34; x. 8; xvii. 18; Mark vii. 29, 30; Luke iv. 33; viii. 27, 30, *et sæpe*. It is of *these* evil spirits that the apostle speaks when he says that they believe. ¶ *Also believe.* That is, particularly, they believe in the existence of the one God. How far their knowledge may extend respecting God, we cannot know; but they are never represented in the Scriptures as denying his existence, or as doubting the great truths of religion. They are never described as *atheists*. That is a sin of this world only   They are not represented as *sceptics*. That, too, is a peculiar sin of the earth; and

20 But wilt thou know, O vain man, that faith without works is dead?

21 Was not Abraham our father justified by works, when ᵃhe had offered Isaac his son upon the altar?

a Ge.22.9,12.

probably, in all the universe besides, there are no beings but those who dwell on this globe, who doubt or deny the existence of God, or the other great truths of religion. ¶ *And tremble.* The word here used (φρίσσω) occurs nowhere else in the New Testament. It means, properly, to be rough, uneven, jaggy, sc., with bristling hair; to bristle, to stand on end, as the hair does in a fright; and then to shudder or quake with fear, &c. Here the meaning is, that there was much more in the case referred to than mere speculative faith. There was a faith that produced *some* effect, and an effect of a very decided character. It did not, indeed, produce good works, or a holy life, but it made it manifest that there *was faith;* and, consequently, it followed that the existence of mere faith was not all that was necessary to save men, or to make it certain that they would be secure, unless it were held that the devils would be justified and saved by it. If they might hold such faith, and still *remain* in perdition, men might hold it, and *go* to perdition. A man should not infer, therefore, because he has faith, even that faith in God which will fill him with alarm, that therefore he is safe. He must have a faith which will produce another effect altogether—that which will lead to a holy life.

20. *But wilt thou know.* Will you have a full demonstration of it will you have the clearest proof in the case. The apostle evidently felt that the instances to which he was about to refer, those of Abraham and Rahab, were decisive. ¶ *O vain man.* The reference by this language is to a man who held an opinion that could not be defended. The word *vain* here used (κενός) means properly *empty,* as opposed to *full*—as empty hands, having nothing in them; then fruitless, or without utility or success; then false, fallacious. The meaning here, properly, would be ' empty,' in the sense of being void of understanding; and this would be a mild and gen-

tle way of saying of one that he was *foolish,* or that he maintained an argument that was *without sense.* James means, doubtless, to represent it as a perfectly plain matter, a matter about which no man of sense could have any reasonable doubt. If we *must* call a man *foolish,* as is sometimes necessary, let us use as mild and inoffensive a term as possible—a term which, while it will convey our meaning, will not unnecessarily wound and irritate. ¶ *That faith without works is dead.* That the faith which does not produce good works is useless in the matter of salvation. He does not mean to say that it would produce *no* effect, for in the case of the demons it *did* produce trembling and alarm; but that it would be valueless in the matter of salvation. The faith of Abraham and of Rahab was entirely different from this.

21. *Was not Abraham our father.* Our progenitor, our ancestor; using the word *father,* as frequently occurs in the Bible, to denote a remote ancestor. Comp. Notes on Matt. i. 1. A reference to his case would have great weight with those who were Jews by birth, and probably most of those to whom this epistle was addressed were of this character. See the Intro. ¶ *Justified by works.* That is, in the sense in which James is maintaining that a man professing religion is to be justified by his works. He does not affirm that the ground of acceptance with God is that we keep the law, or are perfect; or that our good works make an atonement for our sins, and that it is on their account that we are pardoned; nor does he deny that it is necessary that a man should *believe* in order to be saved. In this sense he does not deny that men are justified by faith; and thus he does not contradict the doctrine of the apostle Paul. But he *does* teach that where there are no good works, or where there is not a holy life, there is no true religion; that that faith which is not productive of good works is of no value;

22 ¹ Seest thou how faith ᵃ
1 Or, *Thou seest.*   a He.11.17.

wrought with his works, and by works was faith made perfect?

that if a man has that faith only, it would be impossible that he could be regarded as justified, or could be saved; and that consequently, in that large sense, a man is justified by his works; that is, they are the evidence that he is a justified man, or is regarded and treated as righteous by his Maker. The point on which the apostle has his eye is the nature of saving faith; and his design is to show that a mere faith which would produce no more effect than that of the demons did, could not save. In this he states no doctrine which contradicts that of Paul. The *evidence* to which he appeals in regard to faith, is good works and a holy life; and where that exists it shows that the faith is genuine. The case of Abraham is one directly in point. He showed that he had that kind of faith which was *not* dead. He gave the most affecting evidence that his faith was of such a kind as to lead him to implicit obedience, and to painful sacrifices. Such an act as that referred to—the act of offering up his son—demonstrated, if any thing could, that his faith was genuine, and that his religion was deep and pure. In the sight of heaven and earth it would *justify* him as a righteous man, or would *prove* that he was a righteous man. In regard to the strength of his faith, and the nature of his obedience in this sacrifice, see Notes on Heb. xi. 19. That the apostle here cannot refer to the act of justification as the term is commonly understood, referring by that to the moment when he was accepted of God as a righteous man, is clear from the fact that in a passage of the Scriptures which he himself quotes, that is declared to be consequent on his *believing:* 'Abraham believed God, and it was imputed unto him for righteousness.' The act here referred to occurred long *subsequent* to that, and was thus a fulfilment or confirmation of the declaration of Scripture, which says that 'he *believed* God.' It showed that his faith was not merely speculative, but was an active principle, leading to holy living. See Notes on ver. 23. This demonstrates that what the apostle refers to here is

the evidence by which it is shown that a man's faith is genuine, and that he does not refer to the question whether the act of justification, where a sinner is converted, is solely in consequence of believing. Thus the case proves what James purposes to prove, that the faith which justifies is only that which leads to good works. ¶ *When he had offered Isaac his son upon the altar.* This was long after he believed, and was an act which, if any could, would show that his faith was genuine and sincere. On the meaning of this passage, see Notes on Heb. xi. 17.

22. *Seest thou.* Marg. *Thou seest.* Either rendering is correct, and the sense is the same. The apostle means to say that this was so plain that they could not but see it. ¶ *How faith wrought with his works.* συνήργει. Co-operated with. The meaning of the word is, *to work together with any one; to co operate,* (1 Cor. xvi. 16; 2 Cor. vi. 1); then to aid, or help, (Mark xvi. 20); to contribute to the production of any result, where two or more persons or agents are united. Comp. Rom. viii. 28. The idea here is, that the result in the case of Abraham, that is, his salvation, or his religion, was secured, not by *one* of these things alone, but that *both* contributed to it. The result which *was* reached, to wit, his acceptance with God, could *not* have been obtained by either one of them separately, but both, in some sense, entered into it. The apostle does not say that, in regard to the *merit* which justifies, they came in for an equal share, for he makes no affirmation on that point; he does not deny that in the sight of God, who foresees and knows all things, he was regarded as a justified man the moment he believed, but he looks at the result *as it was,* at Abraham as he appeared under the trial of his faith, and says that *in* that result there was to be seen the co-operation of faith *and* good works Both contributed to the end, as they do now in all cases where there is true religion.

[By the somewhat unhappy term 'merit,' the author clearly means nothing more than 'prin-

23 And the Scripture was ful-
filled which saith, ^aAbraham believed God, and it was imputed

unto him for righteousness : and
he was called ^bthe friend of God.
24 Ye see then how that by works

a Ge.15.6.

b 2 Ch.20 7. Is.41.8.

ciple,' as is obvious from his acute and evange-
lical comment on the verse; as well as from the
admirable reconciliation of Paul and James
below.]

¶ *And by works was faith made perfect.* Made *complete, finished,* or *entire.*
It was so *carried out* as to show its legitimate and fair results. This does not
mean that the faith in itself was defective
before this, and that the defect was *re-
medied* by good works ; or that there is
any deficiency in what the right kind of
faith can do in the matter of justification, which is to be *helped out* by good
works; but that there was that kind of
completion which a thing has when it is
fully developed, or is fairly carried out.
23. *And the Scripture was fulfilled
which saith.* That is, the fair and full
meaning of the language of Scripture
was expressed by this act, showing in
the highest sense that his faith was
genuine; or the declaration that he truly
believed, was *confirmed* or *established*
by this act. His faith was shown to be
genuine ; and the fair meaning of the
declaration that he *believed* God was
carried out in the subsequent act. The
passage here referred to occurs in Gen.
xv. 6. That which it is said Abraham
believed, or in which he believed God,
was this : ' This shall not be thine heir
(viz. Eliezer of Damascus), but he that
shall come forth out of thine own bowels,
shall be thine heir.' And again, ' Look
now toward heaven, and tell the stars,
if thou be able to number them. And
he said unto him, So shall thy seed be,'
vs. 3–5. The act of confiding in these
promises, was that act of which it is
said that ' he believed in the Lord ; and
he counted it to him for righteousness.'
The act of offering his son on the altar,
by which James says this Scripture was
fulfilled, occurred some twenty years
afterwards. That act confirmed or fulfilled the declaration. It showed that
his faith was genuine, and that the
declaration that he believed in God was
true; for what could do more to confirm
that, than a readiness to offer his own
son at the command of God? It cannot

be supposed that James meant to say
that Abraham was justified by *works*
without respect to faith, or to deny that
the primary ground of his justification
in the sight of God was *faith,* for the
very passage which he quotes shows that
faith was the primary consideration :
'Abraham *believed* God, and *it* was imputed,' &c. The meaning, therefore,
can only be, that this declaration received its fair and full expression when
Abraham, by an act of obedience of the
most striking character, long after he
first exercised that faith by which he
was accepted of God, showed that his
faith was genuine. If he had not thus
obeyed, his faith would have been inoperative and of no value. As it was,
his act showed that the declaration of
the Scripture that, he '*believed*' was
well founded. ¶ *Abraham believed God,
and it was imputed,* &c. See this passage fully explained in the Notes on
Rom. iv. 3. ¶ *And he was called the
friend of God.* In virtue of his strong
faith and obedience. See 2 Chron. xx. 7:
'Art not thou our God, who didst drive
out the inhabitants of this land before
thy people Israel, and gavest it to the
seed of Abraham *thy friend* for ever ?'
Isa. xli. 8. ' But thou, Israel, art my
servant, Jacob whom I have chosen, the
seed of Abraham *my friend.*' This was
a most honourable appellation ; but it is
one which, in all cases, will result from
true faith and obedience.
24. *Ye see then.* From the course
of reasoning pursued, and the example
referred to. ¶ *How that by works a
man is justified, and not by faith only.*
Not by a cold, abstract, inoperative faith.
It must be by a faith that shall *produce*
good works, and whose existence will
be shown to men by good works. As
justification takes place in the sight of
God, it is by faith, for he sees that the
faith is genuine, and that it will produce good works if the individual who
exercises faith shall live; and he justifies men in view of *that* faith, and of
no other. If he sees that the faith is
merely speculative; that it is cold and

a a man is justified, and not by faith only.

25 Likewise also was not Rahab *b* the harlot *c* justified by works, when she had received the messen-

a Re.20.12.   b Jos.2.1,&c. He.11.31.
          c Mat.21.31.

gers, and had sent *them* out another way?

26 For as the body without the ¹ spirit is dead, so faith without works is dead also.

1 Or, breath.

dead, and would *not* produce good works, the man is *not* justified in his sight. As a matter of fact, therefore, it is only the faith that produces good works that justifies; and good works, therefore, as the proper expression of the nature of faith, *foreseen* by God as the certain result of faith, and actually *performed* as seen by men, are necessary in order to justification. In other words, no man will be justified who has not a faith which will produce good works, and which is of an operative and practical character. The *ground* of justification in the case is faith, and that only; the *evidence* of it, the carrying it out, the proof of the existence of the faith, is good works; and thus men are justified and saved not by mere abstract and cold faith, but by a faith necessarily connected with good works, and where good works perform an important part. James, therefore, does not contradict Paul, but he contradicts a false explanation of Paul's doctrine. He does not deny that a man is justified in the sight of God by faith, for the very passage which he quotes shows that he believes that; but he *does* deny that a man is justified by a faith which would not produce good works, and which is not expressed by good works; and thus he maintains, as Paul always did, that nothing else than a holy life can show that a man is a true Christian, and is accepted of God.

25. *Likewise also was not Rahab the harlot justified by works?* In the same sense in which Abraham was, as explained above—showing by her act that her faith was genuine, and that it was not a mere cold and speculative assent to the truths of religion. Her act showed that she truly believed God. If that act had not been performed, the fact would have shown that her faith was not genuine, and she could not have been justified. God saw her faith as it was; he saw that it *would* produce acts

of obedience, and he accepted her as righteous. The act which she performed was the public manifestation of her faith, the evidence that she was justified. See the case of Rahab fully explained in the Notes on Heb. xi. 31. It may be observed here, that we are not to suppose that *everything* in the life and character of this woman is commended. She is commended for her *faith*, and for the fair expression of it; a faith which, as it induced her to receive the messengers of the true God, and to send them forth in peace, and as it led her to identify herself with the people of God, was also influential, we have every reason to suppose, in inducing her to abandon her former course of life. When we commend the faith of a man who has been a profane swearer, or an adulterer, or a robber, or a drunkard, we do not commend his former life, or give a sanction to it. We commend that which has induced him to abandon his evil course, and to turn to the ways of righteousness. The more evil his former course has been, the more wonderful, and the more worthy of commendation, is that faith by which he is reformed and saved.

26. *For as the body without the spirit is dead.* Marg. breath. The Greek word πνεῦμα is commonly used to denote *spirit* or *soul*, as referring to the intelligent nature. The meaning here is the obvious one, that the body is animated or kept alive by the presence of the soul, and that when that is withdrawn, hope departs. The body has no life independent of the presence of the soul. ¶ *So faith without works is dead also.* There is as much necessity that faith and works should be united to constitute true religion, as there is that the body and soul should be united to constitute a living man. If good works do not follow, it is clear that there is no true and proper faith; none that justifies and saves. If faith pro-

D

duces no fruit of good living, that fact proves that it is dead, that it has no power, and that it is of no value. This shows that James was not arguing against real and genuine faith, nor against its importance in justification, but against the supposition that mere faith was all that was necessary to save a man, whether it was accompanied by good works or not. *He* maintains that if there is genuine faith it will always be accompanied by good works, and that it is only *that* faith which can justify and save. If it leads to no practical holiness of life, it is like the body without the soul, and is of no value whatever. James and Paul both agree in the necessity of true faith in order to salvation; they both agree that the tendency of true faith is to produce a holy life; they both agree that where there is not a holy life there is no true religion, and that a man cannot be saved. We may learn, then, from the whole doctrine of the New-Testament on the subject, that unless we believe in the Lord Jesus we cannot be justified before God; and that unless our faith is of that kind which will produce holy living, it has no more of the characteristics of true religion than a dead body has of a living man.

Reconciliation of Paul and James.

At the close of the exposition of this chapter, it may be proper to make a few additional remarks on the question in what way the statements of James can be reconciled with those of Paul, on the subject of justification. A difficulty has always been felt to exist on the subject; and there are, perhaps, no readers of the New Testament who are not perplexed with it. Infidels, and particularly Voltaire, have seized the occasion which they supposed they found here to sneer against the Scriptures, and to pronounce them to be contradictory. Luther felt the difficulty to be so great that, in the early part of his career, he regarded it as insuperable, and denied the inspiration of James, though he afterwards changed his opinion, and believed that his epistle was a part of the inspired canon; and one of Luther's followers was so displeased with the statements of James, as to charge him with

wilful falsehood.—Dr. Dwight's Theology, Serm. lxviii. The question is, whether their statements can be so reconciled, or can be shown to be so consistent with each other, that it is proper to regard them both as inspired men? Or, are their statements so opposite and contradictory, that it cannot be believed that both were under the influences of an infallible Spirit? In order to answer these questions, there are two points to be considered: I. What the real difficulty is; and, II. How the statements of the two writers can be reconciled, or whether there is any way of explanation which will remove the difficulty.

I. What the difficulty is. This relates to two points—that James seems to contradict Paul in express terms, and that both writers make use of the same case to illustrate their opposite sentiments.

(1.) That James seems to contradict Paul in express terms. The doctrine of Paul on the subject of justification is stated in such language as the following: 'By the deeds of the law there shall no flesh be justified in his sight,' Rom. iii. 20. 'We conclude that a man is justified by faith without the deeds of the law,' Rom. iii. 28. 'Being justified by faith,' Rom. v. 1. 'Knowing that a man is not justified by the works of the law, but by the faith of Jesus Christ,' Gal. ii. 16. Comp. Rom. iii. 24-26; Gal. iii. 11; Titus iii. 5, 6. On the other hand, the statement of James seems to be equally explicit that a man is *not* justified by faith only, but that good works come in for an important share in the matter. 'Was not Abraham our father justified by works?' ver. 21. 'Seest thou how faith wrought with his works?' ver. 22. 'Ye see then how that by works a man is justified, and not by faith only,' ver. 24.

(2.) Both writers refer to the same case to illustrate their views—the case of Abraham. Thus Paul (Rom. iv. 1–3) refers to it to prove that justification is wholly by faith. 'For if Abraham were justified by works, he hath whereof to glory; but not before God. For what saith the Scripture? Abraham believed God, and it was imputed unto him for righteousness.' And thus James (vs. 21, 22) refers to it to prove that justification is by works : ' Was not Abraham our father justified by works when he had offered Isaac his son upon the altar?'

The difficulty of reconciling these statements would be more clearly seen if they occurred in the writings of the same author; by supposing, for example, that the statements of James were appended to the fourth chapter of the epistle to the Romans, and were to be read in connection with that chapter. Who, the infidel would ask, would not be struck with the contradiction? Who would undertake to harmonize statements so contradictory? Yet the statements are equally contradictory, though they occur in different writers, and especially when it is claimed for both that they wrote under the influence of inspiration.

II. The inquiry then is, how these apparently contradictory statements may be reconciled, or whether there is any way of explanation that will remove the difficulty. This inquiry resolves itself into two—whether there is any theory that can be proposed that would relieve the difficulty, and whether that theory can be shown to be well founded.

(1.) Is there any theory which would remove the difficulty—any explanation which can be given on this point which, if true, would show that the two statements may be in accordance with each other and with truth?

Before suggesting such an explanation, it may be further observed, that, as all history has shown, the statements of Paul on the subject of justification are liable to great abuse. All the forms of Antinomianism have grown out of such abuse, and are only perverted statements of his doctrine. It has been said, that if Christ has freed us from the necessity of obeying the law in order to justification; if he has fulfilled it in our stead, and borne its penalty, then the law is no longer binding on those who are justified, and they are at liberty to live as they please. It has been further said, that if we are saved by faith alone, a man is safe the moment he believes, and good works are therefore not necessary. It is possible that such views as these began to prevail as early as the time of James, and, if so, it was proper that there should be an authoritative

apostolic statement to correct them, and to check these growing abuses. If, therefore, James had, as it has been supposed he had, any reference to the sentiments of Paul, it was not to correct his sentiments, or to controvert them, but it was to correct the *abuses* which began already to flow from his doctrines, and to show that the alleged inferences did not properly follow from the opinions which he held ; or, in other words, to show that the Christian religion required men to lead holy lives, and that the faith by which it was acknowledged that the sinner must be justified, was a faith which was productive of good works.

Now, all that is necessary to reconcile the statements of Paul and James, is to suppose that they contemplate the subject of justification from different points of view, and with reference to different inquiries. Paul looks at it *before* a man is converted, with reference to the question how a sinner may be justified before God ; James *after* a man is converted, with reference to the question how he may show that he has the genuine faith which justifies. Paul affirms that the sinner is justified before God only by faith in the Lord Jesus, and not by his own works ; James affirms that it is not a mere speculative or dead faith which justifies, but only a faith that is productive of good works, and that its genuineness is seen only *by* good works. Paul affirms that whatever else a man has, if he have not faith in the Lord Jesus, he cannot be justified ; James affirms that no matter what pretended faith a man has, if it is not a faith which is adapted to produce good works, it is of no value in the matter of justification. Supposing this to be the true explanation, and that these are the 'stand-points' from which they view the subject, the reconciliation of these two writers is easy: for it was and is still true, that if the question is asked how a sinner is to be justified before God, the answer is to be that of Paul, that it is by faith alone, ' without the works of the law;' if the question be asked, how it can be shown what is the kind of faith that justifies, the answer is that of James, that it is only that which is productive of holy living and practical obedience

(2.) Is this a true theory? Can it be shown to be in accordance with the statements of the two writers? Would it be a proper explanation if the same statements had been made by the same writer? That it is a correct theory, or that it is an explanation founded in truth, will be apparent if (a) the language used by the two writers will warrant it; (b) if it accords with a fair interpretation of the declarations of both writers; and (c) if, in fact, each of the two writers held respectively the same doctrine on the subject.

(a) Will the language bear this explanation? That is, will the word *justify*, as used by the two writers, admit of this explanation? That it will, there need be no reasonable doubt; for both are speaking of the way in which man, who is a sinner, may be regarded and treated by God *as if* he were righteous—the true notion of justification. It is not of justification in the sight *of men* that they speak, but of justification in the sight of God. Both use the word justify in this sense—Paul as affirming that it is only by faith that it can be done; James as affirming, in *addition*, not in *contradiction*, that it is by a faith that produces holiness, and no other.

(b) Does this view accord with the fair interpretation of the declarations of both writers?

In regard to Paul, there can be no doubt that this is the point from which he contemplates the subject, to wit, with reference to the question *how a sinner may be justified.* Thus, in the epistle to the Romans, where his principal statements on the subject occur, he shows, first, that the Gentiles cannot be justified by the works of the law, (ch. i.), and then that the same thing is true in regard to the Jews, (chs. ii., iii.), by demonstrating that both had violated the law given them, and were transgressors, and then (ch. iii. 20) draws his conclusion, 'Therefore by the deeds of the law there shall no flesh be justified in his sight'—the whole argument showing conclusively that he is contemplating the subject *before* a man is justified, and with reference to the question how he *may be.*

In regard to James, there can be as little doubt that the point of view from which he contemplates the subject, is *after* a man professes to have been justified by faith, with reference to the question *what kind of faith justifies,* or *how it may be shown that faith is genuine.* This is clear, (a) because the whole question is introduced by him with almost express reference to that inquiry: 'What doth it *profit,* my brethren, though a man *say* he hath faith, and have not works? Can faith save him?' ver. 14. That is, can *such* faith —can *this* faith (ἡ πίστις) save him? In other words, He must have a different kind of faith in order to save him. The point of James' denial is not that faith, if genuine, would save; but it is, that *such* a faith, or a faith without works, would save. (b) That this is the very point which he discusses, is further shown by his illustrations, vs. 15, 16, 19. He shows (vs. 15, 16) that mere faith in religion would be of no more value in regard to salvation, than if one were naked and destitute of food, it would meet his wants to say, 'Depart in peace, be ye warmed and filled;' and then (ver. 19), that even the demons had a certain kind of faith in one of the cardinal doctrines of religion, but that it was a faith which was valueless—thus showing that his mind was on the question what is true and genuine faith. (c) Then he shows by the case to which he refers (vs. 21–23)—the case of Abraham—that this was the question before his mind. He refers not to the act *when* Abraham first believed—the act by which as a sinner he was justified before God; but to an act that occurred twenty years after—the offering up of his son Isaac. See Notes on those verses. He affirms that the faith of Abraham was of such a kind that it led him to obey the will of God; that is, to good works. Though, as is implied in the objection referred to above, he does refer to the same *case* to which Paul referred—the case of Abraham—yet it is not to the same *act* in Abraham. Paul (Rom. iv. 1–3) refers to him when he first believed, affirming that he was then justified by faith; James refers indeed to an act of the same man, but occurring twenty years after, showing that the faith by which he had been justified was genuine. Abraham was in fact, according to Paul, justified when he believed, and, had he died then, he would have been saved; but according to James, the faith which justified him was not a dead faith, but was living and operative, as was shown by his readiness to offer his son on the altar.

(c) Did each of these two writers in reality hold the same doctrine on the subject? This will be seen, if it can be shown that James held to the doctrine of justification by faith, as really as Paul did; and that Paul held that good works were necessary to show the genuineness of faith, as really as James did. (1.) They both agreed in holding the doctrine of justification by faith. Of Paul's belief there can be no doubt. That *James* held the doctrine is apparent from the fact that he quotes the very passage in Genesis, (xv. 6), and the one on which Paul relies, (Rom. iv. 1–3), as expressing his own views— 'Abraham believed God, and it was imputed unto him for righteousness.' The truth of this, James does not deny, but affirms that the Scripture which made this declaration was fulfilled or confirmed by the act to which he refers. (2.) They both agreed in holding that good works are necessary to show the genuineness of faith. Of *James*' views on that point there can be no doubt. That *Paul* held the same opinion is clear (*a*) from his own life, no man ever having been more solicitous to keep the whole law of God than he was. (*b*) From his constant exhortations and declarations, such as these: 'Created in Christ Jesus unto good works,' (Eph. ii. 10); 'Charge them that are rich, that they be rich in good works,' 1 Tim. vi. 17, 18 ; 'In all things showing thyself a pattern of good works,' (Titus ii. 7); 'Who gave himself for us, that he might purify unto himself a peculiar people, zealous of good works,' (Titus ii. 14); 'These things I will that thou affirm constantly, that they which have believed in God might be careful to maintain good works,' Titus iii. 8. (*c*) It appears from the fact that Paul believed that the rewards of heaven are to be apportioned according to our good works, or according to our character and our attainments in the divine life. The *title* indeed to eternal life is, ac-

cording to him, in consequence of faith; the measure of the reward is to be our holiness, or what we do. Thus he says, (2 Cor. v. 10), 'For we must all appear before the judgment-seat of Christ, that every one may receive the things done in his body.' Thus also he says, (2 Cor. ix. 6), 'He which soweth sparingly, shall reap also sparingly; and he which soweth bountifully, shall reap also bountifully.' And thus also he says, (Rom. ii. 6), that God 'will render to every man according to his deeds.' See also the influence which faith had on Paul personally, as described in the third chapter of his epistle to the Philippians. If these things are so, then these two writers have not contradicted each other, but, viewing the subject from different points, they have together stated important truths which might have been made by any one writer without contradiction ; first, that it is only by faith that a sinner can be justified— and second, that the faith which justifies is that only which leads to a holy life, and that no other is of value in saving the soul. Thus, on the one hand, men would be guarded from depending on their own righteousness for eternal life ; and, on the other, from all the evils of Antinomianism. The great object of religion would be secured—the sinner would be justified, and would become personally holy.

CHAPTER III.

ANALYSIS OF THE CHAPTER.

THE *evil* which the apostle seems to have referred to in this chapter, was a desire, which appears to have prevailed among those to whom he wrote, *to be public teachers* (διδάσκαλοι, ver. 1), and to be such even where there was no proper qualification. It is not easy to see any *connection* between what is said in this chapter, and what is found in other parts of the epistle ; and indeed the plan of the epistle seems to have been to notice such things as the apostle supposed claimed their attention, without particular regard to a logical connection. Some of the errors and improprieties which existed among them had been noticed in the previous chapters, and others are referred to in chs. iv. v. Those which are noticed in this

CHAPTER III.

M Y brethren, be not many
    a masters, knowing that we

shall receive the greater condemnation.[1]

a Mat.23.8,14. 1 Pe.5.3.   1 Or, *judgment.*

chapter grew out of the desire of being
public teachers of religion. It seems
probable that he had this subject in his
eye in the whole of this chapter, and
this will give a clue to the course of
thought which he pursues. Let it be
supposed that there was *a prevailing
desire among those to whom he wrote
to become public teachers, without much
regard for the proper qualifications for
that office,* and the interpretation of the
chapter will become easy. Its design
and drift then may be thus expressed :
I. The general subject of the chapter,
a caution against the desire prevailing
among many to be ranked among public teachers, ver. 1, first clause.
II. Considerations to check and modify that desire, ver. 1 (last clause),
ver. 18. These considerations are the
following :
(1.) The fact that public teachers
must give a more solemn account than
other men, and that they expose themselves to the danger of a deeper condemnation, ver. 1, last clause.
(2.) The evils which grow out of an
improper use of the *tongue;* evils to
which those are particularly liable whose
business is *speaking,* vs. 2–12. This
leads the apostle into a general statement of the importance of the tongue
as a member of the human body ; of the
fact that we are peculiarly liable to offend in that (ver. 2); of the fact that
if that is regulated aright, the whole
man is—as a horse is managed by the
bit, and a ship is steered by the rudder
(vs. 2–4); of the fact that the tongue,
though a little member, is capable of
accomplishing great things, and is peculiarly liable, when not under proper
regulations, to do mischief, (vs. 5, 6);
of the fact that, while every thing else
has been tamed, it has been found impossible to bring the tongue under proper restraints, and that it performs the
most discordant and opposite functions,
(vs. 7–9); and of the impropriety and
absurdity of this, as if the same fountain should bring forth sweet water and
bitter, vs. 10–12. By these considera-

tions, the apostle seems to have designed
to repress the prevailing desire of leaving other employments, and of becoming
public instructors without suitable qualifications.
(3.) The apostle adverts to the importance of *wisdom,* with reference to
the same end ; that is, of suitable qualifications to give public instruction, vs.
13–18. He shows (ver. 13) that if
there was a truly wise man among them,
he should show this by his works, with
'meekness,' and not by obtruding himself upon the attention of others; that
if there was a want of it evinced in a
spirit of rivalry and contention, there
would be confusion and every evil work,
(vs. 14–16); and that where there was
true wisdom, it was unambitious and
unostentatious; it was modest, retiring,
and pure. It would lead to a peaceful
life of virtue, and its existence would
be seen in the 'fruits of righteousness
sown in peace,' vs. 17, 18. It might
be inferred that they who had *this* spirit
would not be ambitious of becoming
public teachers; they would not place
themselves at the head of parties; they
would show the true spirit of religion in
an unobtrusive and humble life. We
are not to suppose, in the interpretation
of this chapter, that the apostle argued
against a desire to enter the ministry,
in itself considered, and where there are
proper qualifications; but he endeavoured to suppress a spirit which has
not been uncommon in the world, to
become public teachers as a means of
more influence and power, and without
any suitable regard to the proper endowments for such an office.
1. *My brethren, be not many masters.*
'Be not many of you teachers.' The
evil referred to is that where *many* desired to be teachers, though but *few*
could be qualified for the office, and
though, in fact, comparatively few were
required. A small number, well qualified, would better discharge the duties of
the office, and do more good, than many
would ; and there would be great evil in
having many crowding themselves un-

CHAPTER III.

qualified into the office. The word here rendered *masters* (διδάσκαλοι) should have been rendered *teachers*. It is so rendered in John iii. 2; Acts xiii. 1; Rom. ii. 20; 1 Cor. xii. 28, 29; Eph. iv. 11; 1 Tim. ii. 11; iv. 3; Heb. v. 12; though it is elsewhere frequently rendered *master*. It has, however, in it primarily the notion of *teaching* (διδάσκω), even when rendered *master;* and the word *master* is often used in the New Testament, as it is with us, to denote an *instructor*—as the 'school-master.' Comp. Matt. x. 24, 25 xxii. 16; Mark x. 17; xii. 19, *et al.* The word is not properly used in the sense of *master*, as distinguished from *a servant*, but as distinguished from *a disciple* or *learner*. Such a position, indeed, implies *authority*, but it is authority based not on power, but on superior qualifications. The connection implies that the word is used in that sense in this place; and the evil reprehended is that of seeking the office of public instructor, especially the sacred office. It would seem that this was a prevailing fault among those to whom the apostle wrote. This desire was common among the Jewish people, who coveted the name and the office of *Rabbi*, equivalent to that here used, (comp. Matt. xxiii. 7), and who were ambitious to be doctors and teachers. See Rom. ii. 19; 1 Tim. i. 7. This fondness for the office of teachers they naturally carried with them into the Christian church when they were converted, and it is this which the apostle here rebukes.* The same spirit the passage before us would rebuke now, and for the same reasons; for although a man should be willing to become a public instructor in religion when called to it by the Spirit and Providence of God, and should esteem it a privilege when so called, yet there would be

scarcely any thing more injurious to the cause of true religion, or that would tend more to produce disorder and confusion, than a prevailing desire of the prominence and importance which a man has in virtue of being a public instructor. If there is any thing which ought to be managed with extreme prudence and caution, it is that of introducing men into the Christian ministry. Comp. 1 Tim. v. 22; Acts i. 15–26; xiii. 2, 3. ¶ *Knowing that we shall receive the greater condemnation,* (μεῖζον κρίμα). Or rather, *a severer judgment;* that is, we shall have a severer trial, and give a stricter account. The word here used does not necessarily mean *condemnation*, but *judgment, trial, account;* and the consideration which the apostle suggests is not that those who were public teachers would be *condemned*, but that there would be a much more solemn account to be rendered by them than by other men, and that they ought duly to reflect on this in seeking the office of the ministry. He would carry them in anticipation before the judgment-seat, and have them determine the question of entering the ministry there. No better 'standpoint' can be taken in making up the mind in regard to this work; and if that had been the position assumed in order to estimate the work, and to make up the mind in regard to the choice of this profession, many a one who has sought the office would have been deterred from it; and it may be added, also, that many a pious and educated youth *would* have sought the office, who has devoted his life to other pursuits. A young man, when about to make choice of a calling in life, should place himself by anticipation at the judgment-bar of Christ, and ask himself how human pursuits and plans will appear there. If *that* were the point of view taken, how many would have been deterred from the ministry who have sought it with a view to honour or emolument! How many, too, who have devoted themselves to the profession of the law, to the army or navy, or to the pursuits of elegant literature, would have felt that it was their duty to serve God in the ministry of reconciliation? How many at the close of life, in the

* A proof of some importance that this prevailed in the early Christian church, among those who had been Jews, is furnished by a passage in the Apocryphal work called 'The Ascension of Isaiah the Prophet;' a work which Dr. Lawrence, the editor, supposes was written not far from the apostolic age. 'In those days (the days of the Messiah) shall many be attached to office, destitute of wisdom; multitudes of iniquitous elders and pastors, injurious to their flocks, and addicted to rapine, nor shall the holy pastors themselves diligently discharge their duty.' Ch. iii. 23, 24

2 For *a* in many things we offend all. If any man offend not in word, *b* the same *is* a perfect man, *and* able also to bridle the whole body.

3 Behold, we put bits *c* in the horses' mouths, that they may obey us; and we turn about their whole body.

4 Behold also the ships, which though *they be* so great, and *are*

a 1 Ki.8.46. Pr.20.9. 1 Jno.1.8. *b* Pr.13.3. *c* Ps.32.9.

ministry and out of it, feel, when too late to make a change, that they have wholly mistaken the purpose for which they should have lived !

2. *For in many things we offend all.* We all offend. The word here rendered *offend*, means to stumble, to fall; then to err, to fail in duty; and the meaning here is, that all were liable to commit error, and that this consideration should induce men to be cautious in seeking an office where an error would be likely to do so much injury. The particular thing, doubtless, which the apostle had in his eye, was the peculiar liability to commit error, or to do wrong with the tongue. Of course, this liability is very great in an office where the *very busi-ness* is public speaking. If anywhere the improper use of the tongue will do mischief, it is in the office of a religious teacher; and to show the danger of this, and the importance of caution in seek-ing that office, the apostle proceeds to show what mischief the *tongue* is capa-ble of effecting. ¶ *If any man offend not in word.* In his speech; in the use of his tongue. ¶ *The same is a perfect man.* Perfect in the sense in which the apostle immediately explains him-self; that he is able to keep every other member of his body in subjection. His object is not to represent the man as absolutely spotless in every sense, and as wholly free from sin, for he had him-self just said that ' all offend in many things;' but the design is to show that if a man can control his tongue, he has complete dominion over himself, as much as a man has over a horse by the bit, or as a steersman has over a ship if he has hold of the rudder. He is perfect in that sense, that he has complete control over himself, and will not be liable to error in any thing. The design is to show the important position which the tongue occupies, as governing the whole man. On the meaning of the word *per-fect*, see Notes on Job i. 1. ¶ *And able*

also to bridle the whole body. To con-trol his whole body, that is, every other part of himself, as a man does a horse by the bridle. The word rendered ' to bridle,' means to lead or guide with a bit; then to rein in, to check, to mode-rate, to restrain. A man always has complete government over himself if he has the entire control of his tongue. It is that by which he gives expression to his thoughts and passions; and if that is kept under proper restraint, all the rest of his members are as easily con-trolled as the horse is by having the control of the bit.

3. *Behold, we put bits in the horses' mouths,* &c. The meaning of this sim-ple illustration is, that as we control a horse by the bit—though the bit is a small thing—so the body is controlled by the tongue. He who has a proper control over his tongue can govern his whole body, as he who holds a bridle governs and turns about the horse.

4. *Behold also the ships.* This illus-tration is equally striking and obvious. A ship is a large object. It seems to be unmanageable by its vastness, and it is also impelled by driving storms. Yet it is easily managed by a small rudder; and he that has control of that, has control of the ship itself. So with the tongue. It is a small member as com-pared with the body; in its size not unlike the rudder as compared with the ship. Yet the proper control of the tongue in respect to its influence on the whole man, is not unlike the control of the rudder in its power over the ship. ¶ *Which though* they be *so great.* So great in themselves, and in comparison with the rudder. Even such bulky and unwieldy objects are controlled by a very small thing. ¶ *And* are *driven of fierce winds.* By winds that would seem to leave the ship beyond control. It is probable that by the ' fierce winds' here as impelling the ship, the apostle meant to illustrate the power of the

driven of fierce winds, yet are they turned about with a very small helm, whithersoever the governor listeth.

5 Even so the tongue is ^{a} a little

a Pr.12,18.

member, and boasteth ^{b} great things. Behold, how great ^{1} a matter a little fire kindleth!

6 And the tongue is a fire, ^{c} a world of iniquity: so is the tongue

b Ps.12.3.   1 Or, wood.   c Pr.16.27.

---

passions in impelling man. Even a man under impetuous passion would be restrained, if the tongue is properly controlled, as the ship driven by the winds is by the helm. ¶ *Yet are they turned about with a very small helm.* The ancient rudder or helm was made in the shape of an oar. This was very small when compared with the size of the vessel— about as small as the tongue is as compared with the body. ¶ *Whithersoever the governor listeth.* As the helmsman pleases. It is entirely under his control.

5. *Even so the tongue is a little member.* Little compared with the body, as the bit or the rudder is, compared with the horse or the ship. ¶ *And boasteth great things.* The design of the apostle is to illustrate the *power* and *influence* of the tongue. This may be done in a great many respects: and the apostle does it by referring to its boasting; to the effects which it produces, resembling that of fire, (ver. 6); to its untameableness, (vs. 8, 9); and to its giving utterance to the most inconsistent and incongruous thoughts, vs. 9, 10. The particular idea here is, that the tongue seems to be conscious of its influence and power, and *boasts* largely of what it can do. The apostle means doubtless to convey the idea that it boasts not *unjustly* of its importance. It *has* all the influence in the world, for good or for evil, which it claims. ¶ *Behold, how great a matter a little fire kindleth!* Marg. *wood.* The Greek word (ὕλη), means a wood, forest, grove; and then fire-wood, fuel. This is the meaning here. The sense is, that a very little fire is sufficient to ignite a large quantity of combustible materials, and that the tongue produces effects similar to that. A spark will kindle a lofty pile ; and a word spoken by the tongue may set a neighbourhood or a village ' in a flame.'

6. *And the tongue* is *a fire.* In this sense, that it produces a ' blaze,' or a great conflagration. It produces a dis-

turbance and an agitation that may be compared with the conflagration often produced by a spark. ¶ *A world of iniquity.* A little world of evil in itself. This is a very expressive phrase, and is similar to one which we often employ, as when we speak of a town as being *a world* in miniature. We mean by it that it is an epitome of the world ; that all that there is in the world is represented there on a small scale. So when the tongue is spoken of as being ' a world of iniquity,' it is meant that all kinds of evil that are in the world are exhibited there in miniature ; it seems to concentrate all sorts of iniquity that exist on the earth. And what evil is there which may not be originated or fomented by the tongue? What else is there that might, with so much propriety, be represented as a little world of iniquity ? With all the good which it does, who can estimate the amount of evil which it causes ? Who can measure the evils which arise from scandal, and slander, and profaneness, and perjury, and falsehood, and blasphemy, and obscenity, and the inculcation of error, by the tongue ? Who can gauge the amount of broils, and contentions, and strifes, and wars, and suspicions, and enmities, and alienations among friends and neighbours, which it produces ? Who can number the evils produced by the ' honeyed' words of the seducer ; or by the tongue of the eloquent in the maintenance of error, and the defence of wrong ? If all men were *dumb*, what a portion of the crimes of the world would soon cease ! If all men would speak only that which *ought* to be spoken, what a change would come over the face of human affairs ! ¶ *So is the tongue among our members, that it defileth the whole body.* It stains or pollutes the whole body. It occupies a position and relation so important in respect to every part of our moral frame, that there is no portion which is not affected by it. Of the truth of this, no

among our members, that it defileth *a* the whole body, and setteth
on fire the ¹ course of nature ; and
it is set on fire of hell.

a Mat.15.11-20.   1 *wheel.*

7 For every ² kind of beasts, and
of birds, and of serpents, and of
things in the sea, is tamed, and hath
been tamed of ³ mankind.

2 *nature.*   3 *nature of man.*

one can have any doubt. There is
nothing else pertaining to us as moral
and intellectual beings, which exerts
such an influence over *ourselves* as the
tongue. A man of pure conversation
is understood and felt to be pure in every
respect; but who has any confidence in
the virtue of the blasphemer, or the
man of obscene lips, or the calumniator
and slanderer? We always regard
such a man as corrupt to the core.
¶ *And setteth on fire the course of nature.* The margin is ' the *wheel* of
nature.' The Greek word also (τροχός)
means *a wheel,* or any thing made for
revolving and running. Then it means
the course run by a wheel; a circular
course or circuit. The word rendered
nature (γίνεσις), means *procreation,
birth, nativity;* and therefore the phrase
means, literally, *the wheel of birth*—that
is, the wheel which is set in motion at
birth, and which runs on through life.
—*Rob. Lex.* sub voce γίνεσις. It may be
a matter of doubt whether this refers to
successive generations, or to the course
of individual life. The more literal
sense would be that which refers to an
individual ; but perhaps the apostle
meant to speak in a popular sense, and
thought of the affairs of the world as
they roll on from age to age, as all
enkindled by the tongue, keeping the
world in a constant blaze of excitement.
Whether applied to an individual life,
or to the world at large, every one can
see the justice of the comparison. One
naturally thinks, when this expression
is used, of a chariot driven on with so
much speed that its wheels by their
rapid motion become self-ignited, and
the chariot moves on amidst flames.
¶ *And it is set on fire of hell.* Hell,
or Gehenna, is represented as a place
where the fires continually burn. See
Notes on Matt. v. 22. The idea here
is, that that which causes the tongue to
do so much evil derives its origin from
hell. Nothing could better characterize
much of that which the tongues does,
than to say that it has its origin in

hell, and has the spirit which reigns
there. The very spirit of that world of
fire and wickedness—a spirit of falsehood, and slander, and blasphemy, and
pollution—seems to inspire the tongue.
The *image* which seems to have been
before the mind of the apostle was that
of a torch which enkindles and burns
every thing as it goes along—a torch
itself lighted at the fires of hell. One
of the most striking descriptions of the
woes and curses which there may be in
hell, would be to pourtray the sorrows
caused on the earth by the tongue.
7. *For every kind of beasts.* The
apostle proceeds to state another thing
showing the power of the tongue, the
fact that it is ungovernable, and that
there is no power of man to keep it under control. Every thing else but this
has been tamed. It is unnecessary to
refine on the expressions used here, by
attempting to prove that it is *literally*
true that every species of beasts, and
birds, and fishes has been tamed. The
apostle is to be understood as speaking
in a general and popular sense, showing
the remarkable power of man over those
things which are by nature savage and
wild. The power of man in taming
wild beasts is wonderful. Indeed, it is
to be remembered that nearly all those
beasts which we now speak of as ' domestic' animals, and which we are accustomed to see only when they are
tame, were once fierce and savage races.
This is the case with the horse, the
ox, the ass, (see Notes on Job xi. 12;
xxxix. 5), the swine, the dog, the cat,
&c. The editor of the Pictorial Bible
well remarks, ' There is perhaps no kind
of creature, to which man has access,
which might not be tamed by him with
proper perseverance. The ancients seem
to have made more exertions to this
end, and with much better success, than
ourselves. The examples given by
Pliny, of creatures tamed by men, relate to elephants, lions, and tigers, among
beasts ; to the eagle, among birds ; to
asps, and other serpents ; and to croco-

8 But the tongue can no man tame ; *it is* an unruly evil, full of deadly *a* poison.

a Ps.140.3. Ro.3.13.

9 Therewith bless we God, even the Father ; and therewith curse we men, which are made after the similitude of God.

---

diles, and various fishes, among the inhabitants of the water. Nat. His. viii. 9, 16, 17 ; x. 5, 44. The lion was very commonly tamed by the ancient Egyptians, and trained to assist both in hunting and in war.' Notes *in loc.* The only animal which it has been supposed has defied the power of man to tame it, is the hyena, and even this, it is said, has been subdued, in modern times. There is a passage in Euripides which has a strong resemblance to this of James:—

Βραχὺ τοι σθένος ἀνέρος
'Αλλὰ ποικιλίαις πραπίδων
Δαμᾶ φῦλα πόντου,
Χθονίων τ' ἀερίων τε παιδεύματα.

' Small is the power which nature has given to man ; but, by various acts of his superior understanding, he has subdued the tribes of the sea, the earth, and the air.' Comp. on this subject, the passages quoted by Pricæus in the Critici Sacri, *in loc.* ¶ *And of birds.* It is a common thing to tame birds, and even the most wild are susceptible of being tamed. A portion of the feathered race, as the hen, the goose, the duck, is thoroughly domesticated. The pigeon, the martin, the hawk, the eagle, may be ; and perhaps there are none of that race which might not be made subject to the will of man. ¶ *And of serpents.* The ancients showed great skill in this art, in reference to asps and other venomous serpents, and it is common now in India. In many instances, indeed, it is known that the fangs of the serpents are extracted ; but even when this is not done, they who practise the art learn to handle them with impunity. ¶ *And of things in the sea.* As the crocodile, mentioned by Pliny. It may be affirmed with confidence that there is no animal which might not, by proper skill and perseverance, be rendered tame, or made obedient to the will of man. It is not necessary, however, to understand the apostle as affirming that literally every animal has been tamed, or ever can be. He evidently speaks in a popular sense

of the great power which man undeniably has over all kinds of wild animals —over the creation beneath him.

8. *But the tongue can no man tame.* This does not mean that it is *never* brought under control, but that it is impossible effectually and certainly to subdue it. It would be possible to subdue and domesticate any kind of beasts, but this could not be done with the tongue. ¶ It is *an unruly evil.* An evil without restraint, to which no certain and effectual check can be applied. Of the truth of this no one can have any doubt, who looks at the condition of the world. ¶ *Full of deadly poison.* That is, it acts on the happiness of man, and on the peace of society, as poison does on the human frame. The allusion here seems to be to the bite of a venomous reptile. Comp. Ps. cxl. 3, 'They have sharpened their tongues like a serpent ; adders' poison is under their lips.' Rom. iii. 13, 'With their tongues they have used deceit ; the poison of asps is under their lips.' Nothing would better describe the mischief that may be done by the tongue. There is no sting of a serpent that does so much evil in the world ; there is no poison more deadly to the frame than the poison of the tongue is to the happiness of man. Who, for example, can stand before the power of the slanderer ? What mischief can be done in society that can be compared with that which he may do ?

'Tis slander ;
Whose edge is sharper than the sword ; whose tongue
Outvenoms all the worms of Nile ; whose breath
Rides on the posting winds, and doth belie
All corners of the world : kings, queens, and states,
Maids, matrons, nay, the secrets of the grave
This viperous slander enters.
Shaks. in Cymbeline.

9. *Therewith bless we God.* We men do this ; that is, all this is done by the tongue. The apostle does not mean that the *same* man does this, but that all this is done by the same organ—the tongue. ¶ *Even the Father.* Who sustains to us the relation of a father.

10 Out of the same mouth proceedeth blessing and cursing. My brethren, these things ought not so to be.

11 Doth a fountain send forth at the same ¹ place sweet *water* and bitter?

1 Or, *hole.*

12 Can the fig-tree, *ᵃ* my brethren, bear olive-berries? either a vine, figs? so *can* no fountain both yield salt water and fresh.

13 Who *ᵇ is* a wise man and endued with knowledge among you? let him show out of a good conver-

a Mat.7.16.　　　b Ps.107.43.

The point in the remark of the apostle is, the absurdity of employing the tongue in such contradictory uses as to bless one who has to us the relation of a *father,* and to *curse* any being, especially those who are made in his image. The word *bless* here is used in the sense of *praise, thank, worship.* ¶ *And therewith curse we men.* That is, it is done by the same organ by which God is praised and honoured. ¶ *Which are made after the similitude of God.* After his image, Gen. i. 26, 27. As we bless God, we ought with the same organ to bless those who are like him. There is an absurdity in cursing men who are thus made, like what there would be in both blessing and cursing the Creator himself.

10. *Out of the same mouth proceedeth blessing and cursing.* The meaning here may be, either that out of the mouth of man two such opposite things proceed, not referring to the same individual, but to different persons; or, out of the mouth of the same individual. Both of these are true; and both are equally incongruous and wrong. No organ should be devoted to uses so unlike, and the mouth should be employed in giving utterance only to that which is just, benevolent, and good. It is true, however, that the mouth *is* devoted to these opposite employments; and that while one part of the race employ it for purposes of praise, the other employ it in uttering maledictions. It is also true of many individuals that at one time they praise their Maker, and then, with the same organ, calumniate, and slander, and revile their fellow-men. After an act of solemn devotion in the house of God, the professed worshipper goes forth with the feelings of malice in his heart, and the language of slander, detraction, or even blasphemy on his lips. ¶ *My brethren, these things ought*

not so to be. They are as incongruous as it would be for the same fountain to send forth both salt water and fresh; or for the same tree to bear different kinds of fruit.

11. *Doth a fountain send forth at the same place.* Marg. *hole.* The Greek word means *opening, fissure,* such as there is in the earth, or in rocks from which a fountain gushes. ¶ *Sweet* water *and bitter.* Fresh water and salt, ver. 12. Such things do not occur in the works of nature, and they should not be found in man.

12. *Can the fig-tree, my brethren, bear olive-berries?* Such a thing is *impossible* in nature, and equally *absurd* in morals. A fig-tree bears only figs; and so the tongue ought to give utterance only to one class of sentiments and emotions. These illustrations are very striking, and show the absurdity of that which the apostle reproves. At the same time, they accomplish the main purpose which he had in view, to repress the desire of becoming public teachers without suitable qualifications. They show the power of the tongue; they show what a dangerous power it is for a man to wield who has not the proper qualifications; they show that no one should put himself in the position where he may wield this power without such a degree of tried prudence, wisdom, discretion, and piety, that there shall be a moral certainty that he will use it aright.

13. *Who* is *a wise man, and endued with knowledge among you?* This is spoken with reference to the work of public teaching; and the meaning of the apostle is, that if there were such persons among them, *they* should be selected for that office. The characteristics here stated as necessary qualifications, are *wisdom* and *knowledge.* Those, it would seem, on which reliance

sation ᵃ his works with meekness of wisdom.

14 But if ye have bitter envying and strife in your hearts, glory not; and lie not against the truth.

15 This ᵇ wisdom descendeth not from above, but *is* earthly, ¹ sensual, devilish.

a Ph.1.27.
b 1Co.3.3.   1 Or, *natural.*

had been placed, were chiefly those which were connected with a ready elocution, or the mere faculty of speaking. The apostle had stated the dangers which would follow if reliance were placed on that alone, and he now says that something more is necessary, that the main qualifications for the office are wisdom and knowledge. No mere power of speaking, however eloquent it might be, was a sufficient qualification. The primary things to be sought in reference to that office were wisdom and knowledge, and they who were endowed with these things should be selected for public instructors. ¶ *Let him show out of a good conversation.* From a correct and consistent life and deportment. On the meaning of the word *conversation*, see Notes on Phil. i. 27. The meaning here is, that there should be an upright *life*, and that this should be the basis in forming the judgment in appointing persons to fill stations of importance, and especially in the office of teaching in the church. ¶ *His works.* His acts of uprightness and piety. He should be a man of a holy life. ¶ *With meekness of wisdom.* With a wise and prudent gentleness of life ; not in a noisy, arrogant, and boastful manner. True wisdom is always meek, mild, gentle ; and that is the wisdom which is needful, if men would become public teachers. It is remarkable that the truly wise man is always characterized by a calm spirit, a mild and placid demeanour, and by a gentle, though firm, enunciation of his sentiments. A noisy, boisterous, and stormy declaimer we never select as a safe counsellor. He may accomplish much in his way by his bold eloquence of manner, but we do not put him in places where we need far-reaching thought, or where we expect the exercise of profound philosophical views. In an eminent degree, the ministry of the gospel should be characterized by a calm, gentle, and thoughtful wisdom—a wisdom which shines in all the actions of the life.

14. *But if ye have bitter envying and strife in your hearts.* If that is your characteristic. There is reference here to a fierce and unholy zeal against each other ; a spirit of ambition and contention. ¶ *Glory not.* Do not boast, in such a case, of your qualifications to be public teachers. Nothing would render you more unfit for such an office than such a spirit. ¶ *And lie not against the truth.* You would lie against what is true by setting up a claim to the requisite qualifications for such an office, if this is your spirit. Men should seek no office or station which they could not properly seek if the whole truth about them were known.

15. *This wisdom descendeth not from above.* Comp. Notes on 1 Cor. iii. 3. The *wisdom* here referred to is that carnal or worldly wisdom which produces strife and contention ; that kind of knowledge which leads to self-conceit, and which prompts a man to defend his opinions with over-heated zeal. In the contentions which are in the world, in church and state, in neighbourhoods and families, at the bar, in political life, and in theological disputes, even where there is the manifestation of enraged and irascible feeling, there is often much of a certain kind of *wisdom.* There is learning, shrewdness, tact, logical skill, subtle and skilful argumentation—'making the worse appear the better reason ;' but all this is often connected with a spirit so narrow, bigoted, and contentious, as to show clearly that it has not its origin in heaven. The spirit which is originated there is always connected with gentleness, calmness, and a love of truth. ¶ *But is earthly.* Has its origin in this world, and partakes of its spirit. It is such as men exhibit who are governed only by worldly maxims and principles. ¶ *Sensual.* Marg. *natural.* The meaning is, that it has its origin in our sensual rather than in our intellectual and moral nature. It is that which takes counsel of our natural appetites and pro-

16 For where envying and strife
is, there *is* [1] confusion and every
evil work.

17 But the wisdom *a* that is from

1 *tumult,* or *unquietness.*　　　*a* 1 Co.2.6,7.

above is first pure, *b* then peaceable, *c* gentle, *d and* easy to be
entreated, full of mercy and good
fruits, without [2] partiality, and
without hypocrisy.

b Ph.4.8. *c* He.12.14. *d* Ga.5.22. 2 Or, *wrangling.*

pensities, and not of high and spiritual
influences. ¶ *Devilish.* Demoniacal
(δαιμονιώδης). Such as the *demons* exhibit. See Notes on ch. ii. 19. There
may be indeed *talent* in it, but there is
the intermingling of malignant passions,
and it leads to contentions, strifes, divisions, and 'every evil work.'

16. *For where envying and strife* is,
there is *confusion.* Marg., *tumult* or
unquietness. Every thing is unsettled
and agitated. There is no mutual confidence ; there is no union of plan and
effort ; there is no co-operation in promoting a common object ; there is no
stability in any plan ; for a purpose,
though for good, formed by one portion,
is defeated by another. ¶ *And every
evil work.* Of the truth of this no one
can have any doubt who has observed
the effects in a family or neighbourhood
where a spirit of strife prevails. All
love and harmony of course are banished;
all happiness disappears ; all prosperity
is at an end. In place of the peaceful
virtues which ought to prevail, there
springs up every evil passion that tends
to mar the peace of a community. Where
this spirit prevails in a church, it is of
course impossible to expect any progress
in divine things ; and in such a church
any effort to do good is vain.

"The Spirit, like a peaceful dove,
　Flies from the realms of noise and strife."

17. *But the wisdom that is from above.*
Comp. Notes on 1 Cor. ii. 6, 7. The
wisdom which has a heavenly origin, or
which is from God. The man who is
characterised by that wisdom will be
pure, peaceable, &c. This does not
refer to the *doctrines* of religion, but to
its *spirit.* ¶ *Is first pure.* That is, the
first effect of it on the mind is to make
it *pure.* The influence on the man is
to make him upright, sincere, candid,
holy. The word here used (ἁγνός) is
that which would be applied to one who
is innocent, or free from crime or blame.

Comp. Phil. iv. 8; 1 Tim. v. 22; 1 John
iii. 3, where the word is rendered, as
here, *pure;* 2 Cor. vii. 11, where it is
rendered *clear,* [in this matter]; 2 Cor.
xi. 2; Titus ii. 5 ; 1 Pet. iii. 2, where
it is rendered *chaste.* The meaning
here is, that the first and immediate
effect of religion is not on the intellect,
to make it more enlightened ; or on the
imagination, to make it more discursive
and brilliant ; or on the memory and
judgment, to make them clearer and
stronger ; but it is to *purify* the heart,
to make the man upright, inoffensive,
and good. This passage should not be
applied, as it often is, to the *doctrines*
of religion, as if it were the first duty
of a church to keep itself free from
errors in doctrine, and that this ought
to be sought even in preference to the
maintenance of peace—as if it meant
that in doctrine a church should be
'*first* pure, *then* peaceable ;' but it
should be applied *to the individual
consciences of men,* as showing the
effect of religion on the heart and life.
The *first* thing which it produces is to
make the man himself pure and good ;
then follows the train of blessings which
the apostle enumerates as flowing from
that. It is true that a church should
be *pure* in doctrinal belief, but that is
not the truth taught here. It is *not*
true that the scripture teaches, here or
elsewhere, that purity of doctrine is to
be preferred to a peaceful spirit ; or that
it always leads to a peaceful spirit; or
that it is proper for professed Christians
and Christian ministers to sacrifice, as
is often done, a peaceful spirit, in an
attempt to preserve purity of doctrine.
Most of the persecutions in the church
have grown out of this maxim. This
led to the establishment of the Inquisi-
tion ; this kindled the fires of Smith-
field; this inspirited Laud and his friends;
this has been the origin of no small part
of the schisms in the church. A pure
spirit is the best promoter of peace, and

will do more than any thing else to secure the prevalence of truth.

[It is but too true that much unseemly strife has had the *aegis* of this text thrown over it. The 'wrath of man' accounts itself zeal for God, and strange fire usurps the place of the true fire of the sanctuary. Yet the author's statement here seems somewhat overcharged; possibly his own personal history may have contributed a little to this result. Although the Greek word ἁγνή, here qualifying the σοφία, or wisdom, refers to purity of *heart*, still it remains true that a pure heart will never relinquish its hold on God's truth for the sake of a peace that at such a price would be too dearly purchased. A pure heart cannot but be faithful to the truth; it could not otherwise be pure, provided *conscientiousness* and *love of truth* form any part of moral purity. Surely, then, an individual solicited to yield up what he believed to be truth, or what were cherished convictions, might properly assign this text as a reason why he could not, and ought not; and if an individual might, why not any number associated into a church? It is true the Scriptures do *not* teach that ' *doctrinal* purity' is to be preferred to a 'peaceful spirit.' However pure a man's doctrine may be, if he has not the peaceful spirit he is none of Christ's. But the common view of this passage. is not chargeable with any such absurdity. It supposes only that there may be circumstances in which the spirit of peace, *though possessed*, cannot be exercised, except in meek submission to wrong for conscience sake; never can it turn traitor to truth, or make any compromise with error. The 'first' of the apostle does not indicate even preference of the pure *spirit* to the peaceful spirit, but only the *order* in which they are to be exercised. There must be no attempts to reach peace by overleaping purity. The maxim that a pure heart ought not to sacrifice truth on any consideration whatever, never gave rise to persecution: it has made many martyrs, but never one persecutor; it has pined in the dungeon, but never immured any there; it has burned amid the flames, but never lighted the faggot; it has ascended scaffolds, but never erected them; it has preserved and bequeathed civil and religious liberty, but never assaulted them; it is a divine principle—the principle by which Christianity became strong, and will ultimately command the homage of the world. There is another principle, with which this has no brotherhood, that denies the right of private judgment, and enforces uniformity by the sword: its progeny are inquisitors, and Lauds and Sharpes; and let it have the credit of its own offspring]

¶ *Then peaceable.* The effect of true religion—the wisdom which is from above—will be to dispose a man to live in peace with all others. See Notes on Rom. xiv. 19. Heb. xii. 14. ¶ *Gentle.* Mild, inoffensive, clement. The word here used (ἐπιεικής) is rendered *moderation* in Phil. iv. 5; *patient* in 1 Tim. iii. 3; and *gentle* in Titus iii. 2; James iii. 17, and 1 Pet. ii. 18. It does not occur elsewhere in the New Testament. Every one has a clear idea of the virtue of *gentleness*—gentleness of spirit, of deportment, and of manners; and every one can see that that is the appropriate spirit of religion. Comp. Notes on 2 Cor. x. 1. It is from this word that we have derived the word *gentleman;* and the effect of true religion is to make every one, in the proper and best sense of the term, a *gentleman.* How can a man have evidence that he is a true Christian, who is not such? The highest title which can be given to a man is, that he is *a Christian gentleman.* ¶ And *easy to be entreated.* The word here used does not elsewhere occur in the New Testament. It means *easily persuaded, compliant.* Of course, this refers only to cases where it is right and proper to be easily persuaded and complying. It cannot refer to things which are in themselves wrong. The sense is, that he who is under the influence of the wisdom which is from above, is not a stiff, stern, obstinate, unyielding man. He does not take a position, and then hold it whether right or wrong; he is not a man on whom no arguments or persuasions can have any influence. He is not one who cannot be affected by any appeals which may be made to him on the grounds of patriotism, justice, or benevolence; but is one who is ready to yield when truth requires him to do it, and who is willing to sacrifice his own convenience for the good of others. See this illustrated in the case of the apostle Paul, in 1 Cor. ix. 20–22. Comp. Notes on that passage. ¶ *Full of mercy.* Merciful; disposed to show compassion to others. This is one of the results of the wisdom that is from above, for it makes us like God, the 'Father of mercies.' See Notes on Matt. v. 7. ¶ *And good fruits.* The fruits of good living; just, benevolent, and kind actions. Notes, Phil. i. 11; 2 Cor. ix. 10. Comp. James ii. 14–26. ¶ *Without partiality.* Marg. 'or *wrangling.*' The word here used (ἀδιάκριτος)

18 And the fruit *a* of righteous- | ness is sown in peace of them that
a He.12.11. | make peace.

occurs nowhere else in the New Testament. It means, properly, *not to be distinguished.* Here it may mean either of the following things : (*a*) not open to distinction or doubt ; that is, unambiguous, so that there shall be no doubt about its origin or nature ; (*b*) making no distinction, that is, in the treatment of others, or *impartial* towards them ; or (*c*) without strife, from διαχρίνω, to contend. The second meaning here suggested seems best to accord with the sense of the passage ; and according to this the idea is, that the wisdom which is from above, or true religion, makes us impartial in our treatment of others : that is, we are not influenced by a regard to dress, rank, or station, but we are disposed to do equal justice to all, according to their moral worth, and to show kindness to all, according to their wants. See ch. ii. 1–4. ¶ *And without hypocrisy.* What it professes to be ; sincere. There is no disguise or mask assumed. What the man pretends to be, he is. This is everywhere the nature of true religion. It has nothing of its own of which to be ashamed, and which needs to be concealed ; its office is not to hide or conceal any thing that is wrong. It neither *is* a mask, nor does it *need* a mask. If such is the nature of the ' wisdom which is from above,' who is there that should be ashamed of it ? Who is there that should not desire that its blessed influence should spread around the world ?

18. *And the fruit of righteousness.* That which the righteousness here referred to produces, or that which is the effect of true religion. The meaning is, that righteousness or true religion produces certain results on the life, like the effects of seed sown in good ground. Righteousness or true religion as certainly produces such effects, as seed that is sown produces a harvest. ¶ *Is sown in peace.* Is scattered over the world in a peaceful manner. That is, it is not done amidst contentions, and brawls, and strifes. The farmer sows his seed in peace. The fields are not

sown amidst the tumults of a mob, or the excitements of a battle or a camp. Nothing is more calm, peaceful, quiet, and composed, than the farmer, as he walks with measured tread over his fields, scattering his seed. So it is in sowing the ' seed of the kingdom,' in preparing for the great harvest of righteousness in the world. It is done by men of peace ; it is done in peaceful scenes, and with a peaceful spirit ; it is not in the tumult of war, or amidst the hoarse brawling of a mob. In a pure and holy life ; in the peaceful scenes of the sanctuary and the Sabbath ; by noiseless and unobtrusive labourers, the seed is scattered over the world, and the result is seen in an abundant harvest in producing peace and order. ¶ *Of them that make peace.* By those who desire to produce peace, or who are of a peaceful temper and disposition. They are engaged everywhere in scattering these blessed seeds of peace, contentment, and order ; and the result shall be a glorious harvest for themselves and for mankind —a harvest rich and abundant on earth and in heaven. The whole effect, therefore, of religion, is to produce peace. It is all peace—peace in its origin and in its results ; in the heart of the individual, and in society ; on earth, and in heaven. The idea with which the apostle commenced this chapter seems to have been that such persons only should be admitted to the office of public teachers. From that, the mind naturally turned to the effect of religion in general ; and he states that in the ministry and out of it ; in the heart of the individual and on society at large ; here and hereafter, the effect of religion is to produce peace. Its nature is peaceful as it exists in the heart, and as it is developed in the world ; and wherever and however it is manifested, it is like seed sown, not amid the storms of war and the contentions of battle, but in the fields of quiet husbandry, producing in rich abundance a harvest of peace. In its origin, and in all its results, it is productive only of contentment, sincerity, goodness, and peace. Happy he who has this religion

CHAPTER IV.

F ROM whence *come* wars and
¹ fightings among you? *come*

they not hence, *even* of your ² lusts
that war *ᵃ* in your members?

1 Or, *brawlings*.   2 Or, *pleasures*.   *a* 1 Pe.2.11.

in his heart; happy he who with liberal
hand scatters its blessings broadcast over
the world!

CHAPTER IV.
ANALYSIS OF THE CHAPTER.

In the previous chapter (vs. 13–18)
the apostle had contrasted the wisdom
which is from above with that which is
from beneath. The former is peaceable,
pure, and gentle, leading to universal
kindness and order; the latter earthly,
sensual, and devilish. The points suggested in this chapter grow directly out
of the remarks made there, and are designed to show the effect of the 'wisdom
which descendeth not from above,' as
evinced in the spirit of this world, and
thus by contrast to show the value of
true wisdom, or of the spirit of religion.
Accordingly, the apostle illustrates the
effects of the wisdom of this world, or
the spirit of this world, by showing what
it produces, or what they do who are
under its influence. We are not to suppose that the persons to whom the apostle addressed this epistle were actually
guilty of the things here referred to
themselves, but such things had an existence in the world, and it gave more
life and spirit to the discussion to represent them as existing 'among them.'
In illustrating the subject, he refers to
the following things as resulting from
the spirit that is opposite to the wisdom
which is from above, viz.: (1.) Wars and
fightings, which are to be traced solely
to the lusts of men, (vs. 1, 2); (2.) The
neglect of prayer, showing the reason
why they did not have the things which
were necessary, (ver. 2); (3.) The fact
that *when* they prayed they did not
obtain what they needed, because they
prayed with improper motives, in order
to have the means of gratifying their
sensual desires, (ver. 3); (4.) The desire
of the friendship of the world as one of
the fruits of being under the influence
of the wisdom which is not from above,
(ver. 4); (5.) *Envy*, as another of these
fruits, ver. 5. In view of these things,
and of the danger to which they were
exposed of acting under their influence,

the apostle proceeds to give them some
solemn cautions and admonitions. He
tells them that God resists all who are
proud, but gives grace to all who are
humble, (ver. 6); he counsels them to
submit to God, (ver. 7), to resist the
devil, (ver. 7), to draw nigh to God, (ver.
8), to cleanse their hands and their
hearts, (ver. 8), to be afflicted and mourn
over their sins, and to become serious
and devout, (ver. 9), and to humble
themselves before God that he might
lift them up (ver. 10); he commands
them not to speak evil one of another,
since by so doing they in fact set themselves up to be judges, and in the circumstances became judges of the law as
well as of their brethren, vs. 11, 12. He
then rebukes the confident spirit which
lays its plans for the future with no just
view of the frailty and uncertainty of
human life, and shows them that all
their plans for the future should be
formed with a distinct recognition of
their dependence on God for success,
and even for the continuance of life, vs.
13–16. The chapter closes with an
affirmation that to him that knows how
to do good and does it not, to him it is
sin, (ver. 17), implying that all he had
said in the chapter might indeed be
obvious, and that they would be ready
to admit that these things were true, and
that if they knew this, and did not do
right, they must be regarded as guilty.

1. *From whence* come *wars and fightings among you?* Marg. *brawlings.*
The reference is to strifes and contentions of all kinds; and the question,
then, as it is now, was an important
one, what was their source or origin?
The answer is given in the succeeding
part of the verse. Some have supposed
that the apostle refers here to the contests and seditions existing among the
Jews, which afterwards broke out in
rebellion against the Roman authority,
and which led to the overthrow of the
Jewish nation. But the more probable
reference is to domestic broils, and to
the strifes of sects and parties; to the
disputes which were carried on among
the Jewish people, and which perhaps

2 Ye lust, and have not: ye [1] kill, and desire to have, and cannot

obtain: ye fight and war, yet ye have not, because ye ask not.

1 Or, *envy.*

led to scenes of violence, and to popular outbreaks among themselves. When the apostle says ' among *you*,' it is not necessary to suppose that he refers to those who were members of the Christian church as actually engaged in these strifes, though he was writing to such; but he speaks of them as a part of the Jewish people, and refers to the contentions which prevailed among them *as a people*—contentions in which those who were Christian converts were in great danger of participating, by being drawn into their controversies, and partaking of the spirit of strife which existed among their countrymen. It is known that such a spirit of contention prevailed among the Jews at that time in an eminent degree, and it was well to put those among them who professed to be Christians on their guard against such a spirit, by stating the causes of *all* wars and contentions. The solution which the apostle has given of the causes of the strifes prevailing then, will apply substantially to all the wars which have ever existed on the earth. ¶ Come they *not hence*, even *of your lusts?* Is not this the true source of all war and contention? The word rendered *lusts* is in the margin rendered *pleasures.* This is the usual meaning of the word (ἡδονὴ); but it is commonly applied to the pleasures of sense, and thence denotes *desire, appetite, lust.* It may be applied to any desire of sensual gratification, and then to the indulgence of any corrupt propensity of the mind. The lust or desire of rapine, of plunder, of ambition, of fame, of a more extended dominion, would be properly embraced in the meaning of the word. The word would equally comprehend the spirit which leads to a brawl in the street, and that which prompted to the conquests of Alexander, Cæsar, or Napoleon. All this is the same spirit evinced on a larger or smaller scale. ¶ *That war in your members.* The word *member* (μέλος) denotes, properly, a limb or member of the body; but it is used in the New Testament to denote the members of the body collectively; that is,

the body itself as the seat of the desires and passions, Rom. vi. 13, 19; vii. 5, 23; Col. iii. 5. The word *war* here refers to the conflict between those passions which have their seat in the flesh, and the better principles of the mind and conscience, producing a state of agitation and conflict. See Notes on Rom. vii. 23. Comp. Gal. v. 17. Those corrupt passions which have their seat in the flesh, the apostle says are the causes of war. Most of the wars which have occurred in the world can be traced to what the apostle here calls *lusts.* The desire of booty, the love of conquest, the ambition for extended rule, the gratification of revenge, these and similar causes have led to all the wars that have desolated the earth. Justice, equity, the fear of God, the spirit of true religion, never originated any war, but the corrupt passions of men have made the earth one great battle-field. If true religion existed among all men, there would be no more war. War always supposes that wrong has been done on one side or the other, and that one party or the other, or both, is indisposed to do right. The spirit of justice, equity, and truth, which the religion of Christ would implant in the human heart, would put an end to war *for ever.*

2. *Ye lust, and have not.* That is, you wish to have something which you do not now possess, and to which you have no just claim, and this prompts to the effort to obtain it by force. You desire extension of territory, fame, booty, the means of luxurious indulgence, or of magnificence and grandeur, and this leads to contest and bloodshed. These are the causes of wars on the large scale among nations, and of the contentions and strifes of individuals. The general reason is, that others have that which we have not, and which we desire to have; and not content with endeavouring to obtain it, if we can, in a peaceful and honest manner, and not willing to content ourselves without its possession, we resolve to secure it by force. Socrates is reported by Plato to have said on the day of his death,

'nothing else but the body and its desires cause wars, seditions, and contests of every kind; for all wars arise through the possession of wealth.' Phædo of Plato, by Taylor, London, 1793, p. 158. The system of wars in general, therefore, has been a system of *great robberies*, no more honest or honourable than the purposes of the foot-pad, and more dignified only because it involves greater skill and talent. It has been said that ' to kill one man makes a murderer, to kill many makes a hero.' So it may be said, that to steal a horse, or to rob a house, makes a man a thief or burglar; to fire a dwelling subjects him to the punishment of arson; but to plunder kingdoms and provinces, and to cause cities, towns, and hamlets to be wrapped in flames, makes an illustrious conqueror, and gives a title to what is deemed a bright page in history. The one enrols the name among felons, and consigns the perpetrator to the dungeon or the gibbet; the other, accompanied with no more justice, and with the same spirit, sends the name down to future times as immortal. Yet in the two the all-discerning eye of God may see no difference except in the magnitude of the crime, and in the extent of the injury which has been inflicted. In his way, and according to the measure of his ability, the felon who ends his life in a dungeon, or on the gibbet, is as worthy of grateful and honoured remembrance as the conqueror triumphing in the spoils of desolated empires. ¶ *Ye kill.* Marg. or *envy.*' The marginal reading ' *envy* ' has been introduced from some doubt as to the correct reading of the text, whether it should be φονυτε, *ye kill*, or φθονειτε, *ye envy*. The latter reading has been adopted by Erasmus, Schmidius, Luther, Beza, and some others, though merely from conjecture. There is no authority from the manuscripts for the change. The correct reading undoubtedly is, *ye kill*. This expression is probably to be taken in the sense o f *having a murderous disposition*, or *fostering a brutal and murderous spirit*. t is not exactly that they killed or committed murder previous to 'desiring to have,' but that they had such a covetous desire of the possessions of others as to produce a murderous and bloody temper. The spirit of *murder* was at the bottom of the whole; or there was such a desire of the possessions of others as to lead to the commission of this crime. Of what aggressive wars which have ever existed is not this true? ¶ *Desire to have.* That is, what is in the possession of others. ¶ *And cannot obtain.* By any fair and honest means; by purchase or negociation: and this leads to bloody conquest. All wars might have been avoided if men had been content with what they had, or could rightfully obtain, and had not desired to have what was in the possession of others, which they could not obtain by honest and honourable means. Every war might have been avoided by fair and honourable negociation. ¶ *Ye fight and war; yet ye have not, because ye ask not.* Notwithstanding you engage in contentions and strifes, you do not obtain what you seek after. If you sought that from God which you truly need. you would obtain it, for he would bestow upon you all that is really necessary. But you seek it by contention and strife, and you have no security of obtaining it. He who seeks to gain anything by war seeks it in an unjust manner, and cannot depend on the Divine help and blessing. The true way of obtaining anything which we really need is to seek it from God by prayer, and then to make use of just and fair means of obtaining it, by industry and honesty, and by a due regard for the rights of others. Thus sought, we shall obtain it if it would be for our good; if it is withheld, it will be because it is best for us that it should not be ours. In all the wars which have been waged on the earth, whether for the settlement of disputed questions, for the adjustment of boundaries, for the vindication of violated rights, or for the permanent extension of empire, how rare has it been that the object which prompted to the war has been secured! The course of events has shown that indisposed as men are to do justice, there is much more probability of obtaining the object by patient negotiation than there is by going to war.

3. *Ye ask, and receive not.* That is, some of you ask, or you ask on some occasions. Though seeking in general

3 Ye ask, and receive not, because ye ask amiss, that ye may
consume *it* upon your [1] lusts.

4 Ye adulterers and adulteresses,

Or, *pleasures.*

know ye not that the friendship [a] of
the world is enmity with God? whosoever therefore will be a friend of
the world, is the enemy of God.

a 1 John 2.15.

what you desire by strife, and without
regard to the rights of others, yet you
sometimes pray. It is not uncommon
for men who go to war to pray, or to
procure the services of a chaplain to
pray for them. It sometimes happens
that the covetous and the quarrelsome;
that those who live to wrong others,
and who are fond of litigation, pray.
Such men may be professors of religion.
They keep up a form of worship in their
families. They pray for success in their
worldly engagements, though those engagements are all based on covetousness.
Instead of seeking property that they
may glorify God, and do good ; that
they may relieve the poor and distressed ;
that they may be the patrons of learning, philanthropy, and religion, they do
it that they may live in splendour, and
be able to pamper their lusts. It is not
indeed *very* common that persons with
such ends and aims of life pray, but
they sometimes do it; for, alas! there
are many professors of religion who have
no higher aims than these, and not a
few such professors feel that consistency
demands that they should observe some
form of prayer. If such persons do not
receive what they ask for, if they are
not prospered in their plans, they should
not set it down as evidence that God
does not hear prayer, but as evidence
that their prayers are offered for improper objects, or with improper motives.
¶ *Because ye ask amiss.* Ye do it with
a view to self-indulgence and carnal
gratification. ¶ *That you may consume
it upon your lusts.* Marg., *pleasures.*
This is the same word which is used in
ver. 1, and rendered *lusts.* The reference is to sensual gratifications ; and the
word would include all that comes under
the name of sensual *pleasure,* or carnal
appetite. It was not that they might
have a decent and comfortable living,
which would not be improper to desire,
but that they might have the means of
luxurious dress and living ; perhaps the
means of gross sensual gratifications.
Prayers offered that we may have the

means of sensuality and voluptuousness,
we have no reason to suppose God will
answer, for he has not promised to hear
such prayers ; and it becomes every one
who prays for worldly prosperity, and
for success in business, to examine his
motives with the closest scrutiny. Nowhere is deception more likely to creep
in than into such prayers ; nowhere are
we more likely to be mistaken in regard
to our real motives, than when we go
before God and ask for success in our
worldly employments.

4. *Ye adulterers and adulteresses.*
These words are frequently used to denote those who are faithless towards
God, and are frequently applied to those
who forsake God for idols, Hos. iii. 1 ;
Isa. lvii. 3, 7; Ezek. xvi., xxiii. It is
not necessary to suppose that the apostle meant that those to whom he wrote
were literally guilty of the sins here referred to; but he rather refers to those
who were unfaithful to their covenant
with God by neglecting their duty to
him, and yielding themselves to the indulgence of their own lusts and passions.
The idea is, ' You have in effect broken
your marriage covenant with God by
loving the world more than him ; and,
by the indulgence of your carnal inclinations, you have violated those obligations to self-mortification and self-denial
to which you were bound by your religious engagements.' To convince them ~
of the evil of this, the apostle shows
them what was the true nature of that
friendship of the world which they
sought. It may be remarked here, that
no terms could have been found which
would have shown more decidedly the
nature of the sin of forgetting the covenant vows of religion for the pleasures
of the world, than those which the apostle uses here. It is a deeper crime to be
unfaithful to God than to any created
being ; and it will yet be seen that even
the violation of the marriage contract,
great as is the sin, is a slight offence
compared with unfaithfulness toward
God. ¶ *Know ye not that the friend-*

ship of the world. Comp. 1 John ii. 15. The term *world* here is to be understood not of the physical world as God made it, for we could not well speak of the *'friendship'* of that, but of the *community*, or *people*, called *'the world*,' in contradistinction from the people of God. Comp. John xii. 31 ; 1 Cor. i. 20 ; iii. 19 ; Gal. iv. 3 ; Col. ii. 8. The *'friendship'* of the world' (φιλία τοῦ κόσμου) is the *love* of that world ; of the maxims which govern it, the principles which reign there, the ends that are sought, the amusements and gratifications which characterize it as distinguished from the church of God. It consists in setting our hearts on those things ; in conforming to them ; in making them the object of our pursuit with the same spirit with which they are sought by those who make no pretensions to religion. See Notes, Rom. xii. 2. ¶ *Is enmity with God.* Is in fact hostility against God, since that world is arrayed against him. It neither obeys his laws, submits to his claims, nor seeks to honour him. To love that world is, therefore, to be arrayed against God ; and the spirit which would lead us to this is, in fact, a spirit of hostility to God. ¶ *Whosoever therefore will be a friend of the world.* 'Whoever' he may be, whether in the church or out of it. The fact of being a member of the church makes no difference in this respect, for it is as easy to be a friend of the world in the church as out of it. The phrase 'whosoever *will*' (βουληθῆ) implies *purpose, intention, design.* It supposes that the *heart* is set on it or that there is a deliberate purpose to seek the friendship of the world. It refers to that strong desire which often exists, even among professing Christians, to secure the friendship of the world ; to copy its fashions and vanities ; to enjoy its pleasures ; and to share its pastimes and its friendships. Wherever there is a manifested purpose to find our chosen friends and associates there rather than among Christians ; wherever there is a greater desire to enjoy the smiles and approbation of the world than there is to enjoy the approbation of God and the blessings of a good conscience ; and wherever there is more conscious pain because we have failed

to win the applause of the world, or have offended its votaries, and have sunk ourselves in its estimation, than there is because we have neglected our duty to our Saviour, and have lost the enjoyment of religion, there is the clearest proof that the heart *wills* or *desires* to be the 'friend of the world.' ¶ *Is the enemy of God.* This is a most solemn declaration, and one of fearful import in its bearing on many who are members of the church. It settles the point that any one, no matter what his professions, who is characteristically a friend of the world, cannot be a true Christian. In regard to the meaning of this important verse, then, it may be remarked, (1.) that there *is* a sense in which the love of this world, or of the physical universe, is not wrong. That kind of love for it as the work of God, which perceives the evidence of his wisdom and goodness and power in the various objects of beauty, usefulness, and grandeur, spread around us, is not evil. The world as such—the physical structure of the earth, of the mountains, forests, flowers, seas, lakes, and vales—is full of illustrations of the Divine character, and it cannot be wrong to contemplate those things with interest, or with warm affection toward their Creator. (2.) When that world, however, becomes our portion ; when we study it only as a matter of science, without 'looking through nature up to nature's God ;' when we seek the wealth which it has to confer, or endeavour to appropriate as our supreme portion its lands, its minerals, its fruits ; when we are satisfied with what it yields, and when in the possession or pursuit of these things, our thoughts never rise to God ; and when we partake of the spirit which rules in the hearts of those who avowedly seek this world as their portion,'though we profess religion, then the love of the world becomes evil, and comes in direct conflict with the spirit of true religion. (3.) The statement in this verse is, therefore, one of most fearful import for many professors of religion. There are many in the church who, so far as human judgment can go, are characteristically *lovers of the world*. This is shown (*a*) by their conformity to it in all in which the world is distinguished

5 Do ye think that the Scripture

1 Or, *enviously*.   *a* Ec.4.4.

saith in vain, The spirit that dwelleth in us lusteth [1] to envy ? *a*

from the church as such; (*b*) in their
seeking the friendship of the world, or
their finding their friends there rather
than among Christians; (*c*) in preferring
the amusements of the world to the
scenes where spiritually-minded Christians find their chief happiness; (*d*) in
pursuing the same pleasures that the
people of the world do, with the same expense, the same extravagance, the same
luxury; (*e*) in making their worldly interests the great object of living, and
everything else subordinate to that.
This spirit exists in all cases where no
worldly interest is sacrificed for religion;
where everything that religion peculiarly requires is sacrificed for the world.
If this be so, then there are many professing Christians who are the 'enemies
of God.' See Notes on Phil. iii. 18.
They have never known what is true
friendship for him, and by their lives
they show that they can be ranked only
among his foes. It becomes every professing Christian, therefore, to examine
himself with the deepest earnestness to
determine whether he is characteristically a friend of the world or of God;
whether he is living for this life only,
or is animated by the high and pure
principles of those who are the friends
of God. The great Searcher of hearts
cannot be deceived, and soon our appropriate place will be assigned us, and our
final Judge will determine to which
class of the two great divisions of the
human family we belong—to those who
are the friends of the world, or to those
who are the friends of God.

5. *Do ye think that the Scripture
saith in vain.* Few passages of the
New Testament have given expositors
more perplexity than this. The difficulty has arisen from the fact that no
such passage as that which seems here
to be quoted is found in the Old Testament; and to meet this difficulty, expositors have resorted to various conjectures and solutions. Some have supposed that the passage is spurious, and
that it was at first a gloss in the margin,
placed there by some transcriber, and
was then introduced into the text; some

that the apostle quotes from an apocryphal book; some, that he quotes the
general spirit of the Old Testament
rather than any particular place; some
regard it not as a quotation, but read
the two members separately, supplying
what is necessary to complete the sense,
thus : ' Do you think that the Scripture
speaks in vain, or without a good reason,
when it condemns such a worldly temper?
No; that you cannot suppose. Do you
imagine that the Spirit of God, which
dwelleth in us Christians, leads to covetousness, pride, envy? No. On the contrary, to such as follow his guidance
and direction, he gives more abundant
grace and favour.' This is the solution
proposed by Benson, and adopted by
Bloomfield. But this solution is by no
means satisfactory. Two things are
clear in regard to the passage: (1.) that
James meant to adduce something that
was *said* somewhere, or which could be
regarded as *a quotation*, or as *authority*
in the case, for he uses the formula by
which such quotations are made; and,
(2.) that he meant to refer, not to an
apocryphal book, but to the inspired
and canonical Scriptures, for he uses a
term (ἡ γραφὴ—*the Scripture*) which is
everywhere employed to denote the Old
Testament, and which is nowhere applied to an apocryphal book, Matt. xxi.
42; xxii. 29; xxvi. 54, 56; John ii. 22;
v. 39; vii. 38, 42; x. 35, *et al.* The
word is used more than fifty times in
the New Testament, and is never applied
to any books but those which were regarded by the Jews as inspired, and
which constitute now the Old Testament, except in 2 Pet. iii. 16, where it
refers to the writings of Paul. The
difficulty in the case arises from the
fact that no such passage as the one
here quoted is found in so many words
in the Old Testament, nor any of which
it can fairly be regarded as a quotation.
The only solution of the difficulty which
seems to me to be at all satisfactory, is
to suppose that the apostle, in the remark made here in the form of a quotation, refers to the Old Testament, but
that he had not his eye on any parti-

cular passage, and did not mean to quote the *words* literally, but meant to refer to what was the current teaching or general spirit of the Old Testament; or that he meant to say that this *sentiment* was found there, and designed himself to embody the sentiment in words, and to put it into a condensed form. His eye was on *envy* as at the bottom of many of the contentions and strifes existing on earth, (chap. iii. 16,) and of the spirit of the world which prevailed everywhere, (chap. iv. 4;) and he refers to the *general teaching* of the Old Testament that the soul is by nature inclined to envy; or that this has a deep lodgement in the heart of man. That truth which was uttered everywhere in the Scriptures, was not taught 'in vain.' The abundant facts which existed showing its developement and operation in contentions, and wars, and a worldly spirit, proved that it was deeply imbedded in the human soul. This general truth, that man is prone to envy, or that there is much in our nature which inclines us to it, is abundantly taught in the Old Testament. Eccl. iv. 4, ' I considered all travail, and every right work, that for this a man is envied of his neighbour.' Job v. 2, 'Wrath killeth, and envy slayeth the silly one.' Prov. xiv. 30, ' Envy is the rottenness of the bones.' Prov. xxvii. 4, ' Who is able to stand before envy ?' For particular *instances* of this, and the effects, see Gen. xxvi. 14 ; xxx. 1 ; xxxvii. 11 ; Psal. cvi. 16 ; lxxiii. 3. These passages prove that there is a strong propensity in human nature to envy, and it was in accordance with the design of the apostle to show this. The effects of envy to which he himself referred evinced the same thing, and demonstrated that the utterance given to this sentiment in the Old Testament was not ' in vain,' or was not false, for the records in the Old Testament on the subject found a strong confirmation in the wars and strifes and worldliness of which he was speaking. ¶ *Saith in vain.* ' Says falsely;' that is, the testimony thus borne is true. The apostle means that what was said in the Old Testament on the subject found abundant confirmation in the facts which were continually occurring, and espe-cially in those to which he was adverting. ¶ *The spirit that dwelleth in us.* Many have supposed that the word *spirit* here refers to the Holy Spirit, or the Christian spirit; but in adopting this interpretation they are obliged to render the passage, ' the spirit that dwells in us lusteth *against* envy,' or tends to check and suppress it. But this interpretation is forced and unnatural, and one which the Greek will not well bear. The more obvious interpretation is to refer it to our spirit or disposition as we are by nature, and it is equivalent to saying that we are naturally prone to envy. ¶ *Lusteth to envy.* Strongly tends to envy. The margin is ' *enviously,*' but the sense is the same. The idea is, that there is in man a strong inclination to look with dissatisfaction on the superior happiness and prosperity of others; to desire to make what they possess our own; or at any rate to deprive them of it by detraction, by fraud, or by robbery. It is this feeling which leads to calumny, to contentions, to wars, and to that strong worldly ambition which makes us anxious to surpass all others, and which is so hostile to the humble and contented spirit of religion. He who could trace all wars and contentions and worldly plans to their source—all the schemes and purposes of even professed Christians, that do so much to mar their religion and to make them worldly-minded, to their real origin—would be surprised to find how much is to be attributed to envy. We are pained that others are more prosperous than we are ; we desire to possess what others have, though we have no right to it; and this leads to the various guilty methods which are pursued to lessen their enjoyment of it, or to obtain it ourselves, or to show that they do not possess as much as they are commonly supposed to. This purpose will be accomplished if we can obtain more than they have ; or if we can diminish what they actually possess; or if by any statements to which we can give currency in society, the general impression shall be that they do *not* possess as much wealth, domestic peace, happiness, or honour, as is commonly supposed—for thus the spirit of envy in our bosoms will be gratified.

6 But he giveth more grace:
Wherefore he saith, *a* God resisteth

a Prov. 29. 23.

the proud, but giveth grace unto
the humble.

---

6. *But he giveth more grace.* The
reference here is undoubtedly to God.
Some have regarded this clause as a
continuation of the quotation in the previous verse, but it is rather to be considered as a declaration of the apostle
himself. The writer had just spoken
of envy, and of the crimes which grew
out of it. He thought of the wars and
commotions of the earth, and of the
various lusts which reigned among men.
In the contemplation of these things, it
seems suddenly to have occurred to him
that *all* were not under the influence
of these things; that there were cases
where men were restrained, and where
a spirit opposite to these things prevailed. Another passage of Scripture
struck his mind, containing the truth
that there was a class of men to whom
God gave grace to restrain these passions, and to subdue these carnal propensities. They were the humble, in
contradistinction to the proud; and
he states the fact that ' God giveth
more grace;' that is, that in some instances he confers more grace than in
the cases referred to; to some he gives
more grace to overcome their evil passions, and to subdue their corrupt inclinations, than he does to others. The
meaning may be thus expressed:—' It
is true that the natural spirit in man is
one that tends to envy, and thus leads
to all the sad consequences of envy.
But there are instances in which higher
grace or favour is conferred; in which
these feelings are subdued, and these
consequences are prevented. They are
not indeed to be found among the
proud, whom God always resists; but
they are to be found among the meek
and the humble. Wherefore submit
yourselves to his arrangements; resist
the devil; draw nigh to God; purify
yourselves, and weep over your past
offences, and you shall find that the
Lord will lift you up, and bestow his
favour upon you,' ver. 10. ¶ *Wherefore
he saith.* The reference here is to
Prov. iii. 34, ' Surely he scorneth the
scorners; but he giveth grace unto the
lowly.' The quotation is made exactly

from the Septuagint, which, though not
entirely literal, expresses the sense of
the Hebrew without essential inaccu-
racy. This passage is also quoted in
1 Pet. v. 5. ¶ *God resisteth the proud.*
The *proud* are those who have an inor-
dinate self-esteem; who have a high
and unreasonable conceit of their own
excellence or importance. This may
extend to any thing; to beauty, or
strength, or attainments, or family, or
country, or equipage, or rank, or even
religion. A man may be proud of any
thing that belongs to him, or which can
in any way be construed as a part of
himself, or as pertaining to him. This
does not, of course, apply to a *correct*
estimate of ourselves, or to the mere
knowledge that we may excel others.
One may *know* that he has more
strength, or higher attainments in learning or in the mechanic arts, or greater
wealth than others, and yet have properly no *pride* in the case. He has
only a *correct* estimate of himself, and
he attaches no undue importance to
himself on account of it. His heart is
not lifted up; he claims no undue deference to himself; he concedes to all
others what is their due; and he is
humble before God, feeling that all that
he has, and is, is nothing in his sight.
He is willing to occupy his appropriate
place in the sight of God and men, and
to be esteemed just as he is. Pride goes
beyond this, and gives to a man a degree of self-estimation which is not war-
ranted by anything that he possesses.
God looks at things as they are; and
hence he abhors and humbles this arrogant claim, Lev. xxvi. 19; Job xxxiii.
17; Ps. lix. 12; Prov. viii. 13; xvi.
18; xxix. 13; Isa. xxiii. 9; xxviii. 1;
Dan. iv. 37; Zech. x. 11. This resistance of pride he shows not only in the
explicit declarations of his word, but in
the arrangements of his providence and
grace. (1.) In his providence, in the
reverses and disappointments which
occur; in the necessity of abandoning
the splendid mansion which we had
built, or in disappointing us in some favourite plan by which our pride was to

7 Submit yourselves therefore to God. Resist *a* the devil, and he will flee from you.

8 Draw *b* nigh to God, and he will draw nigh to you. Cleanse *c* your hands, *ye* sinners; and purify your hearts, *ye* double-minded.

a 1 Pe.5.9.   *b* 2 Ch.15.2.   *c* Is.1.16.

---

be nurtured and gratified. (2.) In sickness, taking away the beauty and strength on which we had so much valued ourselves, and bring us to the sad condition of a sick bed. (3.) In the grave, bringing us down to corruption and worms. Why should one be proud who will soon become so offensive to his best friends that they will gladly hide him in the grave? (4.) In the plan of salvation he opposes our pride. Not a feature of that plan is fitted to foster pride, but all is adapted to make us humble. (*a*) The *necessity* for the plan—that we are guilty and helpless sinners; (*b*) the selection of a Saviour —one who was so poor, and who was so much despised by the world, and who was put to death on a cross; (*c*) our entire dependence on him for salvation, with the assurance that we have no merit of our own, and that salvation is all of grace; (*d*) the fact that we are brought to embrace it only by the agency of the Holy Spirit, and that if we were left to ourselves we should never have one right thought or holy desire—all this is fitted to humble us, and to bring us low before God. God has done nothing to foster the self-estimation of the human heart; but how much has he done to 'stain the pride of all glory!' See Notes on Isa. xxiii. 9. ¶ *But giveth grace unto the humble.* The meaning is, that he shows them *favour;* he bestows upon them the grace needful to secure their salvation. This he does (1,) because they feel their need of his favour; (2,) because they will welcome his teaching and value his friendship; (3,) because all the arrangements of his grace are adapted only to such a state of mind. You cannot *teach* one who is so wise that he already supposes he knows enough; you cannot bestow grace on one who has no sense of the need of it. The arrangements of salvation are adapted only to an humble heart.

7. *Submit yourselves therefore to God.* That is, in his arrangements for obtaining his favour. *Yield* to what he has judged necessary for your welfare in the life that is, and your salvation in the life to come. The duty here enjoined is that of entire acquiescence in the arrangements of God, whether in his providence or grace. All these are for our good, and submission to them is required by the spirit of true humility. The object of the command here, and in the succeeding injunctions to particular duties, is to show them how they might obtain the grace which God is willing to bestow, and how they might overcome the evils against which the apostle had been endeavouring to guard them. The true method of doing this is by submitting ourselves *in all things* to God. ¶ *Resist the devil, and he will flee from you.* While you yield to God in all things, you are to yield to the devil in none. You are to resist and oppose him in whatever way he may approach you, whether by allurements, by flattering promises, by the fascinations of the world, by temptation, or by threats. See 1 Pet. v. 9. Satan makes his way, and secures his triumphs, rather by art, cunning, deception, and threatenings, than by true courage; and when opposed manfully, he flies. The true way of meeting him is by direct resistance, rather than by argument; by steadfastly *refusing* to yield in the slightest degree, rather than by a belief that we can either convince him that he is wrong, or can return to virtue when we have gone a certain length in complying with his demands. No one is safe who yields in the least to the suggestions of the tempter; there is no one who is *not* safe if he does not yield. A man, for example, is always safe from intemperance if he *resists* all allurements to indulgence in strong drink, and never yields in the slightest degree; no one is certainly safe if he drinks even moderately.

8. *Draw nigh to God, and he will draw nigh to you.* Comp. 2 Chron. xv. 2. This declaration contains a great and important principle in religion. If we wish the favour of God, we must

9 Be afflicted, and mourn, and weep: let your laughter be turned to mourning, and *your* joy to heaviness.

come to him; nor can we hope for his mercy, unless we approach him and ask him for it. We cannot come *literally* any nearer to God than we always are, for he is always round about us; but we may come nearer in a spiritual sense. We may address him directly in prayer; we may approach him by meditation on his character; we may draw near to him in the ordinances of religion. We can never hope for his favour while we prefer to remain at a distance from him; none who in fact draw near to him will find him unwilling to bestow on them the blessings which they need. ¶ *Cleanse your hands, ye sinners*. There may possibly be an allusion here to Isa. i. 15, 16: 'Your hands are full of blood; wash you, make you clean; put away the evil of your doings from before mine eyes; cease to do evil.' The *heart* is the seat of motives and intentions—that by which we devise anything; the *hands*, the instruments by which we execute our purposes. The hands here are represented as defiled by blood, or by acts of iniquity. To *wash* or cleanse the hands was, therefore, emblematic of putting away transgression, Mat. xxvii. 24. Comp. Deut. xxi. 6; Psa. xxvi. 6. The heathen and the Jews were accustomed to wash their hands before they engaged in public worship. The particular idea here is, that in order to obtain the favour of God, it is necessary to put away our sins; to approach him with a desire to be pure and holy. The mere washing of the hands, in itself, could not recommend us to his favour; but that of which the washing of the hands would be an emblem, would be acceptable in his sight. It may be inferred from what is said here that no one can hope for the favour of God who does not abandon his transgressions. The *design* of the apostle is, evidently, to state one of the conditions on which we can make an acceptable approach to God. It is indispensable that we come with a purpose and desire to wash ourselves from all iniquity, to put away from us all our transgressions. So David said, 'I will wash my hands in innocency; so will I compass thine altar. O Lord,' Psa. xxvi.6.

['To obtain the favour of God, it is necessary to put away our sins'—is somewhat unguarded phraseology. If the favour of God were not obtained but on this condition, none ever would obtain it. The passage is a strong injunction to holiness and singleness of heart: it does not say, however, that BY these we obtain acceptance with God. Of his favour, holiness is the fruit, the effect, and not the cause. The sinner must not think of getting quit of his sins *to prepare* him for going to God by Jesus; but he must *first* go to Jesus to prepare for laying aside his sins. Yet in every approach to God, it is true there must be a 'desire' to be free from sin; and this doubtless is the view of the commentary; indeed it is so expressed, though some words are objectionable.]

¶ *And purify your hearts*. That is, do not rest satisfied with a mere external reformation; with putting away your outward transgressions. There must be a deeper work than that; a work which shall reach to the heart, and which shall purify the affections. This agrees with all the requisitions of the Bible, and is in accordance with what must be the nature of religion. If the heart is wrong, nothing can be right. If, while we seek an external reformation, we still give indulgence to the secret corruptions of the heart, it is clear that we can have no true religion. ¶ *Ye double-minded*. See Notes on chap. i. 8. The apostle here seems to have had his eye on those who were vacillating in their purposes; whose hearts were not decidedly fixed, but who were halting between good and evil. The *heart* was not right in such persons. It was not settled and determined in favour of religion, but vibrated between that and the world. The proper business of such persons, therefore, was to cleanse the heart from disturbing influences, that it might settle down in unwavering attachment to that which is good.

9. *Be afflicted, and mourn, and weep*. That is, evidently, on account of your sins. The sins to which the apostle refers are those which he had specified in the previous part of the chapter, and which he had spoken of as so evil in their nature, and so dangerous in their tendency. The word rendered 'be afflicted' means, properly, to endure

10 Humble *a* yourselves in the sight of the Lord, and he shall lift you up.

11 Speak *b* not evil one of another, brethren. He that speaketh

a Mat.23.12. *b* Ep.4.31; 1 Pe.2.1.

evil of *his* brother, and judgeth his brother, speaketh evil of the law, and judgeth the law : but if thou judge the law, thou art not a doer of the law, but a judge.

toil or hardship; then to endure affliction or distress; and here means, that they were to *afflict themselves*—that is, they were to feel distressed and sad on account of their transgressions. Comp. Ezra viii. 21. The other words in this clause are those which are expressive of deep grief or sorrow. The language here used shows that the apostle supposed that it was possible that those who had done wrong should voluntarily feel sorrow for it, and that, therefore, it was proper to call upon them to do it.

[All who feel true sorrow for sin, do so *voluntarily;* but it is not intended by this assertion to insinuate that repentance is not the work of the Spirit. He operates on men without destroying their freedom, or doing violence to their will: 'in the day of his power they are willing.' Nor is it improper to call on men to do that for which they require the Spirit's aid. That aid is not withheld in the hour of need; and everywhere the Bible commands sinners to believe and repent.]

¶ *Let your laughter be turned to mourning.* It would seem that the persons referred to, instead of suitable sorrow and humiliation on account of sin, gave themselves to joyousness, mirth, and revelry. See a similar instance in Isa. xxii. 12, 13. It is often the case, that those for whom the deep sorrows of repentance would be peculiarly appropriate, give themselves to mirth and vanity. The apostle here says that such mirth did not become them. Sorrow, deep and unfeigned, was appropriate on account of their sins, and the sound of laughter and of revelry should be changed to notes of lamentation. To how many of the assemblies of the vain, the gay, and the dissipated, might the exhortation in this passage with propriety be now addressed! ¶ *Your joy to heaviness.* The word here rendered *heaviness* occurs nowhere else in the New Testament. It means *dejection, sorrow.* It is not gloom, melancholy, or moroseness, but it is sorrow on

account of sin. God has so made us that we should feel sorrow when we are conscious that we have done wrong, and it is appropriate that we should do so.

10. *Humble yourselves in the sight of the Lord.* Comp. Matt. xxiii. 12. See Notes on ver. 6. That is, be willing to take your appropriate place in the dust on account of your transgressions. This is to be 'in the sight of the Lord,' or before him. Our sins have been committed against him; and their principal aggravation, whoever may have been wronged by them, and great as is their criminality in other respects, arises from that consideration. Psa. li. 4, 'Against thee, thee only, have I sinned, and done this evil in thy sight.' Luke xv. 18, ' I will arise and go to my father, and will say to him, Father, I have sinned *against heaven,* and before thee.' As the Being against whom we have sinned is the only one who can pardon, it is proper that we should humble ourselves before him with penitent confession. ¶ *And he shall lift you up.* He will exalt you from the condition of a broken-hearted penitent to that of a forgiven child ; will wipe away your tears, remove the sadness of your heart, fill you with joy, and clothe you with the garments of salvation. This declaration is in accordance with all the promises in the Bible, and with all the facts which occur on the earth, that God is willing to show mercy to the humble and con-trite, and to receive those who are truly penitent into his favour. Comp. Luke xv. 22.

11. *Speak not evil one of another, brethren.* It is not known to whom the apostle here particularly refers, nor is it necessary to know. It is probable that among those whom he addressed there were some who were less circumspect in regard to speaking of others than they should be, and perhaps this evil prevailed. There are few communities where such an injunction would not be

proper at any time, and few churches where some might not be found to whom the -exhortation would be appropriate. Comp. Notes on Eph. iv. 31; 1 Pet. ii. 1. The evil here referred to is that of *talking against* others—against their actions, their motives, their manner of living, their families, &c. Few things are more common in the world; nothing is more decidedly against the true spirit of religion. ¶ *He that speaketh evil of his brother.* Referring here probably to a Christian brother, or to a fellow Christian. The word *may* however be used in a larger sense to denote any one—a brother of the human race. Religion forbids both, and would restrain us from *all* evil speaking against any human being. ¶ *And judgeth his brother.* His motives, or his conduct. See Notes on Matt. vii. 1. ¶ *Speaketh evil of the law, and judgeth the law.* Instead of manifesting the feelings of a brother, he sets himself up as judge, and not only a judge of his brother, but a judge of *the law.* The *law* here referred to is probably the law of Christ, or the rule which all Christians profess to obey. It is that which James elsewhere calls the 'law of liberty,' (Notes, chap. i. 25;) the law which released men from the servitude of the Jewish rites, and gave them liberty to worship God without the restraint and bondage (Acts **xv.** 10; Gal. iv. 21–31) implied in that ancient system of worship; and the law by which it was contemplated that they should be free from sin. It is not absolutely certain to what the apostle refers here, but it would seem probable that it is to some course of conduct which one portion of the church felt they were at liberty to follow, but which another portion regarded as wrong, and for which they censured them. The explanation which will best suit the expressions here used, is that which supposes that it refers to some difference of opinion which existed among Christians, especially among those of Jewish origin, about the binding nature of the Jewish laws, in regard to circumcision, to holy days, to ceremonial observances, to the distinctions of meats, &c. A part regarded the law on these subjects as still binding, another portion supposed that the obligation in regard to these matters had

ceased by the introduction of the gospel. Those who regarded the obligation of the Mosaic law as still binding, would of course *judge* their brethren, and regard them as guilty of a disregard of the law of God by their conduct. We know that differences of opinion on these points gave rise to contentions, and to the formation of parties in the church, and that it required all the wisdom of Paul and of the other apostles to hush the contending elements to peace. Comp. Notes on Col. ii. 16–18. To some such source of contention the apostle doubtless refers here; and the meaning probably is, that they who held the opinion that all the Jewish ceremonial laws were still binding on Christians, and who judged and condemned their brethren who did not [observe them], by such a course judged and condemned 'the law of liberty' under which they acted—the law of Christianity that had abolished the ceremonial observances, and released men from their obligation. The *judgment* which they passed, therefore, was not only on their brethren, but was on that law of Christianity which had given greater liberty of conscience, and which was intended to abolish the obligation of the Jewish ritual. The same thing now occurs when we judge others for a course which their consciences approve, because they do not deem it necessary to comply with all the rules which *we* think to be binding. Not a few of the harsh judgments which one class of religionists pronounce on others, are in fact judgments on *the laws of Christ.* We set up our own standards, or our own interpretations, and then we judge others for not complying with them, when in fact they may be acting only as the law of Christianity, properly understood, would allow them to do. They who set up a claim to a right to judge the conduct of others, should be certain that they understand the nature of religion themselves. It may be *presumed,* unless there is evidence to the contrary, that others are as conscientious as we are; and it may commonly be supposed that they who differ from us have some *reason* for what they do, and *may be* desirous of glorifying their Lord and Master, and *that they may possibly be*

12 There is one Lawgiver, who ^a is able to save and to destroy: who art thou that judgest another? 13 Go to now, ye that say, To-

day or to-morrow we will go into such a city, and continue there a year, and buy and sell, and get gain :

a Mat.10.28.

right. It is commonly not safe to judge hastily of a man who has turned his attention to a particular subject, or to suppose that he has no reasons to allege for his opinions or conduct. ¶ *But if thou judge the law, thou art not a doer of the law, but a judge.* It is implied here that it is the simple duty of every Christian to *obey* the law. He is not to assume the office of a judge about its propriety or fitness; but he is to do what he supposes the law to require of him, and is to allow others to do the same. Our business in religion is not to make laws, or to declare what they should have been, or to amend those that are made; it is simply to *obey* those which are appointed, and to allow others to do the same, as they understand them. It would be well for all individual Christians, and Christian denominations, to learn this, and to imbibe the spirit of charity to which it would prompt.

12. *There is one lawgiver.* There is but one who has a right to give law. The reference here is undoubtedly to the Lord Jesus Christ, the great Legislator of the church. *This,* too, is a most important and vital principle, though one that has been most imperfectly understood and acted on. The tendency everywhere has been to enact *other* laws than those appointed by Christ —the laws of synods and councils—and to claim that Christians are bound to observe them, and should be punished if they do not. But it is a fundamental principle in Christianity that no laws are binding on the conscience, but those which Christ has ordained; and that all attempts to make other laws pertaining to religion binding on the conscience is a usurpation of his prerogatives. The church is safe while it adheres to this as a settled principle; it is not safe when it submits to any legislation in religious matters as binding the conscience. ¶ *Who is able to save and to destroy.* Comp. Matt. x. 28. The idea

here would seem to be, that he is able to save those whom you condemn, and to destroy you who pronounce a judgment on them. Or, in general, it may mean that he is intrusted with all power, and is abundantly able to administer his government; to restrain where it is necessary to restrain; to save where it is proper to save; to punish where it is just to punish. The whole matter pertaining to *judgment,* therefore, may be safely left in his hands; and, as he is abundantly qualified for it, we should not usurp his prerogatives. ¶ *Who art thou that judgest another?* 'Who art thou, a weak and frail and erring mortal, thyself accountable to that Judge, that thou shouldest interfere, and pronounce judgment on another, especially when he is doing only what that Judge permits him to do?' See this sentiment explained at length in the Notes on Rom. xiv. 4. Comp. Notes, Rom. ii. 1, and Matt. vii. 1. There is nothing more decidedly condemned in the Scriptures than the habit of pronouncing a judgment on the motives and conduct of others. There is nothing in which we are more liable to err, or to indulge in wrong feelings; and there is nothing which God claims more for himself as his peculiar prerogative.

13. *Go to now.* The apostle here introduces a new subject, and refers to another fault which was doubtless prevalent among them, as it is everywhere, that of a presumptuous confidence respecting the future, or of forming plans stretching into the future, without any proper sense of the uncertainty of life, and of our absolute dependence on God. The phrase 'go to now,' (ἄγε νῦν,) is a phrase designed to arrest attention, as if there were something that demanded their notice, and especially, as in this case, with the implied thought that that to which the attention is called is wrong. See ch. v. 1. Comp. Gen. xi. 7; Isa. i. 18. ¶ *Ye that say.* You that form your plans in this manner or that speak

14 Whereas, ye know not what *shall be* on the morrow : For what *is* your life ? It [1] is even a vapour,

a that appeareth for a little time, and then vanisheth away.

thus confidently of what you will do in the future. The word *say* here probably refers to what was in their thoughts, rather than to what was openly expressed. ¶ *To-day or to-morrow we will go into such a city.* That is, they say this without any proper sense of the uncertainty of life, and of their absolute dependence on God. ¶ *And continue there a year.* Fixing a definite time ; designating the exact period during which they would remain, and when they would leave, without any reference to the will of God. The apostle undoubtedly means to refer here to this as a mere *specimen* of what he would reprove. It cannot be supposed that he refers to this single case alone as wrong. All plans are wrong that are formed in the same spirit. ' The practice to which the apostle here alludes,' says the editor of the Pictorial Bible, ' is very common in the East to this day, among a very respectable and intelligent class of merchants. They convey the products of one place to some distant city, where they remain until they have disposed of their own goods and have purchased others suitable for another distant market; and thus the operation is repeated, until, after a number of years, the trader is enabled to return prosperously to his home. Or again, a shopkeeper or a merchant takes only the first step in this process—conveying to a distant town, where the best purchases of his own line are to be made, such goods as are likely to realise a profit, and returning, without any farther stop, with a stock for his own concern. These operations are seldom very rapid, as the adventurer likes to wait opportunities for making advantageous bargains ; and sometimes opens a shop in the place to which he comes, to sell by retail the goods which he has bought.' The practice is common in India. See Roberts' Oriental Illustrations. ¶ *And buy and sell, and get gain.* It is not improbable that there is an allusion here to the commercial habits of the Jews at the time

when the apostle wrote. Many of them were engaged in foreign traffic, and for this purpose made long journeys to distant trading cities, as Alexandria, Antioch, Ephesus, Corinth, etc.—*Bloomfield.*

14. *Whereas, ye know not what* shall be *on the morrow.* They formed their plans as if they knew ; the apostle says it could not be known. They had no means of ascertaining what would occur ; whether they would live or die ; whether they would be prospered, or would be overwhelmed with adversity. Of the *truth* of the remark made by the apostle here, no one can doubt ; but it is amazing how men act as if it were false. We have no power of penetrating the future so as to be able to determine what will occur in a single day or a single hour, and yet we are almost habitually forming our plans as if we saw with certainty all that is to happen. The classic writings abound with beautiful expressions respecting the uncertainty of the future, and the folly of forming our plans as if it were known to us. Many of those passages, some of them almost precisely in the words of James, may be seen in Grotius and Pricæus, *in loc.* Such passages occur in Anacreon, Euripides, Menander, Seneca, Horace, and others, suggesting an obvious but much-neglected thought, that the future is to us all unknown. Man cannot penetrate it ; and his plans of life should be formed in view of the possibility that his life may be cut off and all his plans fail, and consequently in constant preparation for a higher world. ¶ *For what* is *your life ?* All your plans must depend of course on the continuance of your life ; but what a frail and uncertain thing is that ! How transitory and evanescent as a basis on which to build *any* plans for the future ! Who can calculate on the permanence of a vapour ? Who can build any solid hopes on a mist ? ¶ *It is even a vapour.* Marg., *For it is.* The margin is the more correct rendering. The previous question had turned the attention to

15 For that ye *ought* to say, If the Lord will, we shall live, and do this, or that.

16 But now ye rejoice in your

a Lu.12.47.

boastings: all such rejoicing is evil.

17 Therefore *a* to him that knoweth to do good, and doeth *it* not, to him it is sin.

---

life as something peculiarly frail, and as of such a nature that no calculation could be based on its permanence. This expression gives a *reason* for that, to wit, that it is a mere vapour. The word *vapour* (ἀτμὶς,) means a mist, an exhalation, a smoke; such a vapour as we see ascending from a stream, or as lies on the mountain side on the morning, or as floats for a little time in the air, but which is dissipated by the rising sun, leaving not a trace behind. The comparison of life with a vapour is common, and is as beautiful as it is just. Job says,

O remember that my life is wind;
Mine eyes shall no more see good.
Job. vii. 7.

So the Psalmist,

For he remembered that they were but flesh,
A wind that passeth away and that cometh not again.
Ps. lxviii. 39.

Comp. 1 Chron. xxix. 15; Job xiv. 10, 11. ¶ *And then vanisheth away.* Wholly disappears. Like the dissipated vapour, it is entirely gone. There is no remnant, no outline, *nothing* that reminds us that it ever was. So of life. Soon it disappears altogether. The works of art that man has made, the house that he has built, or the book that he has written, remain for a little time, but *the life* has gone. There is nothing of it remaining—any more than there is of the vapour which in the morning climbed silently up the mountain side. The animating principle has vanished for ever. On such a frail and evanescent thing, who can build any substantial hopes?

15. *For that ye* ought *to say.* Instead of what you *do* say, 'we will go into such a city,' you *ought* rather to recognise your absolute dependence on God, and feel that life and success are subject to his will. The meaning is not that we ought always to be *saying* that in so many words, for this might become a mere ostentatious *form*, offensive by constant unmeaning repetition; but

we are, in the proper way, to recognise our dependence on him, and to form all our plans with reference to his will. ¶ *If the Lord will*, etc. This is proper, because we are wholly dependent on him for life, and as dependent on him for success. He alone can keep us, and he only can make our plans prosperous. In a thousand ways he can thwart our best-laid schemes, for all things are under his control. We need not travel far in life to see how completely all that we have is in the hands of God, or to learn how easily he can frustrate us if he pleases. There is nothing on which the success of our plans depends over which we have absolute control; there is nothing, therefore, on which we can base the assurance of success but his favour.

16. *But now ye rejoice in your boastings.* That is, probably, in your boastings of what you can do; your reliance on your own skill and sagacity. You form your plans for the future as if with consummate wisdom, and are confident of success. You do not anticipate a failure; you do not see how plans so skilfully formed *can* fail. You form them as if you were certain that you would live; as if secure from the numberless casualties which may defeat your schemes. ¶ *All such rejoicing is evil.* It is founded on a wrong view of yourselves and of what may occur. It shows a spirit forgetful of our dependence on God; forgetful of the uncertainty of life; forgetful of the many ways by which the best-laid plans may be defeated. We should never boast of any wisdom or skill in regard to the future. A day, an hour may defeat our best-concerted plans, and show us that we have not the slightest power to control coming events.

17. *Therefore to him that knoweth to do good, and doeth* it *not, to him it is sin.* That is, he is guilty of sin if he does not do it. Cotton Mather adopted it as a principle of action, 'that the ability to do good in any case imposes

an obligation to do it.' The proposition in the verse before us is of a general character, but probably the apostle meant that it should refer to the point specified in the previous verses—the forming of plans respecting the future. The particular meaning then would be, ' that he who knows what sort of views he should take in regard to the future, and how he should form his plans in view of the uncertainty of life, and still does *not* do it, but goes on recklessly, forming his plans boastingly and confident of success, is guilty of sin against God.' Still, the proposition will admit of a more general application. It is universally true that if a man knows what is right, and does not do it, he is guilty of sin. If he understands what his duty is ; if he has the means of doing good to others ; if by his name, his influence, his wealth, he can promote a good cause ; if he can, consistently with other duties, relieve the distressed, the poor, the prisoner, the oppressed ; if he can send the gospel to other lands, or can wipe away the tear of the mourner ; if he has talents by which he can lift a voice that shall be heard in favour of temperance, chastity, liberty, and religion, he is under obligations to do it : and if, by indolence, or avarice, or selfishness, or the dread of the loss of popularity, he does not do it, he is guilty of sin before God. No man can be released from the obligation to do good in this world to the extent of his ability; no one should desire to be. The highest privilege conferred on a mortal, besides that of securing the salvation of his own soul, is that of doing good to others—of alleviating sorrow, instructing ignorance, raising up the bowed down, comforting those that mourn, delivering the wronged and the oppressed, supplying the wants of the needy, guiding inquirers into the way of truth, and sending liberty, knowledge, and salvation around the world. If a man does *not* do this when he has the means, he sins against his own soul, against humanity, and against his Maker ; if he does it cheerfully and to the extent of his means, it likens him more than anything else to God.

CHAPTER V.

ANALYSIS OF THE CHAPTER.

THE subjects which are introduced in this chapter are the following :—

I. An address to rich men, and a severe condemnation of the manner in which they lived, vers. 1–6. There have been various opinions in regard to the persons here referred to. (1.) Some have supposed that the address is to unbelieving Jews, and that the punishment which the apostle threatens was that which was about to be brought on the nation by the Roman armies. But, as Benson well observes, it can hardly be presumed that the apostle supposed that his letter would be read by the Jews, and it is not probable, therefore, that he would in this manner directly address them. (2) Another opinion has been, that this, like the rest of the epistle, is addressed to professed Christians who had been Jews, and that the design is to reprove faults which prevailed among them. It is not supposed indeed, by those who hold this opinion, that *all* of those who were rich among them were guilty of the sins here adverted to, nor even that they were very prevalent among them. The rebuke would be proper if the sins here referred to existed at all, and were practised by any who bore the Christian name. As to any improbability that professed Christians would be guilty of these faults, it might be remarked that the period has been rare in the church, if it has occurred at all, in which all that is here said of ' rich men ' would not be applicable to *some* members of the church. Certainly it is applicable in all those countries where slavery prevails ; in countries where religion is allied to the state ; in all places where the mass are poor, and the few are rich. It would be difficult now to find any extended church on earth in relation to which the denunciation here would not be applicable to some of its members. But still it can hardly be supposed that men were tolerated in the church, in the times of the apostles, who were guilty of the oppressions and wrongs here referred to, or who lived in the manner here specified. It is true, indeed, that such men have been, and are still found,

CHAPTER V.

G O to now, *ye* rich *a* men, weep
and howl for your miseries that
shall come upon *you.*

2 Your riches *b* are corrupted,
and your garments are moth-
eaten.*c*

a Pr.11.28; Lu.6.24.   *b* Jer.17.11.   *c* Job 13.28.

in the Christian church; but we should
not, without the clearest proof, suppose
that such cases existed in the times of
the apostles. (3.) The correct opinion
therefore seems to be, that the design of
the apostle in this chapter was to encourage and strengthen poor and oppressed Christians; to impart consolation to
those who, under the exactions of rich
men, were suffering wrong. In doing
this, nothing would be more natural
than for him first to declare his views
in regard to those who were guilty of
these wrongs, and who made use of the
power which wealth gave to injure those
in the humble walks of life. This he
does in the form of an address to rich
men—not perhaps expecting that *they*
would see what he had written, but with
a design to set before those to whom he
wrote, and for whose benefit the statement is made, in a vivid manner, the
nature of the wrongs under which they
were suffering, and the nature of the
punishment which must come upon those
who oppressed them. Nothing would
tend more effectually to reconcile those
to whom he wrote to their own lot, or
do more to encourage them to bear their
trials with patience. At the same time,
nothing would do more to keep them
from envying the lot of the rich, or
desiring the wealth which was connected
with such a mode of life.

II. The apostle exhorts those who
were suffering under these wrongs to
exercise patience, vers. 7–11. He en-
courages them with the hope that the
Lord would come; he refers them to the
example of the farmer, who waits long
for the fruit of the earth; he cautions
them against indulging in hard feelings
and thoughts against others more prospered than they were; he refers them,
as examples of patience, to the prophets,
to the case of Job, and to the Lord Jesus
himself.

III. He adverts to a fault among
them on the subject of *swearing,* ver.
12. This subject is introduced here apparently because they were in danger,

through impatience, of expressing themselves in a severe manner, and even of
uttering imprecations on those who oppressed them. To guard against this,
he exhorts them to control their temper,
and to confine themselves in their conversation to a simple affirmative or
denial.

IV. He refers to the case of those
who were sick and afflicted among them,
and directs them what to do, vers. 14–
18. The duty of those who were sick
was to employ prayer—as the duty of
those who were in health and prosperity
was praise. The afflicted were to pray;
the sick were to call for the elders of the
church, who were to pray over them,
and to anoint them with the oil in the
name of the Lord, not as 'extreme unction,' or *with a view to their dying,* but
with a view to their living. To encourage them thus to call in the aid of
praying men, he refers them to an illustrious instance of the power of prayer in
the case of Elijah.

V. In the close of the chapter and of
the epistle, the apostle adverts to the
possibility that some among them might
err from the truth, and urges the duty
of endeavouring to convert such, vers.
19, 20. To encourage them to do this,
he states the important consequences
which would follow where such an effort
would be successful. He who should do
this, would have the satisfaction of saving a soul from death, and would hide
from the universe a multitude of sins,
which otherwise, in the case of the
erring brother, could not but have been
exposed in the great day of judgment.

1. *Go to now.* Notes on chap. iv. 13.
¶ Ye *rich men.* Not *all* rich men, but
only that class of them who are specified as unjust and oppressive. There is
no sin in merely being rich; where sin
exists peculiarly among the rich, it
arises from the manner in which wealth
is acquired, the spirit which it tends to
engender in the heart, and the way in
which it is used. Comp. Notes on Luke
vi. 24; 1 Tim. vi. 9. ¶ *Weep and*

82 JAMES. [A. D. 60.

3 Your gold and silver is cankered; and the rust of them shall be a witness against you, and shall

eat your flesh as it were fire. Ye have heaped *a* treasure together for the last days.

a Rom.2.5.

howl. Gr., 'Weep howling.' This would be expressive of very deep distress. The language is intensive in a high degree, showing that the calamities which were coming upon them were not only such as would produce tears, but tears accompanied with loud lamentations. In the East, it is customary to give expression to deep sorrow by loud outcries. Comp. Isa. xiii. 6; xiv. 31; xv. 2; xvi. 7; Jer. iv. 8; xlvii. 2; Joel i. 5. ¶ *For your miseries that shall come upon you.* Many expositors, as Benson, Whitby, Macknight, and others, suppose that this refers to the approaching destruction of Jerusalem by the Romans, and to the miseries which would be brought in the siege upon the Jewish people, in which the *rich* would be the peculiar objects of cupidity and vengeance. They refer to passages in Josephus, which describe particularly the sufferings to which the rich were exposed; the searching of their houses by the zealots, and the heavy calamities which came upon them and their families. But there is no reason to suppose that the apostle referred particularly to those events. The poor as well as the rich suffered in that siege, and there were no such special judgments then brought upon the rich as to show that they were the marked objects of the Divine displeasure. It is much more natural to suppose that the apostle means to say that such men as he here refers to exposed themselves always to the wrath of God, and that they had great reason to weep in the anticipation of his vengeance. The sentiments here expressed by the apostle are not applicable merely to the Jews of his time. If there is any class of men which has special reason to dread the wrath of God at all times, it is just the class of men here referred to.

2. *Your riches are corrupted.* The word here rendered *corrupted* (σήπω) does not occur elsewhere in the New Testament. It means, to cause to rot, to corrupt. to destroy. The reference

here is to their hoarded treasures; and the idea is, that they had accumulated more than they needed for their own use; and that, instead of distributing them to do good to others, or employing them in any useful way, they kept them until they rotted or spoiled. It is to be remembered, that a considerable part of the treasures which a man in the East would lay up, consisted of perishable materials, as garments, grain, oil, etc. Such articles of property were often stored up, expecting that they would furnish a supply for many years, in case of the prevalence of famine or wars. Comp. Luke xii. 18, 19. A suitable provision for the time to come cannot be forbidden; but the reference here is to cases in which great quantities had been laid up, perhaps while the poor were suffering, and which were kept until they became worthless. ¶ *Your garments are moth-eaten.* The same idea substantially is expressed here in another form. As the fashions in the East did not change as they do with us, wealth consisted much in the garments that were laid up for show or for future use. See Notes on Matt. vi. 19. Q. Curtius says that when Alexander the Great was going to take Persepolis, the riches of all Asia were gathered there together, which consisted not only of a great abundance of gold and silver, but also of garments, Lib. vi. c. 5. Horace tells us that when Lucullus the Roman was asked if he could lend a hundred garments for the theatre, he replied that he had five thousand in his house, of which they were welcome to take part or all. Of course, such property would be liable to be moth-eaten; and the idea here is, that they had amassed a great amount of this kind of property which was useless to them, and which they kept until it became destroyed.

3. *Your gold and silver is cankered.* That is, that you have heaped together, by injustice and fraud, a large amount, and have kept it from those to whom it

4 Behold, the hire *a* of the labourers who have reaped down your fields, which is of you kept back by

a Jer.22.13; Mal.3.5.

fraud, crieth: and the cries of them which have reaped are entered *b* into the ears of the Lord of sabaoth.

b Ex.22.27.

is due, (ver. 4,) until it has become corroded. The word rendered *is cankered,* (*κατίωται,*) does not occur elsewhere in the New Testament. It properly means, *to cause to rust; to rust out, (Passow;) to be corroded with rust, (Robinson;)* to be spotted with rust. It is true that gold and silver do not properly *rust,* or become *oxidized,* and that they will not be corroded like iron and steel; but by being kept long in a damp place they will contract a dark colour, resembling rust in appearance. This seems to be the idea in the mind of the apostle. He speaks of gold and silver as they *appear* after having been long laid up without use; and undoubtedly the *word* which he uses here is one which would to an ancient have expressed that idea, as well as the mere literal idea of the *rusting* or *oxidizing* of metals. There is no reason to suppose that the word was then used in the strict chemical sense of *rusting,* for there is no reason to suppose that the nature of oxidization was then fully understood. ¶ *And the rust of them.* Another word is used here—*ἰὸς.* This properly denotes something sent out or emitted, (from *ἵημι,*) and is applied to a missile weapon, as an arrow; to poison, as emitted from the tooth of a serpent; and to *rust,* as it seems to be emitted from metals. The word refers to the dark discoloration which appears on gold and silver, when they have remained long without use. ¶ *Shall be a witness against you.* That is, the rust or discoloration shall bear testimony against you that the money is not used as it should be, either in paying those to whom it is due, or in doing good to others. Among the ancients, the gold and silver which any one possessed was laid up in some secret and safe place. Comp. Notes on Isa. xlv. 3. There were no banks then in which money might be deposited; there were few ways of investing money so as to produce regular interest; there were no corporations to employ money in joint operations; and it was not very common to invest money in the purchase of real

estate, and stocks and mortgages were little known. ¶ *And shall eat your flesh as it were fire.* This cannot be taken literally. It must mean that the effect would be *as if* it should corrode or consume their very flesh; that is, the fact of their laying up treasures would be followed by painful consequences. The thought is very striking, and the language in which it is conveyed is singularly bold and energetic. The effect of thus heaping up treasure will be as corroding as fire in the flesh. The reference is to the punishment which God would bring on them for their avarice and injustice—effects that will come on all now for the same offences. ¶ *Ye have heaped treasure together for the last days.* The day of judgment; the closing scenes of this world. You have been heaping up treasure; but it will be treasure of a different kind from what you have supposed. It is treasure not laid up for ostentation, or luxury, or use in future life, but treasure the true worth of which will be seen at the judgment-day. So Paul speaks of 'treasuring up wrath against the day of wrath, and revelation of the righteous judgment of God,' Rom. ii. 5. There are many who suppose they are accumulating property that may be of use to them, or that may secure them the reputation of possessing great wealth, who are in fact accumulating a most fearful treasure against the day of final retribution. Every man who is rich should examine himself closely to see whether there is anything in the manner in which he has gained his property, or in which he now holds it, that will expose him to the wrath of God in the last day. That on which he so much prides himself may yet bring down on him the vengeance of heaven; and in the day of judgment he may curse his own madness and folly in wasting his probation in efforts to amass property.

4. *Behold, the hire of the labourers who have reaped down your fields.* In the previous verses the form of the sin which the apostle specified was that

they had *hoarded* their property. He now states another form of their guilt, that, while doing this, they had withheld what was due from the very labourers who had cultivated their fields, and to whose labour they were indebted for what they had. The phrase ' who have reaped down your fields,' is used to denote labour in general. This particular thing is specified, perhaps, because the reaping of the harvest seems to be more immediately connected with the accumulation of property. What is said here, however, will apply to all kinds of labour. It may be remarked, also, that the sin condemned here is one that may exist not only in reference to those who are hired to cultivate a farm, but to *all* in our employ—to day-labourers, to mechanics, to seamen, etc. It will apply, in an eminent degree, to those who hold others in slavery, and who live by their unrequited toils. The very essence of slavery is, that the slave shall produce by his labour so much *more* than he receives for his own maintenance as to support the master and his family in indolence. The slave is to do the work which the master would otherwise be obliged to do; the advantage of the system is supposed to be that the master is not under a necessity of labouring at all. The amount which the slave receives is not *presumed* to oe what is a fair equivalent for what he does, or what a freeman could be hired for; but so much *less* than his labour is fairly worth, as to be a source of so much *gain* to the master. If slaves were fairly compensated for their labour; if they received what was understood to be a just *price* for what they do, or what they would be willing to bargain for if they were free, the system would at once come to an end. No owner of a slave would keep him if he did not suppose that out of his unrequited toil he might make money, or might be relieved himself from the necessity of labour. He who hires a freeman to reap down his fields pays what the freeman regards as a fair equivalent for what he does; he who employs a slave does *not* give what the slave would regard as an equivalent, and expects that what he gives will be so much *less* than an equivalent, that he may be free alike from the ne-

cessity of labour and of paying him what he has fairly earned. The very *essence* of slavery, therefore, is fraud; and there is nothing to which the remarks of the apostle here are more applicable than to that unjust and oppressive system. ¶ *Which is of you kept back by fraud.* The Greek word here used (ἀποστερέω) is rendered *defraud*, in Mark x. 10; 1 Cor. vi. 7, 8; vii. 5; and *destitute*, in 1 Tim. vi. 5. It occurs nowhere else, except in the passage before us. It means to deprive of, with the notion that that to which it is applied was *due* to one, or that he had a *claim* on it. The *fraud* referred to in keeping it back, may be anything by which the payment is withheld, or the claim evaded—whether it be mere neglect to pay it; or some advantage taken in making the bargain; or some evasion of the law; or mere vexatious delay; or such superior power that he to whom it is due cannot enforce the payment; or such a system that he to whom it is fairly due is supposed in the laws to have no rights, and to be incapable of suing or being sued. Any one of these things would come under the denomination of *fraud.* ¶ *Crieth.* That is, cries out to God for punishment. The voice of this wrong goes up to heaven. ¶ *And the cries of them which have reaped are entered into the ears of the Lord of sabaoth.* That is, he hears them, and he will attend to their cry. Comp. Exod. xxii. 27. They are oppressed and wronged; they have none to regard their cry on earth, and to redress their wrongs, and they go and appeal to that God who *will* regard their cry, and avenge them. On the phrase ' Lord of sabaoth,' or *Lord of hosts*, for so the word *sabaoth* means, see Notes on Isa. i. 9, and Rom. ix. 29. Perhaps by the use of the word here it is implied that the God to whom they cry—the mighty Ruler of all worlds—is *able* to vindicate them. It may be added, that the cry of the oppressed and the wronged is going up constantly from all parts of the earth, and is always heard by God. In his own time he will come forth to vindicate the oppressed, and to punish the oppressor. It may be added, also, that if what is here said were regarded as it should be by all

5 Ye have lived in pleasure ^a on the earth, and been wanton; ye

a Lu.16.19,25.

have nourished your hearts, as in a day of slaughter.

men, slavery, as well as other systems of wrong, would soon come to an end. If everywhere the workman was fairly paid for his earnings; if the poor slave who cultivates the fields of the rich were properly compensated for his toil; if he received what a freeman would contract to do the work for; if there was no *fraud* in withholding what he earns, the system would soon cease in the earth. Slavery could not live a day if this were done. Now there is no such compensation; but the cry of oppressed millions will continue to go up to heaven, and the period must come when the system shall cease. Either the master must be brought to such a sense of right that he will be disposed to do justice, and let the oppressed go free; or God will so impoverish the lands where the system prevails as to make all men see that the system is unprofitable and ruinous as compared with free labour; or the oppressed will somehow become so acquainted with their own strength and their rights that they shall arise and assert their freedom; or under the prevalence of true religion better views will prevail, and oppressors, turned to God, shall relax the yoke of bondage; or God will so bring heavy judgments in his holy providence on the oppresssors, that the system of slavery will everywhere come to an end on the earth. Nothing is more certain than that the whole system is condemned by the passage of Scripture before us; that it is contrary to the genuine spirit of Christianity, and that the prevalence of true religion would bring it to an end. Probably *all* slaveholders feel that to place the Bible in the hands of slaves, and to instruct them to read it, would be inconsistent with the perpetuity of the system. Yet a system which cannot survive the most full and free circulation of the sacred Scriptures, *must* be founded in wrong.

5. *Ye have lived in pleasure on the earth.* One of the things to which the rich are peculiarly addicted. Their wealth is supposed to be of value, because it furnishes them the means of doing it. Comp. Luke xii. 19; xvi. 19.

The word translated 'lived in pleasure, (τρυφάω) occurs only here in the New Testament. It means, to live delicately, luxuriously, at ease. There is not in the word essentially the idea or *vicious* indulgence, but that which characterizes those who live for enjoyment. They lived in ease and affluence on the avails of the labours of others; they indulged in what gratified the taste, and pleased the ear and the eye, while those who contributed the means of this were groaning under oppression. A life of mere indolence and ease, of delicacy and luxury, is nowhere countenanced in the Bible; and even where unconnected with oppression and wrong to others, such a mode of living is regarded as inconsistent with the purpose for which God made man, and placed him on the earth. See Luke xii. 19, 20. Every man has high and solemn duties to perform, and there is enough to be done on earth to give employment to every human being, and to fill up every hour in a profitable and useful way. ¶ *And been wanton.* This word now probably conveys to most minds a sense which is not in the original. Our English word is now commonly used in the sense of *lewd, lustful, lascivious.* It was, however, formerly used in the sense of *sportive, joyous, gay,* and was applied to anything that was variable or fickle. The Greek word used here (σπαταλάω) means, to live luxuriously or voluptuously. Comp. Notes on 1 Tim. v. 6, where the word is explained. It does not refer necessarily to gross criminal pleasures, though the kind of living here referred to often leads to such indulgences. There is a close connection between what the apostle says here, and what he refers to in the previous verses—the oppression of others, and the withholding of what is due to those who labour. Such acts of oppression and wrong are commonly resorted to in order to obtain the means of luxurious living, and the gratification of sensual pleasures. In all countries where slavery exists, the things here referred to are found in close connection. The fraud and wrong by which the re-

6 Ye have condemned *and* killed
  a Mat.5.39.

the just; *and* he doth not resist
a you.

ward of hard toil is withheld from the slave is connected with indolence and sensual indulgence on the part of the master. ¶ *Ye have nourished your hearts.* Or, yourselves—the word *hearts* here being equivalent to *themselves.* The meaning is, that they appeared to have been *fattening* themselves, like stall-fed beasts, for the day of slaughter. As cattle are carefully fed, and are fattened *with a view* to their being slaughtered, so they seemed to have been fattened for the slaughter that was to come on them—the day of vengeance. Thus many now live. They do no work; they contribute nothing to the good of society; they are mere consumers— *fruges, consumere nati;* and, like stall-fed cattle, they seem to live only with reference to the day of slaughter, and to the recompense which awaits them after death. ¶ *As in a day of slaughter.* There has been much variety in the interpretation of this expression. Robinson (*Lex.*) renders it, 'like beasts in the day of slaughter, without care or forethought.' Rosenmüller (*Morgenland*) supposes that it means, *as in a festival;* referring, as he thinks, to the custom among the ancients of having a feast when a part of the animal was consumed in sacrifice, and the rest was eaten by the worshippers. So Benson. On such occasions, indulgence was given to appetite almost without limit; and the idea then would be, that they had given themselves up to a life of pampered luxury. But probably the more correct idea is, that they had fattened themselves as for the day of destruction; that is, as animals are fattened for slaughter. They lived only to eat and drink, and to enjoy life. But, by such a course, they were as certainly preparing for perdition, as cattle were prepared to be killed by being stall-fed.

6. *Ye have condemned* and *killed the just.* τὸν δίκαιον—*the just one,* or *the just man*—for the word used is in the singular number. This may either refer to the condemnation and crucifixion of Christ—meaning that their conduct towards his people had been similar to the treatment of the Saviour, and was in

fact a condemnation and crucifixion of him afresh; or, that by their rejection of him in order to live in sin, they in fact condemned him and his religion; or, that they had condemned and killed *the just man*—meaning that they had persecuted those who were Christians; or, that by their harsh treatment of others in withholding what was due to them, they had deprived them of the means of subsistence, and had, as it were, killed the righteous. Probably the true meaning is, that it was one of their characteristics that they had been guilty of wrong towards good men. Whether it refers, however, to any particular act of violence, or to such a course as would wear out their lives by a system of oppression, injustice, and fraud, cannot now be determined. ¶ And *he doth not resist you.* Some have supposed that this refers to God, meaning that *he* did not oppose them; that is, that he bore with them patiently while they did it. Others suppose that it should be read as a question—'and doth he not resist you?' meaning that God would oppose them, and punish them for their acts of oppression and wrong. But probably the true reference is to the 'just man' whom they condemned and killed; meaning that they were so powerful that all attempts to resist them would be vain, and that the injured and oppressed could do nothing but submit patiently to their acts of injustice and violence. The sense may be either that they could not oppose them—the rich men being so powerful, and they who were oppressed so feeble; or that they bore their wrongs with meekness, and did not attempt it. The sins, therefore, condemned in these verses (1–6), and for which it is said the Divine vengeance would come upon those referred to, are these four: (1,) that of hoarding up money when it was unnecessary for their real support and comfort, and when they might do so much good with it, (comp. Matt. vi. 19;) (2,) that of keeping back the wages which was due to those who cultivated their fields; that is, keeping back what would be a fair compensation for their toil— applicable alike to hired men and to

7 ¹ Be patient therefore, brethren, unto the coming of the Lord. Behold, the husbandman waiteth for the precious fruit of the earth, and hath long patience for it, until he receive the early *a* and latter rain.

1 Or, *Be long patient ; or, Suffer with long patience.*

a De.11.14.

slaves; (3,) that of giving themselves up to a life of ease, luxury, and sensual indulgence; and, (4,) that of wronging and oppressing good and just men—men, perhaps in humble life, who were unable to vindicate their rights, and who had none to undertake their cause; men who were too feeble to offer successful resistance, or who were restrained by their principles from attempting it. It is needless to say that there are multitudes of such persons now on the earth, and that they have the same reason to dread the Divine vengeance which the same class had in the time of the apostle James.

7. *Be patient therefore, brethren.* That is, under such wrongs as the apostle had described in the previous verses. Those whom he addressed were doubtless suffering under those oppressions, and his object was to induce them to bear their wrongs without murmuring and without resistance. One of the methods of doing this was by showing *them,* in an address to their rich oppressors, that those who injured and wronged them would be suitably punished at the day of judgment, or that their cause was in the hands of God; and another method of doing it was by the direct inculcation of the duty of patience. Comp. Notes on Matt. v. 38–41, 43–45. The margin here is, *be long patient,* or *suffer with long patience.* The sense of the Greek is, 'be long-suffering, or let not your patience be exhausted. Your courage, vigour, and forbearance is not to be *short-lived,* but is to be *enduring.* Let it continue as long as there is need of it, even to the coming of the Lord. Then you will be released from sufferings.' ¶ *Unto the coming of the Lord.* The coming of the Lord Jesus—either to remove you by death, or to destroy the city of Jerusalem and bring to an end the Jewish institutions, or to judge the world and receive his people to himself. The 'coming of the Lord' in any way was an event which Christians were taught to expect, and which would be connected with their deliverance from troubles. As the *time* of his appearing was not revealed, it was not improper to refer to that as an event that might *possibly* be near; and as the removal of Christians by death is denoted by the phrase 'the coming of the Lord'—that is, his coming to each one of us—it was not improper to speak of death in that view. On the general subject of the expectations entertained among the early Christians of the second advent of the Saviour, see Notes on 1 Cor. xv. 51; 2 Thess. ii. 2, 3. ¶ *Behold, the husbandman waiteth for the precious fruit of the earth.* The farmer waits patiently for the grain to grow. It requires time to mature the crop, and he does not become impatient. The idea seems to be, that we should wait for things to develope themselves in their proper season, and should not be impatient before that season arrives. In due time we may expect the harvest to be ripened. We cannot hasten it. We cannot control the rain, the sun, the season; and the farmer therefore patiently waits until in the regular course of events he has a harvest. So we cannot control and hasten the events which are in God's own keeping; and we should patiently wait for the developments of his will, and the arrangements of his providence, by which we may obtain what we desire. ¶ *And hath long patience for it.* That is, his patience is not exhausted. It extends through the whole time in which, by the Divine arrangements, he may expect a harvest. ¶ *Until he receive the early and latter rain.* In the climate of Palestine there are two rainy seasons, on which the harvest essentially depends—the autumnal and the spring rains—called here and elsewhere in the Scriptures *the early and the latter rains.* See Deut. xi. 14; Job xxix. 23; Jer. v. 24. The autumnal or early rains of Scripture, usually commence in the latter half of October or the beginning of November; not suddenly, but by degrees, which gives opportunity for the

8 Be ye also patient; stablish your hearts: for *a* the coming of the Lord draweth nigh.

a Re.22.20

---

husbandman to sow his fields of wheat and barley. The rains come mostly from the west or south-west, continuing for two or three days at a time, and falling especially during the nights. The wind then chops round to the north or east, and several days of fine weather succeed. During the months of November and December the rains continue to fall heavily; afterwards they return only at longer intervals, and are less heavy; but at no period during the winter do they entirely cease to occur. Snow often falls in Jerusalem, in January and February, to the depth of a foot or more, but it does not last long. Rain continues to fall more or less through the month of March, but it is rare after that period. At the present time there are not any particular periods of rain, or successions of showers, which might be regarded as distinct rainy seasons. The whole period from October to March now constitutes only one continued rainy season, without any regularly intervening time of prolonged fair weather. Unless, therefore, there has been some change in the climate since the times of the New Testament, the early and the latter rains for which the husbandman waited with longing, seem rather to have implied the first showers of autumn, which revived the parched and thirsty earth, and prepared it for the seed; and the latter showers of spring, which continued to refresh and forward the ripening crops and the vernal products of the fields. In ordinary seasons, from the cessation of the showers in spring until their commencement in October or November, rain never falls, and the sky is usually serene.—*Robinson's Biblical Researches*, vol. ii.,pp. 96–100.

8. *Be ye also patient.* As the farmer is. In due time, as he expects the return of the rain, so you may anticipate deliverance from your trials. ¶ *Stablish your hearts.* Let your purposes and your faith be firm and unwavering. Do not become weary and fretful; but bear with constancy all that is laid upon you, until the time of your deliverance shall come ¶ *For the coming of the Lord*

draweth nigh. Comp. Rev. xxii. 10, 12, 20; Notes, 1 Cor. xv. 51. It is clear, I think, from this place, that the apostle expected that that which *he* understood by 'the coming of the Lord' was soon to occur; for it was to be that by which *they* would obtain deliverance from the trials which they then endured. See ver. 7. Whether it means that he was soon to come to judgment, or to bring to an end the Jewish policy and to set up his kingdom on the earth, or that they would soon be removed by death, cannot be determined from the mere use of the language. The most natural interpretation of the passage, and one which will accord well with the time when the epistle was written, is, that the predicted time of the destruction of Jerusalem (Matt. xxiv.) was at hand; that there were already indications that that would soon occur; and that there was a prevalent expectation among Christians that that event would be a release from many trials of persecution, and would be followed by the setting up of the Redeemer's kingdom. Perhaps many expected that the judgment would occur at that time, and that the Saviour would set up a personal reign on the earth. But the expectation of others might have been merely—what is indeed all that is necessarily implied in the predictions on the subject—that there would be after that a rapid and extensive spread of the principles of the Christian religion in the world. The destruction of Jerusalem and of the temple would contribute to that by bringing to an end the whole system of Jewish types and sacrifices; by convincing Christians that there was not to be one central rallying-point, thus destroying their lingering prejudices in favour of the Jewish mode of worship; and by scattering them abroad through the world to propagate the new religion. The epistle was written, it is supposed, some ten or twelve years before the destruction of Jerusalem, (Intro., § 3,) and it is not improbable that there were already some indications of that approaching event.

9 ¹ Grudge not one against another, brethren, lest ye be condemned : behold, the Judge standeth *ᵃ* before the door.

10 Take, my brethren, the prophets, who have spoken in the name of the Lord, for an example of suffering affliction, *ᵇ* and of patience.

11 Behold, we count them *ᶜ* happy which endure. Ye have heard of the patience *ᵈ* of Job, and have seen the end *ᵉ* of the Lord ; that the Lord is very pitiful, and of tender mercy.

1 Or *Groan ; or, grieve.*　　a Re.3.20.　　b He.11.35-38.
c Ps.94.12; Mat.5.10.　　d Job 1.21,&c.　　e Job 42 10,&c.

9. *Grudge not one against another.* Marg., '*groan, grieve.*' The Greek word (στενάζω) means, *to sigh, to groan,* as of persons in distress, (Rom. viii. 23 ;) and then to sigh or groan through impatience, fretfulness, ill-humour ; and hence *to murmur, to find fault, to complain.* The exact idea here is, not that of *grudging* in the sense of dissatisfaction with what others possess, or of being envious ; it is that of being fretful and impatient—or, to use a common word which more exactly expresses the sense that of *grumbling.* This may arise from many causes ; either because others have advantages which we have not, and we are discontented and unhappy, as if it were *wrong* in them to have such enjoyments ; or because we, without reason, suppose they intend to slight and neglect us ; or because we are ready to take offence at any little thing, and to 'pick a quarrel' with them. There are some persons who are always *grumbling.* They have a sour, dissatisfied, discontented temper ; they see no excellence in other persons ; they are displeased that others are more prospered, honoured, and beloved than they are themselves ; they are always complaining of what others do, not because they are injured, but because others seem to them to be weak and foolish ; they seem to feel that it becomes them to complain if everything is not done precisely as in their estimation it should be. It is needless to say that this spirit —the offspring of pride—will make any man lead a wretched life ; and equally needless to say that it is wholly contrary to the spirit of the gospel. Comp. Luke iii. 14 ; Phil. iv. 11 ; 1 Tim. vi. 8 ; Heb. xiii. 5. ¶ *Lest ye be condemned.* That is, for *judging* others with this spirit—for this spirit is in fact *judging* them. Comp. Notes on Matt. vii. 1. ¶ *Behold, the judge standeth*

before the door. The Lord Jesus, who is soon to come to judge the world. See ver. 8. He is, as it were, even now approaching the door—so near that he can hear all that you say.

10. *Take, my brethren, the prophets.* That is, in your trials and persecutions. To encourage them to the exercise of patience, he points them to the example of those who had trod the same thorny path before them. The prophets were in general a much persecuted race of men : and the argument on which the apostle relies from their example is this :—(1,) that if the prophets were persecuted and tried, it may be expected that other good men will be ; (2,) that they showed such patience in their trials as to be a model for us. ¶ *An example of suffering affliction.* That is, they showed us how evils are to be borne.

11. *Behold, we count them happy which endure.* The word rendered ' we count them happy' (μακαρίζομεν,) occurs only here and in Luke i. 48, where it is rendered '*shall call* me *blessed.*' The word μακάριος (*blessed,* or *happy,*) however, occurs often. See Matt. v. 3–11 ; xi. 6 ; xiii. 6, *et sæpe.* The sense here is, we speak of their patience with commendation. They have done what they ought to do, and their name is honoured and blessed. ¶ *Ye have heard of the patience of Job.* As one of the most illustrious instances of patient sufferers. See Job i. 21. The book of Job was written, among other reasons, to show that true religion would *bear* any form of trial to which it could be subjected. See Job i. 9–11 ; ii. 5, 6. ¶ *And have seen the end of the Lord.* That is, the end or design which the Lord had in the trials of Job, or the result to which he brought the case at last—to wit, that he showed himself to be very merciful to the poor sufferer ; that he met him with the expressions of his approbation

12 But above all things, my brethren, swear *a* not, neither by heaven, neither by the earth, neither

a Mat.5.34,&c.

by any other oath : but let your yea
be yea, and *your* nay, nay ; lest ye
fall into condemnation.

13 Is any among you afflicted?

for the manner in which he bore his trials ; and that he doubled his former possessions, and restored him to more than his former happiness and honour. See Job xlii. Augustine, Luther, Wetstein, and others, understand this as referring to the death of the Lord Jesus, and as meaning that they had seen the manner in which he suffered death, as an example for us. But, though this might strike many as the true interpretation, yet the objections to it are insuperable. (1.) It does not accord with the proper meaning of the word *end*, (τέλος). That word is in no instance applied to *death*, nor does it properly express death. It properly denotes an end, term, termination, completion ; and is used in the following senses :— (*a*) to denote the end, the termination, or the *last* of anything, Mark iii. 26 ; 1 Cor. xv. 24 ; Luke xxi. 9 ; Heb. vii. 3 ; (*b*) an event, issue, or result, Matt. xxvi. 58 ; Rom. vi. 21 ; 2 Cor. xi. 18 ; (*c*) the final purpose, that to which all the parts tend, and in which they terminate, 1 Tim. i. 5 ; (*d*) tax, custom, or tribute — what is paid for public *ends* or purposes, Matt. xvii. 25 ; Rom. xiii. 7. (2) This interpretation, referring it to the death of the Saviour, would not accord with the remark of the apostle in the close of the verse, 'that the Lord is very merciful.' That is, what he says was ' *seen*,' or this was what was particularly illustrated in the case referred to. Yet this was not *particularly* seen in the death of the Lord Jesus. He was indeed most patient and submissive in his death, and it is true that he showed mercy to the penitent malefactor ; but this was not the particular and most prominent trait which he evinced in his death. Besides, if it had been, that would not have been the thing to which the apostle would have referred here. His object was to recommend *patience under trials*, not *mercy shown to others ;* and this he does by showing (*a*) that Job was an eminent instance of it, and (*b*) that the

result was such as to encourage us to be patient. The *end* or the *result* of the Divine dealings in his case was, that the Lord was ' very pitiful and of tender mercy ;' and we may hope that it will be so in our case, and should therefore be encouraged to be patient under our trials. ¶ *That the Lord is very pitiful.* As he showed deep compassion in the case of Job, we have equal reason to suppose that he will in our own.

12. *But above all things.* That is be especially careful on this point ; whatever else is done, let not this be. The manner in which James speaks of the practice referred to here, shows that he regarded it as a sin of a very heinous nature : one that was by all means to be avoided by those whom he addressed. The habit of swearing by various things was a very common one among the Jews, and it was important to guard those who from among them had been converted to Christianity on that subject. ¶ *Swear not.* See this command illustrated in the Notes on Matt. v. 33, 34. Nearly the same things are mentioned here, as objects by which they were accustomed to swear, which are referred to by the Saviour. ¶ *But let your yea be yea.* Let there be a simple affirmation, unaccompanied by any oath or appeal to God or to any of his works. A man who makes that his common method of speech is the man who will be believed. See Notes on Matt. v. 37. ¶ *Lest you fall into condemnation.* That is, for profaning the name of God. ' The Lord will not hold him guiltless that taketh his name in vain,' Exod. xx. 7.

13. *Is any among you afflicted?* By sickness, bereavement, disappointment, persecutions, loss of health or property. The word used here refers to suffering evil of any kind, (κακοπαθεῖ.) ¶ *Let him pray.* That is, prayer is appropriate to trial. The mind naturally resorts to it, and in every way it is proper. God only can remove the source of sorrow ; he can grant unto us 'a happy

let ^ahim pray.   Is any merry? let
him sing   psalms.
   14 Is any sick ^camong you? let

a 2 Ch.33.12; Jonah 2.2,&c.   b Ep.5.19.   c Mar.16.18.

him call for the elders of the church;
and let them pray over him, anointing him with oil in the name of the
Lord :

issue out of all our afflictions;' he can
make them the means of sanctifying
the soul. Comp. 2 Chron. xxxiii. 12 ;
Ps. xxxiv. 4 ; cvii. 6, 13, 28. It matters not what is the form of the trial, it
is a privilege which all have to go to
God in prayer. And it is an inestimable privilege. Health fails, friends
die, property is lost, disappointments
come upon us, danger threatens, death
approaches—and to whom shall we go
but to God? He ever lives. He never
fails us or disappoints us if we trust in
him, and his ear is ever open to our
cries. This would be a sad world indeed, if it were not for the privilege of
prayer. The last resource of millions
who suffer—for millions suffer every
day—would be taken away, if men were
denied the access to the throne of grace.
As it is, there is no one so poor that he
may not pray ; no one so disconsolate
and forsaken that he may not find in
God a friend ; no one so broken-hearted
that he is not able to bind up his spirit.
One of the *designs* of affliction is to
lead us to the throne of grace ; and it
is a happy result of trials if we are led
by our trials to seek God in prayer.
¶ *Is any merry?* The word *merry*
now conveys an idea which is not properly found in the original word here.
It refers now, in common usage, to light
and noisy pleasure ; to that which is
jovial ; to that which is attended with
laughter, or which causes laughter, as
a *merry* jest. In the Scriptures, however, the word properly denotes *cheerful, pleasant, agreeable*, and is applied to a state of mind free from
trouble — the opposite of affliction—
happy, Prov. xv. 13, 15 ; xvii. 22 ;
Isa. xxiv. 7 ; Luke xv. 23, 24, 29, 32.
The Greek word used here (*εὐθυμεῖ*)
means, literally, *to have the mind well*,
(*εὖ* and *θυμὸς* ;) that is, to have it happy,
or free from trouble ; to be cheerful.
¶ *Let him sing psalms.* That is, if any
one is happy ; if he is in health, and is
prospered ; if he has his friends around
him, and there is nothing to produce

anxiety ; if he has the free exercise of
conscience and enjoys religion, it is proper to express that in notes of praise.
Comp. Eph. v. 19, 20. On the meaning of the word here rendered ' sing
psalms,' see Notes, Eph. v. 19, where it
is rendered *making melody*. It does not
mean to sing *psalms* in contradistinction from singing *hymns*, but the reference is to any songs of praise. Praise
is appropriate to such a state of mind.
The heart naturally gives utterance to
its emotions in songs of thanksgiving.
The sentiment in this verse is well expressed in the beautiful stanza,

> In every joy that crowns my days,
>   In every pain I bear,
> My heart shall find delight in praise,
>   Or seek relief in prayer.
>
>   *Mrs. Williams.*

  14. *Is any sick among you?* In the
previous verse the reference was to
affliction in general, and the duty there
urged was one that was applicable to all
forms of trial. The subject of sickness,
however, is so important, since it so
often occurs, that a specific direction
was desirable. That direction is to call
in the aid of others to lead our thoughts,
and to aid us in our devotions, because
one who is sick is less able to direct his
own reflections and to pray for himself
than he is in other forms of trial. Nothing is said here respecting the *degree*
of sickness, whether it is that which
would be fatal if these means were used
or not ; but the direction pertains to
any kind of illness. ¶ *Let him call for
the elders of the church.* Gr. *presbyters.* See Notes on Acts xv. 2 ; xi. 30.
It cannot be supposed that this refers
to the *apostles*, for it could not be that
they would be always accessible ; besides, instructions like this were designed to have a permanent character,
and to be applicable to the church at
all times and in all places. The reference, therefore, is doubtless to the ordinary religious teachers of the congregation ; the officers of the church intrusted
with its spiritual interests. The spirit
of the command would embrace those

who are pastors, and any others to whom the spiritual interests of the congregation are confided—ruling elders, deacons, etc. If the allusion is to the ordinary officers of the church, it is evident that the cure to be hoped for (ver. 15) was not *miraculous*, but was that to be expected in the use of appropriate means accompanied by prayer. It may be added, as worthy of note, that the apostle says they should ' *call*' for the elders of the church; that is, they should *send* for them. They should not *wait* for them to hear of their sickness, as they might happen to, but they should cause them to be informed of it, and give them an opportunity of visiting them and praying with them. Nothing is more common than for persons—even members of the church—to be sick a long time, and to *presume* that their pastor must know all about it ; and then they wonder that he does not come to see them, and think hard of him because he does not. A pastor cannot be supposed to know everything ; nor can it be presumed that he knows when persons are sick, any more than he can know anything else, unless he is apprized of it ; and many hard thoughts, and many suspicions of neglect would be avoided, if, when persons are sick, they would in some way inform their pastor of it. It should always be presumed of a minister of the gospel that he is ready to visit the sick. But how can he go unless he is in some way apprized of the illness of those who need his counsel and his prayers ? The sick *send* for their family physician ; why should they *presume* that their pastor will know of their illness any more than that their physician will ? ¶ *And let them pray over him.* With him, and for him. A man who is sick is often little capable of praying himself ; and it is a privilege to have some one to lead his thoughts in devotion. Besides, the prayer of a good man may be of avail in restoring him to health, ver. 15. Prayer is always one important means of obtaining the Divine favour, and there is no place where it is more appropriate than by the bed-side of sickness. That relief from pain may be granted ; that the mind may be calm and submissive ; that the medicines employed may be blessed to

a restoration to health ; that past sins may be forgiven ; that he who is sick may be sanctified by his trials ; that he may be restored to health, or prepared for his 'last change '—all these are subjects of prayer which we feel to be appropriate in such a case, and every sick man should avail himself of the aid of those who ' have an interest at the throne of grace,' that they may be obtained. ¶ *Anointing him with oil.* Oil, or unguents of various kinds, were much used among the ancients, both in health and in sickness. The oil which was commonly employed was olive oil. See Notes on Isa. i. 6 ; Luke x. 34. The custom of anointing the sick with oil still prevails in the East, for it is believed to have medicinal or healing properties. Niebuhr (Beschrieb. von Arabien, s. 131) says, ' The southern Arabians believe that to anoint with oil strengthens the body, and secures it against the oppressive heat of the sun, as they go nearly naked. They believe that the oil closes the pores of the skin, and thus prevents the effect of the excessive heat by which the body is so much weakened; perhaps also they regard it as contributing to beauty, by giving the skin a glossy appearance. I myself frequently have observed that the sailors in the ships from Dsjidda and Loheia, as well as the common Arabs in Tehama, anointed their bodies with oil, in order to guard themselves against the heat. The Jews in Mocha assured Mr. Forskal, that the Mohammedans as well as the Jews, in Sana, when they were sick, were accustomed to anoint the body with oil.' *Rosenmüller, Morgenland,* in loc. ¶ *In the name of the Lord.* By the authority or direction of the Lord; or as an act in accordance with his will, and that will meet with his approbation. When we do anything that tends to promote virtue, to alleviate misery, to instruct ignorance, to save life, or to prepare others for heaven, it is right to feel that we are doing it in the name of the Lord. Comp., for such uses of the phrase 'in the name of the Lord,' and ' in my name,' Matt. x. 22; xviii. 5, 20 ; xix. 29 ; xxiv. 9 ; Mark. ix. 41 ; xiii. 13; Luke xxi. 12, 17; Rev. ii. 3; Col. iii. 17. There is no reason to think that the phrase is

15 And the prayer of faith shall save the sick, and the Lord shall raise him up ; and if *a* he have com-

mitted sins, they shall be forgiven him.

a Is.33.4.

used here to denote any *peculiar* religious rite or 'sacrament.' It was to be done in the name of the Lord, as any other good deed is.

15. *And the prayer of faith.* The prayer offered in faith, or in the exercise of confidence in God. It is not said that the particular form of the faith exercised shall be that the sick man will certainly recover; but there is to be unwavering confidence in God, a belief that he will do what is best, and a cheerful committing of the cause into his hands. We express our earnest wish, and leave the case with him. The prayer of faith is to accompany the use of means, for all means would be ineffectual without the blessing of God. ¶ *Shall save the sick, and the Lord shall raise him up.* This must be understood, as such promises are everywhere, with this restriction, that they will be restored to health if it shall be the will of God; if he shall deem it for the best. It cannot be taken in the absolute and unconditional sense, for then, if these means were used, the sick person would always recover, no matter how often he might be sick, and he need never die. The design is to encourage them to the use of these means with a strong hope that it would be effectual. It may fairly be inferred from this statement, (1,) that there would be cases in large numbers where these means would be attended with this happy result; and, (2,) that there was so much encouragement to do it that it would be proper in any case of sickness so make use of these means. It may be added, that no one can demonstrate that this promise has not been in numerous instances fulfilled. There *are* instances, not a few, where recovery from sickness *seems* to be in direct answer to prayer, and no one can *prove* that it is not so. Compare the case of Hezekiah, in Isa. xxxviii. 1–5. ¶ *And if he have committed sins, they shall be forgiven him.* Perhaps there may be a particular allusion here to sins which may have brought on the sickness as a punishment. In that case the removal of the

disease in answer to prayer would be an evidence that the sin was pardoned. Comp. Matt. ix. 2. But the promise may be understood in a more general sense as denoting that such sickness would be the means of bringing the sins of the past life to remembrance, especially if the one who was sick had been unfaithful to his Christian vows ; and that the sickness in connection with the prayers offered would bring him to true repentance, and would recover him from his wanderings. On backsliding and erring Christians sickness often has this effect; and the subsequent life is so devoted and consistent as to show that the past unfaithfulness of him who has been afflicted is forgiven.

This passage (vers. 14, 15) is important, not only for the counsel which it gives to the sick, but because it has been employed by the Roman Catholic communion as almost the only portion of the Bible referred to to sustain one of the peculiar rites of their religion—that of 'extreme unction'—a 'sacrament,' as they suppose, to be administered to those who are dying. It is of importance, therefore, to inquire more particularly into its meaning. There can be but three views taken of the passage : I. That it refers to a *miraculous* healing by the apostles, or by other early ministers of religion who were endowed with the power of healing diseases in this manner. This is the interpretation of Doddridge, Macknight, Benson, and others. But to this view the objections seem to me to be insuperable. (*a*) Nothing of this kind is said by the apostle, and this is not necessary to be supposed in order to a fair interpretation of the passage. (*b*) The reference, as already observed, is clearly not to the *apostles*, but to the ordinary officers of the church —for such a reference would be naturally understood by the word *presbyters;* and to suppose that this refers to miracles, would be to suppose that this was a common endowment of the ordinary ministers of religion. But there was no promise of this, and there is no evidence that they possessed it. In regard to the *extent* of the promise, 'they shall lay hands on the sick, and they shall recover,' see Notes on Mark xvi. 17, 18. (*c*) If this referred to the power of working miracles, and if the promise was absolute, then death would not have occurred at all among the early disciples. It would have been easy to secure a restoration to health in any instance where a minister of religion was at hand. II. It is supposed by the Roman Catholics to give sanction to the practice of 'extreme unction,' and to prove that this was practised in the primitive church. But the objections to this are still more obvious. (*a*) It was not to be performed at death, or in the immediate prospect of death, but in sickness at any time. There is no hint that it was to be only when the patient was past all hope of recovery, or in view of the fact that he was to die. But 'extreme unction,' from its very nature, is to be practised only where the patient is past all hope of recovery. (*b*) It was not with a view to his *death*, but to his *living*, that it was to be practised at all. It was not that he might be prepared *to die*, but that he might be restored *to health*—'and the prayer of faith shall save the sick, *and the Lord shall raise him up.*' But 'extreme unction' can be with no such reference, and no such hope. It is *only* with the expectation that the patient is about to die; and if there were any expectation that he would be raised up even by *this* ordinance, it could not be administered as '*extreme* unction.' (*c*) The ordinance practised as 'extreme unction' is a rite wholly unauthorized in the Scriptures, unless it be by this passage. There are instances indeed of persons being embalmed *after* death. It was a fact also that the Saviour said of Mary, when she poured ointment on his body, that she 'did it *for his burial*,' or with reference to his burial, (Notes, Matt. xxvi. 12;) but the Saviour did not say that it was with reference *to his death*, or was designed in any way to prepare him to die, nor is there any instance in the Bible in which such a rite is mentioned. The ceremony of extreme unction has its foundation in two things: first, in superstition, in the desire of something that shall operate as a charm, or that shall possess physical efficiency in calming the apprehensions of a troubled conscience, and in preparing the guilty to die; and, second, in the fact that it gives immense power to the priesthood. Nothing is better adapted to impart such power than a prevalent belief that a minister of religion holds in his hands the ability to alleviate the pangs of the dying, and to furnish a sure passport to a world of bliss. There is deep philosophy in that which has led to the belief of this doctrine—for the dying look around for consolation and support, and they grasp at anything which will promise ease to a troubled conscience, and the hope of heaven. The *gospel* has made arrangements to meet this state of mind in a better way —in the evidence which the guilty may have that by repentance and faith their sins are blotted out through the blood of the cross. III. The remaining supposition, therefore, and, as it seems to me, the true one, is, that the anointing with oil was, in accordance with a common custom, regarded as medicinal, and that a blessing was to be invoked on this as a means of restoration to health. Besides what has been already said, the following suggestions may be made in addition: (*a*) This was, as we have seen, a common usage in the East, and is to this day. (*b*) This interpretation meets all that is demanded to a fair understanding of what is said by the apostle. (*c*) Everything thus directed is rational and proper. It is proper to call in the ministers of religion in time of sickness, and to ask their counsels and their prayers. It is proper to make use of the ordinary means of restoration to health. It was proper then, as it is now, to do this 'in the name of the Lord;' that is, believing that it is in accordance with his benevolent arrangements, and making use of means which he has appointed. And it was proper then, as it is now, having made use of those means, to implore the Divine blessing on them, and to feel that their efficacy depends wholly on him. Thus used, there was ground of *hope* and of *faith* in regard to the recovery of the sufferer; and no one can show that in thousands of instances in the apostles'

16 Confess *your* faults one to another, and pray one for another, that ye may be healed. The effec-

tual fervent prayer of a righteous man availeth much.[b]

a Ae.19.18.   b Ps.145.19

day, and since, the prayer of faith, accompanying the proper use of means, may not have raised up those who were on the borders of the grave, and who *but* for these means would have died.

16. *Confess* your *faults one to another.* This seems primarily to refer to those who were *sick,* since it is added, '*that ye may be healed.*' The fair interpretation is, that it might be supposed that such *confession* would contribute to a restoration to health. The case supposed all along here (see ver. 15) is, that the sickness referred to had been brought upon the patient for his sins, apparently as a punishment for some particular transgressions. Comp. Notes on 1 Cor. xi. 30. In such a case, it is said that if those who were sick would make confession of their sins, it would, in connection with prayer, be an important means of restoration to health. The duty inculcated, and which is equally binding on all now, is, that if we are sick, and are conscious that we have injured any persons, to make confession to them. This indeed is a duty at all times, but in health it is often neglected, and there is a special propriety that such confession should be made when we are sick. The particular *reason* for doing it which is here specified is, that it would contribute to a restoration to health—' that ye may be healed.' In the case specified, this might be supposed to contribute to a restoration to health from one of two causes: (1.) If the sickness had been brought upon them as a *special* act of Divine visitation for sin, it might be hoped that when the confession was made the hand of God would be withdrawn; or (2) in any case, if the mind was troubled by the recollection of guilt, it might be hoped that the calmness and peace resulting from confession would be favourable to a restoration to health. The former case would of course be more applicable to the times of the apostles; the latter would pertain to all times. Disease is often greatly aggravated by the trouble of mind which arises from conscious guilt; and, in such a case,

nothing will contribute more directly to recovery than the restoration of peace to the soul agitated by guilt and by the dread of a judgment to come. This may be secured by *confession*—confession made first to God, and then to those who are wronged. It may be added, that this is a duty to which we are prompted by the very nature of our feelings when we are sick, and by the fact that no one is willing to die with guilt on his conscience; without having done everything that he can to be at peace with all the world. This passage is one on which Roman Catholics rely to demonstrate the propriety of ' *auricular confession,*' or confession made to a priest with a view to an absolution of sin. The doctrine which is held on that point is, that it is a duty to confess to a priest, at certain seasons, *all* our sins, secret and open, of which we have been guilty; all our improper thoughts, desires, words, and actions; and that the priest has power to declare on such confession that the sins are forgiven. But never was any text *less* pertinent to prove a doctrine than this passage to demonstrate that. For, (1.) the confession here enjoined is not to be made by a person in health, that he may obtain salvation, but by a sick person, that he may be healed. (2.) As *mutual* confession is here enjoined, a priest would be as much bound to confess to the people as the people to a priest. (3.) No mention is made of a *priest* at all, or even of a minister of religion, as the one to whom the confession is to be made. (4.) The confession referred to is for ' faults' with reference to ' one another,' that is, where one has injured another; and nothing is said of confessing faults to those whom we have not injured at all. (5.) There is no mention here of *absolution,* either by a priest or any other person. (6.) If anything is meant by *absolution* that is scriptural, it may as well be pronounced by one person as another; by a layman as a clergyman. All that it *can* mean is, that God *promises* pardon to those who are truly penitent, and this fact may as well be stated by one person as another. No priest, no man whatever, is empowered to say to another either that he *is* truly penitent, or to *forgive* sin. 'Who can forgive sins but God only?' None but he whose law has been violated, or who has been wronged, can pardon an offence. No third person can forgive a sin which a man has committed against a neighbour; no one but a parent can pardon the offences of which his own children have been guilty towards him; and who can put himself in the place of God, and presume to pardon the sins which his creatures have committed against him? (7.) The practice of 'auricular confession' is 'evil, and only evil, and that continually.' Nothing gives so much power to a priesthood as the supposition that they have the power of absolution. Nothing serves so much to pollute the soul as to keep impure thoughts before the mind long enough to make the confession, and to *state* them in words. Nothing gives a man so much power over a female as to have it supposed that it is required by religion, and appertains to the sacred office, that all that passes in the mind should be disclosed to him. The thought which but for the necessity of confession would have vanished at once; the image which would have departed as soon as it came before the mind, but for the necessity of retaining it to make confession—these are the things over which a man would seek to have control, and to which he would desire to have access, if he wished to accomplish purposes of villany. *The very thing which a seducer would desire would be the power of knowing all the thoughts of his intended victim; and if the thoughts which pass through the soul could be known, virtue would be safe nowhere.* Nothing probably under the name of religion has ever done more to corrupt the morals of a community than the practice of auricular confession. ¶ *And pray one for another.* One for the other; mutually. Those who have done injury, and those who are injured, should pray for each other. The apostle does not seem here, as in vers. 14, 15, to refer particularly to the prayers of the ministers of religion, or the elders of the church, but refers to it as a duty appertaining to all Christians.

¶ *That ye may be healed.* Not with reference to death, and therefore not relating to 'extreme unction,' but in order that the sick may be restored again to health. This is said in connection with the duty of *confession*, as well as *prayer;* and it seems to be implied that both might contribute to a restoration to health. Of the way in which *prayer* would do this, there can be no doubt; for all healing comes from God, and it is reasonable to suppose that this might be bestowed in answer to prayer. Of the way in which *confession* might do this, see the remarks already made. We should be deciding without evidence if we should say that sickness never comes now as a particular judgment for some forms of sin, and that it might not be removed if the suffering offender would make full confession to God, or to him whom he has wronged, and should resolve to offend no more. Perhaps this is, oftener than we suppose, one of the methods which God takes to bring his offending and backsliding children back to himself, or to warn and reclaim the guilty. When, after being laid on a bed of pain, his children are led to reflect on their violated vows and their unfaithfulness, and resolve to sin no more, they are raised up again to health, and made eminently useful to the church. So calamity, by disease or in other forms, often comes upon the vicious and the abandoned. They are led to reflection and to repentance. They resolve to reform, and the natural effects of their sinful course are arrested, and they become examples of virtue and usefulness in the world.

¶ *The effectual fervent prayer.* The word *effectual* is not the most happy translation here, since it seems to do little more than to state a truism—that a prayer which is *effectual* is *availing*—that is, that it *is* effectual. The Greek word (ἐνεργουμένη) would be better rendered by the word *energetic*, which indeed is derived from it. The word properly refers to that which has power; which in its own nature is fitted to produce an effect. It is not so much that it actually *does* produce an effect, as that it is *fitted* to do it. This is the kind of prayer referred to here. It is not listless, indifferent, cold, lifeless, as

17 Elias was a man subject to like passions as we are, and he [a]prayed [1]earnestly that it might not rain; and it rained not on the earth by the space of three years and six months.

a 1 Ki.17.1.   1 in prayer.

if there were no vitality in it, or power, but that which is adapted to be efficient —earnest, sincere, hearty, persevering. There is but a single word in the original to answer to the translation *effectual fervent.* Macknight and Doddridge suppose that the reference is to a kind of prayer '*inwrought* by the Spirit,' or the '*inwrought* prayer;' but the whole force of the original is expressed by the word *energetic,* or *earnest.* ¶ *Of a righteous man.* The quality on which the success of the prayer depends is not the talent, learning, rank, wealth, or *office* of the man who prays, but the fact that he is a 'righteous man,' that is, a good man; and this may be found in the ranks of the poor, as certainly as the rich; among laymen, as well as among the ministers of religion; among slaves, as well as among their masters. ¶*Availeth much.* ἰσχύει. Is strong; has efficacy; prevails. The idea of *strength* or *power* is that which enters into the word; strength that overcomes resistance and secures the object. Comp. Matt. vii. 28; Acts xix. 16; Rev. xii. 8. It has been said that 'prayer moves the arm that moves the world;' and if there is anything that can prevail with God, it is prayer—humble, fervent, earnest *petitioning.* We have no power to control him; we cannot dictate or prescribe to him; we cannot resist him in the execution of his purposes; but we may ask him for what we desire, and he has graciously said that such asking may effect much for our own good and the good of our fellow-men. Nothing has been more clearly demonstrated in the history of the world than that *prayer* is effectual in obtaining blessings from God, and in accomplishing great and valuable purposes. It has indeed no intrinsic power; but God has graciously purposed that his favour shall be granted to those who call upon him, and that what no mere human power can effect should be produced by *his* power in answer to prayer.

17. *Elias.* The common way of writing the word *Elijah* in the New Testament, Matt. xi. 14; xvi. 14; xvii. 3, etc. ¶ *Was a man subject to like passions as we are.* This does not mean that Elijah was *passionate* in the sense in which that word is now commonly used; that is, that he was excitable or irritable, or that he was the victim of the same corrupt passions and propensities to which other men are subject; but that he was *like affected;* that he was capable of suffering the same things, or being affected in the same manner. In other words, he was a mere man, subject to the same weaknesses and infirmities as other men. Comp. Notes on Acts xiv. 15. The apostle is illustrating the efficacy of prayer. In doing this, he refers to an undoubted case where prayer *had* such efficacy. But to this it might be objected that Elijah was a distinguished prophet, and that it was reasonable to suppose that *his* prayer would be heard. It might be said that his example could not be adduced to prove that the prayers of those who were not favoured with such advantages would be heard; and especially that it could not be argued from his case that the prayers of the ignorant, and of the weak, and of children and of servants, would be answered. To meet this, the apostle says that he was a mere man, with the same natural propensities and infirmities as other men, and that therefore his case is one which should encourage all to pray. It was an instance of the efficacy of *prayer,* and not an illustration of the power of a *prophet.* ¶ *And he prayed earnestly.* Greek, 'He *prayed with prayer*'—a Hebraism, to denote that he prayed earnestly. Comp. Luke xxii. 15. This manner of speaking is common in Hebrew. Comp. 1 Sam. xxvi. 25; Psa. cxviii. 18; Lam. i. 2. The reference here is undoubtedly to 1 Kings xvii. 1. In that place, however, it is not said that Elijah *prayed,* but that he said, 'As the Lord God of Israel liveth, before whom I stand, there shall not be

18 And he prayed again, *a* and
the heaven gave rain, and the earth
brought forth her fruit.

19 Brethren, if any of you do err

from the truth, and one *b* convert
him,

20 Let him know, that he which

a 1 Ki.18.42,45.　　　*b* Mat.18.15.

dew nor rain these three years, but according to my word.' Either James interprets this as a prayer, because it could be accomplished only *by* prayer, or he states what had been handed down by tradition as the way in which the miracle was effected. There can be no reasonable doubt that prayer was employed in the case, for even the miracles of the Saviour were accomplished in connexion with prayer, John xi. 41, 42. ¶ *That it might not rain.* Not to gratify any private resentment of his, but as a punishment on the land for the idolatry which prevailed in the time of Ahab. Famine was one of the principal methods by which God punished his people for their sins. ¶ *And it rained not on the earth.* On the land of Palestine, for so the word *earth* is frequently understood in the Bible. See Notes on Luke ii. 1. There is no reason to suppose that the famine extended beyond the country that was subject to Ahab. ¶ *By the space.* For the time. ¶ *Of three years and six months.* See this explained in the Notes on Luke iv. 25. Comp. Lightfoot, Horæ Hebraicæ, on Luke iv. 25.

18. *And he prayed again.* The allusion here seems to be to 1 Kings xviii. 42, 45, though it is not expressly said there that he *prayed.* Perhaps it might be fairly gathered from the narrative that he *did* pray, or at least that would be the presumption, for he put himself into a natural attitude of prayer. 'He cast himself down upon the earth, and put his face between his knees,' 1 Kings xviii. 42. In such circumstances, it is to be fairly presumed that such a man *would* pray; but it is remarkable that it is not expressly mentioned, and quite as remarkable that James should have made his argument turn on a thing which is *not* expressly mentioned, but which seems to have been a matter of *inference.* It seems probable to me, therefore, that there was some tradition on which he relied, or that it was a common interpretation of the passage in 1 Kings, that Elijah prayed earnestly,

and that this was generally believed by those to whom the apostle wrote. Of the *fact* that Elijah was a man of prayer, no one could doubt; and in these circumstances the tradition and common belief were sufficient to justify the argument which is employed here. ¶ *And the heaven gave rain.* The clouds gave rain. 'The heaven was black with clouds and wind, and there was a great rain,' 1 Kings xviii. 45. ¶ *And the earth brought forth her fruit.* The famine ceased, and the land again became productive. The case referred to here was indeed a miracle, but it was a case of *the power of prayer,* and therefore to the point. If God would work a miracle in answer to prayer, it is reasonable to presume that he will bestow upon us the blessings which we need in the same way.

19. *Brethren, if any of you do err from the truth.* Either doctrinally and speculatively, by embracing error; or practically, by falling into sinful practices. Either of these may be called 'erring from the truth,' because they are contrary to what the truth teaches and requires. What is here said does not appear to have any connexion with what precedes, but the apostle seems to have supposed that such a case *might* occur; and, in the conclusion of the epistle, he called their attention to the importance of endeavouring to save an erring brother, if such an instance should happen. The exhortation would be proper in addressing a letter to any church, or in publicly addressing any congregation. ¶ *And one convert him.* This does not mean *convert him as a sinner,* or *regenerate him,* but turn him from the error of his way; bring him back from his wanderings; re-establish him in the truth, and in the practice of virtue and religion. So far as the word used here is concerned, (ἐπιστρέψῃ,) he who had erred from the truth, and who was to be converted, may have been a true Christian before. The word means simply *to turn,* sc., from his way of error. See Notes on Luke xxii. 32.

20. *Let him know.* Let him who

converteth the sinner from the error of his way shall save a soul from death, and shall hide *a multitude of sins.

a Pr.10.12; 1 Pe.4.8.

converts the other know for his encouragement. ¶ *That he which converteth the sinner from the error of his way.* *Any* sinner; any one who has done wrong. This is a general principle, applicable to this case and to all others of the same kind. It is a universal truth that he who turns a sinner from a wicked path does a work which is acceptable to God, and which will in some way receive tokens of his approbation. Comp. Deut. xii. 3. No work which man can perform is more acceptable to God; none will be followed with higher rewards. In the language which is used here by the apostle, it is evidently intended not to deny that success in converting a sinner, or in reclaiming one from the error of his ways, is to be traced to the grace of God; but the apostle here refers only to the Divine feeling towards the individual who shall attempt it, and the rewards which he may hope to receive. The reward bestowed, the good intended and done, would be the same as if the individual were able to do the work himself. God approves and loves his aims and efforts, though the success is ultimately to be traced to himself. ¶ *Shall save a soul from death.* It has been doubted whether this refers to his own soul, or to the soul of him who is converted. Several manuscripts, and the Vulgate, Syriac, Arabic, and Coptic versions, here read, '*his soul.*' The most natural interpretation of the passage is to refer it to the soul of the one converted, rather than of him who converts him. This accords better with the uniform teaching of the New Testament, since it is nowhere else taught that the method of saving *our* souls is by converting others; and this interpretation will meet all that the scope of the passage demands. The object of the apostle is to present a *motive* for endeavouring to convert one who has wandered away; and assuredly a sufficient motive for that is furnished in the fact, that by this means an immortal soul would be saved from eternal ruin. The word *death* here must refer to eternal death, or to future punishment. There is no other *death* which the soul is in danger of dying. The body dies and moulders away, but the soul is immortal. The apostle cannot mean that he would save the soul from *annihilation*, for it is in no danger of that. This passage proves, then, that there is a death which the soul may die; that there is a condition which may properly be called death as a consequence of sin; and that the soul will suffer that unless it is converted. ¶ *And shall hide a multitude of sins.* Shall cover them over so that they shall not be seen; that is, they shall not be punished. This must mean either the sins which he has committed who is thus converted and saved, or the sins of him who converts him. Whichever is the meaning, a strong *motive* is presented for endeavouring to save a sinner from the error of his ways. It is not easy to determine which is the true sense. Expositors have been about equally divided respecting the meaning. Doddridge adopts substantially *both* interpretations, paraphrasing it, 'not only procuring the pardon of those committed by the convert, but also engaging God to look with greater indulgence on his own character, and to be less ready to mark severely what he has done amiss.' The Jews regarded it as a meritorious act to turn a sinner from the error of his ways, and it is *possible* that James may have had some of their maxims in his eye. Comp. Clarke, *in loc.* Though it may not be possible to determine with certainty whether the apostle here refers to the sins of him who converts another, or of him who is converted, yet it seems to me that the reference is probably to the latter, for the following reasons: (1.) Such an interpretation will meet all that is fairly implied in the language. (2.) This interpretation will furnish a strong motive for what the apostle expects us to do. The motive presented is, according to this, that sin will not be punished. But this is always a good motive for putting forth efforts in the cause of religion, and quite as powerful when drawn from our doing good to others as when applied to ourselves. (3.) This is a *safe* interpretation; the other is attended with danger. According to this, the effort would be one of pure benevolence, and there would be no danger of depending on what we do as a ground of acceptance with God. The other interpretation would seem to teach that our sins might be forgiven on some other ground than that of the atonement—by virtue of some act of our own. And (4) there might be danger, if it be supposed that this refers to the fact that *our* sins are to be covered up by this act, of supposing that by endeavouring to convert others *we* may live in sin with impunity; that however we live, we shall be safe if we lead others to repentance and salvation. If the motive be the simple desire to hide the sins of others—to procure their pardon —to save a soul from death, without any supposition that *by* that we are making an atonement for our own sins —it is a good one, a safe one. But if the idea is that by this act we are making some atonement for our own offences and that we may thus work out a righteousness of our own, the idea is one that is every way dangerous to the great doctrine of justification by faith, and is contrary to the whole teaching of the Bible. For these rea-

sons it seems to me that the true interpretation is, that the passage refers to the sins of others, not our own; and that the simple motive here presented is, that in this way we may save a fellow-sinner from being punished for his sins. It may be added, in the conclusion of the Notes on this epistle, that this motive is one which is sufficient to stimulate us to great and constant efforts to save others. Sin is the source of all the evil in the universe: and the great object which a benevolent heart ought to have, should be that its desolating effects may be stayed; that the sinner may be pardoned; and that the guilty soul may be saved from its consequences in the future world. This is the design of God in the plan of redemption; this was the object of the Saviour in giving himself to die; this is the purpose of the Holy Spirit in renewing and sanctifying the soul; and this is the great end of all those acts of Divine Providence by which the sinner is warned and turned to God. When we come to die, as we shall soon, it will give us more pleasure to be able to recollect that we have been the means of saving one soul from death, than to have enjoyed all the pleasures which sense can furnish, or to have gained all the honour and wealth which the world can give.

THE

FIRST EPISTLE GENERAL OF PETER

INTRODUCTION.

ΓHE first epistle of Peter has never been doubted to be the production of the apostle of that name. While there were doubts respecting the genuineness of the second epistle, (see Intro. to that epistle, § 1,) the unvarying testimony of history, and the uniform belief of the church, ascribe this epistle to him. Indeed, there is no ancient writing whatever of which there is more certainty in regard to the authorship.

The history of Peter is so fully detailed in the New Testament, that it is not necessary to go into any extended statement of his biography in order to an exposition of his epistles. No particular light would be reflected on them from the details of his life; and in order, therefore, to their exposition, it is not necessary to have any farther information of him than what is contained in the New Testament itself. Those who may wish to obtain all the knowledge of his life which can now be had, may find ample details in Lardner, vol. vi. pp. 203–254, ed. London, 1829; Koppe, Proleg.; and Bacon's Lives of the Apostles, pp. 43–286. There are some questions, however, which it is important to consider in order to an intelligent understanding of his epistles.

§ 1. *The persons to whom the first Epistle was addressed.*

THIS epistle purports to have been addressed 'to the strangers scattered throughout Pontus, Galatia, Cappadocia, Asia, and Bithynia.' All these were provinces of Asia Minor; and there is no difficulty, therefore, in regard to the *places* where those to whom the epistle was written resided. The only question is, who they were who are thus designated as 'strangers scattered abroad,' or *strangers of the dispersion*, (παρεπιδήμοις διασπορᾶς.) Comp. Notes on chap. i. 1. In regard to this, various opinions have been held.

(1.) That they were native-born Jews, who had been converted to the Christian faith. Of this opinion were Eusebius, Jerome, Grotius, Beza, Mill, Cave, and others. The principal argument for this opinion is the appellation given to them, (chap. i. 1,) 'strangers scattered abroad,' and what is said in chap. ii. 9; iii. 6, which it is supposed is language which would be applied only to those of Hebrew extraction.

(2.) A second opinion has been that the persons to whom it was sent were all of Gentile origin. Of this opinion were Procopius, Cassiodorus, and more recently Wetstein. This belief is founded chiefly on such passages as the following: chap. i. 18; ii. 10; iv. 3—which are supposed to show that they who were thus addressed were formerly idolaters.

(3.) A third opinion has been that they were Gentiles by birth, but had been Jewish proselytes, or 'proselytes of the gate,' and had then been converted to Christianity. This sentiment was defended by Michaelis, chiefly on the ground that the phrase in chap. i. 1, 'strangers of the dispersion,' when followed by the name of a heathen country or people, in the genitive case, denotes the Jews who were dispersed there, and yet that there is evidence in the epistle that they were not native-born Jews.

(4.) A fourth opinion has been that the persons referred to were not Jews in general, but those of the ten tribes who had wandered from Babylon and the adjacent regions into Asia Minor. This opinion is mentioned by Michaelis as having been entertained by some persons, but no reasons are assigned for it.

(5.) A fifth opinion has been that the persons referred to were Christians, converted from both Jews and Gentiles, with no particular reference to their extraction; that there were those among them who had been converted from the Jews, and those who had been Gentiles, and that the apostle addresses them *as* Christians, though employing language such as the Jews had been accustomed to, when speaking of those of their own nation who were scattered abroad. This is the opinion of Lardner, Estius, Whitby, Wolfius, and Doddridge.

That this last opinion is the correct one, seems to me to be clear from the epistle itself. Nothing can be plainer than that the apostle, while in the main he addresses Christians as such, whether they had been Jews or heathen, yet occasionally makes such allusions, and uses such language, as to show that he had his eye, at one time, on some who had been Jews, and again on some who had been pagans. This is clear, I think, from the following considerations:

(1.) The address of the epistle is general, not directed particularly either to the Jews or to the Gentiles. Thus in chap. v. 14, he says, ' Peace be with you all that are in Christ Jesus.' From this it would seem that the epistle was addressed to *all* true Christians in the region designated in chap. i. 1. But no one can doubt that there were Christians there who had been Jews, and also those who had been Gentiles. The same thing is apparent from the second epistle ; for it is certain, from 2 Pet. iii. 2, that the second epistle was addressed to the same persons as the first. But the address in the second epistle is to Christians residing in Asia Minor, without particular reference to their origin. Thus in chap. i. 1, ' To them that have obtained like precious faith with us through the righteousness of God and our Saviour Jesus Christ.' The same thing is apparent also from the address of the first epistle : ' To the elect strangers scattered throughout Pontus,' etc.; that is, ' to the strangers of the dispersion who are chosen, or who are true Christians, scattered abroad.' The term 'elect' is one which would apply to all who were Christians ; and the phrase, ' the strangers of the dispersion,' is that which one who had been educated as a Hebrew would be likely to apply to those whom he regarded as the people of God dwelling out of Palestine The Jews were accustomed to use this expression to denote their own people who were dispersed among the Gentiles ; and nothing would be more natural than that one who had been educated as a Hebrew, and then converted to Christianity, as Peter had been, should apply this phrase indiscriminately to Christians living out of Palestine. See the Notes on the passage. These considerations make it clear that in writing this epistle he had reference to Christians *as such*, and meant that *all* who were Christians in the parts of Asia Minor which he mentions, (chap. i. 1,) should regard the epistle as addressed to them.

(2.) Yet there are some allusions in the epistle which look as if a part of them at least had been Jews before their conversion, or such as a Jew would better understand than a Gentile would. Indeed, nothing is more probable than that there were Jewish converts in that region. We know that there were many Jews in Asia Minor ; and, from the Acts of the Apostles, it is morally certain that not a few of them had been converted to the Christian faith under the labours of Paul. Of the allusions of the kind referred to in the epistle, the following may be taken as specimens: ' But ye are a chosen generation, a royal priesthood, an holy nation, a peculiar people,' chap. ii. 9. This is such language as was commonly used by the Jews when addressing their own countrymen as the people of God ; and would seem to imply that to some of those at least to whom the epistle was addressed, it was language which would be familiar. See also chap. iii. 6. It should be said, however, that these passages are not *positive* proof that any among them were Hebrews. While it is true that it is such language as would be naturally employed in addressing those who were, and while it supposes an acquaintance among them with the Old Testament, it is also true that it is such language as one who had himself been educated as an Hebrew would not unnaturally employ when addressing any whom he regarded as the people of God.

(3.) The passages in the epistle which imply that many of those to whom it was addressed had been Gentiles or idolaters, are still more clear. Such passages are the following: 'As obedient children, not fashioning yourselves according to your former lusts in your ignorance,' chap. i. 14. 'This,' says Dr. Lardner, 'might be very pertinently said to men converted from Gentilism to Christianity; but no such thing is ever said by the apostles concerning the Jewish people who had been favoured with the Divine revelation, and had the knowledge of the true God.' So in chap. ii. 9, Peter speaks of them as 'having been called out of darkness into marvellous light.' The word 'darkness' is one which would be naturally applied to those who had been heathens, but would not be likely to be applied to those who had had the knowledge of God as revealed in the Jewish Scriptures. So in chap. ii. 10, it is expressly said of them, 'which in time past was not a people, but are now the people of God'—language which would not be applied to those who had been Jews. So also chap. iv. 3, 'For the time past of our life may suffice us to have wrought the will of the Gentiles, when we walked in lasciviousness, lusts, excess of wine, revellings, banquetings, and abominable idolatries.' Though the apostle here uses the word ' *us*,' grouping himself with them, yet it cannot be supposed that he means to charge himself with these things. It is a mild and gentle way of speech, adopted not to give offence, and is such language as a minister of the gospel would now use, who felt that he was himself a sinner, in addressing a church made up of many individuals. Though it might be true that *he* had not been guilty of the particular offences which he specifies, yet in speaking in the name of the church, he would use the term *we*, and use it honestly and correctly. It would be *true* that the church had been formerly guilty of these things ; and this would be a much more mild, proper, and effective method of address, than to say *you*. But the passages adduced here prove conclusively that some of those whom Peter addresses in the epistle had been formerly idolaters, and had been addicted to the sins which idolaters are accustomed to commit.

These considerations make it clear that the epistle was addressed to those Christians in general who were scattered throughout the various provinces of Asia Minor which are specified in chap. i, 1, whether they had been Jews or Gentiles. It is probable that the great body of them had been converted from the heathen, though there were doubtless Jewish converts intermingled with them; and Peter uses such language as would be natural for one who had been a Jew himself in addressing those whom he now regarded as the chosen of God.

§ II.— *The time and place of writing the epistle.*

On this point also there has been no little diversity of opinion. The only designation of the *place* where it was written which occurs in the epistle is in chap. v. 13 : ' The church that is at Babylon, elected together with you, saluteth you.' From this it is clear that it was written at *Babylon*, but still there has been no little difference of opinion as to what place is meant here by Babylon. Some have supposed that it refers to the well-known place of that name on the Euphrates; others to a Babylon situated in Lower Egypt; others to Jerusalem or Rome, represented as Babylon. The claims of each of these places it is proper to examine. The order in which this is done is not material.

(1.) The opinion that the ' Babylon' mentioned in the epistle refers to a place of that name in Egypt, not far from Cairo. This opinion was held by Pearson and Le Clerc, and by most of the *Coptic* interpreters, who have endeavoured to vindicate the honour of their own country, Egypt, as a place where one of the books of Scripture was composed. See Koppe, Proleg. 12. That there *was* such a place in Egypt, there can be no doubt. It was a small town to the north-east of Cairo, where there was a strong castle in the time of Strabo, (i. 17, p. 807,) in which, under Tiberius, there were quartered three Roman legions, designed to keep the Egyptians in order. But there is little reason to suppose that there were many Jews there, or that a church was early collected there. The Jews would have been little likely to resort to a place which was merely a Roman garrison, nor would the apostles have been likely to go early to such a place to preach the gospel. Comp. Basnage, Ant. 36, num. xxvii. As Lardner well remarks, if Peter had written an epistle from Egypt, it would have been likely to have been from Alexandria. Besides, there is not, for the first four centuries, any notice of a church at Babylon in Egypt; a fact which can hardly be accounted for, if it had been supposed that one of the sacred books had been composed there.—Lardner, vol. vi. 265. It may be added, also, that as there was another place of that name on the Euphrates, a place much better known, and which would be naturally supposed to be the one referred to, it is probable that if the epistle had been composed at the Babylon in Egypt, there would have been something said clearly to distinguish it. If the epistle was written at the Babylon on the Euphrates, so well known was that place that no one would be likely to understand that the Babylon in Egypt was the place referred to; on the other supposition, however, nothing would be more likely than that a mistake should occur.

(2.) Others have supposed that Jerusalem is intended, and that the name was given to it on account of its wickedness, and because it resembled Babylon. This was the opinion of Capellus, Spanheim, Hardouin, and some others. But the objections to this are obvious: (*a*) There is no evidence that the name *Babylon* was ever given to Jerusalem, or *so* given to it as to make it commonly understood that that was the place intended when the term was employed. If not so, its use would be likely to lead those to whom the epistle was addressed into a mistake. (*b*) There is every reason to suppose that an apostle in writing a letter, if he mentioned the place at all where it was written, would mention the *real* name. So Paul uniformly does. (*c*) The name Babylon is not one which an apostle would be likely to give to Jerusalem; certainly not as the name by which it was to be familiarly known. (*d*) If the epistle had been written there, there is no conceivable reason why the name of the place should not have been mentioned.

(3.) Others have supposed that *Rome* is intended by the name Babylon. This was the opinion of many of the Fathers, and also of Bede, Valesius, Grotius, Cave, Whitby, and Lardner. The principal reasons for this are, that such is the testimony of Papias, Eusebius, and Jerome; and that at that time Babylon on the Euphrates was destroyed. See Lardner. But the objections to this opinion seem to me to be insuperable. (*a*) There is no evidence that at that early period the name Babylon was given to Rome, nor were there any existing reasons why it should be. The name is generally supposed to have been applied to it by John, in the book of Revelation, (chap. xvi. 19; xvii. 5; xviii. 10, 21;) but this was probably long after this epistle was written, and for reasons which did not exist in the time of Peter. There is no evidence that it was given familiarly to it in the time of Peter, or even at all until after his death. Certain it is, that it was not given so familiarly to it that when the name *Babylon* was mentioned it would be generally understood that Rome was intended. But the only reason which Peter could have had for mentioning the name Babylon at all, was to convey some definite and certain information to those to whom he wrote. (*b*) As has been already observed, the apostles, when they sent an epistle to the churches, and mentioned a place as the one where the epistle was written, were accustomed to mention the real place. (c) It would be hardly consistent with the dignity of an apostle, or any grave writer, to make use of what would be regarded as a *nickname*, when suggesting the name of a place where he then was. (d) If Rome had been meant, it would have been hardly respectful to *the church* there which sent the salutation—' The church that is at Babylon, elected together with you '—to have given it this name. Peter mentions the church with respect and kindness; and yet it would have been scarcely regarded as kind to mention it as a ' Church *in Babylon*,' if he used the term Babylon, as he must have done on such a supposition, to denote a place of eminent depravity. (e) The testimony of the Fathers on this subject does not demonstrate that Rome was the place intended. So far as appears from the extracts relied on by Lardner, they do not give this as *historical testimony*, but as their own interpretation; and, from anything that appears, we are as well qualified to interpret the word as they were. (f) In regard to the objection that Babylon was at that time destroyed, it may be remarked that this is true so far as the original splendour of the city was concerned, but still there may have been a sufficient population there to have constituted a church. The destruction of Babylon was gradual. It had not become an utter desert in the time of the apostles. In the first century of the Christian era a part of it was inhabited, though the greater portion of its former site was a waste. See Notes on Isa. xiii. 19. Comp. Diod. Sic., ii. 27. All that time, there is no improbability in supposing that a Christian church may have existed there. It should be added here, however, that on the supposition that the word Babylon refers to Rome, rests nearly all the evidence which the Roman Catholics can adduce that the apostle Peter was ever at Rome at all. There is nothing else in the New Testament that furnishes the slightest proof that he ever was there. The only passage on which Bellarmine relies to show that Peter was at Rome, is the very passage now under consideration. ' That Peter was one time at Rome,' he says, ' we show first from the testimony of Peter himself, who thus speaks at the end of his first epistle:· " The church that is at Babylon, elected together with you, saluteth you." ' He does not pretend to cite any other evidence from Scripture than this; nor does any other writer.

(4.) There remains the fourth opinion, that the well-known Babylon on the Euphrates was the place where the epistle was written. This was the opinion of Erasmus, Drusius, Lightfoot, Bengel, Wetstein, Basnage, Beausobre, and others. That this is the correct opinion seems to me to be clear from the following considerations : (a) It is the most natural and obvious interpretation. It is that which would occur to the great mass of the readers of the New Testament now, and is that which would have been naturally adopted by those to whom the epistle was sent. The word *Babylon*, without something to give it a different application, would have been understood anywhere to denote the well-known place on the Euphrates. (b) There is, as has been observed already, no improbability that there was a Christian church there, but there are several circumstances which render it probable that this would be the case : 1st. Babylon had been an important place; and its history was such, and its relation to the Jews such, as to make it probable that the attention of the apostles would be turned to it. 2nd. The apostles, according to all the traditions which we have respecting them, travelled extensively in the East, and nothing would be more natural than that they should visit Babylon. 3rd. There were many Jews of the captivity remaining in that region, and it would be in the highest degree probable that they would seek to carry the gospel to their own countrymen there. See Koppe, Proleg., pp. 16–18. Jos. Ant., b. xv., chap. ii., § 2; chap. iii., § 1. Philo. De Virtut., p. 587.

These considerations make it clear that the place where the epistle was written was Babylon on the Euphrates, the place so celebrated in ancient sacred and profane history. If this be the correct view, then this is a fact of much interest, as showing that even in apostolic times there was a true church in a place once so distinguished for splendour and wickedness, and so memorable for its acts in oppressing the ancient people of God. Our information respecting this church, however, ceases here. We know not by whom it was founded; we know not who were its pastors; nor do we know how long it survived. As Babylon, however, continued rapidly to decline, so that in the second century nothing remained but the walls, (comp. Notes on Isa. xiii. 19,) there is no reason to suppose that the church long existed there. Soon the ancient city became a heap of ruins; and excepting that now and then a Christian traveller or missionary has visited it, it is not known that a prayer has been offered there from generation to generation, or that amidst the desolations there has been a single worshipper of the true God. See this subject examined at length in Bacon's Lives of the Apostles, pp. 258—263.

In regard to the *time* when this first epistle was written, nothing certainly can be determined. There are no marks of time in the epistle itself, and there are no certain data from which we can determine when it was composed. Lardner supposes that it was in the year 63, or 64, or at the latest 65; Michaelis, that it was about the year 60. If it was written at Babylon, it was probably some time between the year 58 and 61. The time is not material, and it is impossible now to determine it.

§ 3. *The characteristics of the first Epistle of Peter.*

(1.) THE epistles of Peter are distinguished for great tenderness of manner, and for bringing forward prominently the most consolatory parts of the gospel. He wrote to those who were in affliction; he was himself an old man, (2 Pet. i. 14;) he expected soon to be with his Saviour; he had nearly done with the conflicts and toils of life; and it was natural that he should direct his eye onward, and should dwell on those things in the gospel which were adapted to support and comfort the soul. There is, therefore, scarcely any part of the New Testament where the ripe and mellow Christian will find more that is adapted to his matured feelings, or to which he will more naturally turn.

(2.) There is great compactness and terseness of thought in his epistles. They seem to be composed of a succession of *texts*, each one fitted to constitute the subject of a discourse. There is more that a pastor would like to preach on in a course of expository lectures, and less that he would be disposed to pass over as not so well adapted to the purposes of public instruction, than in almost any other part of the New Testament. There is almost nothing that is local or of temporary interest; there are no discussions about points pertaining to Jewish customs such as we meet with in Paul; there is little that pertains particularly to one age of the world or country. Almost all that he has written is of universal applicability to Christians, and may be read with as much interest and profit now by *us* as by the people to whom his epistles were addressed.

(3.) There is evidence in the epistles of Peter that the author was well acquainted with the writings of the apostle Paul. See this point illustrated at length in Eichhorn, Einleitung in das Neue Tes. viii. 606—618, § 284, and Michaelis, Intro., vol. iv. p. 323, seq. Peter himself speaks of his acquaintance with the epistles of Paul, and ranks them with the inspired writings. 2 Pet. iii. 15, 16, 'Even as our beloved brother Paul also, according to the wisdom given unto him, hath written unto you; as also in all his epistles, speaking in them of these things; in which are some things hard to be understood, which they that are unlearned and unstable wrest, as they do also the other Scriptures, unto their own destruction.' Indeed, to any one who will attentively compare the epistles of Peter with those of Paul, it will be apparent that he was acquainted with the writings of the Apostle of the Gentiles, and had become so familiar with the modes of expression which he employed, that he naturally fell into it. There is that kind of coincidence which would be expected when one was accustomed to read what another had written, and when he had great respect for him, but not that when there was a purpose to *borrow* or *copy* from him.   This will be apparent by a reference to a few parallel passages :—

PAUL.	PETER.
Eph. i. 3. Blessed be the God and Father of our Lord Jesus Christ. See also 2 Cor. i. 3.	1 Pet. i. 3. Blessed be the God and Father of our Lord Christ Jesus.
Col. iii. 8. But now ye also put off all these : anger, wrath, malice, blasphemy, filthy communication out of your mouth.	1 Pet. ii. 1. Wherefore laying aside all malice, and all guile, and all hypocrisies, and envies, and all evil speakings.
Eph. v. 22. Wives, submit yourselves to your own husbands as unto the Lord.	1 Pet. iii. 1. Likewise ye wives, be in subjection to your own husbands.
Eph. v. 21. Submitting yourselves one to another in the fear of God.	1 Pet. v. 5. Yea, all of you be subject one to another.
1 Thess. v. 6. Let us watch and be sober.	1 Pet. v. 8. Be sober: be vigilant. [In the Greek the same words, though the order is reversed.]
1 Cor. xvi. 20. Greet ye one another with an holy kiss. 2 Cor. xiii. 12; Rom. xvi. 16; 1 Thess. v. 26.	1 Pet. v. 14. Greet ye one another with a kiss of love, (ἐν φιλήμασι ἀγάπης.)
Rom. viii. 18. The glory that shall be revealed unto us.	1 Pet. v. 1. The glory that shall be revealed.
Rom. iv. 24. If we believe on him that raised up Jesus our Lord from the dead.	1 Pet. i. 21. Who by him do believe in God, that raised him up from the dead.
Rom. xiii. 1, 3, 4. Let every soul be subject unto the higher powers. For there is no power but of God ; the powers that be are ordained of God....Do that which is good, and thou shalt have praise of the same....For he is a minister of God, a revenger to execute wrath upon him that doeth evil.	1 Pet. ii. 13, 14. Submit yourselves to every ordinance of man for the Lord's sake ; whether it be to the king, as supreme; or unto governors, as unto them that are sent by him for the punishment of evil doers, and for the praise of them that do well.

See also the following passages:

Rom. xii. 6, **7.**   1 Peter iv. 10.
1 Tim. ii. 9.   1 Peter iii. 3.
1 Tim. v. 5.   1 Peter iii. 5.

These coincidences are not such as would occur between two authors when one had no acquaintance with the writings of the other ; and they thus demonstrate, what may be implied in 2 Pet. iii. 15, that Peter was familiar with the epistles of Paul.   This also would seem to imply that the epistles of Paul were in general circulation.

(4.) 'In the structure of his periods,' says Michaelis, 'St. Peter has this peculiarity, that he is fond of beginning a sentence in such a manner that it shall refer to a principal word in the preceding.   The consequence of this structure is, that the sentences, instead of being rounded, according to the manner of the Greeks, are drawn out to a great length ; and in many places where we should expect that a sentence would be closed, a new clause is attached, and another again to this, so that before the whole period comes to an end, it contains parts which, at the commencement of the period, do not appear to have been designed for it.'   This manner of writing is also found often in the epistles of Paul.

The canonical authority of this epistle has never been disputed.   For a view of the contents of it, see the analysis prefixed to the several chapters.

FIRST EPISTLE GENERAL OF PETER.

CHAPTER I.

PETER, an apostle of Jesus Christ, to the strangers scattered [a] throughout Pontus, Galatia, Cappadocia, Asia, and Bithynia,

a Ac.8.4.

CHAPTER I.

ANALYSIS OF THE CHAPTER.

This epistle was evidently addressed to those who were passing through severe trials, and probably to those who were, at that time, enduring persecution, chap. i. 6, 7; iii. 14; vi. 1, 12–19. The main object of this chapter is to comfort them in their trials; to suggest such considerations as would enable them to bear them with the right spirit, and to show the sustaining, elevating, and purifying power of the gospel. In doing this, the apostle adverts to the following considerations:—

(1.) He reminds them that they were the elect of God; that they had been chosen according to his foreknowledge, by the sanctifying agency of the Holy Ghost, and in order that they might be obedient, vers. 1, 2.

(2.) He reminds them of the lively hope to which they had been begotten, and of the inheritance that was reserved for them in heaven. That inheritance was incorruptible, and undefiled, and glorious; it would be certainly theirs, for they would be kept by the power of God unto it, though now they were subjected to severe trials, vers. 3–6.

(3.) Even now they could rejoice in hope of that inheritance, (ver. 6;) their trial was of great importance to themselves in order to test the genuineness of their piety, (ver. 7;) and in the midst of all their sufferings they could rejoice in the love of their unseen Saviour, (ver. 8;) and they would certainly obtain the great object for which they had believed—the salvation of their souls, ver. 9. By these considerations the apostle would reconcile them to their sufferings; for they would thus show the genuineness and value of Christian piety, and would be admitted at last to higher honour.

(4.) The apostle proceeds, in order further to reconcile them to their sufferings, to say that the nature of the salvation which they would receive had been an object of earnest inquiry by the prophets. They had searched diligently to know precisely what the Spirit by which they were inspired meant by the revelations given to them, and they had understood that they ministered to the welfare of those who should come after them, vers. 10–12. Those who thus suffered ought, therefore, to rejoice in a salvation which had been revealed to them in this manner; and in the fact that they had knowledge which had not been vouchsafed even to the prophets; and under these circumstances they ought to be willing to bear the trials which had been brought upon them by a religion so communicated to them.

(5.) In view of these things, the apostle (vers. 13–17) exhorts them to be faithful and persevering to the end. In anticipation of what was to be revealed to them at the final day, they should be sober and obedient; and as he who had called them into his kingdom was holy, so it became them to be holy also.

(6.) This consideration is enforced (vers. 18–21) by a reference to the price that was paid for their redemption. They should remember that they had been redeemed, not with silver and gold, but with the precious blood of Christ. He had been appointed from eternity to be their Redeemer; he had been manifested in those times for them; he had been raised from the dead for them, and their faith and hope were through him. For these reasons they ought to be steadfast in their attachment to him.

(7.) The apostle enjoins on them the especial duty of brotherly love, vers. 22, 23. They had purified their hearts by obeying the truth, and as they were all one family, they should love one another fervently. Thus they would show to their enemies and persecutors the transforming nature of their religion, and furnish an impressive proof of its reality.

(8.) To confirm all these views, the apostle reminds them that all flesh must soon die. The glory of man would fade away. Nothing would abide but the word of the Lord. They themselves would soon die, and be released from their troubles, and they should be willing, therefore, to bear trials for a little time. The great and the rich, and those apparently more favoured in this life, would soon disappear, and all the splendour of their condition would vanish; and they should not envy them, or repine at their own more humble and painful lot, vers. 24, 25. The keenest sufferings here are brief, and the highest honours and splendours of life here soon vanish away; and our main solicitude should be for the eternal inheritance. Having the prospect of that, and building on the sure word of God, which abides for ever, we need not shrink from the trials appointed to us here below.

1. *Peter, an apostle of Jesus Christ.* On the word *apostle*, see Notes on Rom. i. 1; 1 Cor. ix. 1, seq. ¶ *To the strangers.* In the Greek, the word 'elect' (see ver. 2) occurs here : ἐκλεκτοῖς παρεπιδήμοις, 'to the elect strangers.' He here addresses them as elect; in the following verse he shows them in what way they were elected. See the Notes there. The word rendered *strangers* occurs only in three places in the New Testament; Heb. xi. 13, and 1 Pet. ii. 11, where it is rendered *pilgrims*, and in the place before us. See Notes on Heb. xi. 13. The word means, literally, a *by-resident*, a sojourner among a people not one's own.—*Robinson.* There has been much diversity of opinion as to the persons here referred to: some supposing that the epistle was written to those who had been Jews, who were now converted, and who were known by the common appellation among their countrymen as 'the scattered abroad,' or the 'dispersion;' that is, those who were strangers or sojourners away from their native land; others, that the reference is to those who were called, among the Jews, 'proselytes of the gate,' or those who were admitted to certain external privileges among the Jews, (see Notes on Matt. xxiii. 15;) and others, that the allusion is to Christians as such, without reference to their origin, and who are spoken of as strangers and pilgrims. That the apostle did not write merely to those who had been Jews, is clear from chap. iv. 3, 4, (comp. Intro. § 1;) and it seems probable that he means here *Christians as such*, without reference to their origin, who were scattered through the various provinces of Asia Minor. Yet it seems also probable that he did not use the term as denoting that they were 'strangers and pilgrims on the earth,' or with reference to the fact that the earth was not their home, as the word is used in Heb. xi. 13; but that he used the term as a Jew would naturally use it, accustomed, as he was, to employ it as denoting his own countrymen dwelling in distant lands. He would regard them still as the people of God, though dispersed abroad; as those who were away from what was properly the home of their fathers. So Peter addresses these Christians as the people of God, now scattered abroad; as similar in their condition to the Jews who had been dispersed among the Gentiles. Comp. the Intro. § 1. It is not necessarily implied that these persons were strangers to Peter, or that he had never seen them; though this was not improbably the fact in regard to most of them. ¶ *Scattered.* Greek, *of the dispersion,* (διασπορᾶς;) a term which a Jew would be likely to use who spoke of his countrymen dwelling among the heathen. See Notes on John vii. 35, and James i. 1, where the same Greek word is found. It does not elsewhere occur in the New Testament. Here, however, it is applied to Christians as dispersed or scattered abroad. ¶ *Throughout Pontus, &c.* These were provinces of Asia Minor. Their position

2 Elect ^a according to the fore-knowledge ^b of God the Father, through sanctification ^c of the Spirit, unto ^d obedience and sprink-ling ^e of the blood of Jesus Christ Grace unto you, and peace, be multiplied. ^f

a Ep.1.4.　　*b* Rom.8.29.　　*c* 2 Th.2.13.
d Ro.16.26.　　*e* Heb.12.24.　　*f* Jude 2.

may be seen in the map prefixed to the Acts of the Apostles. On the situation of Pontus, see Notes on Acts ii. 9. ¶ *Galatia*. On the situation of this province, and its history, see Intro. to the Notes on Galatians, § 1. ¶ *Cappadocia*. See Notes, Acts ii. 9. ¶ *Asia*. Meaning a province of Asia Minor, of which Ephesus was the capital. Notes, Acts ii. 9. ¶ *And Bithynia*. See Notes on Acts xvi. 7.

2. *Elect*. That is, chosen. The meaning here is, that they were *in fact* chosen. The word does not refer to the *purpose to choose*, but to the fact that they were chosen or selected by God as his people. It is a word commonly applied to the people of God as being *chosen* out of the world, and called to be his. The use of the word does not determine whether God had a previous eternal purpose to choose them or not. That must be determined by something else than the mere use of the term. This word has reference to the *act* of selecting them, without throwing any light on the question why it was done. See Matt. xxiv. 22, 24, 31; Mark xiii. 20; Luke xviii. 7; Rom. viii. 33; Col. iii. 12. Comp. Notes on John xv. 16. The meaning is, that God had, on some account, a preference for them above others as his people, and had chosen them from the midst of others to be heirs of salvation. The word should be properly understood as applied to the *act* of choosing them, not to the *purpose* to choose them ; the *fact* of his selecting them to be his, not the *doctrine* that he would choose them ; and is a word, therefore, which should be freely and gratefully used by all Christians, for it is a word in frequent use in the Bible, and there is nothing for which men should be more grateful than the fact that God has chosen them to salvation. *Elsewhere* we learn that the purpose to choose them was eternal, and that the reason of it was his own good pleasure. See Notes on Eph. i. 4, 5. We are here also informed that it was in accordance with

'the foreknowledge of God the Father.' ¶ *According to the foreknowledge of God the Father*. The Father is regarded, in the Scriptures, as the Author of the plan of salvation, and as having chosen his people to life, and given them to his Son to redeem and save, John vi. 37, 65; xvii. 2, 6, 11. It is affirmed here that the fact that they were elect was in some sense in accordance with the 'foreknowledge of God.' On the meaning of the phrase, see Notes on Rom. viii. 29. The passage does not affirm that *the thing* which God 'foreknew,' and which was the reason of their being chosen, was, that they would of themselves be disposed to embrace the offer of salvation. The foreknowledge referred to might have been of many other things as constituting the reason which operated in the case ; and it is not proper to *assume* that it could have been of this alone. It *may* mean that God foreknew all the events which would ever occur, and that he saw reasons why they should be selected rather than others; or that he foreknew all that could be made to bear on their salvation; or that he foreknew all that he would himself do to secure their salvation; or that he foreknew them as having been designated by his own eternal counsels; or that he foreknew all that could be accomplished by their instrumentality; or that he saw that they would believe ; but it should not be assumed that the word means necessarily any one of these things. The simple fact here affirmed, which no one can deny, is, that there was *foreknowledge* in the case on the part of God. It was not the result of ignorance or of blind chance that they were selected. But if *foreknown*, must it not be *certain* ? How could a thing which is foreknown be contingent or doubtful? The essential idea here is, that the original *choice* was on the part of God, and not on *their* part, and that this choice was founded on what he before knew to be best. He undoubtedly saw good and sufficient *reasons* why the

3 Blessed *a be* the God and Father of our Lord Jesus Christ, which according to his ¹abundant *b* mercy

a 2 Cor.1.3.   1 *much.*   b Ep.2.4.

choice should fall on them. I do not know that the reasons why he did it are revealed, or that they could be fully comprehended by us if they were. I am quite certain that it is *not* stated that it is because they would be more disposed of themselves to embrace the Saviour than others; for the Scriptures abundantly teach, what every regenerated person feels to be true, that the fact that we are disposed to embrace the Saviour is to be traced to a Divine influence on our hearts, and not to ourselves. See John vi. 65; Rom. ix. 16; Titus iii. 5; Psa. cx. 2, 3. ¶ *Through sanctification of the Spirit.* The Holy Spirit, the third person of the Trinity. The Greek is, '*by* (ἐν) sanctification of the Spirit;' that is, it was by this influence or agency. The election that was purposed by the Father was carried into effect by the agency of the Spirit in making them holy. The word rendered *sanctification* (ἀλιασμός) is not used here in its usual and technical sense to denote *the progressive holiness of believers*, but in its more primitive and usual sense of *holiness.* Comp. Notes, 1 Cor. i. 30. It means here *the being made holy;* and the idea is, that we become in fact the chosen or elect of God by a work of the Spirit on our hearts making us holy; that is, renewing us in the Divine image. We are chosen by the Father, but it is necessary that the heart should be renewed and made holy by a work of grace, in order that we may actually *become* his chosen people. Though we are sinners, he proposes to save us; but we are not saved *in* our sins, nor can we regard ourselves as the children of God until we have evidence that we are born again. The purpose of God to save us found us unholy, and we become in fact his friends by being renewed in the temper of our mind A man has reason to think that he is one of the elect of God, **just** so far as he has evidence that he has been renewed by the Holy Spirit, and so far as he has holiness of heart and life, AND NO FARTHER. ¶ *Unto obedience and sprinkling of the blood of Jesus Christ.* This expresses the *design*

for which they had been chosen by the Father, and renewed by the Spirit. It was that they might obey God, and lead holy lives. On the phrase 'unto obedience,' see Notes on Rom. i. 5. The phrase 'unto sprinkling of the blood of Jesus Christ,' means to cleansing from sin, or to holiness, since it was by the sprinkling of that blood that they were to be made holy. See it explained in the Notes on Heb. ix. 18–23; xii. 24. ¶ *Grace unto you, and peace, be multiplied.* Notes, Rom. i. 7. The phrase 'be multiplied' means, 'may it abound, or 'may it be conferred abundantly on you.' From this verse we may learn that they who are chosen should be holy. Just in proportion as they have evidence that God has chosen them at all, they have evidence that he has chosen them to be holy; and, in fact, all the evidence which any man *can* have that he is among the elect, is that he *is* practically a holy man, and desires to become more and more so. No man can penetrate the secret counsels of the Almighty. No one can go up to heaven, and inspect the book of life to see if his name be there. No one should *presume* that his name is there without evidence. No one should depend on dreams, or raptures, or visions, as proof that his name is there. No one should expect a new revelation declaring to him that he is among the elect. All the proof which any man *can* have that he is among the chosen of God, is to be found in the evidences of personal piety; and any man who is willing to be a true Christian may have all that evidence in his own case. If any one, then, wishes to settle the question whether he is among the elect or not, the way is plain. Let him become a true Christian, and the whole matter is determined, for that is all the proof which any one has that *he* is chosen to salvation. Till a man is *willing* to do that, he should not complain of the doctrine of election. If he is not *willing* to become a Christian and to be saved, assuredly he should not complain that those who are think that they have evidence that they are the chosen of God.

hath begotten us again *a* unto a lively hope by the resurrection *b* of Jesus Christ from the dead,

4 To an inheritance *c* incorrup-

tible, and undefiled, and that fadeth *d* not away, reserved *e* in heaven for ¹ you,

a Jn.3.3,5. b 1Co.15.20. c He.9.15.
d 1 Pet.5.4. e Col.1.5. 1 Or, *us.*

---

3. *Blessed* be *the God and Father of our Lord Jesus Christ.* See Notes on 2 Cor. i. 3. ¶ *Which according to his abundant mercy.* Marg., as in the Greek, *much.* The idea is, that there was great mercy shown them in the fact that they were renewed. They had no claim to the favour, and the favour was great. Men are not begotten to the hope of heaven because they have any claim on God, or because it would not be right for him to withhold the favour. See Notes on Eph. ii. 4. ¶ *Hath begotten us again.* The meaning is, that as God is the Author of our life in a natural sense, so he is the Author of our second life by regeneration. The Saviour said, (John iii. 3,) that 'except a man be born again,' or begotten again, (γεννηθῇ ἄνωθεν,) 'he cannot see the kingdom of God.' Peter here affirms that that change *had* occurred in regard to himself and those whom he was addressing. The *word* used here as a compound (ἀναγεννάω) does not elsewhere occur in the New Testament, though it corresponds entirely with the words used by the Saviour in John iii. 3, 5, 7. Perhaps the phrase 'begotten again' would be better in each instance where the word occurs, the sense being rather that of being *begotten again,* than of being *born again.* ¶ *Unto a lively hope.* The word *lively* we now use commonly in the sense of *active, animated, quick;* the word here used, however, means *living,* in contradistinction from that which is *dead.* The hope which they had, had living power. It was not cold, inoperative, dead. It was not a mere form—or a mere speculation—or a mere sentiment; it was that which was vital to their welfare, and which was active and powerful. On the nature of *hope,* see Notes, Rom. 8, 24. Comp. Eph. ii. 12. ¶ *By the resurrection of Jesus Christ from the dead.* The resurrection of the Lord Jesus is the foundation of our hope. It was a confirmation of what he declared as truth when he lived; it was a proof of the doctrine of

the immortality of the soul; it was a pledge that all who are united to him will be raised up. See Notes on 1 Cor. xv. 1–20; 2 Tim. i. 10; 1 Thes. iv. 14. On this verse we may remark, that the fact that Christians are *chosen* to salvation should be a subject of gratitude and praise. Every man should rejoice that *any* of the race may be saved, and the world should be thankful for every new instance of Divine favour in granting to any one a hope of eternal life. Especially should this be a source of joy to true Christians. Well do they know that if God had not chosen them to salvation, they would have remained as thoughtless as others; if he had had no purpose of mercy towards them, they would never have been saved. Assuredly, if there is *anything* for which a man should be grateful, it is that God has so loved him as to give him the hope of eternal life; and if he has had *an eternal purpose* to do this, our gratitude should be proportionally increased.

4. *To an inheritance.* Through the resurrection of the Lord Jesus we now cherish the hope of that future inheritance in heaven. On the word *inheritance,* see Notes on Acts xx. 32; Eph. i. 11, 14, 18; Col. i. 12. Christians are regarded as the adopted children of God, and heaven is spoken of as their *inheritance*—as what their Father will bestow on them as the proof of his love. ¶ *Incorruptible.* It will not fade away and vanish, as that which we inherit in this world does. See the word explained in the Notes on 1 Cor. ix. 25. The meaning here is, that the inheritance will be imperishable, or will endure for ever. Here, to whatever we may be heirs, we must soon part with the inheritance; there it will be eternal. ¶ *And undefiled.* See Notes, Heb. vii. 26; xiii. 4; James i. 27. The word does not elsewhere occur in the New Testament. As applied to an *inheritance,* it means that it will be *pure.* It will not have been obtained by dishonesty, nor will it be held by

5 Who are kept *a* by the power
of God through faith *b* unto salva-

a Jude 1,24.   b Ep.2.8.

tion, ready to be revealed in the
last time.

fraud; it will not be such as will corrupt
the soul, or tempt to extravagance,
sensuality, and lust, as a rich inheritance often does here; it will be such that
its eternal enjoyment will never tend in
any manner to defile the heart. 'How
many estates,' says Benson, 'have been
got by fraudulent and unjust methods;
by poisoning, or in some other way mur-
dering the right heir; by cheating of
helpless orphans; by ruining the fatherless and widows; by oppressing their
neighbours, or grinding the faces of the
poor, and taking their garments or vine-
yards from them! But this future inheritance of the saints is stained by none
of these vices; it is neither got nor de-
tained by any of these methods; nor
shall persons polluted with vice have
any share in it.' Here no one can be
heir to an inheritance of gold or houses
without danger of soon sinking into indolence, effeminacy, or vice; there the
inheritance may be enjoyed for ever,
and the soul continually advance in
knowledge, holiness, and the active service of God. ¶ *And that fadeth not
away.* Gr. ἀμάραντον. This word occurs nowhere else in the New Testament,
though the word ἀμαράντινος (*amaran-
tine*) occurs in chap. v. 4, applied to a
crown or garland. The word is properly
applied to that which does not fade or
wither, in contradistinction from a flower
that fades. It may then denote anything that is enduring, and is applied to
the future inheritance of the saints to
describe its perpetuity *in all its bril-
liance and splendour,* in contrast with
the fading nature of all that is earthly.
The idea here, therefore, is not precisely
the same as is expressed by the word
'incorruptible.' Both words indeed denote *perpetuity,* but that refers to perpetuity in contrast with *decay;* this
denotes perpetuity in the sense that
everything there *will be kept in its
original brightness and beauty.* The
crown of glory, though worn for millions
of ages, will not be dimmed; the golden
streets will lose none of their lustre; the
flowers that bloom on the banks of the
river of life will always be as rich in

colour, and as fragant, as when we first
beheld them. ¶ *Reserved in heaven for
you.* Marg., *us.* The difference in the
text and the margin arises from the
various readings in MSS. The common
reading is 'for *you.*' The sense is not
materially affected. The idea is, that
it is an inheritance appointed for us,
and kept by one who can make it sure
to us, and who will certainly bestow it
upon us. Comp. Notes on Matt. xxv.
34; John xiv. 2; Col. i. 5.

5. *Who are kept by the power of God.*
That is, 'kept' or preserved in the faith
and hope of the gospel; who are preserved from apostacy, or so kept that
you will finally obtain salvation. The
word which is here used, and rendered
kept, (φρουρίω—*phroureo,*) is rendered
in 2 Cor. xi. 32, *kept with a garrison;*
in Gal. iii. 23, and here, *kept;* in Phil.
iv. 7, *shall keep.* It does not elsewhere
occur in the New Testament. It means
to keep, as in a garrison or fortress; or
as with a military watch. The idea is,
that there was a faithful guardianship
exercised over them to save them from
danger, as a castle or garrison is watched
to guard it against the approach of an
enemy. The meaning is, that they were
weak in themselves, and were surrounded
by temptations; and that the only reason
why they were preserved was, that God
exerted his power to keep them. The
only reason which any Christians have
to suppose they will ever reach heaven,
is the fact that God keeps them by his
own power. Comp. Notes, Phil. i. 6;
2 Tim. i. 12; iv. 18. If it were left to
the will of man; to the strength of his
own resolutions; to his power to meet
temptations, and to any probability that
he would of himself continue to walk in
the path of life, there would be no certainty that any one would be saved.
¶ *Through faith.* That is, he does not
keep us by the mere exertion of *power,*
but he excites *faith* in our hearts, and
makes that the *means* of keeping us.
As long as we have faith in God, and in
his promises, we are safe. When that
fails, we are weak; and if it should fail
altogether, we could not be saved. Comp.

6 Wherein ye greatly rejoice, though now for a season, if need *a* be, ye are in heaviness through manifold temptations:

a He.12.7-11.

Notes, Eph. ii. 8. ¶ *Unto salvation.* Not preserved for a little period, and then suffered to fall away, but *so* kept as to be saved. We may remark here that Peter, as well as Paul, believed in the doctrine of the perseverance of the saints. If he did not, how could he have addressed these Christians in this manner, and said that they were 'kept by the power of God *unto salvation?*' What evidence could he have had that they would obtain salvation, unless he believed in the general truth that it was the purpose of God to keep *all* who were truly converted? ¶ *Ready to be revealed in the last time.* That is, when the world shall close. Then it shall be made manifest to assembled worlds that such an inheritance was 'reserved' for you, and that you were 'kept' in order to inherit it. Comp. Matt. xxv. 34. This verse, then, teaches that the doctrine that the saints will *persevere* and be saved, is true. They are 'kept by the power of God to salvation;' and as God has *all* power, and guards them with reference to this end, it cannot be but that they will be saved. It may be added (*a*) that it is very *desirable* that the doctrine should be true. Man is so weak and feeble, so liable to fall, and so exposed to temptation, that it is in itself every way a thing to be wished that his salvation should be in some safer hands than his own. (*b*) If it is *desirable* that it should be true, it is fair to infer that it *is* true, for God has made all the arrangements for the salvation of his people which are really desirable and proper. (*c*) The only *security* for the salvation of any one is founded on that doctrine. If it were left entirely to the hands of men, even the best of men, what assurance could there be that any one could be saved? Did not Adam fall? Did not holy angels fall? Have not some of the best of men fallen into sin? And who has such a strength of holiness that he could certainly confide in it to make his own salvation sure? Any man must know little of himself, and of the human heart, who supposes that he has such a strength of virtue that he would never

fall away if left to himself. But if this be so, then his only hope of salvation is in the fact that God intends to 'keep his people by his own power through faith unto salvation.'

6. *Wherein ye greatly rejoice.* In which hope of salvation. The idea is, that the prospect which they had of the future inheritance was to them a source of the highest joy, even in the midst of their many sufferings and trials. On the *general* grounds for rejoicing, see Notes, Rom. v. 1, 2; Phil. iii. 1; iv. 4; 1 Thess. v. 16. See also the Notes on ver. 8 of this chapter. The *particular* meaning here is, that the hope which they had of their future inheritance enabled them to rejoice *even in the midst of persecutions and trials.* It not only *sustained* them, but it made them *happy.* That must be a valuable religion which will make men *happy* in the midst of persecutions and heavy calamities. ¶ *Though now for a season.* A short period—ὀλίγον. It would be in fact only for a brief period, even if it should continue through the whole of life. Comp. Notes, 2 Cor. iv. 17: 'Our light affliction which is *but for a moment.*' It is possible, however, that Peter supposed that the trials which they then experienced would soon pass over. They may have been suffering persecutions which he hoped would not long continue. ¶ *If need be.* This phrase seems to have been thrown in here to intimate that there was a necessity for their afflictions, or that there was 'need' that they should pass through these trials. There was some good to be accomplished by them, which made it desirable and proper that they should be thus afflicted. The sense is, 'since there is need;' though the apostle expresses it more delicately by suggesting the possibility that there *might* be need of it, instead of saying absolutely that there *was* need. It is the kind of language which we would use in respect to one who was greatly afflicted, by suggesting to him, in the most tender manner, that there *might* be things in his character which God designed to correct

116   I. PETER.   [A. D. 60.

7 That the trial of *a* your faith, being much more precious than of gold that perisheth, though it be

a Ja.1.3,12.   *b* 1 Co.3.13.

tried with *b* fire, might be found unto praise and *c* honour and glory at the appearing *d* of Jesus Christ:

c Ro.2.7,10.   *d* Re·1.7.

by trials, instead of saying roughly and bluntly that such *was* undoubtedly the fact. We would not say to such a person, 'you certainly *needed* this affliction to lead you to amend your life;' but, 'it *may be* that there is something in your character which makes it desirable, or that God intends that some good results shall come from it which will show that it is wisely ordered.' ¶ *Ye are in heaviness.* Gr., ' Ye are sorrowing,' (λυπηθέντες;) you are sad, or grieved, Matt. xiv. 9; xvii. 23. ¶ *Through manifold temptations.* Through many kinds of *trials,* for so the word rendered *temptation* (πειρασμος) means, James i. 2, 12. Notes, Matt. iv. 1; vi. 13. The meaning here is, that they now endured many things which were fitted to *try* or *test* their faith. These might have consisted of poverty, persecution, sickness, or the efforts of others to lead them to renounce their religion, and to go back to their former state of unbelief. Any one or all of these would *try* them, and would show whether their religion was genuine. On the various ways which God has of trying his people, comp. Notes, Isa. xxviii. 23–29.

7. *That the trial of your faith.* The putting of your religion to the test, and showing what is its real nature. Comp. James i. 3, 12. ¶ *Being much more precious than of gold.* This does not mean that their *faith* was much more precious than gold, but that *the testing* of it, (δοκίμιον,) the process of *showing* whether it was or was not genuine, was a much more important and valuable process than that of testing gold in the fire. More important results were to be arrived at by it, and it was more desirable that it should be done. ¶ *That perisheth.* Not that gold perishes by the process of being tried in the fire, for this is not the fact, and the connexion does not demand this interpretation. The idea is, that gold, however valuable it is, is a *perishable* thing. It is not an enduring, imperishable, indestructible thing, like religion. It may not perish in the fire, but it will in some way, for

it will not endure for ever. ¶ *Though it be tried with fire.* This refers to the *gold.* See the Greek. The meaning is, that gold, though it will bear the action of fire, is yet a destructible thing, and will not endure for ever. It is more desirable to *test* religion than it is gold, because it is more valuable. It pertains to that which is eternal and indestructible, and it is therefore of more importance to show its true quality, and to free it from every improper mixture. ¶ *Might be found unto praise.* That is, might be found to be genuine, and such as to meet the praise or commendation of the final judge. ¶ *And honour.* That honour might be done to it before assembled worlds. ¶ *And glory.* That it might be rewarded with that glory which will be then conferred on all who have shown, in the various trials of life, that they had true religion. ¶ *At the appearing of Jesus Christ.* To judge the world. Comp. Matt. xxv. 31; Acts i. 11; 1 Thess. iv. 16; 2 Thess. ii. 8; 1 Tim. vi. 14; 2 Tim. iv. 1, 8; Tit. ii. 13. From these two verses (6 and 7) we may learn : I. That it is desirable that the faith of Christians should be *tried.* (*a*) It is desirable to know whether that which appears to be religion is *genuine,* as it is desirable to know whether that which appears to be gold is genuine. To gold we apply the action of intense heat, that we may know whether it is what it appears to be; and as religion is of more value than gold, so it is more desirable that it should be subjected to the proper tests, that its nature may be ascertained. There is much which *appears* to be gold, which is of no value, as there is much which *appears* to be religion, which is of no value. The one is worth no more than the other, unless it is genuine. (*b*) It is desirable in order to show its true *value.* It is of great importance to know what that which is claimed to be gold is *worth* for the purposes to which gold is usually applied; and so it is in regard to religion. Religion claims to be of more value to man

8 Whom having not *a* seen, ye | love; in whom, though now ye see

a 1 Jn.4.20.

than anything else. It asserts its power to do that for the intellect and the heart which nothing else can do; to impart consolation in the various trials of life which nothing else can impart; and to give a support which nothing else can on the bed of death. It is very desirable, therefore, that in these various situations it should show its power; that is, that its friends should be *in* these various conditions, in order that they may illustrate the true value of religion. (*c*) It is desirable that true religion should be separated from all *alloy*. There is often much alloy in gold, and it is desirable that it should be separated from it, in order that it may be pure. So it is in religion. It is often combined with much that is unholy and impure; much that dims its lustre and mars its beauty; much that prevents its producing the effect which it would otherwise produce. Gold is, indeed, often *better*, for some purposes, for having some alloy mixed with it; but not so with religion. It is never better for having a little pride, or vanity, or selfishness, or meanness, or worldliness, or sensuality mingled with it; and that which will remove these things from our religion will be a favour to us. II. God takes various methods of trying his people, with a design to test the value of their piety, and to separate it from all impure mixtures. (1.) He tries his people by *prosperity*—often as decisive a test of piety as can be applied to it. There is much pretended piety, which will bear adversity, but which will not bear prosperity. The piety of a man is decisively tested by popularity; by the flatteries of the world; by a sudden increase of property; and in such circumstances it is often conclusively shown that there is no true religion in the soul. (2.) He tries his people in adversity. He lays his hand on them heavily, to show (*a*) whether they will *bear up* under their trials, and persevere in his service; (*b*) to show whether their religion will keep them from murmuring or complaining; (*c*) to show whether it is adapted to comfort and sustain the soul. (3.) He tries his people *by sudden transition*

from one to the other. We get accustomed to a uniform course of life, whether it be joy or sorrow; and the religion which is adapted to a uniform course may be little fitted to transitions from one condition of life to another. In *prosperity* we may have shown that we were grateful, and benevolent, and disposed to serve God; but our religion will be subjected to a new test, if we are suddenly reduced to poverty. In sickness and poverty, we learn to be patient and resigned, and perhaps even happy. But the religion which we then cultivated may be little adapted to a sudden transition to prosperity; and in such a transition, there would be a new trial of our faith. That piety which shone so much on a bed of sickness, might be little fitted to shine in circumstances of sudden prosperity. The human frame may become accustomed either to the intense cold of the polar regions, or to the burning heats of the equator; but in neither case might it bear a transition from one to the other. It is such a *transition* that is a more decisive test of its powers of endurance than either intense heat or cold, if steadily prolonged. III. Religion will *bear* any trial which may be applied to it, as gold will bear the action of fire. IV. Religion is *imperishable* in its nature. Even the most fine gold will perish. Time will corrode it, or it will be worn away by use, or it will be destroyed at the universal conflagration; but time and use will not wear out religion, and it will live on through the fires that will consume everything else. V. Christians should be *willing* to pass trough trials. (*a*) They will purify their religion, as the fire will remove dross from gold. (*b*) They will make it shine more brightly, as gold does when it comes out of the furnace. (*c*) They will disclose more fully its value. (*d*) They will furnish an evidence that we shall be saved; for that religion which will bear the tests that God applies to it in the present life, will bear the test of the final trial.

8. *Whom having not seen, ye love.* This epistle was addressed to those

him not, yet believing, ye rejoice

with joy *a* unspeakable and full of glory :

who were 'strangers scattered abroad,' (Notes, ver. 1,) and it is evident that they had not personally seen the Lord Jesus. Yet they had heard of his character, his preaching, his sacrifice for sin, and his resurrection and ascension, and they had learned to love him. (1.) It is possible to love one whom we have not seen. Thus we may love God, whom no ' eye hath seen,' (comp. 1 John iv. 20 ;) and thus we may love a benefactor, from whom we have received important benefits, whom we have never beheld. (2.) We may love the *character* of one whom we have never seen, and from whom we may never have received any particular favours. We may love his uprightness, his patriotism, his benignity, as represented to us. We might love him the more if we should become personally acquainted with him, and if we should receive important favours from him; but it is possible to feel a sense of strong admiration for such a character in itself. (3.) That may be a very *pure* love which we have for one whom we have never seen. It may be based on simple excellence of character; and in such a case there is the least chance for any intermingling of selfishness, or any improper emotion of any kind. (4.) We may love a friend as *really* and as *strongly* when he is absent, as when he is with us. The wide ocean that rolls between us and a child, does not diminish the ardour of our affection for him ; and the Christian friend that has gone to heaven, we may love no less than when he sat with us at the fireside. (5.) Millions, and hundreds of millions, have been led to love the Saviour, who have never seen him. They have seen —not with the bodily eye, but with the eye of faith—the inimitable beauty of his character, and have been brought to love him with an ardour of affection which they never had for any other one. (6.) There is every reason why we *should* love him. (*a*) His character is infinitely lovely. (*b*) He has done more for us than any other one who ever lived among men. He died for us, to redeem our souls. He rose, and brought life and immortality to light. He ever lives to

intercede for us in heaven. He is employed in preparing mansions of rest for us in the skies, and he will come and take us to himself, that we may be with him for ever. Such a Saviour *ought* to be loved, *is* loved, and *will* be loved. The strongest attachments which have ever existed on earth have been for this unseen Saviour. There has been a love for him stronger than that for a father, or mother, or wife, or sister, or home, or country. It has been so strong, that thousands have been willing, on account of it, to bear the torture of the rack or the stake. It has been so strong, that thousands of youth of the finest minds, and the most flattering prospects of distinction, have been willing to leave the comforts of a civilized land, and to go among the benighted heathen, to tell them the story of a Saviour's life and death. It has been so strong, that unnumbered multitudes have longed, more than they have for all other things, that they might see him, and be with him, and abide with him for ever and ever. Comp. Notes, Phil. i. 23. ¶ *In whom, though now ye see* him *not, yet believing.* He is now in heaven, and to mortal eyes now invisible, like his Father. *Faith* in him is the source and fountain of our joy. It makes invisible things real, and enables us to feel and act, in view of them, with the same degree of certainty *as if* we saw them. Indeed, the conviction to the mind of a true believer that there *is* a Saviour, is as certain and as strong as if he saw him ; and the same may be said of his conviction of the existence of heaven, and of eternal realities. If it should be said that faith may deceive us, we may reply, (1,) May not our bodily senses also deceive us ? Does the *eye* never deceive ? Are there no optical illusions ? Does the *ear* never deceive ? Are there no sounds which are mistaken ? Do the *taste* and the *smell* never deceive ? Are we never mistaken in the report which they bring to us ? And does the sense of *feeling* never deceive ? Are we never mistaken in the size, the hardness, the figure of objects which we handle ? But, (2,) for all the practical purposes of life, the senses are

9 Receiving the end of your faith, | *even* the salvation of *your* souls.

correct guides, and do not in general lead us astray. So, (3,) there are objects of faith about which we are never deceived, and where we do act and must act with the same confidence as if we had personally seen them. Are we deceived about the existence of London, or Paris, or Canton, though we may never have seen either? May not a merchant embark with perfect propriety in a commercial enterprise, on the supposition that there *is* such a place as London or Canton, though he has never seen them? Would he not be reputed mad, if he should *refuse* to do it on this ground? And so, may not a man, in believing that there is a heaven, and in forming his plans for it, though he has not yet seen it, act as rationally and as wisely as he who forms his plans on the supposition that there is such a place as Canton? ¶ *Ye rejoice.* Ye *do rejoice;* not merely ye *ought to rejoice.* It may be said of Christians that they *do in fact* rejoice; they *are* happy. The people of the world often suppose that religion makes its professors sad and melancholy. That there are those who have not great comfort in their religion, no one indeed can doubt; but this arises from several causes entirely independent of their religion. Some have melancholy temperaments, and are not happy in anything. Some have little evidence that they are Christians, and their sadness arises not from religion, but from the want of it. But that true religion *does* make its possessors happy, any one may easily satisfy himself by asking any number of sincere Christians, of any denomination, whom he may meet. With one accord they will say to him that they have a happiness which they never found before; that however much they may have possessed of the wealth, the honours, and the pleasures of the world —and they who are now Christians have not all of them been strangers to these things—they never knew solid and substantial peace till they found it in religion. And why should they not be believed? The world would believe them in other things; why will they not when they declare that religion does not

make them gloomy, but happy? ¶ *With joy unspeakable.* A very strong expression, and yet verified in thousands of cases among young converts, and among those in the maturer days of piety. There are thousands who can say that their happiness when they first had evidence that their sins were forgiven, that the burden of guilt was rolled away, and that they were the children of God, was unspeakable. They had no words to express it, it was so full and so new.

> "Tongue can never express
> The sweet comfort and peace
> Of a soul in its earliest love."

And so there have been thousands of mature Christians who can adopt the same language, and who could find no words to express the peace and joy which they have found in the love of Christ; and the hope of heaven. And why are not all Christians enabled to say constantly that they 'rejoice with joy unspeakable?' Is it not a privilege which they might possess? Is there anything in the nature of religion which forbids it? Why should *not* one be filled with constant joy who has the hope of dwelling in a world of glory for ever? Comp. John xiv. 27; xvi. 22. ¶ *And full of glory.* (1.) Of anticipated glory—of the prospect of enjoying the glory of heaven. (2.) Of present glory—with a joy *even now* which is of the same nature as that in heaven; a happiness the same in kind, though not in degree, as that which will be ours in a brighter world. The saints on earth partake of the same *kind* of joy which they will have in heaven; for the happiness of heaven will be but an expansion, a prolongation, and a purifying of that which they have here. Comp. Notes on Eph. i. 14.

9. *Receiving the end of your faith,* even *the salvation of* your *souls.* The *result* or *object* of your faith; that is, what your faith is designed and adapted to secure. Comp. Notes on Rom. x. 4 The word rendered *receiving* is used here as indicating that they would surely obtain that. They even now had such peace and joy in believing, that it furnished undoubted evidence that they

10 Of which salvation the prophets have enquired *a* and searched diligently, who prophesied of the grace *that should come* unto you:

11 Searching what, or what man-

ner of time the Spirit *b* of Christ which was in them did signify, when it testified before-hand the sufferings of Christ, and the glory that should follow:

a Da.9.3.

b 2 Pe.1.21.

would be saved; and such that it might be said that even now they *were* saved. The condition of one who is a true Christian here is so secure that it may even now be called *salvation*.

10. *Of which salvation.* Of the certainty that this system of religion, securing the salvation of the soul, would be revealed. The *object* of this reference to the prophets seems to be to lead them to value the religion which they professed more highly, and to encourage them to bear their trials with patience. They were in a condition, in many respects, far superior to that of the prophets. They had the full light of the gospel. The prophets saw it only at a distance and but dimly, and were obliged to search anxiously that they might understand the nature of that system of which they were appointed to furnish the comparatively obscure prophetic intimations. ¶ *The prophets.* This language would imply that this had been a common and prevalent wish of the prophets. ¶ *Have enquired.* This word is *intensive.* It means that they sought out, or scrutinized with care the revelations made to them, that they might understand exactly what was implied in that which they were appointed to record in respect to the salvation which was to be made known through the Messiah. See the following places where the same word is used which occurs here: Luke xi. 50, 51; Acts xv. 17; Rom. iii. 11; Heb. xi. 6; xii. 17. ¶ *And searched diligently—*ἐξηρεύνάω. Comp. Dan. ix. 2, 3. The word here used means *to search out, to trace out, to explore.* It is not elsewhere used in the New Testament, though one of the words from which this is compounded (ἐρευνάω) occurs. See John v. 39, (Notes;) vii. 52; Rom. viii. 27; 1 Cor. ii. 10; Rev. ii. 23. The idea is, that they perceived that in their communications there were some great and glorious truths which they did not fully comprehend, and that they dili-

gently employed their natural faculties to understand that which they were appointed to impart to succeeding generations. They thus became students and interpreters for themselves of their own predictions. They were not only *prophets,* but *men.* They had souls to be saved in the same way as others. They had hearts to be sanctified by the truth; and it was needful, in order to this, that truth should be applied to their own hearts in the same way as to others. The mere fact that they were the channels or organs for imparting truth to others would not save them, any more than the fact that a man now preaches truth to others will save himself, or than the fact that a sutler delivers bread to an army will nourish and support his own body. ¶ *Who prophesied of the grace* that should come *unto you.* Of the favour that should be shown to you in the gospel. Though the predictions which they uttered appeared to the men of their own times, and perhaps to themselves, obscure, yet they were in fact *prophecies* of what was to come, and of the favours which, under another dispensation, would be bestowed upon the people of God. The apostle does not mean to say that they prophesied particularly of those persons to whom he was then writing, but that their prophecies were *in fact* for their benefit, for the things which they predicted had actually terminated on them. The benefit was as real as though the predictions had been solely on their account.

11. *Searching what.* That is, examining their own predictions with care, to ascertain what they meant. They studied them as we do the predictions which others have made; and though the prophets were the medium through which the truth was made known, yet their own predictions became a subject of careful investigation to themselves. The expression here used in the origi-

nal, rendered 'what,' (εἰς τίνα,) literally, 'unto what,' may mean, so far as the Greek is concerned, either 'what *time*,' or 'what *people*,' or 'what *person*;' that is, with reference to *what person* the prophecies were really uttered. The latter, it seems to me, is the correct interpretation, meaning that they inquired in regard to him, who he would be, what would be his character, and what would be the nature of the work which he would perform. There can be no doubt that they understood that their predictions related to the Messiah ; but still it is not improper to suppose that it was with them an interesting inquiry what sort of a person he would be, and what would be the nature of the work which he would perform. This interpretation of the phrase εἰς τίνα, (*unto what* or *whom*,) it should be observed, however, is not that which is commonly given of the passage. Bloomfield, Rosenmüller, Doddridge, Whitby, Benson, and Grotius suppose it to refer to *time*, meaning that they inquired *at* what time, or *when* these things would occur. Macknight thinks it refers to *people*, (λαον,) meaning that they diligently inquired what people would put him to death. But the most obvious interpretation is that which I have suggested above, meaning that they made particular inquiry to *whom* their prophecies related—what was his rank and character, and what was to be the nature of his work. What would be a more natural inquiry for them than this? What would be more important? And how interesting is the thought that when Isaiah, for example, had given utterance to the sublime predictions which we now have of the Messiah, in his prophecies, he sat himself down with the spirit of a little child, to learn by prayer and study, what was fully implied in the amazing words which the Spirit had taught him to record! How much of mystery might seem still to hang around the subject! And how intent would such a mind be to know what was the full import of those words! ¶ *Or what manner of time.* This phrase, in Greek, (ποῖον καιρον,) would properly relate, not to the exact time *when* these things would occur, but to the *character* or *condition* of the age when they would take place;

perhaps referring to the state of the world at that period, the preparation to receive the gospel, and the probable manner in which the great message would be received. Perhaps, however, the inquiry in their minds pertained to the time *when* the predictions would be fulfilled, as well as to the condition of the world when the event takes place. The meaning of the Greek phrase would not exclude this latter sense. There are not unfrequent indications of time in the prophets, (comp. Dan. ix. 24, seq. ;) and these indications were of so clear a character, that when the Saviour actually appeared there was a general expectation that the event would then occur. See Notes on Matt. ii. 2. ¶ *The Spirit of Christ which was in them.* This does not prove that they *knew* that this was the Spirit of Christ, but is only a declaration of Peter that it was *actually* so. It is not probable that the prophets distinctly understood that the Spirit of inspiration, by which they were led to foretell future events, was peculiarly the Spirit of Christ. They understood that they were inspired; but there is no intimation, with which I am acquainted, in their writings, that they regarded themselves as inspired *by* the Messiah. It was not improper, however, for Peter to say that the Spirit by which they were influenced was in fact the Spirit of Christ, so called because that Spirit which suggested these future events to them was given as the great Medium of all revealed truth to the world. Comp. Heb. i. 3; John i. 9; xiv. 16, 26; xvi. 7; Isa. xlix. 6. It is clear from this passage, (1,) that Christ must have had an existence before his incarnation ; and, (2,) that he must have understood then what would occur to him when he should become incarnate ; that is, it must have been arranged or determined beforehand. ¶ *Did signify.* Meant to intimate or manifest to them, (ἐδήλου ;) or what was *implied* in the communications made to them. ¶ *When it testified beforehand the sufferings of Christ.* As Isaiah, chap. liii; Daniel, chap. ix. 25–27. They saw clearly that the Messiah was *to suffer;* and doubtless this was the common doctrine of the prophets, and the common expectation of the pious part of the Jewish nation. Yet it is not necessary

12 Unto whom it was revealed, that not *a* unto themselves, but unto us they did minister the things, which are now reported unto you by them that have preached the gospel unto you with the Holy Ghost *b* sent down from heaven; which things the angels *c* desire to look into.

a He.2.39,40.   b Ac.2.4; 2 Co.1.22.   c Ep.3.10.

to suppose that they had clear apprehensions of his sufferings, or were able to reconcile all that was said on that subject with what was said of his glory and his triumphs. There was much about those sufferings which *they* wished to learn, as there is much still which *we* desire to know. We have no reason to suppose that there were any views of the sufferings of the Messiah communicated to the prophets except what we now have in the Old Testament; and to see the force of what Peter says, we ought to imagine what would be *our* views of him if all that we have known of Christ as *history* were obliterated, and we had only the knowledge which we could derive from the Old Testament. As has been already intimated, it is probable that they studied their own predictions, just as *we* would study them if we had not the advantage of applying to them the *facts* which have actually occurred. ¶ *And the glory that should follow.* That is, they saw that there *would be* glory which would be the result of his sufferings, but they did not clearly see what it would be. They had some knowledge that he would be raised from the dead, (Psa. xvi. 8–11; Comp. Acts ii. 25–28;) they knew that he would ' see of the travail of his soul, and would be satisfied,' (Isa. liii. 11;) they had some large views of the effects of the gospel on the nations of the earth, Isa. xi; xxv. 7, 8; lx; lxvi. But there were many things respecting his glorification which it cannot be supposed they clearly understood; and it is reasonable to presume that they made the comparatively few and obscure intimations in their own writings in relation to this, the subject of profound and prayerful inquiry.

12. *Unto whom it was revealed.* They were not permitted to know fully the import of the predictions which they were made the instruments of communicating to mankind, but they understood that they were intended for the benefit of future ages. ¶ *That not unto themselves.* We are not to suppose that they derived *no* benefit from their own predictions; for, as far as they understood the truth, it was as much adapted to sanctify and comfort them as it is us now: but the meaning is, that their messages had reference mainly to future times, and that the full benefit of them would be experienced only in distant ages. Comp. Heb. xi. 39, 40. ¶ *Unto us they did minister the things, which are now reported unto you.* Not unto us *by name*, but their ministrations had reference to the times of the Messiah; and those to whom Peter wrote, in common with all Christians, were those who were to enjoy the fruits of the communications which they made. The word *reported* means *announced*, or *made known.* ¶ *By them that have preached the gospel unto you.* The apostles, who have made known unto you, in their true sense, the things which the prophets predicted, the import of which they themselves were so desirous of understanding. ¶ *With the Holy Ghost sent down from heaven.* Accompanied by the influences of the Holy Ghost bearing those truths to the heart, and confirming them to the soul. It was the same Spirit which inspired the prophets which conveyed those truths to the souls of the early Christians, and which discloses them to true believers in every age. Comp. John xvi. 13, 14; Acts ii. 4; x. 44, 45. The *object* of Peter by thus referring to the prophets, and to the interest which they took in the things which those to whom he wrote now enjoyed, seems to have been, to impress on them a deep sense of the value of the gospel, and of the great privileges which they enjoyed. They were reaping the benefit of all the labours of the prophets. They were permitted to see truth clearly, which the prophets themselves saw only obscurely. They were, in many respects, more favoured than even those holy men had been. It was for them that the

prophets had spoken the word of the Lord ; for them and their salvation that a long line of the most holy men that the world ever saw, had lived, and toiled, and suffered ; and while they themselves had not been allowed to understand the full import of their own predictions, the most humble believer was permitted to see what the most distinguished prophet never saw. See Matt. xiii. 17. ¶ *Which things the angels desire to look into.* The object of this reference to the angels is the same as that to the prophets. It is to impress on Christians a sense of the value of that gospel which they had received, and to show them the greatness of their privileges in being made partakers of it. It had excited the deepest interest among the most holy men on earth, and even among the inhabitants of the skies. They were enjoying the full revelation of what even the angels had desired more fully to understand, and to comprehend which they had employed their great powers of investigation. The *things* which are here referred to, (**εἰς ἃ**—*unto which*,) are those which the prophets were so desirous to understand—the great truths respecting the sufferings of Christ, the glory which would follow, and the nature and effects of the gospel. In all the events pertaining to the redemption of a world they felt a deep interest. The word which is rendered ' to look,' (**παρα-κύψαι**,) is rendered *stooping down*, and *stooped down*, in Luke xxiv. 12 ; John xx. 5, 11; *looketh*, in James i. 25; and *look*, in the place before us. It does not elsewhere occur in the New Testament. It properly means, to stoop down near by anything ; to bend forward near, in order to look at anything more closely.—*Robinson, Lex.* It would denote that state where one, who was before at so great a distance that he could not clearly see an object, should draw nearer, stooping down in order that he might observe it more distinctly. It is possible, as Grotius supposes, that there may be an allusion here to the posture of the cherubim over the mercy-seat, represented as looking down with an intense gaze, as if to behold what was in the ark. But it is not necessary to suppose that this is the allusion, nor is it absolutely certain that that was the posture of the cherubim. See Notes on Heb. ix. 5. All that is necessarily implied in the language is, that the angels had an intense desire to look into these things; that they contemplated them with interest and fixed attention, like one who comes near to an object, and looks narrowly upon it. In illustration of this sentiment, we may make the following suggestions: I. The angels, doubtless, desire to look into *all* the manifestations of the character of God, wherever those manifestations are made. (1.) It is not unreasonable to suppose that, to a great degree, they acquire the knowledge of God as all other creatures do. They are not omniscient, and cannot be supposed to comprehend at a glance all his doings. (2.) They doubtless employ their faculties, substantially as we do, in the investigation of truth ; that is, from things known they seek to learn those that are even unknown. (3.) It is not unreasonable to suppose that there are many things in relation to the Divine character and plans, which they do not yet understand. They know, undoubtedly, much more than we do ; but there are plans and purposes of God which are yet made known to none of his creatures. No one can doubt that these plans and purposes must be the object of the attentive study of all holy created minds. (4.) They doubtless feel a great interest in the welfare of other beings—of their fellow-creatures, wherever they are. There is in the universe one great brotherhood, embracing all the creatures of God. (5.) They cannot but feel a deep interest in man—a fallen creature, tempted, suffering, dying, and exposed to eternal death. This they have shown in every period of the world's history. Notes on Heb. i. 14. II. It is probable, that in each one of the worlds which God has made, there is some peculiar manifestation of his glory and character; something which is not to be found at all in any other world, or, if found, not in so great perfection ; and that the angels would feel a deep interest in all these manifestations, and would desire to look into them. (1.) This is probable from the nature of the case, and from the variety which we see in the form, size, movements, and glory of the heavenly orbs. **There is no reason to** suppose, that on *any one* of those worlds *all* the glory of the Divine character would be manifest, which he intends to make known to the universe. (2.) This is probable from what *we* can now see of the worlds which he has made. We know as yet comparatively little of the heavenly bodies, and of the manifestations of the Deity there; and yet, as far as we *can* see, there must be far more striking exhibitions of the power, and wisdom, and glory of God, in many or most of those worlds that roll above us, than there are on our earth. On the body of the sun—on the planets Jupiter and Saturn, so vast in comparison with the earth—there must be far more impressive exhibitions of the glory of the Creator, than there is on our little planet. Saturn, for example, is 82,000 miles in diameter, 1100 times as large as our earth; it moves at the rate of 22,000 miles an hour; it is encircled by two magnificent rings, 5000 miles apart, the innermost of which is 21,000 miles from the body of the planet, and 22,000 miles in breadth, forming a vast illuminated *arch* over the planet above the brightness of our moon, and giving a most beautiful appearance to the heavens there. It is also, doubtless, true of *all* the worlds which God has made, that in each one of them there may be some peculiar manifestation of the glory of the Deity. (3.) The universe, therefore, seems fitted up to give eternal employment to *mind* in contemplating it; and, in the worlds which God has made, there is enough to employ the study of his creatures *for ever.* On our own world, the most diligent and pious student of the works of God might spend many thousand years, and then leave much, very much, which he did not comprehend; and it may yet be the eternal employment of holy minds to range from world to world, and in each new world to find much to study and to admire; much that shall proclaim the wisdom, power, love, and goodness of God, which had not elsewhere been seen. (4.) Our world, therefore, though small, a mere speck in creation, may have something to manifest the glory of the Creator which may not exist in any other. It cannot

be its magnitude; for, in that respect, it is among the smallest which God has made. It may not be the height and the majesty of our mountains, or the length and beauty of our rivers, or the fragrance of our flowers, or the clearness of our sky; for, in these respects, there may be much more to admire in other worlds: it is the exhibition of the character of God in the work of redemption; the illustration of the way in which a sinner may be forgiven; the manifestation of the Deity as incarnate, assuming permanently a union with one of his own creatures. This, so far as we know, is seen in no other part of the universe; *and this is honour enough for one world.* To see this, the angels may be attracted down to earth. When they come, they come not to contemplate our works of art, our painting and our sculpture, or to read our books of science or poetry: they come to gather around the cross, to minister to the Saviour, to attend on his steps while living, and to watch over his body when dead; to witness his resurrection and ascension, and to bless, with their offices of kindness, those whom he died to redeem, Heb. i. 4. III. What, then, is there in our world which we may suppose would attract their attention? What is there which they would not see in other worlds? I answer, that the manifestation of the Divine character in the plan of redemption, is that which would peculiarly attract their attention here, and lead them from heaven down to earth. (1.) The mystery of the incarnation of the Son of God would be to them an object of the deepest interest. This, so far as we know, or have reason to suppose, has occurred nowhere else. There is no evidence that in any other world God has taken upon himself the form of one of his own creatures dwelling there, and stooped to live and act like one of them; to mingle with them; to share their feelings; and to submit to toil, and want, and sacrifice, for their welfare. (2.) The *fact* that the guilty *could* be pardoned would attract their attention, for (*a*) it is elsewhere unknown, no inhabitant of heaven having the need of pardon, and no offer of pardon having been made to a rebel angel. (b) There are great and difficult questions about the whole subject of forgiveness, which an angel could easily *see,* but which he could not so easily *solve.* How could it be done consistently with the justice and truth of God? How could he forgive, and yet maintain the honour of his own law, and the stability of his own throne? There is no more difficult subject in a human administration than that of *pardon;* and there is none which so much perplexes those who are intrusted with executive power. (3.) The *way* in which pardon has been shown to the guilty here would excite their deep attention. It has been in a manner entirely consistent with justice and truth; showing, through the great sacrifice made on the cross, that the attributes of justice and mercy may both be exercised: that, while God may pardon to any extent, he does it in no instance at the expense of justice and truth. This blending of the attributes of the Almighty in beautiful harmony; this manifesting of mercy to the guilty and the lost; this raising up a fallen and rebellious race to the favour and friendship of God; and this opening before a dying creature the hope of immortality, was what could be seen by the angels nowhere else: and hence it is no wonder that they hasten with such interest to our world, to learn the mysteries of redeeming love. Every step in the process of recovering a sinner must be new to them, for it is unseen elsewhere; and the whole work, the atonement, the pardon and renovation of the sinner, the conflict of the child of God with his spiritual foes, the supports of religion in the time of sickness and temptation, the bed of death, the sleep in the tomb, the separate flight of the soul to its final abode, the resurrection of the body, and the solemn scenes of the judgment, all must open new fields of thought to an angelic mind, and attract the heavenly inhabitants to our world, to learn here what they cannot learn in their own abodes, however otherwise bright, where sin, and suffering, and death, and redemption are unknown. In view of these truths we may add: (1.) The work of redemption is worthy of the study of the profoundest minds. Higher talent than *any* earthly talent has been employed in studying it; for, to the most exalted intellects of heaven, it has been a theme of the deepest interest. No mind on earth is too exalted to be engaged in this study; no intellect here is so profound that it would not find in this study a range of inquiry worthy of itself. (2.) This is a study that is peculiarly appropriate to man. The angels have no other interest in it than that which arises from a desire to know God, and from a benevolent regard for the welfare of others; *we* have a personal interest in it of the highest kind. It pertains primarily to us. The plan was formed for us. Our eternal all depends upon it. The angels would be safe and happy if they did *not* fully understand it; if *we* do not understand it, we are lost for ever. It has claims to *their* attention as a wonderful exhibition of the character and purposes of God, and as they are interested in the welfare of *others;* it claims *our* attention because our eternal welfare depends on our accepting the offer of mercy made through a Saviour's blood. (3.) How amazing, then, how wonderful, is the indifference of man to this great and glorious work! How wonderful, that neither as a matter of speculation, nor of personal concern, he can be induced 'to look into these things!' How wonderful that all other subjects engross his attention, and excite inquiry; but that for *this* he feels no concern, and that here he finds nothing to interest him! It is not unreasonable to suppose, that amidst all the other topics of wonder in this plan as seen by angels, this is not the least—that man by nature takes no interest in it; that in so stupendous a work, performed in his own world, he feels no concern; that he is unmoved when he is told that even God became incarnate, and appeared on the earth where he himself dwells; and that, busy and interested as he is in other things, often of a most trifling nature, he has *no* concern for that on which is suspended his own eternal happiness. If heaven was held in mute astonishment when the Son of God left the courts of glory to be poor, to be persecuted, to bleed, and to die, not less must be the astonishment than when, from those lofty heights, the angelic

13 Wherefore gird *a* up the loins of your mind, be sober, *b* and hope 1 to the end *c* for the grace that is to be brought unto you at the revelation of Jesus Christ;

14 As obedient children, not fa-

shioning *d* yourselves according to the former lusts in your ignorance:

15 But as he which hath called you is holy, so be ye holy in all manner of conversation;

a Lu.12.35.   b Lu.21.34.   1 *perfectly.*
c He.10.35.   d Ro.12.2.

hosts look down upon a race unconcerned amidst wonders such as those of the incarnation and the atonement!

13. *Wherefore gird up the loins of your mind.* The allusion here is to the manner in which the Orientals were accustomed to dress. They wear loose, flowing robes, so that, when they wish to run, or to fight, or to apply themselves to any business, they are obliged to bind their garments close around them. See Notes on Matt. v. 38–41. The meaning here is, that they were to have their minds in constant preparation to discharge the duties, or to endure the trials of life—like those who were prepared for labour, for a race, or for a conflict. ¶ *Be sober.* See Notes on 1 Tim. iii. 2; Titus i. 8; ii. 2. ¶ *And hope to the end.* Marg., *perfectly.* The translation in the text is the most correct. It means, that they were not to become faint or weary in their trials. They were not to abandon the hopes of the gospel, but were to cherish those hopes to the end of life, whatever opposition they might meet with, and however much might be done by others to induce them to apostatize. Comp. Notes on Heb. x. 35, 36. ¶ *For the grace that is to be brought unto you.* For the *favour* that shall then be bestowed upon you; to wit, salvation. The word *brought* here means, that this great favour which they hoped for would be borne to them by the Saviour on his return from heaven. ¶ *At the revelation of Jesus Christ.* When the Lord Jesus shall be revealed from heaven in his glory; that is, when he comes to judge the world. See Notes, 2 Thess. i. 7.

14. *As obedient children.* That is, conduct yourselves as becomes the children of God, by obeying his commands; by submitting to his will; and by manifesting unwavering confidence in him as your Father, at all times. ¶ *Not fashioning yourselves.* Not forming or modelling your life. Comp. Notes, Rom.

xii. 2. The idea is, that they were to have *some* model or example, in accordance with which they were to frame their lives, but that they were *not* to make their own former principles and conduct the model. The Christian is to be as different from what he was before conversion as he is from his fellow-men. He is to be governed by new laws, to aim at new objects, and to mould his life in accordance with new principles. Before conversion, he was (*a*) supremely selfish; (*b*) he lived for personal gratification; (*c*) he gave free indulgence to his appetites and passions, restrained only by a respect for the decencies of life, and by a reference to his own health, property, or reputation, without regard to the will of God; (*d*) he conformed himself to the customs and opinions around him, rather than to the requirements of his Maker; (*e*) he lived for worldly aggrandizements, his supreme object being wealth or fame; or (*f*) in many cases, those who are now Christians, gave indulgence to every passion which they wished to gratify, regardless of reputation, health, property, or salvation. Now they are to be governed by a different rule, and their own former standard of morals and of opinions is no longer their guide, but the will of God. ¶ *According to the former lusts in your ignorance.* When you were ignorant of the requirements of the gospel, and gave yourselves up to the unrestrained indulgence of your passions.

15. *But as he which hath called you is holy.* On the word *called,* see Notes on Eph. iv. 1. The meaning here is, that the model or example in accordance with which they were to frame their lives, should be the character of that God who had called them into his kingdom. They were to be like him. Comp. Notes, Matt. v. 48. ¶ *So be ye holy in all manner of conversation.* In all your conduct. On the word *conversation,*

16 Because it is written, *a* Be ye holy; for I am holy.

17 And if ye call on the Father, who without respect of persons judgeth according to every man's work, pass the time of your sojourning *here* in fear: *b*

18 Forasmuch as ye know that ye were not redeemed with corruptible things, *as* silver and gold, from your vain conversation *received* by tradition from your fathers;

a Le.11.44.　　　　*b* Phi.2.12.

---

see Notes on Phil. i. 27. The meaning is, that since God is holy, and we profess to be his followers, we ought also to be holy.

16. *Because it is written, Be ye holy; for I am holy.* Lev. xi. 44. This command was addressed at first to the Israelites, but it is with equal propriety addressed to Christians, as the professed people of God. The foundation of the command is, that they professed to be his people, and that *as* his people they ought to be like their God. Comp. Micah iv. 5. It is a great truth, that men everywhere will imitate the God whom they worship. They will form their character in accordance with his. They will regard what he does as right. They will attempt to rise no higher in virtue than the God whom they adore, and they will practise freely what he is supposed to do or approve. Hence, by knowing what are the characteristics of the gods which are worshipped by any people, we may form a correct estimate of the character of the people themselves; and hence, as the God who is the object of the Christian's worship is perfectly holy, the character of his worshippers *should* also be holy. And hence, also, we may see that the tendency of true religion is to *make* men pure. As the worship of the impure gods of the heathen moulds the character of the worshippers into their image, so the worship of Jehovah moulds the character of his professed friends into his image, and they become like him.

17. *And if ye call on the Father.* That is, if you are true Christians, or truly pious—piety being represented in the Scriptures as calling on God, or as the worship of God. Comp. Acts ix. 11; Gen. iv. 26; 1 Kings xviii. 24; Psa. cxvi. 17; 2 Kings v. 11; 1 Chron. xvi. 8; Joel ii. 32; Rom. x. 13; Zeph. iii. 9; 1 Cor. i. 2; Acts ii. 21. The word 'Father' here is used evidently not to denote the Father in contradistinction to the Son, but as referring to God as the Father of the universe. See ver. 14—'As obedient *children.*' God is often spoken of as the Father of the intelligent beings whom he has made. Christians worship him *as* a Father— as one having all the feelings of a kind and tender parent towards them. Comp. Psa. ciii. 13, seq. ¶ *Who without respect of persons.* Impartiality. Who is not influenced in his treatment of men by a regard to rank, wealth, beauty, or any external distinction. See Notes on Acts x. 34, and Rom. ii. 11. ¶ *Judgeth according to every man's work.* He judges each one according to his character; or to what *he has done,* Rev. xxii. 12. Notes, 2 Cor. v. 10. The meaning is, 'You worship a God who will judge every man according to his real character, and you should therefore lead such lives as he can approve.' ¶ *Pass the time of your sojourning.* 'Of your temporary residence on earth. This is not your permanent home, but you are strangers and sojourners.' See Notes on Heb. xi. 13. ¶ *In fear.* Notes, Phil. ii. 12; Heb. xii. 28. With true reverence or veneration for God and his law. Religion is often represented as the reverent fear of God, Deut. vi. 2, 13, 24; Prov. i. 7; iii. 13; xiv. 26, 27, *et sæpe al.*

18. *Forasmuch as ye know.* This is an argument for a holy life, derived from the fact that they were redeemed, and from the manner in which their redemption had been effected. There is no more effectual way to induce true Christians to consecrate themselves entirely to God, than to refer them to the fact that they are not their own, but have been purchased by the blood of Christ. ¶ *That ye were not redeemed.* On the word rendered *redeemed,* (λυτρόω —*lutroo,*) see Notes, Titus ii. 14. The word occurs in the New Testament only

19 But with the precious blood | of Christ, as of a lamb *a* without blemish and without spot:

a Jn.1.29,36; Re.7.14.

in Luke xxiv. 21; Titus ii. 14, and in this place. The noun (λύτρον—*lutron*) is found in Matt. xx. 28; Mark x. 45, rendered *ransom*. For the meaning of the similar word, (ἀπολύτρωσις—*apolutrosis*,) see Notes on Rom. iii. 24. This word occurs in Luke xxi. 28; Rom. iii. 24; viii. 23; 1 Cor. i. 30; Eph. i. 7, 14; iv. 30; Col. i. 14; Heb. ix. 15, in all which places it is rendered *redemption;* and in Heb. xi. 35, where it is rendered *deliverance.* The word here means that they were rescued from sin and death by the blood of Christ, as *the valuable consideration* on account of which it was done; that is, the blood, or the life of Christ offered as a sacrifice, effected the same purpose in regard to justice and to the maintenance of the principles of moral government, which the punishment of the sinner himself would have done. It was that which God was pleased to accept in the place of the punishment of the sinner, as answering the same great ends in his administration. The principles of his truth and justice could as certainly be maintained in this way as by the punishment of the guilty themselves. If so, then there was no obstacle to their salvation; and they might, on repentance, be consistently pardoned and taken to heaven. ¶ *With corruptible things,* as *silver and gold.* On the word *corruptible,* as applicable to gold, see Notes on ver. 7. Silver and gold usually constitute the price or the valuable consideration paid for the redemption of captives. It is clear that the obligation of one who is redeemed, to love his benefactor, is in proportion to the price which is paid for his ransom. The idea here is, that a price far more valuable than any amount of silver or gold had been paid for the redemption of the people of God, and that they were under proportionate obligation to devote themselves to his service. They were redeemed by the life of the Son of God offered in their behalf; and between the value of that life and silver and gold there could be no comparison. ¶ *From your vain conversation.* Your vain *conduct,* or *manner of*

life. Notes on ver. 15. The word *vain,* applied to conduct, (ματαίας,) means properly *empty, fruitless.* It is a word often applied to the worship of idols, as being *nothing, worthless, unable to help,* (Acts xiv. 15; 1 Kings xvi. 13; 2 Kings xvii. 15; Jer. ii. 5, 8, 19,) and is probably used in a similar sense in this place. The apostle refers to their former worship of idols, and to all the abominations connected with that service, as being vain and unprofitable ; as the worship of nothing real, (comp. 1 Cor. viii. 4, 'We know that an idol is *nothing* in the world;') and as resulting in a course of life that answered none of the proper ends of living. From that they had been redeemed by the blood of Christ. ¶ Received *by tradition from your fathers.* The mode of worship which had been handed down from father to son. The worship of idols depends on no better reason than that it is that which has been practised in ancient times ; and it is kept up now in all lands, in a great degree, only by the fact that it has had the sanction of the venerated men of other generations.

19. *But with the precious blood of Christ.* On the use of the word *blood,* and the reason why the efficacy of the atonement is said to be in the *blood,* see Notes on Rom. iii. 25. The word *precious* (τίμιος) is a word which would be applied to that which is worth much ; which is costly. Comp. for the use of the noun (τιμή) in this sense, Matt. xxvii. 6, ' The *price* of blood;' Acts iv. 34; v. 2, 3; vii. 16. See also for the use of the adjective, (τίμιος,) Rev. xvii. 4, 'gold and *precious* stones.' Rev. xviii. 12. 'vessels of most *precious* wood.' Rev. xxi. 11, ' a stone most *precious.*' The meaning here is, that the blood of Christ had a *value* above silver and gold ; it was *worth* more, to wit, (1,) in itself — being a more valuable thing—and (2,) in effecting our redemption. It accomplished what silver and gold could not do. The universe had nothing more valuable to offer, of which we can conceive, than the blood of the Son of God. ¶ *As of a*

20 Who verily was foreordained before *a* the foundation of the world, but was manifest in these last times for you,

21 Who by him do believe in God,

a Re.13.8.

that raised him up from the dead, and *b* gave him glory; that your faith and hope might be in God.

22 Seeing ye have purified your souls in obeying the truth *c* through

b Mat.28.18; Phi.2.9.　　*c* Jn.17.17,19.

---

lamb. That is, of Christ regarded *as* a lamb offered for sacrifice. Notes on John i. 29. ¶ *Without blemish and without spot.* Such a lamb only was allowed to be offered in sacrifice, Lev. xxii. 20–24; Mal. i. 8. This was required, (1,) because it was *proper* that man should offer that which was regarded as perfect in its kind; and, (2,) because only that would be a proper symbol of the great sacrifice which was to be made by the Son of God. The idea was thus kept up from age to age that he, of whom all these victims were the emblems, would be perfectly pure.

20. *Who verily was foreordained before the foundation of the world.* That is, it was foreordained, or predetermined, that he should be the great atoning Sacrifice for sin. On the meaning of the word *foreordained,* (προγινώσκω,) see Rom. viii. 29. The word is rendered *which knew,* Acts xxvi. 5; *foreknew* and *foreknow,* Rom. viii. 29; xi. 2; *foreordained,* 1 Pet. i. 20; and *know before,* 2 Pet. ii. 17. It does not elsewhere occur in the New Testament. The sense is, that the plan was formed, and the arrangements made for the atonement, before the world was created. ¶ *Before the foundation of the world.* That is, from eternity. It was before man was formed; before the earth was made; before any of the material universe was brought into being; before the angels were created. Comp. Notes on Matt. xxv. 34; John xvii. 24; Eph. i. 4. ¶ *But was manifest.* Was revealed. Notes on 1 Tim. iii. 16. ¶ *In these last times.* In this, the last dispensation of things on the earth. Notes on Heb. i. 2. ¶ *For you.* For your benefit or advantage. See Notes on ver. 12. It follows from what is said in this verse, (1,) that the atonement was not an *after-thought* on the part of God. It entered into his plan when he made the world, and was revolved in his purposes from eternity. (2.) It was not a

device to supply a *defect* in the system; that is, it was not adopted because the system did not work well, or because God had been disappointed. It was arranged *before* man was created, and when none but God could know whether he would stand or fall. (3.) The creation of the earth must have had some reference to this plan of redemption, and that plan must have been regarded as in itself so glorious, and so desirable, that it was deemed best to bring the world into existence that the plan might be developed, though it would involve the certainty that the race would fall, and that many would perish. It was, on the whole, more wise and benevolent that the race should be created with a certainty that they would apostatize, than it would be that the race should *not* be created, and the plan of salvation be unknown to distant worlds. See Notes on ver. 12.

21. *Who by him do believe in God.* Faith is sometimes represented particularly as exercised in God, and sometimes in Christ. It is always a characteristic of true religion that a man has faith in God. Comp. Notes on Mark xi. 22. ¶ *That raised him up from the dead.* Notes on Acts ii. 24; iii. 15, 26; iv. 10; v. 30; xiii. 30; Rom. iv. 24; vi. 4; 1 Cor. xv. 15. ¶ *And gave him glory.* By exalting him at his own right hand in heaven, Phil. ii. 9; 1 Tim. iii. 16; Eph. i. 20, 21. ¶ *That your faith and hope might be in God.* That is, by raising up the Lord Jesus, and exalting him to heaven, he has laid the foundation of confidence in his promises, and of the hope of eternal life. Comp. Notes on ver. 3. Comp. 1 Cor. xv.; Col. i. 27; 1 Thess. i. 3; 1 Tim. i. 1.

22. *Seeing ye have purified your souls.* Greek, 'Having purified your souls.' The apostles were never afraid of referring to human agency as having an important part in saving the soul

the Spirit unto unfeigned love ^a of the brethren, *see that ye* love one another with a pure heart fervently:

a 1 Jn.3.14,18.

Comp. 1 Cor. iv. 15. No one is made pure without personal intention or effort — any more than one becomes accomplished or learned without personal exertion. One of the leading effects of the agency of the Holy Spirit is to excite us to *make* efforts for our own salvation; and there is no true piety which is not the fair result of culture, as really as the learning of a Porson or a Parr, or the harvest of the farmer. The amount of effort which we make 'in purifying our souls' is usually also the *measure* of our attainments in religion. No one can expect to have any true piety *beyond* the amount of effort which he makes to be conformed to God, any more than one can expect wealth, or fame, or learning, without exertion. ¶ *In obeying the truth.* That is, your yielding to the requirements of truth, and to its fair influence on your minds, has been the means of your becoming pure. The *truth* here referred to is, undoubtedly, that which is revealed in the gospel— the great system of truth respecting the redemption of the world. ¶ *Through the Spirit.* By the agency of the Holy Spirit. It is his office to apply truth to the mind; and however precious the truth may be, and however adapted to secure certain results on the soul, it will never produce those effects without the influences of the Holy Spirit. Comp. Titus iii. 5, 6. Notes on John iii. 5. ¶ *Unto unfeigned love of the brethren.* The effect of the influence of the Holy Spirit in applying the truth has been to produce sincere love to all who are true Christians. Comp. Notes on John xiii. 34; 1 Thess. iv. 9. See also 1 John iii. 14–18. ¶ See that ye *love one another with a pure heart fervently.* Comp. Notes on Heb. xiii. 1, John xiii. 34, 35; Eph. v. 2. The phrase ' with a pure heart fervently,' means (1) that it should be *genuine* love, proceeding from a heart in which there is no guile or hypocrisy; and (2) that it should be *intense* affection, (ἐκτενῶς ;) not cold and formal, but ardent and strong. If there is any reason why we should love true Christians at all, there is the same reason why our attachment to them should be intense. This verse establishes the following points : (1.) That *truth* was at the foundation of their piety. They had none of which this was not the proper basis; and in which the foundation was not as broad as the superstructure. There is no religion in the world which is not the fair developement of truth; which the truth is not fitted to produce. (2.) They became Christians as the result of *obeying* the truth; or by yielding to its fair influence on the soul. Their own minds complied with its claims; their own hearts yielded ; there was the exercise of their own volitions. This expresses a doctrine of great importance. (*a*) There is always the exercise of the powers of the mind in true religion; always a yielding to truth ; always a voluntary reception of it into the soul. (*b*) Religion is always of the nature of *obedience*. It consists in yielding to what is true and right ; in laying aside the feelings of opposition, and in allowing the mind to follow where truth and duty lead. (*c*) This would always take place when the truth is presented to the mind, if there were no voluntary resistance. If all men were ready to *yield* to the truth, they would become Christians. The only reason why all men do not love and serve God, is that they refuse to yield to what they know to be true and right. (3.) The agency by which this was accomplished was that of the Holy Ghost. Truth is adapted in itself to a certain end or result, as seed is adapted to produce a harvest. But it will no more of itself produce its appropriate effects on the soul, than seed will produce a harvest without rains, and dews, and suns. In *all* cases, therefore, the proper effect of truth on the soul is to be traced to the influence of the Holy Spirit, as the germination of the seed in the earth is to the foreign cause that acts on it. No man was ever converted by the mere effect of truth without the agency of the Holy Ghost, any more than seed germinates when laid on a hard rock. (4.) The *effect* of this influence of the Holy Spirit in applying

23 Being born *a* again, not of corruptible seed, but of incorruptible, by the word *b* of God, which liveth and abideth for ever.

24 ¹ For *c* all flesh *is* as grass,

and all the glory of man as the flower of grass. The grass withereth, and the flower thereof falleth away;

a Jn.1.13.　　*b* Ja.1.18.　　1 Or, *for that.*　　*c* Is.40.6-8.

the truth is to produce love to all who are Christians. Love to Christian brethren springs up in the soul of every one who is truly converted: and this love is just as certain evidence that the seed of truth has germinated in the soul, as the green and delicate blade that peeps up through the earth is evidence that the seed sown has been quickened into life. Comp. Notes on 1 Thess. iv. 9; 1 John iii. 14. We may learn hence, (*a*) that *truth* is of inestimable value. It is as valuable as religion itself, for all the religion in the world is the result of it. (*b*) Error and falsehood are mischievous and evil in the same degree. There is no true religion which is the fair result of error ; and all the pretended religion that is sustained by error is worthless. (*c*) If a system of religion, or a religious measure or doctrine, cannot be defended by *truth*, it should be at once abandoned. Comp. Notes on Job xiii. 7. (*d*) We should avoid the places where error is taught. Prov. xix. 27, ' Cease, my son, to hear the instruction that causeth to err from the words of knowledge.' (*e*) We should place ourselves under the teachings of truth, for there is truth enough in the world to occupy all our time and attention; and it is only *by* truth that our minds can be benefited.

23. *Being born again.* See Notes on John iii. 3. ¶ *Not of corruptible seed.* ' Not by virtue of any descent from human parents.'—*Doddridge.* The result of such a birth, or of being *begotten* in this way—for so the word rendered *born again* more properly signifies—is only corruption and decay. We are begotten only to die. There is no permanent, enduring life produced by that. It is in this sense that this is spoken of as ' *corruptible* seed,' because it results in decay and death. The word here rendered *seed*—σπορά—occurs nowhere else in the New Testament. ¶ *But of incorruptible.* By *truth*, communicating a living principle to the soul which

can never decay. Comp. 1 John iii. 9 : ' His seed remaineth in him; and he cannot sin, because he is born of God.' ¶ *By the word of God.* See Note on James i. 18: ' Of his own will begat he us with the word of truth, that we should be a kind of first-fruits of his creatures.' Comp. Notes on John i. 13. It is the uniform doctrine of the Scriptures that Divine *truth* is made the instrument of quickening the soul into spiritual life. ¶ *Which liveth and abideth for ever.* This expression may either refer to God, as living for ever, or to the *word* of God, as being for ever true. Critics are about equally divided in the interpretation. The Greek will bear either construction. Most of the recent critics incline to the latter opinion—that it refers to the word of God, or to his doctrine. So Rosenmüller, Doddridge, Bloomfield, Wolf, Macknight, Clarke. It seems to me, however, that the more natural construction of the Greek is to refer it to God, as ever-living or enduring ; and this interpretation agrees well with the connection. The idea then is, that as God is ever-living, that which is produced directly by him in the human soul, by the instrumentality of truth, may be expected also to endure for ever. It will not be like the offspring of human parents, themselves mortal, liable to early and certain decay, but may be expected to be as enduring as its ever-living Creator.

24. *For all flesh* is *as grass.* That is, all human beings, all men. The connection here is this : The apostle, in the previous verse, had been contrasting that which is begotten by man with that which is begotten by God, in reference to its *permanency.* The former was corruptible and decaying; the latter abiding. The latter was produced by God, who lives for ever ; the former by the agency of man, who is himself corruptible and dying. It was not unnatural, then, to dwell upon the feeble, frail, decaying nature of *man,*

25 But the word of the Lord endureth for ever. And this *a* is the word which by the gospel is preached unto you.

a Ja.1.1,14; 2 Pe.1.19.

in contrast with God ; and the apostle, therefore, says that ' *all* flesh, every human being, is like grass. There is no stability in anything that man does or produces. He himself resembles grass that soon fades and withers; but God and his word endure for ever the same.' The comparison of a human being with grass, or with flowers, is very beautiful, and is quite common in the Scriptures. The comparison turns on the fact, that the grass or the flower, however green or beautiful it may be, soon loses its freshness ; is withered ; is cut down, and dies. Thus in Psalm ciii. 15, 16 :—

" As for man, his days are as grass ;
As a flower of the field, so he flourisheth ;
For the wind passeth over it and it is gone,
And the place thereof shall know it no more."

So in Isaiah xl. 6–8 ; a passage which is evidently referred to by Peter in this place :—

" The voice said, Cry.
And he said, What shall I cry ?
All flesh is grass,
And all the goodliness thereof is as the flower of
the field.
The grass withereth,
The flower fadeth,
When the wind of Jehovah bloweth upon it ;
Surely the people is grass,
The grass withereth,
The flower fadeth,
But the word of our God shall stand for ever."

See also James i. 10, 11. This sentiment is beautifully imitated by the great dramatist in the speech of Wolsey :—

" This is the state of man ; to-day he puts forth
The tender leaves of hope, to-morrow blossoms,
And bears his blushing honours thick upon him.
The third day comes a frost, a killing frost,
And—when he thinks, good easy man, full surely
His greatness is a ripening—nips his root,
And then he falls."

Comp. Notes on Isa. xl. 6–8. ¶ *And all the glory of man.* All that man prides himself on—his wealth, rank, talents, beauty, learning, splendour of equipage or apparel. ¶ *As the flower of grass.* The word rendered ' *grass*,' ($\chi\acute{o}\rho\tau o\varsigma$.) properly denotes herbage ; that which furnishes food for animals— pasture, hay. Probably the prophet

Isaiah, from whom this passage is taken, referred rather to the appearance of a meadow or a field, with mingled grass and flowers, constituting a beautiful landscape, than to mere grass. In such a field, the grass soon withers with heat, and with the approach of winter ; and the flowers soon fade and fall. ¶ *The grass withereth, and the flower thereof falleth away.* This is repeated, as is common in the Hebrew writings, for the sake of emphasis, or strong confirmation.

25. *But the word of the Lord.* In Isaiah (xl. 8,) ' the word of our God.' The sense is not materially varied. ¶ *Endureth for ever.* Is unmoved, fixed, permanent. Amidst all the revolutions on earth, the fading glories of natural objects, and the wasting strength of man, his truth remains unaffected. Its beauty never fades ; its power is never enfeebled. The gospel system is as lovely now as it was when it was first revealed to man, and it has as much power to save as it had when first applied to a human heart. We see the grass wither at the coming on of autumn ; we see the flower of the field decay ; we see man, though confident in his strength, and rejoicing in the vigour of his frame, cut down in an instant ; we see cities decline, and kingdoms lose their power : but the word of God is the same now that it was at first, and, amidst all the changes which may ever occur on the earth, that will remain the same. ¶ *And this is the word which by the gospel is preached unto you.* That is, this gospel is the ' word ' which was referred to by Isaiah in the passage which has been quoted. In view, then, of the affecting truth stated in the close of this chapter, (vers. 24, 25,) let us learn habitually to reflect on our feebleness and frailty. ' We all do fade as a leaf,' Isa. lxiv. 6. Our glory is like the flower of the field. Our beauty fades, and our strength disappears, as easily as the beauty and vigour of the flower that grows up in the morning, and that in the evening is cut down, Ps. xc. 6. The rose that blossoms on the cheek of youth

CHAPTER II.

WHEREFORE laying aside
a all malice, and all guile,

and hypocrisies, and envies, and all
evil speakings,

a Ep.4.22,31.

may wither as soon as any other rose ;
the brightness of the eye may become
dim, as readily as the beauty of a field
covered with flowers ; the darkness of
death may come over the brow of manliness and intelligence, as readily as
night settles down on the landscape ;
and our robes of adorning may be laid
aside, as soon as beauty fades in a meadow full of flowers before the scythe of
the mower. There is not an object of
natural beauty on which we pride ourselves that will not decay ; and soon all
our pride and pomp will be laid low in
the tomb. It is sad to look on a beautiful lily, a rose, a magnolia, and to
think how soon all that beauty will disappear. It is more sad to look on a
rosy cheek, a bright eye, a lovely form,
an expressive brow, an open, serene, intelligent countenance, and to think how
soon all that beauty and brilliancy will
fade away. But amidst these changes
which beauty undergoes, and the desolations which disease and death spread
over the world, it is cheering to think
that all is not so. There is that which
does not change, which never loses its
beauty. 'The word of the Lord ' abides.
His cheering promises, his assurances
that there is a brighter and better
world, remain amidst all these changes
the same. The traits which are drawn
on the character by the religion of
Christ, more lovely by far than the
most delicate colouring of the lily, remain for ever. There they abide, aug-
menting in loveliness, when the rose
fades from the cheek; when the brilliancy
departs from the eye ; when the body
moulders away in the sepulchre. The
beauty of religion is the only permanent beauty in the earth ; and he that
has that need not regret that that which
in this mortal frame charms the eye
shall fade away like the flower of the
field.

CHAPTER II.

ANALYSIS OF THE CHAPTER.

THIS chapter may be divided into three
parts :—

I. An exhortation to those whom the
apostle addressed, to lay aside all malice,
and all guile, and to receive the simple
and plain instructions of the word of
God with the earnestness with which
babes desire their appropriate food, vers.
1–3. Religion *reproduces* the traits of
character of children in those whom it
influences, and they ought to regard
themselves as new-born babes, and seek
that kind of spiritual nutriment which
is adapted to their condition as such.

II. The privileges which they had
obtained by becoming Christians, while
so many others had stumbled at the very
truths by which they had been saved,
vers. 4–10. (*a*) They had come to the
Saviour, as the living stone on which
the whole spiritual temple was founded,
though others had rejected him ; they
had become a holy priesthood ; they had
been admitted to the privilege of offering
true sacrifices, acceptable to God, vers.
4, 5. (*b*) To them Christ was precious
as the chief corner-stone, on which all
their hopes rested, and on which the
edifice that was to be reared was safe,
though that foundation of the Christian
hope had been rejected and disallowed
by others, vers. 6–8. (*c*) They were
now a chosen people, an holy nation,
appointed to show forth on earth the
praises of God, though formerly they
were not regarded as the people of God,
and were not within the range of the
methods by which he was accustomed to
show mercy, vers. 9, 10.

III. Various duties growing out of
these privileges, and out of the various
relations which they sustained in life,
vers. 11–25. (*a*) The duty of living as
strangers and pilgrims ; of abstaining
from all those fleshly lusts which war
against the soul; and of leading lives of
entire honesty in relation to the Gentiles, by whom they were surrounded,
vers. 11, 12. (*b*) The duty of submitting to civil rulers, vers. 13–17. (*c*)
The duty of servants to submit to their
masters, though their condition was a
hard one in life, and they were often
called to suffer wrongfully, vers. 18–20.

2 As new-born babes, *a* desire the sincere milk *b* of the word, that ye may grow thereby:

(*d*) This duty was enforced on servants, and on all, from the example of Christ, who was more wronged than any others can be, and who yet bore all his sufferings with entire patience, leaving us an example that we should follow in his steps, ver. 21–25.

1. *Wherefore laying aside.* On the word rendered *laying aside*, see Rom. xiii. 12; Eph. iv. 22, 25; Col. iii. 8. The allusion is to putting off clothes; and the meaning is, that we are to cast off these things entirely; that is, we are no longer to practise them. The word *wherefore* (οὖν) refers to the reasonings in the first chapter. In view of the considerations stated there, we should renounce all evil. ¶ *All malice.* All evil, (κακίαν.) The word *malice* we commonly apply now to a particular kind of evil, denoting extreme enmity of heart, ill-will, a disposition to injure others without cause, from mere personal gratification, or from a spirit of revenge. —*Webster.* The Greek word, however, includes evil of all kinds. See Notes on Rom. i. 29. Comp. Acts viii. 22, where it is rendered *wickedness*, and 1 Cor. v. 8; xiv. 20; Eph. iv. 31; Col. iii. 8; Titus iii. 3. ¶ *And all guile.* Deceit of all kinds. Notes on Rom. i. 29; 2 Cor. xii. 16; 1 Thess. ii. 3. ¶ *And hypocrisies.* Notes on 1 Tim. iv. 2; Matt. xxiii. 28;° Gal. ii. 13, on the word rendered *dissimulation.* The word means, feigning to be what we are not; assuming a false appearance of religion; cloaking a wicked purpose under the appearance of piety. ¶ *And envies.* Hatred of others on account of some excellency which they have, or something which they possess which we do not. See Notes on Rom. i. 29. ¶ *And all evil speaking.* Greek, speaking against others. This word (καταλαλιὰ) occurs only here and in 2 Cor. xii. 20, where it is rendered *backbitings.* It would include all unkind or slanderous speaking against others. This is by no means an uncommon fault in the world, and it is one of the designs of religion to guard against it. Religion teaches us to lay aside whatever guile, insincerity, and false appearances we may have acquired, and to put on the simple honesty and openness of children. We all acquire more or less of guile and insincerity in the course of life. We learn to conceal our sentiments and feelings, and almost unconsciously come to appear different from what we really are. It is not so with children. In the child, every emotion of the bosom appears as it is. *Nature there works well and beautifully.* Every emotion is expressed; every feeling of the heart is developed; and in the cheeks, the open eye, the joyous or sad countenance, we know all that there is in the bosom, as certainly as we know all that there is in the rose by its colour and its fragrance. Now, it is one of the purposes of religion to bring us back to this state, and to *strip off* all the subterfuges which we may have acquired in life; and he in whom this effect is not accomplished has never been converted. A man that is characteristically deceitful, cunning, and crafty, cannot be a Christian. 'Except ye be converted, and become as little children, ye shall not enter into the kingdom of heaven,' Matt. xviii. 3.

2. *As new-born babes.* The phrase here used would properly denote those which were just born, and hence Christians who had just begun the spiritual life. See the word explained in the Notes on 2 Tim. iii. 15. It is not uncommon, in the Scriptures, to compare Christians with little children. See Notes, Matt. xviii. 3, for the reasons of this comparison. Comp. Notes, 1 Cor. iii. 2; Heb. v. 12, 14. ¶ *Desire the sincere milk of the word.* The *pure* milk of the word. On the meaning of the word *sincere*, see Notes, Eph. vi. 24. The Greek word here (ἄδολον) means, properly, that which is without guile or falsehood; then unadulterated, pure, genuine. The Greek adjective rendered 'of the word,' (λογικὸν,) means properly *rational*, pertaining to reason, or mind; and, in the connection here with milk, means that which is adapted to sustain the soul. Comp. Notes, Rom. xii. 1. There is no doubt that there is allusion to the gospel in its purest and most simple form, as adapted to be the nutriment of the new-born soul. Probably

3 If so be ye have tasted *a* that the Lord *is* gracious.

4 To whom coming, *as unto a*

a Ps.34.8

living stone, disallowed *b* indeed of men, but chosen of God, *and* precious,

b Ps.118.22.

there are two ideas here ; one, that the proper aliment of piety is simple truth; the other, that the truths which they were to desire were the more elementary truths of the gospel, such as would be adapted to those who were babes in knowledge. ¶ *That ye may grow thereby.* As babes grow on their proper nutriment. Piety in the heart is susceptible of growth, and is made to grow by its proper aliment, as a plant or a child is, and will grow in proportion as it has the proper kind of nutriment. From this verse we may see, (1,) the reason of the injunction of the Saviour to Peter, to ' feed his lambs,' John xxi. 15; 1 Pet. ii. 1, 2. Young Christians strongly resemble children, babes; and they need watchful care, and kind attention, and appropriate aliment, as much as new-born infants do. Piety receives its form much from its commencement; and the character of the whole Christian life will be determined in a great degree by the views entertained at first, and the kind of instruction which is given to those who are just entering on their Christian course. We may also see, (2,) that it furnishes evidence of conversion, if we have a love for the simple and pure truths of the gospel. It is evidence that we have spiritual life, as really as the desire of appropriate nourishment is evidence that an infant has natural life. The new-born soul loves the truth. It is nourished by it. It perishes without it. The gospel is just what it wants; and without that it could not live. We may also learn from this verse, (3,) that the truths of the gospel which are best adapted to that state, are those which are simple and plain. Comp. Heb. v. 12–14. It is not philosophy that is needed then; it is not the profound and difficult doctrines of the gospel; it is those elementary truths which lie at the foundation of all religion, and which can be comprehended by children. Religion makes every one docile and humble as a child; and whatever may be the age at which one is converted, or whatever attainments he may have made in

science, he relishes the same truths which are loved by the youngest and most unlettered child that is brought into the kingdom of God.

3. *If so be ye have tasted that the Lord is gracious.* Or rather, as Doddridge renders it, ' *Since you have tasted that the Lord is gracious.*' The apostle did not mean to express any doubt on the subject, but to state that, since they had had an experimental acquaintance with the grace of God, they should desire to increase more and more in the knowledge and love of him. On the use of the word *taste*, see Notes on Heb. vi. 4.

4. *To whom coming.* To the Lord Jesus, for so the word ' Lord ' is to be understood in ver. 3. Comp. Notes on Acts i. 24. The idea here is, that *they* had come to him for salvation, while the great mass of men rejected him. Others ' disallowed' him, and turned away from him, but they had seen that he was the one chosen or appointed of God, and had come to him in order to be saved. Salvation is often represented as *coming* to Christ. See Matt. xi. 28. ¶ As unto *a living stone.* The allusion in this passage is to Isa. xxviii. 16, ' Behold, I lay in Zion for a foundation a stone, a tried stone, a precious corner-stone, a sure foundation : he that believeth shall not make haste.' See Notes on that passage. There may be also possibly an allusion to Psa. cxviii. 22, ' The stone which the builders disallowed, is become the head-stone of the corner.' The reference is to Christ as the foundation on which the church is reared. He occupied the same place in regard to the church which a foundation-stone does to the edifice that is reared upon it. Comp. Matt. vii. 24, 25. See Notes on Rom. ix. 33, and Eph. ii. 20–22. The phrase ' *living stone* ' is however unusual, and is not found, I think, except in this place. There seems to be an incongruity in it, in attributing *life* to a stone, yet the meaning is not difficult to be understood. The purpose was not to speak of a temple, like that at

5 Ye also, as lively stones, [1] are built up a spiritual house, [a] an holy priesthood, [b] to offer up spiritual *c* sacrifices, acceptable to God by Jesus Christ.

1 Or, *be ye.* *a* He.3.6. *b* Is.61.6; Re.1.6. *c* Mal.1.11.

Jerusalem, made up of gold and costly stones; but of a temple made up of *living* materials—of redeemed men—in which God now resides. In speaking of that, it was natural to refer to the foundation on which the whole rested, and to speak of that as corresponding to the whole edifice. It was all a *living temple*—a temple composed of living materials—from the foundation to the top. Compare the expression in John iv. 10, 'He would have given thee *living water;*' that is, water which would have imparted life to the soul. So Christ imparts life to the whole spiritual temple that is reared on him as a foundation. ¶ *Disallowed indeed of men.* Rejected by them, first by the Jews, in causing him to be put to death; and then by all men when he is offered to them as their Saviour. See Notes, Isa. liii. 3. Psa. cxviii. 22: 'Which the builders refused.' Comp. Notes, Matt. xxi. 42; Acts iv. 11. ¶ *But chosen of God.* Selected by him as the suitable foundation on which to rear his church. ¶ And *precious.* Valuable. The universe had nothing more valuable on which to rear the spiritual temple.

5. *Ye also, as lively stones.* Gr., '*living* stones.' The word should have been so rendered. The word *lively* with us now has a different meaning from *living*, and denotes *active, quick, sprightly.* The Greek word is the same as that used in the previous verse, and rendered *living.* The meaning is, that the materials of which the temple here referred to was composed, were *living* materials throughout. The foundation is a living foundation, and all the superstructure is composed of living materials. The purpose of the apostle here is to compare the church to a beautiful temple—such as the temple in Jerusalem, and to show that it is complete in all its parts, as that was. It has within itself what corresponds with everything that was valuable in that. It is a beautiful structure like that; and as in that there was a priesthood, and there were real and acceptable sacrifices offered, so it is in

the Christian church. The Jews prided themselves much on their temple. It was a most costly and splendid edifice. It was the place where God was worshipped, and where he was supposed to dwell. It had an imposing service, and there was acceptable worship rendered there. As a new dispensation was introduced; as the tendency of the Christian system was to draw off the worshippers from that temple, and to teach them that God could be worshipped as acceptably elsewhere as at Jerusalem, (John iv. 21–23;) as Christianity did not inculcate the necessity of rearing splendid temples for the worship of God; and as in fact the temple at Jerusalem was about to be destroyed for ever, it was important to show that in the Christian church there might be found all that was truly beautiful and valuable in the temple at Jerusalem; that it had what corresponded to what was in fact most precious there, and that there was still a most magnificent and beautiful temple on the earth. Hence the sacred writers labour to show that all was found in the church that had made the temple at Jerusalem so glorious, and that the great design contemplated by the erection of that splendid edifice—the maintenance of the worship of God—was now accomplished in a more glorious manner than even in the services of that house. For there was a temple, made up of living materials, which was still the peculiar dwelling-place of God on the earth. In that temple there was a holy priesthood—for every Christian was a priest. In that temple there were sacrifices offered, as acceptable to God as in the former—for they were spiritual sacrifices, offered continually. These thoughts were often dwelt upon by the apostle Paul, and are here illustrated by Peter, evidently with the same design, to impart consolation to those who had never been permitted to worship at the temple in Jerusalem, and to comfort those Jews, now converted to Christianity, who saw that that splendid and glorious edifice was about to be destroyed. The peculiar abode of God on the earth was now removed from that temple to the Christian church. The *first* aspect in which this is illustrated here is, that the temple of God was made up of ' living stones ;' that is, that the materials were not inanimate stones, but endued with life, and so much more valuable than those employed in the temple at Jerusalem, as the soul is more precious than any materials of stone. There were living beings which composed that temple, constituting a more beautiful structure, and a more appropriate dwelling-place for God, than any edifice could be made of stone, however costly or valuable. ¶ *A spiritual house.* A spiritual temple, not made of perishable materials, like that at Jerusalem ; not composed of *matter*, as that was, but made up of redeemed souls—a temple more appropriate to be the residence of one who is a pure spirit. Comp. Notes on Eph. ii. 19–22, and 1 Cor. vi. 19, 20. ¶ *An holy priesthood.* In the temple at Jerusalem, the priesthood appointed to minister there, and to offer sacrifices, constituted an essential part of the arrangement. It was important, therefore, to show that this was not overlooked in the spiritual temple that God was raising. Accordingly, the apostle says that this is amply provided for, by constituting *the whole body of Christians* to be in fact a priesthood. Every one is engaged in offering acceptable sacrifice to God. The business is not intrusted to a particular class to be known *as* priests; there is not a particular portion to whom the name is to be peculiarly given ; but *every* Christian is in fact a priest, and is engaged in offering an acceptable sacrifice to God. See Rom. i. 6: ' And hath made us kings and priests unto God.' The Great High Priest in this service is the Lord Jesus Christ, (see the Epistle to the Hebrews, *passim ;*) but besides him there is no one who sustains this office, except as it is borne by all the Christian members. There are *ministers, elders, pastors, evangelists* in the church ; but there is no one who is *a priest*, except in the general sense that *all* are priests —for the great sacrifice has been offered, and there is no expiation now to be made. The name *priest*, therefore,

should never be conferred on a minister of the gospel. It is never so given in the New Testament, and there was a *reason* why it should not be. The proper idea of a *priest* is one who offers sacrifice ; but the ministers of the New Testament have no sacrifices to offer—the one great and perfect oblation for the sins of the world having been made by the Redeemer on the cross. To him, and him alone, under the New Testament dispensation, should the name *priest* be given, as it is uniformly in the New Testament, except in the general sense in which it is given to all Christians. In the Roman Catholic communion it is *consistent* to give the name priest to a minister of the gospel, but it is *wrong* to do it. It is *consistent*, because they claim that a true *sacrifice* of the body and blood of Christ is offered in the mass. It is *wrong*, because that doctrine is wholly contrary to the New Testament, and is derogatory to the one perfect oblation which has been once made for the sins of the world, and in conferring on a class of men a degree of importance and of power to which they have no claim, and which is so liable to abuse. But in a *Protestant* church it is *neither* consistent *nor* right to give the name to a minister of religion. The only sense in which the term can now be used in the Christian church is a sense in which it is applicable to *all* Christians alike—that they ' offer the sacrifice of prayer and praise.' ¶ *To offer up spiritual sacrifices.* Not bloody offerings, the blood of lambs and bullocks, but those which are the offerings of the heart—the sacrifices of prayer and praise. As there is a *priest*, there is also involved the notion of a *sacrifice ;* but that which is offered is such as all Christians offer to God, proceeding from the heart, and breathed forth from the lips, and in a holy life. It is called *sacrifice*, not because it makes an expiation for sin, but because it is of the nature of *worship*. Comp. Notes on Heb. xiii. 15; x. 14. ¶ *Acceptable to God by Jesus Christ.* Comp. Notes on Rom. xii. 1. Through the merits of the great sacrifice made by the Redeemer on the cross. Our prayers and praises are in themselves so imperfect, and proceed from such polluted lips and

6 Wherefore also it is contained in the scripture, *a* Behold I lay in Sion a chief corner-stone, elect, precious: and he that believeth on him shall not be confounded.

7 Unto you therefore which be-

lieve *he is* [1] precious: but unto them which be disobedient, *the* stone *b* which the builders disallowed, the same is made the head of the corner,

a Is.28.16.   1 Or, an honour.   *b* Mat. 21.42.

---

hearts, that they can be acceptable only through him as our intercessor before the throne of God. Comp. Notes on Heb. ix. 24, 25; x. 19–22.

6. *Wherefore also it is contained in the scripture.* Isa. xxviii. 16. The quotation is substantially as it is found in the Septuagint. ¶ *Behold, I lay in Sion.* See Notes, Isa. xxviii. 16, and Rom. ix. 33. ¶ *A chief corner-stone.* The principal stone on which the corner of the edifice rests. A stone is selected for this which is large and solid, and, usually, one which is squared, and wrought with care; and as such a stone is commonly laid with solemn ceremonies, so, perhaps, in allusion to this, it is here said by God that *he would lay* this stone at the foundation. The solemnities attending this were those which accompanied the great work of the Redeemer. See the word explained in the Notes on Eph. ii. 20. ¶ *Elect.* Chosen of God, or selected for this purpose, ver. 4. ¶ *And he that believeth on him shall not be confounded.* Shall not be ashamed. The Hebrew is, 'shall not make haste.' See it explained in the Notes on Rom. ix. 33.

7. *Unto you therefore which believe.* Christians are often called simply *believers,* because faith in the Saviour is one of the prominent characteristics by which they are distinguished from their fellow-men. It sufficiently describes *any* man, to say that he is a *believer* in the Lord Jesus. ¶ He is *precious.* Marg., *an honour.* That is, according to the margin, it is *an honour* to believe on him, and should be so regarded. This is true, but it is very doubtful whether this is the idea of Peter. The Greek is ἡ τιμή; literally, ' esteem, honour, respect, reverence;' then 'value or price.' The noun is probably used in the place of the adjective, in the sense of honourable, valued, precious; and it is not incorrectly rendered in the text, ' he is precious.' The *connection* demands this

interpretation. The apostle was not showing that it was *an honour* to believe on Christ, but was stating the estimate which was put on him by those who believe, as contrasted with the view taken of him by the world. The truth which is taught is, that while the Lord Jesus is rejected by the great mass of men, he is regarded by all Christians as of inestimable value. I. Of the *fact* there can be no doubt. *Somehow,* Christians perceive a value in him which is seen in nothing else. This is evinced (*a*) in their *avowed* estimate of him as their best friend; (*b*) in their being willing so far to honour him as to commit to him the keeping of their souls, resting the whole question of their salvation on him alone; (*c*) in their readiness to keep his commands, and to serve him, while the mass of men disobey him; and (*d*) in their being willing to die for him. II. The *reasons* why he is so precious to them are such as these: (1.) They are brought into a condition where they can appreciate his worth. To see the value of food, we must be hungry; of clothing, we must be exposed to the winter's blast; of home, we must be wanderers without a dwelling-place; of medicine, we must be sick; of competence, we must be poor. So, to see the value of the Saviour, we must see that we are poor, helpless, dying sinners; that the soul is of inestimable worth; that we have no merit of our own; and that unless some one interpose, we must perish. Every one who becomes a true Christian is brought to this condition; and in this state he can appreciate the worth of the Saviour. In this respect the condition of Christians is unlike that of the rest of mankind—for they are in no better state to appreciate the worth of the Saviour, than the man in health is to appreciate the value of the healing art, or than he who has never had a want unsupplied, the kindness of one who comes to us with an abundant

8 And a stone of stumbling, and a rock of offence, *even to them* which stumble at the word, being disobe-

dient: whereunto *a* also they were appointed.

a Jude 4.

supply of food. (2.) The Lord Jesus is *in fact* of more value to them than any other benefactor. We have had benefactors who have done us good, but none who have done us *such* good as he has. We have had parents, teachers, kind friends, who have provided for us, taught us, relieved us; but all that they have done for us is slight, compared with what *he* has done. The fruit of their kindness, for the most part, pertains to the present world; and they have not laid down their lives for us. What *he* has done pertains to our welfare to all eternity; it is the fruit of the sacrifice of his own life. How precious should the name and memory of one be who has laid down his own life to save us! (3.) We owe all our hopes of heaven to him; and in proportion to the value of such a hope, he is precious to us. We have *no* hope of salvation but in him. Take that away—blot out the name and the work of the Redeemer—and we see no way in which we could be saved; we have no prospect of being saved. As our hope of heaven, therefore, is valuable to us; as it supports us in trial; as it comforts us in the hour of death, *so* is the Saviour precious: and the estimate which we form of him is in proportion to the value of such a hope. (4.) There is an intrinsic value and excellency in the character of Christ, apart from his relation to us, which makes him precious to those who can appreciate his worth. In his character, abstractedly considered, there was more to attract, to interest, to love, than in that of any other one who ever lived in our world. There was more purity, more benevolence, more that was great in trying circumstances, more that was generous and self-denying, more that resembled God, than in any other one who ever appeared on earth. In the moral firmament, the character of Christ sustains a pre-eminence above all others who have lived, as great as the glory of the sun is superior to the feeble lights, though so numerous, which glimmer at midnight. With such views of him, it is not to be wondered at that, however he may be

estimated by the world, 'to them who believe, he is PRECIOUS.' ¶ *But unto them which be disobedient.* Literally, *unwilling to be persuaded,* (ἀπειθής;) that is, those who refused to believe; who were obstinate or contumacious, Luke i. 17; Rom. i. 30. The meaning is, that to them he is made a stone against which they impinge, and ruin themselves. Notes, ver. 8. ¶ *The stone which the builders disallowed.* Which they rejected, or refused to make a corner-stone. The allusion here, by the word 'builders,' is primarily to the Jews, represented as raising a temple of salvation, or building with reference to eternal life. They refused to lay this stone, which God had appointed, as the foundation of their hopes, but preferred some other foundation. See this passage explained in the Notes on Matt. xxi. 42; Acts iv. 11; and Rom. ix. 33. ¶ *The same is made the head of the corner.* That is, though it is rejected by the mass of men, yet God has in fact made it the corner-stone on which the whole spiritual temple rests, Acts iv. 11, 12. However men may regard it, there is, in fact, no other hope of heaven than that which is founded on the Lord Jesus. If men are not saved by him, he becomes to them a stone of stumbling, and a rock of offence.

8. *And a stone of stumbling.* A stone over which they stumble, or against which they impinge. The idea seems to be that of a corner-stone which projects from the building, against which they dash themselves, and by which they are made to fall. See Notes on Matt. xxi. 44. The rejection of the Saviour becomes the means of their ruin. They refuse to build on him, and it is *as if* one should run against a solid projecting corner-stone of a house, that would certainly be the means of their destruction. Comp. Notes, Luke i. 34. An idea similar to this occurs in Matt. xxi. 44: 'Whosoever shall fall on this stone shall be broken.' The meaning is, that if this foundation-stone is not the means of their salvation, it will be of their ruin. It is not a matter of indifference

whether they believe on him or not—whether they accept or reject him. They cannot reject him without the most fearful consequences to their souls. ¶ *And a rock of offence.* This expresses substantially the same idea as the phrase ' stone of stumbling.' The word rendered ' *offence,*' (**σκάνδαλον,**) means properly ' a *trap-stick*—a crooked stick on which the bait is fastened, which the animal strikes against, and so springs the trap,' (*Robinson, Lex.;*) then a trap, gin, snare; and then anything which one strikes or stumbles against; a stumbling-block. It then denotes that which is the cause or occasion of ruin. This language would be strictly applicable to the Jews, who rejected the Saviour on account of his humble birth, and whose rejection of him was made the occasion of the destruction of their temple, city, and nation. But it is also applicable to *all* who reject him, from whatever cause; for their rejection of him will be followed with ruin to their souls. It is a crime for which God will judge them as certainly as he did the Jews who disowned him and crucified him, for the offence is substantially the same. What might have been, therefore, the means of their salvation, is made the cause of their deeper condemnation. ¶ *Even to them which stumble at the word.* To *all* who do this. That is, they take the same kind of offence at the gospel which the Jews did at the Saviour himself. It is substantially the same thing, and the consequences must be the same. How does the conduct of the man who rejects the Saviour now, differ from that of him who rejected him when he was on the earth? ¶ *Being disobedient.* Ver. 7. The *reason* why they reject him is, that they are not disposed to obey. They are solemnly commanded to believe the gospel; and a refusal to do it, therefore, is as really an act of *disobedience* as to break any other command of God. ¶ *Whereunto they were appointed.* (**εἰς ὃ καὶ ἐτέθησαν.**) The word ' *whereunto* ' means *unto which.* But unto what? It cannot be supposed that it means that they were ' appointed ' to believe on him and be saved by him; for (1) this would involve all the difficulty which is *ever* felt in the doctrine

of decrees or election; for it would then mean that he had eternally designated them to be saved, which is the doctrine of predestination; and (2) *if* this were the true interpretation, the consequence would follow that God had been foiled in his plan—for the reference here is to those who would *not* be saved, that is, to those who ' stumble at that stumbling-stone,' and are destroyed. Calvin supposes that it means, ' unto which rejection and destruction they were designated in the purpose of God.' So Blcomfield renders it, ' Unto which (disbelief) they were destined,' *(Crit. Digest ;*) meaning, as he supposes, that ' into this stumbling and disobedience they were *permitted* by God to fall.' Doddridge interprets it, ' To which also they were appointed by the righteous sentence of God, long before, even as early as in his first purpose and decree he ordained his Son to be the great foundation of his church.' Rosenmüller gives substantially the same interpretation. Clemens Romanus says it means that ' they were appointed, not that they should *sin,* but that, sinning, they should be *punished.*' See Wetstein. So Macknight · To which *punishment* they were appointed.' Whitby gives the same interpretation of it, that because they were disobedient, (referring, as he supposes, to the Jews who rejected the Messiah,) ' they were appointed, for the punishment of that disobedience, to fall and perish.' Dr. Clark supposes that it means that *they were prophesied of* that they should thus fall; or that, long before, it was predicted that they should thus stumble and fall. In reference to the meaning of this difficult passage, it is proper to observe that there is in the Greek verb necessarily the idea of *designation, appointment, purpose.* There was some agency or intention by which they were put in that condition; some act of *placing* or *appointing,* (the word **τίθημι** meaning *to set, put, lay, lay down, appoint, constitute,*) by which this result was brought about. The fair sense, therefore, and one from which we cannot escape, is, that this did not happen by chance or accident, but that there was a Divine arrangement, appointment, or plan on the part of God in re-

9 But ye *are* a chosen generation, a royal priesthood, an holy nation, a ¹peculiar *a*people; that ye should

1 Or, *purchased.*   *a* De.4.20.

shew forth the ²praises of him who hath called you out of darkness *b* into his marvellous light:

2 Or, *virtues.*   *b* Ac.26.18.

ference to this result, and that the result was in conformity with that. So it is said in Jude 4, of a similar class of men, ' For there are certain men crept in unawares, who were before of old ordained to this condemnation.' The facts were these: (1.) That God appointed his Son to be the corner-stone of his church. (2.) That there was a portion of the world which, from some cause, would embrace him and be saved. (3.) That there was another portion who, it was certain, would *not* embrace him. (4.) That it was known that the appointment of the Lord Jesus as a Saviour would be the occasion of their rejecting him, and of their deeper and more aggravated condemnation. (5.) That the arrangement was nevertheless made, with the understanding that all this *would* be so, and because it was best on the whole that it *should* be so, even *though* this consequence would follow. That is, it was better that the arrangement should be made for the salvation of men even with this result, that a part would sink into deeper condemnation, than that *no* arrangement should be made to save any. The primary and originating arrangement, therefore, did not contemplate *them* or their destruction, but was made with reference to others, and notwithstanding they would reject him, and would fall. The expression *whereunto* (*εις ὃ*) refers to this plan, as involving, under the circumstances, the result which actually followed. Their stumbling and falling was not a matter of chance, or a result which was not contemplated, but entered into the original arrangement; and the *whole*, therefore, might be said to be in accordance with a wise plan and purpose. And, (6.) it might be said in this sense, and in this connection, that those who would reject him were appointed to this stumbling and falling. It was what was foreseen; what entered into the general arrangement; what was involved in the purpose to save any. It was not a matter that was unforeseen, that the consequence of giving a

Saviour would result in the condemnation of those who should crucify and reject him; *but the whole thing*, as it actually occurred, entered into the Divine arrangement. It may be added, that as, in the facts in the case, nothing wrong has been done by God, and no one has been deprived of any rights, or punished more than he deserves, it was not wrong in him to make the arrangement. It was better that the arrangement should be made as it is, even with this consequence, than that none at all should be made for human salvation. Comp. Notes on Rom. ix. 15–18; John xii. 39, 40. This is just a statement, in accordance with what everywhere occurs in the Bible, that all things enter into the eternal plans of God; that nothing happens by chance; that there is nothing that was not foreseen; and that the plan is such as, on the whole, God saw to be best and wise, and therefore adopted it. If there is nothing unjust and wrong in the actual *developement* of the plan, there was nothing in forming it. At the same time, no man who disbelieves and rejects the gospel should take refuge in this as an excuse. He was ' appointed ' to it no otherwise than as it actually occurs; and as they know that they are voluntary in rejecting him, they cannot lay the blame of this on the purposes of God. They are not *forced* or *compelled* to do it; but it was seen that this consequence would follow, and the plan was laid to send the Saviour notwithstanding.

9. *But ye* are *a chosen generation.* In contradistinction from those who, by their disobedience, had rejected the Saviour as the foundation of hope. The people of God are often represented as his *chosen* or *elected* people. See Notes on chap. i. 2. ¶ *A royal priesthood.* See Notes on ver. 5. The meaning of this is, probably, that they ' at once bore the dignity of kings, and the sanctity of priests.'—*Doddridge.* Comp. Rev. i. 6: ' And hath made us kings and priests unto God.' See also Isa. lxi. 6: ' But ye shall be named priests

of the Lord; men shall call ye ministers of our God.' It may be, however, that the word *royal* is used only to denote the dignity of the priestly office which they sustained, or that they constituted, as it were, an entire nation or kingdom of priests. They were a kingdom over which he presided, and they were all priests; so that it might be said they were a kingdom of priests—a kingdom in which all the subjects were engaged in offering sacrifice to God. The expression appears to be taken from Exod. xix. 6—' And ye shall be unto me a kingdom of priests'—and is such language as one who had been educated as a Jew would be likely to employ to set forth the dignity of those whom he regarded as the people of God. ¶ *An holy nation.* This is also taken from Exod. xix. 6. The Hebrews were regarded as a nation consecrated to God; and now that they were cast off or rejected for their disobedience, the same language was properly applied to the people whom God had chosen in their place—the Christian church. ¶ *A peculiar people.* Comp. Notes on Titus ii. 14. The margin here is *purchased.* The word *peculiar,* in its common acceptation now, would mean that they were distinguished from others, or were singular. The reading in the margin would mean that they had been bought or redeemed. Both these things are so, but neither of them expresses the exact sense of the original. The Greek (λαὸς εἰς περιποίησιν) means, ' a people for a possession;' that is, as pertaining to God. They are a people which he has secured as a possession, or as his own; a people, therefore, which belong to him, and to no other. In this sense they are *peculiar* as being his; and, being such, it may be inferred that they *should be* peculiar in the sense of being unlike others in their manner of life. But that idea is not necessarily in the text. There seems to be here also an allusion to Exod. xix. 5: ' Ye shall be a peculiar treasure with me (Sept. λαὸς περιούσιος) above all people.' ¶ *That ye should shew forth the praises of him.* Marg., *virtues.* The Greek word (ἀρετὴ) means properly *good quality, excellence* of any kind. It means here the excellences of God—his goodness, his wondrous deeds,

or those things which make it proper to praise him. This shows one great object for which they were redeemed. It was that they might proclaim the glory of God, and keep up the remembrance of his wondrous deeds in the earth. This is to be done (*a*) by proper ascriptions of praise to him in public, family, and social worship; (*b*) by being always the avowed friends of God, ready ever to vindicate his government and ways; (*c*) by endeavouring to make known his excellences to all those who are ignorant of him; and (*d*) by such a life as shall constantly proclaim his praise—as the sun, the moon, the stars, the hills, the streams, the flowers do, showing what God *does.* The consistent life of a devoted Christian is a constant setting forth of the praise of God, showing to all that the God who has made him such is worthy to be loved. ¶ *Who hath called you out of darkness into his marvellous light.* On the word *called,* see Notes on Eph. iv. 1. *Darkness* is the emblem of ignorance, sin, and misery, and refers here to their condition before their conversion; *light* is the emblem of the opposite, and is a beautiful representation of the state of those who are brought to the knowledge of the gospel. See Notes on Acts xxvi. 18. The word *marvellous* means *wonderful;* and the idea is, that the light of the gospel was such as was unusual, or not to be found elsewhere, as that excites wonder or surprise which we are not accustomed to see. The primary reference here is, undoubtedly, to those who had been heathens, and to the great change which had been produced by their having been brought to the knowledge of the truth as revealed in the gospel; and, in regard to this, no one can doubt that the one state deserved to be characterized as darkness, and the other as light. The contrast was as great as that between midnight and noonday. But what is here said is substantially correct of all who are converted, and is often as strikingly true of those who have been brought up in Christian lands, as of those who have lived among the heathen. The change in conversion is often so great and so rapid, the views and feelings are so different before and after conversion, that it seems like a sudden transition

10 Which *a* in time past *were* not a people, but *are* now the people of God: which had not obtained mercy, but now have obtained mercy.

11 Dearly beloved, I beseech *you* as strangers *b* and pilgrims, abstain from *c* fleshly lusts, which war *d* against the soul;

a Ro.9.25.　　*b* Ps.119.19.　　*c* Ga 5.16-21.　　*d* Ro.8.13; Ja.4.1.

from midnight to noon. In *all* cases, also, of true conversion, though the change may not be so striking, or apparently so sudden, there *is* a change of which this may be regarded as substantially an accurate description. In many cases the convert can adopt this language in all its fulness, as descriptive of his own conversion; in *all* cases of genuine conversion it is true that each one can say that he has been called from a state in which his mind was dark to one in which it is comparatively clear.

10. *Which in time past* were *not a people.* That is, who formerly were not regarded as the people of God. There is an *allusion* here to the passage in Hosea ii. 23, ' And I will have mercy upon her that had not obtained mercy; and I will say to them which were not my people, Thou art my people; and they shall say, Thou art my God.' It is, however, a *mere* allusion, such as one makes who uses the language of another to express his ideas, without meaning to say that both refer to the same subject. In Hosea, the passage refers evidently to the reception of one portion of the Israelites into favour after their rejection; in Peter, it refers mainly to those who had been Gentiles, and who had never been recognised as the people of God. The language of the prophet would exactly express his idea, and he therefore uses it without intending to say that this was its original application. See it explained in the Notes on Rom. ix. 25. Comp. Notes on Eph. ii. 11, 12. ¶ *Which had not obtained mercy.* That is, who had been living unpardoned, having no knowledge of the way by which sinners might be forgiven, and no evidence that your sins were forgiven. They were then in the condition of the whole heathen world, and they had not then been acquainted with the glorious method by which God forgives iniquity.

11. *Dearly beloved, I beseech* you *as strangers and pilgrims.* On the word rendered *strangers,* (παροίκους,) see Notes on Eph. ii. 19, where it is rendered *foreigners.* It means, properly, one dwelling near, neighbouring; then a by-dweller, a sojourner, one without the rights of citizenship, as distinguished from a citizen; and it means here that Christians are not properly citizens of this world, but that their citizenship is in heaven, and that they are here mere sojourners. Comp. Notes on Phil. iii. 20, 'For our conversation [*citizenship*] is in heaven.' On the word rendered *pilgrims,* (παρεπιδήμους,) see Notes on chap. i. 1; Heb. xi. 13. A *pilgrim,* properly, is one who travels to a distance from his own country to visit a holy place, or to pay his devotion to some holy object; then a traveller, a wanderer. The meaning here is, that Christians have no permanent home on earth; their citizenship is not here; they are mere sojourners, and they are passing on to their eternal home in the heavens. They should, therefore, act as become such persons; as sojourners and travellers do. They should not (*a*) *regard* the earth as their home. (*b*) They should not seek to acquire permanent possessions *here,* as if they were to remain here, but should act as travellers do, who merely seek a temporary lodging, without expecting permanently to reside in a place. (*c*) They should not allow any such attachments to be formed, or arrangements to be made, as to *impede* their journey to their final home, as pilgrims seek only a temporary lodging, and steadily pursue their journey. (*d*) Even while engaged here in the necessary callings of life—their studies, their farming, their merchandize—their thoughts and affections should be on other things. One in a strange land thinks much of his country and home; a pilgrim, much of the land to which he goes; and even while his time and attention may be necessarily occupied by the arrangements needful for the journey, his thoughts and affections will be

12 Having your conversation
honest among the Gentiles: that,
¹ whereas they speak against you
as evil doers, they may by *your*

good works, ᵃ which they shall behold, glorify God in the day of visitation.

1 Or, *wherein.*   a Mat.5.16.

---

far away. (*e*) We should not *encumber
ourselves* with much of this world's
goods. Many professed Christians get
so many worldly things around them,
that it is impossible for them to make
a journey to heaven. They burden
themselves as no traveller would, and
they make no progress. A traveller
takes along as few things as possible;
and a staff is often all that a pilgrim
has. We make the most rapid progress
in our journey to our final home when
we are least encumbered with the things
of this world. ¶ *Abstain from fleshly
lusts.* Such desires and passions as the
carnal appetites prompt to. See Notes
on Gal. v. 19–21. A sojourner in a land,
or a pilgrim, does not give himself up
to the indulgence of sensual appetites,
or to the soft pleasures of the soul. All
these would hinder his progress, and
turn him off from his great design.
Comp. Rom. xiii. 4; Gal. v. 24; 2 Tim.
ii. 22; Titus ii. 12; 1 Pet. i. 14.
¶ *Which war against the soul.* Comp.
Notes on Rom. viii. 12, 13. The meaning is, that indulgence in these things
makes war against the nobler faculties
of the soul; against the conscience, the
understanding, the memory, the judgment, the exercise of a pure imagination. Comp. Notes on Gal. v. 17. There
is not a faculty of the mind, however
brilliant in itself, which will not be ultimately ruined by indulgence in the carnal propensities of our nature. The
effect of intemperance on the noble
faculties of the soul is well known; and
alas, there are too many instances in
which the light of genius, in those endowed with splendid gifts, at the bar,
in the pulpit, and in the senate, is extinguished by it, to need a particular
description. But there is one vice pre-
eminently, which prevails all over the
heathen world, (Comp. Notes on Rom.
i. 27–29,) and extensively in Christian lands, which more than all others,
blunts the moral sense, pollutes the memory, defiles the imagination, hardens
the heart, and sends a withering in-

fluence through all the faculties of the
soul.

> ' The soul grows clotted by contagion,
> Embodies, and embrutes, till she quite lose
> The divine property of her first being.'

Of this passion, Burns beautifully and
truly said—

> ' But oh! it hardens a' within,
> And petrifies the feeling.'

From all these passions the Christian
pilgrim is to abstain.

12. *Having your conversation honest.*
Your *conduct.* Notes, Phil. i. 27. That
is, lead upright and consistent lives.
Comp. Notes on Phil. iv. 8. ¶ *Among
the Gentiles.* The heathen by whom
you are surrounded, and who will certainly observe your conduct. Notes on
1 Thess. iv. 12, ' That ye may walk
honestly towards them that are without.'
Comp. Rom. xiii. 13. ¶ *That, whereas
they speak against you as evil doers.*
Marg., *wherein.* Gr. ἐν ᾧ—*in what;*
either referring to *time,* and meaning
that *at the very time* when they speak
against you in this manner they may
be silenced by seeing your upright lives;
or meaning *in respect to which*—that
is, that in respect to the very matters
for which they reproach you they may
see by your meek and upright conduct
that there is really no ground for reproach. Wetstein adopts the former,
but the question which is meant is not
very important. Bloomfield supposes it
to mean *inasmuch, whereas.* The sentiment is a correct one, whichever interpretation is adopted. It should be true
that at the very time when the enemies
of religion reproach us, they should see
that we are actuated by Christian principles, and that in the very matter for
which we are reproached we are conscientious and honest. ¶ *They may, by*
your *good works, which they shall behold.* Gr., 'which they shall closely or
narrowly inspect.' The meaning is,
that upon a close and narrow examination, they may see that you are actuated
by upright principles, and ultimately be

13 Submit yourselves *a* to every ordinance of man for the Lord's

sake: whether it be to the king, as supreme;

a Mat.22.21; Ro.13.1-7.

disposed to do you justice. It is to be remembered that the heathen were very little acquainted with the nature of Christianity; and it is known that in the early ages they charged on Christians the most abominable vices, and even accused them of practices at which human nature revolts. The meaning of Peter is, that while they charged these things on Christians, whether from ignorance or malice, they ought so to live as that a more full acquaintance with them, and a closer inspection of their conduct, would disarm their prejudices, and show that their charges were entirely unfounded. The truth taught here is, *that our conduct as Christians should be such as to bear the strictest scrutiny; such that the closest examination will lead our enemies to the conviction that we are upright and honest.* This *may* be done by every Christian; this his religion solemnly requires him to do. ¶ *Glorify God.* Honour God; that is, that they may be convinced by your conduct of the pure and holy nature of that religion which he has revealed, and be led also to love and worship him. See Notes, Matt. v. 16. ¶ *In the day of visitation.* Many different opinions have been entertained of the meaning of this phrase, some referring it to the day of judgment; some to times of persecution; some to the destruction of Jerusalem; and some to the time when the gospel was preached among the Gentiles, as a period when God visited them with mercy. The word visitation (ἐπισκοπή,) means the act of visiting or being visited for any purpose, usually with the notion of inspecting conduct, of inflicting punishment, or of conferring favours. Comp. Matt. xxv. 36, 43; Luke i. 68, 78; vii. 16; xix. 44. In the sense of visiting for the purpose of punishing, the word is often used in the Septuagint for the Heb. פָּקַד, (*pakad*,) though there is no instance in which the word is so used in the New Testament, unless it be in the verse before us. The 'visitation' here referred to is undoubtedly that of God; and the reference is to some time when he would

make a 'visitation' to men for some purpose, and when the fact that the Gentiles had narrowly inspected the conduct of Christians would lead them to honour him. The only question is, to *what* visitation of that kind the apostle referred. The prevailing use of the word in the New Testament would seem to lead us to suppose that the 'visitation' referred to was designed to confer favours rather than to inflict punishment, and indeed the word seems to have somewhat of a *technical* character, and to have been familiarly used by Christians to denote God's coming to men to bless them; to pour out his Spirit upon them; to revive religion. This seems to me to be its meaning here; and, if so, the sense is, that when God appeared among men to accompany the preaching of the gospel with saving power, the result of the observed conduct of Christians would be to lead those around them to honour him by giving up their hearts to him; that is, their consistent lives would be the means of the revival and extension of true religion. *And is it not always so?* Is not the pure and holy walk of Christians an occasion of his bending his footsteps down to earth to bless dying sinners, and to scatter spiritual blessings with a liberal hand? Comp. Notes, 1 Cor. xiv. 24, 25.

13. *Submit yourselves to every ordinance of man.* Gr., ' to every *creation* of man,' (ἀνθρωπίνη κτίσει.) The meaning is, to every institution or appointment of man; to wit, of those who are in authority, or who are appointed to administer government. The laws, institutes, and appointments of such a government may be spoken of as the *creation* of man; that is, as what man makes. Of course, what is here said must be understood with the limitation everywhere implied, that what is ordained by those in authority is not contrary to the law of God. See Notes on Acts iv. 19. On the general duty here enjoined of subjection to civil authority, see Notes on Rom. xiii. 1-7. ¶ *For the Lord's sake.* Because he has required

14 Or unto governors, as unto them that are sent by him for the punishment of evil doers, and for the praise of them that do well.

15 For so is the will of God, that *a* with well doing ye may put to silence the ignorance of foolish men:

a Tit.2.8.

it, and has intrusted this power to civil rulers. Notes, Rom. xiii. 5. Comp. Notes, Eph. vi. 7. ¶ *Whether it be to the king.* It has been commonly supposed that there is reference here to the Roman emperor, who might be called *king,* because in him the supreme power resided. The common title of the Roman sovereign was, as used by the Greek writers, ἀυτοκράτωρ, and among the Romans themselves, *imperator,* (*emperor;*) but the title *king* was also given to the sovereign. John xix. 15, 'We have no *king* but Cesar.' Acts xvii. 7, 'And these all do contrary to the decrees of Cesar, saying that there is another king, one Jesus.' Peter undoubtedly had particular reference to the Roman emperors, but he uses a general term, which would be applicable to all in whom the supreme power resided, and the injunction here would require submission to such authority, by whatever name it might be called. The meaning is, that we are to be subject to that authority whether exercised by the sovereign in person, or by those who are appointed by him. ¶ *As supreme.* Not supreme in the sense of being superior to God, or not being subject to him, but in the sense of being over all subordinate officers.

14. *Or unto governors.* Subordinate officers, appointed by the chief magistrate, over provinces. Perhaps Roman proconsuls are here particularly intended. ¶ *As unto them that are sent by him.* By the king, or the Roman emperor. They represent the supreme power. ¶ *For the punishment of evil doers.* One of the leading ends of government. 'The Roman governors had the power of life and death in such conquered provinces as those mentioned in chap. i. 1.'—*Doddridge.* Ulpian, the celebrated Roman lawyer, who flourished two hundred years after Christ, thus describes the power of the governors of the Roman provinces: 'It is the duty of a good and vigilant president to see to it that his province be

peaceable and quiet. And that he ought to make diligent search after sacrilegious persons, robbers, man-stealers, and thieves, and to punish every one according to their guilt.' Again, 'They who govern whole provinces, have the power of sending to the mines.' And again, 'The presidents of provinces have the highest authority, next to the emperor.' Peter has described the office of the Roman governors in language nearly resembling that of Ulpian. See Lardner's Credibility, .(Works, i. 77, edit. 8vo., Lond. 1829.) ¶ *And for the praise of them that do well. Praise* here stands opposed to *punishment,* and means commendation, applause, reward. That is, it is a part of their business to reward in a suitable manner those who are upright and virtuous as citizens. This would be by protecting their persons and property; by defending their rights, and, perhaps, by admitting those to share the honours and emoluments of office who showed that they were worthy to be trusted. It is as important a part of the functions of magistracy to protect the innocent, as it is to punish the wicked.

15. *For so is the will of God.* That is, it is in accordance with the Divine will that in this way you should put them to silence. ¶ *That with well doing.* By a life of uprightness and benevolence. ¶ *Ye may put to silence the ignorance of foolish men.* See Notes on Titus ii. 8. The reference here is to men who brought charges against Christians, by accusing them of being inimical to the government, or insubordinate, or guilty of crimes. Such charges, it is well known, were often brought against them by their enemies in the early ages of Christianity. Peter says they were brought by *foolish* men, perhaps using the word *foolish* in the sense of evil-disposed, or wicked, as it is often used in the Bible. Yet, though there might be malice at the bottom, the charges were really based on *ignorance.* They were not thoroughly

16 As free, *a* and not [1] using *your* | liberty for a cloke of maliciousness,

a Ga.5.1,13.   [1] *having.*   but as the servants of God.

acquainted with the principles of the Christian religion; and the way to meet those charges was to act in every way as became good citizens, and so as ' to live them down.' One of the best ways of meeting the accusations of our enemies is to lead a life of strict integrity. It is not easy for the wicked to reply to this argument.

16. *As free.* That is, they were to consider themselves as freemen, as having a right to liberty. The Jews boasted much of their freedom, and regarded it as a birthright privilege that they were free, John viii. 33. They never willingly acknowledged their subjection to any other power, but claimed it as an elementary idea of their civil constitution that God only was their Sovereign. They were indeed conquered by the Romans, and paid tribute, but they did it because they were compelled to do it, and it was even a question much debated among them whether they should do it or not, Matt. xxii. 17. Josephus has often referred to the fact that the Jews rebelled against the Romans under the plea that they were a *free people*, and that they were subject only to God. This idea of essential freedom the Jews had when they became Christians, and every thing in Christianity tended to inspire them with the love of liberty. They who were converted to the Christian faith, whether from among the Jews or the Gentiles, were made to feel that they were the children of God; that his law was the supreme rule of their lives; that in the ultimate resort they were subject to him alone; that they were redeemed, and that, therefore, the yoke of bondage could not be properly imposed on them; that God ' had made of one blood all nations of men, for to dwell on all the face of the earth,' (Acts xvii. 26;) and that, therefore, they were on a level before him. The meaning here is, that they were not to consider themselves as slaves, or to act as slaves. In their subjection to civil authority they were not to forget that they were freemen in the highest sense, and that

liberty was an invaluable blessing. They had been made free by the Son of God, John viii. 32, 36. They were free from sin and condemnation. They acknowledged Christ as their supreme Head, and the whole spirit and tendency of his religion prompted to the exercise of freedom. They were not to submit to the chains of slavery; not to allow their consciences to be bound, or their essential liberty to be interfered with; nor in their subjection to the civil magistrate were they ever to regard themselves otherwise than as freemen. As a matter of fact, Christianity has always been the friend and promoter of liberty. Its influence emancipated the slaves throughout the Roman empire; and all the civil freedom which we enjoy, and which there is in the world, can be traced to the influence of the Christian religion. To spread the gospel in its purity everywhere would be to break every yoke of oppression and bondage, and to make men everywhere free. It is the essential right of every man who is a Christian to be a *freeman* —to be free to worship God; to read the Bible; to enjoy the avails of his own labour; to train up his children in the way in which he shall deem best; to form his own plans of life, and to pursue his own ends, provided only that he does not interfere with the equal rights of others—and every system which prevents this, whether it be that of civil government, of ecclesiastical law, or of domestic slavery, is contrary to the religion of the Saviour. ¶ *And not using* your *liberty for a cloke of maliciousness.* Marg., as in Greek, *having.* Not making your freedom a mere pretext under which to practise all kinds of evil. The word rendered *maliciousness—κακία—*means more than our word *maliciousness* does; for it denotes *evil* of any kind, or all kinds. The word *maliciousness* refers rather to enmity of heart, ill-will, an intention to injure. The apostle has reference to an abuse of freedom, which has often occurred. The pretence of those who have acted in this manner has been,

17 [1] Honour all *men.*[a] Love [b] the brotherhood. Fear [c] God. Honour the king.[d]

1 Or, *esteem.*   a Ro.12.10; Phi.2.3.
b Jn.13.35.   c Ps.111.10.   d Pr.24.21.

that the freedom of the gospel implied deliverance from all kinds of restraint; that they were under *no* yoke, and bound by no laws; that, being the children of God, they had a right to all kinds of enjoyment and indulgence; that even the moral law ceased to bind them, and that they had a right to make the most of liberty in all respects. Hence they have given themselves up to all sorts of sensual indulgence, claiming exemption from the restraints of morality as well as of civil law, and sinking into the deepest abyss of vice. Not a few have done this who have professed to be Christians; and, occasionally, a fanatical sect now appears who make the freedom which they say Christianity confers, a pretext for indulgence in the most base and degrading vices. The apostles saw this tendency in human nature, and in nothing are they more careful than to guard against this abuse. ¶ *But as the servants of God.* Not free from all restraint; not at liberty to indulge in all things, but bound to serve God in the faithful obedience of his laws. Thus bound to obey and serve him, they could not be at liberty to indulge in those things which would be in violation of his laws, and which would dishonour him. See this sentiment explained in the Notes on 1 Cor. vii. 22; ix. 21.

17. *Honour all* men. That is, show them the respect which is due to them according to their personal worth, and to the rank and office which they sustain. Notes, Rom. xiii. 7. ¶ *Love the brotherhood.* The whole fraternity of Christians, regarded as a band of brothers. The word here used occurs only in this place and in chap. v. 9, where it is rendered *brethren.* The *idea* expressed here occurs often in the New Testament. See Notes, John xiii. 34, 35. ¶ *Fear God.* A duty everywhere enjoined in the Bible, as one of the first duties of religion. Comp. Lev. xxv. 17; Psa. xxiii. 18; xxiv. 7; xxv. 14; Prov. i. 7; iii. 13; ix. 10; xxiii. 17; Notes, Rom. iii. 18; 2 Cor. vii. 1. The word *fear,* when used to express our duty to

God, means that we are to reverence and honour him. Religion, in one aspect, is described as the fear of God; in another, as the love of God; in another, as submission to his will, &c. A holy veneration or fear is always an elementary principle of religion. It is the fear, not so much of punishment as of his disapprobation; not so much the dread of suffering as the dread of doing wrong. ¶ *Honour the king.* Referring here primarily to the Roman sovereign, but implying that we are always to respect those who have the rule over us. See Notes, Rom. xiii. 1–7. The doctrine taught in these verses (13–17) is, that we are faithfully to perform all the relative duties of life. There are duties which we owe to ourselves, which are of importance in their place, and which we are by no means at liberty to neglect. But we also owe duties to our fellow-men, to our Christian brethren, and to those who have the rule over us; and religion, while it is honoured by our faithful performance of our duty to ourselves, is more *openly* honoured by our performance of our duties to those to whom we sustain important relations in life. Many of the duties which we owe to ourselves are, from the nature of the case, hidden from public observation. All that pertains to the examination of the heart; to our private devotions; to the subjugation of our evil passions; to our individual communion with God, must be concealed from public view. Not so, however, with those duties which pertain to others. In respect to them, we are open to public view. The eye of the world is upon us. The judgment of the world in regard to us is made up from their observation of the manner in which we perform them. If religion fails there, they judge that it fails altogether; and however devout we may be in private, if it is not seen by the world that our religion leads to the faithful performance of the duties which we owe in the various relations of life, it will be regarded as of little value.

18. *Servants,* be subject to your mas-

18 Servants, ^a *be* subject to *your* masters with all fear ; not only to the good and gentle, but also to the froward.

19 For this *is* ¹thank-worthy, if a man for conscience toward God endure grief, suffering wrongfully.

a Ep.6.5,&c.　　1 Or, *thank*, Lu.6.32.

ters. On the duty here enjoined, see Notes, Eph. vi. 5–9. The Greek word here used (*οἰκέται*) is not the same which is employed in Ephesians, (*δοῦλοι.*) The word here means properly *domestics*—those employed about a house, or living in the same house—from *οἶκος, house.* These persons might have been slaves, or might not. The word would apply to them, whether they were hired, or whether they were owned as slaves. The word should not and cannot be employed to *prove* that slavery existed in the churches to which Peter wrote, and still less to prove that he approved of slavery, or regarded it as a good institution. The exhortation here would be, and still is, strictly applicable to any persons employed as domestics, though they had voluntarily hired themselves out to be such. It would be incumbent on them, while they remained in that condition, to perform with fidelity their duties as Christians, and to bear with Christian meekness all the wrongs which they might suffer from those in whose service they were. Those who are hired, and who are under a necessity of ' going out to service' for a living, are not always free from hard usage, for there are trials incident to that condition of life which cannot be always avoided. It might be better, in many cases, to bear much than to attempt a change of situation, even though they were entirely at liberty to do so. It must be admitted, however, that the exhortation here will have more force if it is supposed that the reference is to slaves, and there can be no doubt that many of this class were early converted to the Christian faith. The word here rendered *masters* (*δεσπόταις*) is not the same which is used in Eph. vi. 5, (*κυρίοις.*) Neither of these words necessarily implies that those who were under them were *slaves.* The word here used is applicable to the head of a family, *whatever* may be the condition of those under him. It is frequently applied to God, and to Christ; and it cannot be maintained that those

to whom God sustains the relation of *δεσπότης,* or *master,* are *slaves.* See Luke ii. 29; Acts iv. 24; 2 Tim. ii. 21; 2 Pet. ii. 1; Jude 4; Rev. vi. 10. The word, indeed, is one that *might* be applied to those who were owners of slaves. If that be the meaning here, it is not said, however, that those to whom it is applied were Christians. It is rather implied that they were pursuing such a course as was inconsistent with real piety. Those who were under them are represented as suffering grievous wrongs. ¶ *With all fear.* That is, with all proper reverence and respect. Notes, Eph. vi. 5. ¶ *Not only to the good and gentle, but also to the froward.* The word rendered *froward* (*σκολιοῖς*) means properly *crooked, bent;* then perverse, wicked, unjust, peevish. Any one who is a servant or domestic is liable to be employed in the service of such a master; but while the relation continues, the servant should perform *his* duty with fidelity, whatever may be the character of the master. *Slaves* are certainly liable to this; and even those who voluntarily engage as servants to others, cannot always be sure that they will have kind employers. Though the *terms* used here do not necessarily imply that those to whom the apostle gave this direction were *slaves,* yet it may be presumed that they probably were, since slavery abounded throughout the Roman empire; but the directions will apply to *all* who are engaged in the service of others, and are therefore of permanent value. Slavery will, sooner or later, under the influence of the gospel, wholly cease in the world, and instructions addressed to masters and slaves will have no permanent value; but it will always be true that there will be those employed as domestics, and it is the duty of all who are thus engaged to evince true fidelity and a Christian spirit themselves, whatever may be the character of their employers.

19. *For this* is *thank-worthy.* Marg., *thank.* Gr., 'This is *grace,*' (*χάρις*).

20 For what glory *is it*, if, when ye be buffeted for your faults, ye shall take it patiently? but if, when ye do well, and suffer *for it*, ye take it patiently, this *a is* [1] acceptable with God.

a Mat.5.10-12.   1 Or, *thank*, Lu.6.32.

Doddridge renders the expression, 'This is *graceful* indeed.' Various interpretations of this expression have been proposed; but the meaning evidently is, that *it is acceptable to God,* (see ver. 20, 'this is acceptable to God'—χάρις παρὰ Θιῶ;) that is, this will be regarded by him with *favour.* It does not mean that it was worthy of *thanks,* or that God would *thank* them for doing it, (comp. Luke xvii. 9, 10;) but that such conduct would meet with his approbation. ¶ *If a man for conscience toward God.* If, in the conscientious discharge of his duty, or if, in the endurance of this wrong, he regards himself as serving God. That is, if he feels that God, by his providence, has placed him in the circumstances in which he is, and that it is a duty which he owes to him to bear every trial incident to that condition with a submissive spirit. If he does this, he will evince the true nature of religion, and will be graciously accepted of God. ¶ *Endure grief.* That is, endure that which is fitted to *produce grief,* or that which is wrong. ¶ *Suffering wrongfully.* Suffering injury, or where there is *injustice,* (πάσχων ἀδίκως.) This, though a general remark, has particular reference to *servants,* and to their duty in the relation which they sustain to their masters. In view of what is here said, we may remark, (1.) that if this has reference to *slaves,* as has been usually supposed, it proves that they are very *liable* to be abused; that they have little or no security against being wronged; and that it was a special and very desirable characteristic of those who were *in* that condition, to be able to bear *wrong* with a proper spirit. It is impossible so to modify slavery that this shall not be the case; for the whole system is one of oppression, and there can be nothing that shall effectually secure the slave from being ill-treated. (2.) It would follow from this passage, if this refers to slavery, that that is a very hard and undesirable condition of life; for that is a very undesirable condition where the principal virtue, which they who are in it are required to exercise, is *patience under wrongs.* Such a condition cannot be in accordance with the gospel, and cannot be designed by God to be *permanent.* The relation of parent and child is never thus represented. It is never said or implied in the Scriptures that the principal virtue to which children are exhorted is *patience under wrongs;* nor, in addressing them, is it ever supposed that the most prominent thing in their condition is, that they would need the exercise of such patience. (3.) It is acceptable to God, if we bear a wrong with a proper spirit, from whatever quarter it may come. Our proper business in life is, to do the will of God; to evince the right spirit, however others may treat us; and to show, even under excessive wrong, the sustaining power and the excellence of true religion. Each one who is oppressed and wronged, therefore, has an eminent opportunity to show a spirit which will honour the gospel; and the slave and the martyr may do more to honour the gospel than if they were both permitted to enjoy liberty and life undisturbed.

20. *For what glory* is it. What honour or credit would it be. ¶ *If, when ye be buffeted for your faults.* That is, if you are punished when you deserve it. The word *buffet* (κολαφίζω) means, to strike with the fist; and then to strike in any way; to maltreat, Matt. xxvi. 67; Mark xiv. 65; 1 Cor. iv. 11; 2 Cor. xii. 7. Perhaps there may be a reference here to the manner in which servants were commonly treated, or the kind of punishment to which they were exposed. They would be likely to be *struck* in sudden anger, either by the hand, or by anything that was accessible. The word rendered 'for your faults,' is *sinning,* (ἁμαρτάνοντες.) That is, 'if being guilty of an offence, or having done wrong.' The idea is, that if they were *justly* punished, and should take it patiently, there would be no credit or honour in it. ¶ *Ye shall take it patiently.* ' If, even then, you evince an uncomplaining

21 For even hereunto *a* were ye called: because Christ also suffered [1] for us, leaving us an example, that ye should follow *b* his steps:

22 Who *c* did no sin, neither was guile found in his mouth:

a Mat.16.24; 1 Th.3.3,4.　　1 Some read, *for you.*
b 1 Jn.3.16; Re.12.11.　　*c* Is.53.9.

spirit, and bear it with the utmost calmness and patience, it would be regarded as comparatively no virtue, and as entitling you to no honour. The feeling of all who saw it would be that you *deserved* it, and there would be nothing to excite their sympathy or compassion. The patience evinced might indeed be as great as in the other case, but there would be the feeling that you *deserved* all that you received, and the spirit evinced in that case could not be regarded as entitled to any particular praise. If your masters are inflicting on you only what you deserve, it would be in the highest degree shameful for you to rise up against them, and resist them, for it would be only adding to the wrong which you had already done.' The expression here is, doubtless, to be understood *comparatively*. The meaning is not that absolutely there would be no more credit due to one who should bear his punishment patiently when he had done wrong, than if he had met it with resistance and murmuring; but that there is *very little* credit in that compared with the patience which an innocent person evinces, who, from regard to the will of God, and by control over all the natural feelings of resentment, meekly endures wrong. This expresses the common feeling of our nature. We attribute no particular credit to one who submits to a just punishment even with a calm temper. We feel that it would be wrong in the highest degree for him to do otherwise. So it is when calamities are brought on a man on account of his sins. If it is *seen* to be the fruit of intemperance or crime, we do not feel that there is any great virtue exhibited if he bears it with a calm temper. But if he is overwhelmed with calamity when it seems to have no particular connection with his sins, or to be a punishment for any particular fault; if he suffers at the hand of man, where there is manifest injustice done him, and yet evinces a calm, submissive, and meek temper, we feel that in such cases

there is eminent virtue. ¶ *This* is *acceptable with God.* Marg., as in ver. 19, *thank.* It is that which is agreeable to him, or with which he is pleased.

21. *For even hereunto were ye called.* Such a spirit is required by the very nature of your Christian vocation ; you were called into the church in order that you might evince it. See Notes, 1 Thess. iii. 3. ¶ *Because Christ also suffered for us.* Marg., 'some read, *for you.*' The latest editions of the Greek Testament adopt the reading ' *for you.*' The sense, however, is not essentially varied. The object is, to hold up the example of Christ to those who were called to suffer, and to say to them that they should bear their trials in the same spirit that he evinced in his. See Notes, Phil. iii. 10. ¶ *Leaving us an example.* The apostle does not say that this was the *only* object for which Christ suffered, but that it was *an* object, and an important one. The word rendered *example* (ὑπογραμμὸν) occurs nowhere else in the New Testament. It means properly *a writing copy,* such as is set for children ; or an outline or sketch for a painter to fill up ; and then, in general, an example, a pattern for imitation. ¶ *That ye should follow his steps.* That we should *follow* him, *as if* we trod exactly along behind him, and should place our feet precisely where his were. The meaning is, that there should be the closest imitation or resemblance. The *things* in which we are to imitate him are specified in the following verses.

22. *Who did no sin.* Who was in all respects perfectly holy. There is an allusion here to Isa. liii. 9 ; and the sense is, that he was entirely innocent, and that he suffered without having committed any crime. In this connection the meaning is, that *we* are to be careful that, if we suffer, it should be without committing any crime. We should so live, as the Saviour did, as not to *deserve* to be punished, and thus only shall we entirely follow his example. It

23 Who, when he was reviled, reviled not again; when he suffered, he threatened not; but committed [1] *himself* to him that judgeth [a] righteously:

1 Or, *his cause.*   a Lu.23.46.

is as much our duty to live so as not to *deserve* the reproaches of others, as it is to bear them with patience when we are called to suffer them. The first thing in regard to hard treatment from others, is so to live that there shall be no just occasion for it; the next is, if reproaches come upon us when we have not deserved them, to bear them as the Saviour did. If he suffered unjustly, we should esteem it to be no strange thing that we should; if he bore the injuries done him with meekness, we should learn that it is *possible* for us to do it also; and should learn also that we have not the spirit of his religion unless we actually do it. On the expression here used, comp. Notes, Isa. liii. 9; Heb. vii. 26. ¶ *Neither was guile found in his mouth.* There was no deceit, hypocrisy, or insincerity. He was in all respects what he professed to be, and he imposed on no one by any false and unfounded claim. All this has reference to the time when the Saviour was put to death; and the sense is, that though he was condemned as an impostor, yet that the charge was wholly unfounded. As in his whole life before he was perfectly sincere, so he was eminently on that solemn occasion.

23. *Who, when he was reviled, reviled not again.* He did not use harsh and opprobrious words in return for those which he received. (1.) He *was* reviled. He . was accused of being a seditious man; spoken of as a deceiver; charged with being in league with Beelzebub, the 'prince of the devils' and condemned as a blasphemer against God. This was done (*a*) by the great and the influential of the land; (*b*) in the most public manner; (*c*) with a design to alienate his friends from him; (*d*) with most cutting and severe sarcasm and irony; and (*e*) in reference to everything that would most affect a man of delicate and tender sensibility. (2.) He did not revile those who had reproached him. He asked that justice might be done. He demanded that if he had spoken evil, they should bear witness of the evil; but beyond that he

did not go. He used no harsh language. He showed no anger. He called for no revenge. He prayed that they might be forgiven. He calmly stood and bore it all, for he came to endure all kinds of suffering in order that he might set us an example, and make an atonement for our sins. ¶ *When he suffered, he threatened not.* That is, when he suffered injustice from others, in his trial and in his death, he did not threaten punishment. He did not call down the wrath of heaven. He did not even *predict* that they would be punished; he expressed no wish that they should be. ¶ *But committed* himself *to him that judgeth righteously.* Marg., *his cause.* The sense is much the same. The meaning is, that he committed his cause, his name, his interests, *the whole case,* to God. The meaning of the phrase 'that judgeth righteously' here is, that God would do him exact justice. Though wronged by men, he felt assured that *he* would do right. He would rescue his name from these reproaches; he would give him the honour in the world which he deserved; and he would bring upon those who had wronged him all that was necessary in order to show his disapprobation of what they had done, and all that would be necessary to give the highest support to the cause of virtue. Comp. Luke xxiii. 46. This is the example which is set before us when we are wronged. The whole example embraces these points: (1.) We should see to it that we ourselves are *guiltless* in the matter for which we are reproached or accused. Before we fancy that we are suffering as Christ did, we should be sure that our lives are such as not to deserve reproach. We cannot indeed hope to be as pure in all things as he was; but we may so live that if we *are* reproached and reviled we may be certain that it is not for any wrong that we have done to others, or that we do not deserve it from our fellow-men. (2.) When we are reproached and reviled, we should feel that we were called to this by our profession; that it was one of the things which we were taught to

24 Who his own self bare *a* our sins in his own body [1] on the tree, that we, being dead to sins, should live *b* unto righteousness : by whose *c* stripes ye were healed.

a Is.53.4,&c.   1 Or, *to.*   *b* Ro.6.11.   *c* Is.53.5,6.

expect when we became Christians; that it is what the prophets and apostles endured, and what the Master himself suffered in an eminent degree ; and that if we meet with the scorn of the great, the gay, the rich, the powerful, it is no more than the Saviour did, and no more than we have been taught to expect will be our portion. It may be well, too, to remember our unworthiness ; and to reflect, that though we have done no wrong to the individual who reviles us, yet that we are sinners, and that such reproaches may not be a useless admonisher of our being guilty before God. So David felt when reproached by Shimei : ' So let him curse, because the Lord hath said unto him, Curse David. Who shall then say, Wherefore hast thou done so ?' 2 Sam. xvi. 10. (3.) When this occurs, we should calmly and confidently commit our cause to God. Our name, our character, our influence, our reputation, while living and after we are dead, we should leave entirely with him. We should not seek nor desire revenge. We should not call down the wrath of God on our persecutors and slanderers. We should calmly feel that God will give us the measure of reputation which we ought to have in the world, and that he will suffer no ultimate injustice to be done us. ' Commit thy way unto the Lord ; trust also in him, and he shall bring it to pass ; and he shall bring forth thy righteousness as the light, and thy judgment as the noon-day,' Ps. xxxvii. 5, 6. The Latin Vulgate has here, ' But he committed himself to him who judged him *unjustly,' judicanti se injusté ;* that is, to Pontius Pilate, meaning that he left himself in his hands, though he knew that the sentence was unjust. But there is no authority for this in the Greek, and this is one of the instances in which that version departs from the original.

24. *Who his own self.* See Notes, Heb i. 3, on the phrase ' when he had *by himself* purged our sins.' The meaning is, that he did it in his own proper person ; he did not make expiation by offering a bloody victim, but was himself the sacrifice. ¶ *Bare our sins.* There is an allusion here undoubtedly to Is. liii. 4, 12. See the meaning of the phrase ' to bear sins ' fully considered in the Notes on those places. As this cannot mean that Christ so took upon himself the sins of men as to become himself a sinner, it must mean that he put himself in the place of sinners, and bore that which those sins deserved ; that is, that he endured in his own person that which, if it had been inflicted on the sinner himself, would have been a proper expression of the Divine displeasure against sin, or would have been a proper punishment for sin. See Notes, 2 Cor. v. 21. He was treated *as if* he had been a sinner, in order that we might be treated *as if* we had not sinned ; that is, as if we were righteous. There is no other way in which we can conceive that one bears the sins of another. They cannot be *literally* transferred to another ; and all that can be meant is, that he should take the consequences on himself, and suffer *as if* he had committed the transgressions himself.

[See also the Supplementary Notes on 2 Cor. v. 21 ; Rom. iv. v.; and Gal. iii· 13, in which the subject of imputation is discussed at large·]

¶ *In his own body.* This alludes undoubtedly to his sufferings. The sufferings which he endured on the cross were such *as if* he had been guilty ; that is, he was treated as *he would have been* if he had been a sinner. He was treated as a malefactor ; crucified as those most guilty were ; endured the same kind of bodily pain- that the guilty do who are punished for their own sins ; and passed through mental sorrows strongly resembling—as much so as the case admitted of—what the guilty themselves experience when they are left to distressing anguish of mind, and are abandoned by God. The sufferings of the Saviour were in all respects made as nearly *like* the sufferings of the most guilty, as the sufferings of a perfectly innocent being could be. ¶ *On the tree.* Marg., ' *to* the tree.'

25 For ye were as sheep going
astray; *a* but are now returned unto

a Ps.119.176.

the Shepherd *b* and Bishop of your
souls.

b Eze.34.23; Jn.10.11-16.

Gr., **ἐπὶ τὸ ξύλον.** The meaning is
rather, as in the text, that while himself *on* the cross, he bore the sorrows
which our sins deserved.   It does not
mean that he conveyed our sorrows
there, but that *while* there he suffered
under the intolerable burden, and was
by that burden crushed in death.   The
phrase ' on the tree,' literally ' on the
wood,' means the cross.   The same
Greek word is used in Acts v. 30 ; x.
39 ; xiii. 29 ; Gal. iii. 13, as applicable
to the cross, in all of which places it is
rendered *tree*. ¶ *That we, being dead
to sins.*   In virtue of his having thus
been suspended on a cross ; that is, his
being put-to death as an atoning sacrifice was *the means* by which we become
dead to sin, and live to God.   The
phrase ' being dead to sins ' is, in the
original, **ταῖς ἁμαρτίαις ἀπογενόμενοι**—
literally, ' *to be absent from sins.*'   The
Greek word was probably used (by an
euphemism) to denote *to die*, that is, *to
be absent from the world.*   This is a
milder and less repulsive word than to
say *to die.*   It is not elsewhere used in
the New Testament.   The meaning is,
that we being *effectually separated*
from sin—that is, being so that it no
longer influences us—should live unto
God.   We are to be, in regard to sin,
as if we were dead ; and it is to have
no more influence over us than if we
were in our graves.   See Notes, Rom.
vi. 2–7.   The *means* by which this is
brought about is the death of Christ,
(Notes, Rom. vi. 8 ;) for as he died
literally on the cross on account of our
sins, the effect has been to lead us to
see the evil of transgression, and to lead
new and holy lives. ¶ *Should live unto
righteousness.*   Though dead in respect
to sin, yet we have real life in another
respect.   We are made alive unto God,
to righteousness, to true holiness.   Notes,
Rom. vi. 11 ; Gal. ii. 20. ¶ *By whose
stripes.*   This is taken from Isa. liii. 5.
See it explained in the Notes on that
verse.   The word rendered *stripes*
(**μώλωπι**) means, properly, the livid and
swollen mark of a blow ; the mark designated by us when we use the expres-

sion ' black and blue.'   It is not properly a bloody wound, but that made
by pinching, beating, scourging.   The
idea seems to be that the Saviour was
scourged or whipped ; and that the
effect on us is the same in producing
spiritual healing, or in recovering us
from our faults, *as if* we had been
scourged ourselves.   By faith we see
the bruises inflicted on him, the black
and blue spots made by beating ; we remember that they were on account of
our sins, and not for his ; and the effect
in reclaiming us is the same as if they
had been inflicted on us. ¶ *Ye were
healed.*   Sin is often spoken of, as a
disease, and redemption from it as a restoration from a deadly malady.   See
this explained in the Notes on Is. liii. 5.
    25. *For ye were as sheep going astray.*
Here also is an allusion to Isa. liii. 6,
' All we like sheep have gone astray.'   See
Notes on that verse.   The figure is plain.
We were like a flock without a shepherd.
We had wandered far away from the
true fold, and were following our own
paths.   We were without a protector,
and were exposed to every kind of danger.   This aptly and forcibly expresses
the condition of the whole race before
God recovers men by the plan of salvation.   A flock thus wandering without
a shepherd, conductor, or guide, is in a
most pitiable condition ; and so was man
in his wanderings before he was sought
out and brought back to the true fold
by the Great Shepherd. ¶ *But are
now returned unto the Shepherd and
Bishop of your souls.*   To Christ, who
thus came to seek and save those who
were lost.   He is often called a *Shepherd.*   See Notes, John x. 1–16.   The
word rendered *bishop*, (**ἐπίσκοπος**,) means
overseer.   It may be applied to one who
inspects or *oversees* anything, as public
works, or the execution of treaties ; to
any one who is an inspector of wares
offered for sale ; or, in general, to any
one who is a superintendent.   It is applied in the New Testament to those
who are appointed to *watch over* the
interests of the church, and especially
to the officers of the church.   Here it

is applied to the Lord Jesus as the great Guardian and Superintendent of his church; and the title of universal Bishop belongs to him alone.

REMARKS.

In the conclusion of this chapter we may remark:—

(1.) That there is something very beautiful in the expression ' *Bishop of souls*.' It implies that the soul is the peculiar care of the Saviour; that it is the object of his special interest; and that it is of great value—so great that it is that which mainly deserves regard. He is the Bishop *of the soul* in a sense quite distinct from any care which he manifests for the *body*. *That* too, in the proper way, is the object of his care; but that has no importance compared with the soul. *Our* care is principally employed in respect to the body; the care of the Redeemer has especial reference to the soul.

(2.) It follows that the welfare of the soul may be committed to him with confidence. It is the object of his special guardianship, and he will not be unfaithful to the trust reposed in him. There is nothing more *safe* than the human soul is when it is committed in faith to the keeping of the Son of God. Comp. 2 Tim. i. 12.

(3.) As, therefore, he has shown his regard for us in seeking us when we were wandering and lost; as he came on the kind and benevolent errand to find us and bring us back to himself, let us show our gratitude to him by resolving to wander no more. As we regard our own safety and happiness, let us commit ourselves to him as our great Shepherd, to follow where he leads us, and to be ever under his pastoral inspection. We had all wandered away. We had gone where there was no happiness and no protector. We had no one to provide for us, to care for us, to pity us. We were exposed to certain ruin. In that state he pitied us, sought us out, brought us back. If we had remained where we were, or had gone farther in our wanderings, we should have gone certainly to destruction. He has sought us out; he has led us back; he has taken us under his own protection and guidance; and we shall be safe as long as we follow where he leads, and no longer. To him then, a Shepherd who never forsakes his flock, let us at all times commit ourselves, following where he leads, feeling that under him our great interests are secure.

(4.) We may learn from this chapter, indeed, as we may from every other part of the New Testament, that in doing this we may be called to suffer. We may be reproached and reviled as the great Shepherd himself was. We may become the objects of public scorn on account of our devoted attachment to him. We may suffer in name, in feeling, in property, in our business, by our honest attachment to the principles of his gospel. Many who are his followers may be in circumstances of poverty or oppression. They may be held in bondage; they may be deprived of their rights; they may feel that their lot in life is a hard one, and that the world seems to have conspired against them to do them wrong; but let us in all these circumstances look to Him ' who made himself of no reputation, and took upon him the form of a servant, and became obedient unto death, even the death of the cross,' (Phil. ii. 7, 8;) and let us remember that it is 'enough for the disciple that he be as his master, and the servant as his lord,' Matt. x. 25. In view of the example of our Master, and of all the promises of support in the Bible, let us bear with patience all the trials of life, whether arising from poverty, an humble condition, or the reproaches of a wicked world. Our trials will soon be ended; and soon, under the direction of the ' Shepherd and Bishop of souls,' we shall be brought to a world where trials and sorrows are unknown.

(5.) In our trials here, let it be our main object so to live that our sufferings shall not be on account of our own faults. See vers. 19–22. Our Saviour so lived. He was persecuted, reviled, mocked, condemned to die. But it was for no fault of his. In all his varied and prolonged sufferings, he had the ever-abiding consciousness that he was innocent; he had the firm conviction that it would yet be seen and confessed by all the world that he was ' holy, harmless, undefiled,' ver. 23. His were not the sufferings produced by a guilty con-

CHAPTER III.

LIKEWISE, ye wives, *a be* in subjection to your own husbands; that, if any obey not the

word, they also may without the word be won by the conversation of the wives;

a Ep.5.22; Tit.2.5,6.

science, or by the recollection that he had wronged any one. So, if we must suffer, let our trials come upon us. Be it our first aim to have a conscience void of offence, to wrong no one, to give no occasion for reproaches and revilings, to do our duty faithfully to God and to men. Then, if trials come, we shall feel that we suffer as our Master did; and then we may, as he did, commit our cause 'to him that judgeth righteously,' assured that in due time 'he will bring forth our righteousness as the light, and our judgment as the noon-day,' Psa. xxxvii. 6.

CHAPTER III.

ANALYSIS OF THE CHAPTER.

THIS chapter embraces the following subjects:—

I. The duty of wives, vers. 1–6. Particularly (*a*) that their conduct should be such as would be adapted to lead their unbelieving husbands to embrace a religion whose happy influence was seen in the pure conduct of their wives, vers. 1, 2. (*b*) In reference to dress and ornaments, that they should not seek that which was external, but rather that which was of the heart, vers. 3, 4. (*c*) For an illustration of the manner in which these duties should be performed, the apostle refers them to the holy example of the wife of Abraham, as one which Christian females should imitate, vers. 5, 6.

II. The duty of husbands, ver. 7. It was their duty to render all proper honour to their wives, and to live with them as fellow-heirs of salvation, that their prayers might not be hindered; implying, (1,) that in the most important respects they were on an equality; (2,) that they *would* pray together, or that there *would be* family prayer; and, (3,) that it was the duty of husband and wife so to live together that their prayers might ascend from united hearts, and that it would be consistent for God to answer them.

III. The general duty of unity and

of kindness, vers. 8–14. They were (*α*) to be of one mind; to have compassion; to love as brèthren, ver. 8. (*b*) They were never to render evil for evil, or railing for railing, ver. 9. (*c*) They were to remember the promises of length of days, and of honour, made to those who were pure in their conversation, and who were the friends of peace, vers. 9, 10. (*d*) They were to remember that the eyes of the Lord were always on the righteous; that they who were good were under his protection, ver. 12; and that if, while they maintained this character, they were called to suffer, they should count it rather an honour than a hardship, vers. 13, 14.

IV. The duty of being ready always to give to every man a reason for the hope they entertained; and, if they were called to suffer persecution and trial in the service of God, of being able still to show good reasons why they professed to be Christians, and of so living that those who wronged them should see that their religion was more than a name, and was founded in such truth as to command the assent even of their persecutors, vers. 15–17.

V. In their persecutions and trials they were to remember the example of Christ, *his* trials, *his* patience, and *his* triumphs, vers. 18–22. Particularly (*a*) the apostle refers them to the fact that he had suffered, though he was innocent, and that he was put to death though he had done no wrong, ver. 18. (*b*) He refers them to the *patience* and *forbearance* of Christ in a former age, an age of great and abounding wickedness, when in the person of his representative and ambassador Noah, he suffered much and long from the opposition of the guilty and perverse men who were finally destroyed, and who are now held in prison, showing us how *patient* we ought to be when offended by others in our attempts to do them good, vers. 19, 20. (*c*) He refers to the fact that notwithstanding all the opposition which Noah met with in bearing a message, as

2 While they behold your chaste | conversation *coupled* with fear.

an ambassador of the Lord, to a wicked generation, he and his family were saved, ver. 21. The *design* of this allusion evidently is to show us, that if we are patient and forbearing in the trials which we meet with in the world, we shall be saved also. Noah, says the apostle, was saved by water. We, too, says he, are saved in a similar manner by water. In his salvation, and in ours, *water* is employed as the means of salvation: in *his* case by bearing up the ark, in *ours* by becoming the emblem of the washing away of sins. (*d*) The apostle refers to the fact that Christ has ascended to heaven, and has been exalted over angels, and principalities, and powers; thus showing that having borne all his trials with patience he ultimately triumphed, and that in like manner we, if we are patient, shall triumph also, ver. 22. He came off a conqueror, and was exalted to the highest honours of heaven; and so, if faithful, we may hope to come off conquerors also, and be exalted to the honours of heaven as he was. The whole argument here is drawn from the example of Christ, first, in his patience and forbearance with the whole world, and then when he was personally on the earth; from the fact, that in the case of that messenger whom he sent to the ungodly race before the flood, and in his own case when personally on earth, there was ultimate triumph after all that they met with from ungodly men; and thus, if we endure opposition and trials in the same way, we may hope also to triumph in heaven with our exalted Saviour.

1. *Likewise, ye wives,* be *in subjection to your own husbands.* On the duty here enjoined, see Notes, 1 Cor. xi. 3–9, and Eph. v. 22. ¶ *That, if any obey not the word.* The word of God; the gospel. That is, if any wives have husbands who are not true Christians. This would be likely to occur when the gospel was first preached, as it does now, by the fact that wives might be converted, though their husbands were not. It cannot be inferred from this, that after they themselves had become Christians they had married unbelieving husbands. The term '*word*' here refers

particularly to the gospel *as preached;* and the idea is, that if they were regardless of that gospel when preached—if they would not attend on preaching, or if they were unaffected by it, or if they openly rejected it, there might be hope still that they would be converted by the Christian influence of a wife at home. In such cases, a duty of special importance devolves on the wife. ¶ *They also may without the word be won.* In some other way than by preaching. This does not mean that they would be converted independently of the influence of *truth*—for truth is always the instrument of conversion, (James i. 18; John xvii. 17;) but that it was to be by another influence than *preaching.* ¶ *By the conversation of the wives.* By the conduct or *deportment* of their wives. See Notes, Phil. i. 27. The word *conversation,* in the Scriptures, is never confined, as it is now with us, to *oral discourse,* but denotes conduct in general. It *includes* indeed 'conversation' as the word is now used, but it embraces also much more—including everything that we *do.* The meaning here is, that the habitual deportment of the wife was to be such as to show the reality and power of religion; to show that it had such influence on her temper, her words, her whole deportment, as to demonstrate that it was from God.

2. *While they behold your chaste conversation.* Your pure conduct. The word *chaste* here (ἀγνὴν) refers to purity of conduct in all respects, and not merely to chastity properly so called. It includes that, but it also embraces much more. The conduct of the wife is to be in all respects *pure;* and this is to be the grand instrumentality in the conversion of her husband. A wife may be strictly *chaste,* and yet there may be many other things in her conduct and temper which would mar the beauty of her piety, and prevent any happy influence on the mind of her husband. ¶ *Coupled with fear.* The word *fear,* in this place, may refer either to the fear of God, or to a proper respect and reverence for their husbands, Eph. v. 33. The trait of character which is referred to is that of proper

3 Whose adorning, *a* let it not be that outward *adorning* of plaiting

a 1 Ti.2.9,10.

the hair, and of wearing of gold, or of putting on of apparel ;

---

respect and reverence in all the relations which she sustained, as opposed to a trifling and frivolous mind.　Leighton suggests that the word *fear* here relates particularly to the other duty enjoined —that of chaste conversation—' fearing the least stain of chastity, or the very appearance of anything not suiting with it.　It is a delicate, timorous grace, afraid of the least air, or shadow of anything that hath but a resemblance of wronging it, in carriage, or speech, or apparel.'

3. *Whose adorning.*　Whose ornament.　The apostle refers here to a propensity which exists in the heart of woman to seek that which would be esteemed ornamental, or that which will *appear well* in the sight of others, and commend us to them.　The desire of this is laid deep in human nature, and therefore, when properly regulated, is not wrong.　The only question is, what is the true and appropriate ornament?　What should be primarily sought as the right kind of adorning? The apostle does not condemn true ornament, nor does he condemn the desire to appear in such a way as to secure the esteem of others.　God does not condemn real ornament.　The universe is full of it.　The colours of the clouds and of the rainbow; the varied hues of flowers; the plumage of birds, and the covering of many of the animals of the forest; the green grass; the variety of hill and dale; the beauty of the human complexion, the ruddy cheek, and the sparkling eye, are all of the nature of *ornament*.　They are something *superadded* to what would be merely useful, *to make them appear well.*　Few or none of these things are absolutely necessary to the things to which they are attached; for the eye could see without the various tints of beauty that are drawn upon it, and the lips and the cheeks could perform their functions without their beautiful tints, and the vegetable world could exist without the variegated colours that are painted on it; but God *meant* that this should be a beautiful world; that it

should *appear well;* that there should be something more than mere utility. The true notion of ornament or adorning is that which will make any person or thing *appear well,* or *beautiful,* to others; and the apostle does not prohibit that which would have this effect in the wife.　The grand thing which she was to seek, was not that which is merely external, but that which is internal, and which God regards as of so great value.　¶ *Let it not be that outward* adorning.　Let not this be the main or principal thing; let not her heart be set on this.　The apostle does not say that she should wholly neglect her personal appearance, for she has no more right to be offensive to her husband by neglecting her personal appearance, than by a finical attention to it.　Religion promotes neatness, and cleanliness, and a proper attention to our external appearance according to our circumstances in life, as certainly as it does to the internal virtue of the soul. On this whole passage, see Notes, 1 Tim. ii. 9, 10.　¶ *Of plaiting the hair.*　See Notes, 1 Tim. ii. 9; Comp. Notes, Isa. iii. 24.　Great attention is paid to this in the East, and it is to this that the apostle here refers.　' The women in the eastern countries,' says Dr. Shaw, (Travels, p. 294,) ' affect to have their hair hang down to the ground, which they collect into one lock, upon the hinder part of the head, binding and plaiting it about with ribbons.　Above this, or on the top of their heads, persons of better fashion wear flexible plates of gold or silver, variously cut through, and engraved in imitation of lace.'　We are not to suppose that a mere braiding or plaiting of the hair is improper, for there may be no more simple or convenient way of disposing of it.　But the allusion here is to the excessive care which then prevailed, and especially to their setting the heart on such ornaments rather than on the adorning which is internal.　It may not be easy to fix the exact limit of propriety about the method of arranging the hair, or about any other ornament ;

4 But *let it be* the hidden man of the heart, *a* in that which is not corruptible, *even the ornament* of a meek *b* and quiet spirit, which is in the sight of God of great price.

a Ps.45.13; Ro.2.29.   b Ps.25.9; 149.4; Mat.5.5.

but those whose *hearts* are right, generally have little difficulty on the subject. Every ornament of the body, however beautiful, is soon to be laid aside; the adorning of the soul will endure for ever. ¶ *And of wearing of gold.* The gold here particularly referred to is probably that which was interwoven in the hair, and which was a common female ornament in ancient times. Thus Virgil says, *crines nodantur in aurum.* And again, *crinem implicat auro.* See Homer, Il., B. 872; Herod. i. 82; and Thucyd. i. 6. The wearing of gold in the hair, however, was more common among women of loose morals than among virtuous females.—Pollux iv. 153. It cannot be supposed that *all* wearing of gold about the person is wrong, for there is nothing evil in gold itself, and there may be some articles connected with apparel made of gold that may in no manner draw off the affections from higher things, and may do nothing to endanger piety. The meaning is, that such ornaments should not be sought; that Christians should be in no way distinguished for them; that they should not engross the time and attention; that Christians should so dress as to show that their minds are occupied with nobler objects, and that in their apparel they should be models of neatness, economy, and plainness. If it should be said that this expression teaches that it is wrong to wear gold *at all,* it may be replied that on the same principle it would follow that the next clause teaches that it is wrong *to put on apparel at all.* There is really no difficulty in such expressions. We are to dress decently, and in the manner that will attract least attention, and we are to show that *our hearts* are interested supremely in more important things than in outward adorning. ¶ *Or of putting on of apparel.* That is, this is not to be the ornament which we principally seek, or for which we are distinguished. We are to desire a richer and more permanent adorning—that of the heart.

4. *But let it be the hidden man of the heart.* This expression is substantially the same as that of Paul in Rom. vii. 22, 'the inward man.' See Notes on that place. The word '*hidden*' here means that which is concealed; that which is not made apparent by the dress, or by ornament It lies within, pertaining to the affections of the soul. ¶ *In that which is not corruptible.* Properly, 'in the incorruptible ornament of a meek and quiet spirit.' This is said to be incorruptible in contradistinction to gold and apparel. They will decay; but the internal ornament is ever enduring. The sense is, that whatever pertains to outward decoration, however beautiful and costly, is fading; but that which pertains to the soul is enduring. As the soul is immortal, so all that tends to adorn that will be immortal too; as the body is mortal, so all with which it can be invested is decaying, and will soon be destroyed. ¶ *The ornament of a meek and quiet spirit.* Of a calm temper; a contented mind; a heart free from passion, pride, envy, and irritability; a soul not subject to the agitations and vexations of those who live for fashion, and who seek to be distinguished for external adorning. The connection here shows that the apostle refers to this, not only as that which would be of great price in the sight of God, but as that which would tend to secure the affection of their husbands, and win them to embrace the true religion, (see vers. 1, 2;) and, in order to this, he recommends them, instead of seeking external ornaments, to seek those of the mind and of the heart, as more agreeable to their husbands; as better adapted to win their hearts to religion; as that which would be most permanently proved. In regard to this point we may observe, (1.) that there are, undoubtedly, *some* husbands who are pleased with excessive ornaments in their wives, and who take a pleasure in seeing them decorated with gold, and pearls, and costly array. (2.) That *all* are pleased and gratified with a suitable attention to personal appear-

ance on the part of their wives. It is as much the duty of a wife to be cleanly in her person, and neat in her habits, in the presence of her husband, as in the presence of strangers; and no wife can hope to secure the permanent affection of her husband who is not attentive to her personal appearance in her own family; especially if, while careless of her personal appearance in the presence of her husband, she makes it a point to appear gaily dressed before others. Yet (3.) the decoration of the body is not all, nor is it the principal thing which a husband desires. He desires primarily in his wife the more permanent adorning which pertains to the heart. Let it be remembered, (a) that a large part of the ornaments on which females value themselves are *lost* to a great extent on the other sex. Many a man cannot tell the difference between diamonds and cut-glass, or paste in the form of diamonds; and few are such connoisseurs in the matter of female ornaments as to appreciate at all the difference in the quality or colour of silks, and shawls, and laces, which might appear so important to a female eye. The fact is, that those personal ornaments which to females appear of so much value, are much less regarded and prized by men than they often suppose. It is a rare thing that a man is so thoroughly skilled in the knowledge of the distinctions that pertain to fashions, as to appreciate that on which the heart of a female often so much prides itself; and it is no great credit to him if he *can* do this. His time usually, unless he is a draper or a jeweller, might have been much better employed than in making those acquisitions which are needful to qualify him to appreciate and admire the peculiarities of gay female apparel. (*b*) But a man has a real interest in what constitutes the ornaments of the heart. His happiness, in his intercourse with his wife, depends on these. He knows what is denoted by a kind temper; by gentle words; by a placid brow; by a modest and patient spirit; by a heart that is calm in trouble, and that is affectionate and pure; by freedom from irritability, fretfulness, and impatience; *and he can fully appreciate the value of these things.* No professional skill is necessary to qua-

lify him to see their worth; and no acquired tact in discrimination is requisite to enable him to estimate them according to their full value. A wife, therefore, if she would permanently please her husband, should seek the adorning of the soul rather than the body; the ornament of the heart rather than gold and jewels. The one can never be a substitute for the other; and whatever outward decorations she may have, unless she have a gentleness of spirit, a calmness of temper, a benevolence and purity of soul, and a cultivation of mind that her husband can love, she cannot calculate on his permanent affection. ¶ *Which is in the sight of God of great price.* Of great value; that being of great value for which a large price is paid. He has shown his sense of its value (·a) by commending it so often in his word; (*b*) by making religion to consist so much in it, rather than in high intellectual endowments, learning, skill in the arts, and valour; and (*c*) by the character of his Son, the Lord Jesus, in whom this was so prominent a characteristic. Sentiments not unlike what is here stated by the apostle, occur not unfrequently in heathen classic writers. There are some remarkable passages in Plutarch, strongly resembling it:—' An ornament, as Crates said, is that which adorns. The proper ornament of a woman is that which becomes her best. This is neither gold, nor pearls, nor scarlet, but those things which are an evident proof of gravity, regularity, and modesty.'— *Conjugalio Præcept.*, c. xxvi. The wife of Phocion, a celebrated Athenian general, receiving a visit from a lady who was elegantly adorned with gold and jewels, and her hair with pearls, took occasion to call the attention of her guest to the elegance and costliness of her dress. ' My ornament,' said the wife of Phocion, ' is my husband, now for the twentieth year general of the Athenians.'--*Plutarch's Life of Phocion.* ' The Sicilian tyrant sent to the daughters of Lysander garments and tissues of great value, but Lysander refused them, saying, " These ornaments will rather put my daughters out of countenance than adorn them." '—*Plutarch.* So in the fragments of Naumachius, as quoted by Benson, there is a precept

5 For after this manner, in the old time, the holy women also, who trusted in God, adorned themselves, being in subjection unto their own husbands:

6 Even as Sara obeyed Abraham, calling him lord: *a*whose ¹ daughters ye are, as long as ye do well, and are not afraid with any amazement.

a Ge.18.12.   1 *children.*

much like this of Peter: ' Be not too fond of gold, neither wear purple hyacinth about your neck, or the green jasper, of which foolish persons are proud. Do not covet such vain ornaments, neither view yourself too often in the glass, nor twist your hair into a multitude of curls,' &c.

5. *For after this manner, in the old time.* The allusion here is particularly to the times of the patriarchs, and the object of the apostle is to state another reason why they should seek that kind of ornament which he had been commending. The reason is, that this characterised the pious and honoured females of ancient times—those females who had been most commended of God, and who were most worthy to be remembered on earth. ¶ *Who trusted in God.* Greek, ' Who *hoped* in God ;' that is, who were truly pious. They were characterised by simple trust or hope in God, rather than by a fondness for external adorning. ¶ *Adorned themselves.* To wit, with a meek and quiet spirit, manifested particularly by the respect evinced for their husbands. ¶ *Being in subjection unto their own husbands.* This was evidently a characteristic of the early periods of the world ; and piety was understood to consist much in proper respect for others, according to the relations sustained towards them.

6. *Even as Sara obeyed Abraham.* Sarah was one of the most distinguished of the wives of the patriarchs, and her case is referred to as furnishing one of the best illustrations of the duty to which the apostle refers. Nothing is said, in the brief records of her life, of any passion for outward adorning ; much is said of her kindness to her husband, and her respect for him. Comp. Gen. xii. 5 ; xviii. 6. ¶ *Calling him Lord.* See Gen. xviii. 12. It was probably inferred from this instance, by the apostle, and not without reason, that Sarah habitually used this respectful appellation.

acknowledging by it that he was her superior, and that he had a right to rule in his own house. The word *lord* has the elementary idea of *ruling*, and this is the sense here—that she acknowledged that he had a right to direct the affairs of his household, and that it was her duty to be in subjection to him as the head of the family. In what respects this is a duty, may be seen by consulting the Notes on Eph. v. 22. Among the Romans, it was quite common for wives to use the appellation *lord*, (*dominus*), when speaking of their husbands. The same custom also prevailed among the Greeks. See Grotius, *in loc.* This passage does not prove that the term *lord* should be the particular appellation by which Christian wives should address their husbands now, but it proves that there should be the same respect and deference which was implied by its use in patriarchal times. The welfare of society, and the happiness of individuals, are not diminished by showing proper respect for all classes of persons in the various relations of life. ¶ *Whose daughters ye are.* That is, you will be worthy to be regarded as her daughters, if you manifest the same spirit that she did. The margin here, as the Greek, is *children.* The sense is, that if they demeaned themselves correctly in the relation of wives, it would be proper to look upon her as their mother, and to feel that they were not unworthy to be regarded as her daughters. ¶ *As long as ye do well.* In respect to the particular matter under consideration. ¶ *And are not afraid with any amazement.* This passage has been variously understood. Some have supposed that this is suggested as an argument to persuade them to *do well*, from the consideration that by so doing they would be preserved from those alarms and terrors which a contest with superior power might bring with it, and which would prove as injurious to their peace as to their character. Rosenmüller explains

7 Likewise, ye husbands, *a* dwell with *them* according to knowledge, giving honour unto the wife, as

a Col.3.19.

unto the weaker vessel, and as being heirs together of the grace of life; that your prayers be not hindered.

---

it, ' If ye do well, terrified by no threats of unbelieving husbands, if they should undertake to compel you to deny the Christian faith.' Doddridge supposes that it means that they were to preserve their peace and fortitude in any time of danger, so as not to act out of character, through amazement or danger. Calvin, Benson, and Bloomfield understand it of that firmness and intrepidity of character which would be necessary to support their religious independence, when united with heathen husbands; meaning that they were not to be deterred from doing their duty by any threats or terrors, either of their unbelieving husbands, or of their enemies and persecutors. Dr. Clarke supposes that it means that if they did well, they would live under no dread of being detected in improprieties of life, or being found out in their *infidelities* to their husbands, as those must always be who are unfaithful to their marriage vows. The word rendered *amazement* (πτόησις) does not elsewhere occur in the New Testament. It means *terror, trepidation, fear;* and the literal translation of the Greek is, 'not fearing any fear.' It seems to me that the following may express the sense of the passage : (1.) There is undoubtedly an allusion to the character of Sarah, and the object of the apostle is to induce them to follow her example. (2.) The thing in Sarah which he would exhort them to imitate, was her pure and upright life, her faithful discharge of her duties as a woman fearing God. This she did constantly wherever she was, regardless of consequences. Among friends and strangers, at home and abroad, she was distinguished for *doing well.* Such was her character, such her fidelity to her husband and her God, such her firm integrity and benevolence, that she at all times lived to do good, and would have done it, unawed by terror, undeterred by threats. To whatever trial her piety was exposed, it bore the trial; and such was her strength of virtue, that it was certain her integrity would be

firm by whatever consequences she might have been threatened for her adherence to her principles. (3.) They were to imitate her in this, and were thus to show that they were worthy to be regarded as her daughters. They were to do well ; to be faithful to their husbands ; to be firm in their principles ; to adhere steadfastly to what was true and good, whatever trials they might pass through, however much they might be threatened with persecution, or however any might attempt to deter them from the performance of their duty. Thus, by a life of Christian fidelity, unawed by fear from any quarter, they would show that they were imbued with the same principles of unbending virtue which characterised the wife of the father of the faithful, and that they were not unworthy to be regarded as her daughters.

7. *Likewise, ye husbands.* On the general duty of husbands, see Notes, Eph. v. 25, seq. ¶ *Dwell with* them. That is, ' Let your manner of living with them be that which is immediately specified.' ¶ *According to knowledge.* In accordance with an intelligent view of the nature of the relation; or, as becomes those who have been instructed in the duties of this relation according to the gospel. The meaning evidently is, that they should seek to obtain just views of what Christianity enjoins in regard to this relation, and that they should allow those intelligent views to control them in all their intercourse with their wives. ¶ *Giving honour unto the wife.* It was an important advance made in society when the Christian religion gave such a direction as this, for everywhere among the heathen, and under all false systems of religion, woman has been regarded as worthy of little honour or respect. She has been considered as a slave, or as a mere instrument to gratify the passions of man. It is one of the elementary doctrines of Christianity, however, that woman is to be treated with respect; and one of the first and most marked effects of religion

on society is to elevate the wife to a condition in which she will be worthy of esteem. The particular reasons for the honour which husbands are directed to show to their wives, here specified, are two: she is to be treated with special kindness as being more feeble than man, and as having a claim therefore to delicate attention; and she is to be honoured as the equal heir of the grace of life. Doddridge, Clarke, and some others, suppose that the word *honour* here refers to maintenance or support; and that the command is, that the husband is to provide for his wife so that she may not want. But it seems to me that the word is to be understood here in its more usual signification, and that it inculcates a higher duty than that of merely providing for the temporal wants of the wife, and strikes at a deeper evil than a mere neglect of meeting her temporal necessities. The *reasons* assigned for doing this seem to imply it. ¶ *As unto the weaker vessel.* It is not uncommon in the Scriptures to compare the body to a *vessel*, (Comp. Notes, 1 Thess. iv. 4,) and thence the comparison is extended to the whole person. This is done either because the body is frail and feeble, like an earthen vessel easily broken; or because it is that in which the soul is lodged; or because, in accordance with a frequent use of the word, (see below,) the body is the *instrument* by which the soul accomplishes its purposes, or is the *helper* of the soul. Comp. Acts ix. 15; Rom. ix. 22, 23; 2 Cor. iv. 7. In the later Hebrew usage it was common to apply the term *vessel* (Heb. כְּלִי, Gr. σκεῦος) to a wife, as is done here. See Schoettgen, Hor. Heb. p. 827. Expressions similar to this, in regard to the comparative *feebleness* of woman, occur frequently in the classic writers. See Wetstein *in loc.* The *reasons* why the term *vessel* was given to a wife, are not very apparent. A not unfrequent sense of the word used here (σκεῦος) in the Greek classics was that of an instrument; a helper; one who was employed by another to accomplish anything, or to aid him, (Passow,) and it seems probable that this was the reason why the term was given to the wife. Comp. Gen. ii. 18. The reason here assigned for the honour that was to be shown to

the wife is, that she is 'the *weaker* vessel.' By this it is not necessarily meant that she is of feebler capacity, or inferior mental endowments, but that she is more tender and delicate; more subject to infirmities and weaknesses; less capable of enduring fatigue and toil; less adapted to the rough and stormy scenes of life. As such, she should be regarded and treated with special kindness and attention. This is a reason, the force of which all can see and appreciate. So we feel toward a sister; so we feel toward a beloved child, if he is of feeble frame and delicate constitution; and so every man should feel in relation to his wife. She may have mental endowments equal to his own; she may have moral qualities in every way superior to his; but the God of nature has made her with a more delicate frame, a more fragile structure, and with a body subject to many infirmities to which the more hardy frame of man is a stranger. ¶*And as being heirs together of the grace of life.* The grace that is connected with eternal life; that is, as fellow-Christians. They were equal heirs of the everlasting inheritance, called in the Scripture '*life;*' and the same ' grace ' connected with that inheritance had been conferred on both. This passage contains a very important truth in regard to the female sex. Under every other system of religion but the Christian system, woman has been regarded as in every way inferior to man. Christianity teaches that, in respect to her higher interests, the interests of religion, *she is every way his equal.* She is entitled to all the hopes and promises which religion imparts. She is redeemed as he is. She is addressed in the same language of tender invitation. She has the same privileges and comforts which religion imparts here, and she will be elevated to the same rank and privileges in heaven. This single truth would raise the female sex everywhere from degradation, and check at once half the social evils of the race. Make her the equal of man in the hope of heaven, and at once she rises to her appropriate place. Home is made what it should be, a place of intelligence and pure friendship; and a world of suffering and sadness smiles under the benefactions of Christian woman. ¶*That*

your prayers be not hindered. It is
fairly implied here, (1.) that it was supposed there would be united or family
prayer. The apostle is speaking of
'dwelling with the wife,' and of the right
manner of treating her; and it is plainly
supposed that united prayer would be
one thing that would characterise their
living together. He does not direct that
there *should* be prayer. He seems to
take it for granted that there *would be;*
and it may be remarked, that where
there is true religion in right exercise,
there is prayer as a matter of course.
The head of a family does not ask
whether he *must* establish family worship; he does it as one of the spontaneous
fruits of religion—as a thing concerning
which no formal command is necessary.
Prayer in the family, as everywhere else,
is a privilege; and the true question to
be asked on the subject is not whether
a man *must*, but whether he *may* pray.
(2.) It is implied that there might be
such a way of living as effectually to
hinder prayer; that is, to prevent its
being offered aright, and to prevent
any answer. This might occur in many
ways. If the husband treated the wife
unkindly; if he did not show her proper respect and affection; if there were
bickerings, and jealousies, and contentions between them, there could be
no hope that acceptable prayer would
be offered. A spirit of strife; irritability and unevenness of temper; harsh
looks and unkind words; a disposition
easily to take offence, and an unwilling-
ness to forgive, all these prevent a
'return of prayers.' Acceptable prayer
never can be offered in the tempest of
passion, and there can be no doubt that
such prayer is often 'hindered' by the
inequalities of temper, and the bickerings and strifes that exist in families.
Yet how desirable is it that husband and
wife should so live together that their
prayers may not be hindered! How
desirable for their own peace and happiness in that relation; how desirable
for the welfare of children! In view of
the exposition in this verse we may remark, (*a*) that Christianity has done
much to elevate the female sex. It has
taught that woman is an heir of the
grace of life as well as man; that, while
she is inferior in bodily vigour, she is

his equal in the most important respect;
that she is a fellow-traveller with him
to a higher world; and that in every
way she is entitled to all the blessings
which redemption confers, as much as
he is. This single truth has done more
than all other things combined to elevate
the female sex, and is all that is needful
to raise her from her degradation all
over the world. (*b*) They, therefore,
who desire the elevation of the female
sex, who see woman ignorant and de-
graded in the dark parts of the earth,
should be the friends of all well-directed
efforts to send the gospel to heathen
lands. Every husband who has a pure
and intelligent wife, and every father
who has an accomplished daughter, and
every brother who has a virtuous sister,
should seek to spread the gospel abroad.
To that gospel only he owes it that he
has such a wife, daughter, sister; and
that gospel, which has given to him
such an intelligent female friend, would
elevate woman everywhere to the same
condition. The obligation which he
owes to religion in this respect can be
discharged in no better way than by
aiding in diffusing that gospel which
would make the wife, the daughter, the
sister, everywhere what she is in his
own dwelling. (*c*) Especially is this
the duty of the Christian female. She
owes her elevation in society to Christianity, and what Christianity has made
her, it would make the sunken and
debased of her own sex all over the
earth; and how can she better show her
gratitude than by aiding in any and
every way in making that same gospel
known in the dark parts of the world?
(*d*) Christianity makes a happy home.
Let the principles reign in any family
which are here enjoined by the apostle,
and that family will be one of intelligence, contentment, and peace. There
is a simple and easy way of being happy
in the family relation. *It is to allow
the spirit of Christ and his gospel to
reign there.* That done, though there
be poverty, and disappointment, and
sickness, and cares, and losses, yet there
will be peace within, for there will be
mutual love, and the cheerful hope of a
brighter world. Where that is wanting,
no outward splendour, no costly furniture, or viands, no gilded equipage, no

8 Finally, *be ye* all of one mind, *having compassion one of another; [1]love *b* as brethren, *be* pitiful, *be* courteous:

9 Not rendering *c* evil for evil, or railing for railing; but contrariwise blessing; knowing that ye are thereunto called, that ye should inherit a blessing.

a Ro.12.16.   1 Or, *loving to the.*   *b* 1 Jn.3.18.
c Mat.5.44.; Ep.4.32.

long train of servants, no wine, or music, or dances, can secure happiness in a dwelling. With all these things there may be the most corroding passions; in the mansion where these things are, pale disease, disappointment, and death may come, and there shall be nothing to console and support.

8. *Finally.* As the last direction, or as general counsel in reference to your conduct in all the relations of life. The apostle had specified most of the important relations which Christians sustain, (chap. ii. 13–25; iii. 1–7;) and he now gives a general direction in regard to their conduct in all those relations. ¶ Be ye *all of one mind.* See Notes, Rom. xii. 16. The word here used (ὁμόφρων) does not elsewhere occur in the New Testament. It means, *of the same mind; like-minded;* and the object is to secure harmony in their views and feelings. ¶ *Having compassion one of another.* Sympathizing, (συμπαθεῖς;) entering into one another's feelings, and evincing a regard for each other's welfare. Notes, Rom. xii. 15. Comp. 1 Cor. xii. 26; John xi. 35. The Greek word here used does not elsewhere occur in the New Testament. It describes that state of mind which exists when we enter into the feelings of others *as if* they were our own, as the different parts of the body are affected by that which affects one. Notes, 1 Cor. xii. 26. ¶ *Love as brethren.* Marg., *loving to the;* i. e., the brethren. The Greek word (φιλάδελφος) does not elsewhere occur in the New Testament. It means *loving one's brethren;* that is, loving each other as Christian brethren.—*Rob. Lex.* Thus it enforces the duty so often enjoined in the New Testament, that of love to Christians as brethren of the same family. Notes, Rom. xii. 10. Comp. Heb. xiii. 1; John xiii. 34. ¶ Be *pitiful.* The word here used (εὔσπλαγχνος) occurs nowhere else in the New Testament, except in Eph. iv. 32, where it is rendered *tender-hearted.* See Notes on

that verse. ¶ *Be courteous.* This word also (φιλόφρων) occurs nowhere else in the New Testament. It means *friendly-minded, kind, courteous.* Later editions of the New Testament, instead of this, read (ταπεινόφρονες) of a lowly or humble mind. See Hahn. The sense is not materially varied. In the one word, the idea of *friendliness* is the one that prevails; in the other, that of *humility.* Christianity requires both of these virtues, and either word enforces an important injunction. The *authority* is in favour of the latter reading; and though Christianity requires that we should be courteous and gentlemanly in our treatment of others, *this* text can hardly be relied on as a proof-text of that point.

9. *Not rendering evil for evil.* See Notes, Matt. v. 39, 44; Rom. xii. 17. ¶ *Or railing for railing.* See Notes, 1 Tim. vi. 4. Comp. Mark xv. 29; Luke xxiii. 39. ¶ *But contrariwise blessing.* In a spirit contrary to this. See Notes, Matt. v. 44. ¶ *Knowing that ye are thereunto called, that ye should inherit a blessing.* 'Knowing that you were called to be Christians in order that you should obtain a blessing infinite and eternal in the heavens. Expecting such a blessing yourselves, you should be ready to scatter blessings on all others. You should be ready to bear all their reproaches, and even to wish them well. The hope of eternal life should make your minds calm; and the prospect that *you* are to be so exalted in heaven should fill your hearts with benignity and love.' There is nothing which is better fitted to cause our hearts to overflow with benignity, to make us ready to forgive all others when they injure us, than the hope of salvation. Cherishing such a hope ourselves, we cannot but wish that all others may share it, and this will lead us to wish for them every blessing   A man who has a hope of heaven should abound in every virtue, and show that he is a sincere well-wisher of the race. Why

10 For he *a* that will love life, and see good days, let him refrain his tongue from evil, and his lips that they speak no guile:

a Ps. 34. 12, &c.

should one who expects soon to be in heaven harbour malice in his bosom? Why should he wish to injure a fellow-worm? How can he?

10. *For he that will love life.* Gr., 'He willing, (θέλων,) or that *wills* to love life.' It implies that there is some positive desire to live; some active wish that life should be prolonged. This whole passage (vers. 10–12) is taken, with some slight variations, from Psalm xxxiv. 12–16. In the Psalm this expression is, 'What man is he that desireth life, and loveth many days, that he may see good?' The sense is substantially the same. It is implied here that it is right to love life, and to desire many days. The desire of this is referred to by the psalmist and by the apostle, without any expression of disapprobation, and the way is shown by which length of days may be secured. Life is a blessing; a precious gift of God. We are taught so to regard it by the instinctive feelings of our nature; for we are so made as to love it, and to dread its extinction. Though we should be prepared to resign it when God commands, yet there are important reasons why we should desire to live. Among them are the following: (1.) Because, as already intimated, life, as such, is to be regarded as a blessing. We instinctively shrink back from death, as one of the greatest evils; we shudder at the thought of annihilation. It is not wrong to love that, in proper degree, which, by our very nature, we are prompted to love; and we are but acting out one of the universal laws which our Creator has impressed on us, when, with proper submission to his will, we seek to lengthen out our days as far as possible. (2.) That we may see the works of God, and survey the wonders of his hand on earth. The world is full of wonders, evincing the wisdom and goodness of the Deity; and the longest life, nay, many such lives as are allotted to us here, could be well employed in studying his works and ways. (3.) That we may make preparation for eternity. Man *may*, indeed, make pre-paration in a very brief period; but the longest life is not too much to examine and settle the question whether we have a well-founded hope of heaven. If man had nothing else to do, the longest life could be well employed in inquiries that grow out of the question whether we are fitted for the world to come. In the possibility, too, of being deceived, and in view of the awful consequences that will result from deception, it is desirable that length of days should be given us that we may bring the subject to the severest test, and so determine it, that we may go sure to the changeless world. (4.) That we may do good to others. We *may*, indeed, do good in another world; but there are ways of doing good which are probably confined to this. What good we may do hereafter to the inhabitants of distant worlds, or what ministrations, in company with angels, or without them, we may exercise towards the friends of God on earth after we leave it, we do not know; but there are certain things which we are morally certain we shall *not* be permitted to do in the future world. We shall not (*a*) personally labour for the salvation of sinners, by conversation and other direct efforts; (*b*) we shall not illustrate the influence of religion by example in sustaining us in trials, subduing and controlling our passions, and making us dead to the world; (*c*) we shall not be permitted to pray for our impenitent friends and kindred, as we may now; (*d*) we shall not have the opportunity of contributing of our substance for the spread of the gospel, or of going personally to preach the gospel to the perishing; (*e*) we shall not be employed in instructing the ignorant, in advocating the cause of the oppressed and the wronged, in seeking to remove the fetters from the slave, in dispensing mercy to the insane, or in visiting the prisoner in his lonely cell; (*f*) we shall not have it in our power to address a kind word to an impenitent child, or seek to guide him in paths of truth, purity, and salvation. What we can do personally and directly for

11 Let him eschew evil, and do good ; let him seek peace, and ensue it.

12 For the eyes of the Lord *are*

over the righteous, and his ears *are open* unto their prayers : but the face of the Lord *is* [1] against them that do evil.

[1] *upon.*

the salvation of others is to be done in this world ; and, considering how much there is to be done, and how useful life may be on the earth, it is an object which we should desire, that our days may, be lengthened out, and should use all proper means that it may be done. While we should ever be ready and willing to depart when God calls us to go ; while we should not wish to linger on these mortal shores beyond the time when we may be useful to others, yet, as long as he permits us to live, we should regard life as a blessing, and should pray that, if it be his will, we may not be cut down in the midst of our way.

"Love not thy life, nor hate; but what thou livest
Live well; how long, or short, permit to heaven."
Paradise Lost.

¶ *And see good days.* In the Psalm (xxxiv. 12) this is, 'and loveth many days, that he may see good.' The quotation by Peter throughout the passage is taken from the Septuagint, excepting that there is a change of the person from the second to the third : in the psalm, e. g., 'refrain thy tongue from evil,' &c.; in the quotation, 'let him refrain his tongue from evil,' &c. 'Good days' are prosperous days ; happy days ; days of usefulness ; days in which we may be respected and loved. ¶ *Let him refrain his tongue from evil.* The general meaning of all that is said here is, 'let him lead an upright and pious life; doing evil to no one, but seeking the good of all men.' To refrain the tongue from evil, is to avoid all slander, falsehood, obscenity, and profaneness, and to abstain from uttering erroneous and false opinions. Comp. James i. 26; iii. 2. ¶ *And his lips that they speak no guile.* No deceit ; nothing that will lead others astray. The words should be an exact representation of the truth. Rosenmüller quotes a passage from the Hebrew book *Musar,* which may be not an inappropriate illustration of this : ' A certain Assyrian

wandering through the city, cried and said, " Who will receive the elixir of life?" The daughter of Rabbi Jodus heard him, and went and told her father. " Call him in," said he. When he came in, Rabbi Jannei said to him, " What is that elixir of life which thou art selling?" He said to him, " Is it not written, What man is he that desireth life, and loveth days that he may see good? Keep thy tongue from evil, and thy lips that they speak no guile. Lo, this is the elixir of life which is in the mouth of a man!" '

11. *Let him eschew evil.* Let him avoid all evil. Comp. Job i. 1. ¶ *And do good.* In any and every way ; by endeavouring to promote the happiness of all. Comp. Notes, Gal. vi. 10. ¶ *Let him seek peace, and ensue it.* Follow it ; that is, practise it. See Notes, Matt. v. 9 ; Rom. xii. 18. The meaning is, that a peaceful spirit will contribute to length of days. (1.) A peaceful spirit—a calm, serene, and equal temper of mind—is favourable to health, avoiding those corroding and distracting passions which do so much to wear out the physical energies of the frame; and (2.) such a spirit will preserve us from those contentions and strifes to which so many owe their death. Let any one reflect on the numbers that are killed in duels, in battles, and in brawls, and he will have no difficulty in seeing how a peaceful spirit will contribute to length of days.

12. *For the eyes of the Lord* are *over the righteous.* That is, he is their Protector. His eyes are indeed on all men, but the language here is that which describes continual guardianship and care. ¶ *And his ears* are open *unto their prayers.* He *hears* their prayers. As he is a hearer of prayer, they are at liberty to go to him at all times, and to pour out their desires before him. This passage is taken from Psa. xxxiv. 15, and it is designed to show the reason why a life of piety will contribute to

13 And who *a is* he that will harm | you, if ye be followers of that which

is good ?

length of days. ¶ *But the face of the Lord* is *against them that do evil.* Marg., *upon.* The sense of the passage, however, is *against.* The Lord sets his face against them : an expression denoting disapprobation, and a determination to punish them. His face is not mild and benignant towards them, as it is towards the righteous. The general sentiment in these verses (10–12) is, that while length of days is desirable, it is to be secured by virtue and religion, or that virtue and religion will contribute to it. This is not to be understood as affirming that *all* who are righteous will enjoy long life, for we know that the righteous are often cut down in the midst of their way ; and that in fire, and flood, and war, and the pestilence, the righteous and the wicked often perish together. But still there is a sense in which it is true that a life of virtue and religion will contribute to length of days, and that the law is so general as *to be a basis of calculation* in reference to the future. I. Religion and virtue contribute to those things which are favourable to length of days, which are conducive to health and to a vigorous constitution. Among those things are the following : (*a*) a calm, peaceful, and contented mind—avoiding the wear and tear of the raging passions of lusts, avarice, and ambition ; (*b*) temperance in eating and drinking—always favourable to length of days ; (*c*) industry—one of the essential means, as a general rule, of promoting long life ; (*d*) prudence and economy—avoiding the extravagancies by which many shorten their days ; and (*e*) a conscientious and careful regard of life itself. Religion makes men feel that life is a blessing, and that it should not be thrown away. Just in proportion as a man is under the influence of religion, does he regard life as of importance, and does he become careful in preserving it. Strange and paradoxical as it may seem, the want of religion often makes men reckless of life, and ready to throw it away for any trifling cause. Religion shows a man what great issues depend on life, and makes him, therefore, desirous of living to

secure his own salvation and the salvation of all others. II. Multitudes lose their lives who would have preserved them if they had been under the influence of religion. To see this, we have only to reflect (*a*) on the millions who are cut off in war as the result of ambition, and the want of religion ; (*b*) on the countless hosts cut down in middle life, or in youth, by intemperance, who would have been saved by religion ; (*c*) on the numbers who are the victims of raging passions, and who are cut off by the diseases which gluttony and licentiousness engender ; (*d*) on the multitude who fall in duels, all of whom would have been saved by religion ; (*e*) on the numbers who, as the result of disappointment in business or in love, close their own lives, who would have been enabled to bear up under their troubles if they had had religion ; and (*f*) on the numbers who are cut off from the earth as the punishment of their crimes, all of whom would have continued to live if they had had true religion. III. God protects the righteous. He does it by saving them from those vices by which the lives of so many are shortened ; and often, we have no reason to doubt, in answer to their prayers, when, but for those prayers, they would have fallen into crimes that would have consigned them to an early grave, or encountered dangers from which they would have had no means of escape. No one can doubt that *in fact* those who are truly religious are saved from the sins which consign millions to the tomb ; nor is there any less reason to doubt that a protecting shield is often thrown before the children of God when in danger. Comp. Psa. xci.

13 *And who* is *he that will harm you, if ye be followers of that which is good?* This question is meant to imply, that as a general thing they need apprehend no evil if they lead an upright and benevolent life. The idea is, that God would in general protect them, though the next verse shows that the apostle did not mean to teach that there would be absolute security, for it is implied there that they *might* be called to suffer

14 But and if ye suffer for righteousness' sake, happy *are ye:* and be *a* not afraid of their terror, neither be troubled ;

15 But sanctify the Lord God in

your hearts ; and *be* ready *b* always to *give* an answer to every man that asketh you a reason of the hope that is in you with meekness and ¹ fear :

a Is. 8.12,13; 51.12.   b Ps. 119.46.   1 Or, *reverence.*

for righteousness' sake. While it is true that the Saviour was persecuted by wicked men, though his life was wholly spent in doing good ; while it is true that the apostles were put to death, though following his example ; and while it is true that good men have often suffered persecution, though labouring only to do good, still it is true as a general thing that a life of integrity and benevolence conduces to safety, even in a wicked world. Men who are upright and pure ; who live to do good to others ; who are characteristically benevolent ; and who are imitators of God—are those who usually pass life in most tranquillity and security, and are often safe when nothing else would give security but confidence in their integrity. A man of a holy and pure life may, under the protection of God, rely on that character to carry him safely through the world, and to bring him at last to an honoured grave. Or should he be calumniated when living, and his sun set under a cloud, still his name will be vindicated, and justice will ultimately be done to him when he is dead. The world ultimately judges right respecting character, and renders ' honour to whom honour is due.' Comp. Psa. xxxvii. 3–6.

14. *But and if ye suffer for righteousness' sake.* Implying that though, in general, a holy character would constitute safety, yet that there was a possibility that they might suffer persecution. Comp. Notes, Matt. v. 10; 2 Tim. iii. 12. ¶ *Happy* are ye. Perhaps alluding to what the Saviour says in Matt. v. 10: ' Blessed are they which are persecuted for righteousness' sake.' On the meaning of the word *happy* or *blessed,* see Notes on Matt. v. 3. The meaning here is, not that they would find positive enjoyment *in* persecution on account of righteousness, but that they were to regard it as *a blessed condition;* that is, as a condition that might be favourable to salvation: and they were not there-

fore, on the whole, to regard it as an evil. ¶ *And be not afraid of their terror.* Of anything which they can do to cause terror. There is evidently an allusion here to Isa. viii. 12, 13 : ' Neither fear ye their fear, nor be afraid. Sanctify the Lord of hosts himself ; and let him be your fear, and let him be your dread.' See Notes on that passage. Comp. Isa. li. 12; Matt. x. 28. ¶ *Neither be troubled.* With apprehension of danger. Comp. Notes, John xiv. 1. If we are true Christians, we have really no reason to be alarmed in view of anything that can happen to us. God is our protector, and he is abundantly able to vanquish all our foes ; to uphold us in all our trials ; to conduct us through the valley of death, and to bring us to heaven. ' All things are yours ; whether Paul, or Apollos, or Cephas, or the world, *or life, or death,* or things present, or things to come,' 1 Cor. iii. 21, 22.

15. *But sanctify the Lord God in your hearts.* In Isaiah (viii. 13) this is, ' sanctify the Lord of hosts himself ;' that is, in that connection, regard him as your Protector, and be afraid of him, and not of what man can do. The sense in the passage before us is, ' In your hearts, or in the affections of the soul, regard the Lord God as holy, and act towards him with that confidence which a proper respect for one so great and so holy demands. In the midst of dangers, be not intimidated ; dread not what man can do, but evince proper reliance on a holy God, and flee to him with the confidence which is due to one so glorious.' This contains, however, a more general direction, applicable to Christians at all times. It is, that in our hearts we are to esteem God as a holy being, and in all our deportment to act towards him as such. The *object* of Peter in quoting the passage from Isaiah, was to lull the fears of those whom he addressed, and preserve them from any alarms in view of the perse-

cutions to which they might be exposed; the trials which would be brought upon them by men. Thus, in entire accordance with the sentiment as employed by Isaiah, he says, 'Be not afraid of their terror, neither be troubled ; but sanctify the Lord God in your hearts.' That is, 'in order to keep the mind calm in trials, sanctify the Lord in your hearts ; regard him as your holy God and Saviour; make him your refuge. This will allay all your fears, and secure you from all that you dread.' The sentiment of the passage then is, that *the sanctifying of the Lord God in our hearts, or proper confidence in him as a holy and righteous God, will deliver us from fear.* As this is a very important sentiment for Christians, it may be proper, in order to a just exposition of the passage, to dwell a moment on it. I. What is meant by our sanctifying the Lord God ? It cannot mean to *make* him holy, for he *is* perfectly holy, whatever may be our estimate of him ; and our views of him evidently can make no change in his character. The meaning therefore must be, that we should regard him as holy in our estimate of him, or in the feelings which we have towards him. This may include the following things : (1.) To *esteem* or *regard* him as a holy being, in contradistinction from all those feelings which rise up in the heart against him—the feelings of complaining and murmuring under his dispensations, as if he were severe and harsh ; the feelings of dissatisfaction with his government, as if it were partial and unequal ; the feelings of rebellion, as if his claims were unfounded or unjust. (2.) To desire that he *may be regarded by others* as holy, in accordance with the petition in the Lord's prayer, (Matt. vi. 9,) 'hallowed be thy name;' that is, 'let thy name be *esteemed to be holy* everywhere ;' a feeling in opposition to that which is regardless of the honour which he may receive in the world. When we esteem a friend, we desire that all due respect should be shown him by others ; we wish that all who know him should have the same views that we have ; we are sensitive to his honour, just in proportion as we love him. (3.) To *act towards him as holy;* that is, to

obey his laws, and acquiesce in all his requirements, as if they were just and good. This implies, (*a*) that we are to speak of him as holy, in opposition to the language of disrespect and irreverence so common among mankind ; (*b*) that we are to flee to him in trouble, in contradistinction from withholding our hearts from him, and flying to other sources of consolation and support. II. What is it to do this in the heart ? 'Sanctify the Lord God *in your hearts ;*' that is, in contradistinction from a mere external service. This may imply the following things : (1.) In contradistinction from a mere intellectual assent to the proposition that he is holy. Many admit the doctrine that God is holy into their creeds, who never suffer the sentiment to find its way to the heart. All is right on this subject in the articles of their faith ; all in their hearts may be murmuring and complaining. In their creeds he is spoken of as just and good ; in their hearts they regard him as partial and unjust, as severe and stern, as unamiable and cruel. (2.) In contradistinction from a mere outward form of devotion In our prayers, and in our hymns, we, of course, 'ascribe holiness to our Maker.' But how much of this is the mere language of form ! How little does the heart accompany it ! And even in the most solemn and sublime ascriptions of praise, how often are the feelings of the heart entirely at variance with what is expressed by the lips ! What would more justly offend us, than for a professed friend to approach us with the language of friendship, when every feeling of his heart belied his expressions, and we knew that his honeyed words were false and hollow ! III. Such a sanctifying of the Lord in our hearts will save us from fear. We dread danger, we dread sickness, we dread death, we dread the eternal world. We are alarmed when our affairs are tending to bankruptcy; we are alarmed when a friend is sick and ready to die; we are alarmed if our country is invaded by a foe, and the enemy already approaches our dwelling. The sentiment in the passage before us is, that if we sanctify the Lord God with proper affections, we shall be delivered from these alarms, and the mind will be calm. (1.) The fear of the Lord, as Leighton (*in loc.*) expresses it, ' as greatest, overtops and nullifies all lesser fears : the heart possessed with this fear hath no room for the other.' It is an absorbing emotion ; making everything else comparatively of no importance. If we fear God, we have nothing else to fear. The highest emotion which there can be in the soul is the fear of God ; and when that exists, the soul will be calm amidst all that might tend otherwise to disturb it. 'What time I am afraid,' says David, ' I will trust in thee,' Psa. lvi. 3. 'We are not careful,' said Daniel and his friends, ' to answer thee, O king. Our God can deliver us; but if not, we will not worship the image,' Dan. iii. 16. (2.) If we sanctify the Lord God in our hearts, there will be a belief that he will do all things *well*, and the mind will be calm. However dark his dispensations may be, we shall be assured that everything is ordered aright. In a storm at sea, a child may be calm when he feels that his father is at the helm, and assures him that there is no danger. In a battle, the mind of a soldier may be calm, if he has confidence in his commander, and he assures him that all is safe. So in anything, if we have the assurance that the *best* thing is done that can be, that the issues will all be right, the mind will be calm. But in this respect the highest confidence that can exist, is that which is reposed in God. (3.) There will be the assurance that all is *safe*. 'Though I walk,' says David, ' through the valley of the shadow of death, I will fear no evil, for thou art with me,' Psa. xxiii. 4. 'The Lord is my light and my salvation ; whom shall I fear ? The Lord is the strength of my life ; of whom shall I be afraid ?' Psa. xxvii. 1. 'God is our refuge and strength, a very present help in trouble : therefore will not we fear, though the earth be removed, and though the mountains be carried into the midst of the sea ; though the waters thereof roar and be troubled, though the mountains shake with the swelling thereof,' Psa. xlvi. 1–3. Let us ever then regard the Lord as holy, just, and good. Let us flee to him in all the trials of the present life, and in the hour of death

repose on his arm. Every other source of trust will fail ; and whatever else may be our reliance, when the hour of anguish approaches, that reliance will fail, and that which we dreaded will overwhelm us. Nor riches, nor honours, nor earthly friends, can save us from those alarms, or be a security for our souls when ' the rains descend, and the floods come, and the winds blow ' upon us. ¶ *And* be *ready always*. That is, (*a*) be always *able* to do it ; have such reasons for the hope that is in you that they *can* be stated ; or, have good and substantial reasons ; and (*b*) be *willing* to state those reasons on all proper occasions. No man ought to entertain opinions for which a good reason cannot be given ; and every man ought to be willing to state the grounds of his hope on all proper occasions. A Christian should have such intelligent views of the truth of his religion, and such constant evidence in his own heart and life that he is a child of God, as to be able at any time to satisfy a candid inquirer that the Bible is a revelation from heaven, and that it is proper for him to cherish the hope of salvation. ¶ *To give an answer*. Greek, An *apology*, (ἀπολογίαν.) This word formerly did not mean, as the word *apology* does now, an *excuse* for anything that is done as if it were wrong, but a *defence* of anything. We apply the word now to denote something written or said in extenuation of what appears to others to be wrong, or what might be construed as wrong—as when we make an apology to others for not fulfilling an engagement, or for some conduct which might be construed as designed neglect. The word originally, however, referred rather to that which was thought not to be *true*, than that which might be construed as *wrong;* and the defence or ' apology ' which Christians were to make of their religion, was not on the supposition that others would regard it as *wrong*, but in order to show them that it was *true*. The word here used is rendered *defence*, Acts xxii. 1; Phil. i. 7, 17; *answer*, Acts xxv. 16; 1 Cor. ix. 3; 2 Tim. iv. 16; 1 Pet. iii. 15; and *clearing of yourselves* in 2 Cor. vii. 11. We are not to hold ourselves ready to make an apology for our religion as if it were a *wrong* thing to be a Christian; but we are always to be ready to give reasons for regarding it as *true*. ¶ *To every man that asketh you.* Any one has a right respectfully to ask another on what grounds he regards his religion as true; for every man has a common interest in religion, and in knowing what is the truth on the subject. If *any* man, therefore, asks us candidly and respectfully by what reasons we have been led to embrace the gospel, and on what grounds we regard it as true, we are under obligation to state those grounds in the best manner that we are able. We should regard it not as an impertinent intrusion into our private affairs, but as an opportunity of doing good to others, and to honour the Master whom we serve. Nay, we should hold ourselves in readiness to state the grounds of our faith and hope, whatever may be the motive of the inquirer, and in whatever manner the request may be made. Those who were persecuted for their religion, were under obligation to make as good a defence of it as they could, and to state to their persecutors the 'reason' of the hope which they entertained. And so now, if a man attacks our religion; if he ridicules us for being Christians; if he tauntingly asks us what reason we have for believing the truth of the Bible, it is better to tell him in a kind manner, and to meet his taunt with a kind and strong argument, than to become angry, or to turn away with contempt. The best way to disarm him, is to show him that by embracing religion we are not fools in understanding; and, by a kind temper, to convince him that the influence of religion over us when we are *abused* and *insulted*, is a 'reason' why we should love our religion, and why *he* should too. ¶ *A reason of the hope that is in you.* Gr., 'an account,' (λόγον.) That is, you are to state on what ground you cherish that hope. This refers to the *whole ground* of our hope, and includes evidently two things: (1.) The reason why we regard Christianity as true, or as furnishing a ground of hope for men; and, (2.) the reason which we have ourselves for cherishing a hope of heaven, or the experimental and practical views which we have of religion,

which constitute a just ground of hope. It is not improbable that the former of these was more directly in the eye of the apostle than the latter, though both seem to be implied in the direction to state the reasons which ought to satisfy others that it is proper for us to cherish the hope of heaven. The *first* part of this duty—that we are to state the reasons why we regard the system of religion which we have embraced as true —implies, that we should be acquainted with the *evidences* of the truth of Christianity, and be able to state them to others. Christianity is founded on *evidence;* and though it cannot be supposed that every Christian will be able to understand *all* that is involved in what are called the *evidences* of Christianity, or to meet all the objections of the enemies of the gospel; yet every man who becomes a Christian should have such intelligent views of religion, and of the evidences of the truth of the Bible, that he can show to others that the religion which he has embraced has claims to their attention, or that it is not a mere matter of education, of tradition, or of feeling. It should also be an object with every Christian to increase his acquaintance with the evidences of the truth of religion, not only for his own stability and comfort in the faith, but that he may be able to defend religion if attacked, or to guide others if they are desirous of knowing what is truth. The *second* part of this duty, that we state the reasons which we have for cherishing the hope of heaven as a personal matter, implies (*a*) that there *should be*, in fact, a well-founded hope of heaven; that is, that we have evidence that we are true Christians, since it is impossible to give a '*reason*' of the hope that is in us unless there are reasons for it; (*b*) that we be able to state in a clear and intelligent manner what constitutes evidence of piety, or what should be reasonably regarded as such; and (*c*) that we be ever *ready* to state these reasons. A Christian should always be willing to converse about his religion. He should have such a deep conviction of its truth, of its importance, and of his personal interest in it; he should have a hope so firm, so cheering, so sustaining, that he

16 Having a good conscience; that, whereas they speak evil of you, as of evil doers, they may be ashamed that falsely accuse your good conversation in Christ.

---

will be always prepared to converse on the prospect of heaven, and to endeavour to lead others to walk in the path to life. ¶ *With meekness*. With modesty; without any spirit of ostentation; with gentleness of manner. This seems to be added on the supposition that they sometimes might be rudely assailed; that the questions might be proposed in a spirit of cavil; that it might be done in a taunting or insulting manner. Even though this should be done, they were not to fall into a passion, to manifest resentment, or to retort in an angry and revengeful manner; but, in a calm and gentle spirit, they were to state the *reasons* of their faith and hope, and leave the matter there. ¶ *And fear*. Marg., *reverence*. The sense seems to be, 'in the fear of God; with a serious and reverent spirit; as in the presence of Him who sees and hears all things.' It evidently does not mean with the fear or dread of those who propose the question, but with that serious and reverent frame of mind which is produced by a deep impression of the importance of the subject, and a conscious sense of the presence of God. It follows, from the injunction of the apostle here, (1,) that every professing Christian should have clear and intelligent views of his own personal interest in religion, or such evidences of piety that they *can* be stated to others, and that they *can* be made satisfactory to other minds; (2,) that every Christian, however humble his rank, or however unlettered he may be, may become a valuable defender of the truth of Christianity; (3,) that we should esteem it a privilege to bear our testimony to the truth and value of religion, and to stand up as the advocates of truth in the world. Though we may be rudely assailed, it is an honour to speak in defence of religion; though we are persecuted and reviled, it is a privilege to be permitted in any way to show our fellow-men that there is such a thing as true religion, and that man *may* cherish the hope of heaven.

16. *Having a good conscience*. That

is, a conscience that does not accuse you of having done wrong. Whatever may be the accusations of your enemies, so live that you may be at all times conscious of uprightness. Whatever you suffer, see that you do not suffer the pangs inflicted by a guilty conscience, the anguish of remorse. On the meaning of the word *conscience*, see Notes on Rom. ii. 15. The word properly means the judgment of the mind respecting right and wrong; or the judgment which the mind passes on the immorality of its own actions, when it instantly approves or condemns them. There is always a feeling of *obligation* connected with operations of conscience, which precedes, attends, and follows our actions. 'Conscience is first occupied in ascertaining our duty, before we proceed to action; then in judging of our actions when performed.' A 'good conscience' implies two things: (1.) That it be properly enlightened to know what is right and wrong, or that it be not under the dominion of ignorance, superstition, or fanaticism, prompting us to do what would be a violation of the Divine law; and (2.) that its dictates be always obeyed. Without the first of these—clear views of that which is right and wrong—conscience becomes an unsafe guide; for it merely prompts us to do what we esteem to be right, and if our views of what is right and wrong are erroneous, we may be prompted to do what may be a direct violation of the law of God. Paul thought he '*ought*' to do many things contrary to the name of Jesus of Nazareth, (Acts xxvi. 9;) the Saviour said, respecting his disciples, that the time would come when whosoever should kill them would think that they were doing God service, (John xvi. 2;) and Solomon says, 'There is a way which seemeth right unto a man, but the end thereof are the ways of death,' (Prov. xiv. 12; xvi. 25.) Under an unenlightened and misguided conscience, with the plea and pretext of religion, the most atrocious crimes have been committed; and no man should infer

17 For *it is* better, if the will of God be so, that ye suffer for well doing than for evil doing.

18 For Christ *a* also hath once suffered for sins, the just *b* for the unjust, that he might bring us to

a 1 Pe.2.21.   *b* 2 Co.5.21.

that he is certainly doing *right*, because he follows the promptings of conscience. No man, indeed, should act *against* the dictates of his conscience; but there may have been a previous *wrong* in not using proper means to ascertain what *is* right. Conscience is not revelation, nor does it answer the purpose of a revelation. It communicates no new truth to the soul, and is a safe guide only so far as the mind has been properly enlightened to see what *is* truth and duty. Its office is *to prompt us to the performance of duty*, not *to determine what is right.* The other thing requisite that we may have a good conscience is, that its decisions *should be obeyed.* Conscience is appointed to be the 'vicegerent' of God in inflicting punishment, if his commands are not obeyed. It pronounces a sentence on our own conduct. Its penalty is remorse; and that penalty will be demanded if its promptings be not regarded. It is an admirable device, as a part of the moral government of God, urging man to the performance of duty, and, in case of disobedience, making the mind its own executioner. There is no penalty that will more certainly be inflicted, sooner or later, than that incurred by a guilty conscience. It needs no witnesses; no process for arresting the offender; no array of judges and executioners; no stripes, imprisonment, or bonds. Its inflictions will follow the offender into the most secluded retreat; overtake him in his most rapid flight; find him out in northern snows, or on the sands of the equator; go into the most splendid palaces, and seek out the victim when he is safe from all the vengeance that man can inflict; pursue him into the dark valley of the shadow of death, or arrest him as a fugitive in distant worlds. No one, therefore, can over-estimate the importance of having a good conscience. A true Christian should aim, by incessant study and prayer, to know what is right, *and then always do it*, no matter what may be the consequences. ¶ *That, whereas they speak evil of you.* They

who are your enemies and persecutors. Christians are not to hope that men will always speak well of them, Matt. v. 11; Luke vi. 26. ¶ *As of evil doers.* Notes, chap. ii. 12. ¶ *They may be ashamed.* They may see that they have misunderstood your conduct, and regret that they have treated you as they have. We should expect, if we are faithful and true, that even our enemies will yet appreciate our motives, and do us justice. Comp. Psa. xxxvii. 5, 6. ¶ *That falsely accuse your good conversation in Christ.* Your good conduct as Christians. They may accuse you of insincerity, hypocrisy, dishonesty; of being enemies of the state, or of monstrous crimes; but the time will come when they will see their error, and do you justice. See Notes on chap. ii. 12.

17. *For* it is *better, if the will of God be so.* That is, if God sees it to be necessary for your good that you should suffer, it is better that you should suffer for doing well than for crime. God often sees it to be necessary that his people should suffer. There are effects to be accomplished by affliction which can be secured in no other way; and some of the happiest results on the soul of a Christian, some of the brightest traits of character, are the effect of trials. But it should be *our* care that our sufferings should not be brought upon us for our own crimes or follies. No man can promote his own highest good by doing wrong, and then enduring the penalty which his sin incurs; and no one should *do* wrong with any expectation that it may be overruled for his own good. If we are to suffer, let it be by the direct hand of God, and not by any fault of our own. If we suffer then, we shall have the testimony of our own conscience in our favour, and the feeling that we may go to God for support. If we suffer for our faults, in addition to the outward pain of body, we shall endure the severest pangs which man can suffer—tho e which the guilty mind inflicts on itself.

18. *For Christ also hath once suffered*

God, being put to death *a* in the flesh, but quickened by the Spirit :

a Ro.4.25.

for sins. Comp. Notes on chap. ii. 21. The *design* of the apostle in this reference to the sufferings of Christ, is evidently to remind them that he suffered as an innocent being, and not for any wrong-doing, and to encourage and comfort them in their sufferings by his example. The reference to his sufferings leads him (vers. 18–22) into a statement of the various ways in which Christ suffered, and of his ultimate triumph. By his example in his sufferings, and by his final triumph, the apostle would encourage those whom he addressed to bear with patience the sorrows to which their religion exposed them. He assumes that all suffering for adhering to the gospel is the result of well-doing ; and for an encouragement in their trials, he refers them to the example of Christ, the highest instance that ever was, or ever will be, both of well-doing, and of suffering on account of it. The expression, 'hath *once* suffered,' in the New Testament, means *once for all;* once, in the sense that it is not to occur again. Comp. Heb. vii. 27. The particular point here, however, is not that he *once* suffered ; it is that he *had* in fact suffered, and that in doing it he had left an example for them to follow. ¶ *The just for the unjust.* The one who was just, (δίκαιος,) on account of, or in the place of, those who were unjust, (ὑπὲρ ἀδίκων:) or one who was righteous, on account of those who were wicked. Comp. Notes, Rom. v. 6; 2 Cor. v. 21; Heb. ix. 28. The idea on which the apostle would particularly fix their attention was, that he was *just* or *innocent.* Thus he was an example to those who suffered for well-doing. ¶ *That he might bring us to God.* That his death might be the means of reconciling sinners to God. Comp. Notes on John iii. 14; xii. 32. It is through that death that mercy is proclaimed to the guilty; it is by that alone that God can be reconciled to men ; and the fact that the Son of God loved men, and gave himself a sacrifice for them, enduring such bitter sorrows, is the most powerful appeal which can be made to mankind to induce them to return to God. There is no appeal which can be made to us more powerful than one drawn from the fact that another *suffers* on our account. We could resist the *argument* which a father, a mother, or a sister would use to reclaim us from a course of sin ; but if we perceive that our conduct involves them in suffering, that fact has a power over us which no mere argument could have. ¶ *Being put to death in the flesh.* As a man; in his human nature. Comp. Notes, Rom. i. 3, 4. There is evidently a contrast here between 'the flesh' in which it is said he was 'put to death,' and 'the Spirit' by which it is said he was 'quickened.' The words '*in the flesh*' are clearly designed to denote something that was *peculiar* in his death ; for it is a departure from the usual method of speaking of *death.* How singular would it be to say of Isaiah, Paul, or Peter, that they were put to death *in the flesh!* How obvious would it be to ask, In what other way are men usually put to death? What was there peculiar in their case, which would distinguish their death from the death of others? The use of this phrase would suggest the thought at once, that though, in regard to that which was properly expressed by the phrase, 'the flesh,' they died, yet that there was something else in respect to which they did not die. Thus, if it were said of a man that he was deprived of his rights *as a father,* it would be implied that in other respects he was not deprived of his rights; and this would be especially true if it were added that he continued to enjoy his rights as a neighbour, or as holding an office under the government. The only proper inquiry, then, in this place is, What is fairly implied in the phrase, *the flesh?* Does it mean simply *his body,* as distinguished from his human soul? or does it refer to him *as a man,* as distinguished from some higher nature, over which death had no power ? Now, that the latter is the meaning seems to me to be apparent, for these reasons : (1.) It is the usual way of denoting the human nature of the Lord Jesus, or of saying that he became incarnate, or was a man, to speak of his being in the flesh. See Rom. i. 2: 'Made of the seed of David according to the flesh.' John i. 14: 'And the Word was made flesh.' 1 Tim. iii. 16: 'God was manifest in the flesh.' 1 John iv. 2: 'Every spirit that confesseth that Jesus Christ is come in the flesh, is of God.' 2 John 7: 'Who confess not that Jesus Christ is come in the flesh.' (2.) So far as appears, the effect of death on the human *soul* of the Redeemer was the same as in the case of the soul of any other person; in other words, the effect of *death* in his case was not confined to the mere body or the flesh. Death, with him, was what death is in any other case—the separation of the soul and body, with all the attendant pain of such dissolution. It is not true that his '*flesh*,' as such, died without the ordinary accompaniments of death on the soul, so that it could be said that the one died, and the other was kept alive. The purposes of the atonement required that he should meet death in the usual form; that the great laws which operate everywhere else in regard to dissolution, should exist in his case; nor is there in the Scriptures any intimation that there was, in this respect, anything peculiar in his case. If his soul had been exempt from whatever there is involved in death in relation to the spirit, it is unaccountable that there is no hint on this point in the sacred narrative. But if this be so, then the expression 'in the flesh' refers to him as a man, and means, that so far as his human nature was concerned, he died. In another important respect, he did *not* die. On the meaning of the word *flesh* in the New Testament, see Notes on Rom. i. 3. ¶ *But quickened.* Made alive—ζωοποιηθείς. This does not mean *kept alive*, but *made alive;* recalled to life; reanimated. The word is never used in the sense of *maintained alive*, or *preserved alive*. Compare the following places, which are the only ones in which it occurs in the New Testament: John v. 21, *twice;* vi. 63; Rom. iv. 17; viii. 11; 1 Cor. xv. 36, 45; 1 Tim. vi. 13; 1 Pet. iii. 18; in all which it is rendered *quickened, quicken, quickeneth;* 1 Cor. xv. 22, *be made alive;* 2 Cor. iii. 6, *giveth life;* and Gal. iii. 21, *have given life.* 'Once the word

refers to God, as he who giveth life to all creatures, 1 Tim. vi. 13; three times it refers to the life-giving power of the Holy Ghost, or of the doctrines of the gospel, John vi. 63; 2 Cor. iii. 6; Gal. iii. 21; seven times it is used with direct reference to the raising of the dead, John v. 21; Rom. iv. 17; viii. 11; 1 Cor. xv. 22, 36, 45; 1 Pet. iii. 18.' See Biblical Repos., April, 1845, p. 269. See also *Passow*, and *Robinson, Lex.* The sense, then, cannot be that, in reference to his soul or spirit, he was *preserved* alive when his body died, but that there was some agency or power *restoring* him to life, or reanimating him after he was dead. ¶ *By the Spirit.* According to the common reading in the Greek, this is τῷ Πνεύματι—with the article *the*—'*the* Spirit.' Hahn, Tittman, and Griesbach omit the article, and then the reading is, 'quickened in spirit;' and thus the reading corresponds with the former expression, 'in flesh' (σαρκί.) where the article also is wanting. The word *spirit*, so far as the mere use of the word is concerned, might refer to his own soul, to his Divine nature, or to the Holy Spirit. It is evident (1.) that it does not refer to his own soul, for, (*a*) as we have seen, the reference in the former clause is to his human nature, including all that pertained to him as a man, body and soul; (*b*) there was no power in his own spirit, regarded as that appertaining to his human nature, to raise him up from the dead, any more than there is such a power in any other human soul. That power does not belong to a human soul in any of its relations or conditions. (2.) It seems equally clear that this does not refer to the Holy Spirit, or the Third Person of the Trinity, for it may be doubted whether the work of raising the dead is anywhere ascribed to that Spirit. His peculiar province is to enlighten, awaken, convict, convert, and sanctify the soul; to apply the work of redemption to the hearts of men, and to lead them to God. This influence is *moral*, not *physical;* an influence accompanying *the truth*, not the exertion of mere physical *power.* (3.) It remains, then, that the reference is to his own Divine nature—a nature by which he was restored to life after he was

19 By which also he went and | preached unto the spirits in prison; [a]

a Is.42.7.

crucified ; to the Son of God, regarded as the Second Person of the Trinity. This appears, not only from the facts above stated, but also (a) from the connection. It is stated that it was in or by this spirit that he went and preached in the days of Noah. But it was not his spirit as a man that did this, for his human soul had then no existence. Yet it seems that he did this personally or directly, and not by the influences of the Holy Spirit, for it is said that ' he went and preached.' The reference, therefore, cannot be to the Holy Ghost, and the fair conclusion is that it refers to his Divine nature. (b) This accords with what the apostle Paul says, (Rom. i. 3, 4,) ' which was made of the seed of David according to the flesh,'—that is, in respect to his human nature,— ' and declared to be the Son of God with power, according to the Spirit of holiness,'—that is, in respect to his Divine nature,—' by the resurrection from the dead.' See Notes on that passage. (c) It accords with what the Saviour himself says, John x. 17, 18: ' I lay down my life, that I might take it again. No man taketh it from me, but I lay it down of myself. I have power to lay it down, and I have power to take it again.' This must refer to his Divine nature, for it is impossible to conceive that a human soul should have the power of restoring its former tenement, the body, to life. See Notes on the passage. The conclusion, then, to which we have come is, that the passage means, that as a man, a human being, he was put to death ; in respect to a higher nature, or by a higher nature, here denominated *Spirit*, (Πνεῦμα,) he was restored to life. As a man, he died ; as the incarnate Son of God, the Messiah, he was made alive again by the power of his own Divine Spirit, and exalted to heaven. Comp. Robinson's Lex. on the word Πνεῦμα, C.

19. *By which*. Evidently by the *Spirit* referred to in the previous verse —ἐν ᾧ—the Divine nature of the Son of God; that by which he was 'quickened ' again, after he had been put to death ; the Son of God regarded as a Divine Being, or in that same nature which afterwards became incarnate, and whose agency was employed in quickening the man Christ Jesus, who had been put to death. The meaning is, that the same ' Spirit' which was efficacious in restoring him to life, after he was put to death, was that by which he preached to the spirits in prison. ¶ *He went*. To wit, in the days of Noah. No particular stress should be laid here on the phrase ' he *went*.' The literal sense is, ' he, *having gone*, preached,' &c.— πορευθείς. It is well known that such expressions are often redundant in Greek writers, as in others. So Herodotus, ' to these things they *spake, saying*'—for they said. ' And he, *speaking, said ;*' that is, he said. So Eph. ii. 17, ' And *came* and preached peace,' &c. Matt. ix. 13, ' But *go* and learn what that meaneth,' &c. So God is often represented as *coming*, as *descending*, &c., when he brings a message to mankind. Thus Gen. xi. 5, ' The Lord *came down* to see the city and the tower.' Exod. xix. 20, ' The Lord *came down* upon Mount Sinai.' Numb. xi. 25, ' The Lord *came down* in a cloud.' 2 Sam. xxii. 10, ' He bowed the heavens and *came down*.' The idea, however, would be conveyed by this language that he did this *personally*, or by *himself*, and not merely by employing the agency of another. It would then be implied here, that though the instrumentality of Noah was employed, yet that it was done not by the Holy Spirit, but by him who afterwards became incarnate. On the supposition, therefore, that this whole passage refers to his preaching to the antediluvians in the time of Noah, and not to the ' spirits' *after* they were confined in prison, this is language which the apostle would have properly and probably used. If that supposition meets the full force of the language, then no *argument* can be based on it in proof that he went to preach to them *after* their death, and while his body was lying in the grave. ¶ *And preached*. The word used here (ἐκήρυξεν) is of a *general* character. meaning to make a proclamation of any kind, as a crier does,

or to deliver a message, and does not necessarily imply that it was the gospel which was preached, nor does it determine anything in regard to the nature of the message. It is not affirmed that he preached *the gospel*, for if that specific idea had been expressed it would have been rather by another word— ευαγγελίζω. The word here used would be appropriate to such a message as Noah brought to his contemporaries, or to *any* communication which God made to men. See Matt. iii. 1; iv. 17; Mark i. 35; v. 20; vii. 36. It is implied in the expression, as already remarked, that he did this himself; that it was the Son of God who subsequently became incarnate, and not the Holy Spirit, that did this; though the language is consistent with the supposition that he did it by the instrumentality of another, to wit, Noah. *Qui facit per ilium, facit per se.* God really proclaims a message to mankind when he does it by the instrumentality of the prophets, or apostles, or other ministers of religion; and all that is necessarily implied in this language would be met by the supposition that Christ delivered a message to the antediluvian race by the agency of Noah. No *argument*, therefore, can be derived from this language to prove that Christ went and *personally* preached to those who were confined in hades or in prison. ¶ *Unto the spirits in prison.* That is, clearly, to the spirits *now* in prison, for this is the fair meaning of the passage. The obvious sense is, that Peter supposed there were 'spirits in prison' at the time when he wrote, and that to those same spirits the Son of God had at some time 'preached,' or had made some proclamation respecting the will of God. As this is the only passage in the New Testament on which the Romish doctrine of purgatory is supposed to rest, it is important to ascertain the fair meaning of the language here employed. There are three obvious inquiries in ascertaining its signification. Who are referred to by *spirits?* What is meant by *in prison?* Was the message brought to them while in the prison, or at some previous period? I. Who are referred to by *spirits?* The specification in the next verse determines this. They were

those 'who were sometimes disobedient, when once the long-suffering of God waited in the days of Noah.' No others are specified; and if it should be maintained that this means that he went down to hell, or to sheol, and preached to those who are confined there, it could be inferred from this passage only that he preached to that portion of the lost spirits confined there which belonged to the particular generation in which Noah lived. *Why* he should do this; or *how* there should be such a separation made in hades that it could be done; or what was the nature of the message which he delivered to that portion, are questions which it is impossible for any man who holds to the opinion that Christ went down to hell after his death *to preach*, to answer. But if it means that he preached to those who lived in the days of Noah, while they were yet alive, the question will be asked why are they called 'spirits?' Were they *spirits* then, or were they men like others? To this the answer is easy. Peter speaks of them as they were when he wrote; not as they *had been*, or were at the time when the message was preached to them. The idea is, that to those spirits who were then in prison who had formerly lived in the days of Noah, the message had been in fact delivered. It was not necessary to speak of them precisely as they were at the *time* when it was delivered, but only in such a way as to *identify* them. We should use similar language now. If we saw a company of men in prison who had seen better days—a multitude now drunken, and debased, and poor, and riotous—it would not be improper to say that 'the prospect of wealth and honour was once held out *to this ragged and wretched multitude.* All that is needful is to *identify* them as the same persons who once had this prospect. In regard to the inquiry, then, who these 'spirits' were, there can be no difference of opinion. *They were that wicked race which lived in the days of Noah.* There is no allusion in this passage to any other; there is no intimation that to any others of those 'in prison' the message here referred to had been delivered. II. What is meant by *prison* here? Purgatory, or the *limbus patrum,* say the Romanists—a place in which departed souls are supposed to be confined, and in which their final destiny may still be effected by the purifying fires which they endure, by the prayers of the living, or by a message in some way conveyed to their gloomy abodes—in which such sins may be expiated as do not deserve eternal damnation. The Syriac here is '*in sheol,*' referring to the abodes of the dead, or the place in which departed spirits are supposed to dwell. The word rendered *prison,* ($\phi v \lambda a x \tilde{\eta}$,) means properly *watch, guard*—the act of keeping watch, or the guard itself; then watch-post, or station; then a place where any one is watched or guarded, as a prison; then a watch in the sense of a division of the night, as the morning watch. It is used in the New Testament, with reference to the future world, only in the following places: 1 Pet. iii. 19, 'Preached unto the spirits *in prison;*' and Rev. xx. 7, 'Satan shall be loosed out of his *prison.*' An *idea* similar to the one here expressed may be found in 2 Pet. ii. 4, though the word *prison* does not there occur: 'God spared not the angels that sinned, but cast them down to hell, and delivered them into chains of darkness, to be reserved unto judgment;' and in Jude 6, 'And the angels which kept not their first estate, but left their own habitation, he hath reserved in everlasting chains, under darkness, unto the judgment of the great day.' The allusion, in the passage before us, is undoubtedly to confinement or imprisonment in the invisible world; and perhaps to those who are reserved there with reference to some future arrangement—for this idea enters commonly into the use of the word prison. There is, however, no specification of the *place* where this is; no intimation that it is *purgatory*—a place where the departed are supposed to undergo purification; no intimation that their condition can be affected by anything that we can do; no intimation that those particularly referred to differ in any sense from the others who are confined in that world; no hint that they can be released by any prayers or sacrifices of ours. This passage, therefore, cannot be adduced to support the Roman Catholic doc-

trine of purgatory, for (1,) the essential ideas which enter into the doctrine of purgatory are not to be found in the word here used; (2,) there is no evidence in the fair interpretation of the passage that any message is borne to them while *in* prison; (3,) there is not the slightest hint that they can be released by any prayers or offerings of those who dwell on the earth. The simple idea is that of persons *confined* as in a prison; and the passage will prove only that in the time when the apostle wrote there *were* those who were thus confined. III. Was the message brought to them while *in* prison, or at some previous period? The Romanists say that it was while *in* prison; that Christ, after he was put to death in the body, was still kept alive in his spirit, and went and proclaimed his gospel to those who were in prison. So Bloomfield maintains, (*in loc.,*) and so Œcumenius and Cyril, as quoted by Bloomfield. But against this view there are plain objections drawn from the language of Peter himself. (1.) As we have seen, the fair interpretation of the passage 'quickened by the Spirit,' is not that he was *kept alive as to his human soul,* but that he, after being dead, was *made alive* by his own Divine energy. (2.) If the meaning be that he went and preached *after* his death, it seems difficult to know why the reference is to those only who 'had been disobedient in the days of Noah.' Why were *they* alone selected for this message? Are they separate from others? Were they the only ones in purgatory who could be beneficially affected by his preaching? On the other method of interpretation, we can suggest a reason why they were particularly specified. But how can we on this? (3.) The language employed does not demand this interpretation. Its full meaning is met by the interpretation that Christ once preached to the spirits then in prison, to wit, in the days of Noah; that is, that he caused a Divine message to be borne to them. Thus it would be proper to say that 'Whitefield came to America, and preached to the souls in perdition;' or to go among the graves of the first settlers of New Haven, and say, 'Davenport came from England to preach to the dead men around us.' (4.) This interpretation accords

20 Which sometime were disobedient, when once *a* the long suffering of God waited in the days of Noah,

a Ge.vi.,&c.

while the ark was a preparing, wherein few, that is, eight souls, were saved by water.

with the design of the apostle in inculcating the duty of patience and forbearance in trials; in encouraging those whom he addressed to be patient in their persecutions. See the analysis of the chapter. With this object in view, there was entire propriety in directing them to the long-suffering and forbearance evinced by the Saviour, through Noah. *He* was opposed, reviled, disbelieved, and, we may suppose, persecuted. It was to the purpose to direct them to the fact that he was saved as the result of his steadfastness to Him who had commanded him to preach to that ungodly generation. But what pertinency would there have been in saying that Christ went down to hell, and delivered some sort of a message there, we know not what, to those who are confined there? 20. *Which sometime were disobedient.* Which were *once,* or *formerly,* (τοτε,) disobedient or rebellious. The language here does not imply that they had *ceased* to be disobedient, or that they had become obedient at the time when the apostle wrote; but the object is to direct the attention to a former race of men characterized by disobedience, and to show the patience evinced under their provocations, in endeavouring to do them good. To say that men were formerly rebellious, or rebellious in a specified age, is no evidence that they are otherwise now. The meaning here is, that they did not obey the command of God when he called them to repentance by the preaching of Noah. Comp. 2 Pet. ii. 5, where Noah is called 'a preacher of righteousness.' ¶ *When once the long suffering of God waited in the days of Noah.* God waited on that guilty race a hundred and twenty years, (Gen. vi. 3,) a period sufficiently protracted to evince his long-suffering toward one generation. It is not improbable that during that whole period Noah was, in various ways, preaching to that wicked generation. Comp. Notes on Heb. xi. 7. ¶ *While the ark was a preparing.* It is probable that preparations were made for building the ark

during a considerable portion of that time. St. Peter's, at Rome, was a much longer time in building; and it is to be remembered that in the age of the world when Noah lived, and with the imperfect knowledge of the arts of naval architecture which must have prevailed, it was a much more serious undertaking to construct an ark that would hold such a variety and such a number of animals as that was designed to, and that would float safely for more than a year in an universal flood, than it was to construct such a fabric as St. Peter's, in the days when that edifice was reared. ¶ *Wherein few, that is, eight souls.* Eight *persons*— Noah and his wife, his three sons and their wives, Gen. vii. 7. The allusion to their being saved here seems to be to encourage those whom Peter addressed to perseverance and fidelity, in the midst of all the opposition which they might experience. Noah was not disheartened. Sustained by the Spirit of Christ—the presence of the Son of God —he continued to preach. He did not abandon his purpose, and the result was that he was saved. True, they were few in number who were saved; the great mass continued to be wicked; but this very fact should be an encouragement to us—that though the great mass of any one generation may be wicked, God **can** protect and save the few who are faithful. ¶ *By water.* They were borne up by the waters, and were thus preserved. The thought on which the apostle makes his remarks turn, and which leads him in the next verse to the suggestions about baptism, is, that *water* was employed in their preservation, or that they owed their safety, in an important sense, to that element. In like manner we owe *our* salvation, in an important sense, **to** water; or, there is an important agency which it is made to perform in our salvation. The apostle does not say that it was in the same way, or that the one was a type *designed* to represent the other, or even that the efficacy **of** water was

21 The like figure whereunto, *even* baptism, *a* doth also now save us, (not the putting away of the

a Ep.5.26.

filth of the flesh, but the answer of a good conscience *b* toward God,) by the resurrection of Jesus Christ:

b Ac.8.37; Ro.10.10.

---

in both cases the same; but he says, that as Noah owed *his* salvation to water, so there is an important sense in which water is employed in *ours.* There is in *certain respects*—he does not say in *all* respects—a resemblance between the agency of water in the salvation of Noah, and the agency of water in our salvation. In both cases water is employed, though it may not be that it is in the same manner, or with precisely the same efficacy.

21. *The like figure whereunto, even baptism, doth also now save us.* There are some various readings here in the Greek text, but the sense is not essentially varied. Some have proposed to read (ᾧ) *to which* instead of (ὅ) *which*, so as to make the sense ' the antitype *to which* baptism now also saves us.' The antecedent to the relative, whichever word is used, is clearly not *the ark*, but *water;* and the idea is, that as Noah was saved by water, so there is a sense in which water is made instrumental in our salvation. The mention of *water* in the case of Noah, in connection with *his* being saved, by an obvious association suggested to the mind of the apostle the use of *water* in our salvation, and hence led him to make the remark about the connection of baptism with our salvation. The Greek word here rendered *figure*—ἀντίτυπον—*antitype* means properly, *resisting a blow* or *impression*, (from ἀντί and τύπος;) that is, *hard, solid.* In the New Testament, however, it is used in a different sense; and (ἀντί) *anti*, in composition, implies resemblance, correspondence; and hence the word means, *formed after a type* or *model; like; corresponding; that which corresponds to a type.*—Rob. Lex. The word occurs only in this place and Heb. ix. 24, rendered *figures.* The meaning here is, that *baptism corresponded to,* or *had a resemblance to,* the water by which Noah was saved; or that there was a use of water in the one case which corresponded in some respects to the water that was used in the other; to wit, *in effecting salvation.*

The apostle does not say that it corresponded *in all respects;* in respect, e. g., to quantity, or to the manner of the application, or to the efficacy; but there is a sense in which water performs an important part in our salvation, as it did in his. ¶ *Baptism.* Not the *mere* application of water, for that idea the apostle expressly disclaims, when he says that it involves not ' putting away the filth of the flesh, but the answer of a good conscience toward God.' The sense is, that baptism, including all that is properly meant by baptism as a religious rite—that is, baptism administered in connection with true repentance, and true faith in the Lord Jesus, and when it is properly a symbol of the putting away of sin, and of the renewing influences of the Holy Spirit, and an act of unreserved dedication to God —now saves us. On the meaning of the word *baptism*, see Notes on Matt. iii. 6. ¶ *Doth also now save us.* The water saved Noah and his family from perishing in the flood ; to wit, by bearing up the ark. Baptism, in the proper sense of the term, as above explained, where the water used is a symbol, in like manner now saves us ; that is, the water is an emblem of that purifying by which we are saved. It may be said to save us, not as the meritorious cause, but as the indispensable condition of salvation. No man can be saved without that regenerated and purified heart of which baptism is the appropriate symbol, and when it would be *proper* to administer that ordinance. The apostle cannot have meant that water saves us *in the same way* in which it saved Noah, for that cannot be true. It is neither the same in quantity, nor is it applied in the same way, nor is it efficacious in the same manner. It is indeed connected with our salvation in its own proper way, as an emblem of that purifying of the heart by which we are saved. Thus it corresponds with the salvation of Noah by water, and is the (ἀντίτυπον) *antitype* of that. Nor does it mean that the salvation of Noah by water was *designed* to be a type of Christian baptism. There is not the least evidence of that; and it should not be affirmed without proof. The apostle saw a *resemblance* in some respects between the one and the other; such a resemblance that the one naturally suggested the other to his mind, and the resemblance was so important as to make it the proper ground of remark.

[But if Noah's preservation in the ark, be the type of that salvation of which baptism is the emblem, who shall say it was not so designed of God? Must we indeed regard the resemblance between Noah's deliverance and ours, as a happy coincidence merely? But the author is wont to deny typical design in very clear cases; and in avoiding one extreme seems to have gone into another. Some will have types everywhere; and, therefore, others will allow them nowhere. See Supp. Note, Heb. vii. 1; M'Knight's Essay, viii. Sect. v., on the laws of typical interpretation, with his commentary *in loco.*]

The points of resemblance in the two cases seem to have been these: (1.) There was *salvation* in both; Noah was saved from death, and we from hell. (2.) *Water* is employed in both cases— in the case of Noah to uphold the ark; in ours to be a symbol of our purification. (3.) The water in both cases is *connected with* salvation: in the case of Noah by sustaining the ark; in ours by being a symbol of salvation, of purity, of cleansing, of that by which we may be brought to God. The meaning of this part of the verse, therefore, may be thus expressed: 'Noah and his family were saved by water, the antitype to which (to wit, that which in important respects corresponds to that) baptism (not the putting away of the filth of the flesh, or the mere application of material water, but that purifying of the heart of which it is the appropriate emblem) now saves us.' ¶ *Not the putting away of the filth of the flesh.* Not a mere external washing, however solemnly done. No outward ablution or purifying saves us, but that which pertains to the conscience. This important clause is thrown in to guard the statement from the abuse to which it would otherwise be liable, the supposition that baptism has of itself a purifying and saving power. To guard against this, the apostle expressly declares that he means much more than

a mere outward application of water. ¶ *But the answer of a good conscience toward God.* The word here rendered *answer* (ἐπερώτημα) means properly *a question, an inquiry.* It is 'spoken of a *question* put to a convert at baptism, or rather of the whole process of question and answer; that is, by implication, *examination, profession.*' — Robinson, Lex. It is designed to mark the spiritual character of the baptismal rite in contrast with a mere external purification, and evidently refers to something that occurred *at* baptism; some question, inquiry, or examination, that took place then; and it would seem to imply, (1,) that when baptism was performed, there was some question or inquiry in regard to the belief of the candidate; (2,) that an answer was expected, implying that there was a good conscience; that is, that the candidate had an enlightened conscience, and was sincere in his profession; and, (3,) that the real efficacy of baptism, or its power in saving, was not in the mere external rite, but in the state of the heart, indicated by the question and answer, of which that was the emblem. On the meaning of the phrase 'a good conscience,' see Notes on ver. 16 of this chapter. Compare on this verse Neander, Geschich der Pflanz. u. Leit. der chr. Kirche, i. p. 203, seq., in Bibl. Reposi. iv. 272, seq. It is in the highest degree probable that questions would be proposed to candidates for baptism respecting their belief, and we have an instance of this fact undoubtedly in the case before us. How extensive such examinations would be, what points would be embraced, how much reference there was to personal experience, we have, of course, no certain means of ascertaining. We may suppose, however, that the examination pertained to what constituted the essential features of the Christian religion, as distinguished from other systems, and to the cordial belief of that system by the candidate. ¶ *By the resurrection of Jesus Christ.* That is, we are saved in this manner through the resurrection of Jesus Christ. The whole efficiency in the case is derived from that. If he had not been raised from the dead, baptism would have been vain, and there would have been no power to save

22 Who is gone into heaven, and is on the right hand of God: angels *and authorities and powers being made subject unto him.

a Ep.1.21.

us. See this illustrated at length in the Notes on Rom. vi. 4, 5. The points, therefore, which are established in regard to baptism by this important passage are these: (1.) That Christian baptism is not a mere *external* rite; a mere outward ablution; a mere application of water to the body. It is not contemplated that it shall be an empty form, and its essence does not consist in a mere ' putting away of the filth of the flesh.' There is a work to be done in respect to the *conscience* which cannot be reached by the application of water. (2.) That there was an examination among the early Christians when a candidate was about to be baptized, and of course such an examination is proper now. Whatever was the ground of the examination, it related to that which existed *before* the baptism was administered. It was not expected that it should be accomplished *by* the baptism. There is, therefore, implied evidence here that there was no reliance placed on that ordinance to *produce* that which constituted the ' answer of a good conscience;' in other words, that it was not supposed to have an efficacy to produce that of itself, and was not a converting or regenerating ordinance. (3.) The 'answer' which was returned in the inquiry, was to be such as indicated a good conscience; that is, as Bloomfield expresses it, (New Test. *in loc.*,) ' that which enables us to return such an answer as springs from a good conscience towards God, which can be no other than the inward change and renovation wrought by the Spirit.' It was supposed, therefore, that there would be an internal work of grace; that there would be much more than an outward rite in the whole transaction. The application of water is, in fact, but an emblem or symbol of that grace in the heart, and is to be administered as denoting that. It does not *convey* grace to the soul by any physical efficacy of the water. It is a symbol of the purifying influences of religion, and is made a means of grace in the same way as obedience to any other of the commands

of God. (4.) There is no efficacy in the mere application of water in any form, or with any ceremonies of religion, to put away sin. It is the ' good conscience,' the renovated heart, the purified soul, of which baptism is the emblem, that furnishes evidence of the Divine acceptance and favour. Comp. Heb. ix. 9, 10. There must be a deep internal work on the soul of man, in order that he may be acceptable to God; and when that is wanting, no external rite is of any avail. Yet, (5,) it does not follow from this that baptism is of no importance. The argument of the apostle here is, that it *is* of great importance. Noah was saved by water; and so baptism has an important connection with our salvation. As water bore up the ark, and was the means of saving Noah, so baptism by water is the emblem of our salvation; and when administered in connection with a ' good conscience,' that is, with a renovated heart, it is as certainly connected with our salvation as the sustaining waters of the flood were with the salvation of Noah. No man can prove from the Bible that baptism has no important connection with salvation; and no man can prove that by neglecting it he will be as likely to obtain the Divine favour as he would by observing it. It is a means of exhibiting great and important truths in an impressive manner to the soul; it is a means of leading the soul to an entire dedication to a God of purity; it is a means through which God manifests himself to the soul, and through which he imparts grace, as he does in all other acts of obedience to his commandments.

22. *Who is gone into heaven.* Notes, Acts i. 9. ¶ *And is on the right hand of God.* Notes, Mark xvi. 19. ¶ *Angels and authorities and powers being made subject unto him.* See Notes, Eph. i. 20, 21. The reason why the apostle here adverts to the fact that the Lord Jesus is raised up to the right hand of God, and is so honoured in heaven, seems to have been to encourage those to whom he wrote to persevere in the service of God, though they were persecuted. The

Lord Jesus was in like manner persecuted. He was reviled, and rejected, and put to death. Yet he ultimately triumphed. He was raised from the dead, and was exalted to the highest place of honour in the universe. Even so they, if they did not faint, might hope to come off in the end triumphant. As Noah, who had been faithful and steadfast when surrounded by a scoffing world, was at last preserved by his faith from ruin, and as the Redeemer, though persecuted and put to death, was at last exalted to the right hand of God, so would it be with them if they bore their trials patiently, and did not faint or fail in the persecutions which they endured.

In view of the exposition in vers. 1 and 2, we may remark, (1,) that it is our duty to seek the conversion and salvation of our impenitent relatives and friends. All Christians have relatives and friends who are impenitent; it is a rare thing that some of the members of their own families are not so. In most families, even Christian families, there is a husband or a wife, a father or a mother, a son or daughter, a brother or sister, who is not converted. To all such, they who are Christians owe important duties, and there is none *more* important than that of seeking their conversion. That this *is* a duty is clearly implied in this passage in reference to a wife, and for the same reason it is a duty in reference to all other persons. It may be further apparent from these considerations : (*a*) It is an important part of the business of *all* Christians to seek the salvation of others. This is clearly the duty of ministers of the gospel; but it is no less the duty of all who profess to be followers of the Saviour, and to take him as their example and guide. Comp. James v. 19, 20. (*b*) It is a duty peculiarly devolving on those who have relatives who are unconverted, on account of the *advantages* which they have for doing it. They are with them constantly; they have their confidence and affection; they can feel more for them than any one else can ; and if *they* are not concerned for their salvation, they cannot hope that any others will be. (*c*) It is not wholly an improper motive to seek their salvation from the happiness which it would confer on those who are already Christians. It is not improper that a wife should be stimulated to desire the conversion of her husband from the increased enjoyment which she would have if her partner in life were united with her in the same hope of heaven, and from the pleasure which it would give to enjoy the privilege of religious worship in the family, and the aid which would be furnished in training up her children in the Lord. A Christian wife and mother has important duties to perform towards her children ; it is not improper that in performing those duties she should earnestly desire the co-operation of her partner in life.

(2.) Those who have impenitent husbands and friends should be *encouraged* in seeking their conversion. It is plainly implied (vers. 1, 2) that it was not to be regarded as a *hopeless* thing, but that in all cases they were to regard it as possible that unbelieving husbands *might* be brought to the knowledge of the truth. If this is true of *husbands*, it is no less true of other friends. We should never despair of the conversion of a friend as long as life lasts, however far he may be from the path of virtue and piety. The grounds of encouragement are such as these : (*a*) You have an *influence* over them which no other one has ; and that influence may be regarded as *capital*, which will give you great advantages in seeking their conversion. (*b*) You have *access* to them at times when their minds are most open to serious impressions. Every man has times when he may be approached on the subject of religion ; when he is pensive and serious ; when he is disappointed and sad ; when the affairs of this world do not go well with him, and his thoughts are drawn along to a better. There are times in the life of every man when he is ready to open his mind to a friend on the subject of religion, and when he would be glad of a word of friendly counsel and encouragement. It is much to have access to a man at such times. (*c*) If all the *facts* were known which have occurred, there would be no lack of encouragement to labour for the conversion of impenitent relatives and friends. Many a husband owes his salvation to the persevering solicitude and prayers of a wife;

many a son will enter heaven because a mother never ceased to pray for his salvation, even when to human view there seemed no hope of it.

(3.) We may learn (vers. 1, 2) what are the principal *means* by which we are to hope to secure the conversion and salvation of impenitent friends. It is to be mainly by a pure life ; by a holy walk ; by a consistent example. *Conversation,* properly so called, is not to be regarded as excluded from those means, but the main dependence is to be on a holy life. This is to be so, because (*a*) most persons form their notions of religion from what they see in the lives of its professed friends. It is not so much what they hear in the pulpit, for they regard preaching as a mere professional business, by which a man gets a living ; not so much by books in defence and explanation of religion, for they seldom or never read them ; not by what religion enabled the martyrs to do, for they may have scarcely heard the names of even the most illustrious of the martyrs ; but by what they see in the walk and conversation of those who profess to be Christians, especially of those who are their near relations. The husband is forming his views of religion constantly from what he sees on the brow and in the eye of his professedly Christian wife ; the brother from what he sees in his sister ; the child from what he sees in the parent. (*b*) Those who profess to be Christians have an opportunity of showing the power of religion in a way which is superior to any abstract argument. It controls their temper ; it makes them kind and gentle ; it sustains them in trial ; it prompts them to deeds of benevolence ; it disposes them to be contented, to be forgiving, to be patient in the reverses of life. Every one may thus be always doing something to make an impression favourable to religion on the minds of others. Yet it is *also* true that much may be done, and should be done for the conversion of others, by *conversation* properly so called, or by direct address and appeal. There is nothing, however, which requires to be managed with more prudence than conversation with those who are not Christians, or direct efforts to lead them to attend to the subject of religion. In

regard to this it may be observed, (*a*,) that it does no good to be *always* talking with them. Such a course only produces disgust. (*b*) It does no good to talk to them at unseasonable and improper times. If they are specially engaged in their business, and would not like to be interrupted—if they are in company with others, or even with their family —it does little good to attempt a conversation with them. It is 'the word that is *fitly* spoken that is like apples of gold in pictures of silver,' Prov. xxv. 11. (*c*) It does no good to *scold* them on the subject of religion, with a view to make them Christians. Ir such a case you show a spirit the very reverse of that religion which you are professedly endeavouring to persuade them to embrace. (*d*) All conversation with impenitent sinners should be kind, and tender, and respectful. It should be addressed to them when they will be disposed to listen; usually when they are alone ; and especially when from trials or other causes they may be in such a state of mind that they will be willing to listen. It may be added, that impenitent sinners are much more frequently in such a state of mind than most Christians suppose, and that they often wonder that their Christian friends do *not* speak to them about the salvation of the soul.

From the exposition given of the important verses 18–21, we may derive the following inferences :—

(1.) The pre-existence of Christ. If he preached to the antediluvians in the time of Noah, he must have had an existence at that time.

(2.) His divinity. If he was 'quickened' or restored to life by his own exalted nature, he must be Divine ; for there is no more inalienable attribute of the Deity than the power of raising the dead.

(3.) If Christ preached to the heathen world in the time of Noah, for the same reason it may be regarded as true that *all* the messages which are brought to men, calling them to repentance, in any age or country, are through him. Thus it was Christ who spake by the prophets and by the apostles ; and thus he speaks now by his ministers.

(4.) If this interpretation is well-founded, it takes away one of the

CHAPTER IV.

FORASMUCH then as Christ hath suffered for us in the flesh, arm yourselves likewise with the same mind : ^a for he ^b that hath suffered in the flesh hath ceased from sin ;

<small>a Phi.2.5.   b Ro.6.2,7</small>

strongest supports of the doctrine of purgatory. There is no *stronger* passage of the Bible in support of this doctrine than the one before us ; and if *this* does not countenance it, it may be safely affirmed that it has not a shadow of proof in the sacred Scriptures.

(5.) It follows that there is no hope or prospect that the gospel will be preached to those who are lost. This is the *only* passage in the Bible that could be supposed to teach any such doctrine ; and if the interpretation above proposed be correct, this furnishes no ground of belief that if a man dies impenitent he will ever be favoured with another offer of mercy. This interpretation also accords with all the other representations in the Bible. 'As the tree falleth, so it lies.' 'He that is holy, let him be holy still ; and he that is filthy, let him be filthy still.' All the representations in the Bible lead us to suppose that the eternal destiny of the soul after death is fixed, and that the only change which can ever occur in the future state is that which will be produced by DEVELOPEMENT : the developement of the principles of piety in heaven ; the developement of the principles of evil in hell.

(6.) It follows, that if there is not a place of *purgatory* in the future world, there is a place of *punishment*. If the word *prison*, in the passage before us, does not mean purgatory, and does not refer to a detention with a prospect or possibility of release, it must refer to detention of another kind, and for another purpose, and that can be only with reference ' to the judgment of the great day,' 2 Pet. ii. 14; Jude 6. From that gloomy prison there is no evidence that any have been, or will be, released.

(7.) Men should embrace the gospel at once. Now it is offered to them ; in the future world it will not be. But even if it could be proved that the gospel would be offered to them in the future world, it would be better to embrace it now. Why should men go down to that world to suffer long before they become reconciled to God? Why choose to taste the sorrows of hell before they embrace the offers of mercy? Why go to that world of woe at all? Are men so in love with suffering and danger that they esteem it wise to go down to that dark prison-house, with the intention or the hope that the gospel may be offered to them there, and that when there they may be disposed to embrace it? Even if it could be shown, therefore, that they *might* again hear the voice of mercy and salvation, how much wiser would it be to hearken to the voice now, and become reconciled to God here, and never experience in any way the pangs of the second death! But of any such offer of mercy in the world of despair, the Bible contains no intimation ; and he who goes to the eternal world unreconciled to God, perishes for ever. The moment when he crosses the line between time and eternity, he goes for ever beyond the boundaries of hope.

CHAPTER IV.

ANALYSIS OF THE CHAPTER.

THIS chapter relates principally to the manner in which those to whom the apostle wrote ought to bear their trials, and to the encouragements to a holy life, notwithstanding their persecutions. He had commenced the subject in the preceding chapter, and had referred them particularly to the example of the Saviour. His great solicitude was, that if they suffered, it should not be for crime, and that their enemies should not be able to bring any well-founded accusation against them He would have them pure and harmless, patient and submissive ; faithful in the performance of their duties, and confidently looking forward to the time when they should be delivered. He exhorts them, therefore, to the following things : (*a*) To arm themselves with the same mind that was in Christ ; to consider that the past time of their lives was enough for them to have wrought

2 That he *a* no longer should live the rest of *his* time in the flesh to the lusts of men, but to the will of God.

3 For the time *b* past of *our* life

a 2 Co.5.15.

may suffice us to have wrought the will of the Gentiles, when we walked in lasciviousness, lusts, excess of wine, revellings, banquetings, and abominable idolatries ;

b 1 Co.6.11; Tit.3.3.

the will of the flesh, and that now it was their duty to be separate from the wicked world, in whatever light the world might regard their conduct—remembering that they who calumniated them must soon give account to God, vers. 1–6. (*b*) He reminds them that the end of all things was at hand, and that it became them to be sober, and watch unto prayer, ver. 7. (*c*) He exhorts them to the exercise of mutual love and hospitality—virtues eminently useful in a time of persecution and afflictions, vers. 8, 9. (*d*) He exhorts them to a performance of every duty with seriousness of manner, and fidelity —whether it were in preaching, or in dispensing alms to the poor and needy, vers. 10, 11. (*e*) He tells them not to think it strange that they were called to pass through fiery trials, nor to suppose that any unusual thing had happened to *them;* reminds them that they only partook of Christ's sufferings, and that it was to be regarded as a favour if any one suffered as a Christian; and presses upon them the thought that they ought to be careful that none of them suffered for crime, vers. 12–16. (*f*) He reminds them that the righteous would be saved with difficulty, and that the wicked would certainly be destroyed; and exhorts them, therefore, to commit the keeping of their souls to a faithful Creator, vers. 18, 19.

1. *Forasmuch then as Christ hath suffered for us in the flesh.* Since he as a man has died for us. Notes, chap. iii. 18. The design was to set the suffering Redeemer before them as an example in their trials. ¶ *Arm yourselves likewise with the same mind.* That is, evidently, the same mind that he evinced —a readiness to suffer in the cause of religion, a readiness to die as he had done. This readiness to suffer and die, the apostle speaks of as *armour,* and having this is represented as being *armed.* Armour is put on for offensive or defensive purposes in war; and the

idea of the apostle here is, that that state of mind when we are *ready* to meet with persecution and trial, and when we are ready to die, will answer the purpose of armour in engaging in the conflicts and strifes which pertain to us as Christians, and especially in meeting with persecutions and trials. We are to put on the same fortitude which the Lord Jesus had, and this will be the best defence against our foes, and the best security of victory. ¶ *For he that hath suffered in the flesh hath ceased from sin.* Comp. Notes, Rom. vi. 7. To 'suffer in the flesh' is *to die.* The expression here has a proverbial aspect, and seems to have meant something like this : ' when a man is dead, he will sin no more ;' referring of course to the present life. So if a Christian becomes *dead* in a moral sense—dead to this world, dead by being crucified with Christ (see Notes, Gal. ii. 20)—he may be expected to cease from sin. The reasoning is based on the idea that there is such a union between Christ and the believer that his death on the cross *secured* the death of the believer to the world. Comp. 2 Tim. ii. 11; Col. ii. 20; iii. 3.

2. *That he no longer should live.* That is, he has become, through the death of Christ, dead to the world and to the former things which influenced him, *in order* that he should hereafter live not to the lusts of the flesh. See Notes, 2 Cor. v. 15. ¶ *The rest of* his *time in the flesh.* The remainder of the time that he is to continue in the flesh; that is, that he is to live on the earth. ¶ *To the lusts of men.* Such lusts as men commonly live for and indulge in. Some of these are enumerated in the following verse. ¶ *But to the will of God.* In such a manner as God commands. The object of redemption is to rescue us from being swayed by wicked lusts, and to bring us to be conformed wholly to the will of God.

3. *For the time past of* our *life may suffice us.* ' We have spent sufficient

time in indulging ourselves, and following our wicked propensities, and we should hereafter live in a different manner.' This does not mean that it was ever *proper* thus to live, but that, as we would say, ' we have had *enough* of these things ; we have tried them ; there is no reason why we should indulge in them any more.' An expression quite similar to this occurs in Horace—I usisti satis, edisti satis, atque bibisti. Tempus abire tibi est, &c.—Epis. ii. 213. ¶ *To have wrought the will of the Gentiles.* This does not mean to be subservient to their will, but to have done what they willed to do ; that is, to live as they did. That the Gentiles or heathen lived in the manner immediately specified, see demonstrated in the Notes on Rom. i. 21–32. ¶ *When we walked in lasciviousness.* When we *lived* in the indulgence of corrupt passions—the word *walk* being often used in the Scriptures to denote the manner of life. On the word *lasciviousness,* see Notes on Rom. xiii. 13. The apostle says *we,* not as meaning that *he* himself had been addicted to these vices, but as speaking of those who were Christians in general. It is common to say that *we* lived so and so, when speaking of a collection of persons, without meaning that each one was guilty of *all* the practices enumerated. See Notes on 1 Thess. iv. 17, for a similar use of the word *we.* The use of the word *we* in this place would show that the apostle did not mean to set himself up as better than they were, but was willing to be identified with them. ¶ *Lusts.* The indulgence of unlawful desires. Notes, Rom. i. 24. ¶ *Excess of wine.* The word here used (οἰνοφλυγία) occurs nowhere else in the New Testament. It properly means *overflowing of wine,* (οἶνος, wine, and φλύω. to overflow ;) then wine-drinking ; drunkenness. That this was a common vice need not be proved. Multitudes of those who became Christians had been drunkards, for intemperance abounded in all the heathen world. Comp. 1 Cor. vi. 9–11 It should not be inferred here from the English translation, ' *excess* of wine,' that wine is improper only when used to excess, or that the moderate use of wine is proper. Whatever may be true on that point, nothing can be de-

termined in regard to it from the use of this word. The apostle had his eye on one thing—on such a use of wine as led to intoxication; such as they had indulged in before their conversion. About the impropriety of that, there could be no doubt. Whether *any* use of wine, by Christians or other persons, was lawful, was another question. It should be added, moreover, that the phrase ' *excess* of wine ' does not precisely convey the meaning of the original. The word *excess* would naturally imply something more than was needful ; or something beyond the proper limit or measure ; but no such idea is in the original word. That refers merely to the *abundance* of wine, without any reference to the inquiry whether there was *more* than was proper or not. Tindal renders it, somewhat better, *drunkenness.* So Luther, *Trunkenheit.* ¶ *Revellings.* Rendered *rioting* in Rom. xiii. 13. See Notes on that verse. The Greek word (κῶμος) occcurs only here, and in Rom. xiii. 13, and Gal. v. 21. It means *feasting, revel ;* ' a carousing or merry-making after supper, the guests often sallying into the streets, and going through the city with torches, music, and songs in honour of Bacchus,' &c. — *Robinson, Lex.* The word would apply to all such noisy and boisterous processions now—scenes wholly inappropriate to the Christian. ¶ *Banquetings.* The word here used (πότος) occurs nowhere else in the New Testament. It means properly *drinking ; an act of drinking; then a drinking bout ; drinking together.* The thing forbidden by it is *an assembling together for the purpose* of *drinking.* There is nothing in this word referring to *eating,* or to *banqueting,* as the term is now commonly employed. The idea in the passage is, that it is improper for Christians to meet together for the purpose of drinking—as wine, toasts, &c. The prohibition would apply to all those assemblages where this is understood to be the main object. It would forbid, therefore, an attendance on all those celebrations in which drinking toasts is understood to be an essential part of the festivities, and all those where hilarity and joyfulness are sought to be produced by the intoxicating bowl. Such are not proper places for Chris-

4 Wherein they think it strange that ye run not with *them* to the same excess of riot, speaking evil [a] of *you:*

tians. ¶ *And abominable idolatries.* Literally, *unlawful idolatries;* that is, unlawful to the Jews, or forbidden by their laws. Then the expression is used in the sense of *wicked, impious,* since what is unlawful is impious and wrong. That the vices here referred to were practised by the heathen world is well known. See Notes on Rom. i. 26–31. That many who became Christians were guilty of them before their conversion is clear from this passage. The fact that *they* were thus converted shows the power of the gospel, and also that we should not despair in regard to those who are indulging in these vices now. They seem indeed almost to be hopeless, but we should remember that many who became Christians when the gospel was first preached, as well as since, were of this character. If *they* were reclaimed; if those who had been addicted to the gross and debasing vices referred to here, were brought into the kingdom of God, we should believe that those who are living in the same manner now may also be recovered. From the statement made in this verse, that 'the time past of our lives may *suffice* to have wrought the will of the Gentiles,' we may remark that the same may be said by all Christians of themselves; the same thing is true of all who are living in sin. (1.) It is true of all who are Christians, and they feel it, that they lived *long enough* in sin. (*a*) They made a fair trial— many of them with ample opportunities; with abundant wealth; with all that the fashionable world can furnish; with all that can be derived from low and gross indulgences. Many who are now Christians had opportunities of living in splendour and ease; many moved in gay and brilliant circles; many occupied stations of influence, or had brilliant prospects of distinction; many gave indulgence to gross propensities; many were the companions of the vile and the abandoned. Those who are *now* Christians, take the church at large, have had ample opportunity of making the fullest trial of what sin and the world can furnish. (*b*) They *all* feel that the past

is enough for this manner of living. It is 'sufficient' to satisfy them that the world cannot furnish what the soul demands. They need a better portion; and they can now see that there is no reason why they should desire to continue the experiment in regard to what the world can furnish. On that unwise and wicked experiment they have expended time enough; and satisfied with that, they desire to return to it no more. (2.) The same thing is true of the wicked —of all who are living for the world. The time past *should* be regarded as sufficient to make an experiment in sinful indulgences; for (*a*) the experiment has been made by millions before them, and has always failed; and they can hope to find in sin only what has always been found—disappointment, mortification, and despair. (*b*) *They* have made a sufficient experiment. They have never found in those indulgences what they flattered themselves they would find, and they have seen enough to satisfy them that what the immortal soul needs can never be obtained there. (*c*) They have spent sufficient *time* in this hopeless experiment. Life is short. Man has no time to waste. He may soon die—and at whatever period of life any one may be who is living in sin, we may say to him that he has already wasted *enough* of life; he has thrown away *enough* of probation in a fruitless attempt to find happiness where it can never be found. For any purpose whatever for which any one could ever suppose it to be desirable to live in sin, the past should suffice. But why should it ever be deemed desirable at all? The fruits of sin are always disappointment, tears, death, despair.

4. *Wherein they think it strange.* In respect to which vices, they who were once your partners and accomplices now think it strange that you no longer unite with them. They do not understand the reasons why you have left them. They regard you as abandoning a course of life which has much to attract and to make life merry, for a severe and gloomy superstition. This is a true account of

the feelings which the people of the world have when their companions and friends leave them and become Christians. It is to them a strange and unaccountable thing, that they give up the pleasures of the world for a course of life which to them seems to promise anything but happiness. Even the kindred of the Saviour regarded him as ' beside himself,' (Mark iii. 21,) and Festus supposed that Paul was mad, Acts xxvi. 24. There is almost nothing which the people of the world so little comprehend as the reasons which influence those with ample means of worldly enjoyment to leave the circles of gaiety and vanity, and to give themselves to the serious employments of religion. The epithets of fool, enthusiast, fanatic, are terms which frequently occur to the heart to denote this, if they are not always allowed to escape from the lips. The *reasons* why they esteem this so strange, are something like the following : (1.) They do not appreciate the *motives* which influence those who leave them. They feel that it is proper to enjoy the world, and to make life cheerful, and they do not understand what it is to act under a deep sense of responsibility to God, and with reference to eternity. They live for themselves. They seek happiness as the end and aim of life. They have never been accustomed to direct the mind onward to another world, and to the account which they must soon render at the bar of God. Unaccustomed to act from any higher motives than those which pertain to the present world, they cannot appreciate the conduct of those who begin to live and act for eternity. (2.) They do not yet see the guilt and folly of sinful pleasures. They are not convinced of the deep sinfulness of the human soul, and they think it strange that others should abandon a course of life which seems to them so innocent. They do not see why those who have been so long accustomed to these indulgences should have changed their opinions, and why they now regard those things as sinful which they once considered to be harmless. (3.) They do not see the force of the argument for religion. Not having the views of the unspeakable importance of religious truth and duty which Christians now

have, they wonder that they should break off from the course of life which they formerly pursued, and separate from the mass of their fellow-men. Hence they sometimes regard the conduct of Christians as amiable weakness ; sometimes as superstition ; sometimes as sheer folly ; sometimes as madness ; and sometimes as sourness and misanthropy. In all respects they esteem it *strange*.

> " Lions and beasts of savage name
> Put on the nature of the lamb,
> While the wide world esteems it strange,
> Gaze, and admire, and hate the change."

¶ *That ye run not with* them. There may be an allusion here to the well-known orgies of Bacchus, in which his votaries *ran* as if excited by the furies, and were urged on as if transported with madness. See Ovid, Metam. iii. 529, thus translated by Addison :

> "For now, through prostrate Greece, young Bacchus rode,
> Whilst howling matrons celebrate the god ;
> All ranks and sexes to his *orgies ran*,
> To mingle in the pomp and fill the train."

The language, however, will well describe revels of any sort, and at any period of the world. ¶ *To the same excess of riot*. The word rendered *excess* (ἀνάχυσις) means, properly, a *pouring out, an affusion;* and the idea here is, that all the sources and forms of riot and disorder were *poured out together*. There was no withholding, no restraint. The most unlimited indulgence was given to the passions. This was the case in the disorder referred to among the ancients, as it is the case now in scenes of midnight revelry. On the meaning of the word *riot*, see Notes on Eph. v. 18; Tit. i. 6. ¶ *Speaking evil of* you. Gr., *blaspheming*. Notes, Matt. ix. 3. The meaning here is, that they used harsh and reproachful epithets of those who would not unite with them in their revelry. They called them fools, fanatics, hypocrites, &c. The idea is not that they blasphemed God, or that they charged Christians with crime, but that they used language fitted to injure the feelings, the character, the reputation of those who would no longer unite with them in the ways of vice and folly.

5. *Who shall give account.* That is, they shall not do this with impunity. They are guilty in this of a great wrong

5 Who shall give account to him that is ready to judge the quick and the dead.

6 For, for this cause was the gos-

pel preached also to them that are dead, that they might be judged *a* according to men in the flesh, but live *b* according to God in the spirit.

a Mat.24.9.　　　　*b* Re.14.13.

and they must answer for it to God. ¶ *That is ready to judge.* That is, 'who is *prepared* to judge'—τῷ ἑτοίμως ἔχοντι. See the phrase used in Acts xxi. 13: 'I am *ready* not to be bound only, but also to die at Jerusalem.' 2 Cor. xii. 14: 'The third time I am *ready* to come to you.' Compare the word *ready*—ἑτοίμος—in Matt. xxii. 4, 8; xxiv. 44; xxv. 10; Luke xii. 40; xxii. 33; 1 Pet. i. 5. The meaning is, not that he was *about* to do it, or that the day of judgment was near at hand —whatever the apostle may have supposed to be true on that point—but that he was *prepared* for it; all the arrangements were made with reference to it; there was nothing to hinder it. ¶ *To judge the quick and the dead.* The *living* and the dead; that is, those who shall be alive when he comes, and those in their graves. This is a common phrase to denote all who shall be brought before the bar of God for judgment. See Notes, Acts x. 42; 1 Thess. iv. 16, 17; 2 Tim. iv. 1. The meaning in this connection seems to be, that they should bear their trials and the opposition which they would meet with patiently, not feeling that they were forgotten, nor attempting to avenge themselves; for the Lord would vindicate them when he should come to judgment, and call those who had injured them to an account for all the wrongs which they had done to the children of God.

6. *For, for this cause.* The expression, 'For, for this cause,' refers to an *end* to be reached, or an *object* to be gained, or a *reason* why anything referred to is done. The end or reason why the thing referred to here, to wit, that 'the gospel was preached to the dead,' was done, is stated in the subsequent part of the verse to have been '*that they might be judged*,' &c. It was with reference to this, or in order that this might be, that the gospel was preached to them. ¶ *Was the gospel preached also to them that are dead.* Many, as Doddridge, Whitby, and others,

understand this of those who are *spiritually dead*, that is, the Gentiles, and suppose that the object for which this was done was that 'they might be brought to such a state of life as their carnal neighbours would look upon as a kind of condemnation and death.'— *Doddridge.* Others have supposed that it refers to those who had suffered martyrdom in the cause of Christianity; others, that it refers to the sinners of the old world, (*Saurin*,) expressing a hope that some of them might be saved; and others, that it means that the Saviour went down and preached to those who are dead, in accordance with one of the interpretations given of chap. iii. 19. It seems to me that the most natural and obvious interpretation is to refer it to those who were *then* dead, to whom the gospel had been preached when living, and who had become true Christians. This is the interpretation proposed by Wetstein, Rosenmüller, Bloomfield, and others. In support of this it may be said, (1.) that this is the natural and obvious meaning of the word *dead*, which should be understood literally, unless there is some good reason in the connection for departing from the common meaning of the word. (2.) The apostle had just used the word in that sense in the previous verse. (3.) This will suit the connection, and accord with the design of the apostle. He was addressing those who were suffering persecution. It was natural, in such a connection, to refer to those who had died in the faith, and to show, for their encouragement, that though they had been put to death, yet they still lived to God. He therefore says, that the design in publishing the gospel to them was, that though they might be judged by men in the usual manner, and put to death, yet that in respect to their higher and nobler nature, *the spirit*, they might live unto God. It was not uncommon nor unnatural for the apostles, in writing to those who were suffering persecution, to refer to those who had been removed

7 But the end *a* of all things is at hand : be ye therefore sober, and watch *b* unto prayer.

a Ja.5,8,9.   b Lu.21.36.

by death, and to make their condition and example an argument for fidelity and perseverance. Compare 1 Thess. iv. 13; Rev. xiv. 13. ¶ *That they might be judged according to men in the flesh.* That is, *so far as men are concerned,* (κατὰ ἀνθρώπους,) or in respect to the treatment which they received from men in the flesh, they were judged and condemned ; in respect to God, and the treatment which they received from him, (κατὰ Θεὸν,) they would live in spirit. Men judged them severely, and put them to death for their religion ; God gave them life, and saved them. By the one they were condemned in the flesh—so far as pain, and sorrow, and death could be inflicted on the body; by the other they were made to live in spirit—to be his, to live with him. The word *judged* here, I suppose, therefore, to refer to a sentence passed on them for their religion, consigning them to death for it. There is a *particle* in the original—μὶν, *indeed*—which has not been retained in the common translation, but which is quite important to the sense : 'that they might *indeed* be judged in the flesh, but live,' &c. The direct object or design of preaching the gospel to them was not that they might be condemned and put to death by man, but this was *indeed* or *in fact* one of the results in the way to a higher object. ¶ *But live according to God.* In respect to God, or so far as he was concerned. By *him* they would not be condemned. By *him* they would be made to live—to have the true life. The gospel was preached to them *in order* that so far as God was concerned, so far as their relation to him was concerned, so far as he would deal with them, they might *live.* The word *live* here seems to refer to the *whole life* that was the consequence of their being brought under the power of the gospel ; (a) that they might have *spiritual* life imparted to them ; (b) that they might live a life of holiness in this world ; (c) that they might live hereafter in the world to come. In one respect, and so far as men were concerned, their embracing the gospel was

followed by *death ;* in another respect, and so far as God was concerned, it was followed by *life.* The value and permanence of the latter, as contrasted with the former, seems to have been the thought in the mind of the apostle in encouraging those to whom he wrote to exercise patience in their trials, and to show fidelity in the service of their Master. ¶ *In the spirit.* In their souls, as contrasted with their body. In respect to that—to the flesh—they were put to death ; in respect to their souls—their higher natures—they were made truly to live. The argument, then, in this verse is, that in the trials which we endure on account of religion, we should remember the example of those who have suffered for it, and should remember why the gospel was preached to them. It was in a subordinate sense, indeed, that they might glorify God by a martyr's death ; but in a higher sense, that in this world and the next they might truly live. The flesh might suffer in consequence of their embracing the gospel that was preached to them, but the soul would live. Animated by their example, we should be willing to suffer in the flesh, if we may for ever live with God.

7. *But the end of all things is at hand.* This declaration is also evidently designed to support and encourage them in their trials, and to excite them to lead a holy life, by the assurance that the end of all things was drawing nigh. The phrase, ' the end of all things,' would naturally refer to the end of the world ; the winding up of human affairs. It is not absolutely certain, however, that the apostle used it here in this sense. It might mean that *so far as they were concerned,* or *in respect to them,* the end of all things drew near. Death is to each one the end of all things here below ; the end of his plans and of his interest in all that pertains to sublunary affairs. Even *if* the phrase did originally and properly refer to the end of the world, it is probable that it would soon come to denote the end of life in relation to the affairs of each individual ; since, if it was be-

lieved that the end of the world was near, it must consequently be believed that the termination of the earthly career of each one also drew near to a close. It is possible that the latter signification may have come ultimately to predominate, and that Peter may have used it in this sense without referring to the other. Comp. Notes on 2 Pet. iii. 8–14, for his views on this subject. See also Notes on Rom. xiii. 11, 12. The word rendered 'is at hand,' (ἤγγικε,) may refer either to proximity of *place* or *time*, and it always denotes that the place or the time referred to was not far off. In the former sense, as referring to nearness of *place*, see Matt. xxi. 1; Mark xi. 1; Luke vii. 12; xv. 25; xviii. 35, 40; xix. 29, 37, 41; xxiv. 15; Acts ix. 3; x. 9; xxi. 33; in the latter sense, as referring to *time* as being near, see Matt. iii. 2; iv. 17; x. 7; xxi. 34; xxvi. 45; Mark i. 15; Luke xxi. 20, 28; Acts vii. 17; Rom. xiii. 12; Heb. x. 25; 1 Pet. iv. 7. The idea as applied to *time*, or to *an approaching event*, is undoubtedly that it is *close by ;* it is not *far off;* it *will soon occur*. If this refers to the end of the world, it would mean that it was soon to occur; if to death, that this was an event which could not be far distant—perhaps an event that was to be hastened by their trials. The fact that it is such language as we now naturally address to men, saying that in respect to them 'the end of all things is at hand,' shows that it cannot be demonstrated that Peter did not use it in the same sense, and consequently that it cannot be proved that he meant to teach that the end of the world was then soon to occur. ¶ *Be ye therefore sober.* Serious; thoughtful; considerate. Let a fact of so much importance make a solemn impression on your mind, and preserve you from frivolity, levity, and vanity. See the word explained in the Notes on 1 Tim. iii. 2. ¶ *And watch unto prayer.* Be looking out for the end of all things in such a manner as to lead you to embrace all proper opportunities for prayer. Comp. Notes on Matt. xxvi. 39, 41. The word rendered *watch*, means to be sober, temperate, abstinent, especially in respect to wine; then watchful, circumspect. The important truth, then, taught by this passage is, that *the near approach of the end of all things should make us serious and prayerful.* I. The *end* may be regarded as approaching. This is true (1) of all things; of the winding up of the affairs of this world. It is constantly drawing nearer and nearer, and no one can tell how soon it will occur. The period is wisely hidden from the knowledge of all men, (see Matt. xxiv. 36; Acts i. 7,) among other reasons, in order that we may be always ready. No man can tell certainly at what time it will come; no man can demonstrate that it *may not* come at any moment. Everywhere in the Scriptures it is represented that it will come at an unexpected hour, as a thief in the night, and when the mass of men shall be slumbering in false security, Matt. xxiv. 37–39, 42, 43; 1 Thess. v. 2; Luke xxi. 34. (2.) It is near in relation to each one of us. The day of our death *cannot be* far distant; it *may be* very near. The very next thing that we may have to do, may be to lie down and die. II. It is proper that such a nearness of the end of all things should lead us to be serious, and to pray. (1.) *To be serious ;* for (*a*) the end of all things, in regard to us, is a most important event. It closes our probation. It fixes our character. It seals up our destiny. It makes all ever onward in character and doom unchangeable. (*b*) We are so made as to be serious in view of such events. God has so constituted the mind, that when we lose property, health, or friends; when we look into a grave, or are beset with dangers; when we are in the room of the dying or the dead, we are serious and thoughtful. It is unnatural *not* to be so. Levity and frivolity on such occasions are as contrary to all the finer and better feelings of our nature as they are to the precepts of the Bible. (*c*) There are *advantages* in seriousness of mind. It enables us to take better views of things, Eccl. vii. 2, 3. A calm, sober, sedate mind is the best for a contemplation of truth, and for looking at things as they are. (2.) *To be watchful unto prayer.* (*a*) Men naturally pray when they suppose that the end of all things is coming. An earthquake induces them to pray. An eclipse, or any other supposed prodigy.

8 And above all things have fervent charity among yourselves: for *a* charity [1] shall cover the multitude of sins.

9 Use hospitality *b* one to another, without grudging.

a 1 Co.13.7.   1 Or. *will.*   *b* He.13.2,16.

leads men to pray if they suppose the end of the world is drawing near. A shipwreck, or any other sudden danger, leads them to pray, Ps. cvii. 28. So men often pray in sickness who have never prayed in days of health. (*b*) It is *proper* to do it. Death is an important event, and in anticipation of such an event we should pray. Who can help us then but God? Who can conduct us through the dark valley but he? Who can save us amidst the wrecks and ruins of the universe but he? Who can dissipate our fears, and make us calm amidst the convulsions of dissolving nature, but God? As that event, therefore, may come upon us at any hour, it should lead us to constant prayer; and the more so because, *when* it comes, we may be in no state of mind to pray. The posture in which we should feel that it would be most appropriate that the messenger of death should find us, would be that of prayer.

8. *And above all things.* More than all things else. ¶ *Have fervent charity among yourselves.* Warm, ardent *love* towards each other. On the nature of *charity*, see Notes on 1 Cor. xiii. 1. The word rendered *fervent*, means properly *extended;* then intent, earnest, fervent. ¶ *For charity shall cover the multitude of sins.* Love to another shall so cover or hide a great many imperfections in him, that you will not notice them. This passage is quoted from Prov. x. 12: 'Love covereth all sins.' For the *truth* of it we have only to appeal to the experience of every one. (*a*) True love to another makes us kind to his imperfections, charitable towards his faults, and often blind even to the existence of faults. We *would not* see the imperfections of those whom we love; and our attachment for what we esteem their real excellencies, makes us insensible to their errors. (*b*) If we love them we are ready to cover over their faults, even those which we may see in them. Of love the Christian poet says—

'Tis gentle, delicate, and kind,
To faults compassionate or blind.

The passage before us is not the same in signification as that in James v. 20, ' He which converteth the sinner from the error of his way shall save a soul from death, and shall hide a multitude of sins.' See Notes on that passage. That passage means, that by the *conversion* of another the sins of him who is converted shall be covered over, or not brought to judgment for condemnation; that is, they shall be covered over so far as *God* is concerned:—this passage means that, under the influence of love, the sins of another shall be covered over so far as *we* are concerned; that is, they shall be unobserved or forgiven. The language here used does not mean, as the Romanists maintain, that ' charity shall procure us pardon for a multitude of sins;' for, besides that such a doctrine is contrary to the uniform teachings of the Scriptures elsewhere, it is a departure from the obvious meaning of the passage. The *subject* on which the apostle is treating is the advantage of *love* in our conduct towards others, and this he enforces by saying that it will make us kind to their imperfections, and lead us to overlook their faults. It is nowhere taught in the Scriptures that our ' charity' to others will be an *atonement* or *expiation* for our own offences. If it could be so, the atonement made by Christ would have been unnecessary. Love, however, is of inestimable value in the treatment of others; and imperfect as we are, and liable to go astray, we all have occasion to cast ourselves on the charity of our brethren, and to avail ourselves much and often of that 'love which covers over *a multitude* of sins.'

9. *Use hospitality one to another.* On the duty of hospitality, see Notes on Rom. xii. 13; Heb. xiii. 2. ¶ *Without grudging.* Greek, 'without *murmurs;*' that is, without complaining of the hardship of doing it; of the time, and expense, and trouble required in doing

10 As every man hath received *a* the gift, *even so* minister the same one to another, as good stewards *b* of the manifold grace of God.

11 If any man speak, *let him speak* as the oracles of God; if any man minister, *let him do it* as of the ability which God giveth: that God in all *c* things may be glorified through Jesus Christ, to *d* whom be praise and dominion for ever and ever. Amen.

a Ro.12.6-8.   *b* Lu.12.42.   *c* 1 Co.10.31.   *d* Re.1.6.

it. The idea of *grudging*, in the common sense of that word—that is, of doing it *unwillingly*, or regretting the expense, and considering it as ill-bestowed, or as not producing an equivalent of any kind—is not exactly the idea here. It is that we are to do it without murmuring or complaining. It greatly enhances the value of hospitality, that it be done on our part with entire cheerfulness. One of the duties involved in it is to make a guest happy; and this can be done in no other way than by showing him that he is welcome.

10. *As every man hath received the gift.* The word rendered *the gift*, (χάρισμα,) in the Greek, without the article, means endowment of any kind, but especially that conferred by the Holy Spirit. Here it seems to refer to every kind of endowment by which we can do good to others; especially every kind of qualification furnished by religion by which we can help others. It does not refer here particularly to the ministry of the word—though it is applicable to that, and includes that—but to all the gifts and graces by which we can contribute to the welfare of others. All this is regarded as a gift, or *charisma*, of God. It is not owing to ourselves, but is to be traced to him. See the word explained in the Notes on 1 Tim. iv. 14. ¶ *Even so minister the same one to another.* In anything by which you can benefit another. Regard what you have and they have not as a *gift* bestowed upon you by God for the common good, and be ready to impart it as the wants of others require. The word *minister* here (διακονοῦντες) would refer to any kind of ministering, whether by counsel, by advice, by the supply of the wants of the poor, or by preaching. It has here no reference to any one of these exclusively; but means, that in whatever God has favoured us more than others, we should be ready to *minister* to their wants. See 2 Tim. i. 18; 2 Cor. iii. 3; viii. 19, 20. ¶ *As good stewards.* Regarding yourselves as the mere *stewards* of God; that is, as appointed by him to do this work for him, and intrusted by him with what is needful to benefit others. *He* intends to do them good, but he means to do it through your instrumentality, and has intrusted to you as a steward what he designed to confer on them. This is the true idea, in respect to any special endowments of talent, property, or grace, which we may have received from God. Comp. Notes on 1 Cor. iv. 1, 2; Luke xvi. 1, 2, 8. ¶ *Of the manifold grace of God.* The grace or favour of God evinced in many ways, or by a variety of gifts. His favours are not confined to one single thing; as, for example, to talent for doing good by preaching; but are extended to a great many things by which we may do good to others—influence, property, reputation, wisdom, experience. All these are to be regarded as his gifts; all to be employed in doing good to others as we have opportunity.

11. *If any man speak.* As a preacher, referring here particularly to the office of the ministry. ¶ Let him speak *as the oracles of God.* As the oracles of God speak; to wit, in accordance with the truth which God has revealed, and with an impressive sense of the responsibility of delivering a message from him. The word rendered *oracles* (λόγια) means, properly, something *spoken* or *uttered*; then anything uttered by God —a Divine communication—a revelation. See Notes, Rom. iii. 2; Heb. v. 12. See the general duty here inculcated illustrated at length in the Notes on Rom. xii. 6-8. The passage here has a strong resemblance to the one in Romans. ¶ *If any man minister.* διακονεῖ. This may refer either, so far as the *word* is concerned, to the office

12 Beloved, think it not strange concerning the fiery ^a trial which is to try you, as though some strange thing happened unto you:

13 But rejoice, ^b inasmuch as ye are partakers of Christ's sufferings; that, when ^c his glory shall be re-

a 1 Co.3.13.   b Ja.1.2.   c 2 Ti.2.12.   d Mat.5.11.

vealed, ye may be glad also with exceeding joy.

14 If ^d ye be reproached for the name of Christ, happy *are ye;* for the spirit of glory and of God resteth upon you: on their part he is evil spoken of, but on your part he is glorified.

of a deacon, or to *any* service which one renders to another. See ver. 10. The word commonly refers to service in general; to attendance on another, or to aid rendered to another; to the distribution of alms, &c. It seems probable that the word here does not refer to the office of a *deacon* as such, because the peculiarity of that office was to take charge of the poor of the church, and of the funds provided for them, (see Acts vi. 2, 3;) but the apostle here says that they to whom he referred should 'minister as of the *ability which God giveth,*' which seems to imply that it was rather to distribute what was their own, than what was committed to them by the church. The word may refer to any aid which we render to others in the church, as distributing alms, attending on the sick, &c. Comp. Notes, Rom. xii. 7, 8. ¶ *As of the ability which God giveth.* In regard to property, talent, strength, influence, &c. This is the limit of all obligation. No one is bound to go *beyond* his ability; every one is required to *come up* to it. Comp. Mark xiv. 8; Luke xvii. 10. ¶ *That God in all things may be glorified.* That he may be honoured; to wit, by our doing all the good we can to others, and thus showing the power of his religion. See Notes, 1 Cor. x. 31. ¶ *Through Jesus Christ.* That is, as the medium through whom all those holy influences come by which God is honoured. ¶ *To whom.* That is, to God; for he is the main subject of the sentence. The apostle says that in all things he is to be glorified by us, and then adds in this doxology that he is *worthy* to be thus honoured. Comp. Rev. i. 6; Notes, 2 Tim. iv. 18. Many, however, suppose that the reference here is to the Son of God. That it would be true of him, and appropriate, see Notes, Rom. ix. 5.

12. *Beloved, think it not strange.* Do

not consider it as anything which you had no reason to expect; as anything which may not happen to others also. ¶ *Concerning the fiery trial which is to try you.* Referring, doubtless, to some severe persecution which was then impending. We have not the means of determining precisely what this was. The word rendered *fiery trial* (πυρώσει) occurs only here and in Rev. xviii. 9, 18; in both of which latter places it is rendered *burning.* It means, properly, *a being on fire, burning, conflagration;* and then any severe trial. It cannot be demonstrated from this word that they were literally to suffer by *fire,* but it is clear that some heavy calamity was before them. ¶ *As though some strange thing happened unto you.* Something unusual; something which did not occur to others.

13. *But rejoice, inasmuch as ye are partakers of Christ's sufferings.* That is, sufferings of the same kind that he endured, and inflicted for the same reasons. Comp. Col. i. 24; James i. 2; Notes, Matt. v. 12. The meaning here is, that they were to regard it as a matter of rejoicing that they were identified with Christ, even in suffering. See this sentiment illustrated at length in the Notes on Phil. iii. 10. ¶ *That, when his glory shall be revealed.* At the day of judgment. See Notes, Matt. xxvi. 30. ¶ *Ye may be glad also with exceeding joy.* Being admitted to the rewards which he will then confer on his people. Comp. 1 Thess. ii. 19. Every good man will have joy when, immediately at death, he is received into the presence of his Saviour; but his joy will be complete only when, in the presence of assembled worlds, he shall hear the sentence which shall confirm him in happiness for ever.

14. *If ye be reproached for the name of Christ, happy are ye.* That is, in

15 But let none of you suffer as a murderer, or *as* a thief, or *as* an evil doer, or as a busy-body in other men's matters.

16 Yet if *any man suffer* as a Christian, let him not be ashamed ; but let him glorify God on this behalf.

his cause, or on his account. See Notes, Matt. v. 11. The sense of the word *happy* here is the same as *blessed* in Matt. v. 3–5, &c. It means that they were to regard their condition or lot as a blessed one; not that they would find personal and positive enjoyment on being reproached and vilified. It would be a blessed condition, because it would be like that of their Saviour; would show that they were his friends ; would be accompanied with rich spiritual influences in the present world; and would be followed by the rewards of heaven. ¶ *For the spirit of glory and of God resteth upon you.* The glorious and Divine Spirit. There is no doubt that there is reference here to the Holy Spirit ; and the meaning is, that they might expect that that Spirit would rest upon them, or abide with them, if they were persecuted for the cause of Christ. There may be some allusion here, in the language, to the fact that the Spirit of God descended and abode on the Saviour at his baptism, (John i. 33;) and, in like manner, they might hope to have the same Spirit resting on them. The essential idea is, that, if they were called to suffer in the cause of the Redeemer, they would not be left or forsaken. They might hope that God would impart his Spirit to them in proportion to their sufferings in behalf of religion, and that they would have augmented joy and peace. This is doubtless the case with those who suffer persecution, and this is the secret reason why they are so sustained in their trials. Their persecutions are made the reason of a much more copious effusion of the Spirit on their souls. The same principle applies, doubtless, to all the forms of trial which the children of God pass through ; and in sickness, bereavement, loss of property, disappointment in their worldly plans, and death itself, they may hope that larger measures of the Spirit's influences will rest upon them. Hence it is often gain to the believer to suffer. ¶ *On their part.* So far as they are

concerned ; or by them. ¶ *He is evil spoken of.* That is, the Holy Spirit. They only *blaspheme* him, (Greek ;) they reproach his sacred influences by their treatment of you and your religion. ¶ *But on your part he is glorified.* By your manner of speaking of him, and by the honour done to him in the patience evinced in your trials, and in your purity of life.

15. *But let none of you suffer as a murderer.* If you must be called to suffer, see that it be not for crime. Comp. Notes, chap. iii. 14, 17. They were to be careful that their sufferings were brought upon them only in consequence of their religion, and not because any crime could be laid to their charge. If even such charges were brought against them, there should be no pretext furnished for them by their lives. ¶ *As an evil doer.* As a wicked man ; or as guilty of injustice and wrong towards others. ¶ *Or as a busy-body in other men's matters.* The Greek word here used (ἀλλοτριοεπίσκοπος) occurs nowhere else in the New Testament. It means, properly, an inspector of strange things, or of the things of others. Professor Robinson (*Lex.*) supposes that the word *may* refer to one who is 'a director of heathenism;' but the more obvious signification, and the one commonly adopted, is that which occurs in our translation —*one who busies himself with what does not concern him;* that is, one who pries into the affairs of another ; who attempts to control or direct them as if they were his own. In respect to the-vice here condemned, see Notes, Phil. ii. 4. Comp. 2 Thess. iii. 11, and 1 Tim. v. 13.

16. *Yet if* any man suffer *as a Christian.* Because he is a Christian ; if he is persecuted on account of his religion. This was often done, and they had reason to expect that it might occur in their own case. Comp. Notes, chap. iii. 17. On the import of the word *Christian,* and the reasons why the name was given to the disciples of the Lord Jesus, see Notes, Acts xi. 26. ¶ *Let him not be*

17 For the time *is come* that judg- | ment must begin *a* at the house of

a Is.10.12; Je.49.12; Eze.9.6.

God: and if *it* first *begin* at us, what shall the end *be* of them that obey not the gospel of God ?

ashamed. (1.) Ashamed of religion so as to refuse to suffer on account of it. (2.) Ashamed that he *is* despised and maltreated. He is to regard his religion as every way honourable, and all that fairly results from it in time and eternity as in every respect desirable. He is not to be ashamed to be called a Christian; he is not to be ashamed of the doctrines taught by his religion; he is not to be ashamed of the Saviour whom he professes to love; he is not to be ashamed of the society and fellowship of those who are true Christians, poor and despised though they may be; he is not to be ashamed to perform any of the duties demanded by his religion; he is not to be ashamed to have his name cast out, and himself subjected to reproach and scorn. A man should be ashamed only of that which is wrong. He should glory in that which is right, whatever may be the consequences to himself. Christians now, though not subjected to open persecution, are frequently reproached by the world on account of their religion; and though the rack may not be employed, and the fires of martyrdom are not enkindled, yet it is often true that one who is a believer is called to 'suffer as a Christian.' He may be reviled and despised. His views may be regarded as bigoted, narrow, severe. Opprobrious epithets, on account of his opinions, may be applied to him. His former friends and companions may leave him because he has become a Christian. A wicked father, or a gay and worldly mother, may oppose a child, or a husband may revile a wife, on account of their religion. In all these cases, the same spirit essentially is required which was enjoined on the early Christian martyrs. We are never to be ashamed of our religion, whatever results may follow from our attachment to it. Comp. Notes, Rom. i. 16. ¶ *But let him glorify God on this behalf.* Let him praise God that he is deemed not unworthy to suffer in such a cause. It is a matter of thankfulness (1.) that they may have *this* evidence that they

are true Christians; (2,) that they may desire the advantages which may result from suffering as Christ did, and in his cause. See Notes, Acts v. 41, where the sentiment here expressed is fully illustrated. Comp. Notes, Phil. iii. 10 ; Col. i. 24.

17. *For the time* is come. That is, this is now to be expected. There is reason to think that this trial will now occur, and there is a propriety that it should be made. Probably the apostle referred to some indications then apparent that this was about to take place. ¶ *That judgment must begin.* The word *judgment* here (κρίμα) seems to mean *the severe trial which would determine character.* It refers to such calamities as would settle the question whether there was any religion, or would test the value of that which was professed. It was to '*begin*' at the house of God, or be applied to the church first, in order that the nature and worth of religion might be seen. The reference is, doubtless, to some fearful calamity which would primarily fall on the 'house of God;' that is, to some form of persecution which was to be let loose upon the church. ¶ *At the house of God.* Benson, Bloomfield, and many others, suppose that this refers to the *Jews,* and to the calamities that were to come around the temple and the holy city about to be destroyed. But the more obvious reference is to *Christians,* spoken of as the *house* or *family* of God. There is probably in the language here an allusion to Ezek. ix. 6 : ' Slay utterly old and young, both maids, and little children, and women; *and begin at my sanctuary.*' Comp. Jer. xxv. 29. But the language used here by the apostle does not denote literally the temple, or the Jews, but those who were in his time regarded as the people of God— Christians—the church. So the phrase (בֵּית יְהֹוָה) *house of Jehovah* is used to denote the family or people of God, Numb. xii. 7; Hos. viii. 1. Comp. also 1 Tim. iii. 15, and the Note on that verse. The sense here is, therefore, that

18 And if *a* the righteous scarcely be saved, where shall the ungodly and the sinner appear?

a Je.25.29; Lu.23.31.

the series of calamities referred to were to commence with the church, or were to come first upon the people of God. Schoettgen here aptly quotes a passage from the writings of the Rabbins : 'Punishments never come into the world unless the wicked are in it; but they do not begin unless they commence first with the righteous.' ¶ *And if it first begin at us, what shall the end be of them that obey not the gospel of God?* If God brings such trials upon us who have obeyed his gospel, what have we not reason to suppose he will bring upon those who are yet in their sins? And if we are selected first as the objects of this visitation, if there is that in us which requires such a method of dealing, what are we to suppose will occur in the end with those who make no pretensions to religion, but are yet living in open transgression? The sentiment is, that if God deals thus strictly with his people ; if there is that in them which makes the visitations of his judgment proper on them, there is a certainty that they who are not his people, but who live in iniquity, will in the end be overwhelmed with the tokens of severer wrath. Their punishment hereafter will be certain ; and who can tell what will be the measure of its severity? Every wicked man, when he sees the trials which God brings upon his own people, should tremble under the apprehension of the deeper calamity which will hereafter come upon himself. We may remark, (1.) that the judgments which God brings upon his own people make it certain that the wicked will be punished. If he does not spare his own people, why should he spare others? (2.) The punishment of the wicked is merely delayed. It *begins* at the house of God. Christians are tried, and are recalled from their wanderings, and are prepared by discipline for the heavenly world. The punishment of the wicked is often delayed to a future world, and in this life they have almost uninterrupted prosperity, but in the end it will be certain. See Psa. lxxiii. 1–19. The punishment will come *in the end.* It

cannot be evaded. Sooner or later justice requires that the wicked should be visited with the expressions of Divine displeasure on account of sin, and in the future world there will be ample time for the infliction of all the punishment which they deserve.

18. *And if the righteous scarcely be saved.* If they are saved *with difficulty.* The word here used (μόλις) occurs in the following places : Acts xiv. 18, '*scarce* restrained they the people;' xxvii. 7, 'and *scarce* were come over against Cnidus ;' ver. 8, 'and *hardly* passing it;' ver. 16, 'we had much work to come by the boat'—literally, we were able *with difficulty* to get the boat; Rom. v. 7, '*scarcely* for a righteous man will one die ;' and in the passage before us. The word implies that there is some difficulty, or obstruction, so that the thing came very near not to happen, or so that there was much risk about it. Compare Luke xiii. 31. The apostle in this passage seems to have had his eye on a verse in Proverbs, (xi. 31,) and he has merely expanded and illustrated it : 'Behold, the righteous shall be recompensed in the earth : much more the wicked and the sinner.' By the question which he employs, he *admits* that the righteous are saved with difficulty, or that there are perils which jeopard their salvation, and which are of such a kind as to make it very near not to happen. They *would* indeed be saved, but it would be in such a manner as to show that the circumstances were such as to render it, to human appearances, doubtful and problematical. This peril may have arisen from many circumstances : (*a*) The difficulty of forming a plan of salvation, involving a degree of wisdom wholly beyond that of man, and of such a character that beforehand it would have been problematical and doubtful whether it could be. There was but one way in which it could be done. But what human wisdom could have devised that, or thought of it? There was but one being who could save. But who would have supposed that the Son of God would have been willing to become a man, and

19 Wherefore, let them that suffer according to the will of God, commit *a* the keeping of their souls to *him* in well-doing, as unto a faithful Creator.

to die on a cross to do it? If *he* had been unwilling to come and die, the righteous could not have been saved. (*b*) The difficulty of bringing those who are saved to a willingness to accept of salvation. All were disposed alike to reject it; and there were many obstacles in the human heart, arising from pride, and selfishness, and unbelief, and the love of sin, which must be overcome before any would accept of the offer of mercy. There was but one agent who could overcome these things, and induce any of the race to embrace the gospel— the Holy Spirit. But who could have anticipated that the Spirit of God would have undertaken to renew and sanctify the polluted human heart? Yet, if *he* had failed, there could have been no salvation for any. (*c*) The difficulty of keeping them from falling away amidst the temptations and allurements of the world. Often it seems to be wholly doubtful whether those who have been converted *will be* kept to eternal life. They have so little religion; they yield so readily to temptation; they conform so much to the world; they have so little strength to bear up under trials, that it seems as if there was no power to preserve them and bring them to heaven. They are saved when they seemed *almost* ready to yield everything. (*d*) The difficulty of rescuing them from the power of the great enemy of souls. The adversary has vast power, and he *means*, if he can, to destroy those who are the children of God. Often they are in most imminent danger, and it seems to be a question of doubtful issue whether they will not be entirely overcome, and perish. It is no small matter to rescue a soul from the dominion of Satan, and to bring it to heaven, so that it shall be eternally safe. Through the internal struggles and the outward conflicts of life, it seems often a matter of doubt whether with all their effort they will be saved; and when they *are* saved, they will feel that they have been rescued from thousands of dangers, and that there has been many a time when they

have stood on the very verge of ruin, and when, to human appearances, it was scarcely possible that they could be saved. ¶ *Where shall the ungodly and the sinner appear?* What hope is there of their salvation? The meaning is, that they would certainly perish; and the doctrine in the passage is, that the fact that the righteous are saved with so much difficulty is proof that the wicked will not be saved at all. This follows, because (*a*) there is the same difficulty in their salvation which there was in the salvation of those who became righteous; the same difficulty arising from the love of sin, the hardness of the heart, and the arts and power of the adversary. (*b*) No one can be saved without effort, and in fact the righteous are saved only by constant and strenuous effort on their part. But the wicked make no effort for their own salvation. They make use of no means for it; they put forth no exertions to obtain it; they do not make it a part of their plan of life. How, then, can they be saved? But *where* will they appear? I answer, (*a*) they will appear *somewhere*. They will not cease to exist when they pass away from this world. Not one of them will be annihilated; and though they vanish from the earth, and will be seen here no more, yet they will make their appearance in some other part of the universe. (*b*) They will appear at the judgment-seat, as all others will, to receive their sentence according to the deeds done in the body. It follows from this, (1.) that the wicked will certainly be destroyed. If the righteous are *scarcely* saved, how can *they* be? (2.) That there will be a state of future punishment, for this refers to what is to occur in the future world. (3.) That the punishment of the wicked will be eternal, for it is the opposite of what is meant by *saved*. The time will never come when it will be said that they are *saved!* But if so, their punishment must be eternal!

19. *Wherefore, let them that suffer according to the will of God.* That is,

CHAPTER V.

THE elders which are among you I exhort, who am also an elder, and a witness of the sufferings of Christ, and also a partaker of the glory *a* that shall be revealed:

a Ro.8.17,18.

---

who endure the kind of sufferings that he, by his Providence, shall appoint. Comp. chap. iii. 17; iv. 15, 16. ¶ *Commit the keeping of their souls* to him. Since there is so much danger; since there is no one else that can keep them; and since he is a Being so faithful, let them commit all their interests to him. Comp. Psa. xxxvii. 5. The word *souls* here (ψυχὰς) is equivalent to *themselves.* They were to leave everything in his hand, faithfully performing every duty, and not being anxious for the result. ¶ *In well doing.* Constantly doing good, or seeking to perform every duty in a proper manner. *Their* business was always to do right; the result was to be left with God. A man who is engaged always in well-doing, may safely commit all his interest to God. ¶ *As unto a faithful Creator.* God may be trusted, or confided in, in all his attributes, and in all the relations which he sustains as Creator, Redeemer, Moral Governor, and Judge. In these, and in all other respects, we may come before him with confidence, and put unwavering trust in him. As *Creator* particularly; as one who has brought us, and all creatures and things into being, we may be sure that he will be 'faithful' to the design which he had in view. From that design he will never depart until it is fully accomplished. He abandons no purpose which he has formed, and we may be assured that he will faithfully pursue it to the end. As *our* Creator we may come to him, and look to him for his protection and care. He made us. He had a design in our creation. He so endowed us that we might live for ever, and so that we might honour and enjoy him. He did not create us that we *might be* miserable; nor does he wish that we *should be.* He formed us in such a way that, if we choose, we may be eternally happy. In that path in which he has appointed us to go, if we pursue it, we may be sure of his aid and protection. If we really aim to accomplish the purposes for which we were

made, we may be certain that he will show himself to be a '*faithful* Creator;' one in whom we may always confide. And even though we have wandered from him, and have long forgotten why we were made, and have loved and served the creature more than the Creator, we may be sure, if we will return to him, that he will not forget the design for which he originally made us. *As* our Creator we may still confide in him. Redeemed by the blood of his Son, and renewed by his Spirit after the image of Him who created us, we may still go to him as our Creator, and may pray that even yet the high and noble ends for which we were made may be accomplished in us. Doing this, we shall find him as true to that purpose as though we had never sinned.

CHAPTER V.

ANALYSIS OF THE CHAPTER.

THIS chapter embraces the following subjects: I. An exhortation to the elders of the churches to be faithful to the flocks committed to their charge, vers. 1–4. II. An exhortation to the younger members of the church to evince all proper submission to those who were older; to occupy the station in which they were placed with a becoming spirit, casting all their care on God, vers. 5–7. III. An exhortation to be sober and vigilant, in view of the dangers which beset them, and the arts and power of their great adversary, the devil, and especially to bear with patience the trials to which they were subjected, in common with their Christian brethren elsewhere, vers. 8–11. IV. Salutations, vers. 12–14.

1. *The elders which are among you I exhort.* The word *elder* means, properly, one who is old; but it is frequently used in the New Testament as applicable to the officers of the church; probably because aged persons were at first commonly appointed to these offices. See Notes on Acts xi. 30; xiv. 23; xv. 2. There is evidently an allusion here to the fact that such persons were selected

2 Feed *a* the flock of God ¹ which is among you, taking the oversight *thereof*, not by constraint, but will-

ingly ; *b* not for filthy lucre, *c* but of a ready mind;

a Jn.21.15-17; Ac.20.28.   1 Or. *as much as in you le.*
b 1Co.9.17.   c 1 Ti.3.3,8.

on account of their *age*, because in the following verses (4, seq.) the apostle addresses particularly *the younger.* It is worthy of remark, that he here refers only to one class of ministers. He does not speak of three 'orders,' of 'bishops, priests, and deacons;' and the evidence from the passage here is quite strong that there *were* no such orders in the churches of Asia Minor, to which this epistle was directed. It is also worthy of remark, that the word '*exhort*' is here used. The language which Peter uses is not that of stern and arbitrary command ; it is that of kind and mild Christian exhortation. Comp. Notes on Philemon, 8, 9. ¶ *Who am also an elder.* Gr., 'a fellow-presbyter,' (συμπρεσβύτερος.) This word occurs nowhere else in the New Testament. It means that he was a co-presbyter with them ; and he makes this one of the grounds of his exhortation to them. He does not put it on the ground of his apostolical authority; or urge it because he was the 'vicegerent of Christ ;' or because he was the head of the church ; or because he had any pre-eminence over others in any way. Would he have used this language if he had been the 'head of the church' on earth ? Would he if he supposed that the distinction between apostles and other ministers was to be perpetuated? Would he if he believed that there were to be distinct orders of clergy ? The whole drift of this passage is adverse to such a supposition. ¶ *And a witness of the sufferings of Christ.* Peter was indeed a witness of the sufferings of Christ when on his trial, and doubtless also when he was scourged and mocked, and when he was crucified. After his denial of his Lord, he wept bitterly, and evidently then followed him to the place where he was crucified, and, in company with others, observed with painful solicitude the last agonies of his Saviour. It is not, so far as I know, expressly said in the Gospels that *Peter* was present at the crucifixion of the Saviour ; but it is said (Luke xxiii. 49) that 'all

his acquaintance, and the women that followed him from Galilee, stood afar off, beholding these things,' and nothing is more probable than that Peter was among them. His warm attachment to his Master, and his recent bitter repentance for having denied him, would lead him to follow him to the place of his death ; for after the painful act of denying him he would not be likely to expose himself to the charge of neglect, or of any want of love again. His own solemn declaration here makes it certain that he was present. He alludes to it now, evidently because it qualified him to exhort those whom he addressed. It would be natural to regard with peculiar respect one who had actually seen the Saviour in his last agony, and nothing would be more impressive than an exhortation falling from the lips of such a man. A son would be likely to listen with great respect to *any* suggestions which should be made by one who had seen his father or mother die. The impression which Peter had of that scene he would desire to have transferred to those whom he addressed, that by a lively view of the sufferings of their Saviour they might be excited to fidelity in his cause. ¶ *And a partaker of the glory that shall be revealed.* Another reason to make his exhortation impressive and solemn. He felt that he was an heir of life. He was about to partake of the glories of heaven. Looking forward, as they did also, to the blessed world before him and them, he had a right to exhort them to the faithful performance of duty. Any one, who is himself an heir of salvation, may appropriately exhort his fellow-Christians to fidelity in the sevice of their common Lord.

2. *Feed the flock of God.* Discharge the duties of a shepherd towards the flock. On the word *feed*, see Notes on John xxi. 15. It is a word which Peter would be likely to remember, from the solemn manner in which the injunction to perform the duty was laid on him by the Saviour. The direction means to

3 Neither as ¹being lords over | God's heritage, but being ensam-
1 Or, *overruling.*　　　　　a 1 Ti.4.12. | ples *ᵃ*to the flock.

take such an oversight of the church as a shepherd is accustomed to take of his flock. See Notes on John x. 1–16. ¶ *Which is among you.* Marg., *as much as in you is.* The translation in the text is the more correct. It means the churches which were among them, or over which they were called to preside. ¶ *Taking the oversight* thereof —ἐπισκοποῦντες. The fair translation of this word is, *discharging the episcopal office;* and the word implies all that is ever implied by the word *bishop* in the New Testament. This idea should have been expressed in the translation. The meaning is not merely *to take the oversight*—for that might be done in a subordinate sense by any one in office ; but it is to take such an oversight as is implied in the episcopate, or by the word *bishop.* The words *episcopate, episcopal,* and *episcopacy,* are merely the Greek word used here and its correlatives transferred to our language. The sense is that of overseeing; taking the oversight of ; looking after, as of a flock ; and the word has originally no reference to what is now spoken of as peculiarly the *episcopal* office. It is a word strictly applicable to *any* minister of religion, or officer of a church. In the passage before us this duty was to be performed by those who, in ver. 1, are called *presbyters,* or *elders;* and this is one of the numerous passages in the New Testament which prove that all that is. properly implied in the performance of the episcopal functions pertained to those who were called *presbyters,* or *elders.* If so, there was no higher grade of ministers to which the peculiar duties of the episcopate were to be intrusted ; that is, there was no class of officers corresponding to those who are now called *bishops.* Comp. Notes, Acts xx. 28. ¶ *Not by constraint, but willingly.* Not as if you felt that a heavy yoke was imposed on you, or a burden from which you would gladly be discharged. Go cheerfully to your duty as a work which you love, and act like a freeman in it, and not as a slave. Arduous are the labours of the ministry, yet there is no work on earth in which a man can and

should labour more cheerfully. ¶ *Not for filthy lucre.* Shameful or dishonourable gain. Notes, 1 Tim. iii. 3. ¶ *But of a ready mind.* Cheerfully, promptly. We are to labour in this work, not under the influence of the desire of gain, but from the promptings of love. There is all the difference conceivable between one who does a thing because he is *paid* for it, and one who does it from *love*—between, for example, the manner in which one attends on us when we are sick who *loves* us, and one who is merely *hired* to do it. Such a difference is there in the spirit with which one who is actuated by mercenary motives, and one whose heart is in the work, will engage in the ministry.

3. *Neither as being lords.* Marg., *overruling.* The word here used (κατακυριεύω) is rendered *exercise dominion over,* in Matt. xx. 25 ; *exercise lordship over,* in Mark x. 42 ; and *overcame,* in Acts xix. 16. It does not elsewhere occur in the New Testament. It refers properly to that kind of jurisdiction which civil rulers or magistrates exercise. This is an exercise of *authority,* as contradistinguished from the influence of reason, persuasion, and example. The latter pertains to the ministers of religion ; the former is forbidden to them. Their dominion is not to be that of temporal lordship; it is to be that of love and truth. This command would prohibit all assumption of temporal power by the ministers of religion, and all conferring of titles of nobility on those who are preachers of the gospel. It needs scarcely to be said that it has been very little regarded in the church. - ¶ *Over God's heritage*—τῶν κλήρων. Vulgate, *in cleris*—over the clergy. The Greek word here (κλῆρος—*kleros*) is that from which the word *clergy* has been derived ; and some have interpreted it here as referring to the *clergy,* that is, to priests and deacons who are under the authority of a bishop. Such an interpretation, however, would hardly be adopted now. The word means properly, (*a,*) *a lot, die,* anything used in determining chances; (*b*) *a part* or *portion,* such as is assigned by lot ; hence (*c*) an *office* to which one

4 And when the chief ^a Shepherd shall appear, ye shall receive a crown ^b of glory that fadeth not away.

5 Likewise, ye younger, submit

<small>a He.13.20.   b 2 Ti.4.8.</small>

yourselves unto the elder: yea, all ^c of you be subject one to another, and be clothed with humility: for God ^d resisteth the proud, and giveth grace to the humble.

<small>c Ep.5.21.   d Ja.4.6.</small>

---

is designated or appointed, by lot or otherwise; and (d) in general any possession or heritage, Acts xxvi. 18; Col. i. 12. The meaning here is, 'not lording it over the possessions or the heritage of God.' The reference is, undoubtedly, to the church, as that which is peculiarly his property; his own in the world. Whitby and others suppose that it refers to the possessions or property of the church; Doddridge explains it—'not assuming dominion over those who fall to your lot,' supposing it to mean that they were not to domineer over the particular congregations committed by Providence to their care. But the other interpretation is most in accordance with the usual meaning of the word. ¶ *But being ensamples to the flock.* Examples. See Notes, 1 Tim. iv. 12. Peter has drawn here with great beauty, the appropriate character of the ministers of the gospel, and described the spirit with which they should be actuated in the discharge of the duties of their office. But how different it is from the character of many who have claimed to be ministers of religion; and especially how different from that corrupt communion which professes in a special manner to recognise Peter as the head, and the vicegerent of Christ. It is well remarked by Benson on this passage, that 'the church of Rome could not well have acted more directly contrary to this injunction of St. Peter's if she had studied to disobey it, and to form herself upon a rule that should be the reverse of this.'

4. *And when the chief Shepherd shall appear.* The prince of the pastors—the Lord Jesus Christ. 'Peter, in the passage above, ranks himself with the *elders;* here he ranks Christ himself with the *pastors.'—Benson.* See Notes, chap. ii. 25. Comp. Heb. xiii. 20. ¶ *Ye shall receive a crown of glory.* A glorious crown or diadem. Comp. Notes, 2 Tim. iv. 8. ¶ *That fadeth not away.* This is essentially the same word, though somewhat different in form, which occurs

in chap. i. 4. See Notes on that verse. The word occurs nowhere else in the New Testament. Comp. Notes, 1 Cor. ix. 25.

5. *Likewise, ye younger.* All younger persons of either sex. ¶ *Submit yourselves unto the elder.* That is, with the respect due to their age, and to the offices which they sustain. There is here, probably, a particular reference to those who sustained the *office* of elders or teachers, as the same word is used here which occurs in ver. 1. As there was an allusion in that verse, by the use of the word, to *age,* so there is in this verse to the fact that they sustained an *office* in the church. The general duty, however, is here implied, as it is everywhere in the Bible, that all suitable respect is to be shown to the aged. Comp. Lev. xix. 32; 1 Tim. v. 1; Acts xxiii. 4; 2 Pet. ii. 9. ¶ *Yea, all of you be subject one to another.* In your proper ranks and relations. You are not to attempt to lord it over one another, but are to treat each other with deference and respect. See Notes, Eph. v. 21; Phil. ii. 3. ¶ *And be clothed with humility.* The word here rendered *be clothed* (ἐγκομβόωσαι) occurs nowhere else in the New Testament. It is derived from κόμβος—a strip, string, or loop to fasten a garment; and then the word refers to a garment that was fastened with strings. The word ἐγκόμβωμα (egkomboma) refers particularly to a long white apron, or outer garment, that was commonly worn by slaves. See *Rob. Lex.; Passow, Lex.* There is, therefore, peculiar force in the use of this word here, as denoting an humble mind. They were to be willing to take any place, and to perform any office, however humble, in order to serve and benefit others. They were not to assume a style and dignity of state and authority, as if they would lord it over others, or as if they were better than others; but they were to be willing to occupy any station, however humble, by which they might honour God. It is known

6 Humble *a* yourselves therefore under the mighty hand of God, that he may exalt you in due time:

7 Casting *b* all your care upon him; for he careth for you.

a Is. 57.15.   *b* Ps. 55.22.

that not a few of the early Christians actually sold themselves as slaves, in order that they might preach the gospel to those who were in bondage. The sense here is, they were to put on humility as a garment bound fast to them, as a servant bound fast to him the apron that was significant of his station. Comp. Col. iii. 13. It is not unusual in the Scriptures, as well as in other writings, to compare the virtues with articles of apparel; as that with which we are clothed, or in which we are seen by others. Comp. Isa. xi. 5; lix. 17. ¶ *For God resisteth the proud*, &c. This passage is quoted from the Greek translation in Prov. iii. 34. See it explained in the Notes on James iv. 6, where it is also quoted.

6. *Humble yourselves therefore.* Be willing to take a low place—a place such as becomes you. Do not arrogate to yourselves what does not belong to you; do not evince pride and haughtiness in your manner; do not exalt yourselves above others. See Notes, Luke xiv. 7–11. Comp. Prov. xv. 33; xviii. 12; xxii. 4; Mic. vi. 8; Phil. ii. 8. ¶ *Under the mighty hand of God.* This refers probably to the calamities which he had brought upon them, or was about to bring upon them; represented here, as often elsewhere, as the infliction *of his hand*—the hand being that by which we accomplish anything. When that hand was upon them they were not to be lifted up with pride and with a spirit of rebellion, but were to take a lowly place before him, and submit to him with a calm mind, believing that he would exalt them in due time. There is no situation in which one will be more likely to feel humility than in scenes of affliction. ¶ *That he may exalt you in due time.* When *he* shall see it to be a proper time. (1.) They might be assured that this would be done at some time. He would not always leave them in this low and depressed condition. He would take off his heavy hand, and raise them up from their state of sadness and suffering. (2.) This would be in due time; that is, in the proper time, in the

best time. (*a*) It might be in the present life. (*b*) It would certainly be in the world to come. There they would be exalted to honours which will be more than an equivalent for all the persecution, poverty, and contempt which are suffered in this world. He may well afford to be humble here who is to be exalted to a throne in heaven.

7. *Casting all your care upon him.* Comp. Psa. lv. 22, from whence this passage was probably taken. ‘Cast thy burden upon the Lord, and he shall sustain thee; he shall never suffer the righteous to be moved.’ Compare, for a similar sentiment, Matt. vi. 25–30. The meaning is, that we are to commit our whole cause to him. If we suffer heavy trials; if we lose our friends, health, or property; if we have arduous and responsible duties to perform; if we feel that we have no strength, and are in danger of being *crushed* by what is laid upon us, we may go and cast all upon the Lord; that is, we may look to him for grace and strength, and feel assured that he will enable us to sustain all that is laid upon us. The *relief* in the case will be as real, and as full of consolation, as if he took the burden and bore it himself. He will enable us to bear with ease what we supposed we could never have done; and the burden which he lays upon us will be light, Matt. xi. 30. Comp. Notes, Phil. iv. 6, 7. ¶ *For he careth for you.* Notes, Matt. x. 29–31. He is not like the gods worshipped by many of the heathen, who were supposed to be so exalted, and so distant, that they did not interest themselves in human affairs; but He condescends to regard the wants of the meanest of his creatures. It is one of the glorious attributes of the true God, that he *can* and *will* thus notice the wants of the mean as well as the mighty; and one of the richest of all consolations when we are afflicted, and are despised by the world, is the thought that we are not forgotten by our heavenly Father. He who remembers the falling sparrow, and who hears the young ravens when they cry, will not be unmindful of us.

8 Be sober, be vigilant; because your adversary the devil, as *a* a roaring lion, walketh about, seeking whom he may devour:

a Re.12.12.

9 Whom resist, *b* steadfast in the faith, knowing that the same afflictions are accomplished in your brethren that are in the world.

b Ja.4.7.

'Yet *the* LORD *thinketh on me*,' was the consolation of David, when he felt that he was 'poor and needy,' Psa. xl. 17. 'When my father and my mother forsake me, then the Lord will take me up,' Psa. xxvii. 10. Comp. Isa. xlix. 15. What more can one wish than to be permitted to feel that the great and merciful Jehovah *thinks* on him? What are we—what have we done, that should be worthy of such condescension? Remember, poor, despised, afflicted child of God, that you will never *be* forgotten. Friends on earth, the great, the gay, the noble, the rich, may forget you ; God never will. Remember that you will never be entirely neglected. Father, mother, neighbour, friend, those whom you have loved, and those to whom you have done good, may neglect you, but God never will. You may become poor, and they may pass by you ; you may lose your office, and flatterers may no longer throng your path ; your beauty may fade, and your admirers may leave you ; you may grow old, and be infirm, and appear to be useless in the world, and no one may seem to care for you ; but it is not thus with the God whom you serve. When he loves, he always loves ; if he regarded you with favour when you were rich, he will not forget you when you are poor ; he who watched over you with a parent's care in the bloom of youth, will not cast you off when you are 'old and grey-headed,' Psa. lxxi. 18. If we are what we should be, we shall never be without a friend as long as there is a God.

8. *Be sober.* While you cast your cares upon God, and have no anxiety on that score, let your solicitude be directed to another point. Do not doubt that he is able and willing to support and befriend you, but be watchful against your foes. See the word used here fully explained in the Notes on 1 Thess. v. 6. ¶ *Be vigilant.* This word (γρηγορέω) is everywhere else in the New Testament rendered *watch.* See Matt. xxiv. 42, 43; xxv. 13; xxvi. 38, 40, 41. It means

that we should exercise careful circumspection, as one does when he is in danger. In reference to the matter here referred to, it means that we are to be on our guard against the wiles and the power of the evil one. ¶ *Your adversary the devil.* Your enemy; he who is opposed to you. Satan opposes man in his best interests. He resists his efforts to do good ; his purposes to return to God ; his attempts to secure his own salvation. There is no more appropriate appellation that can be given to him than to say that he resists all our efforts to obey God and to secure the salvation of our own souls. ¶ *As a roaring lion.* Comp. Rev. xii. 12. Sometimes Satan is represented as transforming himself into an angel of light, (see Notes, 2 Cor. xi. 14;) and sometimes, as here, as a roaring lion : denoting the efforts which he makes to alarm and overpower us. The lion here is not the *crouching* lion —the lion stealthfully creeping towards his foe—but it is the raging monarch of the woods, who by his terrible roar would intimidate all so that they might become an easy prey. The *particular* thing referred to here, doubtless, is *persecution*, resembling in its terrors a roaring lion. When error comes in ; when seductive arts abound ; when the world allures and charms the representation of the character of the foe is not of the roaring lion, but of the silent influence of an enemy that has clothed himself in the garb of an angel of light, 2 Cor. xi. 14. ¶ *Walketh about, seeking whom he may devour.* 'Naturalists have observed that a lion roars when he is roused with hunger, for then he is most fierce, and most eagerly seeks his prey. See Judg. xiv. 5; Psa. xxii. 13; Jer. ii. 15; Ezek. xxii. 25; Hos. xi. 10; Zeph. iii. 3; Zech. xi. 3.'—*Benson.*

9. *Whom resist.* See Notes, James iv. 7. You are in no instance to yield to him, but are in all forms to stand up and oppose him. Feeble in yourselves, you are to confide in the arm of God. No matter in what form of terror he

approaches, you are to fight manfully the fight of faith. Comp. Notes, Eph. vi. 10-17. ¶ *Steadfast in the faith.* Confiding in God. You are to rely on him alone, and the means of successful resistance are to be found in the resources of faith. See Notes, Eph. vi. 16. ¶ *Knowing that the same afflictions are accomplished in your brethren that are in the world.* Comp. for a similar sentiment, 1 Cor. x. 13. The meaning is, that you should be encouraged to endure your trials by the fact that your fellow-Christians suffer the same things. This consideration might furnish consolation to them in their trials in the following ways: (1.) They would feel that they were suffering only the common lot of Christians. There was no evidence that God was peculiarly angry with them, or that he had in a peculiar manner forsaken them. (2.) The fact that others were enabled to bear their trials should be an argument to prove to them that they would also be able. If they looked abroad, and saw that others were sustained, and were brought off triumphant, they might be assured that this would be the case with them. (3.) There would be the support derived from the fact that they were not *alone* in suffering. We can bear pain more easily if we feel that we are not alone—that it is the common lot—that we are in circumstances where we may have sympathy from others. This remark may be of great practical value to *us* in view of persecutions, trials, and death. The consideration suggested here by Peter to sustain those whom he addressed, in the trials of persecution, may be applied now to sustain and comfort *us* in every form of apprehended or real calamity. We are all liable to suffering. We are exposed to sickness, bereavement, death. We often feel as if we could not bear up under the sufferings that may be before us, and especially do we dread *the great trial*—DEATH. It may furnish us some support and consolation to remember, (1.) that this is the common lot of men. There is nothing peculiar in our case. It proves nothing as to the question whether we are accepted of God, and are beloved by him, that we suffer; for those whom he has loved most have

been often among the greatest sufferers. We often think that *our* sufferings are peculiar; that there have been none like them. Yet, if we knew all, we should find that thousands—and among them the most wise, and pure, and good— have endured sufferings of the same *kind* as ours, and perhaps far more intense in *degree.* (2.) Others have been conveyed triumphantly through their trials. We have reason to hope and to believe that we shall also, for (*a*) our trials have been no greater than theirs have been; and (*b*) their natural strength was no greater than ours. Many of them were timid, and shrinking, and trembling, and felt that they had no strength, and that they should fail under the trial. (3.) The grace which sustained them can sustain us. The hand of God is not shortened that it cannot save; his ear is not heavy that it cannot hear. His power is as great, and his grace is as fresh, as it was when the first sufferer was supported by him; and that Divine strength which supported David and Job in their afflictions, and the apostles and martyrs in theirs, is just as powerful as it was when they applied to God to be upheld in their sorrows. (4.) We are especially fearful of death—fearful that our faith will fail, and that we shall be left to die without support or consolation. Yet let us remember that death is the common lot of man. Let us remember *who* have died — tender females; children; the timid and the fearful; those, in immense multitudes, who had no more strength by nature than we have. Let us think of our own kindred who have died. A wife has died, and shall a husband be afraid to die? A child, and shall a father? A sister, and shall a brother? It does much to take away the dread of death, to remember that a mother has gone through the dark valley; that that gloomy vale has been trod by delicate, and timid, and beloved sisters. Shall *I* be afraid to go where they have gone? Shall I apprehend that I shall find no grace that is able to sustain me where they have found it? Must the valley of the shadow of death be dark and gloomy to me, when they found it to be illuminated with the opening light of heaven?

10 But the God of all grace, who hath called us unto his eternal glory by Christ Jesus, after that ye have suffered a while, *a* make you perfect, *b* stablish, *c* strengthen, *d* settle *e* you.

a 2 Co.4.16.   b He.13.21.   c 2 Thess.3.3.
d Zec.10.6,12.   e Ps.138.7,8.

11 To him *be* glory *f* and dominion for ever and ever. Amen.

12 By Silvanus, *g* a faithful brother unto you, as I suppose, I have written briefly, exhorting, and testifying that this is the true grace of God wherein ye *h* stand.

f 1 Pe.4.11.   g 2 Co.1.19.   h 1 Co.15.1.

Above all, it takes away the fear of death when I remember that my Saviour has experienced all the horrors which can ever be in death; that he has slept in the tomb, and made it a hallowed resting-place.

10. *But the God of all grace.* The God who imparts all needful grace. It was proper in their anticipated trials to direct them to God, and to breathe forth in their behalf an earnest and affectionate prayer that they might be supported. A prayer of this kind by an apostle would also be to them a sort of pledge or assurance that the needed grace would be granted them. ¶ *Who hath called us unto his eternal glory.* And who means, therefore, that we shall be saved. As he has called us to his glory, we need not apprehend that he will leave or forsake us. On the meaning of the word *called*, see Notes, Eph. iv. 1. ¶ *After that ye have suffered a while.* After you have suffered as long as he shall appoint. The Greek is, 'having suffered *a little*,' and may refer either to *time* or *degree*. In both respects the declaration concerning afflictions is true. They are *short*, compared with eternity; they are *light*, compared with the exceeding and eternal weight of glory. See Notes, 2 Cor. iv. 16–18. ¶ *Make you perfect.* By means of your trials. The tendency of affliction is to make us perfect. ¶ *Stablish.* The Greek word means *to set fast; to fix firmly; to render immovable*, Luke xvi. 26; ix. 51; xxii. 32; Rom. i. 11; xvi. 25; 1 Thess. iii. 2, 13, *et al.* ¶ *Strengthen.* Give you strength to bear all this. ¶ *Settle you.* Literally, *found you*, or establish you on a firm foundation—θεμελιώσει. The allusion is to a house which is so firmly fixed on a foundation that it will not be moved by winds or floods. Comp. Notes, Matt. vii. 24. seq.

11. *To him* be *glory, &c.* See Notes, chap. iv. 11.
12. *By Silvanus.* Or *Silas.* See Notes, 2 Cor. i. 19; 1 Thess. i. 1. He was the intimate friend and companion of Paul, and had laboured much with him in the regions where the churches were situated to which this epistle was addressed. In what manner he became acquainted with Peter, or why he was now with him in Babylon, is unknown. ¶ *A faithful brother unto you, as I suppose.* The expression ' as I suppose ' —ὡς λογίζομαι—does not imply that there was any doubt on the mind of the apostle, but indicates rather a firm persuasion that what he said was true. Thus. Rom. viii. 18, 'For I *reckon* (λογίζομαι) that the sufferings of this present time are not worthy to be compared,' &c. That is, I am fully persuaded of it; I have no doubt of it. Peter evidently had *no doubt* on this point, but he probably could not speak from any personal knowledge. He had not been with them when Silas was, and perhaps not at all; for they may have been ' strangers ' to him personally —for the word ' strangers,' in chap. i. 1, *may* imply that he had no personal acquaintance with them. Silas, however, had been much with them, (comp. Acts xv. 17–31,) and Peter had no doubt that he had shown himself to be ' a faithful brother ' to them. An epistle conveyed by his hands could not but be welcome. It should be observed, however, that the expression ' I suppose ' has been differently interpreted by some. Wetstein understands it as meaning, ' Not that he supposed Silvanus to be a faithful brother, for who, says he, could doubt that? but that he had written as he understood matters, having carefully considered the subject, and as he regarded things to be true;' and refers for illustration to Rom. viii. 18; Phil. iv.

13 The *church that is* at Babylon, elected together with *you*, saluteth you; and *so doth* Marcus my son.

14 Greet *a* ye one another with a

kiss of charity.   Peace *b* be with you all that are in Christ Jesus. Amen.

a Ro.16.16.   *b* Ep.6.23.

8; Heb. xi. 9.   Grotius understands it as meaning, 'If I remember right;' and supposes that the idea is, that he shows his affection for them by saying that this was not the first time that he had written to them, but that he had written before briefly, and sent the letter, as well as he could remember, by Silvanus.   But there is no evidence that he had written to them before, and the common interpretation is undoubtedly to be preferred.   ¶ *Exhorting.*   No small part of the epistle is taken up with exhortations.   ¶ *And testifying.* Bearing witness.   The main design of the office of the apostles was to bear witness to the truth, (Notes, 1 Cor. ix. 1;) and Peter in this epistle discharged that part of the functions of his office towards the scattered Christians of Asia Minor.   ¶ *That this is the true grace of God wherein ye stand.*   That the religion in which you stand, or which you now hold, is that which is identified with the grace or favour of God.   Christianity, not Judaism, or Paganism, was the true religion.   To show this, and bear continual witness to it, was the leading design of the apostolic office.

13. *The* church that is *at Babylon, elected together with* you.   It will be seen at once that much of this is supplied by our translators; the words 'church that is' not being in the original.   The Greek is, ἡ ἐν Βαβυλῶνι συνεκλεκτὴ; and might refer to a church, or to a female.   Wall, Mill, and some others, suppose that the reference is to

a Christian woman, perhaps the wife of Peter himself.   Comp. 2 John 1.   But the Arabic, Syriac, and Vulgate, as well as the English versions, supply the word *church.*   This interpretation seems to be confirmed by the word rendered *elected together with*—συνεκλεκτὴ.   This word would be properly used in reference to one *individual* if writing to another *individual*, but would *hardly* be appropriate as applied to an individual addressing *a church.*   It could not readily be supposed, moreover, that any one female in Babylon could have such a prominence, or be so well known, that nothing more would be necessary to designate her than merely to say, 'the elect female.'   On the word Babylon here, and the place denoted by it, see the Intro., § 2.   ¶ *And* so doth *Marcus my son.*   Probably John Mark.   See Notes, Acts xii. 12; xv. 37.   Why he was now with Peter is unknown. If this was the Mark referred to, then the word *son* is a title of affection, and is used by Peter with reference to his own superior age.   It is possible, however, that some other Mark may be referred to, in whose conversion Peter had been instrumental.

14. *Greet ye one another with a kiss of charity.*   A kiss of *love;* a common method of affectionate salutation in the times of the apostles.   See Notes, Rom. xvi. 16.   ¶ *Peace* be *with you all that are in Christ Jesus.*   That are true Christians.   Notes, Eph. vi. 23; Phil. iv. 7.

VOL. X.   O

THE

SECOND EPISTLE GENERAL OF PETER.

INTRODUCTION.

§ 1. *Genuineness and authenticity of the Epistle.*

It is well known that at an early period of the Christian history there were doubts respecting the canonical authority of the Second Epistle of Peter. The sole ground of the doubt was, whether Peter was the author of it. Eusebius, in the chapter of his ecclesiastical history where he speaks of the New Testament in general, reckons it among the αντιλεγομενα, (*antilegomena,*) or those books which were not universally admitted to be genuine; literally, '*those which were spoken against,*' b. iii. chap. 25. This does not imply that even he, however, disbelieved its genuineness, but merely that it was numbered among those about which there had not been always entire certainty. Jerome says, ' Peter wrote two epistles, called Catholic; the second of which is denied by many to be his, because of the difference of style from the former.' Origen, before him, had also said, ' Peter, on whom the church is built, has left one epistle [universally] acknowledged. Let it be granted that he also wrote a second. For it is doubted of.' See Lardner, vol. vi., p. 255, Ed. Lond. 1829. Both the epistles of Peter, however, were received as genuine in the fourth and following centuries by all Christians, except the Syrians. The first epistle was never doubted to have been the production of Peter. In regard to the second, as remarked above, it was doubted by some. The principal ground of the doubt, if not the entire ground, was the difference of style between the two, especially in the second chapter, and the fact that the old Syriac translator, though he admitted the Epistle of James, which was also reckoned among the 'doubtful' epistles, did not translate the Second Epistle of Peter. That version was made, probably, at the close of the first century, or in the second; and it is said that it is to be presumed that if this epistle had been then in existence, and had been regarded as genuine, it would also have been translated by him.

It is of importance, therefore, to state briefly the evidence of the genuineness and authenticity of this epistle. In doing this, it is proper to regard the *first* epistle as undoubtedly genuine and canonical, for that was never called in question. That being admitted, the genuineness of this epistle may be argued on the following grounds : (1.) It does not appear to have been *rejected* by any one. It was merely *doubted* whether it was genuine. How far even this *doubt* extended is not mentioned. It is referred to only by Jerome, Origen, and Eusebius, though there is not the least evidence that even *they* had any doubts of its genuineness. They merely state that there were some persons who had doubts on the subject, from the difference of style between this and the former epistle. This fact, indeed, as Wall has remarked, (Critical Notes on the New Testament, pp. 358, 359,) will serve at least to show the care which was evinced in admitting books to be canonical, proving that they were not received without the utmost caution, and that if the slightest doubt existed in the case of any one, it was honestly expressed. (2.) Even all doubt on the subject disappeared as early as the third and fourth centuries, and the epistle was received as being unquestionably the production of Peter. The effect of the examination in the case was to remove all suspicion, and it has never since been doubted that the epistle was written by Peter; at least, no doubt has arisen, except from the fact stated by Jerome and Origen, that it was not universally admitted to be genuine. (3.) This epistle purports to have been written by the author of the former, and has all the internal marks of genuineness which could exist. (*a*) It bears the inscription of the name of the same apostle: 'Simon Peter, a servant and an apostle of Jesus Christ,' chap. i. 1. (*b*) There is an allusion in chap. i. 14, which Peter only could appropriately make, and which an impostor, or forger of an epistle, would hardly have thought of introducing: 'Knowing that shortly I must put off this my tabernacle, even as our Lord Jesus Christ hath showed me.' Here, there is an evident reference to the Saviour's prediction of the death of Peter, recorded in John xxi. 18, 19. It is conceivable, indeed, that an adroit forger of an epistle *might* have introduced such a circumstance; but the supposition that it is genuine is much more natural. It is such an allusion as Peter would naturally make; it would have required much skill and tact in another to have introduced it so as not to be easily detected, even if it had occurred to him to personate Peter at all. Would not a forger of an epistle have been likely to mention particularly what *kind* of death was predicted by the Saviour, and not to have made a mere allusion? (*c*) In chap. i. 16–18, there is another allusion of a similar kind. The writer claims to have been one of the 'eye-witnesses of the majesty' of the Lord Jesus when he was transfigured in the holy mount. It was natural for Peter to refer to this, for he was with him; and he has mentioned it just as one would be likely to do who had actually been with him, and who was writing from personal recollection. A forger of the epistle would have been likely to be more particular, and would have described the scene more minutely, and the place where it occurred, and would have dwelt more on the nature of the evidence furnished there of the Divine mission of the Saviour. (*d*) In chap. iii. 1, it is stated that this is a second epistle written to the same persons, as a former one had been; and that the writer aimed at substantially the same object in both. Here the plain reference is to the first epistle of Peter, which has always been acknowledged to be genuine. It may be said that one who forged the epistle might have made this allusion. This is true, but it may be doubtful whether he *would* do it. It would have increased the liability to detection, for it would not be easy to imitate the manner, and to carry out the views of the apostle. (4.) To these considerations it may be added, that there is clear internal evidence of another kind to show that it was written by Peter. This evidence, too long to be introduced here, may be seen in Michaelis' Introduction, iv. 349–356. The sum of this internal evidence is, that it would not have been practicable for a writer of the first or second century to have imitated Peter so as to have escaped detection; and that, in general, it is not difficult to detect the books that were forged in imitation of, and in the name of, the apostles.

As to the alleged objection in regard to the difference of the style in the second chapter, see Michaelis, iv. 352–356. Why it was not inserted in the old Syriac version is not known. It is probable that the author of that version was exceedingly cautious, and did not admit any books about which *he* had any doubt. The fact that this was doubted by some, and that these doubts were not removed from his mind, as in the case of the epistle of James, was a good reason for his not inserting it, though it by no means proves that it is not genuine. It came, however, to be acknowledged afterwards by the Syrians as genuine and canonical Ephrem the Syrian, a writer of the fourth century, not only quotes several passages of it, but expressly ascribes it to Peter. Thus, in the second volume of his Greek works, p. 387, he says, 'The blessed Peter, also, the Coryphæus of the apostles, cries, concerning that day, saying, The day of the Lord cometh as a thief in the night, in which the heavens being on fire shall be dissolved, and the elements shall melt with fervent heat.' This is literally quoted (in the Greek) from

2 Pet. iii. 12. See Michaelis, as above, p. 348. And Asseman, in his catalogue of the Vatican Manuscripts, gives an account of a Syriac book of Lessons, to be read, in which is one taken from this epistle. See Michaelis.

These considerations remove all reasonable doubt as to the propriety of admitting this epistle into the canon, as the production of Peter.

§ 2. *The time when the Epistle was written.*

In regard to the *time* when this epistle was written, nothing can be determined with absolute certainty. All that appears on that subject from the epistle itself, is, that at the time of writing it the author was expecting soon to die. Chap. i. 14, ' Knowing that shortly I must put off this my tabernacle, even as our Lord Jesus Christ hath showed me.' What evidence he had that he was soon to die he has not informed us; nor is it known even what he meant precisely by the word *shortly.* The Greek word (ταχινή) is indeed one that would imply that the event was expected not to be far off; but a man would not unnaturally use it who felt that he was growing old, even though he should in fact live several years afterwards. The Saviour (John xxi. 18) did not state to Peter *when* his death would occur, except that it would be when he should be ' *old;*' and the probability is, that the fact that he was growing *old* was the only intimation that he had that he was soon to die. Ecclesiastical history informs us that he died at Rome, A.D. 66. in the 12th year of the reign of Nero. See Calmet, *Art.* Peter. Comp. Notes, John xxi. 18, 19. Lardner supposes, from chap. i. 13–15 of this epistle, that this was written not long after the first, as he then says that he ' would not be *negligent* to put them in remembrance of these things.' The two epistles he supposes were written in the year 63 or 64, or at the latest 65. Michaelis supposes it was in the year 64; Calmet that it was in the year of Christ 68, or according to the Vulgar Era, A.D. 65. Probably the year 64 or 65 would not be far from the real date of this epistle. If so, it was, according to Calmet, one year only before the martyrdom of Peter, (A.D. 66,) and six years before the destruction of Jerusalem by Titus, A.D. 71.

§ 3. *The persons to whom this Epistle was written, and the place where.*

On this subject there is no room for doubt. In chap. iii. 1, the writer says, ' this second epistle, beloved, I now write unto you; in both which I stir up your pure minds by way of remembrance.' This epistle was written, therefore, to the same persons as the former. On the question to whom that was addressed, see the Introduction to that epistle, § 1. The epistles were addressed to persons who resided in Asia Minor, and in both they are regarded as in the midst of trials. No certain intimation of the *place* where this epistle was written is given in the epistle itself. It is probable that it was at the same place as the former, as, if it had not been, we may presume that there would have been some reference to the fact that he had changed his residence, or some local allusion which would have enabled us to determine the fact. If he wrote this epistle from Babylon, as he did the former one, (see Intro. to that epistle, § 2,) it is not known why he was so soon removed to Rome, and became a martyr there. Indeed, everything respecting the last days of this apostle is involved in great uncertainty. See the article *Peter* in Calmet's Dictionary. See these questions examined also in Bacon's Lives of the Apostles, pp. 258–279.

§ 4.— *The occasion on which the Epistle was written.*

The first epistle was written in view of the trials which those to whom it was addressed were then enduring, and the persecutions which they had reason to anticipate, chap. i. 6, 7; iv. 12–19; v. 8–11. The main object of that epistle was to comfort them in their trials, and to encourage them to bear them with a Christian spirit, imitating the example of the Lord Jesus. This epistle appears to have been written, not so much in view of persecutions and bodily sufferings, real or prospective, as in view of the fact that there were teachers of error among them, the tendency of whose doctrine was to turn them away from the gospel. To those teachers of error, and to the dangers to which they were exposed on that account, there is no allusion in the first epistle, and it would seem not to be improbable that Peter had been informed that there were such teachers among them after he had written and despatched that. Or, if he was not thus *informed* of it, it seems to have occurred to him that this was a point of great importance which had not been noticed in the former epistle, and that an effort should be made by apostolic influence and authority to arrest the progress of error, to counteract the influence of the false teachers, and to confirm the Christians of Asia Minor in the belief of the truth. A large part of the epistle, therefore, is occupied in characterising the teachers of error, in showing that they would certainly be destroyed, and in stating the true doctrine in opposition to what they held. It is evident that Peter supposed that the danger to which Christians in Asia Minor were exposed from these errors, was not less than that to which they were exposed from persecution, and that it was of as much importance to guard them from those errors as it was to sustain them in their trials.

The characteristics of the teachers referred to in this epistle, and the doctrines which they taught, were the following :—

(1.) One of the prominent errors was a denial of the Lord that bought them, chap. ii. 1.   On the nature of this error, see Notes on that verse.

(2.) They gave indulgence to carnal appetites, and were sensual, corrupt, beastly, lewd, vers. 10, 12, 13, 14, 19. Comp. Jude 4, 8, 16. It is remarkable that so many professed *reformers* have been men who have been sensual and lewd—men who have taken advantage of their character as professed religious teachers, and as *reformers*, to corrupt and betray others.   Such reformers often begin with pure intentions, but a constant familiarity with a certain class of vices tends to corrupt the mind, and to awaken in the soul passions which would otherwise have slept ; and they fall into the same vices which they attempt to reform. It should be said, however, that many professed reformers are corrupt at heart, and only make use of their pretended zeal in the cause of reformation to give them the opportunity to indulge their base propensities.

(3.) They were disorderly in their views, and '*radical*' in their movements. The tendency of their doctrines was to unsettle the foundations of order and government ; to take away all restraint from the indulgence of carnal propensities, and to break up the very foundations of good order in society, chap. ii. 10–12. They 'walked after the flesh in the lust of uncleanness ;' they 'despised government' or authority ; they were 'presumptuous and self-willed ;' they 'were not afraid to speak evil of dignities ;' they were like 'natural brute beasts ;' they 'spoke evil of the subjects which they did not understand.' It is by no means an uncommon thing for professed reformers to become anti-government men, or to suppose that all the restraints of law stand in their way, and that they must be removed in order to success.   They fix the mind on *one* thing to be accomplished.   That thing magnifies itself until it fills all the field of vision.   Everything which *seems* to oppose their efforts, or to uphold the evil which they seek to remove, they regard as an evil itself ; and as the laws and the government of a country often seem to sustain the evil, they become opposed to the government itself, and denounce it as an evil.   Instead of endeavouring to enlighten the public mind, and to modify the laws by a course of patient effort, they array themselves against them, and seek to overturn them. For the same reason, also, they suppose that *the church* upholds the evil, and become the deadly foe of all church organizations.

(4.) They were seductive and artful, and adopted a course of teaching that was fitted to beguile the weak, and especially to produce licentiousness of living, chap. ii. 14. They were characterised by 'adulterous' desires; and they practised their arts particularly on the 'unstable,' those who were easily led away by any new and plausible doctrine that went to unsettle the foundations of rigid morality.

(5.) They adopted a pompous mode of teaching, distinguished for sound rather than for sense, and proclaimed themselves to be the special friends of liberal views, and of a liberal Christianity, chap. ii. 17–19. They were like 'wells without water;' 'clouds that were carried about with a tempest;' they spake 'great swelling words of vanity,' and they promised 'liberty' to those who would embrace their views, or freedom from the restraints of bigotry and of a narrow and gloomy religion. This appeal is usually made by the advocates of error.

(6.) They had been professed Christians, and had formerly embraced the more strict views on morals and religion which were held by Christians in general, chap. ii. 20–22. From this, however, they had departed, and had fallen into practices quite as abominable as those of which they had been guilty before their pretended conversion.

(7.) They denied the doctrines which the apostles had stated respecting the end of the world. The *argument* on which they based this denial was the fact that all things continued unchanged as they had been from the beginning, and that it might be inferred from that that the world would be stable, chap. iii. 3, 4. They saw no change in the laws of nature; they saw no indications that the world was drawing to a close, and they *inferred* that laws so stable and settled as those were which existed in nature would continue to operate, and that the changes predicted by the apostles were impossible.

A large part of the epistle is occupied in meeting these errors, and in so portraying the characters of their advocates as to show what degree of reliance was to be placed on their preaching. For a particular view of the manner in which these errors are met, see the analyses to chapters ii. iii.

This epistle is characterised by the same earnest and tender manner as the first, and by a peculiarly 'solemn grandeur of imagery and diction.' The apostle in the last two chapters had to meet great and dangerous errors, and the style of rebuke was appropriate to the occasion. He felt that he himself was soon to die, and, in the prospect of death, his own mind was peculiarly impressed with the solemnity and importance of coming events. He believed that the errors which were broached tended to sap the very foundations of the Christian faith and of good morals, and his whole soul is roused to meet and counteract them. The occasion required that he should state in a solemn manner what *was* the truth in regard to the second advent of the Lord Jesus; what great changes *were* to occur; what the Christian *might* look for hereafter; and his soul kindles with the sublime theme, and he describes in glowing imagery, and in impassioned language, the end of all things, and exhorts them to live as became those who were looking forward to so important events. The practical effect of the whole epistle is to make the mind intensely solemn, and to put it into a position of waiting for the coming of the Lord. On the similarity between this epistle (chap. ii.) and the epistle of Jude, see Introduction to Jude.

THE

SECOND EPISTLE GENERAL OF PETER.

CHAPTER I.

SIMON [1] Peter, a servant and an apostle of Jesus Christ, to them that have obtained like *a* precious faith with us through the righteousness of [2] God and our Saviour Jesus Christ:

1 Or, *Symeon.*   a Ep.4.5.   2 *our God and Saviour.*

CHAPTER I.

ANALYSIS OF THE CHAPTER.

THIS chapter comprises the following subjects:—

I. The usual salutations, vers. 1, 2.

II. A statement that all the mercies which they enjoyed pertaining to life and godliness, had been conferred by the power of God, and that he had given them exceeding great and precious promises, vers. 3, 4. It was mainly with reference to these 'promises' that the epistle was written, for they had been assailed by the advocates of error, (chaps. ii. iii.,) and it was important that Christians should see that they *had* the promise of a future life. Comp. chap. iii. 5–14.

III. An exhortation to abound in Christian virtues; to go on making constant attainments in knowledge, and temperance, and patience, and godliness, and brotherly kindness, and charity, vers. 5–9.

IV. An exhortation to endeavour to make their calling and election sure, that so an entrance might be ministered unto them abundantly into the kingdom of the Redeemer, vers. 10, 11.

V. The apostle says that he will endeavour to keep these things before their minds, vers. 12–15. He knew well that they were then established in the truth, (ver. 12,) but he evidently felt that they were in danger of being shaken in the faith by the seductive influence of error, and he says therefore, (vers. 13,) that it was proper, as long as he remained on earth, to endeavour to excite in their minds a lively remembrance of the truths which they had believed;

that the opportunity for his doing this must soon cease, as the period was approaching when he must be removed to eternity, in accordance with the prediction of the Saviour, (ver. 14,) but that he would endeavour to make so permanent a record of his views on these important subjects that they might always have them in remembrance, ver. 15.

VI. A solemn statement that the doctrines which had been taught them, and which they had embraced, were not cunningly-devised fables, but were true, vers. 16–21. In support of this the apostle appeals to the following things:—

(*a*) The testimony to the fact that Jesus was the Son of God, which Peter had himself heard given on the mount of transfiguration, vers. 17, 18.

(*b*) Prophecy. These truths, on which he expected them to rely, had been the subject of distinct prediction, and they should be held, whatever were the plausible arguments of the false teachers, vers. 19, 20.

The general object, therefore, of this chapter is to affirm the truth of the great facts of religion, on which their hopes were based, and thus to prepare the way to combat the errors by which these truths were assailed. He first assures them that the doctrines which they held were true, and then, in chaps. ii. and iii., meets the errors by which they were assailed.

1. *Simon Peter.* Marg., *Symeon.* The name is written either *Simon* or *Simeon*—Σίμων or Συμεών. Either word properly means *hearing;* and perhaps, like other names, was at first significant. The first epistle (chap. i. 1) begins simply, 'Peter, an apostle,' &c. The name

2 Grace and peace [a] be multiplied unto you through the knowledge of God, and of Jesus our Lord.

3 According as his divine power hath given unto us all [b] things that pertain unto life and godliness, through the knowledge of him that hath called us [1] to glory and virtue: [c]

a Da.4.1; 6.25.　　　b Ps.84.11; 1 Ti.4.8.
1 Or, by.　　　c 2 Ti.1.9.

Simon, however, was, his proper name—*Peter*, or *Cephas*, having been added to it by the Saviour, John i. 42. Comp. Matt. xvi. 18. ¶ *A servant and an apostle of Jesus Christ.* In the first epistle the word *apostle* only is used. Paul, however, uses the word *servant* as applicable to himself in Rom. i. 1, and to himself and Timothy in the commencement of the epistle to the Philippians, chap. i. 1. See Notes, Rom. i. 1. ¶ *To them that have obtained like precious faith with us.* With us who are of Jewish origin. This epistle was evidently written to the same persons as the former, (Intro., § 3,) and that was intended to embrace many who were of Gentile origin. Notes, 1 Pet. i. 1. The apostle addresses them all now, whatever was their origin, as heirs of the common faith, and as in all respects brethren. ¶ *Through the righteousness of God.* Through the method of justification which God has adopted. See this fully explained in the Notes on Rom. i. 17.

[The original is ἐν δικαιοσύνῃ, IN the righteousness, &c., which makes the righteousness the *object* of faith. We cannot but regard the author's rendering of the famous phrase here used by Peter, and by Paul, Rom. i. 17; iii. 21, as singularly unhappy. That Archbishop Newcome used it and the Socinian version adopted it, would not make us reject it; but when the apostles state *specially* the GROUND of justification, why should they be made to speak *indefinitely* of its general 'plan,' or method. The rendering of Stuart, viz., 'justification of God,' is not more successful; it confounds the *thing itself* with the *ground* of it. Why not prefer the apostle's own words to any change or periphrasis? See Supplementary Note, Rom. i. 17.]

¶ *God and our Saviour Jesus Christ.* Marg., *our God and Saviour.* The Greek will undoubtedly *bear* the construction given in the margin; and if this be the true rendering, it furnishes an argument for the divinity of the Lord Jesus Christ. Bishop Middleton, Slade, Valpy, Bloomfield, and others, contend that this is the true and proper render-ing. It is doubted, however, by Wetstein, Grotius, and others. Erasmus supposes that it may be taken in either sense. The construction, though certainly not a violation of the laws of the Greek language, is not so free from all doubt as to make it proper to use the passage as a proof-text in an argument for the divinity of the Saviour. It is easier to prove the doctrine from other texts that are plain, than to show that this *must* be the meaning here.

2. *Grace and peace be multiplied unto you through the knowledge of God, and of Jesus our Lord.* That is, grace and peace *abound* to us, or may be expected to be conferred on us abundantly, if we have a true knowledge of God and of the Saviour. Such a knowledge constitutes true religion: for in that we find *grace*—the grace that pardons and sanctifies; and *peace*—peace of conscience, reconciliation with God, and calmness in the trials of life. See Notes, John xvii. 3.

3. *According as his divine power hath given unto us.* All the effects of the gospel on the human heart are, in the Scriptures, traced to the *power* of God. See Notes, Rom. i. 16. There are no moral means which have ever been used that have such *power* as the gospel; none through which God has done so much in changing the character and affecting the destiny of man. ¶ *All things that* pertain *unto life and godliness.* The reference here in the word *life* is undoubtedly to the life of religion; the life of the soul imparted by the gospel. The word *godliness* is synonymous with piety. The phrase ' according as ' (ὡς) seems to be connected with the sentence in ver. 5, ' Forasmuch as he has conferred on us these privileges and promises connected with life and godliness, we are bound, in order to obtain all that is implied in these things, to give all diligence to add to our faith, knowledge,' &c. ¶ *Through the knowledge of him.* By a proper acquaintance

4 Whereby are given unto us exceeding great and precious promises; *a* that by these ye might be

a 2 Co.7.1.

partakers *b* of the divine nature, having escaped *c* the corruption that is in the world through lust.

b He.12.10.   *c* 2 Pe.2.18,20.

with him, or by the right kind of knowledge of him. Notes, John xvii. 3. ¶ *That hath called us to glory and virtue.* Margin, *by.* Greek, '*through* glory,' &c. Doddridge supposes that it means that he has done this 'by the strengthening virtue and energy of his spirit.' Rosenmüller renders it, '*by* glorious benignity.' Dr. Robinson (*Lex.*) renders it, 'through a glorious display of his efficiency.' The *objection* which any one feels to this rendering arises solely from the word *virtue,* from the fact that we are not accustomed to apply that word to God. But the original word (ἀρετή) is not as limited in its signification as the English word is, but is rather a word which denotes a good quality or excellence of any kind. In the ancient classics it is used to denote manliness, vigour, courage, valour, fortitude; and the word would rather denote *energy* or *power* of some kind, than what we commonly understand by virtue, and would be, therefore, properly applied to the *energy* or *efficiency* which God has displayed in the work of our salvation. Indeed, when applied to moral excellence at all, as it is in ver. 5, of this chapter, and often elsewhere, it is perhaps with a reference to the *energy, boldness, vigour,* or *courage* which is evinced in overcoming our evil propensities, and resisting allurements and temptations. According to this interpretation, the passage teaches that it is *by a glorious Divine efficiency* that we are called into the kingdom of God.

4. *Whereby.* Δἰ ὧν. 'Through which' —in the plural number, referring either to the *glory* and *virtue* in the previous verse, and meaning that it was by that glorious Divine efficiency that these promises were given; or, to all the things mentioned in the previous verse, meaning that it was through those arrangements, and in order to their completion, that these great and glorious promises were made. The promises given are in connection with the plan of securing 'life and godliness,' and are a part of the gracious arrangements for that ob-

ject. ¶ *Exceeding great and precious promises.* A *promise* is an assurance on the part of another of some good for which we are dependent on him. It implies, (1,) that the thing is in his power; (2,) that he may bestow it or not, as he pleases; (3,) that we cannot infer from any process of reasoning that it is his purpose to bestow it on us; (4,) that it is a favour which we can obtain *only* from him, and not by any independent effort of our own. The promises here referred to are those which pertain to salvation. Peter had in his eye probably all that then had been revealed which contemplated the salvation of the people of God. They are called 'exceeding great and precious,' because of their value in supporting and comforting the soul, and of the honour and felicity which they unfold to us. The promises referred to are doubtless those which are made in connection with the plan of salvation revealed in the gospel, for there are no *other* promises made to man. They refer to the pardon of sin; strength, comfort, and support in trial; a glorious resurrection; and a happy immortality. If we look at the greatness and glory of the objects, we shall see that the promises are in fact exceedingly precious; or if we look at their influence in supporting and elevating the soul, we shall have as distinct a view of their value. The promise goes beyond our reasoning powers; enters a field which we could not otherwise penetrate—the distant future; and relates to what we could not otherwise obtain. All that we need in trial, is the simple *promise* of God that he will sustain us; all that we need in the hour of death, is the assurance of our God that we shall be happy for ever. What would this world be without a *promise?* How impossible to penetrate the future! How dark that which is to come would be! How bereft we should be of consolation! The past has gone, and its departed joys and hopes can never be recalled to cheer us again; the present may be an hour of pain, and sadness, and disappointment, and gloom, with perhaps not a ray of comfort; the future only opens fields of happiness to our vision, and everything there depends on the will of God, and all that we can know of it is from his promises. Cut off from these, we have no way either of obtaining the blessings which we desire, or of ascertaining that they can be ours. For the promises of God, therefore, we should be in the highest degree grateful, and in the trials of life we should cling to them with unwavering confidence as the only things which can be an anchor to the soul. ¶ *That by these.* Greek, '*through* these.' That is, these constitute the basis of your hopes of becoming partakers of the divine nature. Comp. Notes on 2 Cor. vii. 1. ¶ *Partakers of the divine nature.* This is a very important and a difficult phrase. An expression somewhat similar occurs in Heb. xii. 10: 'That we might be partakers of his holiness.' See Notes on that verse. In regard to the language here used, it may be observed, (1,) that it is directly contrary to all the notions of *Pantheism*—or the belief that all things are *now* God, or a part of God—for it is said that the object of the promise is, that we '*may become* partakers of the divine nature,' not that we are now. (2.) It cannot be taken in so literal a sense as to mean that we can ever partake of the divine *essence*, or that we shall be *absorbed* into the divine nature so as to lose our individuality. This idea is held by the Budhists; and the perfection of being is supposed by them to consist in such absorption, or in losing their own individuality, and their ideas of happiness are graduated by the approximation which may be made to that state. But this cannot be the meaning here, because (*a*) it is in the nature of the case impossible. There must be for ever an essential difference between a created and an uncreated mind. (*b*) This would argue that the Divine Mind is not perfect. If this absorption was necessary to the completeness of the character and happiness of the Divine Being, then he was imperfect before; if before perfect, he would *not* be after the absorption of an infinite number of finite and imperfect minds. (*c*) In all

the representations of heaven in the Bible, the idea of *individuality* is one that is prominent. *Individuals* are represented everywhere as worshippers there, and there is no intimation that the separate existence of the redeemed is to be absorbed and lost in the essence of the Deity. Whatever is to be the condition of man hereafter, he is to have a separate and individual existence, and the *number* of intelligent beings is never to be diminished either by annihilation, or by their being united to any other spirit so that they shall become *one*. The reference then, in this place, must be to the *moral* nature of God; and the meaning is, that they who are renewed become participants of the same *moral* nature; that is, of the same views, feelings, thoughts, purposes, principles of action. Their nature as they are born, is sinful, and prone to evil, (Eph. ii. 3;) their nature as they are born again, becomes like that of God. They are made *like* God; and this resemblance will increase more and more for ever, until in a much higher sense than can be true in this world, they may be said to have become 'partakers of the divine nature.' Let us remark, then, (*a*) that *man* only, of all the dwellers on the earth, is capable of rising to this condition. The nature of all the other orders of creatures here below is incapable of any such transformation that it can be said that they become 'partakers of the divine nature.' (*b*) It is impossible now to estimate the degree of approximation to which man may yet rise towards God, or the exalted sense in which the term may yet be applicable to him; but the prospect before the believer in this respect is most glorious. Two or three circumstances may be referred to here as mere *hints* of what we may yet be : (1.) Let any one reflect on the amazing advances made by himself since the period of infancy. But a few, very few years ago, he knew *nothing*. He was in his cradle, a poor, helpless infant. He knew not the use of eyes, or ears, or hands, or feet. He knew not the name or use of anything, not even the name of father or mother. He could neither walk, nor talk, nor creep. He knew not even that a candle would burn him if he put his finger there. He

5 And beside this, giving all diligence, add to your faith virtue; [a]
and to virtue knowledge; [b]

a Phi.4.8.   b Phi.1.9.

knew not how to grasp or hold a rattle, or what was its sound, or whence that sound or any other sound came. Let him think what he is at twenty, or forty, in comparison with this; and then, if his improvement in every similar number of years hereafter *should* be equal to this, who can tell the height to which he will rise? (2.) We are here limited in our own powers of learning about God or his works. We become acquainted with him *through* his works —by means of *the senses.* But by the appointment of this method of becoming acquainted with the external world, the design seems to have been to accomplish a double work quite contradictory—one to help us, and the other to hinder us. One is to give us the means of communicating with the external world—by the sight, the hearing, the smell, the touch, the taste; the other is to shut us *out* from the external world, except by these. The body is a *casement*, an enclosure, a prison in which the soul is incarcerated, from which we can *look out* on the universe only through these organs. But suppose, as may be the case in a future state, there shall be *no* such enclosure, and that the whole soul may look directly on the works of God—on spiritual existences, on God himself— who can then calculate the height to which man may attain in becoming a 'partaker of the divine nature?' (3.) We shall have an *eternity* before us to grow in knowledge, and in holiness, and in conformity to God. Here, we attempt to climb the hill of knowledge, and having gone a few steps—while the top is still lost in the clouds—we lie down and die. We look at a few things; become acquainted with a few elementary principles; make a little progress in virtue, and then all our studies and efforts are suspended, and 'we fly away.' In the future world we shall have an *eternity* before us to make progress in knowledge, and virtue, and holiness, uninterrupted; and who can tell in what exalted sense it may yet be true that we shall be 'partakers of the divine nature,' or what attainments we may yet make? ¶ *Having escaped the cor-*

ruption *that is in the world through lust.* The world is full of corruption. It is the design of the Christian plan of redemption to deliver us from that, and to make us holy; and the means by which we are to be made like God, is by rescuing us from its dominion.

5. *And beside this.* Καὶ αὐτὸ τοῦτο. Something here is necessary to be understood in order to complete the sense. The *reference* is to ver. 3; and the connection is, 'since (ver. 3) God has given us these exalted privileges and hopes, *in respect to this,* (κατὰ or διὰ being understood,) or as a *consequence* fairly flowing from this, we ought to give all diligence that we may make good use of these advantages, and secure as high attainments as we possibly can. We should add one virtue to another, that we may reach the highest possible elevation in holiness.' ¶ *Giving all diligence.* Greek, 'Bringing in all zeal or effort.' The meaning is, that we ought to make this a distinct and definite object, and to apply ourselves to it as a thing to be accomplished. ¶ *Add to your faith virtue.* It is not meant in this verse and the following that we are to endeavour particularly to add these things one to another *in the order* in which they are specified, or that we are to seek first to have faith, and then to add to *that* virtue, and then to add knowledge to virtue rather than to faith, &c. The *order* in which this is to be done, the *relation* which one of these things may have to another, is not the point aimed at; nor are we to suppose that any other order of the words would not have answered the purpose of the apostle as well, or that any one of the virtues specified would not sustain as direct a relation to any other, as the one which I.e has specified. The design of the apostle is to say, in an emphatic manner, that we are to strive to possess and exhibit all these virtues; in other words, we are not to content ourselves with a single grace, but are to cultivate *all* the virtues, and to endeavour to make our piety complete in all the relations which we sustain. The essential idea in the passage before us seems to be, that in our

6 And to knowledge temperance; *a* and to temperance patience; *b* and to patience godliness; *c*

7 And to godliness brotherly kindness; *d* and to brotherly kindness charity. *e*

8 For if these things be in you, and abound, they make *you that ye shall* neither *be* [1] barren nor unfruitful *f* in the knowledge of our Lord Jesus Christ.

a 1 Co.9.25.	*b* Ja.1.4.	*c* 1 Ti.4.7.
d Jn.13.34,35.	*e* 1 Co.13.1-3.	1 *idle.*	*f* Jn.15.2-6.

religion we are not to be satisfied with one virtue, or one class of virtues, but that there is to be (1,) a diligent CULTIVATION of our religion, since the graces of religion are as susceptible of cultivation as any other virtues; (2,) that there is to be PROGRESS made from one virtue to another, seeking to reach the highest possible point in our religion; and, (3,) that there is to be an ACCUMULATION of virtues and graces—or we are not to be satisfied with one class, or with the attainments which we can make in one class. We are to endeavour to *add on* one after another until we have become possessed of all. Faith, perhaps, is mentioned first, because that is the foundation of all Christian virtues; and the other virtues are required to be added to that, because, from the place which faith occupies in the plan of justification, many might be in danger of supposing that if they had that they had all that was necessary. Comp. James ii. 14, seq. In the Greek word rendered '*add,*' (ἐπιχορηγήσατε,) there is an allusion to a *chorus-leader* among the Greeks, and the sense is well expressed by Doddridge: ' Be careful to accompany that belief with all the lovely train of attendant graces.' Or, in other words, ' let faith lead on as at the head of the choir or the graces, and let all the others follow in their order.' The word here rendered *virtue* is the same which is used in ver. 3; and there is included in it, probably, the same general idea which was noticed there. All the things which the apostle specifies, unless *knowledge* be an exception, are *virtues* in the sense in which that word is commonly used; and it can hardly be supposed that the apostle here meant to use a *general* term which would include all of the others. The probability is, therefore, that by the word here he has reference to the common meaning of the Greek word, as referring to manliness, courage,

vigour, energy; and the sense is, that he wished them to evince whatever firmness or courage might be necessary in maintaining the principles of their religion, and in enduring the trials to which their faith might be subjected. True *virtue* is not a tame and passive thing. It requires great energy and boldness, for its very essence is firmness, manliness, and independence. ¶ *And to virtue knowledge.* The knowledge of God and of the way of salvation through the Redeemer, ver. 3. Comp. chap. iii. 8. It is the duty of every Christian to make the highest possible attainments in *knowledge.*

6. *And to knowledge temperance.* On the meaning of the word *temperance*, see Notes on Acts xxiv. 25, and 1 Cor. ix. 25. The word here refers to the mastery over all our evil inclinations and appetites. We are to allow none of them to obtain control over us. See Notes on 1 Cor. vi. 12. This would include, of course, abstinence from intoxicating drinks; but it would also embrace *all* evil passions and propensities. Everything is to be confined within proper limits, and to no propensity of our nature are we to give indulgence beyond the limits which the law of God allows. ¶ *And to temperance patience.* Notes on James i. 4. ¶ *And to patience godliness.* True piety. Notes on ver. 3. Comp. 1 Tim. ii. 2; iii. 16; iv. 7, 8; vi. 3, 5, 6, 11.

7. *And to godliness brotherly kindness.* Love to Christians as such. See Notes on John xiii. 34; Heb. xiii. 1. ¶ *And to brotherly kindness charity.* Love to all mankind. There is to be a peculiar affection for Christians as of the same family; there is to be a true and warm love, however, for all the race. See Notes on 1 Cor. xiii.

8. *For if these things be in you, and abound.* If they are in you in rich abundance; if you are eminent for these

9 But he that lacketh these things is blind,[a] and cannot see afar off, and hath forgotten that he was purged from his old sins.

10 Wherefore the rather, bre-

thren, give diligence [b] to make your calling and election sure : for [c] if ye do these things, ye shall never fall :

a 1 Jn.2.9-11.   b 2 Pe.3.17.   c 1 Jn.3.19; Re.22.14.

things. ¶ *They make* you that ye shall *neither* be *barren nor unfruitful.* They will show that you are not barren or unfruitful. The word rendered *barren,* is, in the margin, *idle.* The word *idle* more accurately expresses the sense of the original. The meaning is, that if they evinced these things, it would show (1) that they were diligent in cultivating the Christian graces, and (2) that it was not a vain thing to attempt to grow in knowledge and virtue. Their efforts would be followed by such happy results as to be an encouragement to exertion. In nothing is there, in fact, more encouragement than in the attempt to become eminent in piety. On no other efforts does God smile more propitiously than on the attempt to secure the salvation of the soul and to do good. A small part of the exertions which men put forth to become rich, or learned, or celebrated for oratory or heroism, would secure the salvation of the soul. In the former, also, men often fail ; in the latter, never.

9. *But he that lacketh these things is blind.* He has no clear views of the nature and the requirements of religion. ¶ *And cannot see afar off.* The word used here, which does not occur elsewhere in the New Testament, (μυωπάζω,) means to shut the eyes ; i. e., to contract the eyelids, to blink, to twinkle, as one who cannot see clearly, and hence to be *near-sighted.* The meaning here is, that he is like one who has an indistinct vision ; one who can see only the objects that are near him, but who has no correct apprehension of objects that are more remote. He sees but a little way into the true nature and design of the gospel. He does not take those large and clear views which would enable him to comprehend the whole system at a glance. ¶ *And hath forgotten that he was purged from his old sins.* He does not remember the obligation which grows out of the fact that a system has been devised to purify the heart, and that he

has been so far brought under the power of that system as to have his sins forgiven. If he had any just view of that, he would see that he was under obligation to make as high attainments as possible, and to cultivate to the utmost extent the Christian graces.

10. *Wherefore the rather, brethren, give diligence.* Ver. 5. 'In view of these things, give the greater diligence to secure your salvation.' The considerations on which Peter based this appeal seem to have been the fact that such promises are made to us, and such hopes held out before us ; the degree of uncertainty thrown over the whole matter of our personal salvation by low attainments in the divine life, and the dreadful condemnation which will ensue if in the end it shall be found that we are destitute of all real piety. The general thought is, that religion is of sufficient importance to claim our highest diligence, and to arouse us to the most earnest efforts to obtain the assurance of salvation. ¶ *To make your calling and election sure.* On the meaning of the word *calling,* see Notes on Eph. iv. 1. On the meaning of the word *election,* see Notes on Rom. ix. 11; 1 Thess. i. 4. Comp. Eph. i. 5. The word rendered election here, (ἐκλογή,) occurs only in this place and in Acts ix. 15; Rom. ix. 11; xi. 5, 7, 28; 1 Thess. i. 4; though corresponding words from the same root denoting *the elect, to elect, to choose,* frequently occur. The word here used means *election,* referring to the act of God, by which those who are saved are *chosen* to eternal life. As the word *calling* must refer to the act of God, so the word *election* must ; for it is God who both *calls* and *chooses* those who shall be saved. The word in the Scriptures usually refers to the actual *choosing* of those who shall be saved; that is, referring to the time when they, in fact, *become* the children of God, rather than to the *purpose* of God that it shall be done; but still there must have been an

eternal purpose, for God makes no choice which he did not always intend to make. The word *sure*, means firm, steadfast, secure, (βεβαίαν.) Here the reference must be to *themselves;* that is, they were so to act as to make it certain to themselves that they had been chosen, and were truly called into the kingdom of God. It cannot refer to God, for no act of theirs could make it more certain on his part, if they had been actually chosen to eternal life. Still, God everywhere treats men as moral agents; and what may be absolutely certain in his mind from the mere purpose that it *shall* be so, is to be made certain to us only by evidence, and in the free exercise of our own powers. The meaning here is, that they were to obtain such evidences of personal piety as to put the question whether they were *called* and *chosen*, so far as their own minds were concerned, to rest; or so as to have undoubted evidence on this point. The Syriac, the Vulgate, and some Greek manuscripts, insert here the expression 'by your good works;' that is, they were to make their calling sure *by* their good works, or by holy living. This clause, as Calvin remarks, is not authorized by the best authority, but it does not materially affect the sense. It was undoubtedly by their 'good works' in the sense of holy living, or of lives consecrated to the service of God, that they were to obtain the evidence that they were true Christians; that is, that they had been really called into the kingdom of God, for there is nothing else on which we can depend for such evidence. God has given no assurance to us by name that he intends to save us. We can rely on no voice, or vision, or new revelation, to prove that it is so. No internal feeling of itself, no raptures, no animal excitement, no confident persuasion in our own minds that we are elected, can be proof in the case; and the only certain *evidence* on which we can rely is that which is found in a life of sincere piety. In view of the important statement of Peter in this verse, then, we may remark, (1.) that he believed in the doctrine of election, for he uses language which obviously implies this, or such as they are accustomed to use who believe the doctrine. (2.) The fact that God has chosen

those who shall be saved, does not make our own efforts unnecessary to make that salvation sure to us. It can be made sure to our own minds only by our own exertions; by obtaining evidence that we are in fact the children of God. There can be no evidence that salvation will be ours, unless there is a holy life; that is, unless there is true religion. Whatever may be the secret purpose of God in regard to us, the only evidence that we have that we shall be saved is to be found in the fact that we are sincere Christians, and are honestly endeavouring to do his will. (3.) It is possible to make our calling and election sure; that is, to have such evidence on the subject that the mind shall be calm, and that there will be no danger of deception. If we can determine the point that we are *in fact* true Christians, that settles the matter—for then the unfailing promise of God meets us that we shall be saved. In making our salvation sure to our own minds, if we are in fact true Christians, we have not to go into an argument to prove that we have sufficient strength to resist temptation, or that we shall be able in any way to keep ourselves. All that matter is settled by the promise of God, that if we are Christians we shall be kept *by him* to salvation. The only question that is to be settled is, whether we are in fact true Christians, and all beyond that may be regarded as determined immutably. But assuredly it is possible for a man to determine the question whether he is or is not a true Christian. (4.) If it *can* be done, it *should* be. Nothing is more important for us to do than this; and to this great inquiry we should apply our minds with unfaltering diligence, until by the grace of God we can say that there are no lingering doubts in regard to our final salvation. ¶ *For if ye do these things.* The things referred to in the previous verses. If you use all diligence to make as high attainments as possible in piety, and *it* you practise the virtues demanded by religion, vers. 5–7. ¶ *Ye shall never fall.* You shall never fall into perdition. That is, you shall certainly be saved.

11. *For so an entrance.* In this manner you shall be admitted into the kingdom of God. ¶ *Shall be ministered*

11 For so an entrance shall be ministered unto you abundantly into the everlasting kingdom of our Lord and Saviour Jesus Christ.

12 Wherefore I will not be negligent to put you always in remembrance of these things, though ye know *them*, and be established in the present truth.

13 Yea, I think it meet, as long as I am in this tabernacle, to stir *a*

unto you. The same Greek word is here used which occurs in ver. 5, and which is there rendered *add.* See Notes on that verse. There was not improbably in the mind of the apostle a recollection of that word; and the sense may be, that 'if they would lead on the virtues and graces referred to in their beautiful order, those graces would attend them in a radiant train to the mansions of immortal glory and blessedness.' See Doddridge *in loc.* ¶ *Abundantly.* Gr., *richly.* That is, the most ample entrance would be furnished; there would be no doubt about their admission there. The gates of glory would be thrown wide open, and they, adorned with all the bright train of graces, would be admitted there. ¶ *Into the everlasting kingdom,* &c. Heaven. It is here called *everlasting*, not because the Lord Jesus shall preside over it as the Mediator, (comp. Notes, 1 Cor. xv. 24,) but because, in the form which shall be established when 'he shall have given it up to the Father,' it will endure for ever. The empire of God which the Redeemer shall set up over the souls of his people shall endure to all eternity. The object of the plan of redemption was to secure their allegiance to God, and that will never terminate.

12. *Wherefore I will not be negligent.* That is, in view of the importance of these things. ¶ *To put you always in remembrance.* To give you the means of having them always in remembrance; to wit, by his writings. ¶ *Though ye know* them. It was of importance for Peter, as it is for ministers of the gospel now, to bring known truths to remembrance. Men are liable to forget them, and they do not exert the influence over them which they ought. It is the office of the ministry not only to impart to a people truths which they did not know before, but a large part of their work is to bring to recollection well-known truths, and to seek that they may exert

a proper influence on the life. Amidst the cares, the business, the amusements, and the temptations of the world, even true Christians are prone to forget them; and the ministers of the gospel render them an essential service, even if they should do nothing more than remind them of truths which are well understood, and which they have known before. A pastor, in order to be useful, need not always aim at originality, or deem it necessary always to present truths which have never been heard of before. He renders an essential service to mankind who *reminds* them of what they know but are prone to forget, and who endeavours to impress plain and familiar truths on the heart and conscience, for these truths are most important for man. ¶ *And be established in the present truth.* That is, the truth which is with you, or which you have received.—*Rob. Lex.* on the word παριμι. The apostle did not doubt that they were now confirmed in the truth as far as it had been made known to them, but he felt that amidst their trials, and especially as they were liable to be drawn away by false teachers, there was need of reminding them of the grounds on which the truths which they had embraced rested, and of adding his own testimony to confirm their Divine origin. Though we may be very firm in our belief of the truth, yet there is a propriety that the grounds of our faith should be stated to us frequently, that they may be always in our remembrance. The mere fact that at present we are firm in the belief of the truth, is no certain evidence that we shall always continue to be; nor because we are thus firm should we deem it improper for our religious teachers to state the grounds on which our faith rests, or to guard us against the arts of those who would attempt to subvert our faith.

13. *Yea, I think it meet.* I think it becomes me as an apostle. It is my

you up, by putting *you* in remembrance;

14 Knowing that shortly I must put off *this* my tabernacle, even as

a Jn.21.18,19.

our Lord Jesus Christ hath shewed me.[a]

15 Moreover, I will endeavour that ye may be able after my decease to have these things always in remembrance.

appropriate duty; a duty which is felt the more as the close of life draws near. ¶ *As long as I am in this tabernacle.* As long as I live ; as long as I am in the body. The body is called a tabernacle, or *tent,* as that in which the soul resides for a little time. See Notes, 2 Cor. v. 1. ¶ *To stir you up, by putting you in remembrance.* To excite or arouse you to a diligent performance of your duties; to keep up in your minds a lively sense of Divine things. Religion becomes more important to a man's mind always as he draws near the close of life, and feels that he is soon to enter the eternal world.

14. *Knowing that shortly I must put off* this *my tabernacle.* That I must die. This he knew, probably, because he was growing old, and was reaching the outer period of human life. It does not appear that he had any express revelation on the point. ¶ *Even as our Lord Jesus Christ hath shewed me.* See Notes, John xxi. 18, 19. This does not mean that he had any new revelation on the subject, showing him that he was soon to die, as many of the ancients supposed ; but the idea is, that the time drew near when he was to die *in the manner* in which the Saviour had told him that he would. He had said (John xxi. 18) that this would occur when he should be 'old,' and as he was now becoming old, he felt that the predicted event was drawing near. Many years had now elapsed since this remarkable prophecy was uttered. It would seem that Peter had never doubted the truth of it, and during all that time he had had before him the distinct assurance that he must die by violence; by having ' his hands stretched forth ;' and by being conveyed by force to some place of death to which he would not of himself go, (John xxi. 18;) but, though the prospect of such a death must have been painful, he never turned away from it ; never sought to abandon his Master's cause ;

and never doubted that it would be so. This is one of the few instances that have occurred in the world, where a man knew distinctly, long beforehand, what would be the manner of his own death, and where he could have it constantly in his eye. *We* cannot foresee this in regard to ourselves, but we may learn to feel that death is not far distant, and may accustom ourselves to think upon it in whatever manner it may come upon us, as Peter did, and endeavour to prepare for it. Peter would naturally seek to prepare himself for death in the particular form in which he knew it would occur to him; we should prepare for it in whatever way it may occur to us. The subject of crucifixion would be one of peculiar interest to him ; to us death itself should be the subject of peculiar interest—the manner is to be left to God. Whatever may be the signs of its approach, whether sickness or grey hairs, we should meditate much upon an event so solemn to us; and as these indications thicken we should be more diligent, as Peter was, in doing the work that God has given us to do. Our days, like the fabled Sybil's leaves, become more valuable as they are diminished in number; and as the 'inevitable hour' draws nearer to us, we should labour more diligently in our Master's cause, gird our loins more closely, and trim our lamps. Peter thought of the cross, for it was such a death that he was led to anticipate. Let us think of the bed of languishing on which we may die, or of the blow that may strike us suddenly down in the midst of our way, calling us without a moment's warning into the presence of our Judge.

15. *Moreover, I will endeavour.* I will leave such a permanent record of my views on these subjects that you may not forget them. He meant not only to declare his sentiments orally, but to record them that they might be

perused when he was dead. He had such a firm conviction of the truth and value of the sentiments which he held, that he would use all the means in his power that the church and the world should not forget them. ¶ *After my decease.* My *exode,* (ἔξοδον;) my journey out; my departure; my exit from life. This is not the usual word to denote death, but is rather a word denoting that he was going on a journey *out* of this world. He did not expect to cease to be, but he expected to go on his travels to a distant abode. This idea runs through all this beautiful description of the feelings of Peter as he contemplated death. Hence he speaks of taking down the 'tabernacle' or *tent,* the temporary abode of the soul, that his spirit might be removed to another place, (ver. 13;) and hence he speaks of an *exode* from the present life—a journey to another world. This is the true notion of death; and if so, two things follow from it: (1,) we should make preparation for it, as we do for a journey, and the more in proportion to the distance that we are to travel, and the time that we are to be absent; and (2,) when the preparation is made, we should not be unwilling to enter on the journey, as we are not now when we are prepared to leave our homes to visit some remote part of our own country, or a distant land. ¶ *To have these things always in remembrance.* By his writings. We may learn from this, (1.) that when a Christian grows old, and draws near to death, his sense of the value of Divine truth by no means diminishes. As he approaches the eternal world; as from its borders he surveys the past, and looks on to what is to come; as he remembers what benefit the truths of religion have conferred on him in life, and sees what a miserable being he would now be if he had no such hope as the gospel inspires; as he looks on the whole influence of those truths on his family and friends, on his country and the world, their value rises before him with a magnitude which he never saw before, and he desires most earnestly that they should be seen and embraced by all. A man on the borders of eternity is likely to have a very deep sense of the value of the Christian religion; and is he not then in favourable circumstances to estimate this matter aright? Let any one place himself in imagination in the situation of one who is on the borders of the eternal world, as all in fact soon will be, and can he have any doubt about the value of religious truth? (2.) We may learn from what Peter says here, that it is the *duty* of those who are drawing near to the eternal world, and who are the friends of religion, to do all they can that the truths of Christianity 'may be always had in remembrance.' Every man's experience of the value of religion, and the results of his examination and observation, should be regarded as the property of the world, and should not be lost. As he is about to die, he should seek, by all the means in his power, that those truths should be perpetuated and propagated. This duty may be discharged by some in counsels offered to the young, as they are about to enter on life, giving them the results of their own experience, observation, and reflections on the subject of religion; by some, by an example so consistent that it cannot be soon forgotten—a legacy to friends and to the world of much more value than accumulated silver and gold; by some, by solemn warnings or exhortations on the bed of death; in other cases, by a recorded experience of the conviction and value of religion, and a written defence of its truth, and illustration of its nature—for every man who can write a good book owes it to the church and the world to do it; by others, in leaving the means of publishing and spreading good books in the world. He does a good service to his own age, and to future ages, who records the results of his observations and his reflections in favour of the truth in a book that shall be readable; and though the book itself may be ultimately forgotten, it may have saved some persons from ruin, and may have accomplished its part in keeping up the knowledge of the truth in his own generation. Peter, as a minister of the gospel, felt himself bound to do this, and no men have so good an opportunity of doing this now as ministers of the gospel; no men have more ready access to the press; no men have so much certainty that they will have the public attention, if they will write anything worth reading; no men, commonly, in a

16 For we have not followed cunningly devised fables, *a* when we made known unto you the power

a 2 Co.4.2.

and coming of our Lord Jesus Christ, but were eye-witnesses *b* of his majesty.

b Mat.17.1-5; Jn.1.14.

community are better educated, or are more accustomed to write ; no men, by their profession, seem to be so much called to address their fellow-men in any way in favour of the truth ; and it is matter of great marvel that men who have such opportunities, and who seem especially called to the work, do not do more of this kind of service in the cause of religion. Themselves soon to die, how can they help desiring that they may leave *something* that shall bear an honourable, though humble, testimony to truths which they so much prize, and which they are appointed to defend ? A tract may live long after the author is in the grave ; and who can calculate the results which have followed the efforts of Baxter and Edwards to keep up in the world the remembrance of the truths which they deemed of so much value ? This little epistle of Peter has shed light on the path of men now for eighteen hundred years, and will continue to do it until the second coming of the Saviour.

16. *For we have not followed cunningly devised fables.* That is, fictions or stories invented by artful men, and resting on no solid foundation. The doctrines which they held about the coming of the Saviour were not, like many of the opinions of the Greeks, defended by weak and sophistical reasoning, but were based on solid evidence—evidence furnished by the personal observation of competent witnesses. It is true of the gospel, in general, that it is not founded on cunningly devised fables; but the particular point referred to here is the promised coming of the Saviour. The evidence of that fact Peter proposes now to adduce. ¶ *When we made known unto you.* Probably Peter here refers particularly to statements respecting the coming of the Saviour in his first epistle, (chap. i. 5, 13; iv. 13;) but this was a common topic in the preaching, and in the epistles, of the apostles. It may, therefore, have referred to statements made to them at some time in his preaching, as well as to what he said in his former epistle. The apostles laid

great stress on the second coming of the Saviour, and often dwelt upon it. Comp. 1 Thess. iv. 16; Notes, Acts i. 11. ¶ *The power and coming.* These two words refer to the same thing; and the meaning is, his *powerful coming*, or his *coming in power.* The advent of the Saviour is commonly represented as connected with the exhibition of power. Matt. xxiv. 30, 'Coming in the clouds of heaven, with power.' See Notes on that verse. Comp. Luke xxii. 69 ; Mark iii. 9. The *power* evinced will be by raising the dead ; summoning the world to judgment; determining the destiny of men, &c. When the coming of the Saviour, therefore, was referred to by the apostles in their preaching, it was probably always in connection with the declaration that it would be accompanied by exhibitions of great power and glory—as it undoubtedly will be. The fact that the Lord Jesus would thus return, it is clear, had been denied by some among those to whom this epistle was addressed, and it was important to state the evidence on which it was to be believed. The *grounds* on which they denied it (chap. iii. 4) were, that there were no appearances of his approach ; that the promise had not been fulfilled ; that all things continued as they had been ; and that the affairs of the world moved on as they always had done. To meet and counteract this error—an error which so prevailed that many were in danger of ' falling from their own steadfastness,' (chap. iii. 17,)—Peter states the proof on which he believed in the coming of the Saviour. ¶ *But were eye-witnesses of his majesty.* On the mount of transfiguration, Matt. xvii. 1—5. See Notes on that passage. That transfiguration was witnessed only by Peter, James, and John. But it may be asked, how the facts there witnessed demonstrate the point under consideration—that the Lord Jesus will come with power ? To this it may be replied, (1,) that these apostles had there such a view of the Saviour in his glory as to convince them beyond doubt

17 For he received from God the Father honour and glory, when there came such a voice to him from the excellent glory, This is my beloved Son, in whom I am well pleased.

18 And this voice which came

a Ps.119.105; Pr.6.23.　　　b Re.2.28; 22.16.

from heaven we heard, when we were with him in the holy mount.

19 We have also a more sure word of prophecy; whereunto ye do well that ye take heed, as unto a light *a* that shineth in a dark place, until the day dawn, and the day-star *b* arise in your hearts:

---

that he was the Messiah. (2.) That there was a direct attestation given to that fact by a voice from heaven, declaring that he was the beloved Son of God. (3.) That that transfiguration was understood to have an important reference to the coming of the Saviour in his kingdom and his glory, and was designed to be a representation of the manner in which he would then appear. This is referred to distinctly by each one of the three evangelists who have mentioned the transfiguration. Matt. xvi. 28, 'There be some standing here which shall not taste of death till they see the Son of man coming in his kingdom;' Mark ix. 1, 2; Luke ix. 27, 28. The transfiguration which occurred soon after these words were spoken was *designed* to show them what he would be in his glory, and to furnish to them a demonstration which they could never forget, that he would yet set up his kingdom in the world. (4.) They had in fact such a view of him as he would be in his kingdom, that they could entertain no doubt on the point; and the fact, as it impressed their own minds, they made known to others. The evidence as it lay in Peter's mind was, that that transfiguration was *designed* to furnish proof to them that the Messiah would certainly appear in glory, and to give them a view of him as coming to reign which would never fade from their memory. As that had not yet been accomplished, he maintained that the evidence was clear that it must occur at some future time. As the transfiguration was *with reference* to his coming in his kingdom, it was proper for Peter to use it with that reference, or as bearing on that point.

17. *For he received from God the Father honour and glory.* He was honoured by God in being thus addressed. ¶ *When there came such a voice*

to him from the excellent glory. The magnificent splendour; the bright cloud which overshadowed them, Matt. xvii. 5. ¶ *This is my beloved Son, in whom I am well pleased.* See Notes, Matt. xvii. 5; iii. 17. This demonstrated that he was the Messiah. Those who heard that voice could not doubt this; they never did afterwards doubt.

18. *And this voice which came from heaven we heard.* To wit, Peter, and James, and John. ¶ *When we were with him in the holy mount.* Called holy on account of the extraordinary manifestation of the Redeemer's glory there. It is not certainly known what mountain this was, but it has commonly been supposed to be Mount Tabor. See Notes, Matt. xvii. 1.

19. *We have also a more sure word of prophecy.* That is, a prophecy pertaining to the coming of the Lord Jesus; for that is the point under discussion. There has been considerable diversity of opinion in regard to the meaning of this passage. Some have supposed that the apostle, when he says, 'a *more sure* word,' did not intend to make any comparison between the miracle of the transfiguration and prophecy, but that he meant to say merely that the word of prophecy was *very* sure, and could certainly be relied on. Others have supposed that the meaning is, that the prophecies which foretold his coming into the world having been confirmed by the fact of his advent, are rendered more sure and undoubted than when they were uttered, and may now be confidently appealed to. So Rosenmüller, Benson, Macknight, Clarke, Wetstein, and Grotius. Luther renders it, ' we have a firm prophetic word;' omitting the comparison. A literal translation of the passage would be, ' and we have the prophetic word more firm.' If a *com-parison* is intended, it may be either

that the prophecy was more sure than the *fables* referred to in ver. 16; or than the miracle of the transfiguration; or than the word which was heard in the holy mount; or than the prophecies even in the time when they were first spoken. If such a comparison was designed, the most obvious of these interpretations would be, that the prophecy was more certain proof than was furnished in the mount of transfiguration. But it seems probable that no *comparison* was intended, and that the thing on which Peter intended to fix the eye was not that the prophecy was a *better* evidence respecting the advent of the Messiah than other evidences, but that it was a *strong* proof which demanded their particular attention, as being of a firm and decided character. There can be no doubt that the apostle refers here to what is contained in the Old Testament; for, in ver. 21, he speaks of the prophecy as that which was spoken 'in old time, by men that were moved by the Holy Ghost.' The *point* to which the prophecies related, and to which Peter referred, was the great doctrine respecting the coming of the Messiah, embracing perhaps all that pertained to his work, or all that he designed to do by his advent. They had had one illustrious proof respecting his advent as a glorious Saviour by his transfiguration on the mount; and the apostle here says that the prophecies abounded with truths on these points, and that they ought to give earnest heed to the disclosures which they made, and to compare them diligently with facts as they occurred, that they might be confirmed more and more in the truth. If, however, as the more obvious sense of this passage *seems* to be, and as many suppose to be the correct interpretation, (see Doddridge, *in loc.*, and Professor Stuart, on the canon of the Old Test., p. 329,) it means that the prophecy was more sure, more steadfast, more to be depended on than even what the three disciples had seen and heard in the mount of transfiguration, this may be regarded as true in the following respects: (1.) The prophecies are *numerous*, and by their number they furnish a stronger proof than could be afforded by a single manifestation, however clear

and glorious. (2.) They were *recorded*, and might be the subject of careful comparison with the events as they occurred. (3.) They were written long beforehand, and it could not be urged that the testimony which the prophets bore was owing to any illusion on their minds, or to any agreement among the different writers to impose on the world. Though Peter regarded the testimony which he and James and John bore to the glory of the Saviour, from what they saw on the holy mount, as strong and clear confirmation that he was the Son of God, yet he could not but be aware that it might be suggested by a caviller that they might have *agreed* to impose on others, or that they might have been dazzled and deceived by some natural phenomenon occurring there. Comp. Kuinoel on Matt. xvii. 1, seq. (4.) Even supposing that there was a miracle in the case, the evidence of the prophecies, embracing many points in the same general subject, and extending through a long series of years, would be more satisfactory than any single miracle whatever. See Doddridge, *in loc.* The general meaning is, that the fact that he had come as the Messiah was disclosed in the mount by such a manifestation of his glory, and of what he would be, that they who saw it could not doubt it; the same thing the apostle says was more fully shown also in the prophecies, and these prophecies demanded their close and prolonged attention. ¶ *Whereunto ye do well that ye take heed.* They are worthy of your study, of your close and careful investigation. There is perhaps no study more worthy of the attention of Christians than that of the prophecies. ¶ *As unto a light that shineth in a dark place.* That is, the prophecies resemble a candle, lamp, or torch, in a dark room, or in an obscure road at night. They make objects distinct which were before unseen; they enable us to behold many things which would be otherwise invisible. The object of the apostle in this representation seems to have been, to state that the prophecies do not give a *perfect* light, or that they do not remove *all* obscurity, but that they shed some light on objects which would otherwise be *entirely* dark, and that the light which they furnished

20 Knowing this first, that no prophecy of the scripture is of any private interpretation.

was so valuable that we ought by all means to endeavour to avail ourselves of it. Until the day shall dawn, and we shall see objects by the clear light of the sun, they are to be our guide. A lamp is of great value in a dark night, though it may not disclose objects so clearly as the light of the sun. But it may be a safe and sure guide ; and a man who has to travel in dark and dangerous places, does 'well' to 'take heed' to his lamp. ¶ *Until the day dawn.* Until you have the clearer light which shall result from the dawning of the day. The reference here is to the morning light as compared with a lamp ; and the meaning is, that we should attend to the light furnished by the prophecies until the truth shall be rendered more distinct by the events as they shall actually be disclosed—until the brighter light which shall be shed on all things by the glory of the second advent of the Saviour, and the clearing up of what is now obscure in the splendours of the heavenly world. The point of comparison is between the necessary obscurity of prophecy, and the clearness of events when they actually occur—a difference like that which is observable in the objects around us when seen by the shining of the lamp and by the light of the sun. The apostle directs the mind onward to a period when all shall be clear—to that glorious time when the Saviour shall return to receive his people to himself in that heaven where all shall be light. Comp. Rev. xxi. 23—25 ; xxii. 5. Meantime we should avail ourselves of all the light which we have, and should apply ourselves diligently to the study of the prophecies of the Old Testament which are still unfulfilled, and of those in the New Testament which direct the mind onward to brighter and more glorious scenes than this world has yet witnessed. In our darkness they are a cheering lamp to guide our feet, till that illustrious day shall dawn. Comp. Notes, 1 Cor. xiii. 9, 10. ¶ *And the day-star.* The morning star —the bright star that at certain periods of the year leads on the day, and which

is a pledge that the morning is about to dawn. Comp. Rev. ii. 28; xxii. 16. ¶ *Arise in your hearts. On* your hearts ; that is, sheds its beams on your hearts. Till you see the indications of that approaching day in which all is light. The period referred to here by the approaching day that is to diffuse this light, is when the Saviour shall return in the full revelation of his glory—the splendour of his kingdom. Then all will be clear. Till that time, we should search the prophetic records, and strengthen our faith, and comfort our hearts, by the predictions of the future glory of his reign. Whether this refers, as some suppose, to his reign on earth, either personally or by the principles of his religion universally prevailing, or, as others suppose, to the brighter revelations of heaven when he shall come to receive his people to himself, it is equally clear that a brighter time than any that has yet occurred is to dawn on our race, and equally true that we should regard the prophecies, as we do the morning star, as the cheering harbinger of day.

20. *Knowing this first.* Bearing this steadily in mind as a primary and most important truth. ¶ *That no prophecy of the Scripture.* No prophecy contained in the inspired records. The word *scripture* here shows that the apostle referred particularly to the prophecies recorded in the Old Testament. The remark which he makes about prophecy is general, though it is designed to bear on a particular class of the prophecies. ¶ *Is of any private interpretation.* The expression here used (ἰδίας ἐπιλύσεως) has given rise to as great a diversity of interpretation, and to as much discussion, as perhaps any phrase in the New Testament; and to the present time there is no general agreement among expositors as to its meaning. It would be foreign to the design of these Notes, and would be of little utility, to enumerate the different interpretations which have been given of the passage, or to examine them in detail. It will be sufficient to remark, preparatory to endeavouring to ascertain the true sense

of the passage, that some have held that it teaches that no prophecy can be interpreted of itself, but can be understood only by comparing it with the event; others, that it teaches that the prophets did not themselves understand what they wrote, but were mere passive organs under the dictation of the Holy Spirit to communicate to future times what they could not themselves explain; others, that it teaches that 'no prophecy is of self-interpretation,' *(Horsley;)* others, that it teaches that the prophecies, besides having a literal signification, have also a hidden and mystical sense which cannot be learned from the prophecies themselves, but is to be perceived by a peculiar power of insight imparted by the Holy Ghost, enabling men to understand their recondite mysteries. It would be easy to show that some of these opinions are absurd, and that none of them are sustained by the fair interpretation of the language used, and by the drift of the passage. The more correct interpretation, as it seems to me, is that which supposes that the apostle teaches that the truths which the prophets communicated were not originated by themselves; were not of their own suggestion or invention; were not their own opinions, but were of higher origin, and were imparted by God; and according to this the passage may be explained, ' knowing this as a point of first importance when you approach the prophecies, or always bearing this in mind, that it is a great principle in regard to the prophets, that what they communicated *was not of their own disclosure;* that is, was not revealed or originated by them.' That this is the correct interpretation will be apparent from the following considerations: (1.) It accords with the *design* of the apostle, which is to produce an impressive sense of the importance and value of the prophecies, and to lead those to whom he wrote to study them with diligence. This could be secured in no way so well as by assuring them that the writings which he wished them to study did not contain truths originated by the human mind, but that they were of higher origin. (2.) This interpretation accords with what is said in the following verse, and is the only one of all those proposed that is

consistent with that, or in connection with which that verse will have any force. In that verse (21,) a *reason* is given for what is said here: ' For (γὰρ) the prophecy came not in old time *by the will of man,'* &c. But this can be a good reason for what is said here only on the supposition that the apostle meant to say that what they communicated was not originated by themselves; that it was of a higher than human origin; that the prophets spake 'as they were moved by the Holy Ghost.' This fact was a good reason why they should show profound respect for the prophecies, and study them with attention. But how could the fact that *they were moved by the Holy Ghost* be a reason for studying them, if the meaning here is that the prophets could not understand their own language, or that the prophecy could be understood only by the event, or that the prophecy had a double meaning, &c.? If the prophecies were of Divine origin, then *that* was a good reason why they should be approached with reverence, and should be profoundly studied. (3.) This interpretation accords as well, to say the least, with the fair meaning of the language employed, as either of the other opinions proposed. The word rendered *interpretation* (ἐπί-λυσις) occurs nowhere else in the New Testament. It properly means *solution,* (Rob. Lex.,) *disclosure,* (Prof. Stuart on the Old Testament, p. 328,) *making free (Passow,)* with the notion that what is thus released or loosed was before bound, entangled, obscure. The verb from which this word is derived (ἐπιλύω) means, *to let loose upon,* as dogs upon a hare,(Xen. Mem. 7,8; *ib* 9,10;) to loose or open letters; to loosen a band; to loose or disclose a riddle or a dark saying, and then to enlighten, illustrate, &c.—*Passow.* It is twice used in the New Testament. Mark iv. 34, 'He *expounded* all things to his disciples; Acts xix. 39, 'It shall be *determined* in a lawful assembly.' The verb would be applicable to loosing anything which is bound or confined, and thence to the explanation of a mysterious doctrine or a parable, or to a disclosure of what was before unknown. The word, according to this, in the place before us, would mean the disclosure of what was before

21 For the prophecy came not [1] in ^aold time by the will of man : but holy men of God spake *as they were* moved by ^bthe Holy Ghost.

1 Or, *at any.*   a Lu.1.70.   b 2 Ti.3.16.

bound, or retained, or unknown ; either what had never been communicated at all, or what had been communicated obscurely ; and the idea is, ' no prophecy recorded in the Scripture is of, or comes from, any exposition or disclosure of the will and purposes of God by the prophets themselves.' It is not a thing of their own, or a private matter originating with themselves, but it is to be traced to a higher source. If this be the true interpretation, then it follows that the prophecies are to be regarded as of higher than any human origin ; and then, also, it follows that this passage should not be used to prove that the prophets did not understand the nature of their own communications, or that they were mere unconscious and passive instruments in the hand of God to make known his will. Whatever may be the truth on those points, this passage proves nothing in regard to them, any more than the fact that a minister of religion now declares truth which he did not originate, but which is to be traced to God as its author, proves that he does not understand what he himself says. It follows, also, that this passage cannot be adduced by the Papists to prove that the people at large should not have free access to the word of God, and should not be allowed to interpret it for themselves. It makes no affirmation on that point, and does not even contain any *principle* of which such a use can be made ; for, (1.) whatever it means, it is confined to *prophecy ;* it does not embrace the whole Bible. (2.) Whatever it means, it merely states a *fact ;* it does not enjoin a *duty.* It states, as a fact, that there was *something* about the prophecies which was not of private solution, but it does not state that it is the duty of the church to *prevent* any private explanation or opinion even of the prophecies. (3.) It says nothing about *the church* as empowered to give a public or authorized interpretation of the prophecies. There is not a hint, or an intimation of any kind, that the church is intrusted with any such power whatever. There never was any greater perversion of a passage of Scripture than to suppose that this teaches that any class of men is not to have free access to the Bible. The effect of the passage, properly interpreted, should be to lead us to study the Bible with profound reverence, as having a higher than any human origin, not to turn away from it as if it were unintelligible, nor to lead us to suppose that it can be interpreted only by one class of men. The fact that it discloses truths which the human mind could not of itself have originated, is a good reason for studying it with diligence and with prayer—not for supposing that it is unlawful for us to attempt to understand it ; a good reason for reverence and veneration for it—not for sanctified neglect.

21. *For the prophecy came not in old time.* Marg., ' or, *at any.*' The Greek word (ποτὲ) will bear either construction. It would be true in either sense, but the reference is particularly to the recorded prophecies in the Old Testament. What was true of them, however, is true of all prophecy, that it is not by the will of man. The word *prophecy* here is without the article, meaning prophecy in general—all that is prophetic in the Old Testament ; or, in a more general sense still, all that the prophets taught, whether relating to future events or not. ¶ *By the will of man.* It was not of human origin ; not discovered by the human mind. The word *will,* here seems to be used in the sense of *prompting* or *suggestion ;* men did not speak by their own suggestion, but as truth was brought to them by God. ¶ *But holy men of God.* Pious men commissioned by God, or employed by him as his messengers to mankind. ¶ *Spake* as they were *moved by the Holy Ghost.* Comp. 2 Tim. iii. 16. The Greek phrase here (ὑπὸ Πνεύματος ἁγίου φερόμενοι) means *borne along, moved, influenced* by the Holy Ghost. The idea is, that in what they spake they were *carried along* by an influence from above. They moved in the case

CHAPTER II.

BUT there *a* were false prophets also among the people even as there shall be false teachers among you, *b* who privily shall bring in damnable heresies, even denying the Lord that bought them, and bring upon themselves swift destruction.

a De.13.1,&c.　　*b* Mat.24.5,24; Ac.20.29,30; 1 Ti.4.1.

only as they were moved ; they spake only as the influence of the Holy Ghost was upon them. They were no more self-moved than a vessel at sea is that is impelled by the wind ; and as the progress made by the vessel is to be measured by the impulse bearing upon it, so the statements made by the prophets are to be traced to the impulse which bore upon their minds. They were not, indeed, in all respects like such a vessel, but only in regard to the fact that all they said as prophets was to be traced to the foreign influence that bore upon their minds. There could not be, therefore, a more decided declaration than this in proof that the prophets were inspired. If the authority of Peter is admitted, his positive and explicit assertion settles the question. If this be so, also, then the point with reference to which he makes this observation is abundantly confirmed, that the prophecies demand our earnest attention, and that we should give all the heed to them which we would to a light or lamp when travelling in a dangerous way, and in a dark night. In a still more general sense, the remark here made may also be applied to the whole of the Scriptures. We are in a dark world. We see few things clearly ; and all around us, on a thousand questions, there is the obscurity of midnight. By nature there is nothing to cast light on those questions, and we are perplexed, bewildered, embarrassed. The Bible is given to us to shed light on our way. It is the *only* light which we have respecting the future, and though it does not give *all* the information which we might desire in regard to what is to come, yet it gives us sufficient light to guide us to heaven. It teaches us what it is necessary to know about God, about our duty, and about the way of salvation, in order to conduct us safely ; and no one who has committed himself to its direction, has been suffered to wander finally away from the paths of salva-

tion. It is, therefore, a duty to attend to the instructions which the Bible imparts, and to commit ourselves to its holy guidance in our journey to a better world : for soon, if we are faithful to its teachings, the light of eternity will dawn upon us, and there, amidst its cloudless splendour, we shall see as we are seen, and know as we are known ; then we shall ' need no candle, neither light of the sun; for the Lord God shall give us light, and we shall reign for ever and ever.' Comp. Rev. xxi. 22–24 ; xxii. 5.

CHAPTER II.

ANALYSIS OF THE CHAPTER.

THE general subject of this chapter is stated in the first verse, and it embraces these points : (1,) that it might be expected that there would be false teachers among Christians, as there were false prophets in ancient times ; (2,) that they would introduce destructive errors, leading many astray ; and, (3,) that they would be certainly punished. The design of the chapter is to illustrate and defend these points.

I. That there would be such false teachers the apostle expressly states in ver. 1 ; and incidentally in that verse, and elsewhere in the chapter, he notices some of their characteristics, or some of the doctrines which they would hold. (*a*) They would deny the Lord that bought them, ver. 1. See Notes on that verse. (*b*) They would be influenced by covetousness, and their object in their attempting to seduce others from the faith, and to induce them to become followers of themselves, would be to make money, ver. 3. (*c*) They would be corrupt, beastly, and licentious in their conduct ; and it would be one design of their teaching to show that the indulgence of gross passions was not inconsistent with religion ; ver. 10, ' that walk after the flesh, in the lust of uncleanness ;' ver. 12, ' as natural brute beasts ;' ' shall perish in their own corruption ;' ver. 14, ' having eyes full of adultery, and that cannot cease from sin ;' ver. 22, ' the dog has returned to his own vomit again.' (d) They would be proud, arrogant, and self-willed; men who would despise all proper government, and who would be thoroughly '*radical*' in their views ; ver. 10, ' and despise government ; presumptuous are they and self-willed, they are not afraid to speak evil of dignities ;' ver. 18, ' they speak great swelling words of vanity.' (e) They were persons who had been formerly of corrupt lives, but who had become professing Christians. This is implied in vers. 20–22. They are spoken of as having ' escaped the pollutions of the world, through the knowledge of the Lord and Saviour Jesus Christ ;' as ' having known the ways of righteousness,' but as having turned again to their former corrupt practices and lusts ; ' it has happened to them according to the true proverb,' &c. There were various classes of persons in primitive times, coming under the general appellation of the term *Gnostic*, to whom this description would apply, and it is probable that they had begun to broach their doctrines in the times of the apostles. Among those persons were the Ebionites, Corinthians, Nicolaitanes, &c.

II. These false teachers would obtain followers, and their teachings would be likely to allure many. This is intimated more than once in the chapter : ver. 2, ' and many shall follow their pernicious ways ;' ver. 3, ' and through covetousness shall they with feigned words make merchandise of you ;' ver. 14, ' beguiling unstable souls.' Comp. ver. 18.

III. They would certainly be punished. A large part of the chapter is taken up in proving this point, and especially in showing from the examples of others who had erred in a similar manner, that they could not escape destruction. In doing this, the apostle refers to the following facts and illustrations : (1.) The case of the angels that sinned, and that were cast down to hell, ver. 4. If God brought such dreadful punishment on those who were once before his throne, wicked men could have no hope of escape. (2.) The case of the wicked in the time of Noah, who were

cut off by the flood, ver. 5. (3.) The case of Sodom and Gomorrah, ver. 6. (4.) The *character* of the persons referred to was such that they could have no hope of escape. (a) They were corrupt, sensual, presumptuous, and self-willed, and were even worse than the rebel angels had been—men that seemed to be made to be taken and destroyed, vers. 10–12. (b) They were spots and blemishes, sensual and adulterers, emulating the example of Balaam, who was rebuked by even a dumb ass for his iniquity, vers. 13–16. (c) They allured others to sin under the specious promise of liberty, while they were themselves the slaves of debased appetites, and gross and sensual passions, vers. 17–19. From the entire description in this chapter, it is clear that the persons referred to, though once professors of religion, had become eminently abandoned and corrupt. It may not, indeed, be easy to identify them with any particular sect or class then existing and now known in history, though not a few of the sects in the early Christian church bore a strong resemblance to this description ; but there have been those in every age who have strongly resembled these persons ; and this chapter, therefore, possesses great value as containing important warnings against the arts of false teachers, and the danger of being seduced by them from the truth. Compare Introduction to the Epistle of Jude, § 3, 4.

1. *But there were false prophets also among the people.* In the previous chapter, (vers. 19–21,) Peter had appealed to the prophecies as containing unanswerable proofs of the truth of the Christian religion. He says, however, that he did not mean to say that all who claimed to be prophets were true messengers of God. There were many who pretended to be such, who only led the people astray. It is unnecessary to say, that such men have abounded in all ages where there have been true prophets. ¶ *Even as there shall be false teachers among you.* The fact that false teachers would arise in the church is often adverted to in the New Testament. Compare Matt. xxiv. 5. 24 ; Acts xx. 29, 30. ¶ *Who privily* That is, in a secret manner, or under

plausible arts and pretences. They would not at first make an open avowal of their doctrines, but would, in fact, while their teachings *seemed* to be in accordance with truth, covertly maintain opinions which would sap the very foundations of religion. The Greek word here used, and which is rendered ' who privily shall bring in,' (παρεισάγω,) means properly *to lead in by the side of others ; to lead in along with others.* Nothing could better express the usual way in which error is introduced. It is *by the side,* or *along with,* other doctrines which are true ; that is, while the mind is turned mainly to other subjects, and is off its guard, gently and silently to lay down some principle, which, being admitted, would lead to the error, or from which the error would follow as a natural consequence. Those who inculcate error rarely do it openly. If they would at once boldly ' deny the Lord that bought them,' it would be easy to meet them, and the mass of professed Christians would be in no danger of embracing the error. But when principles are laid down which may lead to that ; when doubts on remote points are suggested which may involve it ; or when a long train of reasoning is pursued which may secretly tend to it ; there is much more probability that the mind will be corrupted from the truth. ¶ *Damnable heresies.* αἱρέσεις ἀπωλείας. ' Heresies of destruction ;' that is, heresies that will be followed by destruction. The Greek word which is rendered *damnable,* is the same which in the close of the verse is rendered *destruction* It is so rendered also in Matt. vii. 13 ; Rom. ix. 22 ; Phil. iii. 19 ; 2 Pet. iii. 16—in all of which places it refers to the future loss of the soul. The same word also is rendered *perdition* in John xvii. 12 ; Phil. i. 28 ; 1 Tim. vi. 9 ; Heb. x. 39 ; 2 Pet. iii. 7 ; Rev. xvii. 8, 11—in all which places it has the same reference. On the meaning of the word rendered ' *heresies,*' see Notes on Acts xxiv. 14 ; 1 Cor. xi. 19. The idea of *sect* or *party* is that which is conveyed by this word, rather than doctrinal errors ; but it is evident that in this case the formation of the sect or party, as is the fact in most cases, would be founded on error of doctrine.

The thing which these false teachers would attempt would be divisions, alienations, or parties, in the church, but these would be based on the erroneous doctrines which they would promulgate. What would be the particular doctrine in this case is immediately specified, to wit, that they 'would deny the Lord that bought them.' The idea then is, that these false teachers would form sects or parties in the church, of a destructive or ruinous nature, founded on a denial of the Lord that bought them. Such a formation of sects would be ruinous to piety, to good morals, and to the soul. The authors of these sects, holding the views which they did, and influenced by the motives which they would be, and practising the morals which they would practise, as growing out of their principles, would bring upon themselves swift and certain destruction. It is not possible now to determine to what particular class of errorists the apostle had reference here, but it is generally supposed that it was to some form of the Gnostic belief. There were many early sects of so-called *heretics* to whom what he here says would be applicable. ¶ *Even denying the Lord that bought them.* This must mean that they held doctrines which were *in fact* a denial of the Lord, or the tendency of which would be a denial of the Lord, for it cannot be supposed that, while they professed to be Christians, they would openly and avowedly deny him. To 'deny the Lord' may be either to deny his existence, his claims, or his attributes ; it is to withhold from him, in our belief and profession, anything which is essential to a proper conception of him. The particular thing, however, which is mentioned here as entering into that self-denial, is something connected with the fact that he had ' *bought* ' them. It was such a denial of the Lord *as having bought them,* as to be in fact a renunciation of the peculiarity of the Christian religion. There has been much difference of opinion as to the meaning of the word *Lord* in this place —whether it refers to God the Father, or to the Lord Jesus Christ. The Greek word is Δεσπότης — *despotes.* Many expositors have maintained that it refers to the Father, and that when it is said that he had *bought* them, it means in a general sense that he was the Author of the plan of redemption, and had *caused* them to be purchased or redeemed. Michaelis supposes that the Gnostics are referred to as denying the Father by asserting that he was not the Creator of the universe, maintaining that it was created by an inferior being.—Intro. to New Testament, iv. 360. Whitby, Benson, Slade, and many others, maintain that this refers to the Father as having originated the plan by which men are redeemed; and the same opinion is held, of necessity, by those who deny the doctrine of general atonement. The only *arguments* to show that it refers to God the Father would be, (1,) that the word used here ($\Delta\epsilon\sigma\pi\acute{o}\tau\eta\varsigma$) is not the usual term ($\kappa\acute{v}\rho\iota\sigma\varsigma$) by which the Lord Jesus is designated in the New Testament; and (2,) that the admission that it refers to the Lord Jesus would lead inevitably to the conclusion that some will perish for whom Christ died. That it *does*, however, refer to the Lord Jesus, seems to me to be plain from the following considerations: (1.) It is the obvious interpretation; that which would be given by the great mass of Christians, and about which there could never have been any hesitancy if it had not been supposed that it would lead to the doctrine of general atonement. As to the alleged fact that the word used (*Despotes*) is not that which is commonly applied to the Lord Jesus, that may be admitted to be true, but still the word here may be understood as applied to him. It properly means *a master* as opposed to a servant; then it is used as denoting supreme authority, and is thus applied to God, and may be in that sense to the Lord Jesus Christ, as head over all things, or as having supreme authority over the church. It occurs in the New Testament only in the following places: 1 Tim. vi. 1, 2; Titus ii. 9; 1 Pet. ii. 18, where it is rendered *masters;* Luke ii. 29; Acts iv. 24; Rev. vi. 10, where it is rendered *Lord*, and is applied to God; and in Jude 4, and in the passage before us, in both which places it is rendered *Lord*, and is probably to be regarded as applied to the Lord Jesus. There is nothing in the proper signification of the word which would forbid this. (2.) The phrase is one that is properly applicable to the Lord Jesus as having *bought* us with his blood. The Greek word is $\dot{\alpha}\gamma\sigma\rho\acute{\alpha}\zeta\omega$—a word which means properly *to market, to buy, to purchase*, and then to redeem, or acquire for one's self by a price paid, or by a ransom. It is rendered *buy* or *bought* in the following places in the New Testament: Matt. xiii. 44, 46; xiv. 15; xxi. 12; xxv. 9, 10; xxvii. 7; Mark. vi. 36, 37; xi. 15; xv. 46; xvi. 1; Luke ix. 13; xiv. 18, 19; xvii. 28; xix. 45; xxii. 36; John iv. 8; vi. 5; xiii. 29; 1 Cor. vii. 30; Rev. iii. 18; xiii. 17; xviii. 11,—in all which places it is applicable to ordinary transactions of *buying*. In the following places it is also rendered *bought*, as applicable to the redeemed, as being bought or purchased by the Lord Jesus: 1 Cor. vi. 20; vii. 23, 'Ye are *bought* with a price;' and in the following places it is rendered *redeemed*, Rev. v. 9; xiv. 3, 4. It does not elsewhere occur in the New Testament. It is true that in a large sense this word might be applied to the Father as having caused his people to be redeemed, or as being the Author of the plan of redemption; but it is also true that the word is more properly applicable to the Lord Jesus, and that, when used with reference to redemption, it is uniformly given to him in the New Testament. Compare the passages referred to above. It is strictly and properly true only of the Son of God that he has '*bought*' us. The Father indeed is represented as making the arrangement, as giving his Son to die, and as the great Source of all the blessings secured by redemption; but the *purchase* was actually made by the Son of God by his sacrifice on the cross. Whatever there was of the nature of *a price* was paid by him; and whatever obligations may grow out of the fact that we are purchased or ransomed are due particularly to him; 2 Cor. v. 15. These considerations seem to me to make it clear that Peter referred here to the Lord Jesus Christ, and that he meant to say that the false teachers mentioned held doctrines which were in fact a *denial* of that Saviour. He does not specify particularly what constituted

2 And many shall follow their
¹ pernicious ways; by reason of

whom the way of truth shall be evil
spoken of.

1 Or, *lascivious*, as some copies read.

such a denial; but it is plain that any
doctrine which represented him, his
person, or his work, as essentially
different from what was the truth, would
amount to such a denial. If he was
Divine, and that fact was denied, making
him wholly a different being; if he
actually made an expiatory sacrifice by
his death, and that fact was denied,
and he was held to be a mere religious
teacher, changing essentially the character of the work which he came to
perform; if he, in some proper sense,
'bought' them with his blood, and that
fact was denied in such a way that according to their views it was not strictly
proper to speak of him as having *bought*
them at all, which would be the case if
he were a mere prophet or religious
teacher, then it is clear that such a representation would be in fact a denial
of his true nature and work. That some
of these views entered into their *denial*
of him is clear, for it was with reference
to the fact that he had 'bought' them,
or redeemed them, that they denied him.
¶ *And bring upon themselves swift destruction.* The *destruction* here referred
to can be only that which will occur in
the future world, for there can be no
evidence that Peter meant to say that
this would destroy their health, their
property, or their lives. The Greek
word (ἀπώλειαν) is the same which is
used in the former part of the verse, in
the phrase '*damnable heresies.*' See
Notes. In regard, then, to this important passage, we may remark, (1.) that
the apostle evidently believed that some
would perish for whom Christ died. (2.)
If this be so, then the same truth may
be expressed by saying that he died for
others besides those who will be saved;
that is, that the atonement was not
confined merely to the elect. This one
passage, therefore, demonstrates the doctrine of general atonement. This conclusion would be drawn from it by the
great mass of readers, and it may be
presumed, therefore, that this is the
fair interpretation of the passage.

[See the Supplementary Notes on 2 Cor. v. 14;
Heb. ii. 9 for a general view of the question re-

garding the extent of the atonement. On this
text Scott has well observed: 'Doubtless Christ
intended to redeem those, and those only, who
he foresaw would *eventually* be saved by faith
in him; yet his ransom was of infinite sufficiency,
and men are continually addressed according to
their profession.' Christ has indeed laid down
such a price as that all the human family may
claim and find salvation in him. An unhappy
ambiguity of terms has made this controversy
very much a war of words. When the author
here says, 'Christ died for others besides those
who will be saved,' he does not use the words
in the common sense of an actual *design* on the
part of Christ to save all. The reader will see,
by consulting the Notes above referred to, how
much disputing might be saved by a careful definition of terms.]
(3.) It follows that men may destroy
themselves by a denial of the great and
vital *doctrines* of religion. It cannot be
a harmless thing, then, to hold erroneous
opinions; nor can men be safe who deny
the fundamental doctrines of Christianity. It is truth, not error, that saves
the soul; and an erroneous opinion on
any subject may be as dangerous to a
man's ultimate peace, happiness, and
prosperity, as a wrong course of life.
How many men have been ruined in
their worldly prospects, their health,
and their lives, by holding false sentiments on the subject of morals, or in
regard to medical treatment! Who
would regard it as a harmless thing if a
son should deny in respect to his father
that he was a man of truth, probity,
and honesty, or should attribute to him
a character which does not belong to
him—a character just the reverse of
truth? Can the same thing be innocent
in regard to God our Saviour? (4.) Men
bring destruction '*on themselves.*' No
one *compels* them to deny the Lord that
bought them; no one *forces* them to
embrace any dangerous error. If men
perish, they perish by their own fault,
for (*a*) ample provision was made for
their salvation as well as for others, (*b*)
they were freely invited to be saved;
(*c*) it was, in itself, just as easy for
them to embrace the truth as it was for
others; and (*d*) it was as easy to embrace the truth as to embrace error.

2. *And many shall follow their per-*

3 And through covetousness shall they with feigned words make merchandise of you : whose judgment

a now of a long time lingereth not, and their damnation slumbereth not.

nicious ways. Marg., *lascivious.* A large number of manuscripts and versions read *lascivious* here—ἀσιλγείαις— instead of *pernicious*—ἀπωλείαις, (see Wetstein,) and this reading is adopted in the editions of the Greek Testament by Tittman, Griesbach, and Hahn, and it seems probable that this is the correct reading. This will agree well with the account elsewhere given of these teachers, that their doctrines tended to licentiousness, vers. 10, 14, 18, 19. It is a very remarkable circumstance, that those who have denied the essential doctrines of the gospel have been so frequently licentious in their own conduct, and have inculcated opinions which tended to licentiousness. Many of the forms of religious error have somehow had a connection with this vice. Men who are corrupt at heart often seek to obtain for their corruptions the sanction of religion. ¶ *By reason of whom the way of truth shall be evil spoken of.* (1.) Because they were professors of religion, and religion would seem to be held responsible for their conduct ; and, (2.) because they were professed teachers of religion, and, by many, would be understood as expounding the true doctrines of the gospel.

3. *And through covetousness.* This shows what *one* of the things was by which they were influenced—a thing which, like licentiousness, usually exerts a powerful influence over the teachers of error. The religious principle is the strongest that is implanted in the human bosom ; and men who can obtain a livelihood in no other way, or who are too unprincipled or too indolent to labour for an honest living, often turn public teachers of religion, and adopt the kind of doctrines that will be likely to give them the greatest power over the purses of others. True religion, indeed, requires of its friends to devote all that they have to the service of God and to the promotion of his cause ; but it is very easy to pervert this requirement, so that the teacher of error shall take advantage of it for his own aggrandizement. ¶ *Shall they with feigned words.* Gr. formed,

fashioned ; then those which are *formed* for the occasion—feigned, false, deceitful. The idea is, that the doctrines which they would defend were not maintained by solid and substantial arguments, but that they would make use of plausible reasoning *made up* for the occasion. ¶ *Make merchandise of you.* Treat you not as rational beings but as a bale of goods, or any other article of traffic. That is, they would endeavour to make money out of them, and regard them only as fitted to promote that object. ¶ *Whose judgment.* Whose condemnation. ¶ *Now of a long time lingereth not.* Greek, 'of old ; long since.' The idea seems to be, that justice had been long attentive to their movements, and was on its way to their destruction. It was not a new thing—that is, there was no new principle involved in their destruction ; but it was a principle which had always been in operation, and which would certainly be applicable to them, and of a long time justice had been impatient to do the work which it was accustomed to do. What had occurred to the angels that sinned, (ver. 4,) to the old world, (ver. 5,) and to Sodom and Gomorrah, (ver 6,) would occur to them ; and the same justice which had overthrown them might be regarded as on its way to effect their destruction. Comp. Notes, Isa. xviii. 4. ¶ *And their damnation slumbereth not.* Their condemnation, (Notes, 1 Cor. xi. 29,) yet here referring to future punishment. 'Mr. Blackwell observes, that this is a most beautiful figure, representing the vengeance that shall destroy such incorrigible sinners as an angel of judgment pursuing them on the wing, continually approaching nearer and nearer, and in the mean time keeping a watchful eye upon them, that he may at length discharge an unerring blow.'—*Doddridge.* It is not uncommon to speak of 'sleepless justice ;' and the idea here is, that however justice may have *seemed* to slumber or to linger, it was not really so, but that it had on them an everwatchful eye, and was on its way to do that which was right in regard to them.

4 For if God spared not the angels that sinned, but cast *them* down to hell, and delivered *them* into chains of darkness. to be reserved unto judgment ;

5 And spared not the old world,

A sinner should never forget that there is an eye of unslumbering vigilance always upon him, and that everything that he does is witnessed by one who will yet render exact justice to all men. No man, however careful to conceal his sins, or however bold in transgression, or however unconcerned he may seem to be, can hope that justice will always linger, or destruction always slumber.

4. *For if God spared not the angels that sinned.* The apostle now proceeds to the *proof* of the proposition that these persons would be punished. It is to be remembered that they had been, or were even then, professing Christians, though they had really, if not in form, apostatized from the faith, (vers. 20–22 ;) and a part of the proofs, therefore, are derived from the cases of those who had apostatized from the service of God. He appeals, therefore, to the case of the angels that had revolted. Neither their former rank, their dignity, nor their holiness, saved them from being thrust down to hell ; and if God punished them so severely, then false teachers could not hope to escape. The apostle, by the *angels* here, refers undoubtedly to a revolt in heaven—an event referred to in Jude 6, and everywhere implied in the Scriptures. *When* that occurred, however—*why* they revolted, or what was the number of the apostates—we have not the slightest information, and on these points conjecture would be useless. In the supposition that it occurred, there is no improbability ; for there is nothing more absurd in the belief that angels have revolted than that men have ; and if there are evil angels, as there is no more reason to doubt than that there are evil men, it is morally certain that they must have fallen at some period from a state of holiness, for it cannot be believed that God *made* them wicked. ¶ *But cast* them *down to hell.* Gr., ταρταρώσας—'thrusting them down to Tartarus.' The word here used occurs nowhere else in the New Testament, though it is common in the classical writers. It is a verb formed from Τάρταρος *(Tartarus,)* which in Greek my-

thology was the lower part, or abyss of hades where the shades of the wicked were supposed to be imprisoned and tormented, and answered to the Jewish word Γέεννα—*Gehenna.* It was regarded, commonly, as beneath the earth ; as entered through the grave ; as dark, dismal, gloomy ; and as a place of punishment. Comp. Notes, Job x. 21, 22, and Matt. v. 22. The word here is one that properly refers to a place of punishment, since the whole argument relates to that, and since it cannot be pretended that the 'angels that sinned' were removed to a place of happiness on account of their transgression. It must also refer to punishment in some other world than this, for there is no evidence that *this* world is made a place of punishment for fallen angels. ¶ *And delivered* them *into chains of darkness.* 'Where darkness lies like chains upon them.'—*Rob. Lex.* The meaning seems to be, that they are confined in that dark prison-house *as if* by chains. We are not to suppose that spirits are literally bound ; but it was common to bind or fetter prisoners who were in dungeons, and the representation here is taken from that fact. This representation that the mass of fallen angels are confined in *Tartarus,* or in hell, is not inconsistent with the representations which elsewhere occur that their leader is permitted to roam the earth, and that even many of those spirits are allowed to tempt men. It may be still true that the mass are confined within the limits of their dark abode ; and it may even be true also that Satan and those who are permitted to roam the earth are under bondage, and are permitted to range only within certain bounds, and that they are so secured that they will be brought to trial at the last day. ¶ *To be reserved unto judgment :* Jude 6, 'to the judgment of the great day.' They will then, with the revolted inhabitants of this world, be brought to trial for their crimes. That the fallen angels will be punished *after* the judgment is apparent from Rev. xx. 10. The argument in this verse is, that if God punished the angels who revolted

but saved Noah [a] the eighth *person,* a preacher of righteousness, bringing in the flood upon the world of the ungodly;

6 And turning the cities of [b] Sodom and Gomorrha into ashes, con-

demned *them* with an overthrow, making [c] *them* an ensample unto those that after should live ungodly;

7 And delivered just Lot, [d] vexed with the filthy conversation of the wicked;

a Ge.7.1,&c.　　　b Ge.19.24,25.　　　c De.29.23.　　　d Ge.19.16.

from him, it is a fair inference that he will punish wicked men, though they were once professors of religion.

5. *And spared not the old world.* The world before the flood. The argument here is, that he cut off that wicked race, and thus showed that he would punish the guilty. By that awful act of sweeping away the inhabitants of a world, he showed that men could not sin with impunity, and that the incorrigibly wicked must perish. ¶ *But saved Noah the eighth* person. This reference to Noah, like the reference to Lot in ver. 7, seems to have been thrown in in the progress of the argument as an incidental remark, to show that the righteous, however few in number, would be saved when the wicked were cut off. The phrase 'Noah the eighth,' means Noah, one of eight; that is, Noah and seven others. This idiom is found, says Dr. Bloomfield, in the best writers—from Herodotus and Thucydides downwards. See examples in Wetstein. The meaning in this place then is, that eight persons, and eight only of that race, were saved; thus showing, that while the wicked would be punished, however numerous they might be, the righteous, however few, would be saved. ¶ *A preacher of righteousness.* In Gen. vi. 9, it is said of Noah that he was ' a just man and perfect in his generations, and Noah walked with God;' and it may be presumed that during his long life he was faithful in reproving the wickedness of his age, and warned the world of the judgment that was preparing for it. Compare Notes, Heb. xi. 7. ¶ *Bringing in the flood upon the world of the ungodly.* Upon all the world besides that pious family. The argument here is, that if God would cut off a wicked race in this manner, the principle is settled that the wicked will not escape.

6. *And turning the cities of Sodom and Gomorrha into ashes.* Gen. xix.

24, 25. This is a third example to demonstrate that God will punish the wicked. Comp. Notes, Jude 7. The word here rendered 'turning into ashes,' (τεφρώσας,) occurs nowhere else in the New Testament. It is from τέφρα, *(ashes,)* and means to reduce to ashes, and then to consume or destroy. ¶ *Condemned* them *with an overthrow.* By the fact of their being overthrown, he showed that they were to be condemned, or that he disapproved their conduct. Their calamity came expressly on account of their enormous sins; as it is frequently the case now that the awful judgments that come upon the licentious and the intemperate, are as plain a proof of the Divine disapprobation as were the calamities that came upon Sodom and Gomorrah. ¶ *Making* them *an ensample,* &c. That is, they were a demonstration that God disapproved of the crimes for which they were punished, and would disapprove of the same crimes in every age and in every land. The punishment of one wicked man or people always becomes a warning to all others.

7. *And delivered just Lot.* Gen. xix. 16. This case is incidentally referred to, to show that God makes a distinction between the righteous and the wicked; and that while the latter will be destroyed, the former will be saved. See ver. 9. Lot is called *just,* because he preserved himself uncontaminated amidst the surrounding wickedness. As long as he lived in Sodom he maintained the character of an upright and holy man. ¶ *Vexed with the filthy conversation of the wicked.* By the corrupt and licentious conduct of the wicked around him. On the word *conversation,* see Notes, Phil. i. 27. The original phrase, which is rendered *filthy,* has reference to licentiousness. The corruption of Sodom was open and shameless; and as Lot was compelled to see much of it, his

8 (For that righteous man dwelling among them, in seeing and hearing, vexed *his* righteous soul from

day to day with *their* unlawful
deeds;)
9 The Lord knoweth how to *a* de-
a Ps.34.15–18.

heart was pained. The word here rendered *vexed*, means that he was wearied
or burdened. The crimes of those around
him he found it hard to bear with.
8. *For that righteous man dwelling
among them.* The Latin Vulgate
renders this, ' For in seeing and hearing he was just;' meaning that he
maintained his uprightness, or that he
did not become contaminated by the
vices of Sodom. Many expositors have
supposed that this is the correct rendering; but the most natural and the most
common explanation is that which is
found in our version. According to
that, the meaning is, that compelled as
he was, while living among them, to
see and to hear what was going on, his
soul was constantly troubled. ¶ *In seeing and hearing.* Seeing their open
acts of depravity, and hearing their vile
conversation. The effect which this
had on the mind of Lot is not mentioned
in Genesis, but nothing is more probable than the statement here made by
Peter. Whether this statement was
founded on tradition, or whether it is a
suggestion of inspiration to the mind of
Peter, cannot be determined. The
words rendered *seeing* and *hearing* may
refer to the *act* of seeing, or to the *object* seen. Wetstein and Robinson suppose that they refer here to the latter,
and that the sense is, that he was
troubled by what he saw and heard.
The meaning is not materially different.
Those who live among the wicked are
compelled to see and hear much that
pains their hearts, and it is well if they
do not become indifferent to it, or contaminated by it. *Vexed* his *righteous
soul from day to day with* their *unlawful deeds.* Tortured or tormented his
soul—*ἐβασάνιζεν.* Comp. Matt. viii. 6,
29; Luke viii. 28; Rev. ix. 5; xi. 10;
xiv. 10; xx. 10, where the same word
is rendered *tormented*. The use of this
word would seem to imply that there
was something *active* on the part of Lot
which produced this distress on account
of their conduct. He was not merely
troubled as if his soul were passively

acted on, but there were strong mental
exercises of a positive kind, arising perhaps from anxious solicitude how he
might prevent their evil conduct, or from
painful reflections on the consequences of
their deeds to themselves, or from earnest
pleadings in their behalf before God, or
from reproofs and warnings of the wicked. At all events, the language is such
as would seem to indicate that he was not
a mere passive observer of their conduct.
This, it would seem, was ' from day to
day;' that is, it was constant. There
were doubtless reasons why Lot should
remain among such a people, and why,
when he might so easily have done it,
he did not remove to another place.
Perhaps it was one purpose of his remaining to endeavour to do them good,
as it is often the duty of good men now
to reside among the wicked for the
same purpose. Lot is supposed to have
resided in Sodom—then probably the
most corrupt place on the earth—for
sixteen years; and we have in that fact
an instructive demonstration that a
good man *may* maintain the life of religion in his soul when surrounded by
the wicked, and an illustration of the
effects which the conduct of the wicked
will have on a man of true piety when
he is compelled to witness it constantly.
We may learn from the record made of
Lot what those effects will be, and what
is evidence that one *is* truly pious who
lives among the wicked. (1.) He will
not be *contaminated* with their wickedness, or will not conform to their evil
customs. (2.) He will not become *indifferent* to it, but his heart will be
more and more affected by their depravity. Comp. Psa. cxix. 136; Luke xix.
41; Acts xvii. 16. (3.) He will have
not only constant, but growing solicitude in regard to it—solicitude that
will be felt every day: ' He vexed his
soul *from day to day.*' It will not only
be at intervals that his mind will be
affected by their conduct, but it will be
an habitual and constant thing. True
piety is not fitful, periodical, and spas-
modic; it is constant and steady. It

liver the godly out of temptations, and to reserve *a* the unjust unto the day of judgment to be punished:

10 But chiefly them *b* that walk after the flesh in the lust of unclean-

ness, and despise [1] government: presumptuous *are they,* self-willed; they are not afraid to speak evil of dignities. *c*

a Jude 14,15.　　*b* He.13.4.　　1 Or, *dominion.*
c Jude 8,10.

---

is not a *jet* that occasionally bursts out; it is a fountain always flowing. (4.) He will seek to do them good. We may suppose that this was the case with Lot; we are certain that it is a characteristic of true religion to seek to do good to all, however wicked they may be. (5.) He will secure their confidence. He will practise no improper arts to do this, but it will be one of the usual results of a life of integrity, that a good man will secure the confidence of even the wicked. It does not appear that Lot lost that confidence, and the whole narrative in Genesis leads us to suppose that even the inhabitants of Sodom regarded him as a good man. The wicked may *hate* a good man because he is good; but if a man lives as he should, they will regard him as upright, and they will give him the credit of it when he dies, if they should withhold it while he lives.

9. *The Lord knoweth,* &c. That is, the cases referred to show that God is able to deliver his people when tempted, and understands the best way in which it should be done. He sees a way to do it when we cannot, though it is often a way which we should not have thought of. He can send an angel to take his tempted people by the hand; he can interpose and destroy the power of the tempter; he can raise up earthly friends; he can deliver his people completely and for ever from temptation, by their removal to heaven. ¶ *And to reserve the unjust.* As he does the rebel angels, ver. 4. The case of the angels shows that God can keep wicked men, as if under bonds, reserved for their final trial at his bar. Though they seem to go at large, yet they are under his control, and are kept by him with reference to their ultimate arraignment.

10. *But chiefly.* That is, it may be presumed that the principles just laid down would be applicable in an eminent degree to such persons as he proceeds to designate. ¶ *That walk after the flesh.* That live for the indulgence of their

carnal appetites. Notes, Rom. viii. 1. ¶ *In the lust of uncleanness.* In polluted pleasures. Comp. Notes, ver. 2. ¶ *And despise government.* Marg., *dominion.* That is, they regard all government in the state, the church, and the family, as an evil. Advocates for unbridled freedom of all sorts; declaimers on liberty and on the evils of oppression; defenders of what they regard as the rights of injured man, and yet secretly themselves lusting for the exercise of the very power which they would deny to others—they make no just distinctions about what constitutes true freedom, and in their zeal array themselves against government in all forms. No topic of declamation would be more popular than this, and from none would they hope to secure more followers; for if they could succeed in removing all respect for the just restraints of law, the way would be open for the accomplishment of their own purposes, in setting up a dominion over the minds of others. It is a common result of such views, that men of this description become impatient of the government of God himself, and seek to throw off *all* authority, and to live in the unrestrained indulgence of their vicious propensities. ¶ *Presumptuous are they.* Τολμηταί—daring, bold, audacious, presumptuous men. ¶ *Self-willed*—αὐθάδεις. See Notes, Titus i. 7. ¶ *They are not afraid to speak evil of dignities.* The word rendered *dignities* here, (δόξας,) means properly honour, glory, splendour; then that which is fitted to inspire respect; that which is dignified or exalted. It is applied here to men of exalted rank; and the meaning is, that they did not regard rank, or station, or office—thus violating the plainest rules of propriety and of religion. See Notes, Acts xxiii. 4, 5. Jude, between whose language and that of Peter in this chapter there is a remarkable resemblance, has expressed this more fully. He says, (ver.

11 Whereas angels, which are greater in power and might, bring not railing accusation [1]against them before the Lord.

12 But these, as natural brute

1 Some read, *against themselves.*

a beasts, made to be taken and destroyed, speak evil of the things that they understand not; and shall utterly perish in their own corruption ;

a Je.12.3.

8,) ' These filthy dreamers defile the flesh, despise dominion, and speak evil of dignities.' It is one of the effects of religion to produce respect for superiors; but when men are self-willed, and when they purpose to give indulgence to corrupt propensities, it is natural for them to dislike all government. Accordingly, it is by no means an unfrequent effect of certain forms of error to lead men to speak disrespectfully of those in authority, and to attempt to throw off all the restraints of law. It is a very certain indication that men hold wrong opinions when they show disrespect to those in authority, and despise the restraints of law.

11. *Whereas angels.* The object, by the reference to angels here, is to show that they, even when manifesting the greatest zeal in a righteous cause, and even when opposing others, did not make use of reproachful terms, or of harsh and violent language. It is not known precisely to what Peter alludes here, nor on what the statement here is based. There can be little doubt, however, as Benson has remarked, that, from the strong resemblance between what Peter says and what Jude says, (Jude 9, 10,) there is allusion to the same thing, and probably both referred to some common tradition among the Jews respecting the contention of the archangel Michael with the devil about the body of Moses. See Notes, Jude 9. As the statement in Jude is the most full, it is proper to explain the passage before us by a reference to that; and we may suppose that, though Peter uses the plural term, and speaks of *angels,* yet that he really had the case of Michael in his eye, and meant to refer to that as an example of what the angels do. Whatever may have been the origin of this tradition, no one can doubt that what is here said of the angels accords with probability, and no one can prove that it is not true. ¶ *Which are greater in power and*

might. And who might, therefore, if it were in any case proper, speak freely of things of an exalted rank and dignity. It would be more becoming for them than for men. On this difficult passage, see Notes on Jude 9. ¶ *Bring not railing accusation.* They simply say, ' The Lord rebuke thee,' Jude 9. Comp. Zech. iii. 2. The Greek here is, ' bring not blasphemous or reproachful judgment, or condemnation'—βλάσφη- μον κρίσιν. They abhor all scurrility and violence of language ; they simply state matters as they are. No one can doubt that this accords with what we should expect of the angels; and that if they had occasion to speak of those who were opposers, it would be in a calm and serious manner, not seeking to overwhelm them by reproaches. ¶ *Against them.* Margin, *against themselves.* So the Vulgate. The more correct reading is *against them ;* that is, against those who might be regarded as their adversaries, (Jude 9,) or those of their own rank who had done wrong—the fallen angels. ¶ *Before the Lord.* When standing before the Lord ; or when represented as reporting the conduct of evil spirits. Comp. Zech. iii. 1, 2. This phrase, however, is wanting in many manuscripts. See Wetstein.

12. *But these, as natural brute beasts.* These persons, who resemble so much irrational animals which are made to be taken and destroyed. The *point* of the comparison is, that they are like fierce and savage beasts that exercise no control over their appetites, and that *seem* to be made only to be destroyed. These persons, by their fierce and ungovernable passions, appear to be made only for destruction, and rush blindly on to it. The word rendered *natural,* (which, however, is wanting in several manuscripts,) means *as they are by nature,* following the bent of their natural appetites and passions. The idea is, that they exercised no more restraint over their passions than beasts

13 And shall receive the reward of unrighteousness, *as* they *a* that count it pleasure to riot in the day-

a Phi.3.19; Jude 12,&c.

time. Spots *they are* and blemishes, sporting themselves with their own deceivings, while they feast with you;

---

do over their propensities. They were entirely under the dominion of their natural appetites, and did not allow their reason or conscience to exert any constraint. The word rendered *brute*, means without reason ; irrational. Man *has* reason, and should allow it to control his passions ; the brutes have no rational nature, and it is to be expected that they will act out their propensities without restraint. Man, as an animal, has many passions and appetites resembling those of the brute creation, but he is also endowed with a higher nature, which is designed to regulate and control his inferior propensities, and to keep them in subordination to the requirements of law. If a man sinks himself to the level of brutes, he must expect to be treated like brutes ; and as wild and savage animals—lions, and panthers, and wolves, and bears—are regarded as dangerous, and as ' made to be taken and destroyed,' so the same destiny must come upon men who make themselves like them. ¶ *Made to be taken and destroyed.* They are not only useless to society, but destructive ; and men feel that it is right to destroy them. We are not to suppose that this teaches that the only object which *God* had in view in making wild animals was that they *might be* destroyed ; but that *men* so regard them. ¶ *Speak evil of the things that they understand not.* Of objects whose worth and value they cannot appreciate. This is no uncommon thing among men, especially in regard to the works and ways of God. ¶ *And shall utterly perish in their own corruption.* Their views will be the means of their ruin ; and they render them fit for it, just as much as the fierce passions of the wild animals do.

13. *And shall receive the reward of unrighteousness.* The appropriate recompense of their wickedness in the future world. Such men do not always receive the due recompense of their deeds in the present life ; and as it is a great and immutable principle that all will be

treated, under the government of God, as they deserve, or that justice will be rendered to every rational being, it follows that there must be punishment in the future state. ¶ As *they that count it pleasure to riot in the day-time.* As men peculiarly wicked, shameless, and abandoned ; for only such revel in open day. Comp. Notes, Acts ii. 15; 1 Thess. v. 7. ¶ *Spots* they are *and blemishes.* That is, they are like a dark spot on a pure garment, or like a deformity on an otherwise beautiful person. They are a scandal and disgrace to the Christian profession. ¶ *Sporting themselves.* The Greek word here means to live delicately or luxuriously; to revel. The idea is not exactly that of *sporting*, or playing, or amusing themselves ; but it is that they take advantage of their views to live in riot and luxury. Under the garb of the Christian profession, they give indulgence to the most corrupt passions. ¶ *With their own deceivings.* Jude, in the parallel place, (ver. 12,) has, ' These are spots in your feasts of charity, when they feast with you.' Several versions, and a few manuscripts also, here read *feasts* instead of *deceivings*, (ἀγάπαις for ἀπάταις.) The common reading, however, is undoubtedly the correct one, (see Wetstein, *in loc.;*) and the meaning is, that they took advantage of their false views to turn even the sacred feasts of charity, or perhaps the Lord's Supper itself, into an occasion of sensual indulgence. Comp. Notes, 1 Cor. xi. 20–22. The difference between these persons, and those in the church at Corinth, seems to have been that these did it of design, and for the purpose of leading others into sin ; those who were in the church at Corinth erred through ignorance. ¶ *While they feast with you.* συνευωχούμενοι. This word means to feast several together; to feast with any one; and the reference seems to be to some festival which was celebrated by Christians, where men and women were assembled together, (ver. 14,) and where they could convert the festival into a

14 Having eyes full of ¹ adultery, and that cannot cease from sin; beguiling unstable souls: an heart they have exercised with covetous practices; cursed children;

¹ *an adulteress.*

15 Which have forsaken the right way, and are gone astray, following the way of Balaam *a* *the son* of Bosor, who loved the wages of unrighteousness;

a Nu.22.5,&c.

---

scene of riot and disorder. If the Lord's Supper was celebrated by them as it was at Corinth, that would furnish such an occasion; or if it was preceded by a 'feast of charity,' (Notes, Jude 12,) that would furnish such an occasion. It would seem to be probable that a festival of some kind was connected with the observance of the Lord's Supper, (Notes, 1 Cor. xi. 21,) and that this was converted by these persons into a scene of riot and disorder.

14. *Having eyes full of adultery.* Marg., as in the Greek, *an adulteress;* that is, gazing with desire after such persons. The word *full* is designed to denote that the corrupt passion referred to had wholly seized and occupied their minds. The eye was, as it were, full of this passion; it saw nothing else but some occasion for its indulgence; it expressed nothing else but the desire. The reference here is to the sacred festival mentioned in the previous verse; and the meaning is, that they celebrated that festival with licentious feelings, giving free indulgence to their corrupt desires by gazing on the females who were assembled with them. In the passion here referred to, the *eye* is usually the first offender, the inlet to corrupt desires, and the medium by which they are expressed. Comp. Notes, Matt. v. 28. The wanton glance is a principal occasion of exciting the sin; and there is much often in dress, and mien, and gesture, to charm the eye and to deepen the debasing passion. ¶ *And that cannot cease from sin.* They cannot look on the females who may be present without sinning. Comp. Matt. v. 28. There are many men in whom the presence of the most virtuous woman only excites impure and corrupt desires. The expression here does not mean that they have no natural ability to cease from sin, or that they are impelled to it by any physical necessity, but only that they are so corrupt and unprincipled that they certainly will sin always.

¶ *Beguiling unstable souls.* Those who are not strong in Christian principle, or who are naturally fluctuating and irresolute. The word rendered *beguiling* means to bait, to entrap, and would be applicable to the methods practised in hunting. Here it means that it was one of their arts to place specious allurements before those who were known not to have settled principles or firmness, in order to allure them to sin. Comp. 2 Tim. iii. 6. ¶ *An heart they have exercised with covetous practices.* Skilled in the arts which covetous men adopt in order to cheat others out of their property. A leading purpose which influenced these men was to obtain money. One of the most certain ways for dishonest men to do this is to make use of the religious principle; to corrupt and control the conscience; to make others believe that they are eminently holy, or that they are the special favourites of heaven; and when they can do this, they have the purses of others at command. For the religious principle is the most powerful of all principles; and he who can control that, can control all that a man possesses. The idea here is, that these persons had made this their study, and had learned the ways in which men could be induced to part with their money under religious pretences. We should always be on our guard when professedly religious teachers propose to have much to do with money matters While we should always be ready to aid every good cause, yet we should remember that unprincipled and indolent men often assume the mask of religion that they may practise their arts on the credulity of others, and that their real aim is to obtain their property, not to save their souls. ¶ *Cursed children.* This is a Hebraism, meaning literally, 'children of the curse;' that is, persons devoted to the curse, or who will certainly be destroyed.

15. *Which have forsaken the right way.* The straight path of honesty and

16 But was rebuked for his iniquity : the dumb ass, speaking with man's voice, forbad the madness of the prophet.

integrity. Religion is often represented as a straight path, and to do wrong is to go out of that path in a crooked way. ¶ *Following the way of Balaam the son of Bosor.* See Numb. xxii. 5, seq. In the Book of Numbers, Balaam is called the son of *Beor.* Perhaps the name Beor was corrupted into Bosor; or, as Rosenmüller suggests, the father of Balaam may have had two names. Schleusner (*Lex.*) supposes that it was changed by the Greeks because it was more easily pronounced. The Seventy, however, read it Βεωρ — *Beor.* The meaning here is, that they *imitated* Balaam. The particular point to which Peter refers in which they imitated him, seems to have been the love of gain, or covetousness. Possibly, however, he might have designed to refer to a more general resemblance, for *in fact* they imitated him in the following things : (1,) in being professed religious teachers, or the servants of God ; (2,) in their covetousness ; (3,) in inducing others to sin, referring to the same kind of sins in both cases. Balaam counselled the Moabites to entice the children of Israel to illicit connection with their women, thus introducing licentiousness into the camp of the Hebrews, (Numb. xxxi. 16 ; comp. Numb. xxv. 1–9 ;) and in like manner these teachers led others into licentiousness, thus corrupting the church. ¶ *Who loved the wages of unrighteousness.* Who was supremely influenced by the love of gain, and was capable of being employed, for a price, in a wicked design ; thus prostituting his high office, as a professed prophet of the Most High, to base and ignoble ends. That Balaam, though he professed to be influenced by a supreme regard to the will of God, (Numb. xxii. 18, 38,) was really influenced by the desire of reward, and was willing to prostitute his great office to secure such a reward, there can be no doubt. (1.) The elders of Moab and of Midian came to Balaam with ' the rewards of divination in their hand,' (Numb. xxii. 7,) and with promises from Balak of promoting him to great honour, if he would curse the children of Israel, Numb. xxii. 17.

(2.) Balaam was disposed to go with them, and was restrained from going at once only by a direct and solemn prohibition from the Lord, Numb. xxii. 11. (3.) Notwithstanding this solemn prohibition, and notwithstanding he said to the ambassadors from Balak that he would do only as God directed, though Balak should give him his house full of silver and gold, (Numb. xxii. 18,) yet he did not regard the matter as settled, but proposed to them that they should wait another night, with the hope that the Lord would give a more favourable direction in reference to their request, thus showing that his *heart* was in the service which they required, and that his inclination was to avail himself of their offer, Numb. xxii. 19. (4.) When he *did* obtain permission to go, it was only to say that which the Lord should direct him to say, (Numb. xxii. 20 ;) but he went with a ' perverse ' heart, with a secret wish to comply with the desire of Balak, and with a knowledge that he was doing wrong, (Numb. xxii. 34,) and was restrained from uttering the curse which Balak desired only by an influence from above which he could not control. Balaam was undoubtedly a wicked man, and was constrained by a power from on high to utter sentiments which God *meant* should be uttered, but which Balaam would never have expressed of his own accord.

16. *But was rebuked for his iniquity* The object of Peter in this seems to be to show that God employed the very extraordinary means of causing the ass on which he rode to speak, because his iniquity was so monstrous. The guilt of thus debasing his high office, and going forth to curse the people of God— a people who had done him no wrong, and given no occasion for his malediction—was so extraordinary, that means as extraordinary were proper to express it. If God employed means so extraordinary to rebuke *his* depravity, it was to be expected that in some appropriate way he would express his sense of the wickedness of those who resembled him. ¶ *The dumb ass, speaking with man's voice.* Numb. xxii. 28. God seems to

17 These are wells without water, clouds *a* that are carried with a

a Ep.4.14.

tempest; to whom the mist of darkness is reserved for ever.

have designed that both Balaam and Balak should be convinced that the children of Israel were his people; and so important was it that this conviction should rest fully on the minds of the nations through whom they passed, that he would not suffer even a pretended prophet to make use of his influence to curse them. He designed that all that influence should be in favour of the cause of truth, thus furnishing a striking instance of the use which he often makes of wicked men. To convince Balaam of the error of his course, and to make him sensible that God was an observer of his conduct, and to induce him to utter only what he should direct, nothing would be better fitted than this miracle. The very animal on which he rode, dumb and naturally stupid, was made to utter a reproof; a reproof as directly from heaven as though the stones had cried out beneath his feet, or the trees of the wood had uttered the language of remonstrance. As to the nature of the miracle here referred to, it may be remarked, (1,) that it was as easy for God to perform this miracle as any other; and (2,) that it was a miracle that would be as likely to be effectual, and to answer the purpose, as any other. No man can show that it could *not* have occurred; and the occasion was one in which some decided rebuke, in language beyond that of conscience, was necessary. ¶ *Forbade the madness of the prophet.* That is, the mad or perverse design of the prophet. The word here rendered *madness* means, properly, being aside from a right mind. It is not found elsewhere in the New Testament. It is used here to denote that Balaam was engaged in an enterprise which indicated a headstrong disposition; an acting contrary to reason and sober sense. He was so much under the influence of avarice and ambition that his sober sense was blinded, and he acted like a madman. He knew indeed what was right, and had professed a purpose to do what was right, but he did not allow that to control him; but, for the sake of gain, went against his own sober conviction,

and against what he knew to be the will of God. He was so mad or infatuated that he allowed neither reason, nor conscience, nor the will of God, to control him.

17. *These are wells without water.* Jude (12, 13) employs several other epithets to describe the same class of persons. The language employed both by Peter and Jude is singularly terse, pointed, and emphatic. Nothing to an oriental mind would be more expressive than to say of professed religious teachers, that they were 'wells without water.' It was always a sad disappointment to a traveller in the hot sands of the desert to come to a well where it was expected that water might be found, and to find it dry. It only aggravated the trials of the thirsty and weary traveller. Such were these religious teachers. In a world, not unaptly compared, in regard to its real comforts, to the wastes and sands of the desert, they would only grievously disappoint the expectations of all those who were seeking for the refreshing influences of the truths of the gospel. There are many such teachers in the world. ¶ *Clouds that are carried with a tempest.* Clouds that are driven about by the wind, and that send down no rain upon the earth. They promise rain, only to be followed by disappointment. Substantially the same idea is conveyed by this as by the previous phrase. 'The Arabs compare persons who put on the appearance of virtue, when yet they are destitute of all goodness, to a light cloud which makes a show of rain, and afterwards vanishes.'—*Benson.* The sense is this: The cloud, as it rises, promises rain. The expectation of the farmer is excited that the thirsty earth is to be refreshed with needful showers. Instead of this, however, the wind 'gets into' the cloud; it is driven about, and no rain falls, or it ends in a destructive tornado which sweeps everything before it. So of these religious teachers. Instruction in regard to the way of salvation was expected from them; but, instead of that, they disappointed the expectations of those who were desirous of

18 For when they speak *a* great swelling *words* of vanity, they allure through the lusts of the flesh, *through*

a Ps.73.8.

much wantonness, those that were clean[1] escaped from them who live in error.

1 Or, *for a little while*, as some read.

---

knowing the way of life, and their doctrines only tended to destroy. ¶ *To whom the mist of darkness is reserved for ever.* The word rendered *mist* here, (ζόφος,) means properly muskiness, thick gloom, darkness, (see ver. 4;) and the phrase 'mist of darkness' is designed to denote *intense* darkness, or the thickest darkness. It refers undoubtedly to the place of future punishment, which is often represented as a place of intense darkness. See Notes, Matt. viii. 12. When it is said that this is *reserved* for them, it means that it is *prepared* for them, or is kept in a state of readiness to receive them. It is like a jail or penitentiary which is built in anticipation that there will be criminals, and with the expectation that there will be use for it. So God has constructed the great prison-house of the universe, the world where the wicked are to dwell, with the knowledge that there would be occasion for it; and so he keeps it from age to age that it may be ready to receive the wicked when the sentence of condemnation shall be passed upon them. Comp. Matt. xxv. 41. The word *for ever* is a word which denotes properly eternity· (εἰς αἰῶνα,) and is such a word as could *not* have been used if it had been meant that they would not suffer for ever. Comp. Notes, Matt. xxv. 46.

18. *For when they speak great swelling* words *of vanity.* When they make pretensions to wisdom and learning, or seem to attach great importance to what they say, and urge it in a pompous and positive manner. Truth is simple, and delights in simple statements. It expects to make its way by its own intrinsic force, and is willing to pass for what it is worth. Error is noisy and declamatory, and hopes to succeed by substituting sound for sense, and by such tones and arts as shall induce men to believe that what is said is true, when it is known by the speaker to be false. ¶ *They allure through the lusts of the flesh.* The same word is used here which in ver. 14 is rendered *beguiling*, and in James i. 14 *enticed.* It does not else-

where occur in the New Testament. It means that they make use of deceitful arts to allure, ensnare, or beguile others. The *means* which it is here said they employed, were *the lusts of the flesh;* that is, they promised unlimited indulgence to the carnal appetites, or taught such doctrines that their followers would feel themselves free to give unrestrained liberty to such propensities. This has been quite a common method in the world, of inducing men to embrace false doctrines. ¶ Through much *wantonness.* See Notes, 2 Tim. iii. 6. The meaning here is, that they made use of every variety of lascivious arts to beguile others under religious pretences. This has been often done in the world; for religion has been abused to give seducers access to the confidence of the innocent, only that they might betray and ruin them. It is *right* that for all such the 'mist of darkness should be reserved for ever;' and if there were *not* a place of punishment prepared for such men, there would be defect in the moral administration of the universe. ¶ *Those that were clean escaped from them who live in error.* Marg., *for a little while.* The difference between the margin and the text here arises from a difference of reading in the Greek. Most of the later editions of the Greek Testament coincide with the reading in the margin, (ὀλίγως,) meaning *little, but a little, scarcely.* This accords better with the scope of the passage; and, according to this, it means that they had *almost escaped* from the snares and influences of those who live in error and sin. They had begun to think of their ways; they had broken off many of their evil habits; and there was hope that they would be entirely reformed, and would become decided Christians, but they were allured again to the sins in which they had so long indulged. This seems to me to accord with the design of the passage, and it certainly accords with what frequently occurs, that those who are addicted to habits of vice become apparently in-

19 While they promise them liberty, they themselves are the servants of corruption : for *a* of whom a man is overcome, of the same is he brought in bondage

20 For if after they have escaped

a Jn.8.34; Ro.6.16.

the pollutions of the world, through the knowledge of the Lord and Saviour Jesus Christ, they are again *b* entangled therein and overcome, the latter end is worse with them than the beginning.

b Lu.11.26; Heb.6.4,&c.; 10.26,27

terested in religion, and abandon many of their evil practices, but are again allured by the seductive influences of sin, and relapse into their former habits. In the case referred to here it was by professedly religious teachers—and is this never done now? Are there none, for example, who have been addicted to habits of intemperance, who had been almost reformed, but who are led back again by the influence of religious teachers? Not directly and openly, indeed, would they lead them into habits of intemperance. But, when their reformation is begun, its success and its completion depend on total abstinence from all that intoxicates. In this condition, nothing more is necessary to secure their entire reformation and safety than mere abstinence; and nothing more may be necessary to lead them into their former practices than the example of others who indulge in moderate drinking, or than the doctrine inculcated by a religious teacher that such moderate drinking is not contrary to the spirit of the Bible.

19. *While they promise them liberty.* True religion always promises and produces liberty, (see Notes, John viii. 36;) but the particular liberty which these persons seem to have promised, was freedom from what they regarded as needless restraint, or from strict and narrow views of religion. ¶ *They themselves are the servants of corruption.* They are the slaves of gross and corrupt passions, themselves utter strangers to freedom, and bound in the chains of servitude. These passions and appetites have obtained the entire mastery over them, and brought them into the severest bondage. This is often the case with those who deride the restraints of serious piety. They are themselves the slaves of appetite, or of the rules of fashionable life, or of the laws of honour, or of vicious indulgences. ' He

is a freeman whom the truth makes free, and all are slaves besides.' Comp. Notes, 2 Cor. iii. 17. ¶ *For of whom a man is overcome,* &c. Or rather ' by *what* (ᾧ) any one is overcome;' that is, *whatever* gets the mastery of him, whether it be avarice, or sensuality, or pride, or any form of error. See Notes, Rom. vi. 16, where this sentiment is explained.

20. *For if after they have escaped the pollutions of the world.* This does not necessarily mean that they had been true Christians, and had fallen from grace. Men may outwardly reform, and escape from the open corruptions which prevail around them, or which they had themselves practised, and still have no true grace at heart. ¶ *Through the knowledge of the Lord and Saviour Jesus Christ.* Neither does *this* imply that they were true Christians, or that they had ever had any saving knowledge of the Redeemer. There is a knowledge of the doctrines and duties of religion which may lead sinners to abandon their outward vices, which has no connection with saving grace. They may profess religion, and may *know* enough of religion to understand that it requires them to abandon their vicious habits, and still never be true Christians. ¶ *They are again entangled therein and overcome.* The word rendered *entangled,* (ἐμπλέκω,) from which is derived our word *implicate,* means to braid in, to interweave; then to involve in, to entangle. It means here that they become implicated in those vices like an animal that is entangled in a net. ¶ *The latter end is worse with them than the beginning.* This is usually the case. Apostates become worse than they were before their professed conversion. Reformed drunkards, if they go back to their ' cups' again, become more abandoned than ever. Thus it is with these who

21 For it had been better *a* for them not to have known the way of *b* righteousness, than, after they have known *it*, to turn from the holy commandment delivered unto them.

a Mat.11.23,24; Lu.12.47,48.

22 But it is happened unto them according to the true proverb, *c* The dog *is* turned to his own vomit again ; and the sow that was washed, to her wallowing in the mire.

b Pr.12.28.   *c* Pr.26.11.

have been addicted to any habits of vice, and who profess to become religious, and then fall away. The *reasons* of this may be, (1,) that they are willing now to show to others that they are no longer under the restraints by which they had professedly bound themselves ; (2,) that God gives them up to indulgence with fewer restraints than formerly ; and (3,) their old companions in sin may be at special pains to court their society, and to lead them into temptation, in order to obtain a triumph over virtue and religion.

21. *For it had been better for them,* &c. Comp. Notes on Matt. xxvi. 24. It would have been better for them, for (1) then they would not have dishonoured the cause of religion as they have now done ; (2) they would not have sunk so deep in profligacy as they now have ; and (3) they would not have incurred so aggravated a condemnation in the world of woe. If men are resolved on being wicked, they had better never pretend to be good. If they are to be cast off at last, it had better not be as apostates from the cause of virtue and religion.

22. *But it is happened unto them according to the true proverb.* The *meaning* of the proverbs here quoted is, that they have returned to their former vile manner of life. Under all the appearances of reformation, still their evil nature remained, as really as that of the dog or the swine, and that nature finally prevailed. There was no thorough internal change, any more than there is in the swine when it is washed, or in the dog. This passage, therefore, would seem to demonstrate that there never had been any real change of heart, and of course there had been no falling away from true religion. It should not, therefore, be quoted to prove that true Christians may fall from grace and perish. The dog and the swine had never been anything else than the dog and the swine, and these persons had never been

anything else than sinners. ¶ *The dog is turned to his own vomit again.* That is, to eat it up. The passage would seem to imply, that whatever pains should be taken to change the habits of the dog, he would return to them again. The quotation here is from Prov. xxvi. 11 : ' As a dog returneth to his vomit, so a fool returneth to his folly.' A similar proverb is found in the Rabbinical writers. Of the truth of the disgusting *fact* here affirmed of the dog, there can be no doubt. Phaedrus (Fab. 27.) states a fact still more offensive respecting its habits. In the view of the Orientals, the dog was reckoned among the most vile and disgusting of all animals. Comp. Deut. xxiii. 18 ; 1 Sam. xvii. 43 ; 2 Sam. iii. 8 ; ix. 8 ; xvi. 9 ; Matt. vii. 6 ; Phil. iii. 2. See also Horace, II. Epis. 1, 26 :—

Vixisset canis immundus, vel amica luto sus.

On the use of this proverb, see Wetstein, *in loc.* ¶ *And the sow that was washed,* &c. This proverb is not found in the Old Testament, but it was common in the Rabbinical writings, and is found in the Greek classics. See Wetstein, *in loc.* Its meaning is plain, and of the truth of what is affirmed no one can have any doubt. No matter how clean the swine is made by washing, this would not prevent it, in the slightest degree, from rolling in filth again. It will act out its real nature. So it is with the sinner. No external reformation will certainly prevent his returning to his former habits ; and when he *does* return, we can only say that he is acting according to his real nature—a nature which has never been changed, any more than the nature of the dog or the swine. On the *characteristics* of the persons referred to in this chapter, (vers. 9–19,) see the Introduction, § 3.

This passage is often quoted to prove ' the possibility of falling from grace, and from a very high degree of it too.' But it is one of the last passages in the

CHAPTER III.

THIS second epistle, beloved, I now write unto you; in *both*

Bible that should be adduced to prove that doctrine. The true point of this passage is to show that the persons referred to never *were* changed; that whatever external reformation might have occurred, their nature remained the same; and that when they apostatized from their outward profession, they merely acted out their nature, and showed that in fact there had been *no* real change. This passage will prove—what there are abundant facts to confirm —that persons may reform externally, and then return again to their former corrupt habits; it can never be made to prove that one *true* Christian will fall away and perish. It will also prove that we should rely on no mere external reformation, no outward cleansing, as certain evidence of piety. Thousands who have been externally reformed have ultimately shown that they had no religion, and there is nothing in mere outward reformation that can fit us for heaven. God looks upon the heart; and it is only the religion that has its seat there, that can secure our final salvation.

CHAPTER III.

ANALYSIS OF THE CHAPTER.

THE principal design of this chapter is to demonstrate, in opposition to the objections of scoffers, that the Lord Jesus will return again to this world; that the world will be destroyed by fire, and that there will be a new heaven and a new earth; and to show what effect this should have on the minds of Christians. The chapter, without any very exact arrangement by the author, essentially consists of two parts.

I. The argument of the objectors to the doctrine that the Lord Jesus will return to the world, and that it will be destroyed, vers. 1–4. In doing this, the apostle (vers. 1, 2) calls their attention to the importance of attending diligently to the things which had been spoken by the prophets, and to the commands of the apostles, reminding them that it was to be expected that in the last days there would be scoffers who

which I stir up your pure minds by way of remembrance:

2 That *a* ye may be mindful of

a Jude 17,18.

would deride the doctrines of religion, and who would maintain that there was no evidence that what had been predicted would be fulfilled, ver. 3. He then (ver. 4) adverts to the *argument* on which they professed to rely, that there were no signs or indications that those events were to take place; that there were no natural causes in operation which could lead to such results; and that the fact of the stability of the earth since the time of the creation, demonstrated that the predicted destruction of the world could not occur.

II. The argument of Peter, in reply to this objection; a strong affirmation of the truth of the doctrine that the Lord Jesus will return; that the earth and all which it contains will be burned up; that there will be a new heaven and a new earth; and the effect which the prospect of the coming of the Lord Jesus, and of the destruction of the world by fire, should have on the minds of Christians, vers. 5–18.

(1.) The arguments of Peter, in reply to the objection from the long-continued stability of the earth, are the following: (*a*) He refers to the destruction of the old world by the flood—a fact against which the same objections could have been urged, beforehand, which are urged against the predicted destruction of the world by fire, vers. 5–7. With just as much plausibility it might have been urged then that the earth had stood for thousands of years, and that there were no natural causes at work to produce that change. It might have been asked where the immense amount of water necessary to drown a world could come from; and perhaps it might have been argued that God was too *good* to destroy a world by a flood. Every objection which could be urged to the destruction of the world by fire, could have been urged to its destruction by water; and as, in fact, those objections, as the event showed, would have had no real force, so they should be regarded as having no real force now. (*b*) No argument against this predicted event can be

the words which were spoken before by *a* the holy prophets, and of the

a 1 Ti.4.1; 2 Ti.3.1.

commandment of us the apostles of the Lord and Saviour:

derived from the fact that hundreds and thousands of years are suffered to elapse before the fulfilment of the predictions, vers. 8, 9. What seems long to men is not long to God. A thousand years with him, in reference to this point, are as one day. He does not measure time as men do. They soon die; and if they cannot execute their purpose in a brief period, they cannot at all. But this cannot apply to God. He has infinite ages in which to execute his purposes, and therefore no argument can be derived from the fact that his purposes are long delayed, to prove that he will not execute them at all. (*c*) Peter says (ver. 15, seq.) that the delay which was observed in executing the plans of God should not be interpreted as a proof that they would *never* be accomplished, but as an evidence of his long-suffering and patience; and, in illustration of this, he refers to the writings of Paul, in which he says that the same sentiments were advanced. There were indeed, he says, in those writings, some things which were hard to be understood; but on this point they were plain.

(2.) A strong affirmation of the truth of the doctrine, vers. 9, 10, 13. He declares that these events will certainly occur, and that they should be expected to take place suddenly, and without any preintimations of their approach—as the thief comes at night without announcing his coming.

(3.) The practical suggestions which Peter intersperses in the argument illustrative of the effect which these considerations should have on the mind, are among the most important parts of the chapter : (1.) We should be holy, devout, and serious, ver. 11. (2.) We should look forward with deep interest to the new heavens and earth which are to succeed the present, ver. 12. (3.) We should be diligent and watchful, that we may be found on the return of the Saviour 'without spot and blameless,' ver. 14. (4.) We should be cautious that we be not seduced and led away by the errors which deny these great doctrines, (ver. 17;) and (5) we

should grow in grace, and in the knowledge of the Lord Jesus Christ, ver. 18.

1. *This second epistle, beloved, I now write unto you.* This expression proves that he had written a former epistle, and that it was addressed to the same persons as this. Comp. Intro., § 3. ¶ *In* both *which I stir up your pure minds, &c.* That is, the main object of both epistles is the same—to call to your remembrance important truths which you have before heard, but which you are in danger of forgetting, or from which you are in danger of being turned away by prevailing errors. Comp. Notes, chap. i. 12–15. The word rendered *pure* (*εἰλικρινής*) occurs only here and in Phil. i. 10, where it is rendered *sincere.* The word properly refers to *that which may be judged of in sunshine;* then it means *clear, manifest;* and then *sincere, pure*—as that in which there is no obscurity. The idea here perhaps is, that their minds were open, frank, candid, sincere, rather than that they were *pure.* The apostle regarded them as *disposed* to see the truth, and yet as liable to be led astray by the plausible errors of others. Such minds need to have truths often brought fresh to their remembrance, though they are truths with which they had before been familiar.

2. *That ye may be mindful of the words.* Of the doctrines; the truths; the prophetic statements. Jude (ver. 18) says that it had been foretold by the apostles, that in the last days there would be scoffers. Peter refers to the instructions of the apostles and prophets in general, though evidently designing that his remarks should bear particularly on the fact that there would be scoffers. ¶ *Which were spoken before by the holy prophets.* The predictions of the prophets before the advent of the Saviour, respecting his character and work. Peter had before appealed to them, (chap. i. 19–21,) as furnishing important evidence in regard to the truth of the Christian religion, and valuable instruction in reference to its nature. See Notes on that passage.

3 Knowing this first, that there shall come in the last days scoffers, walking *a* after their own lusts,

4 And saying, Where *b* is the promise of his coming? for since the fathers fell asleep, all things continue as *they were* from the beginning of the creation.

a Is.5.19.

b Je.17.15; Eze.12.22-27; Mat.24.48.

Many of the most important doctrines respecting the kingdom of the Messiah are stated as clearly in the Old Testament as in the New, (comp. Isa. liii.,) and the prophecies therefore deserve to be studied as an important part of Divine revelation. It should be added here, however, that when Peter wrote there was this special reason why he referred to the prophets, that the canon of the New Testament was not then completed, and he could not make his appeal to that. To some parts of the writings of Paul he could and did appeal, (vers. 15, 16,) but probably a very small part of what is now the New Testament was known to those to whom this epistle was addressed. ¶ *And of the commandment of us the apostles of the Lord and Saviour.* As being equally entitled with the prophets to state and enforce the doctrines and duties of religion. It may be observed, that no man would have used this language who did not regard himself and his fellow-apostles as inspired, and as on a level with the prophets.

3. *Knowing this first.* As among the first and most important things to be attended to—as one of the predictions which demand your special regard. Jude (ver. 18) says that the fact that there would be 'mockers in the last time,' had been particularly foretold by them. It is probable that Peter refers to the same thing, and we may suppose that this was so well understood by all the apostles that they made it a common subject of preaching. ¶ *That there shall come in the last days.* In the last dispensation; in the period during which the affairs of the world shall be wound up. The apostle does not say that that was the last time in the sense that the world was about to come to an end; nor is it implied that the period called 'the last day' might not be a very long period, longer in fact than either of the previous periods of the world. He says that during that pe-

riod it had been predicted there would arise those whom he here calls *scoffers*. On the meaning of the phrase ' in the last days,' as used in the Scriptures, see Notes, Acts ii. 17; Heb. i. 2; Isa. ii. 2. ¶ *Scoffers.* In Jude (ver. 18) the same Greek word is rendered *mockers*. The word means those who deride, reproach, ridicule. There is usually in the word the idea of contempt or malignity towards an object. Here the sense seems to be that they would treat with derision or contempt the predictions respecting the advent of the Saviour, and the end of the world. It would appear probable that there was a particular or definite class of men referred to; a class who would hold peculiar opinions, and who would urge plausible objections against the fulfilment of the predictions respecting the end of the world, and the second coming of the Saviour—for those are the points to which Peter particularly refers. It scarcely required inspiration to foresee that there would be *scoffers* in the general sense of the term—for they have so abounded in every age, that no one would hazard much in saying that they would be found at any particular time; but the eye of the apostle is evidently on a particular class of men, the special form of whose reproaches would be the ridicule of the doctrines that the Lord Jesus would return; that there would be a day of judgment; that the world would be consumed by fire, &c. Archbishop Tillotson explains this of the Carpocratians, a large sect of the Gnostics, who denied the resurrection of the dead, and the future judgment. ¶ *Walking after their own lusts.* Living in the free indulgence of their sensual appetites See Notes, chap. ii. 10, 12, 14, 18, 19.

4. *And saying, Where is the promise of his coming?* That is, either, Where is the *fulfilment* of that promise; or, Where are the *indications* or *signs* that he will come? They evidently meant

5 For this they willingly are ignorant of, that *a* by the word of God the heavens were of old, and the earth ¹ standing out of the water *b* and in the water ;

a Ge.1.6,9.   1 consisting.   b Ps.24.2.

to imply that the promise had utterly failed ; that there was not the slightest evidence that it would be accomplished ; that they who had believed this were entirely deluded. It is possible that some of the early Christians, even in the time of the apostles, had undertaken to fix the time when these events would occur, as many have done since ; and that as *that* time had passed by, they inferred that the prediction had utterly failed. But whether this were so or not, it was easy to allege that the predictions respecting the second coming of the Saviour *seemed* to imply that the end of the world was near, and that there were no indications that they would be fulfilled. The laws of nature were uniform, as they had always been, and the alleged promises had failed. ¶ *For since the fathers fell asleep.* Since they *died*—death being often, in the Scriptures, as elsewhere, represented as sleep. Notes, John xi. 11 ; 1 Cor. xi. 30. This reference to the 'fathers,' by such scoffers, was probably designed to be ironical and contemptuous. Perhaps the meaning may be thus expressed: 'Those old men, the prophets, indeed foretold this event. They were much concerned and troubled about it ; and their predictions alarmed others, and filled their bosoms with dread. They looked out for the signs of the end of the world, and expected that that day was drawing near. But those good men have died. They lived to old age, and then died as others ; and since they have departed, the affairs of the world have gone on very much as they did before. The earth is suffered to have rest, and the laws of nature operate in the same way that they always did.' It seems not improbable that the immediate reference in the word *fathers* is not to the prophets of former times, but to aged and pious men of the times of the apostles, who had dwelt much on this subject, and who had made it a subject of conversation and of preaching. Those old men, said the scoffing objector, have died like others ; and, notwithstanding their confident predic-

tions, things now move on as they did from the beginning. ¶ *All things continue as* they were *from the beginning of the creation.* That is, the laws of nature are fixed and settled. The *argument* here—for it was doubtless designed to be an argument—is based on the stability of the laws of nature, and the uniformity of the course of events. Thus far all these predictions had failed. Things continued to go on as they had always done. The sun rose and set ; the tides ebbed and flowed ; the seasons followed each other in the usual order ; one generation succeeded another, as had always been the case ; and there was every indication that those laws would continue to operate as they had always done. This argument for the stability of the earth, and against the prospect of the fulfilment of the predictions of the Bible, would have more force with many minds now than it had then, for eighteen hundred years more have rolled away, and the laws of nature remain the same. Meantime, the expectations of those who have believed that the world was coming to an end have been disappointed ; the time set for this by many interpreters of Scripture has passed by ; men have looked out in vain for the coming of the Saviour, and sublunary affairs move on as they always have done. Still there are no indications of the coming of the Saviour; and perhaps it would be said that the farther men search, by the aid of science, into the laws of nature, the more they become impressed with their stability, and the more firmly they are convinced of the improbability that the world will be destroyed in the manner in which it is predicted in the Scriptures that it will be. The specious and plausible objection arising from this source, the apostle proposes to meet in the following verses.

5. *For this they willingly are ignorant of.* Λανθάνει γὰρ αὐτοὺς τοῦτο θέλοντας. There is some considerable variety in the translation of this passage. In our common version the Greek word (θέλον-

ϝαϛ) is rendered as if it were an adverb, or as if it referred to their *ignorance* in regard to the event ; meaning, that while they might have known this fact, they took no pains to do it, or that they preferred to have its recollection far from their minds. So Beza and Luther render it. Others, however, take it as referring to what follows, meaning, 'being so minded ; being of that opinion , or affirming.' So Bloomfield, Robinson, (*Lex.*,) Mede, Rosenmüller, &c. According to this interpretation the sense is, ' They who thus *will* or think ; that is, they who hold the opinion that all things will continue to remain as they were, are ignorant of this fact that things have *not* always thus remained ; that there has been a destruction of the world once by water.' The Greek seems rather to demand this interpretation ; and then the sense of the passage will be, 'It is concealed or hidden from those who hold this opinion, that the earth has been once destroyed.' It is implied, whichever interpretation is adopted, that the *will* was concerned in it ; that they were influenced by that rather than by sober judgment and by reason ; and whether the word refers to their *ignorance*, or to their *holding that opinion*, there was obstinacy and perverseness about it. The *will* has usually more to do in the denial and rejection of the doctrines of the Bible than the *understanding* has. The argument which the apostle appeals to in reply to this objection is a simple one. The adversaries of the doctrine affirmed that the laws of nature had always remained the same, and they affirmed that they always would. The apostle denies the fact which they assumed, in the sense in which they affirmed it, and maintains that those laws have *not* been so stable and uniform that the world has never been destroyed by an overwhelming visitation from God. It has been destroyed by a flood ; it may be again by fire. There was the same improbability that the event would occur, so far as the argument from the stability of the laws of nature is concerned, in the one case that there is in the other, and consequently the objection is of no force. ¶ *That by the word of God.* By the command of God. 'He *spake*, and it

was done.' Comp. Gen. i. 6, 9; Psa. xxxiii. 9. The idea here is, that everything depends on his word or will. As the heavens and the earth were originally *made* by his command, so by the same command they can be destroyed. ¶ *The heavens were of old.* The heavens were formerly made, Gen. i. 1. The word *heaven* in the Scriptures sometimes refers to the atmosphere, sometimes to the starry worlds as they appear above us, and sometimes to the exalted place where God dwells. Here it is used, doubtless, in the popular signification, as denoting the heavens as they *appear*, embracing the sun, moon, and stars. ¶ *And the earth standing out of the water and in the water.* Marg., *consisting.* Gr., συνιστῶσα. The Greek word, when used in an intransitive sense, means *to stand with*, or *together;* then tropically, *to place together*, to constitute, place, bring into existence.—*Robinson*. The idea which our translators seem to have had is, that, in the formation of the earth, a part was out of the water, and a part under the water; and that the former, or the inhabited portion, became entirely submerged, and that thus the inhabitants perished. This was not, however, probably the idea of Peter. He doubtless has reference to the account given in Gen. i. of the creation of the earth, in which *water* performed so important a part. The thought in his mind seems to have been, that *water* entered materially into the formation of the earth, and that in its very origin there existed the means by which it was afterwards destroyed. The word which is rendered '*standing*' should rather be rendered *consisting of*, or *constituted of;* and the meaning is, that the creation of the earth was the result of the Divine agency acting on the mass of elements which in Genesis is called *waters*, Gen. i. 2, 6, 7, 9. There was at first a vast fluid, an immense unformed collection of materials, called *waters*, and from that the earth arose. The point of time, therefore, in which Peter looks at the earth here, is not when the mountains, and continents, and islands, seem to be standing partly out of the water and partly in the water, but when there was a vast mass of materials called *waters* from which the

6 Whereby the world that then was, being overflowed with water, *a* perished :

7 But the heavens and the earth

a Ge.7.11.

which are now, by the same word are kept in store, reserved unto fire *b* against the day of judgment and perdition of ungodly men.

b Ps.50.3; Zep.3.8; 2 Thess.1.8.

---

earth was formed. The phrase ' *out of the water* ' (ἰξ ὕδατος) refers to the *origin* of the earth. It was formed *from*, or *out of*, that mass. The phrase ' *in the water* ' (δι' ὕδατος) more properly means *through* or *by*. It does not mean that the earth stood *in* the water in the sense that it was partly submerged ; but it means not only that the earth arose *from* that mass that is called *water* in Gen. i., but that that mass called *water* was in fact the grand material out of which the earth was formed. It was *through* or *by means of* that vast mass of mingled elements that the earth was made as it was. Everything arose out of that chaotic mass ; through that, or by means of that, all things were formed, and from the fact that the earth was thus formed out of the water, or that water entered so essentially into its formation, there existed causes which ultimately resulted in the deluge.

6. *Whereby.* Δι' ὧν. Through which, or by means of which. The pronoun here is in the plural number, and there has been much difference of opinion as to what it refers. Some suppose that it refers to the heavens mentioned in the preceding verse, and to the fact that the windows of heaven were opened in the deluge, (*Doddridge;*) others that the Greek phrase is taken in the sense of (δὶ) *whence.* Wetstein supposes that it refers to the ' heavens and the earth.' But the most obvious reference, though the plural number is used, and the word *water* in the antecedent is in the singular, is to *water.* The fact seems to be that the apostle had the *waters* mentioned in Genesis prominently in his eye, and meant to describe the effect produced *by* those waters. He has also twice, in the same sentence, referred to *water*—' out of the *water* and in the *water.*' It is evidently to these *waters* mentioned in Genesis, out of which the world was originally made, that he refers here. The world was formed from that fluid mass ; by these waters which ex-

isted when the earth was made, and out of which it arose, it was destroyed. The antecedent to the word in the plural number is rather that which was in the mind of the writer, or that of which he was thinking, than the *word* which he had used. ¶ *The world that then was, &c.* Including all its inhabitants. Rosenmüller supposes that the reference here is to some universal catastrophe which occurred before the deluge in the time of Noah, and indeed before the earth was fitted up in its present form, as described by Moses in Gen. i. It is rendered more than probable, by the researches of geologists in modern times, that such changes have occurred ; but there is no evidence that Peter was acquainted with them, and his purpose did not require that he should refer to them. All that his argument demanded was the fact that the world had been once destroyed, and that therefore there was no improbability in believing that it would be again. They who maintained that the prediction that the earth would be destroyed was improbable, affirmed that there were no signs of such an event ; that the laws of nature were stable and uniform ; and that as those laws had been so long and so uniformly unbroken, it was absurd to believe that such an event could occur. To meet this, all that was necessary was to show that, in a case where the same objections substantially might be urged, it had actually occurred that the world had been destroyed. There was, in itself considered, as much improbability in believing that the world could be destroyed by water as that it would be destroyed by fire, and consequently the objection had no real force. Notwithstanding the apparent stability of the laws of nature, the world had been once destroyed ; and there is, therefore, no improbability that it may be again. On the objections which *might* have been plausibly urged against the flood, see Notes on Heb. xi. 7.

7. *But the heavens and the earth which are now.* As they now exist. There is no difficulty here respecting what is meant by the word *earth*, but it is not so easy to determine precisely how much is included in the word *heavens.* It cannot be supposed to mean *heaven* as the place where God dwells ; nor is it necessary to suppose that Peter understood by the word all that would now be implied in it, as used by a modern astronomer. The word is doubtless employed in a popular signification, referring to the *heavens as they appear to the eye;* and the idea is, that the conflagration would not only destroy the earth, but would change the heavens as they now appear to us. If, in fact, the earth with its atmosphere should be subjected to an universal conflagration, all that is properly implied in what is here said by Peter would occur. ¶ *By the same word.* Dependent solely on the will of God. He has only to give command, and all will be destroyed. The laws of nature have no stability independent of his will, and at his pleasure all things could be reduced to nothing, as easily as they were made. A single word, a breath of command, from one Being, a Being over whom we have no control, would spread universal desolation through the heavens and the earth. Notwithstanding the laws of nature, as they are called, and the precision, uniformity, and power with which they operate, the dependence of the universe on the Creator is as entire as though there were no such laws, and as though all were conducted by the mere will of the Most High, irrespective of such laws. In fact, those laws have no efficiency of their own, but are a mere statement of the way in which God produces the changes which occur, the methods by which He operates who 'works all in all.' At any moment he could suspend them ; that is, he could cease to act, or withdraw his efficiency, and the universe would cease to be. ¶ *Are kept in store.* Gr., '*Are treasured up.*' The allusion in the Greek word is to anything that is treasured up, or reserved for future use. The apostle does not say that this is the *only* purpose for which the heavens and the earth are preserved, but that this is *one* object, or

this is *one* aspect in which the subject may be viewed. They are like treasure reserved for future use. ¶ *Reserved unto fire.* Reserved or kept to be burned up. See Notes on ver. 10. The first mode of destroying the world was by water, the next will be by fire. That the world would at some period be destroyed by fire was a common opinion among the ancient philosophers, especially the Greek Stoics. What was the foundation of that opinion, or whence it was derived, it is impossible now to determine ; but it is remarkable that it should have accorded so entirely with the statements of the New Testament. The authorities in proof that this opinion was entertained may be seen in Wetstein, *in loc.* See Seneca, N. Q. iii. 28 ; Cic. N. D. ii. 46 ; Simplicius in Arist. de Cœlo i. 9 ; Eusebius, P. xv. 18. It is quite remarkable that there have been among the heathen in ancient and modern times so many opinions that accord with the statements of revelation —opinions, many of them, which could not have been founded on any investigations of science among them, and which must, therefore, have been either the result of conjecture, or handed down by tradition. Whatever may have been their origin, the fact that such opinions prevailed and were believed, may be allowed to have some weight in showing that the statements in the Bible are not improbable. ¶ *Against the day of judgment and perdition of ungodly men.* The world was destroyed by a flood on account of the wickedness of its inhabitants. It would seem from this passage that it will be destroyed by fire with reference to the same cause ; at least, that its destruction by fire will involve the perdition of wicked men. It cannot be inferred from this passage that the world will be *as* wicked at the general conflagration as it was in the time of Noah ; but the idea in the mind of Peter seems to have been, that in the destruction of the world by fire the perdition of the wicked will be involved, or will at that time occur. It also seems to be implied that the fire will accomplish an important agency in that destruction, as the water did on the old world. It is not said, in the passage before us, whether those to be destroyed will be

8 But, beloved, be not ignorant of this one thing, that one day *is* with the Lord as a thousand years, and a *a* thousand years as one day.

9 The Lord is not slack *b* con-

cerning his promise, as some men count slackness; but is long-suffer-ing *c* to us-ward, not willing *d* that any should perish, but that all should *e* come to repentance.

a Ps.90.4.　　*b* Ha.2.3.

c Ps.86.15; Is.30.18.　*d* Eze. 33.11.　*e* 1 Ti.2.4.

living at that time, or will be raised up from the dead, nor have we any means of determining what was the idea of Peter on that point. All that the passage essentially teaches is, that the world is reserved now with reference to such a consummation by fire; that is, that there are elements kept in store that may be enkindled into an universal conflagration, and that such a conflagra-tion will be attended with the destruc-tion of the wicked.

8. *But, beloved, be not ignorant of this one thing, that one day* is *with the Lord as a thousand years.* This (vers. 8, 9) is the second consideration by which the apostle meets the objection of scoffers against the doctrine of the second coming of the Saviour. The objection was, that much time, and perhaps the time which had been supposed to be set for his coming, had passed away, and still all things remained as they were. The reply of the apostle is, that no argument could be drawn from this, for that which may seem to be a long time to us is a brief period with God. In the infinity of his own duration there is abundant time to accomplish his designs, and it can make no difference with him whether they are accomplished in one day or extended to a thousand years. Man has but a short time to live, and if he does not accomplish his purposes in a very brief period, he never will. But it is not so with God. He always lives ; and we cannot therefore infer, because the execution of his purposes seems to be delayed, that they are abandoned. With Him who always lives it will be as easy to accomplish them at a far distant period as now. If it is his pleasure to accomplish them in a single day, he can do it; if he chooses that the execution shall be deferred to a thousand years, or that a thousand years shall be consumed in executing them, he has power to carry them onward through what seems to us to be so vast a duration. The

wicked, therefore, cannot infer that they will escape because their punish-ment is delayed; nor should the right-eous fear that the Divine promises will fail because ages pass away before they are accomplished. The expression here used, that 'one day is with the Lord as a thousand years,' &c., is common in the Rabbinical writings. See Wetstein *in loc.* A similar thought occurs in Psa. xc. 4 : 'For a thousand years in thy sight are but as yesterday when it is past, and as a watch in the night.'

9. *The Lord is not slack concerning his promise.* That is, it should not be inferred because his promise seems to be long delayed that therefore it will fail. When *men*, after a considerable lapse of time, fail to fulfil their engage-ments, we infer that it is because they have changed their plans, or because they have forgotten their promises, or because they have no ability to perform them, or because there is a want of principle which makes them regardless of their obligations. But no such in-ference can be drawn from the apparent delay of the fulfilment of the Divine purposes. Whatever may be the rea-sons why they seem to be deferred, we may be sure that it is from no such causes as these. ¶ *As some men count slackness.* It is probable that the apos-tle here had his eye on some professing Christians who had become disheart-ened and impatient, and who, from the delay in regard to the coming of the Lord Jesus, and from the representa-tions of those who denied the truth of the Christian religion, arguing from that delay that it was false, began to fear that his promised coming would indeed never occur. To such he says that it should not be inferred from his delay that he would not return, but that the delay should be regarded as an evi-dence of his desire that men should have space for repentance, and an op-portunity to secure their salvation. See

Notes on ver. 15. ¶ *But is long-suffer-ing to us-ward.* Toward us. The delay should be regarded as a proof of his forbearance, and of his desire that men should be saved. Every sinner should consider the fact that he is not cut down in his sins, not as a proof that God will not punish the wicked, but as a demonstration that he is now forbearing, and is willing that he should have an ample opportunity to obtain eternal life. No man should infer that God will not execute his threatenings, unless he can look into the most distant parts of a coming eternity, and demonstrate that there is no suffering appointed for the sinner there ; any man who sins, and who is spared even for a moment, should regard the respite as a proof that God is merciful and forbearing now. ¶ *Not willing that any should perish.* That is, he does not *desire* it or *wish* it. His nature is benevolent, and he sincerely desires the eternal happiness of all, and his patience towards sinners *proves* that he is willing that they should be saved. If he were not willing, it would be easy for him to cut them off, and exclude them from hope at once. This passage, however, should not be adduced to prove (1) that sinners never *will* in fact perish ; for (*a*) the passage does not refer to what God will do as the final Judge of mankind, but to what are his feelings and desires now towards men. (*b*) One may have a sincere desire that others should not perish, and yet it may be that, in entire consistency with that, they will perish. A parent has a sincere *wish* that his children should not be punished, and yet he himself may be under a moral necessity to punish them. A lawgiver may have a sincere wish that no one should ever break the laws, or be punished, and yet he himself may build a prison, and construct a gallows, and cause the law to be executed in a most rigorous manner. A judge on the bench may have a sincere desire that no man should be executed, and that every one arraigned before him should be found to be innocent, and yet even he, in entire accordance with that wish, and with a most benevolent heart, even with tears in his eyes, may pronounce the sentence of the law. (*c*) It cannot be inferred that all that the heart of infinite benevolence would desire will be accomplished by his mere *will*. It is evidently as much in accordance with the benevolence of God that no man should be miserable in this world, as it is that no one should suffer in the next, since the difficulty is not in the question *where* one shall suffer, but in the fact itself that *any* should suffer ; and it is just as much in accordance with his nature that all should be happy *here*, as that they should be happy hereafter. And yet no man can maintain that the fact that God is benevolent proves that no one will suffer here. As little will that fact prove that none will suffer in the world to come. (2.) The passage should not be adduced to prove that God has no *purpose*, and has formed no *plan*, in regard to the destruction of the wicked ; for (*a*) the word here used has reference rather to his disposition, or to his nature, than to any act or plan. (*b*) There is a sense, as is admitted by all, in which he does will the destruction of the wicked—to wit, if they do not repent—that is, if they deserve it. (*c*) Such an act is as inconsistent with his general benevolence as an eternal purpose in the matter, since his eternal purpose can only have been to do what he actually does ; and if it be consistent with a sincere desire that sinners should be saved to *do* this, then it is consistent to *determine* beforehand to do it—for to determine beforehand to do what is in fact right, cannot but be a lovely trait in the character of any one. (3.) The passage then proves (*a*) that God has a sincere *desire* that men should be saved ; (*b*) that any purpose in regard to the destruction of sinners is not founded on mere will, or is not arbitrary ; (*c*) that it would be agreeable to the nature of God, and to his arrangements in the plan of salvation, if all men should come to repentance, and accept the offers of mercy ; (*d*) that if any come to him truly penitent, and desirous to be saved, they will not be cast off ; (*e*) that, since it is in accordance with his nature that he should desire that all men may be saved, it may be presumed that he has made an arrangement by which it is possible that they should be ; and (*f*) that, since this is his desire, it is proper for the ministers of religion to

10 But the day of the Lord will come as a thief *a* in the night; in the which the heavens *b* shall pass away with a great noise, and the elements shall melt with fervent heat: the earth also, and the works that are therein, shall be burned up.

a Mat.24.42,43; Re.16.15.
b Ps.102.26; Is.51.6 ; Re.20.11.

offer salvation to every human being. Comp. Ezek. xxxiii. 11.

10. *But the day of the Lord.* The day of the Lord Jesus. That is, the day in which he will be manifested. It is called *his* day, because he will then be the grand and prominent object as the Judge of all. Comp. Luke xvii. 27. ¶ *Will come as a thief in the night.* Unexpectedly; suddenly. See Notes, 1 Thess. v. 2. ¶ *In the which the heavens shall pass away with a great noise.* That is, what seems to *us* to be the heavens. It cannot mean that the holy abode where God dwells will pass away; nor need we suppose that this declaration extends to the starry worlds and systems as disclosed by the modern astronomy. The word is doubtless used in a popular sense—that is, as things appear to us; and the *fair* interpretation of the passage would demand only such a change as would occur by the destruction of this world by fire. If a conflagration should take place, embracing the earth and its surrounding atmosphere, all the phenomena would occur which are here described; and, if this would be so, then this is all that can be proved to be meant by the passage. Such a destruction of the elements could not occur without 'a great noise.' ¶ *And the elements shall melt with fervent heat.* Gr., 'the elements being burned, or burning, (*καυσούμενα*,) shall be dissolved.' The idea is, that the *cause* of their being 'dissolved' shall be fire ; or that there will be a conflagration extending to what are here called the 'elements,' that shall produce the effects here described by the word 'dissolved.' There has been much difference of opinion in regard to the meaning of the word here rendered *elements*, (*στοιχεῖα*.) The word occurs in the New Testament only in the following places: Gal. iv. 3, 9 ; 2 Pet. iii. 10, 12, in which it is rendered *elements;* Col. ii. 8, 20, in which it is rendered *rudiments;* and in Heb. v. 12, where it is rendered *principles.* For the general meaning of the word, see Notes, Gal. iv. 3. The word denotes the *rudiments* of anything; the minute parts or portions of which anything is composed, or which constitutes the simple portions out of which anything grows, or of which it is compounded. Here it would properly denote the component parts of the material world; or those which enter into its composition, and of which it is made up. It is not to be supposed that the apostle used the term with the same exact signification with which a chemist would use it now, but in accordance with the popular use of the term in his day. In all ages, and in all languages, some such word, with more or less of scientific accuracy, has been employed to denote the primary materials out of which others were formed, just as, in most languages, there have been characters or letters to denote the elementary sounds of which language is composed. The ancients in general supposed that the elements out of which all things were formed were four—air, earth, fire, and water. Modern science has entirely overturned this theory, and has shown that these, so far from being simple elements, are themselves compounds; but the tendency of modern science is still to show that the elements of all things are in fact few in number. The word, as here used by Peter, would refer to the elements of things as then understood in a popular sense ; it would now not be an improper word to be applied to the few elements of which all things are composed, as disclosed by modern chemistry. In either case the use of the word would be correct. Whether applied to the one or the other, science has shown that all are capable of combustion. Water, in its component parts, is inflammable in a high degree; and even the diamond has been shown to be combustible. The idea contained in the word 'dissolved,' is, properly, only the change which *heat* produces. Heat changes the *forms* of things ; dissolves them into their elements ; dissipates those which were solid by driving

them off into gases, and produces new compounds, but it *annihilates* nothing. It could not be demonstrated from this phrase that the world would be annihilated by fire; it could be proved only that it will undergo important changes. So far as the action of fire is concerned, the *form* of the earth may pass away, and its aspect be changed; but unless the direct power which created it interposes to annihilate it, the *matter* which now composes it will still be in existence. ¶ *The earth also, and the works that are therein, shall be burned up.* That is, whether they are the works of God or man—the whole vegetable and animal creation, and all the towers, the towns, the palaces, the productions of genius, the paintings, the statuary, the books, which man has made.

" The cloud-capp'd towers, the gorgeous palaces,
The solemn temples, the great globe itself,
And all that it inherits, shall *dissolve*,
And, like the baseless fabric of a vision,
Leave not one wreck behind."

The word rendered 'burned up,' like the word just before used and rendered *fervent heat*—a word of the same origin, but here *intensive*—means that they will undergo such a change as fire will produce ; not, necessarily, that the matter composing them will be annihilated. If the matter composing the earth is ever to be destroyed entirely, it must be by the immediate power of God, for only He who created can destroy. There is not the least evidence that a particle of matter originally made has been *annihilated* since the world began ; and there are no fires so intense, no chemical powers so mighty, as to cause a particle of matter to cease wholly to be. So far as the power of man is concerned, and so far as one portion of matter can prey on another, matter is as imperishable as mind, and neither can be destroyed unless *God* destroys it. Whether it is his purpose to *annihilate* any portion of the matter which he has made, does not appear from his word; but it is clear that he intends that the universe shall undergo important *changes*. As to the possibility or probability of such a destruction by fire as is here predicted, no one can have any doubt who is acquainted with the disclosures of modern science in regard to the internal struc-

ture of the earth. Even the ancient philosophers, from some cause, supposed that the earth would yet be destroyed by fire, (Notes, ver. 7;) and modern science has made it probable that the interior of the earth is a melted and intensely heated mass of burning materials; that the habitable world is but a comparatively thin crust or shell over those internal fires; that earthquakes are caused by the vapours engendered by that heated mass when water comes in contact with it; and that volcanoes are but openings and vent-holes through which those internal flames make their way to the surface. Whether these fires will everywhere make their way to the surface, and produce an universal conflagration, perhaps could not be determined by science; but no one can doubt that the simple command of God would be all that is necessary to pour those burning floods over the earth, as he once caused the waters to roll over every mountain and through every valley. As to the question whether it is probable that such a change produced by fire, and bringing the present order of things to a close, will occur, it may be remarked farther, that there is reason to believe that such changes are in fact taking place in other worlds. ' During the last two or three centuries, upwards of thirteen fixed stars have disappeared. One of them, situated in the northern hemisphere, presented a peculiar brilliancy, and was so bright as to be seen by the naked eye at mid-day. It seemed to be on fire, appearing at first of a dazzling white, then of a reddish yellow, and lastly of an ashy pale colour. La Place supposes that it was burned up, as it has never been seen since. The conflagration was visible about sixteen months.' The well-known astronomer, Von Littrow, in the section of his work on ' New and Missing Stars,' (entitled Die Wunder der Himmels oder Gemeinfassliche Darstellung der Weltsystems, Stuttgard, 1843, § 227,) observes : ' Great as may be the revolutions which take place on the surface of those fixed stars, which are subject to this alternation of light, what entirely different changes may those others have experienced, which in regions of the firmament where no star had ever been be-

11 *Seeing* then *that* all these things shall be dissolved, what manner *of persons* ought ye to be in *all* holy conversation and godliness;

12 Looking for *a* and [1] hasting

<small>*a* Tit.2.13.   1 Or, *hasting the coming.*</small>

unto the coming of the day of God, wherein the heavens, being on fire, shall be dissolved, and the elements shall melt *b* with fervent heat?

13 Nevertheless we, according to

<small>*b* Is.34.4,   Mic.1.4.</small>

fore, appeared to blaze up in clear flames, and then to disappear, perhaps for ever.' He then gives a brief history of those stars which have excited the particular attention of astronomers. ' In the year 1572, on the 11th of November,' says he, 'Tycho, on passing from his chemical laboratory to the observatory, through the court of his house, observed in the constellation Cassiopeia, at a place where before he had only seen very small stars, a new star of uncommon magnitude. It was so bright that it surpassed even Jupiter and Venus in splendour, and was visible even in the day-time. During the whole time in which it was visible, Tycho could observe no parallax or change of position. At the end of the year, however, it gradually diminished; and at length, in March 1574, sixteen months after its discovery, entirely disappeared, since which all traces of it have been lost. When it first appeared, its light was of a dazzling white colour ; in January 1573, two months after its reviving, it became yellowish; in a few months it assumed a reddish hue, like Mars or Aldebaran; and in the beginning of the year 1574, two or three months before its total disappearance, it glimmered only with a gray or lead-coloured light, similar to that of Saturn.' See Bibliotheca Sacra, III., p. 181. If such things occur in other worlds, there is nothing improbable or absurd in the supposition that they may yet occur on the earth.

11. Seeing *then* that *all these things shall be dissolved.* Since this is an undoubted truth. ¶ *What manner* of persons *ought ye to be in* all *holy conversation and godliness.* In holy conduct and piety. That is, this fact ought to be allowed to exert a deep and abiding influence on us, to induce us to lead holy lives. We should feel that there is nothing permanent on the earth; that this is not our abiding home; and that our great interests are in another world. We should be serious, humble,

and prayerful; and should make it our great object to be prepared for the solemn scenes through which we are soon to pass. An habitual contemplation of the truth, that all that we see is soon to pass away, would produce a most salutary effect on the mind. It would make us serious. It would repress ambition. It would lead us not to desire to accumulate what must so soon be destroyed. It would prompt us to lay up our treasures in heaven. It would cause us to ask with deep earnestness whether we are prepared for these amazing scenes, should they suddenly burst upon us.

12. *Looking for.* Not knowing *when* this may occur, the mind should be in that state which constitutes *expectation;* that is, a belief that it will occur, and a condition of mind in which we would not be taken by surprise should it happen at any moment. See Notes, Titus ii. 13. ¶ *And hasting unto the coming.* Marg., as in Greek, '*hasting the coming.*' The Greek word rendered *hasting,* (σπεύδω,) means to urge on, to hasten; and then to hasten after anything, to await with eager desire. This is evidently the sense here.— *Wetstein* and *Robinson.* The state of mind which is indicated by the word is that when we are anxiously desirous that anything should occur, and when we would hasten or accelerate it if we could. The true Christian does not dread the coming of that day. He looks forward to it as the period of his redemption, and would welcome, at any time, the return of his Lord and Saviour. While he is willing to wait as long as it shall please God for the advent of his Redeemer, yet to him the brightest prospect in the future is that hour when he shall come to take him to himself. ¶ *The coming of the day of God.* Called ' the day of God,' because God will then be manifested in his power and glory.

13. *Nevertheless we, according to his promise.* The allusion here seems to

his promise, look for new *ᵃ* heavens | and a new earth, wherein dwelleth

ᵃ Re.21.1,27. | righteousness.

be, beyond a doubt, to two passages in Isaiah, in which a promise of this kind is found. Isa. lxv. 17: 'For, behold, I create new heavens, and a new earth: and the former shall not be remembered, nor come into mind.' Isa. lxvi. 22: ' For as the new heavens and the new earth, which I will make, shall remain before me, saith the Lord,' &c. Comp. Rev. xxi. 1, where John says he had a vision of the new heaven and the new earth which was promised : ' And I saw a new heaven and a new earth; for the first heaven and the first earth were passed away, and there was no more sea.' See Notes, Isa. lxv. 17. ¶ *Look for new heavens and a new earth.* It may not be easy to answer many of the questions which might be asked respecting the 'new heaven and earth' here mentioned. One of those which are most naturally asked is, whether the apostle meant to say that this earth, after being purified by fire, would be fitted up again for the abode of the redeemed ; but this question it is impossible to answer with certainty. The following remarks may perhaps embrace all that is known, or that can be shown to be probable, on the meaning of the passage before us. I. The ' new heavens and the new earth' referred to will be such as will exist *after* the world shall have been destroyed by fire ; that is, *after* the general judgment. There is not a word expressed, and not a hint given, of any ' new heaven and earth' *previous* to this, in which the Saviour will reign personally over his saints, in such a renovated world, through a long millennial period. The *order* of events stated by Peter, is (*a*) that the heavens and earth which are now, are ' kept in store, reserved unto fire *against the day of judgment,* and perdition of ungodly men,' ver. 7 ; (*b*) that the day of the Lord will come suddenly and unexpectedly, ver. 10 ; that *then* the heavens and earth will pass away with a great noise, the elements will melt, and the earth with all its works be burned up, ver. 10 ; and (*c*) that *after* this (ver. 13) we are to expect the ' new heavens and

new earth.' Nothing is said of a personal reign of Christ ; nothing of the resurrection of the saints to dwell with him on the earth ; nothing of the world's being fitted up for their abode *previous* to the final judgment. If Peter had any knowledge of such events, and believed that they would occur, it is remarkable that he did not even allude to them here. The passage before us is one of the very few places in the New Testament where allusion is made to the manner in which the affairs of the world will be closed ; and it cannot be explained why, if he looked for such a glorious personal reign of the Saviour, the subject should have been passed over in total silence. II. The word ' new,' applied to the heavens and the earth that are to succeed the present, might express one of the following three things —that is, either of these things would correspond with all that is fairly implied in that word : (*a*) If a new world was literally created out of nothing after this world is destroyed ; for that would be in the strictest sense *new.* That such an event is possible no one can doubt, though it is not revealed. (*b*) If an inhabitant of the earth should dwell after death on any other of the worlds now existing, it would be to him a ' new' abode, and everything would appear new. Let him, for instance, be removed to the planet *Saturn,* with its wonderful ring, and its seven moons, and the whole aspect of the heavens, and of the world on which he would then dwell, would be *new* to him. The same thing would occur if he were to dwell on any other of the heavenly bodies, or if he were to pass from world to world. See this illustrated at length in the works of Thomas Dick, LL.D.—' Celestial Scenery,' &c. Comp. Notes, 1 Pet. i. 12. (*c*) *If* the earth should be renovated, and fitted up for the abode of man *after* the universal conflagration, it would then be a new abode. III. This world, thus renovated, may be from time to time the temporary abode of the redeemed, after the final judgment. No one can prove that this may not be, though there is no evidence that it will be their permanent and eternal abode, or that even all the redeemed will at any one time find a home on this globe, for no one can suppose that the earth is spacious enough to furnish a dwelling-place for all the unnumbered millions that are to be saved. But that the earth *may* again be revisited from time to time by the redeemed ; that in a purified and renovated form it may be *one* of the 'many mansions' which are to be fitted up for them, (John xiv. 2,) may not appear wholly improbable from the following suggestions : (1.) It seems to have been a law of the earth that in its progress it should be *prepared* at one period for the dwelling-place of a higher order of beings at another period. Thus, according to the disclosures of geology, it existed perhaps for countless ages before it was fitted to be an abode for man ; and that it was occupied by the monsters of an inferior order of existence, who have now passed away to make room for a nobler race. Who can tell but the present order of things may pass away to make place for the manifestations of a more exalted mode of being ? (2.) There is no certain evidence that any world has been *annihilated*, though some have disappeared from human view. Indeed, as observed above, (Notes, ver. 10,) there is no proof that a single particle of matter ever has been annihilated, or ever will be. It may change its form, but it may still exist. (3.) It seems also to accord most with probability, that, though the earth may undergo important changes by flood or fire, it will not be annihilated. It seems difficult to suppose that, as a world, it will be wholly displaced from the system of which it is now a part, or that the system itself will disappear. The earth, as one of the worlds of God, has occupied too important a position in the history of the universe to make it to be easily believed that the place where the Son of God became incarnate and died, shall be utterly swept away. It would, certainly, accord more with all the *feelings* which we can have on such a subject, to suppose that a world once so beautiful when it came from the hand of its Maker, should be restored to primitive loveliness; that a world which seems to have been *made* primarily (see Notes, 1 Pet. i. 12) with a view to illustrate the glory of God in redemption, should be preserved in some appropriate form to be the theatre of the exhibition of the developement of that plan in far distant ages to come. (4.) To the redeemed, it would be most interesting again to visit the spot where the great work of their redemption was accomplished ; where the Son of God became incarnate and made atonement for sin ; and where there would be so many interesting recollections and associations, even after the purification by fire, connected with the infancy of their existence, and their preparation for eternity. Piety would at least *wish* that the world where Gethsemane and Calvary are should never be blotted out from the universe. But (5.) if, after their resurrection and reception into heaven, the redeemed shall ever revisit a world so full of interesting recollections and associations, where they began their being, where their Redeemer lived and died, where they were renewed and sanctified, and where their bodies once rested in the grave, there is no reason to suppose that this will be their permanent and unchanging abode. It may be mere speculation, but it seems to accord best with the goodness of God, and with the manner in which the universe is made, to suppose that every portion of it may be visited, and become successively the abode of the redeemed ; that they may pass from world to world, and survey the wonders and the works of God as they are displayed in different worlds. The universe, so vast, seems to have been fitted up for such a purpose, and nothing else that we can conceive of will be so adapted to give employment without weariness to the minds that God has made, in the interminable duration before them. IV. The new heavens and earth will be *holy*. They will be the abode of righteousness for ever. (*a*) This fact is clearly revealed in the verse before us ; 'wherein dwelleth righteousness.' It is also the correct statement of the Scriptures, Rev. xxi. 27; 1 Cor. vi. 9, 10; Heb. xii. 14. (*b*) This will be in strong contrast with what has occurred

14 Wherefore, beloved, seeing that ye look for such things, be diligent *a* that ye may be found of him in peace, without spot, and blameless.

a 1 Co. 15.58; 1 Th.5.23.

15 And account *that* the long-suffering of our Lord *is* salvation; *b* even as our beloved brother Paul also, according to the wisdom given unto him, hath written unto you;

b Ro.2.4.

on earth. The history of this world has been almost entirely a history of *sin* —of its nature, developements, results. There have been no perfectly holy beings on the earth, except the Saviour, and the angels who have occasionally visited it. There has been no perfectly holy place—city, village, hamlet; no perfectly holy community. But the future world, in strong contrast with this, will be perfectly pure, and will be a fair illustration of what religion in its perfect form will do. (*c*) It is for this that the Christian desires to dwell in that world, and waits for the coming of his Saviour. It is not primarily that he may be happy, desirable as that is, but that he may be in a world where he himself will be perfectly pure, and where all around him will be pure; where every being that he meets shall be 'holy as God is holy,' and every place on which his eye rests, or his foot treads, shall be uncontaminated by sin. To the eye of faith and hope, how blessed is the prospect of such a world!

14. *Wherefore, beloved, seeing that ye look for such things, be diligent.* That is, in securing your salvation. The effect of such hopes and prospects should be to lead us to an earnest inquiry whether we are prepared to dwell in a holy world, and to make us diligent in performing the duties, and patient in bearing the trials of life. He who has such hopes set before him, should seek earnestly that he may be enabled truly to avail himself of them, and should make their-attainment the great object of his life. He who is so soon to come to an end of all weary toil, should be willing to labour diligently and faithfully while life lasts. He who is so soon to be relieved from all temptation and trial, should be willing to bear a little longer the sorrows of the present world. What are all these compared with the glory that awaits us? Comp. Notes, 1 Cor. xv. 58; Rom. viii. 18, seq.; 2 Cor. iv. 16-18. ¶ *That ye may be*

found of him in peace. Found by him when he returns in such a state as to secure your eternal peace. ¶ *Without spot, and blameless.* See Notes, Eph. v. 27. It should be an object of earnest effort with us to have the last stain of sin and pollution removed from our souls. A deep feeling that we are soon to stand in the presence of a holy God, our final Judge, cannot but have a happy influence in making us pure.

15. *And account* that *the long-suffering of our Lord* is *salvation.* Regard his delay in coming to judge the world, not as an evidence that he never will come, but as a proof of his desire that we should be saved. Many had drawn a different inference from the fact that the Saviour did not return, and had supposed that it was a proof that he would never come, and that his promises had failed. Peter says that that conclusion was not authorized, but that we should rather regard it as an evidence of his mercy, and of his desire that we should be saved. This conclusion is as proper now as it was then. Wicked men should not infer, because God does not cut them down, that therefore they never will be punished, or that God is not faithful to his threatenings. They should rather regard it as a proof that he is willing to save them; for (1) he might justly cut them off for their sins; (2) the only reason of which we have knowledge why he spares the wicked is to give them space for repentance; and (3) as long as life is prolonged a sinner has the opportunity to repent, and may turn to God. We may therefore, in our own case, look on all the delays of God to punish—on all his patience and forbearance towards us, notwithstanding our sins and provocations—on the numberless tokens of his kindness scattered along our way, as evidence that he is not willing that we should perish. What an accumulated argument in any case would this afford of the willingness of God to save! Let any man look on

16 As also in all *his* epistles, *a* speaking in them of these things; in which are some things hard to be understood, which they that are

unlearned and unstable wrest, as *they do* also the other scriptures, unto their own destruction.

a Ro.8.19; 1 Co.15.24; 1 Th.iv.,v.; 2 Th.1.5-10.

---

his own sins, his pride, and selfishness, and sensuality; let him contemplate the fact that he has sinned through many years, and against many mercies; let him endeavour to estimate the number and magnitude of his offences, and upon God's patience in bearing with him while these have been committed, and who can overrate the force of such an argument in proof that God is slow to anger, and is willing to save? Comp. Notes, Rom. ii. 4. ¶ *Even as our beloved brother Paul also.* From this reference to Paul the following things are clear: (1) that Peter was acquainted with his writings; (2) that he presumed that those to whom he wrote were also acquainted with them; (3) that Peter regarded Paul as a 'beloved brother,' notwithstanding the solemn rebuke which Paul had had occasion to administer to him, Gal. ii. 2, seq.; (4) that he regarded him as authority in inculcating the doctrines and duties of religion; and (5) that he regarded him as an inspired man, and his writings as a part of Divine truth. See Notes, ver. 16. That Peter has shown in his epistles that he was acquainted with the writings of Paul, has been abundantly proved by Eichhorn, (Einleitung in das N. Tes. viii. 606, seq.,) and will be apparent by a comparison of the following passages : Eph. i. 3, with 1 Pet. iii. 1 ; Col. iii. 8, with 1 Pet. ii. 1 ; Eph. v. 22, with 1 Pet. iii. 1 ; Eph. v. 21, with 1 Pet. v. 5 ; 1 Thess. v. 6, with 1 Pet. v. 8 ; 1 Cor. xvi. 20, with 1 Pet. v. 14 ; Rom. viii. 18, with 1 Pet. v. 1; Rom. iv. 24, with 1 Pet. i. 21 ; Rom. xiii. 1, 3, 4, with 1 Pet. ii. 13, 14 ; 1 Tim. ii. 9, with 1 Pet. iii. 3 ; 1 Tim. v. 5, with 1 Pet. iii. 5. The writings of the apostles were doubtless extensively circulated ; and one apostle, though himself inspired, could not but feel a deep interest in the writings of another. There would be cases also, as in the instance before us, in which one would wish to confirm his own sentiments by the acknowledged wisdom, experience, and authority of another. ¶ *According to the wisdom given unto him.* Peter evidently did not mean to disparage that wisdom, or to express a doubt that Paul was endowed with wisdom ; he meant undoubtedly that, in regard to Paul, the same thing was true which he would have affirmed of himself or of any other man, that whatever wisdom he had was to be traced to a higher than human origin. This would at the same time tend to secure more respect for the opinion of Paul than if he had said it was his own, and would keep up in the minds of those to whom he wrote a sense of the truth that *all* wisdom is from above. In reference to ourselves, to our friends, to our teachers, and to all men, it is proper to bear in remembrance the fact that *all* true wisdom is from the 'Father of lights.' Comp. Notes, James i. 5, 17. ¶ *Hath written unto you.* It is not necessary to suppose that Paul had written any epistles addressed specifically, and by name, to the persons to whom Peter wrote. It is rather to be supposed that the persons to whom Peter wrote (1 Pet. i. 1) lived in the regions to which some of Paul's epistles were addressed, and that they might be regarded as addressed to them. The epistles to the Galatians, Ephesians, and Colossians were of this description, all addressed to churches in Asia Minor, and all, therefore, having reference to the same people to whom Peter addressed his epistles.

16. *As also in all his epistles.* Not only in those which he addressed to the churches in Asia Minor, but in his epistles generally. It is to be presumed that they might have had an acquaintance with some of the other epistles of Paul, as well as those sent to the churches in their immediate vicinity. ¶ *Speaking in them of these things.* The things which Peter had dwelt upon in his two epistles. The great doctrines of the cross; of the depravity of man; of the Divine purposes; of the new birth; of the consummation of all things;

of the return of the Saviour to judge the world, and to receive his people to himself; the duty of a serious, devout, and prayerful life, and of being prepared for the heavenly world. These things are constantly dwelt upon by Paul, and to his authority in these respects Peter might appeal with the utmost confidence. ¶ *In which.* The common reading in this passage is **ἐν οἷς,** and according to this the reference is to the *subjects* treated of—'in which *things*'—referring to what he had just spoken of —'speaking of these *things.*' This reading is found in the common editions of the New Testament, and is supported by far the greater number of mss., and by most commentators and critics. It is found in Griesbach, Tittman, and Hahn, and has every evidence of being the genuine reading. Another reading, however, (**ἐν αἷς,**) is found in some valuable mss., and is supported by the Syriac and Arabic versions, and adopted by Mill, (Proleg. 1484,) and by Beza. According to this, the reference is to the *epistles* themselves—as would seem to be implied in our common version. The true construction, so far as the evidence goes, is to refer it not directly to the *epistles,* but to the *things* of which Peter says Paul wrote; that is, not to the style and language of Paul, but to the great truths and doctrines which he taught. Those doctrines were indeed contained in his epistles, but still, according to the fair construction of the passage before us, Peter should not be understood as accusing Paul of obscurity of *style.* He refers not to the difficulty of understanding what Paul *meant,* but to the difficulty of comprehending the great *truths* which he taught. This is, generally, the greatest difficulty in regard to the statements of Paul. The difficulty is not that the meaning of the writer is not plain, but it is either (*a*) that the mind is overpowered by the grandeur of the thought, and the incomprehensible nature of the theme, or (*b*) that the truth is so unpalatable, and the mind is so prejudiced against it, that we are *unwilling* to receive it. Many a man knows well enough what Paul means, and would *receive* his doctrines without hesitation if the heart was not opposed to it; and in this state

of mind Paul is charged with obscurity, when the real difficulty lies only in the *heart* of him who makes the complaint. If this be the true interpretation of this passage, then it should not be adduced to prove that Paul is an obscure writer, whatever may be true on that point. There *are,* undoubtedly, obscure things in his writings, as there are in all other ancient compositions, but this passage should not be adduced to prove that he had not the faculty of making himself understood. An honest heart, a willingness to receive the truth, is one of the best qualifications for understanding the writings of Paul; and when this exists, no one will fail to find truth that may be comprehended, and that will be eminently adapted to sanctify and save the soul. ¶ *Are some things hard to be understood.* Things pertaining to high and difficult subjects, and which are not easy to be comprehended. Peter does not call in question the truth of what Paul had written; he does not intimate that he himself would differ from him His language is rather that which a man would use who regarded the writings to which he referred as true, and what he says here is an honourable testimony to the authority of Paul. It may be added, (1,) that Peter does not say that *all* the doctrines of the Bible, or even *all* the doctrines of Paul, are hard to be understood, or that nothing is plain. (2.) He says nothing about withholding the Bible, or even the writings of Paul, from the mass of Christians, on the ground of the difficulty of understanding the Scriptures; nor does he intimate that that was the design of the Author of the Bible. (3.) It is perfectly manifest, from this very passage, that the writings of Paul were in fact in the hands of the people, else how could they wrest and pervert them? (4.) Peter says nothing about an infallible interpreter of any kind, nor does he intimate that either he or his 'successors' were authorized to interpret them for the church. (5.) With what propriety can the *pretended* successor of Peter—the pope—undertake to expound those difficult doctrines in the writings of Paul, when even Peter himself did not undertake it, and when he did not profess to be able to comprehend them?

Is the pope more skilled in the knowledge of divine things than the apostle Peter? Is he better qualified to interpret the sacred writings than an inspired apostle was? (6.) Those portions of the writings of Paul, for anything that appears to the contrary, are just as 'hard to be understood' now, as they were before the 'infallible' church undertook to explain them. The world is little indebted to any claims of infallibility in explaining the meaning of the oracles of God. It remains yet to be seen that any portion of the Bible has been made clearer by *any* mere authoritative explanation. And (7.) it should be added, that without any such exposition, the humble inquirer after truth may find enough in the Bible to guide his feet in the paths of salvation. No one ever approached the sacred Scriptures with a teachable heart, who did not find them '*able* to make him wise unto salvation.' Comp. Notes on 2 Tim. iii. 15. ¶ *Which they that are unlearned.* The evil here adverted to is that which arises in cases where those without competent knowledge undertake to become expounders of the word of God. It is not said that it is not proper for them to attempt to become instructed by the aid of the sacred writings; but the danger is, that without proper views of interpretation, of language, and of ancient customs, they might be in danger of perverting and abusing certain portions of the writings of Paul. Intelligence among the people is everywhere in the Bible presumed to be proper in understanding the sacred Scriptures; and ignorance may produce the same effects in interpreting the Bible which it will produce in interpreting other writings. Every good thing is liable to abuse; but the proper way to correct this evil, and to remove this danger, is not to *keep* the people in ignorance, or to appoint some one to be an infallible interpreter; it is to remove the ignorance itself by enlightening the people, and rendering them better qualified to understand the sacred oracles. The way to remove error is not to perpetuate ignorance; it is to enlighten the mind, so that it may be qualified to appreciate the truth. ¶ *And unstable.* Who have no settled principles and views. The evil here

adverted to is that which arises where those undertake to interpret the Bible who have no established principles They regard nothing as settled. They have no landmarks set up to guide their inquiries. They have no stability in their character, and of course nothing can be regarded as settled in their methods of interpreting the Bible. They are under the control of feeling and emotion, and are liable to embrace one opinion to-day, and another directly opposite to-morrow. But the way to prevent *this* evil is not by attempting to give to a community an authoritative interpretation of the Bible; it is to diffuse abroad just principles, that men may obtain from the Bible an intelligent view of what it means. ¶ *Wrest.* Pervert—στρεβλοῦσιν. The word here used occurs nowhere else in the New Testament. It is derived from a word meaning a windlass, winch, instrument of torture, (στρεβλή,) and means to roll or wind on a windlass; then to wrench, or turn away, as by the force of a windlass; and then to wrest or pervert. It implies a turning out of the way by the application of force. Here the meaning is, that they apply those portions of the Bible to a purpose for which they were never intended. It is doubtless true that this may occur. Men may abuse and pervert anything that is good. But the way to prevent this is not to set up a pretended infallible interpreter. With all the perversities arising from ignorance in the interpretation of the Bible; in all the crude, and weak, and fanciful expositions which could be found among those who have interpreted the Scriptures for themselves—and they are many—if they were all collected together, there would not be found so many adapted to corrupt and ruin the soul, as have come from the interpretations attempted to be palmed upon the world by the one church that claims to be the infallible expounder of the word of God. ¶ *As* they do *also the other scriptures.* This is an unequivocal declaration of Peter that he regarded the writings of Paul as a part of the holy Scriptures, and of course that he considered him as inspired. The word 'Scriptures,' as used by a Jew, had a technical signification—meaning the in-

17 Ye therefore, beloved, seeing ye know *these things* before, beware lest ye also, being led away with the error of the wicked, fall from your own steadfastness.

a Col.1.10.

18 But grow *a* in grace, and *ir* the knowledge of our Lord and Saviour Jesus Christ. To him *b be* glory, both now and for ever. Amen.

b 2 Ti.4.18.

spired writings, and was the common word which was applied to the sacred writings of the Old Testament. As Peter uses this language, it implies that he regarded the writings of Paul as on a level with the Old Testament; and as far as the testimony of one apostle can go to confirm the claim of another to inspiration, it proves that the writings of Paul are entitled to a place in the sacred canon. It should be remarked, also, that Peter evidently speaks here of the *common estimate* in which the writings of Paul were held. He addresses those to whom he wrote, not in such a way as to declare to them that the writings of Paul were to be regarded as a part of the inspired volume, but as if this were already known, and were an admitted point. ¶ *Unto their own destruction.* By embracing false doctrines. Error destroys the soul; and it is very possible for a man so to read the Bible as only to confirm himself in error. He may find passages which, by a perverted interpretation, shall seem to sustain his own views; and, instead of embracing the truth, may live always under delusion, and perish at last. It is not to be inferred that every man who reads the Bible, or even every one who undertakes to be its public expounder, will certainly be saved.

17. *Seeing that ye know* these things *before.* Being aware of this danger, and knowing that such results may follow. Men should read the Bible with the feeling that it is *possible* that they may fall into error, and be deceived at last. This apprehension will do much to make them diligent, and candid, and prayerful, in studying the word of God. ¶ *With the error of the wicked.* Wicked men. Such as he had referred to in chap. ii., who became public teachers of religion. ¶ *Fall from your own steadfastness.* Your firm adherence to the truth. The particular danger here referred to is not that of falling from grace, or from true religion, but from

the firm and settled principles of religious truth into error.

18. *But grow in grace.* Comp. Col. i. 10. Religion in general is often represented as *grace*, since every part of it is the result of grace, or of unmerited favour; and to ' grow in grace' is to increase in that which constitutes true religion. Religion is as susceptible of cultivation and of growth as any other virtue of the soul. It is feeble in its beginnings, like the grain of mustard seed, or like the germ or blade of the plant, and it increases as it is cultivated. There is no piety in the world which is not the result of cultivation, and which cannot be measured by the degree of care and attention bestowed upon it. No one becomes eminently pious, any more than one becomes eminently learned or rich, who does not intend to; and ordinarily men in religion are what they design to be. They have about as much religion as they wish, and possess about the character which they intend to possess. When men reach extraordinary elevations in religion, like Baxter, Payson, and Edwards, they have gained only what they *meant* to gain; and the gay and worldly professors of religion, who have little comfort and peace, have in fact the characters which they designed to have. If these things are so, then we may see the propriety of the injunction ' to grow in grace ;' and then too we may see the reason why so feeble attainments are made in piety by the great mass of those who profess religion. ¶ *And* in *the knowledge of our Lord and Saviour Jesus Christ.* See Notes, John xvii. 3. Comp. Notes on Col. i. 10. To know the Lord Jesus Christ—to possess just views of his person, character, and work —is the sum and essence of the Christian religion; and with this injunction, therefore, the apostle appropriately closes this epistle. He who has a saving knowledge of Christ, has in fact all that is essential to his welfare in the life that is, and in that which is to come; he who has not this knowledge, though he may be distinguished in the learning of the schools, and may be profoundly skilled in the sciences, has in reality no knowledge that will avail him in the great matters pertaining to his eternal welfare. ¶ *To him* be *glory*, &c. Comp. Notes, Rom. xvi. 27; 2 Tim. iv.

18. With the desire that honour and glory should be rendered to the Redeemer, all the aspirations of true Christians appropriately close. There is no wish more deeply cherished in their hearts than this; there is nothing that will enter more into their worship in heaven. Compare Rev. i. 5, 6; v. 12, 13.

THE

FIRST EPISTLE GENERAL OF JOHN.

INTRODUCTION.

§ 1. *The authenticity of the Epistle.*

LITTLE need be said respecting the authenticity of this epistle, or the evidence that it was written by the apostle John. There are, in general, two sources of evidence in regard to ancient writings: the external evidence, or that which may be derived from the testimony of other writers; and the evidence which may be derived from some marks of the authorship in the writing itself, which is called the internal evidence. Both of these are remarkably clear in regard to this epistle.

(1.) The external evidence. (*a*) It is quoted or referred to by the early Christian writers as the undoubted production of the apostle John. It is referred to by Polycarp in the beginning of the second century; it is quoted by Papias, and also by Irenæus. Origen says, ' John, beside the Gospel and Revelation, has left us an epistle of a few lines. Grant also a second, and a third; for all do not allow these to be genuine.' See Lardner, vi. 275, and Lücke, Einlei. i. Dionysius of Alexandria admitted the genuineness of John's first epistle; so also did Cyprian. All the three epistles were received by Athanasius, by Cyril of Jerusalem, and by Epiphanius. Eusebius says, ' Beside his Gospel, his first epistle is universally acknowledged by those of the present time, and by the ancients; but the other two are contradicted.' (*b*) It is found in the old Syriac version, probably made in the first century, though the second and third epistles are not there. (*c*) The genuineness of the first epistle was never extensively called in question, and it was never reckoned among the doubtful or disputed epistles. (*d*) It was rejected or doubted only by those who rejected his Gospel, and for the same reasons. Some small sects of those who were called ' heretics,' rejected *all* the writings of John, because they conflicted with their peculiar views; but this was confined to a small number of persons, and never affected the general belief of the church. See Lücke, Einlei. 9, seq.

(2.) There is strong internal evidence that the same person wrote this epistle who was the author of the Gospel which bears the same name. The resemblance in the mode of expression, and in the topics referred to, are numerous, and at the same time are not such as would be made by one who was *attempting* to imitate the language of another. The allusions of this kind, moreover, are to what is *peculiar* in the Gospel of John, and not to what is common to that Gospel and the other three. There is nothing in the epistle which would particularly remind us of the Gospel of Matthew, or Mark, or Luke; but it is impossible to read it and not be reminded constantly of the Gospel by John. Among those passages and expressions the following may be referred to:

EPISTLE.		GOSPEL.
Chapter i. 1	compared with	Chapter i. 1, 4, 14.
ii. 5	....	xiv. 23.
ii. 6	....	xv. 4.
ii. 8; iii. 11	....	xiii. 34.
ii. 8, 10	....	i. 5, 9; xi. 10.
ii. 13, 14	....	xvii. 3.
iii. 1	....	i. 12.
iii. 2	....	xvii. 24.
iii. 8	....	viii. 44.
iii. 13	....	xv. 20.
iv. 9	....	iii. 16.
iv. 12	....	i. 18.
v. 13	....	xx. 31.
v. 14	....	xiv. 14.
v. 20	....	xvii. 2.

This language in the epistle, as will be easily seen by a comparison, is such as the real author of the Gospel by John would be likely to use if he wrote an epistle. The passages referred to are in his style; they show that the mind of the author of both was turned to the same points, and those not such points as might be found in all writers, but such as indicated a peculiar mode of thinking. They are not such expressions as Matthew, or Mark, or Luke, or Paul would have used in an epistle, but just such as we should expect from the writer of the Gospel of John. It must be clear to any one that either the author of the Gospel was also the author of this epistle, or that the author of the epistle *meant* to imitate the author of the Gospel, and to leave the impression that the apostle John was the author. But there are several things which make it clear that this is not a forgery. (*a*) The passages where the resemblance is found are not exact quotations, and are not such as a man would make if he *designed* to imitate another. They are rather such as the same man would use if he were writing twice on the same subject, and should express himself the second time without intending to copy what he had said the first. (*b*) If it had been an intentional fraud or forgery, there would have been some allusion to the name or authority of the author; or, in other words, the author of the epistle would have endeavoured to sustain himself by some distinct reference to the apostle, or to his authority, or to his well-known characteristics as a teller of truth. See John xix. 35; xxi. 24. Compare 3 John 12. But nothing of the kind occurs in this epistle. It is written without disclosing the name of the author, or the place where he lived, or the persons to whom it was addressed, and with no allusions to the Gospel, except such as show that the author thought in the same manner, and had the same things in his eye, and was intent on the same object. It is, throughout, the style and manner of one who felt that his method of expressing himself was so well understood, that he did not need even to mention his own name; as if, without anything further, it would be apparent from the very epistle itself who had written it, and what right he had to speak. But this would be a device too refined for forgery. It bears all the marks of sincerity and truth.

§ 2. *The time and place of writing the Epistle.*

Almost nothing is known of the time and place of writing the epistle, and nearly all that is said on this point is mere conjecture. Some recent critics have supposed that it was in fact a part of the Gospel, though in some way it afterwards became detached from it; others, that it was sent *as an epistle* at the same time with the Gospel, and to the same persons. Some have supposed that it was written before the destruction of Jerusalem, and some long after, when John was very aged; and these last suppose that they find evidences of the very advanced age of the author in the epistle itself, in such characteristics as commonly mark the conversation and writings of an old man. An examination of these opinions may be found in Lücke, Einlei. Kap. 2; and in Hug, Introduction, p. 456, seq., p. 732, seq.

There are *very few* marks of time in the epistle, and none that can determine the time of writing it with any degree of certainty. Nor is it of much importance that we should be able to determine it. The truths which it contains are, in the main, as applicable to one age as to another, though it cannot be denied (see § 3) that the author had some prevailing forms of error in his eye. The only marks of time in the epistle by which we can form any conjecture as to the period when it was written are the following: (1.) It was in what the author calls *the last time,* (ἐσχάτη ὥρα,) ch. ii. 18. From this expression it might perhaps be inferred by some that it was just before the destruction of Jerusalem, or that the writer supposed that the end of the world was near. But nothing can be certainly determined from this expression in regard to the exact period when the epistle was written. This phrase, as used in the Scriptures, denotes no more than, the last dispensation or economy of things, the dispensation under which the affairs of the world would be wound up, though that period might be in fact much longer than any one that had preceded it. See Notes on Isa. ii. 2; Acts ii. 17; Heb. i. 2. The object of the writer of this epistle, in the passage referred to, (chap. ii. 18,) is merely to show that the closing dispensation of the world had actually come; that is, that there were certain things which it was known would mark that dispensation, which actually existed then, and by which it could be known that they were living under the last or closing period of the world. (2.) It is quite evident that the epistle was composed *after* the Gospel by John was published. Of this no one can have any doubt who will compare the two together, or even the parallel passages referred to above, § 1. The Gospel is manifestly the original; and it was evidently presumed by the writer of the epistle that the Gospel was in the hands of those to whom he wrote. The statements there made are much more full; the circumstances in which many of the peculiar doctrines adverted to were first advanced are detailed; and the writer of the epistle clearly supposed that all that was necessary in order to an understanding of these doctrines was to state them in the briefest manner, and almost by mere allusion. On this point Lücke well remarks, 'the more brief and condensed expression of the same sentiment by the same author, especially in regard to peculiarities of idea and language, is always the later one; the more extended statement, the unfolding of the idea, is an evidence of an earlier composition,' Einlei. p. 21. Yet while this is clear, it determines little or nothing about the time when the epistle was written, for it is a matter of great uncertainty when the Gospel itself was composed. Wetstein supposes that it was soon after the ascension of the Saviour; Dr. Lardner that it was about the year 68; and Mill and Le Clerc that it was about the year 97. In this uncertainty, therefore, nothing can be determined absolutely from this circumstance in regard to the time of writing the epistle. (3.) The only other note of time on which any reliance has been placed is the supposed fact that there were indications in the epistle itself of the *great age* of the author, or evidences that he was an old man, and that consequently it was written near the close of the life of John. There *is* some evidence in the epistle that it was written when the author was an old man, though none that he was in his *dotage*, as Eichhorn and some others have maintained. The evidence that he was even an old man is not positive, but there is a certain air and manner in the epistle, in its repetitions, and its want of exact order, and especially in the style in which he addresses those to whom he wrote, as *little children*—τεκνία—(chap. ii. 1, 12, 28; iii. 7,

18; iv. 4; v. 21)—which would seem to be appropriate only to an aged man. Comp. Lücke, Einlei. pp. 23, 25, and Stuart in Hug's Introduction, pp. 732, 733.

As little is known about the *place* where the epistle was written as about the *time*. There are no local references in it; no allusions to persons or opinions which can help us to determine where it was written. As John spent the latter part of his life, however, in Ephesus and its vicinity, there is no impropriety in supposing that it was written there. Nothing, in the interpretation of the epistle, depends on our being able to ascertain the place of its composition. Hug supposes that it was written in Patmos, and was sent as a letter accompanying his Gospel, to the church at Ephesus.—Intro. § 69. Lücke supposes that it was a circular epistle addressed to the churches in Asia Minor, and sent from Ephesus. —Einlei. p. 27.

To *whom* the epistle was written is also unknown. It bears no inscription, as many of the other epistles of the New Testament do, and as even the second and third of John do, and there is no reference to any particular class of persons by which it can be determined for whom it was designed. Nor is it known why the name of the author was not attached to it, or why the persons for whom it was designed were not designated. All that can be determined on this subject from the epistle itself is the following: (1.) It seems to have been addressed to no particular church, but rather to have been of a circular character, designed for the churches in a region of country where certain dangerous opinions prevailed. (2.) The author presumed that it would be known who wrote it, either by the style, or by the sentiments, or by its resemblance to his other writings, or by the messenger who bore it, so that it was unnecessary to affix his name to it. (3.) It appears to have been so composed as to be adapted to *any* people where those errors prevailed; and hence it was thought better to give it a *general* direction, that all might feel themselves to be addressed, than to designate any particular place or church. There is, indeed, an ancient tradition that it was written to the *Parthians*. Since the time of Augustine this has been the uniform opinion in the Latin church. Venerable Bede remarks, that 'many of the ecclesiastical writers, among whom is St. Athanasius, testify that the first epistle of John was written to the Parthians.' Various conjectures have been made as to the origin of this opinion, and of the title which the epistle bears in many of the Latin mss., (*ad Parthos,*) but none of them are satisfactory. No such title is found in the epistle itself, nor is there any intimation in it to whom it was directed. Those who are disposed to examine the conjectures which have been made in regard to the origin of the title may consult Lücke, Enlei. p. 28, seq. No reason can be assigned why it should have been sent to the Parthians, nor is there any sufficient evidence to suppose that it was.

§ 3. *The object of the Epistle.*

It is evident from the epistle itself that there were some prevailing errors among those to whom it was written, and that one design of the writer was to counteract those errors. Yet very various opinions have been entertained in regard to the nature of the errors that were opposed, and the persons whom the writer had in his eye. Loeffler supposes that *Jews* and *Judaizers* are the persons opposed; Semler, Tittman, Knapp, and Lange suppose that they were *Judaizing Christians*, and especially *Ebionites*, or apostate Christians; Michaelis, Kleuker, Paulus, and others, suppose that the *Gnostics* are referred to; others, as Schmidt, Lücke, Vitringa, Bertholdt, Prof. Stuart, suppose that the *Docetæ* was the sect that was principally opposed.

It is impossible now to determine with accuracy to whom particularly the writer referred, nor could it be well done without a more accurate knowledge than we now have of the peculiarities of the errors which prevailed in the time of the author, and among the people to whom he wrote. All that we can learn on the

subject that is certain, is to be derived from the epistle itself; and there the intimations are few, but they are so clear that we may obtain some knowledge to
guide us.

(1.) The persons referred to had been professing Christians, and were now
apostates from the faith. This is clear from ch. ii. 19, 'They went out from us,
but they were not of us,' &c. They had been members of the church, but they
had now become teachers of error.

(2.) They were probably of the sect of the *Docetæ;* or if that sect had not then
formally sprung up, and was not organized, they held the opinions which they
afterwards embraced. This sect was a branch of the great Gnostic family; and
the peculiarity of the opinion which they held was that Christ was only in appearance and seemingly, but not in reality, a man; that though he seemed to
converse, to eat, to suffer, and to die, yet this was merely an *appearance* assumed
by the Son of God for important purposes in regard to man. He had, according
to this view, no *real humanity;* but though the Son of God had actually appeared
in the world, yet all this was only an assumed form for the purpose of a manifestation to men. The opinions of the *Docetes* are thus represented by Gibbon :
'They denied the truth and authenticity of the Gospels, as far as they relate the
conception of Mary, the birth of Christ, and the thirty years which preceded the
first exercise of his ministry. He first appeared on the banks of the Jordan in
the form of perfect manhood; but it was a form only, and not a substance; a
human figure created by the hand of Omnipotence to imitate the faculties and
actions of a man, and to impose a perpetual illusion on the senses of his friends
and enemies. Articulate sounds vibrated on the ears of his disciples; but the
image which was impressed on their optic nerve, eluded the more stubborn evidence of the touch, and they enjoyed the spiritual, but not the corporeal presence
of the Son of God. The rage of the Jews was idly wasted against an impassive
phantom, and the mystic scenes of the passion and death, the resurrection and
ascension of Christ, were represented on the theatre of Jerusalem for the benefit
of mankind.'—Decl. and Fall, vol. iii. p. 245, Ed. New York, 1829. Comp. vol,
i. 440.

That these views began to prevail in the latter part of the first century there
can be no reason to doubt ; and there can be as little doubt that the author of
this epistle had this doctrine in his eye, and that he deemed it to be of special
importance in this epistle, as he had done in his Gospel, to show that the Son of
God had actually *come in the flesh;* that he was truly and properly a man; that
he lived and died in reality, and not in appearance only. Hence the allusion
to these views in such passages as the following: 'That which was from the
beginning, which we have heard, which we have seen with our eyes, which we
have looked upon, and *our hands have handled,* of the Word of life—that which
we have seen and heard declare we unto you,' chap. i. 1, 3. 'Many false prophets are gone out into the world. Hereby know we the Spirit of God : Every
spirit that confesseth that Jesus Christ *is come in the flesh* is of God; and every
spirit that confesseth not that Jesus Christ is come in the flesh is not of God ;
and this is that spirit of antichrist, whereof ye have heard that it should come,'
chap. iv. 1–3. Comp. vers. 9, 14, 15; v. 1, 6, 10–12. John had written his
Gospel to show that Jesus was the Christ, (chap. xx. 31;) he had furnished ample
proof that he was Divine, or was equal with the Father, (chap. i. 1–14,) and also
that he was truly a man, (chap. xv. 25–28;) but still it seemed proper to furnish
a more unequivocal statement that he had actually appeared *in the flesh*, not in
appearance only but in reality, and this purpose evidently was a leading design
of this epistle.

The main scope of the epistle the author has himself stated in chap. v. 13:
'These things have I written unto you that believe on the name of the Son of
God ; that ye may know that ye have eternal life, and that ye may believe on
the name of the Son of God ;' that is, that you may have just views of him, and
exercise an intelligent faith.

In connection with this general design, and keeping in view the errors to which they to whom the epistle was written were exposed, there are two leading trains of thought, though often intermingled, in the epistle. (*a*) The author treats of the doctrine that Jesus is the Christ, and (*b*) the importance of *love* as an evidence of being united to him, or of being true Christians. Both these things are characteristic of John; they agree with the design for which he wrote his gospel, and they were in accordance with his peculiarity of mind as 'the *beloved* disciple,' the disciple whose heart was full of love, and who made religion consist much in that.

The main characteristics of this epistle are these: (1.) It is full of love. The writer dwells on it; places it in a variety of attitudes; enforces the duty of loving one another by a great variety of considerations, and shows that it is essential to the very nature of religion. (2.) The epistle abounds with statements on the evidences of piety, or the characteristics of true religion. The author seems to have felt that those to whom he wrote were in danger of embracing false notions of religion, and of being seduced by the abettors of error. He is therefore careful to lay down the characteristics of real piety, and to show in what it essentially consists. A large part of the epistle is occupied with this, and there is perhaps no portion of the New Testament which one could study to more advantage who is desirous of ascertaining whether he himself is a true Christian. An anxious inquirer, a man who wishes to know what true religion is, could be directed to no portion of the New Testament where he would more readily find the instruction that he needs, than to this portion of the writings of the aged and experienced disciple whom Jesus loved. A true Christian can find nowhere else a more clear statement of the nature of his religion, and of the evidences of real piety, than in this epistle.

THE

FIRST EPISTLE GENERAL OF JOHN.

CHAPTER I.

THAT which was from the *a* beginning, which we have heard, which we have seen *b* with our eyes, which we have looked upon, and our hands have *c* handled, of the Word of life ;

a Jn.1.1,&c.   *b* 2 Pe.1.16.   *c* Lu.24.39.

CHAPTER I.
ANALYSIS OF THE CHAPTER.

THIS short chapter embraces the following subjects : I. A strong affirmation that the Son of God, or the 'Life,' had appeared in the flesh, vers. 1—3. The evidence of this, the writer says, was that he had seen him, heard him, handled him ; that is, he had had all the evidence which could be furnished by the senses. His declaration on this point he repeats, by putting the statement into a variety of forms, for he seems to regard it as essential to true religion. II. He says that he wrote to them, in order that they might have fellowship with him in the belief of this truth, and might partake of the joy which flows from the doctrine that the Son of God has actually come in the flesh, vers. 3, 4. III. He states that the sum and substance of the whole message which he had to bring to them was, that God is light, and that if we profess to have fellowship with him we must walk in the light, vers. 5—10. (*a*) In God is no darkness, no impurity, no sin, ver. 5. (*b*) If we are in darkness, if we are ignorant and sinful, it proves that we cannot have any fellowship with him, ver. 6. (*c*) If we walk in the light as he is in the light, if we partake of his character and spirit, then we shall have fellowship one with another, and we may believe that the blood of Christ will cleanse us from all sin, ver. 7. (*d*) Yet we are to guard ourselves from one point of danger, we are not to allow ourselves to feel that we have *no* sin. We are to bear with us the constant recollection that we are sinners, and are to permit that fact to produce its proper impression on our minds, vers. 8, 10. (*e*) Yet we are not to be desponding though we do feel this, but are to remember, that if we will truly confess our sins he will be found faithful to his promises, and just to the general arrangements of grace, by which our sins may be forgiven, ver. 9.

1. *That which was from the beginning.* There can be no doubt that the reference here is to the Lord Jesus Christ, or the 'Word' that was made flesh. See Notes, John i. 1. This is such language as John would use respecting him, and indeed the phrase 'the beginning,' as applicable to the Lord Jesus, is peculiar to John in the writings of the New Testament : and the language here may be regarded as one proof that this epistle was written by him, for it is just such an expression as *he* would use, but not such as one would be likely to adopt who should attempt to palm off his own writings as those of John. One who should have attempted that would have been likely to introduce the name *John* in the beginning of the epistle, or in some way to have claimed his authority. The apostle, in speaking of '*that which* was from the beginning,' uses a word in the neuter gender instead of the masculine, (*ὅ.*) It is not to be supposed, I think, that he meant to apply this term *directly* to the Son of God, for if he had he would have used the masculine pronoun ; but though he had the Son of God in view, and meant to make a strong affirmation respecting him, yet the particular thing here referred to was *whatever* there was respecting that

incarnate Saviour that furnished testimony to any of the senses, or that pertained to his character and doctrine, he had borne witness to. He was looking rather at the *evidence* that he was incarnate; the *proofs* that he was manifested; and he says that those proofs had been subjected to the trial of the senses, and he had borne witness to them, and now did it again. This is what is referred to, it seems to me, by the phrase 'that which,' (δ.) The sense may be this: 'Whatever there was respecting the Word of life, or him who is the living Word, the incarnate Son of God, from the very beginning, from the time when he was first manifested in the flesh; whatever there was respecting his exalted nature, his dignity, his character, that could be subjected to the testimony of the senses, to be the object of sight, or hearing, or touch, *that* I was permitted to see, and that I declare to you respecting him.' John claims to be a competent witness in reference to everything which occurred as a *manifestation* of what the Son of God was. If this be the correct interpretation, then the phrase 'from the beginning' (ἀπ' ἀρχῆς) does not here refer to his eternity, or his being *in* the beginning of all things, as the phrase '*in* the beginning' (ἐν ἀρχῇ) does in John i. 1; but rather means from the very commencement of his *manifestation* as the Son of God, the very first indications on earth of what he was as the Messiah. When the writer says (ver. 3) that he 'declares' this to them, it seems to me that he has not reference merely to what he *would* say in this epistle, for he does not go extensively into it here, but that he supposes that they had his Gospel in their possession, and that he also means to refer to that, or presumes that they were familiar with the testimony which he had borne *in* that Gospel respecting the evidence that the 'Word became flesh.' Many have indeed supposed that this epistle accompanied the Gospel when it was published, and was either a part of it that became subsequently detached from it, or was a letter that accompanied it. See *Hug*, Intro. P. II. § 68. There is, it seems to me, no certain evidence of that; but no one can doubt

that he supposed that those to whom he wrote had access to that Gospel, and that he refers here to the testimony which he had borne in that respecting the incarnate Word. ¶ *Which we have heard.* John was with the Saviour through the whole of his ministry, and he has recorded more that the Saviour *said* than either of the other evangelists. It is on what he *said* of himself that he grounds much of the evidence that he was the Son of God. ¶ *Which we have seen with our eyes.* That is, pertaining to his person, and to what he did. 'I have seen *him*; seen what he was as a man; how he appeared on earth; and I have seen whatever there was in his works to indicate his character and origin.' John professes here to have seen enough in this respect to furnish evidence that he was the Son of God. It is not hearsay on which he relies, but he had the testimony of his own eyes in the case. Comp. Notes, 2 Pet. i. 16. ¶ *Which we have looked upon.* The word here used seems designed to be more emphatic or intensive than the one before occurring. He had just said that he had 'seen him with his eyes,' but he evidently designs to include an idea in this word which would imply something more than *mere* beholding or seeing. The additional idea which is couched in this word seems to be that of *desire* or *pleasure;* that is, that he had looked on him with desire, or satisfaction, or with the pleasure with which one beholds a beloved object. Comp. Matt. xi. 7; Luke vii. 24; John i. 14; x. 45. See *Rob. Lex.* There was an intense and earnest gaze, as when we behold one whom we have desired to see, or when one goes out purposely to look·on an object. The evidences of the incarnation of the Son of God had been subjected to such an intense and earnest gaze. ¶ *And our hands have handled.* That is, the evidence that he was *a man* was subjected to the sense of *touch*. It was not merely that he had been seen by the eye, for then it might be pretended that this was a mere *appearance* assumed without reality; or that what occurred might have been a mere optical illusion; but the evidence that he appeared in the flesh was subjected to more senses than one; to the fact that

2 (For the life was manifested, and we have seen *it*, and bear witness, and shew unto you that eternal life, *a* which was with the Father, and was manifested unto us;)

a Jn.17.3.

his voice was heard; that he was seen with the eyes; that the most intense scrutiny had been employed; and, lastly, that he had been actually *touched* and *handled*, showing that it could not have been a mere *appearance*, an assumed form, but that it was a reality. This kind of proof that the Son of God had appeared *in the flesh*, or that he was truly and properly *a man*, is repeatedly referred to in the New Testament. Luke xxiv. 39: ' Behold my hands and my feet, that it is I myself: handle me and see; for a spirit hath not flesh and bones as ye see me have.' Comp. John xx. 25–27. There is evident allusion here to the opinion which early prevailed, which was held by the *Docetes*, that the Son of God did not truly and really become a man, but that there was only an *appearance* assumed, or that he *seemed* to be a man. See the Intro., § 3. It was evidently with reference to this opinion, which began early to prevail, that the apostle dwells on this point, and repeats the idea so much, and shows by a reference to all the senses which could take any cognizance in the case, that he was truly and properly a man. The amount of it is, that we have the same evidence that he was properly a man which we can have in the case of any other human being; the evidence on which we constantly act, and in which we cannot believe that our senses deceive us. ¶ *Of the Word of life.* Respecting, or pertaining to, the Word of life. ' That is, whatever there was pertaining to the Word of life, which was manifested from the beginning in his speech and actions, of which the senses could take cognizance, and which would furnish the evidence that he was truly incarnate, that we have declared unto you.' The phrase ' the Word of life,' means the Word in which life resided, or which was the source and fountain of life. See Notes, John i. 1, 3. The reference is undoubtedly to the Lord Jesus Christ.

2. *For the life was manifested.* Was made manifest or visible unto us. He who was the life was made known to men by the incarnation. He appeared among men so that they could see him and hear him. Though originally with God, and dwelling with him, (John i. 1, 2,) yet he came forth and appeared among men. Comp. Notes, Rom. i. 3; 1 Tim. iii. 16. He is the great source of all life, and he appeared on the earth, and we had an opportunity of seeing and knowing what he was. ¶ *And we have seen* it. This repetition, or turning over the thought, is designed to express the idea with emphasis, and is much in the manner of John. See John i. 1–3. He is particularly desirous of impressing on them the thought that he had been a personal *witness* of what the Saviour was, having had every opportunity of knowing it from long and familiar intercourse with him. ¶ *And bear witness.* We testify in regard to it. John was satisfied that his own character was known to be such that credit would be given to what he said. He felt that he was known to be a man of truth, and hence he never doubts that faith would be put in all his statements. See John xix. 35; xxi. 24; Rev. i. 2; 3 John 12. ¶ *And shew unto you that eternal life.* That is, we declare unto you what that life was—what was the nature and rank of him who was the life, and how he appeared when on earth. He here attributes *eternity* to the Son of God—implying that he had always been with the Father. ¶ *Which was with the Father.* Always before the manifestation on the earth. See John i. 1. ' The word was with God.' This passage demonstrates the pre-existence of the Son of God, and proves that he was eternal. Before he was manifested on earth he had an existence to which the word *life* could be applied, and that was *eternal*. He is the Author of eternal life to us. ¶ *And was manifested unto us.* In the flesh; as a man. He who was the *life* appeared unto men. The idea of John evidently is, (1,) that the Being here referred to was for ever with God; (2,) that it was proper before the incarnation that the word *life* should be given to him as descriptive of his nature; (3,) that there was a manifestation of

3 That which we have seen and heard declare we unto you, that ye also may have fellowship with us :

and truly our fellowship *a is* with the Father, and with his Son Jesus Christ.

him who was thus called *life*, on earth; that he appeared among men; that he had a real existence here, and not a merely *assumed* appearance; and (4,) that the true characteristics of this incarnate Being could be borne testimony to by those who had seen him, and who had been long with him. This second verse should be regarded as a parenthesis.

3. *That which we have seen and heard declare we unto you.* We *announce* it, or make it known unto you—referring either to what he purposes to say in this epistle, or more probably embracing *all* that he had written respecting him, and supposing that his Gospel was in their hands. He means to call their attention to *all* the testimony which he had borne on the subject, in order to counteract the errors which began to prevail. ¶ *That ye may have fellowship with us.* With us the apostles ; with us who actually saw him, and conversed with him. That is, he wished that they might have the same belief, and the same hope, and the same joy which he himself had, arising from the fact that the Son of God had become incarnate, and had appeared among men. To 'have fellowship,' means to have anything *in common* with others; to partake of it; to share it with them, (see Notes, Acts ii. 42;) and the idea here is, that the apostle wished that they might *share* with him all the peace and happiness which resulted from the fact that the Son of God had appeared in human form in behalf of men. The *object* of the apostle in what he wrote was, that they might have the same views of the Saviour which he had, and partake of the same hope and joy. This is the true notion of *fellowship* in religion. ¶ *And truly our fellowship is with the Father.* With God the Father. That is, there was something *in common* with him and God; something of which he and God partook together, or which they shared. This cannot, of course, mean that his *nature* was the same as that of God, or that in *all things* he shared with God, or that in *anything* he was *equal* with God; but

it means that he partook, in some respects, of the feelings, the views, the aims, the joys which God has. There was a union in feeling, and affection, and desire, and plan, and this was to him a source of joy. He had an attachment to the same things, loved the same truth, desired the same objects, and was engaged in the same work ; and the *consciousness* of this, and the *joy* which attended it, was what was meant by *fellowship.* Comp. Notes on 1 Cor. x. 16; 2 Cor. xii. 14. The fellowship which Christians have with God relates to the following points: (1.) Attachment to the same truths, and the same objects; love for the same principles, and the same beings. (2.) The same *kind* of happiness, though not in the same *degree.* The happiness of God is found in holiness, truth, purity, justice, mercy, benevolence. The happiness of the Christian is of the same kind that God has ; the same kind that angels have : the same kind that he will himself have in heaven—for the joy of heaven is only that which the Christian has now, expanded to the utmost capacity of the soul, and freed from all that now interferes with it, and prolonged to eternity. (3.) Employment, or co-operation with God. There *is* a sphere in which God works alone, and in which we can have no co-operation, no fellowship with him. In the work of creation; in upholding all things; in the government of the universe ; in the transmission of light from world to world; in the return of the seasons, the rising and setting of the sun, the storms, the tides, the flight of the comet, we can have no joint agency, no co-operation with him. There God works alone. But there is also a large sphere in which he admits us graciously to a co-operation with him, and in which, unless *we* work, his agency will not be put forth. This is seen when the farmer sows his grain ; when the surgeon binds up a wound ; when we take the medicine which God has appointed as a means of restoration to health. So in the moral world. In

4 And these things write we unto
you, that *a* your joy may be full.

5 This then is the message which

a Jn.15.11.

we have heard of him, and declare
unto you, that God is light, *b* and in
him is no darkness at all.

b Jn.1.4,9; 1 Ti.6.16.

our efforts to save our own souls and the
souls of others, God graciously works
with us; and unless *we* work, the object
is not accomplished. This co-operation
is referred to in such passages as these:
'We are labourers together (συνεργοί)
with God,' 1 Cor. iii. 9. 'The Lord
working *with them*,' Mark xvi. 20. 'We
then as workers together with him,' 2
Cor. vi. 1. 'That we might be fellow-
helpers to the truth,' 3 John 8. In all
such cases, while the *efficiency* is of God
—alike in exciting us to effort, and in
crowning the effort with success—it is
still true that if *our* efforts were not put
forth, the work would not be done. In
this department God would not work by
himself alone; he would not secure the
result by miracle. (4.) We have fellowship with God by direct communion
with him, in prayer, in meditation, and
in the ordinances of religion. Of this
all true Christians are sensible, and this
constitutes no small part of their peculiar joy. The nature of this, and the
happiness resulting from it, is much of
the same nature as the communion of
friend with friend—of one mind with
another kindred mind—that to which
we owe no small part of our happiness
in this world. (5.) The Christian will
have fellowship with his God and Saviour in the triumphs of the latter day,
when the scenes of the judgment shall
occur, and when the Redeemer shall
appear, that he may be admired and
adored by assembled worlds. Comp.
Notes, 2 Thess. i. 10. See also Matt.
xix. 28; Rev. iii. 21. ¶ *And with his
Son Jesus Christ.* That is, in like
manner there is much which we have *in
common* with the Saviour—in character,
in feeling, in desire, in spirit, in plan.
There is a *union* with him in these
things—and the consciousness of this
gives peace and joy.

[There is a *real* union between Christ and his
people, which lies at the foundation of this fellowship. Without *this* union there can be no communion. But a 'union with Christ in these
things, *i. e.*, in character and feeling, &c,' is
nothing more than the union which subsists

between any chief and his followers; and why
the apostle Paul, or others after him, should
reckon this a great mystery, is not easily comprehended. Eph. v. 32; Col. i. 27. For a full
view of the subject, see the Author's Notes, with
the Supplementary Note, Rom. viii. 10.]

4. *And these things write we unto
you.* These things respecting him who
was manifested in the flesh, and respecting the results which flow from that.
¶ *That your joy may be full.* This is
almost the same language which the
Saviour used when addressing his disciples as he was about to leave them,
(John xv. 11;) and there can be little
doubt that John had that declaration in
remembrance when he uttered this remark. See Notes on that passage. The
sense here is, that full and clear views
of the Lord Jesus, and the fellowship
with him and with each other, which
would follow from that, would be a
source of happiness. Their joy would
be complete if they had that; for their
real happiness was to be found in their
Saviour. The best editions of the Greek
Testament now read '*your* joy,' instead
of the common reading '*our* joy.'

5. *This then is the message which we
have heard of him.* This is the substance of the announcement (ἐπαγγελία)
which we have received of him, or which
he made to us. The *message* here refers
to what he communicated as the sum of
the revelation which he made to man.
The phrase '*of him*' (ἀπ' αὐτου) does
not mean *respecting him*, or *about him*,
but *from him;* that is, this is what we
received from his preaching; from all
that he said. The peculiarity, the substance of all that he said, may be summed
up in the declaration that God is light,
and in the consequences which follow
from this doctrine. He came as the
messenger of Him who is *light;* he came
to inculcate and defend the truths which
flow from that central doctrine, in regard
to sin, to the danger and duty of man,
to the way of recovery, and to the rules
by which men ought to live. ¶ *That
God is light.* Light, in the Scriptures,
is the emblem of purity, truth, know-

6 If we say that we have fellowship with him, and walk in darkness, we lie, and do not the truth:

ledge, prosperity, and happiness—as darkness is of the opposite. John here says that ' God is *light*'—φῶς—not *the* light, or *a* light, but *light itself*; that is, he is himself all light, and is the source and fountain of light in all worlds. He is perfectly pure, without any admixture of sin. He has all knowledge, with no admixture of ignorance on any subject. He is infinitely happy, with nothing to make him miserable. He is infinitely true, never stating or countenancing error; he is blessed in all his ways, never knowing the darkness of disappointment and adversity. Comp. Notes on James i. 17; John i. 4, 5; 1 Tim. vi. 16. ¶ *And in him is no darkness at all.* This language is much in the manner of John, not only affirming that a thing is so, but guarding it so that no mistake could possibly be made as to what he meant. Comp. John i. 1–3. The expression here is designed to affirm that God is absolutely perfect; that there is nothing in him which is in any way imperfect, or which would dim or mar the pure splendour of his character, not even as much as the smallest spot would on the sun. The language is probably designed to guard the mind from an error to which it is prone, that of charging God with being the Author of the sin and misery which exist on the earth; and the apostle seems to design to teach that whatever was the source of sin and misery, it was not in any sense to be charged on God. This doctrine that God is a pure light, John lays down as the substance of all that he had to teach; of all that he had learned from him who was made flesh. It is, in fact, the fountain of all just views of truth on the subject of religion, and all proper views of religion take their origin from this.

6. *If we say that we have fellowship with him.* If we reckon ourselves among his friends, or, in other words, if we profess to be like him: for a profession of religion involves the idea of having *fellowship* with God, (comp. Notes on ver. 3,) and he who professes that should be like him. ¶ *And walk in darkness.* Live in sin and error. To ' walk in darkness ' now commonly denotes to be

in doubt about our religious state, in contradistinction from living in the enjoyment of religion. That is not, however, probably the whole idea here. The leading thought is, that if we live in sin, it is a proof that our profession of religion is false. Desirable as it is to have the comforts of religion, yet it is not always true that they who do not are not true Christians, nor is it true by any means that they intend to deceive the world. ¶ *We lie.* We are false professors; we are deceived if we think that we can have fellowship with God, and yet live in the practice of sin. As God is pure, so must we be, if we would be his friends. This does not mean necessarily that they *meant* to deceive, but that there was an irreconcilable contradiction between a life of sin and fellowship with God. ¶ *And do not the truth.* Do not act truly. The profession is a false one. Comp. Notes on John iii. 22. To *do the truth* is to act in accordance with truth; and the expression here means that such an one could not be a Christian. And yet how many there are who are living in known sin who profess to be Christians! How many whose minds are dark on the whole subject of religion, who have never known anything of the real peace and joy which it imparts, who nevertheless entertain the belief that they are the friends of God, and are going to heaven! They trust in a name, in forms, in conformity to external rites, and have never known anything of the internal peace and purity which religion imparts, and in fact have never had any true fellowship with that God who is light, and in whom there is no darkness at all. Religion is light; religion is peace, purity, joy; and though there are cases where for a time a true Christian may be left to darkness, and have no spiritual joy, and be in doubt about his salvation, yet still it is a great truth, that unless we know by personal experience what it is to walk habitually in the light, to have the comforts of religion, and to experience in our own souls the influences which make the heart pure, and which bring us into conformity to the God who

7 But if we walk *a* in the light, as he is in the light, we have fellowship one with another, and the blood *b* of Jesus Christ his Son cleanseth us from all sin.

8 If we say that we have no sin, *c* we deceive ourselves, and the truth is not in us.

a Jn.12.35.   *b* Ep.1.7; He.9.14; 1 Pe.1.19; Re.1.5.
         c 1 Ki.8.46; Job 25.4; Ec.7.20; Ja.3.2.

---

is light, we can have no true religion. All else is but a name, which will not avail us on the final day.

7. *But if we walk in the light.* Comp. Notes on ver. 5. Walking in the light may include the three following things: (1.) Leading lives of holiness and purity; that is, the Christian must be characteristically a holy man, a light in the world, by his example. (2.) Walking in the truth; that is, embracing the truth in opposition to all error of heathenism and infidelity, and having clear, spiritual views of truth, such as the unrenewed never have. See 2 Cor. iv. 6; 1 Cor. ii. 9–15; Eph. i. 18. (3.) Enjoying the comforts of religion; that is, having the joy which religion is fitted to impart, and which it does impart to its true friends, Psa. xciv. 19; Isa. lvii. 8; 2 Cor. i. 3; xiii. 11. Comp. Notes on John xii. 35. ¶ *As he is in the light.* In the same kind of light that he has. The measure of light which we may have is not the same in *degree*, but it is of the same *kind*. The true Christian in his character and feelings resembles God. ¶ *We have fellowship one with another.* As we all partake of his feelings and views, we shall resemble each other. Loving the same God, embracing the same views of religion, and living for the same ends, we shall of course have much that is *common* to us all, and thus shall have fellowship with each other. ¶ *And the blood of Jesus Christ his Son cleanseth us from all sin.* See the sentiment here expressed fully explained in the Notes on Heb. ix. 14. When it is said that his blood cleanses us from *all* sin, the expression must mean one of two things—either that it is through that blood that all past sin is forgiven, or that that blood will ultimately purify us from all transgression, and make us perfectly holy. The general meaning is plain, that in regard to any and every sin of which we may be conscious, there is efficacy in that blood to remove it, and to make us wholly pure.

There is no stain made by sin so deep that the blood of Christ cannot take it entirely away from the soul. The *connection* here, or the reason why this is introduced here, seems to be this: The apostle is stating the substance of the message which he had received, ver. 5. The first or leading part of it was, that God is light, and in him is no darkness, and that his religion requires that all his friends should resemble him by their walking in the light. Another, and a material part of the same message was, that provision was made in his religion for cleansing the soul from sin, and making it like God. No system of religion intended for man could be adapted to his condition which did not contain this provision, and this *did* contain it in the most full and ample manner. Of course, however, it is meant that that blood cleanses from all sin only on the conditions on which its efficacy can be made available to man—by repentance for the past, and by a cordial reception of the Saviour through faith.

8. *If we say that we have no sin.* It is not improbable that the apostle here makes allusion to some error which was then beginning to prevail in the church. Some have supposed that the allusion is to the sect of the Nicolaitanes, and to the views which they maintained, particularly that nothing was forbidden to the children of God under the gospel, and that in the freedom conferred on Christians they were at liberty to do what they pleased, Rev. ii. 6, 15. It is not certain, however, that the allusion is to them, and it is not necessary to suppose that there is reference to *any* particular sect that existed at that time. The object of the apostle is to show that it is implied in the very nature of the gospel that we are sinners, and that if, on any pretence, we denied that fact, we utterly deceived ourselves. In all ages there have been those who have attempted, on some pretence, to justify their conduct; who have felt that they

9 If we confess ^a our sins, he is faithful and just to forgive us *our*

a Job 33.27,28; Ps.32.5; Pr.28.13.

sins, and to cleanse ^b us from all unrighteousness.

b Ps.51.2; 1 Co.6.11.

did not need a Saviour ; who have maintained that they had a right to do what they pleased; or who, on pretence of being perfectly sanctified, have held that they live without the commission of sin. To meet these, and all similar cases, the apostle affirms that it is a great elementary truth, which on no pretence is to be denied, that we are all sinners. We are at all times, and in all circumstances, to admit the painful and humiliating truth that we are transgressors of the law of God, and that we need, even in our best services, the cleansing of the blood of Jesus Christ. The fair interpretation of the declaration here will apply not only to those who maintain that they have not been guilty of sin in the past, but also to those who profess to have become perfectly sanctified, and to live without sin. In any and every way, if we say that we have no sin, we deceive ourselves. Compare Notes on James iii. 2. ¶ *We deceive ourselves.* We have wrong views about our character. This does not mean that the self-deception is wilful, but that it in fact exists. No man knows himself who supposes that in all respects he is perfectly pure. ¶ *And the truth is not in us.* On this subject. A man who should maintain that he had never committed sin, could have no just views of the truth in regard to himself, and would show that he was in utter error. In like manner, according to the obvious interpretation of this passage, he who maintains that he is wholly sanctified, and lives without any sin, shows that he is deceived in regard to himself, and that the truth, in this respect, is not in him. He may hold the truth on other subjects, but he does not on this. The very nature of the Christian religion supposes that we feel ourselves to be sinners, and that we should be ever ready to acknowledge it. A man who claims that he is absolutely perfect, that he is holy as God is holy, must know little of his own heart. Who, after all his reasoning on the subject, would **dare to go out** under the open heaven, at midnight, and lift up

his hands and his eyes towards the stars, and say that he had no sin to confess— that he was as pure as the God that made those stars ?

9. *If we confess our sins.* Pardon in the Scriptures, always supposes that there is confession, and there is no promise that it will be imparted unless a full acknowledgment has been made. Compare Psa. li. ; xxxii. ; Luke xv. 18, seq. ; vii. 41, seq. ; Prov. xxviii. 13. ¶ *He is faithful.* To his promises. He will do what he has assured us he will do in remitting them. ¶ *And just to forgive us our sins.* The word *just* here cannot be used in a strict and proper sense, since the forgiveness of sins is never an act of *justice,* but is an act of *mercy.* If it were an act of justice it could be demanded or enforced, and that is the same as to say that it is not forgiveness, for in that case there could have been no sin to be pardoned. But the word *just* is often used in a larger sense, as denoting upright, equitable, acting properly in the circumstances of the case, &c. Comp. Notes on Matt. i. 19. Here the word may be used in one of the following senses : (1.) Either as referring to his general excellence of character, or his disposition to do what is proper ; that is, he is one who will act in every way as becomes God ; or, (2,) that he will be just in the sense that he will be true to his promises ; or that, since he has *promised* to pardon sinners, he will be found faithfully to adhere to those engagements ; or perhaps, (3,) that he will be just to his Son in the covenant of redemption, since, now that an atonement has been made by him, and a way has been opened through his sufferings by which God can consistently pardon, and with a view and an understanding that he might and would pardon, it would be an act of injustice to *him* if he did not pardon those who believe on him. Viewed in either aspect, we may have the fullest assurance that God is ready to pardon us if we exercise true repentance and faith. No one can come to God without finding him ready to do

10 If we say that we have not sinned, we make him a liar, and his word is not in us.

all that is appropriate for a God to do in pardoning transgressors; no one who will not, in fact, receive forgiveness if he repents, and believes, and makes confession; no one who will not find that God is just to his Son in the covenant of redemption, in pardoning and saving all who put their trust in the merits of his sacrifice. ¶ *And to cleanse us from all unrighteousness.* By forgiving all that is past, treating us as if we were righteous, and ultimately by removing all the stains of guilt from the soul.

10. *If we say that we have not sinned.* In times that are past. Some perhaps might be disposed to say this; and as the apostle is careful to guard every point, he here states that if a man should take the ground that his past life had been wholly upright, it would prove that he had no true religion. The statement here respecting the *past* seems to prove that when, in ver. 8, he refers to the present—' if we say we *have* no sin '—he meant to say that if a man should claim to be perfect, or to be wholly sanctified, it would demonstrate that he deceived himself; and the two statements go to prove that neither in reference to the past nor the present can any one lay claim to perfection. ¶ *We make him a liar.* Because he has everywhere affirmed the depravity of all the race. Compare Notes on Rom. i. ii. iii. On no point have his declarations been more positive and uniform than on the fact of the universal sinfulness of man. Comp. Gen. vi. 11, 12; Job xiv. 4; xv. 16; Psa. xiv. 1, 2, 3; li. 5; lviii. 3; Rom. iii. 9–20; Gal. iii. 21. ¶ *And his word is not in us.* His truth; that is, we have no true religion. The whole system of Christianity is based on the fact that man is a fallen being, and needs a Saviour; and unless a man admits that, of course he cannot be a Christian.

REMARKS.

(1.) The importance of the doctrine of the incarnation of the Son of God, vers. 1, 2. On that doctrine the apostle lays great stress; begins his epistle with it; presents it in a great variety of forms; dwells upon it as if he would not have it forgotten or misunderstood. It *has* all the importance which he attached to it, for (*a*) it is the most wonderful of all the events of which we have any knowledge; (*b*) it is the most deeply connected with our welfare.

(2.) The intense interest which true piety always takes in this doctrine, vers. 1, 2. The feelings of John on the subject are substantially the feelings of all true Christians. The world passes it by in unbelief, or as if it were of no importance; but no true Christian can look at the fact that the Son of God became incarnate but with the deepest emotion.

(3.) It is an object of ardent desire with true Christians that all others should share their joys, vers. 3, 4. There is nothing selfish, or narrow, or exclusive in true religion; but every sincere Christian who is happy desires that all others should be happy too.

(4.) Wherever there is true fellowship with God, there is with all true Christians, vers. 3, 4. There is but one church, one family of God; and as all true Christians have fellowship with God, they must have with each other.

(5.) Wherever there is true fellowship with Christians, there is with God himself, vers. 3, 4. If we love his people, share their joys, labour with them in promoting his cause, and love the things which they love, we shall show that we love him. There is but one God, and one church; and if all the members love each other, they will love their common God and Saviour. An evidence, therefore, that we love Christians, becomes an evidence that we love God.

(6.) It is a great privilege to be a Christian, vers. 3, 4. If we are Christians, we are associated with (*a*) God the Father; (*b*) with his Son Jesus Christ; (*c*) with all his redeemed on earth and in heaven; (*d*) with all holy angels. There is one bond of fellowship that unites all together; and what a privilege it is to be united in the eternal bonds of friendship with all the holy minds in the universe!

(7.) If God is *light*, (ver. 5,) then all that occurs is reconcilable with the idea that he is worthy of confidence. What he does may *seem* to be dark to us, but we may be assured that it is all light with him. A cloud may come between us and the sun, but beyond the cloud the sun shines with undimmed splendour, and soon the cloud itself will pass away. At midnight it is dark to us, but it is not because the sun is shorn of his beams, or is extinguished. He will rise again upon our hemisphere in the fulness of his glory, and all the darkness of the cloud and of midnight is reconcilable with the idea that the sun is a bright orb, and that in him is no darkness at all. So with God. We may be under a cloud of sorrow and of trouble, but above that the glory of God shines with splendour, and soon that cloud will pass away, and reveal him in the fulness of his beauty and truth.

(8.) We should, therefore, at all times exercise a cheerful confidence in God, ver. 5. Who supposes that the sun is never again to shine when the cloud passes over it, or when the shades of midnight have settled down upon the world? We confide in that sun that it will shine again when the cloud has passed off, and when the shades of night have been driven away. So let us confide in God, for with more absolute certainty we shall yet see him to be light, and shall come to a world where there is no cloud.

(9.) We may look cheerfully onward to heaven, ver. 5. There all is light. There we shall see God as he is. Well may we then bear with our darkness a little longer, for soon we shall be ushered into a world where there is no need of the sun or the stars; where there is no darkness, no night.

(10.) Religion is elevating in its nature, vers. 6, 7. It brings us from a world of darkness to a world of light. It scatters the rays of light on a thousand dark subjects, and gives promise that all that is now obscure will yet become clear as noonday. Wherever there is true religion, the mind emerges more and more into light; the scales of ignorance and error pass away.

(11.) There is no sin so great that it may not be removed by the blood of the atonement, ver. 7, *last clause*. This blood has shown its efficacy in the pardon of all the great sinners who have applied to it, and its efficacy is as great now as it was when it was applied to the first sinner that was saved. No one, therefore, however great his sins, need hesitate about applying to the blood of the cross, or fear that his sins are so great that they cannot be taken away.

(12.) The Christian will yet be made wholly pure, ver. 7, *last clause*. It is of the nature of that blood which the Redeemer shed that it ultimately cleanses the soul entirely from sin. The prospect before the true Christian that he will become perfectly holy is absolute; and whatever else may befall him, he is sure that he will yet be holy as God is holy.

(13.) There is no use in attempting to conceal our offences, ver. 8. They are known, all known, to one Being, and they will at some future period all be disclosed. We cannot hope to evade punishment by hiding them; we cannot hope for impunity because we suppose they may be passed over *as if* unobserved. No man can escape on the presumption either that his sins are unknown, or that they are unworthy of notice.

(14.) It is manly to make confession when we have sinned, vers. 9, 10. All *meanness* was in doing the wrong, not in confessing it; what we should be ashamed of is that we are guilty, not that confession is to be made. When a wrong has been done, there is no nobleness in trying to conceal it; and as there is no nobleness in such an attempt, so there could be no safety.

(15.) Peace of mind, when wrong has been done, can be found only in confession, vers. 9, 10. That is what nature prompts to when we have done wrong, if we would find peace, and that the religion of grace demands. When a man has done wrong, the least that he can do is to make confession; and when that is done and the wrong is pardoned, all is done that *can* be to restore peace to the soul.

(16.) The *ease* of salvation, ver. 9. What more easy terms of salvation could we desire than an acknowledgment of

CHAPTER II.

MY little children, these things
write I unto you, that ye sin

our sins? No painful sacrifice is demanded; no penance, pilgrimage, or
voluntary scourging; all that is required
is that there should be an acknowledgment of sin at the foot of the cross, and
if this is done with a true heart the
offender will be saved. If a man is not
willing to do this, why should he be
saved? How can he be?

CHAPTER II.

ANALYSIS OF THE CHAPTER.

THE *subjects* which are introduced
into this chapter are the following:
I. A statement of the apostle that the
great object which he had in writing to
them was that they should not sin; and
yet if they sinned, and were conscious
that they were guilty before God, they
should not despair, for they had an
Advocate with the Father who had made
propitiation for the sins of the world,
vers. 1, 2. This is properly a continuation of what he had said in the close of
the previous chapter, and should not
have been separated from that. II.
The evidence that we know God, or that
we are his true friends, is to be found
in the fact that we keep his commandments, vers. 3–6. III. The apostle says
that what he had been saying was no
new commandment, but was what they
had always heard concerning the nature
of the gospel; but though in this respect
the law of love which he meant particularly to enforce was no new commandment, none which they had not heard
before, yet in another respect it *was* a
new commandment, for it was one which
in its peculiarity was originated by the
Saviour, and which he meant to make
the characteristic of his religion, vers.
7–11. A large part of the epistle is
taken up in explaining and enforcing
this commandment requiring love to the
brethren. IV. The apostle specifies
(vers. 12–14) various reasons why he
had written to them—reasons derived
from the peculiar character of different
classes among them — little children,
fathers, young men. V. Each of these
classes he solemnly commands not to love

not. And if any man sin, we have
an advocate *a* with the Father,
Jesus Christ the righteous:

a Ro.8.34; He.7.25.

the world, or the things that are in the
world, for that which constitutes the
peculiarity of the ' world ' as such is not
of the Father, and all ' that there is in
the world is soon to pass away,' vers. 15
–17. VI. He calls their attention to
the fact that the closing dispensation of
the world had come, vers. 18–20. The
evidence of this was, that antichrist had
appeared. VII. He calls their attention
to the characteristics of the antichrist.
The essential thing would be that antichrist would deny that Jesus was the
Christ, involving a practical denial of
both the Father and the Son. Persons
of this character were abroad, and they
were in great danger of being seduced
by their arts from the way of truth and
duty, vers. 21–26. VIII. The apostle,
in the close of the chapter, (vers. 27–
29,) expresses the belief that they would
not be seduced, but that they had an
anointing from above which would keep
them from the arts of those who would
lead them astray. He earnestly exhorts
them to abide in God the Saviour, that
when he should appear they might have
confidence and not be ashamed at his
coming.

1. *My little children.* Τεκνία μου.
This is such language as an aged apostle
would be likely to use when addressing
a church, and its use in this epistle may
be regarded as one evidence that John
had reached an advanced period of life
when he wrote the epistle. ¶ *These
things write I unto you.* To wit, the
things stated in chap. i. ¶ *That ye sin
not.* To keep you from sin, or to induce
you to lead a holy life. ¶ *And if any
man sin.* As all are liable, with hearts
as corrupt as ours, and amidst the temptations of a world like this, to do. This,
of course, does not imply that it is *proper* or *right* to sin, or that Christians
should have no concern about it; but
the meaning is, that all are liable to sin,
and when we are conscious of sin the
mind should not yield to despondency
and despair. It *might* be supposed,
perhaps, that if one sinned after baptism,
or after being converted, there could be

no forgiveness. The apostle designs to guard against any such supposition, and to show that the atonement made by the Redeemer had respect to all kinds of sin, and that under the deepest consciousness of guilt and of personal unworthiness, we may feel that we have an advocate on high. ¶ *We have an advocate with the Father.* God only can forgive sin; and though we have no claim on him, yet there is one with him who can plead our cause, and on whom we can rely to manage our interests there. The word rendered *advocate* (παράκλητος —*paraclete*) is elsewhere applied to the Holy Spirit, and is in every other place where it occurs in the New Testament rendered *comforter*, John xiv. 16, 26; xv. 26; xvi. 7. On the meaning of the word, see Notes on John xiv. 16. As used with reference to the Holy Spirit (John xiv. 16, *et al.*) it is employed in the more general sense of *helper*, or *aid;* and the particular manner in which the Holy Spirit aids us, may be seen stated in the Notes on John xiv. 16. As usual here with reference to the Lord Jesus, it is employed in the more limited sense of the word *advocate*, as the word is frequently used in the Greek writers to denote an advocate in court; that is, one whom we *call to our aid;* or *to stand by us*, to defend our suit. Where it is applied to the Lord Jesus, the language is evidently figurative, since there can be no *literal* pleading for us in heaven; but it is expressive of the great truth that he has undertaken our cause with God, and that he performs for us all that we expect of an advocate and counsellor. It is not to be supposed, however, that he manages our cause in the same way, or on the same principles on which an advocate in a human tribunal does. An advocate in court is employed to *defend* his client. He does not begin by admitting his guilt, or in any way basing his plea on the conceded fact that he *is* guilty; his proper business is to show that he is *not* guilty, or, if he be proved to be so, to see that no injustice shall be done him. The proper business of an advocate in a human court, therefore, embraces two things: (1.) To show that his client is not guilty in the form and manner charged on him.

This he may do in one of two ways, either, (*a*) by showing that he did not do the act charged on him, as when he is charged with murder, and can prove an *alibi*, or show that he was not present at the time the murder was committed; or (*b*) by proving that he had a *right* to do the deed—as, if he is charged with murder, he may admit the fact of the killing, but may show that it was in self-defence. (2.) In case his client is convicted, his office is to see that no injustice is done to him in the sentence; to stand by him still; to avail himself of all that the law allows in his favour, or to state any circumstance of age, or sex, or former service, or bodily health, which would in any way mitigate the sentence. The advocacy of the Lord Jesus in our behalf, however, is wholly different from this, though the same general object is pursued and sought, the good of those for whom he becomes an advocate. The nature of his advocacy may be stated in the following particulars: (1.) He admits the guilt of those for whom he becomes the advocate, to the full extent charged on them by the law of God, and by their own consciences. He does not attempt to hide or conceal it. He makes no apology for it. He neither attempts to deny *the fact*, nor to show that they had *a right* to do as they have done. He could not do this, for it would not be true; and any plea before the throne of God which shoud be based on a denial of our guilt would be fatal to our cause. (2.) As our advocate, he undertakes to be security that no wrong shall be done to the universe if we are *not* punished as we deserve; that is, if we are pardoned, and treated *as if* we had not sinned. This he does by pleading what he has done in behalf of men; that is, by the plea that his sufferings and death in behalf of sinners have done as much to honour the law, and to maintain the truth and justice of God, and to prevent the extension of apostasy, as if the offenders themselves had suffered the full penalty of the law. If sinners are punished in hell, there will be some object to be accomplished by it; and the simple account of the atonement by Christ is, that his death will secure all the good results to the uni-

2 And he is the propitiation *a* for our sins: and not for ours only,

a Ro.3.25.

but also for *the sins of* the whole world.

---

verse which would be secured by the punishment of the offender himself. It has done as much to maintain the honour of the law, and to impress the universe with the truth that sin cannot be committed with impunity. If all the good results can be secured by substituted sufferings which there would be by the punishment of the offender himself, then it is clear that the guilty may be acquitted and saved. Why should they not be? The Saviour, as our advocate, undertakes to be security that this shall be. (3.) As our advocate, he becomes a *surety* for our good behaviour ; gives a pledge to justice that we will obey the laws of God, and that he will keep us in the paths of obedience and truth; that, *if* pardoned, we will not continue to rebel. This pledge or surety can be given in no human court of justice. No man, advocate or friend, can give security when one is pardoned who has been convicted of stealing a horse, that he will not steal a horse again; when one who has been guilty of murder is pardoned, that he will never be guilty of it again ; when one who has been guilty of forgery is pardoned, that he will not be guilty of it again. If he *could* do this, the subject of pardon would be attended with much fewer difficulties than it is now. But the Lord Jesus becomes such a pledge or surety for us, (Heb. vii. 22,) and hence he becomes such an advocate with the Father as we need. ¶ *Jesus Christ the righteous.* One who is eminently righteous himself, and who possesses the means of rendering others righteous. It is an appropriate feeling when we come before God in his name, that we come pleading the merits of one who is eminently righteous, and on account of whose righteousness we may be justified and saved.

2. *And he is the propitiation for our sins.* The word rendered *propitiation* (ἱλασμός) occurs nowhere else in the New Testament, except in chap. iv. 10 of this epistle ; though words of the same derivation, and having the same essential meaning, frequently occur.

The corresponding word ἱλαστήριον (*hilasterion*) occurs in Rom. iii. 25, rendered *propitiation*—'whom God hath set forth to be a *propitiation* through faith in his blood;' and in Heb. ix. 5, rendered *mercy-seat*—'shadowing the *mercy-seat*.' The verb ἱλάσκομαι (*hilaskomai*) occurs also in Luke xviii. 3—'God *be merciful* to me a sinner;' and Heb. ii. 17—'to *make reconciliation* for the sins of the people.' For the idea expressed by these words, see Notes on Rom. iii. 25. The proper meaning of the word is that of reconciling, appeasing, turning away anger, rendering propitious or favourable. The idea is, that there is anger or wrath, or that something has been done to offend, and that it is needful to turn away that wrath, or to appease. This may be done by a sacrifice, by songs, by services rendered, or by bloody offerings. So the word is often used in Homer.— *Passow.* We have similar words in common use, as when we say of one that he has been offended, and that something must be done to appease him, or to turn away his wrath. This is commonly done with us by making restitution ; or by an acknowledgment ; or by yielding the point in controversy ; or by an expression of regret ; or by different conduct in time to come. But this idea must not be applied too literally to God ; nor should it be explained away. The essential thoughts in regard to him, as implied in this word, are, (1,) that his will has been disregarded, and his law violated, and that he has reason to be offended with us ; (2,) that in that condition he cannot, consistently with his perfections, and the good of the universe, treat us as if we had not done it; (3,) that it is proper that, in some way, he should show his displeasure at our conduct, either by punishing us, or by something that shall answer the same purpose ; and, (4,) that the means of propitiation come in here, and accomplish this end, and make it proper that he should treat us as if we had not sinned ; that is, he is reconciled, or appeased, and his anger is turned away. This is done, it is supposed, by the death of the Lord Jesus, accomplishing, in most important respects, what would be accomplished by the punishment of the offender himself. In regard to this, in order to a proper understanding of what is accomplished, it is necessary to observe two things—what is *not* done, and what *is*. I. There are certain things which do *not* enter into the idea of propitiation. They are such as these: (*a*) That it does not change the fact that the wrong was done. That is a fact which cannot be denied, and he who undertakes to make a propitiation for sin does not deny it. (*b*) It does not change God ; it does not make him a different being from what he was before; it does not *buy him over* to a willingness to show mercy; it does not change an inexorable being to one who is compassionate and kind. (*c*) The offering that is made to secure reconciliation does not necessarily produce reconciliation in fact. It prepares the way for it on the part of God, but whether they for whom it is made will be disposed to accept it is another question. When two men are alienated from each other, you may go to B and say to him that all obstacles to reconciliation on the part of A are removed, and that he is disposed to be at peace, but whether B will be willing to be at peace is quite another matter. The mere fact that his adversary is disposed to be at peace, determines nothing in regard to his disposition in the matter. So in regard to the controversy between man and God. It may be true that all obstacles to reconciliation on the part of God are taken away, and still it may be quite a separate question whether man will be willing to lay aside his opposition, and embrace the terms of mercy. In itself considered, one does not necessarily determine the other, or throw any light on it. II. The amount, then, in regard to the propitiation made for sin is, that it removes all obstacles to reconciliation on the part of God; it does whatever is necessary to be done to maintain the honour of his law, his justice, and his truth ; it makes it consistent for him to offer pardon— that is, it removes whatever there was that made it necessary to inflict punish-

ment, and thus, so far as the word can be applied to God, it appeases him, or turns away his anger, or renders him propitious. This it does, not in respect to producing any *change* in God, but in respect to the fact that it removes whatever there was in the nature of the case that prevented the free and full offer of pardon. The idea of the apostle in the passage before us is, that when we sin we may be assured that this has been done, and that pardon may now be freely extended to us. ¶ *And not for our's only.* Not only for the sins of us who are Christians, for the apostle was writing to such. The idea which he intends to convey seems to be, that when we come before God we should take the most liberal and large views of the atonement ; we should feel that the most ample provision has been made for our pardon, and that in no respect is there any limit as to the sufficiency of that work to remove *all* sin. It is sufficient for us; sufficient for all the world. ¶ *But also for* the sins of *the whole world.* The phrase ' *the sins of* ' is not in the original, but is not improperly supplied, for the connection demands it. This is one of the expressions occurring in the New Testament which demonstrate that the atonement was made for all men, and which cannot be reconciled with any other opinion. If he had died only for a part of the race, this language *could not* have been used. The phrase, ' the whole world,' is one which naturally embraces all men ; is such as would be used if it be supposed that the apostle *meant* to teach that Christ died for all men ; and is such as cannot be explained on any other supposition. If he died only for the elect, it is not true that he is the ' propitiation for the sins of the whole world ' in any proper sense, nor would it be possible then to assign a sense in which it could be true. This passage, interpreted in its plain and obvious meaning, teaches the following things : (1.) That the atonement in its own nature is *adapted* to all men, or that it is as much fitted to one individual, or one class, as another ; (2,) that it is *sufficient* in merit for all ; that is, that if any more should be saved than actually will be, there would be no need of any additional suffering in order to save

3 And hereby we do know that we know him, if we keep *a* his commandments.

4 He that saith, I know him, and keepeth not his commandments, is a liar, and the truth is not in him.

a Lu.6.46; Jn.14.15,23.

5 But whoso keepeth his word, in him verily is the love of God perfected: hereby know we that we are in him.

6 He that saith, he abideth *b* in him, ought himself also so to walk, *c* even as he walked.

b Jn.15.4,5.   c Jn.13.15.

them; (3,) that it has no *special* adaptedness to one person or class more than another; that is, that in its own nature it did not render the salvation of one more easy than that of another. It so magnified the law, so honoured God, so fully expressed the Divine sense of the evil of sin in respect to all men, that the offer of salvation might be made as freely to one as to another, and that any and all might take shelter under it and be safe. Whether, however, God might not, for wise reasons, resolve that its benefits should be applied to a part only, is another question, and one which does not affect the inquiry about the intrinsic nature of the atonement. On the evidence that the atonement was made for all, see Notes on 2 Cor. v. 14, and Heb. ii. 9.

[See also the Supplementary Notes on these passages, for a general review of the argument regarding the extent of atonement.]

3. *And hereby we do know that we know him.* To wit, by that which follows, we have evidence that we are truly acquainted with him, and with the requirements of his religion; that is, that we are truly his friends. The word *him*, in this verse, seems to refer to the Saviour. On the meaning of the word *know*, see Notes, John xvii. 3. The apostle had stated in the previous part of this epistle some of the leading points revealed by the Christian religion, and he here enters on the consideration of the nature of the evidence required to show that we are personally interested in it, or that we are true Christians. A large part of the epistle is occupied with this subject. The first, the grand evidence—that without which all others would be vain—he says is, that we keep his commandments. ¶ *If we keep his commandments.* See Notes, John xiv. 15. Comp. John xiv. 23, 24; xv. 10, 14.

4. *He that saith, I know him.* He

who professes to be acquainted with the Saviour, or who professes to be a Christian. ¶ *And keepeth not his commandments.* What he has appointed to be observed by his people; that is, he who does not *obey* him. ¶ *Is a liar.* Makes a false profession; professes to have that which he really has not. Such a profession is a falsehood, because there can be no true religion where one does not obey the law of God.

5. *But whoso keepeth his word.* That is, what he has spoken or commanded. The term *word* here will include all that he has made known to us as his will in regard to our conduct. ¶ *In him verily is the love of God perfected.* He professes to have the love of God in his heart, and that love receives its *completion* or *filling up* by obedience to the will of God. That obedience is the proper carrying out, or the exponent of the love which exists in the heart. Love to the Saviour would be defective without that, for it is never complete without obedience. If this be the true interpretation, then the passage does not make any affirmation about sinless *perfection*, but it only affirms that if true love exists in the heart, it will be carried out in the life; or that love and obedience are parts of the same thing; that one will be manifested by the other; and that where obedience exists, it is the completion or perfecting of love. Besides, the apostle does not say that either the love or the obedience would be in themselves absolutely perfect; but he says that one cannot fully develope itself without the other. ¶ *Hereby know we that we are in him.* That is, by having in fact such love as shall insure obedience. To be *in* him, is to be united to him; to be his friends. Comp. Notes, John vi. 56; Rom. xiii. 14.

6. *He that saith, he abideth in him.* Gr., *remains* in him; that is, abides or

7 Brethren, I write no new commandment unto you, but an old
commandment, which ye had from
the beginning. The old command-

ment is the word which ye have
heard from the beginning.

8 Again, a new ^a commandment

^a Jn.13.34.

remains in the belief of his doctrines,
and in the comfort and practice of
religion. The expression is one of those
which refer to the intimate union between Christ and his people. A great
variety of phrase is employed to denote
that. For the meaning of this word in
John, see Notes, chap. iii. 6. ¶ *Ought
himself also so to walk, even as he
walked.* Ought to live and act as he
did. If he is *one* with him, or professes
to be united to him, he ought to imitate
him in all things. Comp. John xiii. 15.
See also Notes, chap. i. 6.

7. *Brethren, I write no new commandment unto you.* That is, what I
am now enjoining is not new. It is the
same doctrine which you have always
heard. There has been much difference
of opinion as to what is referred to by
the word *commandment,* whether it is
the injunction in the previous verse to
live as Christ lived, or whether it is
what he refers to in the following verses,
the duty of brotherly love. Perhaps
neither of these is exactly the idea of
the apostle, but he may mean in this
verse to put in a *general* disclaimer
against the charge that what he enjoined
was *new.* In respect to *all* that he
taught, the views of truth which he held,
the duties which he enjoined, the course
of life which he would prescribe as proper for a Christian to live, he meant to
say that it was not at all *new;* it was
nothing which he had originated himself, but it was in fact the same system
of doctrines which they had always received since they became Christians.
He might have been induced to say
this because he apprehended that some
of those whom he had in his eye, and
whose doctrines he meant to oppose,
might say that this was all new; that
it was not the nature of religion as it
had been commonly understood, and as
it was laid down by the Saviour. In a
somewhat different sense, indeed, he
admits (ver. 8) that there *was* a 'new'
commandment which it was proper to
enjoin—for he did not forget that the
Saviour himself called that '*new;*' and

though that commandment had also
been all along inculcated under the
gospel, yet there was a sense in which
it was proper to call *that* new, for it had
been so called by the Saviour. But in
respect to *all* the doctrines which he
maintained, and in respect to *all* the
duties which he enjoined, he said that
they were not new in the sense that he
had originated them, or that they had
not been enjoined from the beginning.
Perhaps, also, the apostle here may have
some allusion to false teachers who were
in fact scattering new doctrines among
the people, things before unheard of, and
attractive by their novelty; and he may
mean to say that *he* made no pretensions
to any such novelty, but was content to
repeat the old and familiar truths which
they had always received. Thus, if *he*
was charged with broaching new opinions,
he denies it fully ; if *they* were advancing new opinions, and were even 'making
capital' out of them, he says that he
attempted no such thing, but was content with the old and established opinions
which they had always received. ¶ *But
an old commandment.* Old, in the
sense that it has always been inculcated ;
that religion has always enjoined it.
¶ *Which ye had from the beginning.*
Which you have always received ever
since you heard anything about the
gospel. It was preached when the
gospel was first preached ; it has always
been promulgated when that has been
promulgated ; it is what you first heard
when you were made acquainted with
the gospel. Compare Notes, chap. i. 1.
¶ *The old commandment is the word
which ye have heard from the beginning.*
Is the *doctrine;* or is what was enjoined.
John is often in the habit of putting a
truth in a new form or aspect in order
to make it emphatic, and to prevent the
possibility of misapprehension See
John i. 1, 2. The sense here is, All
that I am saying to you is in fact an
old commandment, or one which you
have always had. There is nothing
new in what I am enjoining on you.'

8. *Again, a new commandment I*

I write unto you ; which thing is true in him and in you, because the darkness *a* is past, and the true light now shineth.

9 He that saith he is in the light,

a Ro.13.12.

and hateth his brother, is in darkness *b* even until now.

10 He that loveth his brother abideth in the light, and there is none 1 occasion of stumbling in him.

b 2 Pe.1.9.   1 *scandal.*

write unto you. ' And yet, that which I write to you, and particularly enjoin on you, deserves in another sense to be called a new commandment, though it has been also inculcated from the beginning, for it was called *new* by the Saviour himself.' Or the meaning may be, ' In addition to the general precepts which I have referred to, I do now call your attention to *the new* commandment of the Saviour, that which he himself called new.' There can be no doubt here that John refers to the commandment to ' love one another,' (see vers. 9–11,) and that it is here called *new,* not in the sense that *John* inculcated it as a novel doctrine, but in the sense that the Saviour called it such. For the reasons why it was so called by him, see Notes, John xiii. 34. ¶ *Which thing is true in him.* In the Lord Jesus. That is, which commandment or law of love was illustrated in him, or was manifested by him in his intercourse with his disciples. That which was most prominent in him was this very love which he enjoined on all his followers. ¶ *And in you.* Among you. That is, you have manifested it in your intercourse with each other. It is not new in the sense that you have never heard of it, and have never evinced it, but in the sense only that he called it new. ¶ *Because the darkness is past, and the true light now shineth.* The ancient systems of error, under which men hated each other, have passed away, and you are brought into the light of the true religion. Once you were in darkness, like others ; now the light of the pure gospel shines around you, and that requires, as its distinguishing characteristic, *love.* Religion is often represented as *light ;* and Christ spoke of himself, and was spoken of, as the light of the world. See Notes, John i. 4, 5. Comp. John viii. 12 ; xii. 35, 36, 46 ; Isa. ix. 2.

9. *He that saith he is in the light.* That he has true religion, or is a Christian. See chap. i. 7. ¶ *And hateth his*

brother. The word *brother* seems here to refer to those who professed the same religion. The word is indeed sometimes used in a larger sense, but the reference here appears to be to that which is properly brotherly love among Christians. Comp. Lücke, *in loc.* ¶ *Is in darkness even until now.* That is, he cannot have true religion unless he has love to the brethren. The command to love one another was one of the most solemn and earnest which Christ ever enjoined, (John xv. 17;) he made it the peculiar badge of discipleship, or that by which his followers were to be everywhere known, (John xiii. 35;) and it is, therefore, impossible to have any true religion without love to those who are sincerely and truly his followers. If a man has not that, he is in deep darkness, whatever else he may have, on the whole subject of religion. Comp. Notes, 1 Thess. iv. 9.

10. *He that loveth his brother abideth in the light.* Has true religion, and enjoys it. ¶ *And there is none occasion of stumbling in him.* Marg., *scandal.* Greek, ' and there is no stumbling ' [or scandal—σκάνδαλον—in him.] The word here used, means anything against which one strikes or stumbles ; and then a stumbling-block, an impediment, or anything which occasions a fall. Then it is used in a moral or spiritual sense, as denoting that which is the occasion of falling into sin. See Notes, Matt. v. 29, and Rom. xiv. 13. Here it refers to an individual in respect to his treatment of others, and means that there is nothing, so far as he is concerned, to lead him into sin.—*Rob. Lex.* If he has love to the brethren, he has true religion ; and there is, so far as the influence of this shall extend, nothing that will be the occasion of his falling into sin in his conduct towards them, for ' love worketh no ill to his neighbour,' Rom. xiii. 10. His course will be just, and upright, and benevolent. He will have no envy towards them in their

11 But he that hateth his brother is in darkness, and walketh ^a in darkness, and knoweth not whither he goeth, because that darkness hath blinded his eyes.

12 I write unto you, little children, because your sins are forgiven you for his ^b name's sake.

^a Pr.4.15; Jn.12.35.
^b Ps.25.11; Lu.24.47; Ac.10.43.

prosperity, and will not be disposed to detract from their reputation in adversity; he will have no feelings of exultation when they fall, and will not be disposed to take advantage of their misfortunes; and, loving them as brethren, he will be in no respect under temptation to do them wrong. In the bosom of one who loves his brother, the baleful passions of envy, malice, hatred, and uncharitableness, can have no place. At the same time, this love of the brethren would have an important effect on his whole Christian life and walk, for there are few things that will have more influence on a man's character in keeping him from doing wrong, than the love of the good and the pure. He who truly loves good men, will not be likely in any respect to go astray from the paths of virtue.

11. *But he that hateth his brother.* The word here used would, in this connection, include both the mere absence of love, and positive hatred. It is designed to include the whole of that state of mind where there is not love for the brethren. ¶ *Is in darkness.* Ver. 9. ¶ *And walketh in darkness.* He is like one who walks in the dark, and who sees no object distinctly. See Notes, John xii. 35. ¶ *And knoweth not whither he goeth.* Like one in the dark. He wanders about not knowing what direction he shall take, or where the course which he is on will lead. The general meaning is, that he is ignorant of the whole nature of religion; or, in other words, love to the brethren is a central virtue in religion, and when a man has not that, his mind is entirely clouded on the whole subject, and he shows that he knows nothing of its nature. There is no virtue that is designed to be made more prominent in Christianity; and there is none that will throw its influence farther over a man's life.

12. *I write unto you, little children.* There has been much difference of opinion among commentators in regard to this verse and the three following verses, on account of their apparent tautology. Even Doddridge supposes that considerable error has here crept into the text, and that a portion of these verses should be omitted in order to avoid the repetition. But there is no authority for omitting any portion of the text, and the passage is very much in accordance with the general style of the apostle John. The author of this epistle was evidently accustomed to express his thoughts in a great variety of ways, having even the appearance of tautology, that the exact idea might be before his readers, and that his meaning might not be misapprehended. In order to show that the truths which he was uttering in this epistle pertained to all, and to secure the interest of all in them, he addresses himself to different classes, and says that there were reasons existing in regard to each class why he wrote to them. In the expressions 'I write,' and 'I have written,' he refers to what is found in the epistle itself, and the statements in these verses are designed to be *reasons* why he brought these truths before their minds. The word here rendered *little children* (τεκνία) is different from that used in ver. 13, and rendered there *little children*, (παιδία;) but there can be little doubt that the same class of persons is intended. Some have indeed supposed that by the term *little children* here, as in ver. 1, the apostle means to address all believers—speaking to them as a father; but it seems more appropriate to suppose that he means in these verses to divide the body of Christians whom he addressed into three classes—children, young men, and the aged, and to state particular reasons why he wrote to each. If the term (τεκνία) *little children* here means the same as the term (παιδία) *little children* in ver. 13, then he addresses each of these classes *twice* in these two verses, giving each time somewhat varied reasons why he addressed them. That, by

the term 'little children' here, he means children literally, seems to me to be clear, (1,) because this is the usual meaning of the word, and should be understood to be the meaning here, unless there is something in the connection to show that it is used in a metaphorical sense; (2,) because it seems necessary to understand the other expressions, 'young men,' and 'fathers,' in a literal sense, as denoting those more advanced in life; (3,) because this would be quite in character for the apostle John. He had recorded, and would doubtless remember the solemn injunction of the Saviour to Peter, (John xxi. 15,) to 'feed his lambs,' and the aged apostle could not but feel that what was worthy of so solemn an injunction from the Lord, was worthy of his attention and care as an apostle; and (4,) because in that case, each class, fathers, young men, and children, would be twice addressed in these two verses; whereas if we understood this of Christians in general, then fathers and young men would be twice addressed, and children but once. If this be so, it may be remarked, (1,) that there were probably quite young children in the church in the time of the apostle John, for the word would naturally convey that idea. (2,) The *exact* age cannot be indeed determined, but two things are clear: (*a*) one is, that they were undoubtedly under twenty years of age, since they were younger than the 'young men'—νεανίσκοι—a word usually applied to those who were in the vigour of life, from about the period of twenty up to forty years, (Notes, ver. 13,) and this word would embrace all who were younger than that class; and (*b*) the other is, that the word itself would convey the idea that they were in quite early life, as the word *children*—a fair translation of it—does now with us. It is not possible to determine, from the use of this word, *precisely* of what age the class here referred to was, but the word would imply that they were in quite early life. No rule is laid down in the New Testament as to the age in which children may be admitted to the communion. The whole subject is left to the wise discretion of the church, and is safely left there. Cases must vary so much

that no rule could be laid down; and little or no evil has arisen from leaving the point undetermined in the Scriptures. It may be doubted, however, whether the church has not been rather in danger of erring by having it deferred too late, than by admitting children too early. (3.) Such children, if worthy the attention of an aged apostle, should receive the particular notice of pastors now. Comp. Notes, John xxi. 15. There are reasons in all cases now, as there were then, why this part of a congregation should receive the special attention of a minister of religion. The hopes of a church are in them. Their minds are susceptible to impression. The character of the piety in the next age will depend on their views of religion. All that there is of value in the church and the world will soon pass into their hands. The houses, farms, factories; the pulpits, and the chairs of professors in colleges; the seats of senators and the benches of judges; the great offices of state, and all the offices in the church; the interests of learning, and of benevolence and liberty, are all soon to be under their control. Everything valuable in this world will soon depend on their conduct and character; and who, therefore, can over-estimate the importance of training them up in just views of religion. As John *wrote* to this class, should not pastors *preach* to them? ¶ *Because—ὅτι.* This particle may be rendered *for,* or *because;* and the meaning may be either that the fact that their sins were forgiven was a *reason* for writing to them, since it would be proper, on that ground, to exhort them to a holy life; or that he wrote to them because it was a privilege to address them as those who were forgiven, for he felt that, in speaking to *them,* he could address them as such. It seems to me that it is to be taken as a *causal* particle, and that the apostle, in the various specifications which he makes, designs to assign particular *reasons* why he wrote to each class, enjoining on them the duties of a holy life. Comp. ver. 21. ¶ *Your sins are forgiven you.* That is, this is a *reason* why he wrote to them, and enjoined these things on them. The meaning seems to be, that the fact that our past sins are blotted

13 I write unto you, fathers, because ye have known him *a that is* from the beginning. I write unto you, young men, because ye have overcome the wicked one. I write unto you, little children, because ye have known the Father. *b*

a 1 Jn.1.1.   b Jn.14.7,9.

out furnishes a strong *reason* why we should be holy. That reason is founded on the goodness of God in doing it, and on the obligation under which we are brought by the fact that God has had mercy on us. This is a consideration which children will feel as well as others ; for there is nothing which will tend more to make a child obedient hereafter, than the fact that a parent freely forgives the past. ¶ *For his name's sake.* On account of the name of Christ ; that is, in virtue of what he has done for us. In ver. 13, he states another reason why he wrote to this same class—"because they had known the Father."

13. *I write unto you, fathers.* As there were special reasons for writing to children, so there were also for writing to those who were more mature in life. The class here addressed would embrace all those who were in advance of the *νεανίσκοι*, or *young men*, and would properly include those who were at the head of families. ¶ *Because ye have known him* that is *from the beginning.* That is, the Lord Jesus Christ. Notes, chap. i. 1. The argument is, that they had been long acquainted with the principles of his religion, and understood well its doctrines and duties. It cannot be certainly inferred from this that they had had a *personal* acquaintance with the Lord Jesus: yet that this might have been is not impossible, for John had himself personally known him, and there may have been some among those to whom he wrote who had also seen and known him. If this were so, it would give additional impressiveness to the reason assigned here for writing to them, and for reminding them of the principles of that religion which they had learned from his own lips and example. But perhaps all that is necessarily implied in this passage is, that they had had long opportunity of becoming acquainted with the religion of the Son of God, and that having understood that thoroughly, it was proper to address them as aged and established Christians,

and to call on them to maintain the true doctrines of the gospel, against the specious but dangerous errors which then prevailed. ¶ *I write unto you, young men.* *νεανίσκοι.* This word would properly embrace those who were in the vigour of life, midway between children and old men. It is uniformly rendered *young men* in the New Testament: Matt. xix. 20, 22 ; Mark xiv. 51; xvi. 5 ; Luke vii. 14 ; Acts ii. 17 ; v. 10 ; and in the passages before us. It does not elsewhere occur. It is commonly understood as embracing those in the prime and vigour of manhood up to the period of about forty years.—*Robinson.* ¶ *Because ye have overcome the wicked one.* That is, because you have vigour, (see the next verse,) and that vigour you have shown by overcoming the assaults of the wicked one—the devil. You have triumphed over the passions which prevail in early life ; you have combated the allurements of vice, ambition, covetousness, and sensuality; and you have shown that there is a strength of character and of piety on which reliance can be placed in promoting religion. It is proper, therefore, to exhort you not to disgrace the victory which you have already gained, but to employ your vigour of character in maintaining the cause of the Saviour. The thing to which John appeals here is the energy of those at this period of life, and it is proper at all times to make this the ground of appeal in addressing a church. It is right to call on those who are in the prime of life, and who are endowed with energy of character, to employ their talents in the service of the Lord Jesus, and to stand up as the open advocates of truth. Thus the apostle calls on the three great classes into which a community or a church may be considered as divided : *youth,* because their sins were already forgiven, and, though young, they had actually entered on a career of virtue and religion, a career which by all means they ought to be exhorted to pursue; *fathers,* or

14 I have written unto you, fathers, because ye have known him *that is* from the beginning. I have written unto you, young men, because ye are strong, *a* and the word of God abideth *b* in you, and ye have overcome *c* the wicked one.

a Ep.6.10.   *b* Jn.15.7.   *c* Re.2.7,&c.

aged men, because they had had long experience in religion, and had a thorough acquaintance with the doctrines and duties of the gospel, and they might be expected to stand steadfastly as examples to others; and *young men*, those who were in the vigour and prime of life, because they had shown that they had power to resist evil, and were endowed with strength, and it was proper to call on them to exert their vigour in the sacred cause of religion. ¶ *I write unto you, little children.* Many MSS. read here, *I have written*—ἔγραψα—instead of *I write*—γράφω. This reading is found in both the ancient Syriac versions, and in the Coptic; it was followed by Origen, Cyril, Photius, and Œcumenius; and it is adopted by Grotius, Mill, and Hahn, and is probably the true reading. The connection seems to demand this. In vers. 12, 13, the apostle uses the word γράφω—*I write*—in relation to children, fathers, and young men; in the passage before us, and in the next verse, he again addresses children, fathers, and young men, and in relation to the two latter, he says ἔγραψα—*I have written.* The connection, therefore, seems to demand that the same word should be employed here also. Some persons have supposed that the whole passage is spurious, but of that there is no evidence; and, as we have elsewhere seen, it is not uncommon for John to repeat a sentiment, and to place it in a variety of lights, in order that he might make it certain that he was not misapprehended. Some have supposed, also, that the expression ' I *have* written,' refers to some former epistle which is now lost, or to the Gospel by the same author, which had been sent to them, (*Hug.*) and that he means here to remind them that he had written to them on some former occasion, inculcating the same sentiments which he now expressed. But there is no evidence of this, and this supposition is not necessary in order to a correct understanding of the passage. In the former expression, ' *I write*,' the state of mind would be that of one who

fixed his attention on what he was *then* doing, and the particular reason *why* he did it—and the apostle states these reasons in vers. 12, 13. Yet it would not be unnatural for him immediately to throw his mind into the past, and to state the reasons why he had resolved to write to them at all, and then to look at what he had purposed to say as already done, and to state the reasons why that was done. Thus one who sat down to write a letter to a friend might appropriately state in any part of the letter the reasons which had induced him to write at all to him on the subject. If he fixed his attention on the fact that he was *actually* writing, and on the reasons why he wrote, he would express himself in the present tense— *I write ;* if on the previous purpose, or the reasons which induced him to write at all, he would use the past tense—*I have written* for such and such reasons. So John seems here, in order to make what he says emphatic, to refer to two states of his own mind: the one when he *resolved* to write, and the reasons which occurred to him then; and the other when he was *actually* writing, and the reasons which occurred to him then. The reasons are indeed substantially the same, but they are contemplated from different points of view, and that fact shows that what he did was done with deliberation, and from a deep sense of duty. ¶ *Because ye have known the Father.* In verse 12, the reason assigned for writing to this class is, that their sins were forgiven. The reason assigned here is, that in early life they had become acquainted with God as a Father. He desires that they would show themselves dutiful and faithful children in this relation which they sustained to him. Even children may learn to regard God as their Father, and may have towards him all the affectionate interest which grows out of this relation.

14. *I have written unto you, fathers, because,* &c. The reason assigned here for writing to fathers is the same which is given in the previous verse. It would

15 Love *a* not the world, neither *b* any man love the world, the love the things *that are* in the world. If of the Father is not in him.

a Ro.12.2.   *b* Mat.6.24; Ga.1.10; Ja.4.4.

seem that, in respect to them, the apostle regarded this as a sufficient reason for writing to them, and only meant to enforce it by repeating it. The fact that they had through many years been acquainted with the doctrines and duties of the true religion, seemed to him a sufficient reason for writing to them, and for exhorting them to a steadfast adherence to those principles and duties. ¶ *I have written unto you, young men, because ye are strong,* &c. The two additional circumstances which he here mentions as reasons for writing to young men are, that they are strong, and that the word of God abides in them. The first of these reasons is, that they were strong; that is, that they were qualified for active and useful service in the cause of the Redeemer. Children were yet too young and feeble to appeal to them by this motive, and the powers of the aged were exhausted; but those who were in the vigour of life might be called upon for active service in the cause of the Lord Jesus. The same appeal may be made now to the same class; and the fact that they *are* thus vigorous is a proper ground of exhortation, for the church needs their active services, and they are bound to devote their powers to the cause of truth. The other additional ground of appeal is, that the word of God abode in them; that is, that those of this class to whom he wrote had showed, perhaps in time of temptation, that they adhered firmly to the principles of religion. They had not flinched from an open defence of the truths of religion when assailed; they had not been seduced by the plausible arts of the advocates of error, but they had had strength to overcome the wicked one. The reason here for appealing to this class is, that in fact they *had* showed that they could be relied on, and it was proper to depend on them to advocate the great principles of Christianity.

15. *Love not the world.* The term *world* seems to be used in the Scriptures in three senses: (1.) As denoting the physical universe; the world as it appears to the eve; the world considered as the work of God, as a material creation. (2.) The world as applied to the *people* that reside in it—'the world of mankind.' (3.) As the dwellers on the earth are by nature without religion, and act under a set of maxims, aims, and principles that have reference only to this life, the term comes to be used with reference to that community; that is, to the objects which *they* peculiarly seek, and the principles by which they are actuated. Considered with reference to the first sense of the word, it is not improper to love the world as the work of God, and as illustrating his perfections; for we may suppose that God loves his own works, and it is not wrong that we should find pleasure in their contemplation. Considered with reference to the second sense of the word, it is not wrong to love the *people* of the world with a love of benevolence, and to have attachment to our kindred and friends who constitute a part of it, though they are not Christians. It is only with reference to the word as used in the third sense that the command here can be understood to be applicable, or that the love of the world is forbidden; with reference to the objects sought, the maxims that prevail, the principles that reign in that community that lives for this world as contradistinguished from the world to come. The meaning is, that we are not to fix our affections on worldly objects—on what the world can furnish—as our portion, with the spirit with which they do who live only for this world, regardless of the life to come. We are not to make this world the object of our chief affection; we are not to be influenced by the maxims and feelings which prevail among those who do. Comp. Notes, Rom. xii. 2, and James iv. 4. See also Matt. xvi. 26; Luke ix. 25; 1 Cor. i. 20; iii. 19; Gal. iv. 3; Col. ii. 8. ¶ *Neither the things that are in the world.* Referred to in the next verse as 'the lust of the flesh, the lust of the eyes, and the pride of life.' This explanation shows what John meant by 'the things that are in the world.' He does not say that we are in

16 For all that *is* in the world, the lust of the flesh, *a* and the lust of the *b* eyes, and the pride *c* of life, is not of the Father, but is of the world.

17 And *d* the world passeth away, and the lust thereof : but he that doeth the will of God abideth for ever.

a 2Pe.2.10.   *b* Ps.119.37.   *c* Ps.73.6.
d Ps.39.6; 1 Co.7.31.

no sense to love *anything* that is in the material world ; that we are to feel no interest in flowers, and streams, and forests, and fountains ; that we are to have no admiration for what God has done as the Creator of all things ; that we are to cherish no love for any of the inhabitants of the world, our friends and kindred ; or that we are to pursue none of the objects of this life in making provision for our families ; but that we are *not* to love the things which are sought merely to pamper the appetite, to please the eye, or to promote pride in living. These are the objects sought by the people of the world ; these are not the objects to be sought by the Christian. ¶ *If any man love the world,* &c. If, in this sense, a man loves the world, it shows that he has no true religion ; that is, if characteristically he loves the world as his portion, and lives for that ; if it is the ruling principle of his life to gain and enjoy that, it shows that his heart has never been renewed, and that he has no part with the children of God. See Notes, James iv. 4; Matt. vi. 24.

16. *For all that* is *in the world.* That is, all that really constitutes the world, or that enters into the aims and purposes of those who live for this life. All that that community lives for may be comprised under the following things. ¶ *The lust of the flesh.* The word *lust* is used here in the general sense of *desire,* or that which is the object of desire —not in the narrow sense in which it is now commonly used to denote libidinous passion. See Notes, James i. 14. The phrase, ' the lust *of the flesh,*' here denotes that which pampers the appetites, or all that is connected with the indulgence of the mere animal propensities. A large part of the world lives for little more than this. This is the lowest form of worldly indulgence ; those which are immediately specified being of a higher order, though still merely worldly. ¶ *And the lust of the eyes.* That which is designed merely to gratify the sight.

This would include, of course, costly raiment, jewels, gorgeous furniture, splendid palaces, pleasure-grounds, &c. The object is to refer to the gay vanities of this world, the thing on which the eye delights to rest where there is no higher object of life. It does not, of course, mean that the eye is never to be gratified, or that we can find as much pleasure in an ugly as in a handsome object, or that it is sinful to find pleasure in beholding objects of real beauty—for the world, as formed by its Creator, is full of such things, and he could not but have intended that pleasure should enter the soul through the eye, or that the beauties which he has shed so lavishly over his works should contribute to the happiness of his creatures; but the apostle refers to this when it is the great and leading object of life—when it is sought without any connection with religion or reference to the world to come. ¶ *And the pride of life.* The word here used means, properly, ostentation or boasting, and then arrogance or pride. —*Robinson.* It refers to whatever there is that tends to promote pride, or that is an index of pride, such as the ostentatious display of dress, equipage, furniture, &c. ¶ *Is not of the Father.* Does not proceed from God, or meet with his approbation. It is not of the nature of true religion to seek these things, nor can their pursuit be reconciled with the existence of real piety in the heart. The sincere Christian has nobler ends ; and he who has not any higher ends, and whose conduct and feelings can all be accounted for by a desire for these things, cannot be a true Christian. ¶ *But is of the world.* Is originated solely by the objects and purposes of this life, where religion and the life to come are excluded.

17. *And the world passeth away.* Everything properly constituting this world where religion is excluded. The reference here does not seem to be so much to the material world, as to the

18 Little children, it is the last *a* time: and as ye have heard *b* that antichrist shall come, even now are there many antichrists; whereby we know that it is the last time.

a He.1.2. *b* Mat.24.24; 1 Ti.4.1.

scenes of show and vanity which make up the world. These things are passing away like the shifting scenes of the stage. See Notes, 1 Cor. vii. 31. ¶ *And the lust thereof.* All that is here so much the object of desire. These things are like a pageant, which only amuses the eye for a moment, and then disappears for ever. ¶ *But he that doeth the will of God abideth for ever.* This cannot mean that he will never die ; but it means that he has built his happiness on a basis which is secure, and which can never pass away. Comp. Notes, Matt. vii. 24–27.

18. *Little children.* See ver. 1. ¶ *It is the last time.* The closing period or dispensation ; that dispensation in which the affairs of the world are ultimately to be wound up. The apostle does not, however, say that the end of the world would soon occur, nor does he intimate how long this dispensation would be. That period might continue through many ages or centuries, and still be the last dispensation, or that in which the affairs of the world would be finally closed. See Notes, Isa. ii. 2 ; Acts ii. 17 ; Heb. i. 2. Some have supposed that the 'last time' here refers to the destruction of Jerusalem, and the end of the Jewish economy ; but the more natural interpretation is to refer it to the last dispensation of the world, and to suppose that the apostle meant to say that there were clear evidences that that period had arrived. ¶ *And as ye have heard that antichrist shall come.* The word *antichrist* occurs in the New Testament only in these epistles of John, 1 John ii. 18, 22 ; iv. 3 ; 2 John 7. The proper meaning of *anti* (ἀντί) in composition is, (1,) *over-against,* as ἀντιτάσσειν ; (2,) *contrary to,* as ἀντιλέγειν ; (3,) reciprocity, as ἀνταποδίδωμι ; (4,) *substitution,* as ἀντιβασιλεύς ; (5,) the place of the king, or ἀνθύπατος—*proconsul.* The word *antichrist,* therefore, might denote any one who either was or claimed to be in the place of Christ, or one who, for any cause, was in opposition to him. The word, further, would apply to one opposed to him, on whatever ground the opposition might be ; whether it were open and avowed, or whether it were only *in fact,* as resulting from certain claims which were adverse to his, or which were inconsistent with his. A *vice-functionary,* or an *opposing functionary,* would be the idea which the word would naturally suggest. If the word stood alone, and there were nothing said further to explain its meaning, we should think, when the word *antichrist* was used, either of one who claimed to be the Christ, and who thus was a rival ; or of one who stood in opposition to him on some other ground. That which constituted the characteristics of antichrist, according to John, who only has used the word, he has himself stated. Ver. 22, 'Who is a liar, but he that denieth that Jesus is the Christ? He is antichrist, that denieth the Father and the Son.' Chap. iv. 3, 'And every spirit that confesseth not that Jesus Christ is come in the flesh, is not of God ; and this is that spirit of antichrist.' 2 John 7, 'For many deceivers are entered into the world, who confess not that Jesus Christ is come in the flesh. This is a deceiver and an antichrist.' From this it is clear, that John understood by the word all those that denied that Jesus is the Messiah, or that the Messiah has come in the flesh. If they held that Jesus was a deceiver, and that he was not the Christ, or if they maintained that, though Christ had come, he had not come in the flesh, that is, with a proper human nature, this showed that such persons had the spirit of antichrist. They arrayed themselves against him, and held doctrines which were in fact in entire opposition to the Son of God. It would appear then that John does not use the word in the sense which it *would* bear as denoting one who set up a rival claim, or who came in the place of Christ, but in the sense of those who were opposed to him by denying essential doctrines in regard to his person and advent. It is not certainly known to what persons he refers, but it would

seem not improbable to Jewish adversaries, (see Suicer's Thesaur. s. voc.,) or to some forms of the Gnostic belief. See Notes, chap. iv. 2. The doctrine respecting antichrist, as stated in the New Testament, may be summed up in the following particulars: (1.) That there would be those, perhaps in considerable numbers, who would openly claim to be the Christ, or the true Messiah, Matt. xxiv. 5, 24. (2.) That there would be a spirit, which would manifest itself early in the church, that would strongly tend to some great apostasy under some one head or leader, or to a concentration on an individual, or a succession of individuals, who would have eminently the spirit of antichrist, though for a time the developement of that spirit would be hindered or restrained. See Notes, 2 Thess. ii. 1-7. (3.) That this would be ultimately concentrated on a single leader—'the man of sin'—and embodied under some great apostasy, at the head of which would be that 'man of sin,' 2 Thess. ii. 3, 4, 8, 9, 10. It is to this that *Paul* particularly refers, or this is the view which he took of this apostacy, and it is this which *he* particularly describes. (4.) That, in the mean time, and before the elements of the great apostasy should be concentrated and embodied, there might not be a few who would partake of the same general spirit, and who would be equally opposed to Christ in their doctrines and aims; that is, who would embody in themselves the essential spirit of antichrist, and by whose appearing it might be known that the last dispensation had come. It is to these that *John* refers, and these he found in his own age. *Paul* fixed the eye on future times, when the spirit of antichrist should be embodied under a distinct and mighty organization; *John* on his own time, and found then essentially what it had been predicted would occur in the church. He here says that they had been taught to expect that antichrist would come under the last dispensation; and it is implied that it could be ascertained that it was the last time, from the fact that the predicted opposer of Christ had come. The reference is probably to the language of the Saviour, that before the end should be, and as a sign

that it was coming, many would arise claiming to be Christ, and, of course, practically denying that he was the Christ. Matt. xxiv. 5, 'Many shall come in my name, saying, *I am Christ*; and shall deceive many.' Ver. 24, 'And there shall arise false Christs, and false prophets; and they shall show great signs and wonders, insomuch that, if it were possible, they shall deceive the very elect.' This prediction it is probable the apostles had referred to wherever they had preached, so that there was a general expectation that one or more persons would appear claiming to be the Christ, or maintaining such opinions as to be inconsistent with the true doctrine that Jesus was the Messiah. Such persons, John says, had then in fact appeared, by which it could be known that they were living under the closing dispensations of the world referred to by the Saviour. Comp. Notes, 2 Thess. ii. 2-5. ¶ *Even now are there many antichrists.* There are many who have the characteristics which it was predicted that antichrist would have; that is, as explained above, there are many who deny that Jesus is the Messiah, or who deny that he has come in the flesh. If they maintained that Jesus was an impostor and not the true Messiah, or if, though they admitted that the Messiah had come, they affirmed, as the *Docetæ* did, (Note on chap. iv. 2,) that he had come in *appearance* only, and not really come in the flesh, this was the spirit of antichrist. John says that there were many such persons in fact in his time. It would seem from this that John did not refer to a single individual, or to a succession of individuals who should come previous to the winding up of the affairs of the world, as Paul did, (2 Thess. ii. 2, seq.,) but that he understood that there might be many at the same time who would evince the spirit of antichrist. Both he and Paul, however, refer to the expectation that before the coming of the Saviour to judge the world there would be prominent adversaries of the Christian religion, and that the end would not come until such adversaries appeared. Paul goes more into detail, and describes the characteristics of the great apostasy more at length, (2 Thess. ii. 2, seq.; 1

19 They went out from us, but they were not of us: for *a* if they had been of us, they would *no doubt* have continued with us: but *they went out*, that they might be made manifest *b* that they were not all of us.

a 2 Ti.2.19.   *b* 2 Ti.3.9.

Tim. iv. 1, seq.; 2 Tim. iii. 1, seq.;) John says, not that the appearing of these persons indicated that the end of the world was near, but that they had such characteristics as to show that they were living in the last dispensation. Paul so describes them as to show that the end of the world was not to be immediately expected, (Notes, 2 Thess. ii. 1, seq.;) John, without referring to that point, says that there were enough of that character then to prove that the last dispensation had come, though he does not say how long it would continue. ¶ *Whereby we know it is the last time.* They have the characteristics which it was predicted many would have before the end of the world should come. The evidence that it was 'the last time,' or the closing dispensation of the world, derived from the appearing of these persons, consists simply in the fact that it was predicted that such persons would appear under the Christian, or the last dispensation, Matt. xxiv. 5, 24–27. Their appearance was to precede the coming of the Saviour, though it is not said *how long* it would precede that; but at any time the appearing of such persons would be an evidence that it was the closing dispensation of the world, for the Saviour, in his predictions respecting them, had said that they would appear before he should return to judgment. It cannot now be determined precisely to what classes of persons there is reference here, because we know too little of the religious state of the times to which the apostle refers. No one can prove, however, that there were *not* persons at that time who so fully corresponded to the predictions of the Saviour as to be a complete fulfilment of what he said, and to demonstrate that the last age had truly come. It would seem probable that there may have been reference to some Jewish adversaries, who denied that Jesus was the Messiah, (*Rob. Lex.*,) or to some persons who had already broached the doctrine of the *Docetæ*, that though Jesus was the Mes-

siah, yet that he was a man in appearance only, and had not really come in the flesh. Classes of persons of each description abounded in the early ages of the church.

19. *They went out from us.* From the church. That is, they had once been professors of the religion of the Saviour, though their apostasy showed that they never had any true piety. John refers to the fact that they had once been in the church, perhaps to remind those to whom he wrote that they knew them well, and could readily appreciate their character. It was a humiliating statement that those who showed themselves to be so utterly opposed to religion had once been members of the Christian church; but this is a statement which we are often compelled to make. ¶ *But they were not of us.* That is, they did not really belong to us, or were not true Christians. See Notes, Matt. vii. 23. This passage proves that these persons, whatever their pretensions and professions may have been, were never sincere Christians. The same remark may be made of all who apostatize from the faith, and become teachers of error. They never were truly converted; never belonged really to the spiritual church of Christ. ¶ *For if they had been of us.* If they had been sincere and true Christians. ¶ *They would* no doubt *have continued with us.* The words '*no doubt*' are supplied by our translators, but the affirmation is equally strong without them: 'they would have remained with us.' This affirms, without any ambiguity or qualification, that if they had been true Christians they *would* have remained in the church; that is, they would not have apostatized. There could not be a more positive affirmation than that which is implied here, that those who are true Christians will continue to be such; or that the saints will not fall away from grace. John affirms it of these persons, that if they had been true Christians they would

never have departed from the church. He makes the declaration so general that it may be regarded as a universal truth, that if *any* are truly ' of us,' that is, if they are true Christians, they will continue in the church, or will never fall away. The statement is so made also as to teach that if any *do* fall away from the church, the fact is full proof that they never had any religion, for if they had had they would have remained steadfast in the church. ¶ *But* they went out, *that they might be made manifest that they were not all of us.* It was suffered or permitted in the providence of God that this should occur, *in order* that it might be seen and known that they were not true Christians, or in order that their real character might be developed. It was desirable that this should be done, (*a*,) in order that the church might be purified from their influence—comp. Notes, John xv. 2 ; (*b*) in order that it might not be responsible for their conduct, or reproached on account of it ; (*c*) in order that their real character might be developed, and they might themselves see that they were not true Christians ; (*d*) in order that, being seen and known as apostates, their opinions and conduct might have less influence than if they were connected with the church ; (*e*) in order that they might themselves understand their own true character, and no longer live under the delusive opinion that they were Christians and were safe, but that, seeing themselves in their true light, they might be brought to repentance. For there is only a most slender prospect that any who are deceived *in* the church will ever be brought to true repentance there ; and slight as is the hope that one who apostatizes will be, such an event is much more probable than it would be if he remained in the church. Men are more likely to be converted when their character is known and understood, than they are when playing a game of deception, or are themselves deceived. What is here affirmed of these persons often occurs now ; and those who have no true religion are often suffered to apostatize from their profession for the same purposes. It is better that they should

cease to have any connection with the church than that they should remain in it ; and God often suffers them to fall away even from the profession of religion, in order that they may not do injury as professing Christians. This very important passage, then, teaches the following things : (1.) That when men apostatize from the profession of religion, and embrace fatal error, or live in sin, it proves that they never had any true piety. (2.) The fact that such persons fall away cannot be adduced to prove that Christians ever fall from grace, for it demonstrates nothing on that point, but proves only that these persons never had any real piety. They may have had much that seemed to be religion; they may have been zealous, and apparently devoted to God, and may even have had much comfort and peace in what they took to be piety; they may have been eminently ' gifted' in prayer, or may have even been successful preachers of the gospel, but all this does not prove that they ever had any piety, nor does the fact that such persons apostatize from their profession throw any light on a question quite foreign to this—whether true Christians ever fall from grace. Comp. Matt. vii. 22, 23. (3.) The passage before us proves that if any are true Christians they will remain in the church, or will certainly persevere and be saved. They may indeed backslide grievously; they may wander far away, and pain the hearts of their brethren, and give occasion to the enemies of religion to speak reproachfully; but the apostle says, ' if they had been of us, they would have continued with us.' (4.) One of the best evidences of true piety is found in the fact of continuing with the church. I do not mean nominally and formally, but really and spiritually, having the heart with the church ; loving its peace and promoting its welfare ; identifying ourselves with real Christians, and showing that we are ready to co-operate with those who love the Lord Jesus and its cause. (5.) The main reason why professing Christians are suffered to apostatize is to show that they had no true religion. It is desirable that they should see it themselves; desirable that others should

20 But ye have an unction *a* from the Holy One, and ye know *b* all things.

see it also. It is better that it should be known that they had no true religion than that they should remain in the church to be a burden on its movements, and a reproach to the cause. By being allowed thus to separate themselves from the church, they *may* be brought to remember their violated vows, and the church will be free from the reproach of having those in its bosom who are a dishonour to the Christian name. We are not to wonder, then, if persons apostatize who have been professors of true religion; and we are not to suppose that the greatest injury is done to the cause when they do it. A *greater* injury by far is done when such persons remain in the church.

20. *But ye have an unction from the Holy One.* The apostle in this verse evidently intends to say that he had no apprehension in regard to those to whom he wrote that *they* would thus apostatize, and bring dishonour on their religion. They had been so anointed by the Holy Spirit that they understood the true nature of religion, and it might be confidently expected that they would persevere. The word *unction* or *anointing* (χρίσμα) means, properly, 'something rubbed in or ointed;' oil for anointing, *ointment;* then it means an anointing. The allusion is to the anointing of kings and priests, or their inauguration or coronation, (1 Sam. x. 1; xvi. 13; Exod. xxviii. 41; xl. 15; comp. Notes on Matt. i. 1;) and the idea seems to have been that the oil thus used was emblematic of the gifts and graces of the Holy Spirit as qualifying them for the discharge of the duties of their office. Christians, in the New Testament, are described as 'kings and priests,' (Rev. i. 6; v. 10,) and as a 'royal priesthood,' (Notes, 1 Pet. ii. 5, 9;) and hence they are represented as *anointed,* or as endowed with those graces of the Spirit, of which anointing was the emblem. The phrase 'the Holy One' refers here, doubtless, to the Holy Spirit, that Spirit whose influences are imparted to the people of God, to enlighten, to sanctify, and to comfort them in their trials. The particular reference here is to the influences of that Spirit as giving them clear and just views of the nature of religion, and thus securing them from error and apostasy. ¶ *And ye know all things.* That is, all things which it is essential that you should know on the subject of religion. See Notes, John xvi. 13; 1 Cor. ii. 15. The meaning cannot be that they knew all things pertaining to history, to science, to literature, and to the arts; but that, under the influences of the Holy Spirit, they had been made so thoroughly acquainted with the truths and duties of the Christian religion, that they might be regarded as safe from the danger of fatal error. The same may be said of all true Christians now, that they are so taught by the Spirit of God, that they have a practical acquaintance with what religion is, and with what it requires, and are secure from falling into fatal error. In regard to the general meaning of this verse, then, it may be observed : I. That it does *not* mean any one of the following things: (1.) That Christians are literally instructed by the Holy Spirit in *all* things, or that they literally understand all subjects. The teaching, whatever it may be, refers only to religion. (2.) It is not meant that any new faculties of mind are conferred on them, or any increased intellectual endowments, by their religion. It is not a fact that Christians, as such, are superior in mental endowments to others; nor that by their religion they have any mental traits which they had not before their conversion. Paul, Peter, and John had essentially the same mental characteristics after their conversion which they had before; and the same is true of all Christians. (3.) It is not meant that any new truth is revealed to the mind by the Holy Spirit. All the truth that is brought before the mind of the Christian is to be found in the word of God, and *revelation,* as such, was completed when the Bible was finished. (4.) It is not meant that anything is perceived by Christians which they had not the natural faculty for

21 I have not written unto you because ye know not the truth, but

because ye know it, and that no lie is of the truth.

perceiving before their conversion, or which other men have not also the natural faculty for perceiving. The difficulty with men is not a defect of natural faculties, it is in the blindness of the heart. II. The statement here made by John *does* imply, it is supposed, the following things: (1.) That the minds of Christians are so enlightened that they have a new perception of the truth. They see it in a light in which they did not before. They see it *as* truth. They see its beauty, its force, its adaptedness to their condition and wants. They understand the subject of religion better than they once did, and better than others do. What was once dark appears now plain; what once had no beauty to their minds now appears beautiful; what was once repellant is now attractive. (2.) They see this *to be* true; that is, they see it in such a light that they cannot doubt that it *is* true. They have such views of the doctrines of religion, that they have no doubt that they are true, and are willing on the belief of their truth to lay down their lives, and stake their eternal interests. (3.) Their knowledge of truth is enlarged. They become acquainted with *more* truths than they would have known if they had not been under the teaching of the Holy Spirit. Their range of thought is greater; their vision more extended, as well as more clear. III. The *evidence* that this is so is found in the following things: (1.) The express statements of Scripture. See 1 Cor. ii. 14, 15, and the Notes on that passage. Comp. John xvi. 13, 14. (2.) It is a matter of fact that it is so. (*a*) Men by nature do not perceive any beauty in the truths of religion. They are distasteful to them, or they are repulsive and offensive. 'The doctrine of the cross is to the Jew a stumbling-block, and to the Greek foolishness.' They may see indeed the force of an argument, but they do not see the beauty of the way of salvation. (*b*) When they are converted they do. These things appear to them to be changed, and they see them in a new light, and perceive a beauty in them which they never did

before. (*c*) There is often a surprising *developement* of religious knowledge when persons are converted. They seem to understand the way of salvation, and the whole subject of religion, in a manner and to an extent which cannot be accounted for, except on the supposition of a teaching from above. (*d*) This is manifest also in the knowledge which persons otherwise ignorant exhibit on the subject of religion. With few advantages for education, and with no remarkable talents, they show an acquaintance with the truth, a knowledge of religion, an ability to defend the doctrines of Christianity, and to instruct others in the way of salvation, which could have been derived only from some source superior to themselves. Comp John vii. 15; Acts iv. 13. (*e*) The same thing is shown by their *adherence to truth* in the midst of persecution, and simply because they perceive that for which they die to be the truth. And is there anything incredible in this? May not the mind see what truth is? How do we judge of an axiom in mathematics, or of a proposition that is demonstrated, but by the fact that the mind *perceives* it to be true, and cannot doubt it? And may it not be so in regard to religious truth—especially when that truth is seen to accord with what we know of ourselves, our lost condition as sinners, and our need of a Saviour, and when we see that the truths revealed in the Scriptures are exactly adapted to our wants?

[See also the Supplementary Note under 1 Cor. ii. 14.]

21. *I have not written unto you because ye know not the truth.* You are not to regard my writing to you in this earnest manner as any evidence that I do not suppose you to be acquainted with religion and its duties. Some, perhaps, might have been disposed to put this construction on what he had said, but he assures them that that was not the reason why he had thus addressed them. The very fact that they *did* understand the subject of religion, he says, was rather the reason why he

22 Who is a liar, but he that *a* denieth that Jesus is the Christ? He is antichrist, that denieth the Father and the Son.

a 1 Jn.4.3.

wrote to them. ¶ *But because ye know it.* This was the ground of his hope that his appeal would be effectual. If they had never known what religion was, if they were ignorant of its nature and its claims, he would have had much less hope of being able to guard them against error, and of securing their steady walk in the path of piety. We may always make a strong and confident appeal to those who really understand what the nature of religion is, and what are the evidences of its truth. ¶ *And that no lie is of the truth.* No form of error, however plausible it may appear, however ingeniously it may be defended, and however much it may seem to be favourable to human virtue and happiness, can be founded in truth. What the apostle says here has somewhat the aspect of a truism, but it contains a real truth of vital importance, and one which should have great influence in determining our minds in regard to any proposed opinion or doctrine. Error often appears plausible. It seems to be adapted to relieve the mind of many difficulties which perplex and embarrass it on the subject of religion. It seems to be adapted to promote religion. It seems to make those who embrace it happy, and for a time they apparently enjoy religion. But John says that however plausible all this may be, however much it may seem to prove that the doctrines thus embraced are of God, it is a great and vital maxim that *no* error can have its foundation in truth, and, of course, that it must be worthless. The grand question is, *what is truth;* and when that is determined, we can easily settle the inquiries which come up about the various doctrines that are abroad in the world. Mere plausible appearances, or temporary good results that may grow out of a doctrine, do not prove that it is based on truth; for whatever those results may be, it is impossible that any error, however plausible, should have its origin in the truth.

22. *Who is a liar.* That is, who is false; who maintains an erroneous doctrine; who is an impostor, if he is not?

The object of the apostle is to specify one of the prevailing forms of error, and to show that, however plausible the arguments might be by which it was defended, it was impossible that it should be true. Their own knowledge of the nature of religion must convince them at once that this opinion was false. ¶ *That denieth that Jesus is the Christ.* It would seem that the apostle referred to a class who admitted that Jesus lived, but who denied that he was the true Messiah. On what grounds they did this is unknown : but to maintain this was, of course, the same as to maintain that he was an impostor. The ground taken may have been that he had not the characteristics ascribed to the Messiah in the prophets; or that he did not furnish evidence that he was sent from God; or that he was an enthusiast. Or perhaps some peculiar form of error may be referred to, like that which is said to have been held by Corinthus, who in his doctrine separated Jesus from Christ, maintaining them to be two distinct persons.—*Doddridge.* ¶ *He is antichrist.* Notes, ver. 18. He has all the characteristics and attributes of antichrist ; or, a doctrine which practically involves the denial of both the Father and the Son, must be that of antichrist. ¶ *That denieth the Father and the Son.* That denies the peculiar truths pertaining to God the Father, and to the Son of God. The charge here is not that they entertained incorrect views of God *as such*—as almighty, eternal, most wise, and good ; but that they denied the doctrines which religion taught respecting God *as* Father and Son. Their opinions tended to a denial of what was revealed respecting God as a Father—not in the general sense of being the *Father* of the universe, but in the particular sense of his relation to the Son. It cannot be supposed that they denied the existence and perfections of God as such, nor that they denied that God is a *Father* in the relation which he sustains to the universe ; but the meaning must be that what they held went to a practical

23 Whosoever *a* denieth the Son, the same hath not the Father: [*but*] *he that acknowledgeth the Son, hath the Father also.*

24 Let *b* that therefore abide in you, which ye have heard from the beginning.   If that which ye have

heard from the beginning shall remain in you, ye also shall continue in the Son, and in the Father.

25 And this is the promise that he hath promised us, *even* eternal *c* life.

a Jn.15.23.   *b* 2 Jn.6.   *c* Jn.17.3.

denial of that which is peculiar to the true God, considered as sustaining the relation of a Father to his Son Jesus Christ.   Correct views of the Father could not be held without correct views of the Son ; correct views of the Son could not be held without correct views of the Father.   The doctrines respecting the Father and the Son were so connected that one could not be held without holding the other, and one could not be denied without denying the other. Compare Notes, Matt. xi. 27 ; John v. 23.   No man can have just views of God the Father who has not right apprehensions of the Son.   As a matter of fact in the world, men have right apprehensions of God only when they have correct views of the character of the Lord Jesus Christ.

23. *Whosoever denieth the Son, the same hath not the Father.*   That is, has no just views of the Father, and has no evidence of his friendship.   It is only by the Son of God that the Father is made known to men, (Matt. xi. 27 ; Heb. i. 2, 3,) and it is only through him that we can become reconciled to God, and obtain evidence of his favour. Notes on John v. 23.   ¶ *But he that acknowledges the Son, hath the Father also.* This passage, in the common version of the New Testament, is printed in Italics, as if it were not in the original, but was supplied by the translators.   It is true that it is not found in all the MSS. and versions ; but it is found in a large number of MSS., and in the Vulgate, the Syriac, the Æthiopic, the Coptic, the Armenian, and the Arabic versions, and in the critical editions of Griesbach, Tittmann, and Hahn.   It is probable, therefore, that it should be regarded as a genuine portion of the sacred text.   It is much in the style of John, and though not necessary to complete the sense, yet it well suits the connection.   As it was true that if one denied the Son of God

he could have no pretensions to any proper acquaintance with the Father, so it seemed to follow that if any one had any proper knowledge of the Son of God, and made a suitable confession of him, he had evidence that he was acquainted with the Father.   Compare John xvii. 3 ; Rom. x. 9.   Though, therefore, this passage was wanting in many of the MSS. consulted by the translators of the Bible, and though in printing it in the manner in which they have they showed the great caution with which they acted in admitting anything doubtful into their translation, yet this passage should be restored to the text, and be regarded as a genuine portion of the word of God.   The great truth can never be too clearly stated, or too often inculcated, that it is only by a knowledge of the Lord Jesus Christ that we can have any true acquaintance with God, and that all who have just views of the Saviour are in fact acquainted with the true God, and are heirs of eternal life.

24. *Let that therefore abide in you.* Adhere steadfastly to it ; let the truth obtain a permanent lodgement in the soul.   In view of its great importance, and its influence on your happiness here and hereafter, let it never depart from you.   ¶ *Which ye have heard from the beginning.*   That is, the same doctrines which you have always been taught respecting the Son of God and the way or salvation.   Notes, ver. 7.   ¶ *Ye also shall continue in the Son, and in the Father.*   Truly united to the Son and to the Father ; or having evidence of the favour and friendship of the Son and the Father.

25. *And this is the promise that he hath promised us,* even *eternal life.* This is evidently added to encourage them in adhering to the truths which they had embraced respecting the Son of God.   In maintaining these truths they had the promise of eternal life ; in

26 These *things* have I written unto you concerning them that seduce you.

27 But the anointing which ye have received of him abideth in you, and ye need not that any man teach you: but as the same anointing teacheth *a* you of all things, and is truth, and is no lie, and even as it hath taught you, ye shall abide in ¹ him.

28 And now, little children, abide in him; that, when he shall appear,

a Jn.14.26.　　　1 Or, *it.*

departing from them they had none, for the *promise* of heaven in our world is made only to those who embrace one class of doctrines or opinions. No one can show that any *promise* of heaven is made to the mere possessor of beauty, or wealth, or talent; to the accomplished or the gay; to those who are distinguished for science, or skill in the arts; to rank, or birth, or blood; to courage or strength. Whatever expectation of heaven any one may entertain on account of any of these things, must be traced to something else than a *promise*, for there is none in the Bible to that effect. The *promise* of heaven to men is limited to those who repent of their sins, who believe in the Lord Jesus Christ, and who lead a holy life; and if any one will base his hope of heaven *on a promise*, it must be limited to these things. And yet what well-founded hope of heaven *can* there be, except that which is based *on a promise?* How does any one know that he can be saved, unless he has some assurance from God that it may and shall be so? Is not heaven his home? How does any one know that he may dwell there, without some assurance from him that he may? Is not the crown of life his gift? How can any one know that he will possess it, unless he has some promise from him? However men may reason, or conjecture, or hope, the only *promise* of eternal life is found in the Bible; and the fact that we have such a promise should surely be a sufficient inducement to us to hold fast the truth. On the promise of life in the gospel, see John xvii. 2; Rom. ii. 6, 7; Mark xvi. 16; Matt. xxv. 46.

26. *These* things *have I written unto* you concerning them that *seduce you.* Respecting their character, and in order to guard you against their arts. The word *seduce* means to lead astray; and it here refers to those who would seduce them *from the truth,* or lead them into dangerous error. The apostle does not mean that they had actually seduced them, for he states in the following verse that they were yet safe; but he refers to the fact that there was danger that they might be led into error.

27. *But the anointing which ye have received of him.* See Notes on ver. 20. ¶ *Abideth in you.* The meaning is, that the influence on your heart and life, which results from the fact that you are anointed of God, permanently abides with you, and will keep you from dangerous error. The apostle evidently meant to say that he felt assured that they would not be seduced from the truth, and that his confidence in regard to this was placed in the fact that they had been truly anointed unto God as kings and priests. Thus understood, what he here says is equivalent to the expression of a firm conviction that those who are true Christians will not fall away. Comp. Notes on vers. 19, 20. ¶ *And ye need not that any man teach you.* That is, what are the things essential to true religion. See Notes on ver. 20. ¶ *But as the same anointing teacheth you of all things.* This cannot mean that the mere act of *anointing,* if that had been performed in their case, would *teach* them; but it refers to what John includes in what he calls the anointing—that is, in the solemn consecrating to the duties of religion under the influences of the Holy Spirit. ¶ *And is truth, and is no lie.* Leads to truth, and not to error. No man was ever led into error by those influences which result from the fact that he has been consecrated to the service of God. ¶ *Ye shall abide in him.* Marg., 'or *it.*' The Greek will bear either construction. The connection, however, seems to demand that it should be understood as referring to *him* —that is, to the Saviour.

28. *And now, little children.* Notes,

we may have confidence, and not be ashamed before him at his coming. 29 If ye know that he is righ-

teous, [1] ye know that *a* every one that doeth righteousness is born of him.

1 Or, *know ye.*

a Je.13. 23; Mat.7.16-18.

ver. 1. ¶ *Abide in him; that, when he shall appear.* In the end of the world, to receive his people to himself. Notes, John xiv. 2, 3. ¶ *We may have confidence.* Greek, *boldness—παῤῥησίαν.* This word is commonly used to denote openness, plainness, or boldness in speaking, Mark viii. 32; John vii. 4, 13, 26; Acts ii. 29; iv. 13, 29; 2 Cor. iii. 12; vii. 4. Here it means the kind of boldness, or calm assurance, which arises from evidence of piety, and of preparation for heaven. It means that they would not be overwhelmed and confounded at the coming of the Saviour, by its being then found that all their hopes were fallacious. ¶ *And not be ashamed before him at his coming.* By having all our hopes taken away; by being held up to the universe as guilty and condemned. We feel ashamed when our hopes are disappointed; when it is shown that we have a character different from what we professed to have; when our pretensions to goodness are stripped off, and the heart is made bare. Many will thus be ashamed in the last day, (Matt. vii. 21–23;) but it is one of the promises made to those who truly believe on the Saviour, that they shall never be ashamed or confounded. See Notes on 1 Pet. ii. 6. Comp. Isa. xlv. 17; Rom. v. 5; 1 Pet. iv. 16; Mark viii. 38.

29. *If ye know that he is righteous.* This is not said as if there could be any doubt on the subject, but merely to call their attention to it as a well-known truth, and to state what followed from it. Every one who has any true acquaintance with God, must have the fullest conviction that he is a righteous Being. But, if this be so, John says, then it must follow that only those who are truly righteous can regard themselves as begotten of him. ¶ *Ye know.* Marg., *know ye.* The Greek will bear either construction, and either would make good sense. Assuming that God is righteous, it would be proper to state, as in the text, that it followed from this that they must know that only those who are righteous can be regarded as

begotten of him; or, assuming this to be true, it was proper to exhort them *to be* righteous, as in the margin. Whichever interpretation is adopted, the great truth is taught, that only those who are truly righteous can regard themselves as the children of God. ¶ *That every one that doeth righteousness is born of him.* Or rather, is *begotten* of him; is truly a child of God. This truth is everywhere taught in the Bible, and is worthy of being often repeated. No one who is not, in the proper sense of the term, a righteous man, can have any well-founded pretensions to being regarded as a child of God. If this be so, then it is not difficult to determine whether we are the children of God. (1.) If we are unjust, false, dishonest, we cannot be his children. (2.) If we are indulging in any known sin, we cannot be. (3.) If we are not truly righteous, all visions and rapture, all zeal and ardour, though in the cause of religion, all that we may pride ourselves on in being fervent in prayer, or eloquent in preaching, is vain. (4.) If we *are* righteous, in the true and proper sense, doing that which is *right* toward God and toward men, to ourselves, to our families, to our neighbours, to the world at large, to the Saviour who died for us, then we are true Christians; and then, no matter how soon he may appear, or how solemn and overwhelming the scenes that shall close the world, we shall not be ashamed or confounded, for we shall hail him as our Saviour, and rejoice that the time has come that we may go and dwell with him for ever.

CHAPTER III.

ANALYSIS OF THE CHAPTER.

This chapter embraces the following subjects :—

I. The fact that Christians are now the sons of God, vers. 1-3. (1.) We are the sons of God, and this will explain the reason why the world does not appreciate our character, or understand the reasons of our conduct, ver. 1. (2.) The consequences of sustaining that re-

CHAPTER III.

BEHOLD, what manner of love ^a the Father hath bestowed upon us, that we should be called the sons ^b of God ! therefore the world ^c knoweth us not, because it knew him not.

a Ep.2.4,5.   b Jn.1.12; Re.21.7.   c Jn.17.23.

lation to God, or of being regarded as his sons. (a) We shall be like him when he appears, ver. 2. (b) We shall purify ourselves under the influence of this hope, ver. 3.

II. The fact that he who is an adopted child of God does not commit sin, vers. 4–10. (1.) All sin is the transgression of the law, ver. 4; (2.) Christ was manifested to take away our sins, ver. 5; (3.) he that commits sin is of the devil, ver. 8; and, (4.) as a matter of fact, he who is of God does *not* commit sin, vers. 7, 9, 10.

III. True religion will be manifested by love to the Christian brotherhood, vers. 10–18. (1.) As a man who is not righteous cannot be a true Christian, neither can he who does not love his brother, ver. 10. (2.) It is the solemn command of the Saviour that his followers should love one another, ver. 11. (3.) The importance of this is seen by the opposite conduct of Cain, ver. 12. (4.) Love to the brethren furnishes the most certain evidence that we have passed from death unto life, ver. 14. (5.) A man who hates another is in fact a murderer, and, of course, cannot be a true child of God, ver. 15. (6.) We should be stimulated to the love of the brethren by the example of the Saviour, who laid down his life for us, ver. 16. (7.) If we see a brother in want, and have the means of aiding him, and do not do it, we cannot have the love of God dwelling in us, vers. 17, 18.

IV. We may have evidence that we love God by the consciousness of our feelings towards him, as well as by outward acts towards his friends, vers. 19–21.

V. If we keep his commandments our prayers will be answered, vers. 22, 23. (1.) There is an assurance that we shall receive what we need if we ask it, and keep his commandments, ver. 22. (2.) The particular commandments on which the efficacy of prayer so much depends, are (a) that we believe on the name of the Saviour, and (b) that we love the Christian brotherhood, ver. 23.

VI. We may know that we abide in God by the spirit which he has given us, as well as by keeping his commandments, ver. 24.

This chapter, therefore, is occupied mainly with stating what are the evidences of true piety; and, in order to determine this question, there is perhaps no part of the Bible that may be studied with more profit than this portion of the writings of John.

1. *Behold, what manner of love.* What love, in *kind* and in *degree.* In *kind* the most tender and the most ennobling, in adopting us into his family, and in permitting us to address him as our Father ; in *degree* the most exalted, since there is no higher love that can be shown than in adopting a poor and friendless orphan, and giving him a parent and a home. Even God could bestow upon us no more valuable token of affection than that we should be adopted into his family, and permitted to regard him as our Father. When we remember how insignificant we are as creatures, and how ungrateful, rebellious, and vile we have been as sinners, we may well be amazed at the love which would adopt us into the holy family of God, so that we may be regarded and treated as the children of the Most High. A prince could manifest no higher love for a wandering, ragged, vicious orphan boy, found in the streets, than by adopting him into his own family, and admitting him to the same privileges and honours as his own sons ; and yet this would be a trifle compared with the honour which God has bestowed on us. ¶ *The Father hath bestowed upon us.* God, regarded as a Father, or as at the head of the universe considered as one family. ¶ *That we should be called the sons of God.* That is, that we should be the sons of God—the word *called* being often used in the sense of *to be.* On the nature and privileges of adoption, see Notes, Rom. viii. 15–17, and 2 Cor. vi. 18, and practical remarks on that chapter, 19 20 ¶ *Therefore the*

2 Beloved, now are we the sons *a* of God; and it doth not yet appear what we shall be: but we know that, when he shall appear, we shall be

a Ro.8.14,18.   *b* 1 Co.15.49; Phi.3.21; 2 Pe.1.4.
c Job 19.26; Ps.17.15; Mat.5.8: 1 Co.13.12.

like him; *b* for we shall see *c* him as he is.

3 And every man that hath this hope in him purifieth himself, even as he is pure.

world knoweth us not. Does not understand our principles; the reasons of our conduct; the sources of our comforts and joys. The people of the world regard us as fanatics or enthusiasts; as foolish in abandoning the pleasures and pursuits which they engage in; as renouncing certain happiness for that which is uncertain; as cherishing false and delusive hopes in regard to the future, and as practising needless austerities, with nothing to compensate for the pleasures which are abandoned. There is nothing which the gay, the ambitious, and the selfish *less* understand than they do the elements which go into the Christian's character, and the nature and source of the Christian's joys. ¶ *Because it knew him not.* Did not know the Lord Jesus Christ. That is, the world had no right views of the real character of the Lord Jesus when he was on the earth. They mistook him for an enthusiast or an impostor; and it is no wonder that, having wholly mistaken his character, they should mistake ours. On the fact that the world did not know him, see Notes, 1 Cor. ii. 8; Acts iii. 17. Comp. John xvii. 25. On the fact that Christians may be expected to be regarded and treated as their Saviour was, see Notes on John xv. 18–20. Comp. Matt. x. 24, 25.

2. *Beloved, now are we the sons of God.* We now in fact sustain this rank and dignity, and on that we may reflect with pleasure and gratitude. It is in itself an exalted honour, and may be contemplated as such, whatever may be true in regard to what is to come. · In the dignity and the privileges which we now enjoy, we may find a grateful subject of reflection, and a cause of thankfulness, even if we should look to nothing beyond, or when we contemplate the fact by itself. ¶ *And it doth not yet appear what we shall be.* It is not fully revealed what we shall be hereafter; what will be the full result of being regarded as the children of

God. There are, indeed, certain things which may be inferred as following from this. There is enough to animate us with hope, and to sustain us in the trials of life. There is *one* thing which is clear, that we shall be like the Son of God; but what is fully involved in this is not made known. Perhaps (1) it could not be so revealed that we could understand it, for that. state may be so unlike the present that no words would fully convey the conception to our minds. Perhaps (2) it may be necessary to our condition here, as on probation, that no more light should be furnished in regard to the future than to stimulate us to make efforts to reach a world where all is light. For an illustration of the sentiment expressed here by the apostle, comp. Notes on 2 Pet. i. 4. ¶ *But we know that, when he shall appear, we shall be like him.* It is revealed to us that we shall be made like Christ; that is, in the bodies with which we shall be raised up, in character, in happiness, in glory. Comp. Notes, Phil. iii. 21; 2 Cor. iii. 18. This is enough to satisfy the Christian in his prospects for the future world. To be like Christ is the object of his supreme aim. For that he lives, and all his aspirations in regard to the coming world may be summed up in this—that he wishes to be like the glorified Son of God, and to share his honours and his joys. See Notes, Phil. iii. 10. ¶ *For we shall see him as he is.* It is clearly implied here that there will be an influence in beholding the Saviour as he is, which will tend to make us like him, or to transform us into his likeness. See the nature of this influence explained in the Notes on 2 Cor. iii. 18.

3. *And every man that hath this hope in him.* This hope of seeing the Saviour, and of being made like him; that is, every true Christian. On the nature and influence of hope, see Notes on Rom. viii. 24, 25. ¶ *Purifieth him-*

4 Whosoever committeth sin transgresseth also the law: for sin is the transgression of the law.

self. Makes himself holy. That is, under the influence of this hope of being like the Saviour, he puts forth those efforts in struggling against sin, and in overcoming his evil propensities, which are necessary to make him pure. The apostle would not deny that for the success of these efforts we are dependent on Divine aid ; but he brings into view, as is often done in the sacred writings, the agency of man himself as essentially connected with success. Comp. Phil. ii. 12. The particular thought here is, that the hope of being like Christ, and of being permitted to dwell with him, will lead a man to earnest efforts to become holy, and will be actually followed by such a result. ¶ *Even as he is pure.* The same *kind* of purity here, the same *degree* hereafter. That is, the tendency of such a hope is to make him holy now, though he may be imperfect ; the effect will be to make him *perfectly* holy in the world to come. It cannot be shown from this passage that the apostle meant to teach that any one actually becomes as pure in the present life as the Saviour is, that is, becomes perfectly holy ; for all that is fairly implied in it, is, that those who have this hope in them *aim* at the same purity, and will *ultimately* obtain it. But the apostle does not say that it is attained in this world. If the passage *did* teach this, it would teach it respecting *every one* who has this hope, and then the doctrine would be that no one can be a Christian who does not become absolutely perfect on earth ; that is, not that some Christians *may* become perfect here, but that all actually *do.* But none, it is presumed, will hold this to be a true doctrine. A true Christian does not, indeed, habitually and wilfully sin ; but no one can pretend that all Christians attain to a state of sinless perfection on earth, or are, in fact, *as pure* as the Saviour was. But unless the passage proves that *every* Christian becomes absolutely perfect in the present life, it does not prove that in fact *any* do. It proves (1) that the tendency, or the fair influence of this hope, **is to** make the Christian pure ; (2)

that all who cherish it will, in fact, *aim* to become as holy as the Saviour was ; and (3) that this object will, at some future period, be accomplished. There is a world where all who are redeemed shall be perfectly holy.

4. *Whosoever committeth sin transgresseth also the law.* The law of God given to man as a rule of life. The object of the apostle here is to excite them to holiness, and to deter them from committing sin, perhaps in view of the fact stated in ver. 3, that every one who has the hope of heaven will aim to be holy like the Saviour. To confirm this, he shows them that, as a matter of fact, those who are born of God *do* lead lives of obedience, (vers. 5—10 ;) and this he introduces by showing what is the nature of sin, in the verse before us. The considerations by which he would deter them from indulging in sin are the following : (*a*) all sin is a violation of the law of God, ver. 4 ; (*b*) the very object of the coming of Christ was to deliver men from sin, ver. 5 ; (*c*) those who are true Christians do not habitually sin, ver. 6 ; (*d*) those who sin cannot be true Christians, but are of the devil, ver. 8; and (*e*) he who is born of God has a germ or principle of true piety in him, and cannot sin, ver. 9. It seems evident that the apostle is here combating an opinion which then existed that men might sin, and yet be true Christians, (ver. 7 ;) and he apprehended that there was danger that this opinion would become prevalent. On what *ground* this opinion was held is unknown. Perhaps it was held that all that was necessary to constitute religion was to embrace the doctrines of Christianity, or to be orthodox in the faith ; perhaps that it was not expected that men would become holy in this life, and therefore they might indulge in acts of sin ; perhaps that Christ came to modify and relax the law, and that the *freedom* which he procured for them was freedom to indulge in whatever men chose ; perhaps that, since Christians were heirs of all things, they had a right to enjoy all things ; perhaps that the passions of

men were so strong that they could not be restrained, and that therefore it was not wrong to give indulgence to the propensities with which our Creator has formed us. All these opinions have been held under various forms of Antinomianism, and it is not at all improbable that some or all of them prevailed in the time of John. The argument which he urges would be applicable to any of them. The consideration which he here states is, that all sin is a transgression of law, and that he who commits it, under whatever pretence, is to be held as a transgressor of the law. The literal rendering of this passage is, 'He who doeth sin (ἁμαρτίαν) doeth also transgression'—ἀνομίαν. Sin is the generic term embracing all that would be wrong. The word transgression (ἀνομία) is a specific term, showing where the wrong lay, to wit, in violating the law. ¶ *For sin is the transgression of the law.* That is, all sin involves this as a consequence that it is a violation of the law. The object of the apostle is not so much to define sin, as to deter from its commission by stating what is its essential nature— though he has in fact given the best definition of it that could be given. The essential idea is, that God has given a law to men to regulate their conduct, and that whatever is a departure from that law in any way is held to be sin. The law measures our duty, and measures therefore the degree of guilt when it is not obeyed. The law determines what is right in all cases, and, of course, what is wrong when it is not complied with. The law is the expression of what is the will of God as to what we shall do; and when that is not done, there is sin. The law determines what we shall love or not love; when our passions and appetites shall be bounded and restrained, and to what extent they may be indulged; what shall be our motives and aims in living; how we shall act toward God and toward men;- and whenever, in any of these respects, its requirements are not complied with, there is sin. This will include everything in relation to which the law is given, and will embrace what we *omit* to do when the law has commanded a thing to be done, as well as a

positive act of transgression where the law has forbidden a thing. This idea is properly found in the original word rendered *transgression of the law*— ἀνομία. This word occurs in the New Testament only in the following places: Matt. vii. 23; xiii. 41; xxiii. 28; xxiv. 12; Rom. iv. 7; vi. 19; 2 Thess. ii. 7; Titus ii. 14; Heb. i. 9; vili. 12; x. 17, in all which places it is rendered *iniquity* and *iniquities;* in 2 Cor. vi. 14, where it is rendered *unrighteousness ;* and in the verse before us twice. It properly means *lawlessness*, in the sense that the requirements of the law are not conformed to, or complied with; that is, either by not obeying it, or by positively violating it. When a parent commands a child to do a thing, and he does not do it, he is as really guilty of violating the law as when he does a thing which is positively forbidden. This important verse, therefore, may be considered in two aspects—as a definition of the nature of sin, and as an argument against indulgence in it, or against committing it. I. As a definition of the nature of sin. It teaches (*a*) that there is a rule of law by which the conduct of mankind is to be regulated and governed, and to which it is to be conformed. (*b*) That there is sin in all cases where that law is not complied with; and that all who do *not* comply with it are guilty before God. (*c*) That the particular thing which determines the guilt of sin, and which measures it, is that it is a departure from law, and consequently that there is no sin where there is no departure from law. The essential thing is, that the law has not been respected and obeyed, and sin derives its character and aggravation from that fact. No one can reasonably doubt as to the *accuracy* of this definition of sin. It is founded on the fact (*a*) that God has an absolute right to prescribe what we may and may not do; (*b*) that it is to be presumed that what he prescribes will be in accordance with what is right; and (*c*) that nothing else in fact constitutes sin. Sin can consist in nothing else. It does not consist of a particular height of stature, or a particular complexion; of a feeble intellect, or an intellect *made* feeble, as the

5 And ye know *a* that he was manifested to take away our sins; and in him is no sin.

a He.9.26,28.

result of any former apostasy ; of any constitutional propensity, or any disposition founded in our nature as creatures. For none of these things do our consciences condemn us; and however we may lament them, we have no consciousness of wrong.

[In these remarks the author has in view the doctrine of original sin, or imputed sin, which he thinks as absurd as sin of stature or complexion. His views will be found at large in the Notes on Rom. v. throughout, and by comparing these with the Supplementary Notes on the same place, the reader will be able to form his own opinion. There does not seem to be anything affecting the point in this passage.]

II. As an argument against the commission of sin. This argument may be considered as consisting of two things— the wrong that is done by the violation of law, and the exposure to the penalty. (1.) The wrong itself. This wrong, as an argument to deter from sin, arises mainly from two things : (*a*) because sin is a violation of the will of God, and it is in itself wrong to disregard that will ; and (*b*) because it is to be presumed that when God has given law there is a good reason why he has done it. (2.) The fact that the law has a penalty is an argument for not violating the law. All law has a penalty ; that is, there is some suffering, disadvantage, forfeit of privileges, &c., which the violation of law draws in its train, and which is to be regarded as an expression of the sense which the lawgiver entertains of the value of his law, and of the evil of disobeying it. Many of these penalties of the violation of the Divine law are seen in this life, and all will be certain to occur sooner or later, in this world or in the world to come. With such views of the law and of sin— of his obligations, and of the evils of disobedience—a Christian should not, and will not, deliberately and habitually violate the law of God.

5. *And ye know that he was manifested.* The Lord Jesus, the Son of God. ' You know that he became incarnate, or appeared among men, for the very purpose of putting an end to

sin,' Matt. i. 21. Comp. Notes, 1 Tim. iii. 16. This is the *second* argument in this paragraph, (vers. 4–10,) by which the apostle would deter us from sin. The argument is a clear one, and is perhaps the strongest that can be made to bear on the mind of a true Christian —that the Lord Jesus saw sin to be so great an evil, that he came into our world, and gave himself to the bitter sorrows of death on the cross, to redeem us from it. ¶ *To take away our sins.* The essential argument here is, that the whole work of Christ was designed to deliver us from the dominion of sin, not to furnish us the means of indulgence in it ; and that, therefore, we should be deterred from it by all that Christ has done and suffered for us. He perverts the whole design of the coming of the Saviour who supposes that his work was in any degree designed to procure for his followers the indulgences of sin, or who so interprets the methods of his grace as to suppose that it is now lawful for him to indulge his guilty passions. The argument essentially is this : (1.) That we profess to be the followers of Christ, and should carry out his ends and views in coming into the world ; (2,) that the great and leading purpose of his coming was to set us free from the bondage of transgression; (3,) that in doing this he gave himself up to a life of poverty, and shame, and sorrow, and'to a most bitter death on the cross ; and, (4,) that we should not indulge in that from which he came to deliver us, and which cost him so much toil and such a death. How could we indulge in that which has brought heavy calamity on the head of a father, or which has pierced a sister's heart with many sorrows ? Still more, how can we be so ungrateful and hardhearted as to indulge in that which crushed our Redeemer in deatl. ? ¶ *And in him is no sin.* An additional consideration to show that we should be holy. As he was perfectly pure and spotless,so should all his followers aim to be; and none can truly pretend to be his who do not desire and design to become like him. On the

6 Whosoever abideth in him sin-

a 3 Jn. 11.

neth not: whosoever *a* sinneth, hath not seen him, neither known him.

---

personal holiness of the Lord Jesus, see Notes on Heb. vii. 26, and 1 Pet. ii. 23. 6. *Whosoever abideth in him.* See chap. ii. 6. The word here employed (μίνων) properly means to remain, to continue, to abide. It is used of persons remaining or dwelling in a place, in the sense of abiding there permanently, or lodging there, and this is the common meaning of the word, Matt. x. 11; xxvi. 38; Mark vi. 10; Luke i. 56, *et sœpe.* In the writings of John, however, it is quite a favourite word to denote the *relation* which one sustains to another, in the sense of being united to him, or remaining with him in affection and love; being with him in heart and mind and will, as one makes his home in a dwelling. The sense seems to be that we have some sort of relation to him similar to that which we have to our home; that is, some fixed and permanent attachment to him. We live in him; we remain steadfast in our attachment to him, as we do to our own home. For the use of the word in John, in whose writings it so frequently occurs, see John v. 38; vi. 56; xiv. 10, 17; xv. 4–7, 9; 1 John ii. 6, 10, 14, 17, 27, 28; iii. 6, 24; iv. 12, 13, 15, 16. In the passage before us, as in his writings generally, it refers to one who lives the life of a Christian, as if he were always with Christ, and abode with him. It refers to the Christian considered as adhering steadfastly to the Saviour, and not as following him with transitory feelings, emotions, and raptures.

[See the Supplementary Note, Rom. viii. 10. We abide in Christ by union with him. The phrase expresses the *continuance* of the union; of which see in the Note as above. Scott explains, 'whoever abides in Christ *as one with him* and as maintaining communion with him.']

It does not of itself necessarily mean that he will always do this; that is, it does not *prove* the doctrine of the perseverance of the saints, but it refers to the adherence to the Saviour as a *continuous* state of mind, or as having permanency; meaning that there is a life of continued faith in him. It is of a person thus attached to the Saviour that

the apostle makes the important declaration in the passage before us, that he does not sin. This is the *third* argument to show that the child of God should be pure; and the substance of the argument is, that *as a matter of fact* the child of God is not a sinner. ¶ *Sinneth not.* There has been much difference of opinion in regard to this expression, and the similar declaration in ver. 9. Not a few have maintained that it teaches the 'doctrine of perfection,' or that Christians may live entirely without sin; and some have held that the apostle meant to teach that this is always the characteristic of the true Christian. Against the interpretation, however, which supposes that it teaches that the Christian is absolutely perfect, and lives wholly without sin, there are three insuperable objections: (1.) If it teaches that doctrine at all, it teaches that *all* Christians are perfect; '*whosoever* abideth in him,' '*whosoever* is born of God,' 'he *cannot* sin,' ver. 9. (2.) This is not true, and cannot be held to be true by those who have any just views of what the children of God have been and are. Who can maintain that Abraham, or Isaac, or Jacob; that Moses, David, or Job;. that Peter, John, or Paul, were absolutely perfect, and were never, after their regeneration, guilty of an act of sin? Certainly they never affirmed it of themselves, nor does the sacred record attribute to them any such perfection. And who can affirm this of *all* who give evidence of true piety in the world? Who can of themselves? Are we to come to the painful conclusion that all who are not absolutely perfect in thought, word, and deed, are destitute of any religion, and are to be set down as hypocrites or self-deceivers? And yet, unless this passage proves that *all* who have been born again are absolutely perfect, it will not prove it of any one, for the affirmation is not made of a part, or of what any favoured individual may be, but of what every one is in fact who is born of God. (3.) This interpretation is not necessary to a fair exposition of the passage. The language used is such

7 Little children, let no man deceive you: he *a* that doeth righ-

teousness is righteous, even as he is righteous.

a Eze.18.5-9; Ro.2.13.

as would be employed by any writer if he designed to say of one that he is not characteristically a sinner; that he is a good man; that he does not commit habitual and wilful transgression. Such language is common throughout the Bible, when it is said of one man that he is a saint, and of another that he is a sinner; of one that he is righteous, and of another that he is wicked; of one that he obeys the law of God, and of another that he does not. John expresses it strongly, but he affirms no more in fact than is affirmed elsewhere. The passage teaches, indeed, most important truths in regard to the true Christian; and the fair and proper meaning may be summed up in the following particulars: (*a*) He who is born again does not sin *habitually*, or is not *habitually* a sinner. If he does wrong, it is when he is overtaken by temptation, and the act is against the habitual inclination and purpose of his soul. If a man sins habitually, it proves that he has never been renewed. (*b*) That he who is born again does not do wrong *deliberately* and of *design*. He means to do right. He is not wilfully and deliberately a sinner. If a man deliberately and intentionally does wrong, he shows that he is not actuated by the spirit of religion. It is true that when one does wrong, or commits sin, there is a momentary assent of the will; but it is under the influence of passion, or excitement, or temptation, or provocation, and not as the result of a deliberate plan or purpose of the soul. A man who deliberately and intentionally does a wrong thing, shows that he is not a true Christian; and if this were all that is understood by *perfection*, then there would be many who are perfect, for there are many, very many Christians, who cannot recollect an instance for many years in which they have intentionally and deliberately done a wrong thing. Yet these very Christians see much corruption in their own hearts over which to mourn, and against which they earnestly strive; in comparing themselves with the perfect law of God, and

with the perfect example of the Saviour, they see much in which they come short. (*c*) He who is born again will not sin *finally*, or will not fall away. 'His seed remaineth in him,' ver. 9. See Notes on that verse. There is a principle of grace by which he will ultimately be restrained and recovered. This, it seems to me, is fairly implied in the language used by John; for if a man might be a Christian, and yet wholly fall away and perish, how could it be said with any truth that such a man 'sinneth not;' how that 'he doth not commit sin;' how that 'his seed remaineth in him, and he cannot sin?' Just the contrary would be true if this were so. ¶ *Whosoever sinneth.* That is, as explained above, habitually, deliberately, characteristically, and finally. —*Doddridge.* 'Who habitually and avowedly sinneth.' ¶ *Hath not seen him, nor known him.* Has had no just views of the Saviour, or of the nature of true religion. In other words, cannot be a true Christian.

7. *Little children.* Notes on chap. ii. 1. ¶ *Let no man deceive you.* That is, in the matter under consideration; to wit, by persuading you that a man may live in sinful practices, and yet be a true child of God. From this it is clear that the apostle supposed there were some who would attempt to do this, and it was to counteract their arts that he made these positive statements in regard to the nature of true religion. ¶ *He that doeth righteousness is righteous.* This is laid down as a great and undeniable principle in religion— a maxim which none could dispute, and as important as it is plain. And it is worthy of all the emphasis which the apostle lays on it. The man who does righteousness, or leads an upright life, is a righteous man, and no other one is. No matter how any one may claim that he is justified by faith; no matter how he may conform to the external duties and rites of religion; no matter how zealous he may be for orthodoxy, or for the order of the church; no matter what visions and raptures he may have,

8 He *a* that committeth sin is of the devil; for the devil sinneth from the beginning. For this purpose the Son of God was manifested, that *b* he might destroy the works of the devil.

9 Whosoever *c* is born of God doth not commit sin; for his seed *d* remaineth in him: and he cannot sin, because he is born of God.

a Jn.8.44.   *b* He.2.14.   *c* 1Jn.5.18.
d 1Pe.1.23.

---

or of what peace and joy in his soul he may boast; no matter how little he may fear death, or hope for heaven— unless he is in fact a righteous man, in the proper sense of the term, he cannot be a child of God. Compare Matt. vii. 16—23. If he is, in the proper sense of the word, a man who keeps the law of God, and leads a holy life, he is righteous, for that is religion. Such a man, however, will always feel that his claim to be regarded as a righteous man is not to be traced to what he is in himself, but to what he owes to the grace of God. ¶ *Even as he is righteous.* See notes on ver. 3. Not necessarily in this world to the same *degree*, but with the same *kind* of righteousness. Hereafter he will become wholly free from all sin, like his God and Saviour, ver. 2.

8. *He that committeth sin.* Habitually, wilfully, characteristically. ¶ *Is of the devil.* This cannot mean that no one who commits *any* sin, or who is not absolutely perfect, can be a Christian, for this would cut off the great mass, even according to the belief of those who hold that the Christian may be perfectly holy, from all claim to the Christian character. But what the apostle here says is true in two senses: (1.) That all who commit sin, even true believers, so far as they are imperfect, in this respect resemble Satan, and are under his influence, since sin, just so far as it exists at all, makes us resemble him. (2.) All who habitually and characteristically sin are of the devil. This latter was evidently the principal idea in the mind of the apostle. His *object* here is to show that those who sinned, in the sense in which it would seem some maintained that the children of God might sin, could have no real evidence of piety, but really belonged to Satan. ¶ *For the devil sinneth from the beginning.* The beginning of the world; or from the first account we have of him. It does not

mean that he sinned from the beginning of his existence, for he was made holy like the other angels. Notes, Jude 6. The meaning is, that he introduced sin into the universe, and that he has continued to practise it ever since. The word *sinneth* here implies *continued* and *habitual* sin. He did not commit one act of sin and then reform; but he has continued, and still continues, his course of sin. This may confirm what has been already said about the kind of sin that John refers to. He speaks of sinning habitually, continuously, wilfully; and any one who does this shows that he is under the influence of him whose characteristic it has been and is to sin. ¶ *For this purpose the Son of God was manifested.* Became incarnate, and appeared among men, ver. 5. Comp. Notes on 1 Tim. iii. 16. ¶ *That he might destroy the works of the devil.* All his plans of wickedness, and his control over the hearts of men. Compare notes on Matt. viii. 39; Mark i. 24; Heb. ii. 14. The *argument* here is, that as the Son of God came to destroy all the works of the devil, he cannot be his true follower who lives in sin.

9. *Whosoever is born of God doth not commit sin.* This passage must either mean that they who are born of God, that is, who are true Christians, do not sin habitually and characteristically, or that every one who is a true Christian is absolutely perfect, and never commits any sin. If it can be used as referring to the doctrine of absolute perfection at all, it proves, not that Christians *may* be perfect, or that *a portion* of them are, but that *all* are. But who can maintain this? Who can believe that John meant to affirm this? Nothing can be clearer than that the passage has *not* this meaning, and that John did not teach a doctrine so contrary to the current strain of the Scriptures, and to fact; and if he did not teach this,

10 In this the children of God are manifest, and the children of the

then in this whole passage he refers to those who are habitually and characteristically righteous. ¶ *For his seed remaineth in him.* There is much obscurity in this expression, though the general sense is clear, which is, that there is something abiding in the heart of the true Christian which the apostle here calls *seed*, which will prevent his sinning. The word '*his*' in this phrase, '*his* seed,' may refer either to the individual himself—in the sense that this can now be properly called *his*, inasmuch as it is a part of himself, or a principle abiding in him; or it may refer to God—in the sense that what is here called 'seed' is *his*, that is, he has implanted it, or it is a germ of Divine origin. Robinson (*Lex.*) understands it in the latter sense, and so also do Macknight, Doddridge, Lücke, and others, and this is probably the true interpretation. The word *seed* (σπέρμα) means properly seed sown, as of grain, plants, trees; then anything that resembles it, anything which germinates, or which springs up, or is produced. It is applied in the New Testament to the word of God, or the gospel, as that which produces effects in the heart and life similar to what seed that is sown does. Comp. Matt. xiii. 26, 37, 38. Augustin, Clemens, (*Alex.*,) Grotius, Rosenmüller, Benson, and Bloomfield, suppose that this is the signification of the word here. The proper idea, according to this, is that the seed referred to is truth, which God has implanted or sown in the heart, from which it may be expected that the fruits of righteousness will grow. But that which abides in the heart of a Christian is not the naked word of God; the mere gospel, or mere truth; it is rather that word as made vital and efficacious by the influences of his Spirit; the germ of the Divine life; the principles of true piety in the soul. Comp. the words of Virgil:—Igneus est illi vigor et cœlestis origo semini. The exact idea here, as it seems to me, is not that the 'seed' refers to *the word of God*, as Augustin and others suppose, or to *the Spirit of God*, but to the germ of piety which has been produced in the heart *by* the word and

Spirit of God, and which may be regarded as having been implanted there by God himself, and which may be expected to produce holiness in the life. There is, probably, as Lücke supposes, an allusion in the word to the fact that we are *begotten* (ὁ γεγεννημένος) of God. The word *remaineth*—μένει, comp. Notes on ver. 6—is a favourite expression of John. The expression here used by John, thus explained, would seem to imply two things: (1,) that the germ or seed of religion implanted in the soul abides there as a constant, vital principle, so that he who is born of God cannot become habitually a sinner; and, (2,) that it will so continue to live there that he will not fall away and perish. The idea is clearly that the germ or principle of piety so permanently abides in the soul, that he who is renewed never can become again characteristically a sinner. ¶ *And he cannot sin.* Not merely he will not, but he cannot; that is, in the sense referred to. This cannot mean that one who is renewed has not physical ability to do wrong, for every moral agent has; nor can it mean that no one who is a true Christian never does, in fact, do wrong in thought, word, or deed, for no one could seriously maintain that: but it must mean that there is somehow a certainty as absolute *as if* it were physically impossible, that those who are born of God will not be characteristically and habitually sinners; that they will not sin in such a sense as to lose all true religion and be numbered with transgressors; that they will not fall away and perish. Unless this passage teaches that no one who is renewed ever *can* sin in any sense; or that every one who becomes a Christian is, and must be, absolutely and always perfect, no words could more clearly prove that true Christians will never fall from grace and perish. How can what the apostle here says be true, if a real Christian can fall away and become again a sinner? ¶ *Because he is born of God.* Or begotten of God. God has given him, by the new birth, real, spiritual life, and that life can never become extinct.

10. *In this the children of God are manifest,* &c. That is, this furnishes a

devil: whosoever doeth not righteousness, is not of God, neither he that loveth not his brother.

11 For this is the ¹message that ye heard from the beginning, that *ᵃ* we should love one another.

12 Not as Cain, *ᵇ* who was of that

wicked one, and slew his brother. And wherefore slew he him? Because his own works were evil, and his brother's righteous.

13 Marvel not, my brethren, if the world *ᶜ* hate you.

1 Or, *commandment.*   *a* Jn.15.12.   *b* Ge.4.4-8.
c Jn.15.18,19.

test of their true character. The test is found in doing righteousness, and in the love of the brethren. The former he had illustrated ; the latter he now proceeds to illustrate. The general idea is, that if a man is not truly a righteous man, and does not love the brethren, he cannot be a child of God. Perhaps by the phrase ' *in this,*' using a pronoun in the singular number, he means to intimate that an important part of righteousness consists in brotherly love. ¶ *Whosoever doeth not righteousness, is not of God.* In ver. 7, he had said that ' he that doeth righteousness *is* of God.'

If that is true, then what he here affirms must be true also, that a man who does *not* righteousness is not of God. The general idea is the same, that no one can be a true Christian who is not in fact a righteous man. ¶ *Neither he that loveth not his brother.* The illustration of this point continues to ver. 18. The general sense is, that brotherly love is essential to the Christian character, and that he who does not possess it cannot be a Christian. On the nature and importance of brotherly love as an evidence of piety, see Notes on John xiii. 34, 35.

11. *For this is the message.* Marg., *commandment.* In the received text, this is ἀγγελία—*a message brought ;* in several mss., and in later editions, it is ἐπαγγελία — *annunciation, announcement ;* an order given, or a commandment, Acts xxiii. 21. It is not very material which reading is followed. The word *command* or *rule* would express the sense with sufficient clearness. The reference is to the law given by the Saviour as a permanent direction to his disciples. ¶ *That ye heard from the beginning, that we should love one another.* See Notes, John xiii. 34, 35 ; 1 John ii. 7.

12. *Not as Cain.* Not manifesting

the spirit which Cain did. His was a most remarkable and striking instance of a want of love to a brother, and the case was well adapted to illustrate the propriety of the duty which the apostle is enjoining. See Gen. iv. 4-8. ¶ Who *was of that wicked one.* Of the devil : that is, he was under his influence, and acted from his instigation. ¶ *And wherefore slew he him ? Because his own works were evil, and his brother's righteous.* He acted under the influence of envy. He was dissatisfied that his own offering was not accepted, and that his brother's was. The apostle seems desirous to guard those to whom he wrote against the indulgence of *any* feelings that were the opposite of love ; from anything like envy toward more highly favoured brethren, by showing to what this would lead if fairly acted out, as in the case of Cain. A large part of the crimes of the earth have been caused, as in the murder of Abel, by the want of brotherly love. Nothing but love would be necessary to put an end to the crimes, and consequently to a large part of the misery, of the world.

13. *Marvel not.* Do not think it so unusual, or so little to be expected, as to excite astonishment. ¶ *If the world hate you.* The emphasis here is to be placed on the word *you.* The apostle had just adverted to the fact that Cain hated Abel, his brother, without cause, and he says that they were not to deem it strange if the world hated *them* in like manner. The Saviour (John xv. 17, 18) introduced these subjects in the same connection. In enjoining the duty of brotherly love on his disciples, he adverts to the fact that they must expect to be hated by the world, and tells them to remember that the world hated him before it hated them. The object of all this was to show more clearly the necessity of strong and tender mutual affec-

14 We know that we have passed from death unto life, because we love the brethren. He [a] that loveth not *his* brother abideth in death.

15 Whosoever [b] hateth his brother is a murderer: and ye know that

no murderer hath eternal life abiding in him.

16 Hereby [c] perceive we the love *of God*, because he laid down his life for us: and we ought to lay down *our* lives for the brethren.

[a] 1 Jn. 2. 9, 11.   [b] Mat. 5. 21, 22.   [c] Jn. 15. 13; Ro. 5. 8.

tion among Christians, since they could hope for none from the world. See Notes, John xv. 18, 19.

14. *We know that we have passed from death unto life.* From spiritual death (Notes, Eph. ii. 1) to spiritual life; that is, that we are true Christians. ¶ *Because we love the brethren.* The sentiment here is, that it is an infallible evidence of true piety if we love the followers of Christ as such. See this sentiment illustrated in the Notes on John xiii. 35. But how easy it would seem to be to apply such a test of piety as this! Who cannot judge accurately of his own feelings, and determine whether he loves a Christian because he bears the name and image of the Saviour—loves him the more just in proportion as he bears that image? Who cannot, if he chooses, look beyond the narrow bounds of his own sect, and determine whether he is pleased with the true Christian character wherever it may be found, and whether he would prefer to find his friends among those who bear the name and the image of the Son of God, than among the people of the world? The Saviour meant that his followers should be known by this badge of discipleship all over the world, John xiii. 34, 35. John says, in carrying out the sentiment, that Christians, by this test, may know *among themselves* whether they have any true religion. ¶ *He that loveth not his brother abideth in death.* He remains dead in sins; that is, he has never been converted. Comp. Notes, ver. 6. As love to the Christian brotherhood is essential to true piety, it follows that he who has not that remains unconverted, or is in a state of spiritual death. He is by nature dead in sin, and unless he has evidence that he is brought out of that state, he *remains* or *abides* in it.

15. *Whosoever hateth his brother is a murderer,* &c. That is, he has the

spirit of a murderer; he has that which, if it were acted out, would lead him to commit murder, as it did Cain. The private malice, the secret grudge, the envy which is cherished in the heart, is murderous in its tendency, and were it not for the outward restraints of human laws, and the dread of punishment, it would often lead to the act of murder. The apostle does not say that he who hates his brother, though he does not in fact commit murder, is guilty to the same degree as if he had actually done it; but he evidently means to say that the spirit which would lead to murder is there, and that God will hold him responsible for it. Nothing is wanting but the removal of outward restraints to lead to the commission of the open deed, and God judges men as he sees them to be *in their hearts.* What a fearful declaration, then, is this! How many real murderers there are on the earth besides those who are detected and punished, and besides those open violators of the laws of God and man who go at large! And who is there that should not feel humbled and penitent in view of his own heart, and grateful for that sovereign mercy which has restrained him from open acts of guilt? —for who is there who has not at some period of his life, and perhaps often, indulged in feelings of hatred, and envy, and malice towards others, which, if acted out, would have led to the commission of the awful crime of taking human life? Any man may well shudder at the remembrance of the secret sins of his own heart, and at the thought of what he *would* have been but for the restraining grace of God. And how wonderful is that grace which, in the case of the true Christian, not only restrains and checks, but which effectually subdues all these feelings, and implants in their place the principles of love!

16. *Hereby perceive we the love of*

God. The words '*of God*' are not in the original, and should not have been introduced into the translation, though they are found in the Latin Vulgate, and in the Genevan versions, and in one manuscript. They would naturally convey the idea that *God* laid down his life for us; or that God himself, in his Divine nature, suffered. But this idea is not expressed in this passage as it is in the original, and of course no argument can be derived from it either to prove that Christ is God, or that the Divine nature is capable of suffering. The original is much more expressive and emphatic than it is with this addition : ' By this we know love ;' that is, we know what true love is ; we see a most affecting and striking illustration of its nature. *Love itself*—its real nature, its power, its sacrifices, its influences—was seen in its highest form, when the Son of God gave himself to die on a cross. For an illustration of the sentiment, see Notes on John iii. 16, and xv. 13. ¶ *Because he laid down his life for us.* There can be no doubt that the Saviour is here referred to, though his name is not mentioned particularly. There are several instances in the New Testament where he is mentioned under the general appellation '*he*,' as one who was well known, and about whom the writers were accustomed to speak. ¶ *And we ought to lay down* our *lives for the brethren.* For the good of our fellow-Christians, if it be necessary. That is, circumstances may occur where it would be proper to do it, and we ought always to be ready to do it. The spirit which led the Saviour to sacrifice his life for the good of the church, should lead us to do the same thing for our brethren if circumstances should require it. That this is a correct principle no one can doubt; for (1) the Saviour did it, and we are bound to imitate his example, and to possess his spirit ; (2) the prophets, apostles, and martyrs did it, laying down their lives in the cause of truth, and for the good of the church and the world ; and (3) it has always been held that it is right and proper, in certain circumstances, for a man to lay down his life for the good of others. So we speak of the patriot who sacrifices his life for the good of his country;

so we feel in the case of a shipwreck, that it may be the duty of a captain to sacrifice his life for the good of his passengers and crew ; so in case of a pestilential disease, a physician should not regard his own life, if he may save others ; and so we always hold the man up to honour who is willing to jeopard his own life on noble principles of self-denial for the good of his fellow-men. In what cases this should occur the apostle does not state ; but the general principle would seem to be, that it is to be done when a greater good would result from our self-sacrifice than from carefully guarding our own lives. Thus, in the case of a patriot, his death, in the circumstances, might be of greater value to his country than his life would be ; or, his exposing himself to death would be a greater service to his country, than if that should not be done. Thus the Saviour laid down his life for the good of mankind ; thus the apostles exposed their lives to constant peril in extending the principles of religion ; and thus the martyrs surrendered their lives in the cause of the church and of truth. In like manner we ought to be ready to hazard our lives, and even to lay them down, if in that way we may promote the cause of truth, and the salvation of sinners, or serve our Christian brethren. In what way this injunction was understood by the primitive Christians, may be perceived from what the world is reported to have said of them, ' Behold, how they love one another ; they are ready to die for one another.' —Tertull. Apol. c. 39. So Eusebius (Eccl. His. vii. 22) says of Christians, that ' in a time of plague they visited one another, and not only hazarded their lives, but actually lost them in their zeal to preserve the lives of others.' We are not indeed to throw away our lives; we are not to expose them in a rash, reckless, imprudent manner ; but when, in the discharge of duty, we are placed in a situation where life is exposed to danger, we are not to shrink from the duty, or to run away from it. Perhaps the following would embrace the principal instances of the duty here enjoined by the apostle: (1.) We ought to have such love for the church that we should be *willing* to die for it, as a

17 But *a* whoso hath this world's good, and seeth his brother have need, and shutteth up his bowels *of compassion* from him, how *b* dwelleth the love of God in him?

18 My little children, let *c* us not love in word, neither in tongue; but in deed and in truth.

19 And hereby *d* we know that we are of the truth, and shall ¹ assure our hearts before him.

a De.15.7. *b* 1 Jn.4.20. *c* Eze.33.31; Ro.12.9; Ja.2.15,16; 1 Pe.1.22. *d* Jn.13.35. 1 Or, *persuade.*

patriot is willing to die for his country. (2.) We ought to have such love for Christians as to be willing to jeopard our lives to aid them—as in case of a pestilence or plague, or when they are in danger by fire, or flood, or foes. (3.) We ought to have such love for the truth as to be willing to sacrifice our lives rather than deny it. (4.) We ought to have such love for the cause of our Master as to be willing to cross oceans, and snows, and sands; to visit distant and barbarous regions, though at imminent risk of our lives, and though with the prospect that we shall never see our country again. (5.) We ought to have such love for the church that we shall engage heartily and constantly in services of labour and self-sacrifice on its account, until, our work being done, exhausted nature shall sink to rest in the grave. In one word, we should regard ourselves as devoted to the service of the Redeemer, living or dying to be found engaged in his cause. If a case should actually occur where the question would arise whether a man would abandon his Christian brother or die, he ought not to hesitate; in all cases he should regard his life as consecrated to the cause of Sion and its friends. Once, in the times of primitive piety, there was much of this spirit in the world; how little, it is to be feared, does it prevail now!

17. *But whoso hath this world's good.* Has property—called 'this world's good,' or a good pertaining to this world, because it is of value to us only as it meets our wants this side of the grave; and perhaps also because it is sought supremely by the men of the world. The general meaning of this verse, in connection with the previous verse, is, that if we ought to be willing to lay down our lives for others, we ought to be willing to make those comparatively smaller sacrifices which are necessary to relieve them in their distresses; and that if we are unwilling to do this, we can have no evidence that the love of God dwells in us. ¶ *And seeth his brother have need.* Need of food, of raiment, of shelter; or sick, and poor, and unable to provide for his own wants and those of his family. ¶ *And shutteth up his bowels* of compassion *from him.* The bowels, or *upper viscera,* embracing the heart, and the region of the chest generally, are in the Scriptures represented as the seat of mercy, piety, and compassion, because when the mind feels compassion it is that part which is affected. Comp. Notes, Isa. xvi. 11. ¶ *How dwelleth the love of God in him?* How can a man love God who does not love those who bear his image? See Notes, chap. iv. 20. On the general sentiment here, see Notes on James ii. 14—16. The meaning is plain, that we cannot have evidence of piety unless we are ready to do good to others, especially to our Christian brethren. See Notes, Matt. xxv. 45; Gal. vi. 10.

18. *My little children, let us not love in word, neither in tongue.* By mere profession; by merely *saying* that we love each other. See 1 Pet. i. 22. ¶ *But in deed and in truth.* In such acts as shall show that our professed love is sincere and real. Let us do the deed of love, whether anything is said about it or not. See Notes on Matt. vi. 3.

19. *And hereby.* Gr., *by this;* that is, by the fact that we have true love to others, and that we manifest it by a readiness to make sacrifices to do them good. ¶ *We know that we are of the truth.* That we are not deceived in what we profess to be; that is, that we are true Christians. To be of the truth stands opposed to cherishing false and delusive hopes. ¶ *And shall assure our hearts before him.* Before God, or before the Saviour. In the margin, as in the Greek, the word rendered *shall assure,* is *persuade.* The Greek word

20 For if our heart condemn us, God is greater than our heart, and knoweth all things.

a Job 27.6; Ps.101.2.

21 Beloved, if our heart *a* condemn us not, *then* have we confidence *b* toward God.

b He.10.22.

is used as meaning to *persuade*, e. g., to the reception and belief of truth; then to persuade any one who has unkind or prejudiced feelings towards us, or to bring over to kind feelings, *to conciliate*, and thus to pacify or quiet. The meaning here seems to be, that we shall in this way allay the doubts and trouble of our minds, and produce a state of quiet and peace, to wit, by the evidence that we are of the truth. Our consciences are often restless and troubled in view of past guilt; but, in thus furnishing the evidence of true piety by love to others, we shall pacify an accusing mind, and conciliate our own hearts, and persuade or convince ourselves that we are truly the children of God. See Rob. Lex. sub voce πειθω, I. *b.* In other words, though a man's heart may condemn him as guilty, and though he knows that God sees and condemns the sins of his past life, yet the agitations and alarms of his mind may be calmed down and soothed by evidence that he is a child of God, and that he will not be finally condemned. A true Christian does not attempt to conceal the fact that there is much for which his own heart and conscience might justly accuse him; but he finds, notwithstanding all this, evidence that he is a child of God, and he is persuaded that all will be well.

20. *For if our heart condemn us.* We cannot hope for peace from any expectation that our own hearts will never accuse us, or that we ourselves can approve of all that we have done. The reference here is not so much to our past lives, as to our present conduct and deportment. The object is to induce Christians so to live that their hearts will not condemn them for any secret sins, while the outward deportment may be unsullied. The general sentiment is, that if they should so live that their own hearts would condemn them for present insincerity and hypocrisy, they could have no hope of peace, for God knows all that is in the heart. In view of the past—when the heart accuses us of what we *have* done—we may find

peace by such evidences of piety as shall allay the troubles of an agitated soul, (ver. 9,) but we cannot have such peace if our hearts condemn us for the indulgence of secret sins, now that we profess to be Christians. If our hearts condemn us for present insincerity, and for secret sins, we can never 'persuade' or soothe them by any external act of piety. In view of the consciousness of past guilt, we may find peace; we can find none if there is a present purpose to indulge in sin. ¶ *God is greater than our heart, and knoweth all things.* We cannot hope to find peace by hiding anything from his view, or by any supposition that he is not acquainted with the sins for which our consciences trouble us. He knows all the sins of which we are conscious, and sees all their guilt and aggravation as clearly as we do. He knows more than this. He knows all the sins which we have forgotten; all those acts which we endeavour to persuade ourselves are not sinful, but which are evil in his sight; and all those aggravations attending our sins which it is impossible for us fully and distinctly to conceive. He is more disposed to condemn sin than we are; he looks on it with less allowance than we do. We cannot hope, then, for a calm mind in any supposition that God does not see our sins as clearly as we do, or in any hope that he will look on them with more favour and indulgence. Peace cannot be found in the indulgence of sin in the hope that God will not perceive or regard it, for we can sooner deceive ourselves than we can him; and while therefore, (ver. 19,) in reference to the past, we can only 'persuade' our hearts, or soothe their agitated feelings by evidence that we are of the truth now, and that our sins are forgiven; in reference to the present and the future, the heart can be kept calm only by such a course of life that our own hearts and our God shall approve the manner in which we live.

21. *Beloved, if our heart condemn us not.* If we so live as to have an ap-

22 And whatsoever *a* we ask, we receive of him, because we keep his commandments, and do those things that are pleasing in his sight.

23 And this *b* is his commandment, That we should believe on the name of his Son Jesus Christ,

a Ps.145.18,19; Pr.15.29; Mar.11.24.
b De.18.15-19; Jn.14.1.

and love one another, as he gave us commandment.

24 And he *c* that keepeth his commandments dwelleth in him, and he in him. And hereby *d* we know that he abideth in us, by the Spirit which he hath given us.

c Jn.14.23; 15.10.　　　*d* Ro.8.9,14.

proving conscience—that is, if we indulge in no secret sin ; if we discharge faithfully every known duty ; if we submit without murmuring to all the allotments of Divine Providence. ¶ Then *have we confidence toward God.* Comp. Notes, ver. 19; chap. i. 28; Acts xxiv. 16. The apostle evidently does not mean that we have confidence towards God on the ground of what we do, as if it were meritorious, or as if it constituted a claim to his favour; but that we may so live as to have evidence of personal piety, and that we may look forward with a confident hope that we shall be accepted of him in the great day. The word here rendered *confidence*—παρρησίαν—means properly *boldness;* usually boldness or openness in speaking our sentiments. See Notes, chap. ii. 28. The confidence or boldness which we have towards our Maker is founded solely on the evidence that he will graciously accept us as pardoned sinners; not in the belief that we deserve his favour.

22. *And whatsoever we ask, we receive of him.* If we are truly his children, and ask in a proper manner. See Notes, Matt. vii. 7. Comp. Mark xi. 24; Luke xi. 9; xviii. 1, seq.; John xiv. 13; xv. 7; 1 John v. 14. The declaration here made must be understood with these limitations : (1,) that we ask in a proper manner, James iv. 3; and, (2,) that the thing asked shall be such as will be consistent for God to give; that is, such as he shall see to be best for us, 1 John v. 14. See Notes on this latter passage. ¶ *Because we keep his commandments.* Not that this is the meritorious ground of our being heard, but that it furnishes evidence that we are his children, and he hears his children as such. ¶ *And do those things that are pleasing in his sight.* As a parent is disposed to bestow favours on obedient,

affectionate, and dutiful children, so God is on those who please him by their obedience and submission to his will. We can have no hope that he will hear us unless we do so live as to please him.

23. *And this is his commandment.* His commandment, by way of eminence; the leading, principal thing which he enjoins on us ; the commandment which lies at the foundation of all true obedience. ¶ *That we should believe on the name of his Son Jesus Christ.* See Notes, Mark xvi. 16. Comp. John xvi. 1; Acts xvi. 31. ¶ *And love one another*, &c. This follows from the other, and hence they are mentioned as together constituting his commandment. Notes, John xiii. 35.

24. *And he that keepeth his commandments*, &c. See Notes, John xiv. 23. ¶ *And hereby we know that he abideth in us.* That is, this is another certain evidence that we are true Christians. The Saviour had promised (John xiv. 23) that he would come and take up his abode with his people. John says that we have proof that he does this by the Spirit which he has given us. That is, the Holy Spirit is imparted to his people to enlighten their minds ; to elevate their affections ; to sustain them in times of trial ; to quicken them in the performance of duty ; and to imbue them with the temper and spirit of the Lord Jesus. When these effects exist, we may be certain that the Spirit of God is with us; for these are the 'fruits' of that Spirit, or these are the effects which he produces in the lives of men. Comp. Notes, Gal. v. 22, 23. On the evidence of piety here referred to, see Notes on Rom. viii. 9, 14, 16. No man can be a true Christian in whom that Spirit does not constantly dwell, or to whom he is not 'given.' And yet no one can determine that the Spirit dwells in him, except by the *effects* produced

CHAPTER IV.

BELOVED, believe ^a not every spirit, but try ^b the spirits

^a Je.29.8; Mat.24.4.   ^b 1 Th.5.31; Re.2.2.

in his heart and life. In the following chapter, the apostle pursues the subject suggested here, and shows that we should examine ourselves closely, to see whether the 'Spirit' to which we trust, as furnishing evidence of piety, is truly the Spirit of God, or is a spirit of delusion.

CHAPTER IV.

ANALYSIS OF THE CHAPTER.

THERE are two principal subjects discussed in this chapter:—

I. The method by which we may determine that we have the Spirit of God, vers. 1—6. The apostle had said (chap. iii. 24) that it could be determined that God dwells in them by the Spirit which he has given them; but as it is probable that the teachers of error, the persons whom John regarded as 'antichrist,' (chap. ii. 18, 19,) would lay claim to the same thing, it was important to know how it could be ascertained that the Spirit of God had been really given to them, or how it could be determined that the spirit that was in them was not the spirit of antichrist, the very thing against which he would guard them. In doing this, he (1) cautions them against trusting to every kind of spirit, or supposing that every spirit which animated even the professed friends of religion was the Spirit of God, ver. 1; and (2) he shows them how it might be determined that they had really the Spirit of God, or what would be the effect of the influences of the Spirit on the mind. This evidence consisted of the following things: (*a*) they had the Spirit of God who confessed that Jesus Christ had come in the flesh, ver. 2; (*b*) they who denied that, had not the Spirit of God, and the denial of this was the real spirit of antichrist, ver. 3; (*c*) they who had the Spirit of God had not the spirit of this world, vers. 4, 5; and (*d*) they who had the Spirit of God would hear those who were his apostles, or who were sent by him, ver. 6.

II. The duty, power, and influence of love, vers. 7—21. This is a favourite

whether they are of God: because ^c many false prophets are gone out into the world.

^c 2 Pe.2.8.

subject with John, and he here considers it at length, as a subject that was essential in determining the evidences of piety. The duty and value of love are enforced by the following considerations: (1.) Love has its origin in God, and every one who has true love is born of God, vers. 7, 8. (2.) God has shown his great love to us by having given his Son to die for us; and as he has so loved us, we ought also to love one another, vers. 9—11. (3.) If we love one another, it furnishes the best evidence that God dwells in us, vers. 12—15. (4.) God is love, and if we have true love we dwell in him, and he dwells in us, ver. 16. (5.) Love will furnish us great advantage in the day of judgment, by giving us confidence when we come before him, ver. 17. (6.) Love will cast out all fear, and will make our minds calm in view of the events which are to come, ver. 18. (7.) The very fact that he has first manifested his love to us should lead us to the exercise of love, ver. 19. (8.) A man cannot truly love God and yet hate his brother, ver. 20; and (9) it is the solemn command of God that he who loves God should love his brother also.

1. *Beloved, believe not every spirit.* Do not confide implicitly in every one who professes to be under the influences of the Holy Spirit. Comp. Matt. xxiv. 4, 5. The true and the false teachers of religion alike claimed to be under the influence of the Spirit of God, and it was of importance that all such pretensions should be examined. It was not to be admitted because any one claimed to have been sent from God that therefore he was sent. Every such claim should be subjected to the proper proof before it was conceded. All pretensions to divine inspiration, or to being authorised teachers of religion, were to be examined by the proper tests, because there were many false and delusive teachers who set up such claims in the world. ¶ *But try the spirits whether they are of God.* There were those in the early Christian church who had the

2 Hereby know ye the Spirit of God: Every *a* spirit that confesseth

a 1 Co. 12. 3.

gift of 'discerning spirits,' (see Notes, 1 Cor. xii. 10,) but it is not certain that the apostle refers here to any such supernatural power. It is more probable, as he addresses this command to Christians in general, that he refers to the ability of doing this by a comparison of the doctrines which they professed to hold with what was revealed, and by the fruits of their doctrines in their lives. If they taught what God had taught in his word, and if their lives corresponded with his requirements, and if their doctrines agreed with what had been inculcated by those who were admitted to be true apostles, (ver. 6,) they were to receive them as what they professed to be. If not, they were to reject them, and hold them to be impostors. It may be remarked, that it is just as proper and as important now to examine the claims of all who profess to be teachers of religion, as it was then. In a matter so momentous as religion, and where there is so much at stake, it is important that *all* pretensions of this kind should be subjected to a rigid examination. No man should be received as a religious teacher without the clearest evidence that he has come in accordance with the will of God, nor unless he inculcates the very truth which God has revealed. See Notes on Isa. viii. 20, and Acts xvii. 11. ¶ *Because many false prophets are gone out into the world.* The word *prophet* is often used in the New Testament to denote religious instructors or preachers. See Notes, Rom. xii. 6. Compare Notes, 2 Pet. ii. 1. Such false teachers evidently abounded in the times here referred to. See Notes, chap. ii. 18. The meaning is, that many had gone out into the world pretending to be true teachers of religion, but who inculcated most dangerous doctrines; and it was their duty to be on their guard against them, for they had the very spirit of antichrist, ver. 3.

2. *Hereby.* Gr., 'By this;' that is, by the test which is immediately specified. ¶ *Know ye the Spirit of God.* You may discern who are actuated by the Spirit of God. ¶ *Every spirit.*

that Jesus Christ is come in the flesh, is of God:

Every one professing to be under the influence of the Spirit of God. The apostle uses the word *spirit* here with reference to the person who made the claim, on the supposition that every one professing to be a religious teacher was animated by some spirit or foreign influence, good or bad. If the Spirit of God influenced them, they would confess that Jesus Christ had come in the flesh; if some other spirit, the spirit of error and deceit, they would deny this. ¶ *That confesseth.* That is, that makes a proper acknowledgment of this; that inculcates this doctrine, and that gives it a due place and prominence in his instructions. It cannot be supposed that a mere statement of this in words would show that they were of God in the sense that they were true Christians; but the sense is, that if this constituted one of the doctrines which they held and taught, it would show that they were advocates of truth, and not apostles of error. If they did not do this, (ver. 3,) it would be decisive in regard to their character and claims. ¶ *That Jesus Christ is come in the flesh.* Benson and some others propose to render this, 'That Jesus, who came in the flesh, is the Christ.' But this is liable to serious objections. (1.) It is not the obvious interpretation. (2.) It is unusual to say that '*Jesus*' had come in the flesh, though the expression 'the Son of God has come in the flesh,' or 'God was manifested in the flesh,' would be in accordance with the usage of the New Testament. (3.) This would not, probably, meet the real point in the case. The thing denied does not appear to have been that Jesus was the Messiah, for their pretending to be Christian teachers at all implied that they admitted this; but that the Son of God was *really a man*, or that he actually assumed human nature in permanent union with the Divine. The point of the remark made by the apostle is, that the acknowledgment was to be that Christ assumed human nature; that he was really a man as he appeared to be; or that there was a real incar-

3 And every spirit that confesseth not that Jesus Christ is come
in the flesh, is not of God : and this
is that *spirit* of antichrist, whereof

ye have heard that it should come;
and even now already is it in the
world.

4 Ye are of God, little children,

---

nation, in opposition to the opinion that
he came in *appearance* only, or that he
merely *seemed* to be a man, and to
suffer and die. That this opinion was
held by many, see the Intro. § III. 2.
It is quite probable that the apostle
here refers to such sentiments as those
which were held by the *Docetæ;* and
that he meant to teach that it was indispensable to proper evidence that any
one came from God, that he should
maintain that Jesus was truly *a man,*
or that there was a real *incarnation* of
the Son of God. John always regarded
this as a very important point, and often
refers to it, John xix. 34, 35 ; xx. 25—
27; 1 John v. 6. It is as important to
be held now as it was then, for the fact
that there was a real incarnation is
essential to all just views of the atonement. If he was *not* truly a man, if he
did not literally shed his blood on the
cross, of course all that was done was in
appearance only, and the whole system
of redemption as revealed was merely a
splendid illusion. There is little danger
that this opinion will be held now, for
those who depart from the doctrine laid
down in the New Testament in regard
to the person and work of Christ, are
more disposed to embrace the opinion
that he was a mere man ; but still it is
important that the truth that he was
truly incarnate should be held up constantly before the mind, for in no other
way can we obtain just views of the
atonement. ¶ *Is of God.* This does
not necessarily mean that every one
who confessed this was personally a true
Christian, for it is clear that a doctrine
might be acknowledged to be true, and
yet that the heart might not be changed;
nor does it mean that the acknowledgment of this truth was *all* which it was
essential to be believed in order that one
might be recognised as a Christian ; but
it means that it was *essential* that this
truth should be admitted by every one
who truly came from God. They who
taught this held a truth which he had
revealed, and which was essential to be
held ; and they thus showed that they

did not belong to those to whom the
name 'antichrist' could be properly
given. Still, whether they held this
doctrine in such a sense, and in such
connection with other doctrines, as to
show that they were sincere Christians,
was quite another question, for it is
plain that a man may hold and teach
the true doctrines of religion, and yet
have no evidence that he is a child of
God.

3. *And every spirit that confesseth
not,* &c. That is, this doctrine is *essential* to the Christian system ; and he
who does not hold it cannot be regarded
either as a Christian, or recognised as
a Christian teacher. If he was not a
man, then all that occurred in his life,
in Gethsemane, and on the cross, was
in *appearance* only, and was assumed
only to delude the senses. There were
no real sufferings ; there was no shedding
of blood; there was no death on the
cross ; and, of course, there was no atonement. A mere show, an appearance
assumed, a vision, could not make atonement for sin ; and a denial, therefore, of
the doctrine that the Son of God had
come in the flesh, was in fact a denial
of the doctrine of expiation for sin. The
Latin Vulgate here reads *qui solvit
Jesum,* 'who dissolves or divides Jesus ;'
and Socrates (H. E. vii. 32) says that
in the old copies of the New Testament
it is written ὅ λίει τὸν Ἰησοῦν, 'who dissolves or divides Jesus ;' that is, who
separates his true nature or person, or
who supposes that there were *two* Christs,
one in appearance, and one in reality.
This reading was early found in some
MSS., and is referred to by many of the
Fathers, (see Wetstein,) but it has no
real authority, and was evidently introduced, perhaps at first from a marginal note, to oppose the prevailing
errors of the times. The common reading, 'who confesseth not,' is found in all
the Gr. MSS., in the Syriac versions, in
the Arabic ; and, as Lücke says, the
other reading is manifestly of Latin
origin. The common reading in the
text is that which is sustained by

and have overcome *a* them: because greater is he that is in you, than he that is in the world.

5 They are of the world: *b* therefore speak they of the world, and the world heareth them.

6 We are of God: he that knoweth God, heareth us; he that is not of God, heareth not us. Hereby *c* know we the spirit of truth, and the spirit of error.

a Ro.8.37.   *b* Jn.3.31.   *c* Is.8.20.

authority, and is entirely in accordance with the manner of John. ¶ *And this is that* spirit *of antichrist.* This is one of the things which characterize antichrist. John here refers not to an *individual* who should be known as antichrist, but to a class of persons. This does not, however, forbid the idea that there might be some one individual, or a succession of persons in the church, to whom the name might be applied by way of eminence. See Notes, chap. ii. 18. Comp. Notes, 2 Thess. ii. 3, seq. ¶ *Whereof ye have heard that it should come.* See Notes, chap. ii. 18.

4. *Ye are of God.* You are of his family; you have embraced his truth, and imbibed his Spirit. ¶ *Little children.* Notes, chap. ii. 1. ¶ *And have overcome them.* Have triumphed over their arts and temptations; their endeavours to draw you into error and sin. The word '*them*' in this place seems to refer to the false prophets or teachers who collectively constituted antichrist. The meaning is, that they had frustrated or thwarted all their attempts to turn them away from the truth. ¶ *Because greater is he that is in you, than he that is in the world.* God, who dwells in your hearts, and by whose strength and grace alone you have been enabled to achieve this victory, is more mighty than Satan, who rules in the hearts of the people of this world, and whose seductive arts are seen in the efforts of these false teachers. The apostle meant to say that it was by no power of their own that they achieved this victory, but it was to be traced solely to the fact that God dwelt among them, and had preserved them by his grace. What was true then is true now. He who dwells in the hearts of Christians by his Spirit, is infinitely more mighty than Satan, 'the ruler of the darkness of this world;' and victory, therefore, over all his arts and temptations may be sure. In his conflicts with

sin, temptation, and error, the Christian should never despair, for his God will insure him the victory.

5. *They are of the world.* This was one of the marks by which those who had the spirit of antichrist might be known. They belonged not to the church of God, but to the world. They had its spirit; they acted on its principles; they lived for it. Comp. Notes, chap. ii. 15. ¶ *Therefore speak they of the world.* Comp. Notes, chap. iii. 31. This may mean either that their conversation pertained to the things of this world, or that they were wholly influenced by the love of the world, and not by the Spirit of God, in the doctrines which they taught. The general sense is, that they had no higher ends and aims than they have who are influenced only by worldly plans and expectations. It is not difficult to distinguish, even among professed Christians and Christian teachers, those who are heavenly in their conversation from those who are influenced solely by the spirit of the world. 'Out of the abundance of the heart the mouth speaketh,' and the general turn of a man's conversation will show what 'spirit is within him.' ¶ *And the world heareth them.* The people of the world—the gay, the rich, the proud, the ambitious, the sensual—receive their instructions, and recognize them as teachers and guides, for their views accord with their own. See Notes, John xv. 19. A professedly religious teacher may always determine much about himself by knowing what class of people are pleased with him. A professed Christian of any station in life may determine much about his evidences of piety, by asking himself what kind of persons desire his friendship, and wish him for a companion.

6. *We are of God.* John here, doubtless, refers to himself, and to those who taught the same doctrines which he did. He takes it for granted that those to whom he wrote would admit this, and

7 Beloved, let us love *a* one another: for love is of God ; and

a 1 Jn.3.11,23.

every one that loveth, is born of God, and knoweth God.

argues from it as an indisputable truth. He had given them such evidence of this, as to establish his character and claims beyond a doubt ; and he often refers to the fact that he was what he claimed to be, as a point which was so well established that no one would call it in question. See John xix. 35 ; xxi. 24 ; 3 John 12. Paul, also, not unfrequently refers to the same thing respecting himself ; to the fact—a fact which no one would presume to call in question, and which might be regarded as the basis of an argument—that he and his fellow-apostles were what they claimed to be. See 1 Cor. xv. 14, 15 ; 1 Thess. ii. 1—11. Might not, and ought not, all Christians, and all Christian ministers, so to live that the same thing might be assumed in regard to them in their intercourse with their fellow-men; that their characters for integrity and purity might be so clear that no one would be disposed to call them in question? There *are* such men in the church and in the ministry now ; why might not all be such ? ¶ *He that knoweth God, heareth us.* Every one that has a true acquaintance with the character of God will receive our doctrine. John might assume this, for it was not doubted, he presumed, that he was an apostle and a good man ; and if this were admitted, it would follow that those who feared and loved God would receive what he taught. ¶ *Hereby.* By this; to wit, by the manner in which they receive the doctrines which we have taught. ¶ *Know we the spirit of truth, and the spirit of error.* We can distinguish those who embrace the truth from those who do not. Whatever pretensions they might set up for piety, it was clear that if they did not embrace the doctrines taught by the true apostles of God, they could not be regarded as his friends ; that is, as true Christians. It may be added that the same test is applicable now. They who do not receive the plain doctrines laid down in the word of God, whatever pretensions they may make to piety, or whatever zeal they may evince in the cause which they have espoused, can have no well-founded

claims to the name Christian. One of the clearest evidences of true piety is a readiness to receive all that God has taught. Comp. Matt. xviii. 1–3 ; Mark x. 15 ; James i. 19–21.

7. *Beloved, let us love one another.* This verse introduces a new topic, the consideration of which occupies the remainder of the chapter. See the Analysis. The subject is one on which John dwells more than on any other—that of love. His own character peculiarly inclined him to the exercise of love ; and the remarkable affection which the Lord Jesus had shown for him, seems to have had the effect to give this grace a peculiar prominence in his views of what constituted true religion. Compare John xiii. 23. On the duty here enjoined, see Notes on John xiii. 34, 35, and 1 John iii. 11, 23. ¶ *For love is of God.* (1.) All true love has its origin in God. (2.) Real love shows that we have his Spirit, and that we belong to him. (3.) It assimilates us to God, or makes us more and more like him. What is here said by the apostle is based on the truth of what he elsewhere affirms, (ver. 8,) that God is love. Hatred, envy, wrath, malice, all have their source in something else than God. He neither originates them, commends them, nor approves them. ¶ *And every one that loveth, is born of God.* Is a regenerated man. That is, every one who has true love to Christians as such, or true brotherly love, is a true Christian. This cannot mean that every one that loves his wife and children, his classmate, his partner in business, or his friend—his house, or his farms, or his horses, or his hounds, is a child of God ; it must be understood as referring to the point under discussion. A man may have a great deal of natural affection towards his kindred ; a great deal of benevolence in his character towards the poor and needy, and still he may have none of the love to which John refers. He may have no real love to God, to the Saviour, or to the children of God as such ; and it would be absurd for such a one to argue because he loves his wife and children

8 He that loveth not, knoweth not God ; for God is love. *a*

9 In this *b* was manifested the love of God toward us, because that God sent his only begotten Son

into the world, that *c* we might live through him.

10 Herein is love, not that we loved God, but that he loved us, and sent his Son *to be* the propitiation *d* for our sins.

a ver.16; 2Co.13.11. *b* Jn.3.16. *c* Jn.6.51. *d* 1Jn.2.2.

that *therefore* he loves God, or is born again.

8. *He that loveth not, knoweth not God.* Has no true acquaintance with God ; has no just views of him, and no right feelings towards him. The reason for this is implied in what is immediately stated, that ' God is love,' and of course if they have no love reigning in their hearts, they cannot pretend to be like him. ¶ *For God is love.* He is not merely benevolent, he is benevolence itself. Compare Notes, 2 Cor. xiii. 11. Never was a more important declaration made than this ; never was more meaning crowded into a few words than in this short sentence—*God is love.* In the darkness of this world of sin—in all the sorrows that come now upon the race, and that will come upon the wicked hereafter—we have the assurance that a God of infinite benevolence rules over all ; and though we may not be able to reconcile all that occurs with this declaration, or see how the things which he has permitted to take place are consistent with it, yet in the exercise of faith on his own declarations we may find consolation in *believing* that it is so, and may look forward to a period when all his universe shall *see* it to be so. In the midst of all that occurs on the earth of sadness, sin, and sorrow, there are abundant evidences that God is love. In the original structure of things before sin entered, when all was pronounced ' good ;' in the things designed to promote happiness, where the only thing contemplated is happiness, and where it would have been as easy to have caused pain ; in the preservation of a guilty race, and in granting that race the opportunity of another trial ; in the ceaseless provision which God is making in his providence for the wants of unnumbered millions of his creatures ; in the arrangements made to alleviate sorrow, and to put an end to it ; in the gift of a Saviour more than all, and in the

offer of eternal life on terms simple and easy to be complied with—in all these things, which are the *mere* expressions of love, not *one* of which would have been found under the government of a malignant being, we see illustrations of the sublime and glorious sentiment before us, that ' God is love.' Even in this world of confusion, disorder, and darkness, we have evidence sufficient to prove that he is benevolent, but the full glory and meaning of that truth will be seen only in heaven. Meantime let us hold on to the truth that he is love. Let us believe that he sincerely desires our good, and that what seems dark to us may be designed for our welfare ; and amidst all the sorrows and disappointments of the present life, let us feel that our interests and our destiny are in the hands of the God of love.

9. *In this was manifested the love of God.* That is, in an eminent manner, or this was a most signal proof of it. The apostle does not mean to say that it has been manifested in no other way, but that this was so prominent an instance of his love, that all the other manifestations of it seemed absorbed and lost in this. ¶ *Because that God sent his only begotten Son,* &c. See Notes on John iii. 16. ¶ *That we might live through him.* He died that we might have eternal life through the merits of his sacrifice. The *measure* of that love, then, which was manifested in the gift of a Saviour, is to be found, (1,) in the worth of the soul ; (2,) in its exposure to eternal death ; (3,) in the greatness of the gift ; (4,) in the greatness of his sorrows for us ; and, (5,) in the immortal blessedness and joy to which he will raise us. Who can estimate all this ? All these things will magnify themselves as we draw near to eternity ; and *in* that eternity to which we go, whether saved or lost, we shall have an ever-expanding view of the wonderful love of God.

11 Beloved, if *a* God so loved us, we ought also to love one another.

12 No *b* man hath seen God at

any time. If we love one another, God dwelleth in us, and his love is perfected *c* in us.

a Mat.18.33; Jn.15.12,13.　　　*b* 1Ti.6.16.

c 1 Co.13.13.

10. *Herein is love.* In this great gift is the highest expression of love, as if it had done all that it can do. ¶ *Not that we loved God.* Not that we were in such a state that we might suppose he would make such a sacrifice for us, but just the opposite. If we had loved and obeyed him, we might have had reason to believe that he would be willing to show his love to us in a corresponding manner. But we were alienated from him. We had even no desire for his friendship and favour. In *this* state he showed the greatness of his love for us by giving his Son to die for his enemies. See Notes on Rom. v. 7, 8. ¶ *But that he loved us.* Not that he approved our character, but that he desired our welfare. He loved us not with the love of complacency, but with the love of benevolence. ¶ *And sent his Son* to be *the propitiation for our sins.* On the meaning of the word *propitiation*, see Notes on Rom. iii. 25. Comp. Notes, 1 John ii. 2.

11. *Beloved, if God so loved us, we ought also to love one another.* (1.) Because he is so much exalted above us, and if he has loved those who were so inferior and so unworthy, we ought to love those who are on a level with us; (2,) because it is only in this way that we can show that we have his Spirit; and, (3,) because it is the nature of love to seek the happiness of all. There are much stronger reasons why we should love one another than there were why God should love us; and unless we do this, we can have no evidence that we are his children.

12. *No man hath seen God at any time.* See Notes, John i. 18, where the same declaration occurs. The statement seems to be made here in order to introduce a remark to show in what way we may know that we have any true knowledge of God. The idea is, 'He has never indeed been seen by mortal eyes. We are not, then, to expect to become acquainted with what he is in that way. But there is a method by which we may be assured that we have

a true knowledge of him, and that is, by evidence that we love another, and by the presence of his Spirit in our hearts. We cannot become acquainted with him by sight, but we may by love.' ¶ *If we love one another, God dwelleth in us.* Though we cannot see him, yet there is a way by which we may be assured that he is near us, and that he even dwells in us. That way is by the exercise of love. Comp. Notes, John xiv. 23, 24. ¶ *And his love is perfected in us.* Is carried out to completion. That is, our love for each other is the proper exponent of love to him reigning in our hearts. The idea here is not that we are absolutely perfect, or even that our love is perfect, whatever may be true on those points, but that this love to others is the proper carrying out of our love towards him; that is, without this our love to him would not have accomplished what it was adapted and designed to do. Unless it produced this effect, it would be defective or incomplete. Comp. ver. 17. The general sense is this: 'We claim to have the love of God in our hearts, or that we are influenced and controlled by love. But however high and exalted that may seem to be as exercised toward God, it would be defective; it would not exert a fair influence over us, unless it led us to love our Christian brethren. It would be like the love which we might profess to have for a father, if it did not lead us to love our brothers and sisters. True love will diffuse itself over all who come within its range, and will thus become complete and entire.' This passage, therefore, cannot be adduced to demonstrate the doctrine of sinless perfection, or to prove that Christians are ever absolutely perfect in this life. It proves only that love to God is not complete, or fully developed, unless it leads those who profess to have it to love each other. See Notes on Job i. 1. On the meaning of the Greek word here used, (τελειόω,) see Notes on Phil. iii. 12. Comp. Notes, Heb. ii. 10.

13. *Hereby know we that we dwell in*

13 Hereby *a* know we that we dwell in him, and he in us, because he hath given us of his Spirit.

14 And we have seen, and do testify, that the Father sent the Son *to be* the Saviour of the world.

15 Whosoever *b* shall confess that

Jesus is the Son of God, God dwelleth in him, and he in God.

16 And we have known and believed the love that God hath to us. God *c* is love ; and he that dwelleth in love dwelleth in God, and God in him.

a Jn.14.20; 1Jn.3.24.   *b* Ro.10.9.   *c* ver.8.

him. Here is another, or an additional evidence of it. ¶ *Because he hath given us of his Spirit.* He has imparted the influences of that Spirit to our souls, producing ' love, joy, peace, long-suffering, gentleness, goodness, faith,' &c., Gal. v. 22, 23. It was one of the promises which the Lord Jesus made to his disciples that he would send the Holy Spirit to be with them after he should be withdrawn from them, (John xiv. 16, 17, 26; xv. 26; xvi. 7,) and one of the clearest evidences which we can have that we are the children of God, is derived from the influences of that Spirit on our hearts. See this sentiment illustrated in the Notes on Rom. viii. 16.

14. *And we have seen.* Notes on chap. i. 1. ¶ *And do testify.* Notes on chap. i. 3. That is, we who are apostles bear witness to you of this great truth, that God has sent his Son to be a Saviour. Comp. Notes, John xx. 31. The reason why this is referred to here is not quite apparent, but the train of thought in this passage would seem to be this : The writer is discoursing of the love of God, and of its manifestation in the gift of the Saviour, and of the proper influence which it should have on us. Struck with the greatness and importance of the subject, his mind adverts to the *evidence* on which what he was saying rested—the evidence that the Father had *really* thus manifested his love. That evidence he repeats, that he had actually *seen* him who had been sent, and had the clearest demonstration that what he deemed so important had really occurred.

15. *Whosoever shall confess that Jesus is the Son of God.* In the true sense, and from the heart. This will *always* prove that a man is a Christian. But the passage cannot mean that if he merely says so in words, or if he does it insincerely or without any proper

sense of the truth, it will prove that he is a Christian. On the meaning of the sentiment here expressed, see Notes on ver. 2. Comp. Notes, Rom. x. 10.

16. *And we have known and believed,* &c. We all have assurance that God has loved us, and the fullest belief in the great fact of redemption by which he has manifested his love to us. ¶ *God is love.* Notes on ver. 8. It is not uncommon for John to repeat an important truth. He delights to dwell on such a truth as that which is here expressed ; and who should not ? What truth is there on which the mind can dwell with more pleasure ; what is there that is better fitted to win the heart to holiness; what that will do more to sustain the soul in the sorrows and trials of this life ? In our trials; in the darkness which is around us; in the perplexities which meet and embarrass us in regard to the Divine administration ; in all that seems to us incomprehensible in this world, and in the prospect of the next, let us learn to repeat this declaration of the favoured disciple, ' *God is love.*' What trials may we not bear, if we feel assured of that ! What dark cloud that seems to hang over our way, and to involve all things in gloom, will not be bright, if from the depths of our souls we can always say, ' *God is love !* ' ¶ *And he that dwelleth in love,* &c. Religion is all love. God is love ; he has loved us ; we are to love him ; we are to love one another; we are to love the whole world. Heaven is filled with love, and there is nothing else there. The earth is filled with love just as far as religion prevails, and would be entirely if it should prevail everywhere. Love would remove all the corrupt passions, the crimes, the jealousies, the wars on the earth, and would diffuse around the globe the bliss of heaven. If a man, therefore, is actuated by this, he has

17 Herein is [1] our love made perfect, that we may have boldness in the day of judgment: because as he is, so are we in this world.

18 There is no fear in love; but

1 *love with us.*

perfect love casteth out fear; because fear hath torment. He that feareth, is not made perfect in love.

19 We love him, because he [a] first loved us.

a Jn.15.16.

the spirit of the heavenly world reigning in his soul, and lives in an atmosphere of love.

17. *Herein is our love made perfect.* Marg., *love with us.* The margin accords with the Greek—μεθ' ἡμῶν. The meaning is, ' the love that is within us, or in us, is made perfect.' The expression is unusual; but the general idea is, that *love* is rendered complete or entire in the manner in which the apostle specifies. In this way love becomes what it should be, and will prepare us to appear with confidence before the judgment-seat. Comp. Notes on ver. 12. ¶ *That we may have boldness in the day of judgment.* By the influence of love in delivering us from the fear of the wrath to come, ver. 18. The idea is, that he who has true love to God will have nothing to fear in the day of judgment, and may even approach the awful tribunal where he is to receive the sentence which shall determine his everlasting destiny without alarm. ¶ *Because as he is, so are we in this world.* That is, we have the same traits of character which the Saviour had, and, resembling him, we need not be alarmed at the prospect of meeting him.

18. *There is no fear in love.* Love is not an affection which produces fear. In the love which we have for a parent, a child, a friend, there is no fear. If a man had perfect love to God, he would have no fear of anything—for what would he have to dread? He would have no fear of death, for he would have nothing to dread beyond the grave. It is guilt that makes men fear what is to come; but he whose sins are pardoned, and whose heart is filled with the love of God, has nothing to dread in this world or the world to come. The angels in heaven, who have always loved God and one another, have no fear, for they have nothing to dread in the future; the redeemed in heaven, rescued from all danger, and filled with the love of God, have nothing to dread; and as far as

that same loves operates on earth, it delivers the soul now from all apprehension of what is to come. ¶ *But perfect love casteth out fear.* That is, love that is complete, or that is allowed to exert its proper influence on the soul. As far as it exists, its tendency is to deliver the mind from alarms. If it should exist in any soul in an absolutely perfect state, that soul would be entirely free from all dread in regard to the future. ¶ *Because fear hath torment.* It is a painful and distressing emotion. Thus men suffer from the fear of poverty, of losses, of bereavement, of sickness, of death, and of future woe. From all these distressing apprehensions, that love of God which furnishes an evidence of true piety delivers us. ¶ *He that feareth, is not made perfect in love.* He about whose mind there lingers the apprehension of future wrath, shows that love in his soul has not accomplished its full work. Perhaps it never will on any soul until we reach the heavenly world, though there are many minds so full of love to God, as to be prevailingly delivered from fear.

19. *We love him, because he first loved us.* This passage is susceptible of two explanations; either (1) that the fact that he first loved us is the *ground* or *reason* why we love him, or (2) that as a matter of fact we have been brought to love him in consequence of the love which he has manifested towards us, though the real ground of our love may be the excellency of his own character. If the former be the meaning, and if that were the *only* ground of love, then it would be mere selfishness, (comp. Matt. v. 46, 47;) and it cannot be believed that John meant to teach that that is the *only* reason of our love to God. It is true, indeed, that that is *a* proper ground of love, or that we are bound to love God in proportion to the benefits which we have received from his hand; but still genuine love to God is something which cannot be explained by

20 If a man say, I love God, and hateth his brother, he is a liar : for he that loveth not his brother whom he hath seen, how ^acan he love God whom he hath not seen?

21 And this commandment have we from him, That ^bhe who loveth God love his brother also.

CHAPTER V.

WHOSOEVER ^c believeth that Jesus is the Christ, is born of God : and every one that loveth him that begat, loveth him also that is begotten of him.

a 1Jn.3.17.   b Jn.13.34.   c Jn.1.12,13.

the mere fact that we have received favours from him. The true, the original ground of love to God, is *the excellence of his own character,* apart from the question whether we are to be benefited or not. There is that in the Divine nature which a holy being will love, apart from the benefits which he is to receive, and from any thought even of his own destiny. It seems to me, therefore, that John must have meant here, in accordance with the second interpretation suggested above, that *the fact* that we love God is to be traced to the means which he has used to bring us to himself, but without saying that this is the sole or even the main *reason* why we love him. It was his love manifested to us by sending his Son to redeem us which will explain *the fact* that we now love him ; but still the real ground or reason why we love him is the infinite excellence of his own character. It should be added here, that many suppose that the Greek words rendered ' we love ' (ἡμεῖς ἀγαπῶμεν) are not in the indicative, but in the subjunctive ; and that this is an exhortation—' let us love him, because he first loved us.' So the Syriac, the Arabic, and the Vulgate read it ; and so it is understood by Benson, Grotius, and Bloomfield. The main idea would not be essentially different ; and it is a proper ground of exhortation to love God because he has loved us, though the highest ground is, because his character is infinitely worthy of love. 20. *If a man say, I love God, and hateth his brother.* His Christian brother ; or, in a larger sense, any man. The sense is, that no man, whatever may be his professions and pretensions, can have any true love to God, unless he love his brethren. ¶ *He is a liar.* Comp. Notes, chap. i. 6. It is not necessary, in order to a proper interpretation of this passage, to suppose that

he *intentionally* deceives. The sense is, that this must be a false profession. ¶ *For he that loveth not his brother whom he hath seen, &c.* It is more reasonable to expect that we should love one whom we have seen and known personally, than that we should love one whom we have not seen. The apostle is arguing from human nature as it is, and every one feels that we are more likely to love one with whom we are familiar than one who is a stranger. If a professed Christian, therefore, does not love one who bears the Divine image, whom he sees and knows, how can he love that God whose image he bears, whom he has not seen? Comp. Notes on chap. iii. 17.

21. *And this commandment have we from him.* That is, the command to love a brother is as obligatory as that to love God. If one is obeyed, the other ought to be also ; if a man feels that one is binding on him, he should feel that the other is also ; and he can never have evidence that he is a true Christian, unless he manifests love to his brethren as well as love to God. See Notes on James ii. 10. ¶ *That he who loveth God love his brother also.* See Notes, John xiii. 34, 35. Comp. John xv. 12, 17.

CHAPTER V.

ANALYSIS OF THE CHAPTER.

This chapter embraces the following subjects : I. A continuance of the discussion about *love,* vers. 1—3. These verses should have been attached to the previous chapter. II. The victory which is achieved over the world by those who are born of God. The grand instrumentality by which this is done, is by the belief that Jesus is the Son of God, vers. 4, 5. III. The evidence that Jesus *is* the Son of God ; or the means by which that truth is so believed as to secure a victory over the world, vers. 6—12. In this part of the chapter the apostle goes

2 By this we know that we love the children of God, when we love God, and keep his commandments.

fully into the nature of this evidence, or the ways in which the Christian becomes so thoroughly convinced of it as to give to faith this power. He refers to these sources of evidence : (*a*) The witness of the Spirit, ver. 6. (*b*) The record borne in heaven, ver. 7—if that verse be genuine. (*c*) The evidence borne on earth, by the Spirit, the water, and the blood —all bearing witness to that one truth. (*d*) The credit which is due to the testimony of God, or which the soul pays to it, ver. 8. (*e*) The fact that he who believes on the Son of God has the witness in himself, ver. 10. (*f*) The amount of the record, that God has given to us eternal life through his Son, vers. 11, 12. IV. The reason why all this was written by the apostle, ver. 13. It was that they might know that they had eternal life, and might believe on the name of the Saviour. V. The effect of this in leading us to the throne of grace, with the assurance that God will hear us, and will grant our requests, vers. 14, 15. VI. The power of prayer, and the duty of praying for those who have sinned. The encouragement to this is, that there are many sins which are not unto death, and that we may hope that God will be merciful to those who have not committed the unpardonable offence, vers. 16, 17. VII. A *summary* of all that the apostle had said to them, or of the points of which they were sure in the matter of salvation, vers. 18–20. They knew that those who are born of God do not sin ; that the wicked one cannot permanently injure them ; that they were of God, while all the world lay in wickedness ; that the Son of God had come, and that they were truly united to that Saviour who is the true God, and who is eternal life. VIII. An exhortation to keep themselves from all idolatry, ver. 21.

1. *Whosoever believeth that Jesus is the Christ.* Is the Messiah ; the anointed of God. On the meaning of the word *Christ*, see Notes on Matt. i. 1. Of course it is meant here that the proposition, that ' Jesus is the Christ,' should be believed or received in the true and proper sense, in order to fur-

nish evidence that any one is born of God. Comp. Notes on chap. iv. 3. It cannot be supposed that a mere intellectual acknowledgment of the proposition that Jesus is the Messiah is all that is meant, for that is not the proper meaning of the word *believe* in the Scriptures. That word, in its just sense, implies that the truth which is believed should make its fair and legitimate impression on the mind, or that we should feel and act *as if* it were true. See Notes, Mark xvi. 16. If, in the proper sense of the phrase, a man does believe that Jesus *is the Christ*, receiving him as he is revealed as the Anointed of God, and a Saviour, it is undoubtedly true that that constitutes him a Christian, for that is what is required of a man in order that he may be saved. See Notes, Acts viii. 37. ¶ *Is born of God.* Or rather, 'is begotten of God.' See Notes, John iii. 3. ¶ *And every one that loveth him that begat.* That loves that God who has thus begotten those whom he has received as his children, and to whom he sustains the endearing relation of Father. ¶ *Loveth him also that is begotten of him.* That is, he will love all the true children of God ; all Christians. See Notes on chap. iv. 20. The general idea is, that as all Christians are the children of the same Father ; as they constitute one family ; as they all bear the same image ; as they share his favour alike ; as they are under the same obligation of gratitude to him, and are bound to promote the same common cause, and are to dwell together in the same home for ever, they should therefore love one another. As all the children in a family love their common father, so it should be in the great family of which God is the Head.

2. *By this we know that we love the children of God, &c.* This is repeating the same truth in another form. ' As it is universally true that if we love him who has begotten us, we shall also love his children, or our Christian brethren, so it is true also that if we love his children it will follow that we love him.' In other places, the apostle

3 For this is the love of God, that *a* we keep his commandments: and his commandments are not *b* grievous.

a Jn.14.15,21.　　b Ps.119.45; Mat.11.30.

4 For whatsoever is born of God overcometh *c* the world : and this is the victory that overcometh the world, *even* our faith.

c 1Co.15.57.

says that we may know that we love God if we love those who bear his image, chap. iii. 14. He here says, that there is another way of determining what we are. We may have undoubted evidence that we love *God*, and from that, as the basis of an argument, we may infer that we have true love to his children. Of the fact that we may have evidence that we love God, apart from that which we derive from our love to his children, there can be no doubt. We may be conscious of it; we may find pleasure in meditating on his perfections; we may feel sure that we are moved to obey him by true attachment to him, as a child may in reference to a father. But, it may be asked, how can it be inferred from this that we truly love his children? Is it not more easy to ascertain this of itself than it is to determine whether we love God? Comp. chap. iv. 20. To this it may be answered, that we may love Christians from many motives: we may love them as personal friends; we may love them because they belong to our church, or sect, or party; we may love them because they are naturally amiable: but the apostle says here, that when we are conscious that an attachment *does* exist towards Christians, we may ascertain that it is genuine, or that it does not proceed from any improper motive, by the fact that we love God. We shall then love him *as* his children, whatever *other* grounds of affection there may be towards them. ¶ *And keep his commandments.* See Notes, John xiv. 15.

3. *For this is the love of God, that we keep his commandments.* This constitutes true love; this furnishes the evidence of it. ¶ *And his commandments are not grievous.* Greek, heavy—βαρεῖαι; that is, difficult to be borne as a burden. See Matt. xi. 30. The meaning is, that his laws are not unreasonable; the duties which he requires are not beyond our ability; his government is not oppressive. It is

easy to obey God when the heart is right; and those who endeavour in sincerity to keep his commandments do not complain that they are hard. All complaints of this kind come from those who are not disposed to keep his commandments. *They*, indeed, object that his laws are unreasonable; that they impose improper restraints; that they are not easily complied with; and that the Divine government is one of severity and injustice. But no such complaints come from true Christians. They find *his* service easier than the service of sin, and the laws of God more mild and easy to be complied with than were those of fashion and honour, which they once endeavoured to obey. The service of God is freedom; the service of the world is bondage. No man ever yet heard a true Christian say that the laws of God, requiring him to lead a holy life, were stern and ' grievous.' But who has not felt this in regard to the inexorable laws of sin? What votary of the world would not say this if he spoke his real sentiments? Comp. Notes, John viii. 32.

4. *For whatsoever is born of God overcometh the world.* The world, in its maxims, and precepts, and customs, does not rule him, but he is a freeman. The idea is, that there is a conflict between religion and the world, and that in the heart of every true Christian religion secures the victory, or triumphs. In John xvi. 33, the Saviour says, ' Be of good cheer; I have overcome the world.' See Notes on that verse. He obtained a complete triumph over him ' who rules the darkness of the world,' and laid the foundation for a victory by his people over all vice, error, and sin. John makes this affirmation of *all* who are born of God. ' Whatsoever,' or, as the Greek is, ' Everything which is begotten of God,' (πᾶν τὸ γεγεννημένον;) meaning to affirm, undoubtedly, that *in every instance* where one is truly regenerated, there is this victory over the world. See Notes, James iv. 4 ; 1 John

VOL. X.　　　　Y

5 Who is he that overcometh the world, but he that believeth that Jesus is the Son of God?

6 This is he that came *a* by water and blood, *even* Jesus Christ; not

a Jn.19.34.

ii. 15, 16. It is one of the settled maxims of religion, that every man who is a true Christian gains a victory over the world; and consequently a maxim *as* settled, that where the spirit of the world reigns supremely in the heart, there is no true religion. But, if this be a true principle, how many professed Christians are there who are strangers to all claims of piety—for how many are there who are wholly governed by the spirit of this world! ¶ *And this is the victory.* This is the source or means of the victory which is thus achieved. ¶ Even *our faith.* Faith in the Lord Jesus Christ, ver. 5. He overcame the world, (John xvi. 33,) and it is by that faith which makes us one with him, and that imbues us with his Spirit, that we are able to do it also.

5. *Who is he, &c.* Where is there one who can pretend to have obtained a victory over the world, except he who believes in the Saviour? All else are worldly, and are governed by worldly aims and principles. It is true that a man may gain a victory over *one* worldly passion; he may subdue some one evil propensity; he may abandon the gay circle, may break away from habits of profaneness, may leave the company of the unprincipled and polluted; but still, unless he has faith in the Son of God, the spirit of the world will reign supreme in his soul in some form. The appeal which John so confidently made in his time may be as confidently made now. *We* may ask, as *he* did, where is there one who shows that he has obtained a complete victory over the world, except the true Christian? Where is there one whose end and aim is not the present life? Where is there one who shows that all his purposes in regard to this world are made subordinate to the world to come? There are those now, as there were then, who break away from one form of sin, and from one circle of sinful companions; there are those who change the ardent passions of youth for the soberness of middle or advanced life;

there are those who see the folly of profaneness, and of gaiety, and intemperance; there are those who are disappointed in some scheme of ambition, and who withdraw from political conflicts; there are those who are satiated with pageantry, and who, oppressed with the cares of state, as Diocletian and Charles V. were, retire from public life; and there are those whose hearts are crushed and broken by losses, and by the death, or what is worse than death, by the ingratitude of their children, and who cease to cherish the fond hope that their family will be honoured, and their name perpetuated in those whom they tenderly loved—but still there is no victory over the world. Their deep dejection, their sadness, their brokenness of spirit, their lamentations, and their want of cheerfulness, all show that the spirit of the world still reigns in their hearts. If the calamities which have come upon them could be withdrawn; if the days of prosperity could be restored, they would show as much of the spirit of the world as ever they did, and would pursue its follies and its vanities as greedily as they had done before. Not many years or months elapse before the worldly mother who has followed one daughter to the grave, will introduce another into the gay world with all the brilliancy which fashion prescribes; not long will a worldly father mourn over the death of a son before, in the whirl of business and the exciting scenes of ambition, he will show that his heart is as much wedded to the world as it ever was. If such sorrows and disappointments conduct to the Saviour, as they sometimes do; if they lead the troubled mind to seek peace in his blood, and support in the hope of heaven, then a real victory is obtained over the world; and then, when the hand of affliction is withdrawn, it is seen that there has been a work of grace in the soul that has effectually changed all its feelings, and secured a triumph that shall be eternal.

6. *This is he.* This Son of God re-

by water only, but by water and blood. And it is the Spirit *a* that

beareth witness, because the Spirit is truth.

a Jn.14.17.

ferred to in the previous verse. The object of the apostle in this verse, in connection with verse 8, is to state the nature of the evidence that Jesus is the Son of God. He refers to three well-known things on which he probably had insisted much in his preaching—the water, and the blood, and the Spirit. These, he says, furnished evidence on the very point which he was illus-trating, by showing that that Jesus on whom they believed was the Son of God. 'This,' says he, 'is the same one, the very person, to whom the well-known and important testimony is borne; to him, and him alone, these undisputed things appertain, and not to any other who should claim to be the Messiah; and they all agree on the same one point,' ver. 8. ¶ *That came.* ὁ ἐλθὼν. This does not mean that when he came into the world he was accompanied in some way by water and blood; but the idea is, that the water and the blood were clearly manifest during his ap-pearing on earth, or that they were remarkable testimonials in some way to his character and work. An ambas-sador might be said to *come* with cre-dentials; a warrior might be said to *come* with the spoils of victory; a prince might be said to *come* with the insignia of royalty; a prophet *comes* with signs and wonders; and the Lord Jesus might also be said to have come with power to raise the dead, and to heal disease, and to cast out devils; but John here fixes the attention on a fact so impressive and remarkable in his view as to be worthy of special remark, that he *came* by water and blood. ¶ *By water.* There have been many opinions in re-gard to the meaning of this phrase. See Pool's Synopsis. Compare also Lücke, *in loc.* A mere reference to some of these opinions may aid in as-certaining the true interpretation. (1.) Clement of Alexandria supposes that by *water* regeneration and faith were denoted, and by *blood* the public ac-knowledgment of that. (2.) Some, and among them Wetstein, have held that the words are used to denote the fact

that the Lord Jesus was truly a man, in contradistinction from the doctrine of the *Docetæ;* and that the apostle means to say that he had all the pro-perties of a human being—a spirit or soul, blood, and the watery humours of the body. (3.) Grotius supposes that by his coming 'by water,' there is refer-ence to his pure life, as water is the emblem of purity; and he refers to Ezek. xxxvi. 25; Isa. i. 16; Jer. iv. 14. As a sign of that purity, he says that John baptized him, John i. 28. A suf-ficient objection to this view is, that as in the corresponding word *blood* there is undoubted reference to blood literally, it cannot be supposed that the word *water* in the same connection would be used figuratively. Moreover, as Lücke (p. 287) has remarked, water, though a *symbol* of purity, is never used to denote *purity itself,* and therefore can-not here refer to the pure life of Jesus. (4.) Many expositors suppose that the reference is to the baptism of Jesus, and that by his 'coming by water and blood,' as by the latter there is un-doubted reference to his death, so by the former there is reference to his baptism, or to his entrance on his public work. Of this opinion were Tertullian, Œcumenius, Theophylact, among the fathers, and Capellus, Heumann, Stroth, Lange, Ziegler, A. Clarke, Bengel, Rosenmüller, Macknight, and others, among the moderns. A leading ar-gument for this opinion, as alleged, has been that it was then that the Spirit bare witness to him, (Matt. iii. 16,) and that this is what John here refers to when he says, 'It is the Spirit that beareth witness,' &c. To this view, Lücke urges substantially the following objections: (*a*) That if it refers to bap-tism, the phrase would much more ap-propriately express the fact that Jesus came baptizing others, if that were so, than that he was baptized himself. The phrase would be strictly applicable to John the Baptist, who came baptizing, and whose ministry was distinguished for that, (Matt. iii. 1;) and if Jesus had baptized in the same manner, or if this had been a prominent characteristic of his ministry, it would be applicable to him. Comp. John iv. 2. But if it means that he was *baptized*, and that he came in that way ' by water,' it was equally true of all the apostles who were baptized, and of all others, and there was nothing *so* remarkable in the fact that he was baptized as to justify the prominence given to the phrase in this place. (*b*) If reference be had here, as is supposed in this view of the passage, to the ' witness ' that was borne to the Lord Jesus on the occasion of his baptism, then the reference should have been not to the ' *water* ' as the witness, but to the ' voice that came from heaven,' (Matt. iii. 17,) for it was that which was the witness in the case. Though this occurred at the *time* of the baptism, yet it was quite an independent thing, and was important enough to have been referred to. See Lücke, *Com. in loc.* These objections, however, are not insuperable. Though Jesus did not come baptizing others himself, (John iv. 2,) and though the phrase would have expressed that if he had, yet, as Christian baptism began with him ; as this was the first act in his entrance on public life ; as it was by this that he was set apart to his work ; and as he designed that this should be always the initiatory rite of his religion, there was no impropriety in saying that his ' coming,' or his advent in this world, was at the beginning characterized by water, and at the close by blood. Moreover, though the ' witness ' at his baptism was really borne by a voice from heaven, yet his baptism was the prominent thing ; and if we take the baptism to denote *all* that in fact occurred when he was baptized, all the objections made by Lücke here vanish. (5.) Some, by the ' water ' here, have understood the ordinance of baptism as it is appointed by the Saviour to be administered to his people, meaning that the ordinance was instituted by him. So Beza, Calvin, Piscator, Calovius, Wolf, Beausobre, Knapp, Lücke, and others understand it. According to this the meaning would be, that he appointed baptism by water as a symbol of the cleansing of the heart, and shed his blood to effect the ransom of man, and that thus it might be said that he ' came

by water and blood;' to wit, by these two things as effecting the salvation of men. But it seems improbable that the apostle should have grouped these things together in this way. For (*a*) the ' blood ' is that which he shed ; which pertained to him personally ; which he poured out for the redemption of man ; and it is clear that, whatever is meant by the phrase ' *he came*,' his coming by ' water ' is to be understood in some sense similar to his coming by ' blood ;' and it seems incredible that the apostle should have joined a mere *ordinance* of religion in this way with the shedding of his blood, and placed them in this manner on an equality. (*b*) It cannot be supposed that John meant to attach so much importance to baptism as would be implied by this. The shedding of his blood was essential to the redemption of men ; can it be supposed that the apostle meant to teach that baptism by water is equally necessary ? (*c*) If this be understood of baptism, there is no natural connection between that and the ' blood ' referred to ; nothing by which the one would suggest the other ; no reason why they should be united. If he had said that he ' came ' by the appointment of two ordinances for the edification of the church, ' baptism and *the supper*,' however singular such a statement might be in some respects, yet there would be a connection, a reason why they should be suggested together. But why should baptism and the blood shed by the Saviour on the cross be grouped together as designating the principal things which characterized his coming into the world ? (6.) There remains, then, but one other interpretation ; to wit, that he refers to the ' water and the blood ' which flowed from the side of the Saviour when he was pierced by the spear of the Roman soldier. John had himself laid great stress on this occurrence, and on the fact that he had himself witnessed it, (see Notes on John xix. 34, 35 ;) and as, in these epistles, he is accustomed to allude to more full statements made in his Gospel, it would seem most natural to refer the phrase to that event as furnishing a clear and undoubted proof of the death of the Saviour. This would be the obvious interpretation, and would be

7 For there are three that bear record in heaven, the Father, *a* the

a Jn.8.18.

Word, *b* and the Holy Ghost : *c* and these three are one.

b He.4.12,13; Re.19.13.   *c* Jn.10.30.

entirely clear, if John did not immediately speak of the ' water ' and the 'blood' as *separate* witnesses, each as bearing witness to an important point, *as* separate as the ' Spirit ' and the 'water,' or the ' Spirit' and the 'blood;' whereas, if he refers to the mingled water and blood flowing from his side, they both witness only the same fact, to wit, his death. There was no *special* significancy in the water, no distinct testifying to anything different from the flowing of the blood; but together they bore witness to the *one* fact that he actually died. But here he seems to suppose that there is some special significancy in each. ' Not by water *only,* but by water *and* blood.' ' There are *three* that bear witness, the Spirit, *and* the water, *and* the blood, and these three agree in one.' These considerations seem to me to make it probable, on the whole, that the fourth opinion, above referred to, and that which has been commonly held in the Christian church, is correct, and that by the ' water ' the *baptism* of the Saviour is intended ; his baptism as an emblem of his own purity; as significant of the nature of his religion ; as a rite which was to be observed in his church at all times. That furnished an important attestation to the fact that he was the Messiah, (comp. Notes on Matt. iii. 15,) for it was by that that he entered on his public work, and it was then that a remarkable testimony was borne to his being the Son of God. He himself ' *came* ' thus by water as an emblem of purity ; and the water used in his church in all ages in baptism, together with the ' blood ' and the ' Spirit,' bears public testimony to the pure nature of his religion. It is *possible* that the mention of the ' water ' in his baptism suggested to John also the water which flowed from the side of the Saviour at his death, intermingled with blood ; and that though the primary thought in his mind was the fact that Jesus was baptized, and that an important attestation was then given to his Messiahship, yet he *may* have instantly adverted to the fact that *water* per-

formed so important a part, and was so important a symbol through all his work ; water at his introduction to his work, as an ordinance in his church, as symbolical of the nature of his religion, and even at his death, as a public attestation, in connection with flowing blood, to the fact that he truly *died*, in reality, and not, as the *Docetæ* pretended, in appearance only, thus completing the work of the Messiah, and making an atonement for the sins of the world. Comp. Notes, John xix. 34, 35. ¶ *And blood.* Referring, doubtless, to the shedding of his blood on the cross. He ' *came* ' by that ; that is, he was manifested by that to men, or that was one of the forms in which he appeared to men, or by which his coming into the world was characterized. The apostle means to say that the blood shed at his death furnished an important evidence or ' witness ' of what he was. In what way this was done, see Notes on ver. 8. ¶ *Not by water only, but by water and blood.* John the Baptist came ' by water only ;' that is, he came to baptize the people, and to prepare them for the coming of the Messiah. Jesus was distinguished from him in the fact that his ministry was characterized by the shedding of blood, or the shedding of his blood constituted one of the peculiarities of his work. ¶ *And it is the Spirit.* Evidently the Holy Spirit. ¶ *That beareth witness.* That is, he is the *great* witness in the matter, confirming all others. He bears witness to the soul that Jesus came ' by water and blood,' for that would not be received by us without his agency. In what way he does this, see Notes on ver. 8. ¶ *Because the Spirit is truth.* Is so eminently *true* that he may be called *truth itself,* as God is so eminently benevolent that he may be called *love itself.* See Notes on chap. iv. 8.

7. *For there are three that bear record in heaven,* &c. There are three that *witness*, or that *bear witness*—the same Greek word which, in ver. 8, is rendered *bear witness — μαρτυροῦντες.* There is no passage of the New Testa-

ment which has given rise to so much discussion in regard to its genuineness as this. The supposed importance of the verse in its bearing on the doctrine of the Trinity has contributed to this, and has given to the discussion a degree of consequence which has pertained to the examination of the genuineness of no other passage of the New Testament. On the one hand, the clear testimony which it seems to bear to the doctrine of the Trinity, has made that portion of the Christian church which holds the doctrine reluctant in the highest degree to abandon it; and on the other hand, the same clearness of the testimony to that doctrine, has made those who deny it not less reluctant to admit the genuineness of the passage. It is not consistent with the design of these Notes to go into a full investigation of a question of this sort. And all that can be done is to state, in a brief way, the *results* which have been reached, in an examination of the question. Those who are disposed to pursue the investigation further, can find all that is to be said in the works referred to at the bottom of the page.✱ The portion of the passage, in vers. 7, 8, whose genuineness is disputed, is included in brackets in the following quotation, as it stands in the common editions of the New Testament : ' For there are three that bear record [in heaven, the Father, the Word, and the Holy Ghost: and these three are one. And there are three that bear witness on earth,] the Spirit, and the water, and the blood; and these three agree in one.' If the disputed passage, therefore, be omitted as spurious, the whole passage will read, ' For there are three that bear record, the Spirit, and the water, and the blood; and these three agree in one.' The reasons which seem to me to prove that the passage included in brackets is spurious, and should not be regarded as a part of the inspired

writings, are briefly the following : I. It is wanting in all the earlier Greek manuscripts, for it is found in *no* Greek MS. written before the sixteenth century. Indeed, it is found in only two Greek manuscripts of any age—one the Codex Montfortianus, or Britannicus, written in the beginning of the sixteenth century, and the other the Codex Ravianus, which is a mere transcript of the text, taken partly from the third edition of Stephen's New Testament, and partly from the Complutensian Polyglott. But it is incredible that a genuine passage of the New Testament should be wanting in *all* the early Greek manuscripts. II. It is wanting in the earliest versions, and, indeed, in a large part of the versions of the New Testament which have been made in all former times. It is wanting in both the Syriac versions— one of which was made probably in the first century; in the Coptic, Armenian, Sclavonic, Ethiopic, and Arabic. III. It is never quoted by the Greek fathers in their controversies on the doctrine of the Trinity—a passage which would be so much in point, and which could not have failed to be quoted if it were genuine ; and it is not referred to by the Latin fathers until the time of Vigilius, at the end of the fifth century. If the passage were believed to be genuine—nay, if it were known at all to be in existence, and to have any probability in its favour—it is incredible that in all the controversies which occurred in regard to the Divine nature, and in all the efforts to define the doctrine of the Trinity, this passage should never have been referred to. But it never was; for it must be plain to any one who examines the subject with an unbiassed mind, that the passages which are relied on to prove that it was quoted by Athanasius, Cyprian, Augustin, &c., (Wetstein, II., p. 725,) are not taken from this place, and are not such as they would have made if they had been acquainted with this passage, and had designed to quote it. IV. The argument against the passage from the external proof is confirmed by internal evidence, which makes it morally certain that it cannot be genuine. (*a*) The connection does not demand it. It does not contribute to advance what the

* Mill. New Test., pp. 379-386 ; Wetstein, II. 721-727 ; Father Simon, Crit Hist. New Test. ; Michaelis, Intro. New Test., iv. 412 seq.; Semler, Histor. und Krit. Sammlungen über die sogenannten Beweistellen der Dogmatik. Erstes Stuck über, 1 John v. 7; Griesbach, Diatribe in locum, 1 John v. 7, 8, second edit., New Test., vol. II., appendix 1; and Lucke's Commentary *in loc.*

apostle is saying, but breaks the thread of his argument entirely. He is speaking of certain things which bear 'witness' to the fact that Jesus is the Messiah; certain things which were well known to those to whom he was writing—the Spirit, and the water, and the blood. How does it contribute to strengthen the force of this to say that *in heaven* there are 'three that bear witness'—three not before referred to, and having no connection with the matter under consideration? (*b*) The *language* is not such as John would use. He does, indeed, elsewhere use the term *Logos*, or *Word*—ὁ Λόγος, (John i. 1, 14; 1 John i. 1,) but it is never in this form, 'The Father, and the Word;' that is, the terms '*Father*' and '*Word*' are never used by him, or by any of the other sacred writers, as correlative. The word *Son*—ὁ Υἱός—is the term which is correlative to the *Father* in every other place as used by John, as well as by the other sacred writers. See 1 John i. 3; ii. 22—24; iv. 14; 2 John iii. 9; and the Gospel of John, *passim*. Besides, the correlative of the term *Logos*, or *Word*, with John, is not *Father*, but *God*. See John i. 1. Comp. Rev. xix. 13. (*c*) Without this passage, the sense of the argument is clear and appropriate. There are three, says John, which bear witness that Jesus is the Messiah. These are referred to in ver. 6; and in immediate connection with this, in the argument, (ver. 8,) it is affirmed that their testimony goes to one point, and is harmonious. To say that there are *other* witnesses elsewhere, to say that they are one, contributes nothing to illustrate the nature of the testimony of these three—the water, and the blood, and the Spirit; and the internal sense of the passage, therefore, furnishes as little evidence of its genuineness as the external proof. V. It is easy to imagine how the passage found a place in the New Testament. It was at first written, perhaps, in the margin of some Latin manuscript, as expressing the belief of the writer of what was true in heaven, as well as on earth, and with no more intention to deceive than we have when we make a marginal note in a book. Some transcriber copied it into the body of the text, perhaps with

a sincere belief that it was a genuine passage, omitted by accident; and then it became too important a passage in the argument for the Trinity, ever to be displaced but by the most clear critical evidence. It was rendered into Greek, and inserted in one Greek manuscript of the 16th century, while it was wanting in all the earlier manuscripts. VI. The passage is now omitted in the best editions of the Greek Testament, and regarded as spurious by the ablest critics. See Griesbach and Hahn. On the whole, therefore, the evidence seems to me to be clear that this passage is not a genuine portion of the inspired writings, and should not be appealed to in proof of the doctrine of the Trinity. One or two remarks may be made, in addition, in regard to its use. (1.) Even on the supposition that it *is* genuine, as Bengel believed it was, and as he believed that some Greek manuscript *would* yet be found which would contain it;[*] yet it is not wise to adduce it as a proof-text. It would be much easier to prove the doctrine of the Trinity from other texts, than to demonstrate the genuineness of this. (2.) It is not *necessary* as a proof-text. The doctrine which it contains can be abundantly established from other parts of the New Testament, by passages about which there can be no doubt. (3.) The removal of this text does nothing to weaken the evidence for the doctrine of the Trinity, or to modify that doctrine. As it was never used to shape the early belief of the Christian world on the subject, so its rejection, and its removal from the New Testament, will do nothing to modify that doctrine. The doctrine was embraced, and held, and successfully defended without it, and it can and will be so still.

8. *And there are three that bear witness in earth.*—This is a part of the text, which, if the reasoning above is correct, is to be omitted. The genuine passage reads, (ver. 7,) 'For there are three that bear record, [or witness—

---

[*] Et tamen etiam atque etiam sperare licet, si non autographum Joanneum, at alios vetustissimos codices Græcos, qui hanc periocham habeant, in occultis providentiæ divinæ forulis adhuc latentes suo tempore productum iri.

8 And there are three that bear witness in earth, the Spirit, [a] and

a Jn.15.26; Ac.2.2–4; 2 Co.1.22.

the water, [b] and the blood: [c] and these three agree in one.

b 1Pe.3.21.   *c* He.13.12.

μαρτυροῦντες,] the Spirit, and the water, and the blood.' There is no reference to the fact that it is done '*in earth.*' The phrase was introduced to correspond with what was said in the interpolated passage, that there are three that bear record '*in heaven.*' ¶ *The Spirit.* Evidently the Holy Spirit. The assertion here is, that that Spirit bears witness to the fact that Jesus is the Son of God, ver. 5. The testimony of the Holy Ghost to this fact is contained in the following things: (1.) He did it at the baptism of Jesus. Notes, Matt. iii. 16, 17. (2.) Christ was eminently *endowed* with the influences of the Holy Spirit; as it was predicted that the Messiah would be, and as it was appropriate he should be, Isa. xi. 2; lxi. 1. Compare Luke iv. 18; Notes, John iii. 34. (3.) The Holy Spirit bore witness to his Messiahship, after his ascension, by descending, according to his promise, on his apostles, and by accompanying the message which they delivered with saving power to thousands in Jerusalem, Acts ii. (4.) He still bears the same testimony on every revival of religion, and in the conversion of every individual who becomes a Christian, convincing them that Jesus is the Son of God. Comp. John xvi. 14, 15. (5.) He does it in the hearts of all true Christians, for ' no man can say that Jesus is Lord but by the Holy Ghost,' 1 Cor. xii. 3. See Notes on that passage. The Spirit of God has thus always borne witness to the fact that Jesus is the Christ, and he will continue to do it to the end of time, convincing yet countless millions that he was sent from God to redeem and save lost men. ¶ *And the water.* See Notes, ver. 6. That is, the baptism of Jesus, and the scenes which occurred when he was baptized, furnished evidence that he was the Messiah. This was done in these ways: (1.) It was proper that the Messiah should be baptized when he entered on his work, and perhaps it was expected; and the fact that he was baptized showed that he had *in fact* entered on his work as

Redeemer. See Notes, Matt. iii. 15. (2.) An undoubted attestation was then furnished to the fact that he was 'the Son of God,' by the descent of the Holy Spirit in the form of a dove, and by the voice that addressed him from heaven, Matt. iii. 16, 17. (3.) His baptism with water was an emblem of the purity of his own character, and of the nature of his religion. (4.) Perhaps it may be implied here, also, that water used in baptism now bears witness to the same thing, (*a*,) as it is the ordinance appointed by the Saviour; (*b*) as it keeps up his religion in the world; (*c*) as it is a public symbol of the purity of his religion; (*d*) and as, in every case where it is administered, it is connected with the public expression of a belief that Jesus is the Son of God. ¶ *And the blood.* There is undoubted allusion here to the blood shed on the cross; and the meaning is, that that blood bore witness also to the fact that he was the Son of God. This it did in the following respects: (1.) The shedding of the blood showed that he was truly dead—that his work was complete—that he died in *reality*, and not in *appearance* only. See Notes, John xix. 34, 35. (2.) The remarkable circumstances that attended the shedding of this blood—the darkened sun, the earthquake, the rending of the veil of the temple—showed in a manner that convinced even the Roman centurion that he was the Son of God. See Notes, Matt. xxvii. 54. (3.) The fact that an *atonement* was thus made for sin was an important ' witness ' for the Saviour, showing that he had done that which the Son of God only could do, by disclosing a way by which the sinner may be pardoned, and the polluted soul be made pure. (4.) Perhaps, also, there *may* be here an allusion to the Lord's Supper, as designed to set forth the shedding of this blood; and the apostle may mean to have it implied that the representation of the shedding of the blood in this ordinance is intended to keep up the conviction that Jesus is the Son of God. If so, then the general

9 If we receive the witness of men, the witness of God is greater: for this is the witness of God, which he hath testified of his Son.

10 He that believeth on the Son of God hath the witness *a* in himself : he that believeth not God hath made him a liar ; because he believeth not the record that God gave of his Son.

a Ro.8.16.

sense is, that that blood—however set before the eyes and the hearts of men—on the cross, or by the representation of its shedding in the Lord's Supper—is a witness in the world to the truth that Jesus is the Son of God, and to the nature of his religion. Comp. Notes, 1 Cor. xi. 26. ¶ *And these three agree in one.* εἰς τὸ ἕν εἰσι. They agree in one thing; they bear on one and the same point, to wit, the fact that Jesus is the Son of God. All are appointed by God as witnesses of this fact ; and all harmonize in the testimony which is borne. The apostle does not say that there are no other witnesses to the same thing ; nor does he even say that these are the most important or decisive which have been furnished ; but he says that these *are* important witnesses, and are entirely harmonious in their testimony.

9. *If we receive the witness of men.* As we are accustomed to do, and as we must do in courts of justice, and in the ordinary daily transactions of life. We are constantly acting on the belief that what others say is true ; that what the members of our families, and our neighbours say, is true ; that what is reported by travellers is true ; that what we read in books, and what is sworn to in courts of justice, is true. We could not get along a single day if we did not act on this belief ; nor are we accustomed to call it in question, unless we have reason to suspect that it is false. The mind is so made that it must credit the testimony borne by others; and if this should cease even for a single day, the affairs of the world would come to a pause. ¶ *The witness of God is greater.* Is more worthy of belief ; as God is more true, and wise, and good than men. Men may be deceived, and may undesignedly bear witness to that which is not true —God never can be ; men may, for sinister and base purposes, intend to deceive—God never can ; men may act from partial observation, from rumours unworthy of credence—God never can ;

men may desire to excite admiration by the marvellous—God never can ; men have deceived—God never has ; and though, from these causes, there are many instances where we are not certain that the testimony borne by men is true, yet we are always certain that that which is borne by God is not false. The only question on which the mind ever hesitates is, whether we actually *have* his testimony, or certainly *know* what he bears witness to; when that is ascertained, the human mind is so made that it *cannot* believe that God would deliberately deceive a world. See Notes, Heb. vi. 18. Comp. Titus i. 2. ¶ *For this is the witness of God,* &c. The testimony above referred to—that borne by the Spirit, and the water, and the blood. Who that saw his baptism, and heard the voice from heaven, (Matt. iii. 16, 17,) could doubt that he was the Son of God ? Who that saw his death on the cross, and that witnessed the amazing scenes which occurred there, could fail to join with the Roman centurion in saying that this was the Son of God ? Who that has felt the influences of the Eternal Spirit on his heart, ever doubted that Jesus was the Son of God? Comp. Notes, 1 Cor. xii. 3. Any one of these is sufficient to convince the soul of this ; all combined bear on the same point, and confirm it from age to age.

10. *He that believeth on the Son of God hath the witness in himself.* The evidence that Jesus is the Son of God. Comp. Notes, Rom. viii. 16. This cannot refer to any distinct and immediate *revelation* of that fact, that Jesus is the Christ, to the soul of the individual, and is not to be understood as independent of the external evidence of that truth, or as superseding the necessity of that evidence ; but the 'witness' here referred to is the fruit of *all* the evidence, external and internal, on the heart, producing this result ; that is, there is the deepest conviction of the truth that Jesus is the Son of God. There is the evi-

11 And this is the record, that God hath given to us eternal life, and this life *a* is in his Son.

12 He *b* that hath the Son, hath life ; *and* he that hath not the Son of God, hath not life.

13 These things have I written unto you that believe on the name of the Son of God ; that ye *c* may know that ye have eternal life, and that ye may believe on the name of the Son of God.

a Jn.1.4.	*b* Jn.5.24.	*c* Jn.20.31.

dence derived from the fact that the soul has found peace by believing on him ; from the fact that the troubles and anxieties of the mind on account of sin have been removed by faith in Christ ; from the new views of God and heaven which have resulted from faith in the Lord Jesus ; from the effect of this in disarming death of its terrors ; and from the whole influence of the gospel on the intellect and the affections—on the heart and the life. These things constitute a mass of evidence for the truth of the Christian religion, whose force the believer cannot resist, and make the sincere Christian ready to sacrifice anything rather than his religion ; ready to go to the stake rather than to renounce his Saviour. Comp. Notes, 1 Pet. iii. 15. ¶ *He that believeth not God hath made him a liar.* Comp. Notes, chap. i. 10. ¶ *Because he believeth not the record,* &c. The idea is, that in various ways—at his baptism, at his death, by the influences of the Holy Spirit, by the miracles of Jesus, &c.—God had become a *witness* that the Lord Jesus was sent by him as a Saviour, and that to doubt or deny this partook of the same character as doubting or denying any other testimony ; that is, it was practically charging him who bore the testimony with falsehood.

11. *And this is the record.* This is the *sum,* or the *amount,* of the testimony (μαρτυρία) which God has given respecting him. ¶ *That God hath given to us eternal life.* Has provided, through the Saviour, the means of obtaining eternal life. See Notes, John v. 24 ; xvii. 2, 3. ¶ *And this life is in his Son.* Is treasured up in him, or is to be obtained through him. See Notes, John i. 4 ; xi. 25 ; xiv. 6 ; Col. iii. 3.

12. *He that hath the Son, hath life.* See Notes, John v. 24. John evidently designs to refer to that passage in the verse before us, and to state a principle laid down by the Saviour himself. This is the sense of all the important testimony that had ever been borne by God on the subject of salvation, that he who believes in the Lord Jesus already *has* the elements of eternal life in his soul, and will certainly obtain salvation. Comp. Notes, John xvii. 3. ¶ And *he that hath not the Son of God, hath not life.* He that does not believe on him will not attain to eternal life. See Notes, John iii. 36 ; Mark xvi. 16.

13. *These things have I written unto you.* The things in this epistle respecting the testimony borne to the Lord Jesus. ¶ *That believe on the name of the Son of God.* To believe on his *name,* is to believe on himself—the word *name* often being used to denote the person. See Notes, Matt. xxviii. 19. ¶ *That ye may know that ye have eternal life.* That you may see the evidence that eternal life has been provided, and that you may be able, by self-examination, to determine whether you possess it. Comp. Notes, John xx. 31. ¶ *And that ye may believe,* &c. That you may *continue* to believe, or may *persevere* in believing. He was assured that they actually *did* believe on him then ; but he was desirous of so setting before them the nature of religion, that they would *continue* to exercise faith in him. It is often one of the most important duties of ministers of the gospel, to present to real Christians such views of the nature, the claims, the evidences, and the hopes of religion, as shall be adapted to secure their perseverance in the faith. In the human heart, even when converted, there is such a proneness to unbelief ; the religious affections so easily become cold ; there are so many cares pertaining to the world that are fitted to distract the mind ; there are so many allurements of sin to draw the affections away from the Saviour ; that there is need of being constantly reminded of the nature of re-

14 And this is the confidence
that we have ¹in him, that, if we

1 *concerning.*

ask any thing according to his will,
he heareth us:

ligion, in order that the heart may not
be wholly estranged from the Saviour.
No small part of preaching, therefore,
must consist of the re-statement of arguments with which the mind has been
before fully convinced; of motives whose
force has been once felt and acknowledged; and of the grounds of hope and
peace and joy which have already, on former occasions, diffused comfort through
the soul. It is not less important to
keep the soul, than it is to *convert* it;
to save it from coldness, and deadness,
and formality, than it was to impart to
it the elements of spiritual life at first.
It may be as important to trim a vine,
if one would have grapes, as it is to set
it out; to keep a garden from being
overrun with weeds in the summer, as
it was to plant it in the spring.

14. *And this is the confidence that we
have in him.* Marg., *concerning.* Greek,
'towards him,' or in respect to him—
πρὸς αὐτόν. The confidence referred to
here is that which relates to the answer
to prayer. The apostle does not say
that this is the *only* thing in respect to
which there is to be confidence in him,
but that it is one which is worthy of
special consideration. The sense is, that
one of the effects of believing on the
Lord Jesus (ver. 13) is, that we have
the assurance that our prayers will be
answered. On the word *confidence,* see
Notes on chap. iii. 21; iv. 17. ¶ *That,
if we ask any thing according to his
will, he heareth us.* This is the proper
and the necessary limitation in all prayer.
God has not promised to grant anything
that shall be contrary to his will, and
it could not be right that he should do
it. We ought not to wish to receive
anything that should be contrary to
what he judges to be best. No man
could hope for good who should esteem
his own wishes to be a better guide than
the will of God; and it is one of the
most desirable of all arrangements that
the promise of any blessing to be obtained
by prayer should be limited and bounded
by the will of God. The limitation here,
'according to his will,' probably implies
the following things: (1.) In accordance

with what he has *declared* that he is
willing to grant. Here the range is
large, for there are many things which
we know to be in accordance with his
will, if they are sought in a proper manner—as the forgiveness of sins, the sanctification of the soul, (1 Thess. iv. 3,)
comfort in trial, the needful supply of
our wants, grace that we may do our
duty, wisdom to direct and guide us,
(James i. 5,) deliverance from the evils
which beset us, the influences of his
Spirit to promote the cause of religion
in the world, and our final salvation.
Here is a range of subjects of petition
that may gratify the largest wishes of
prayer. (2.) The expression, 'according
to his will,' must limit the answer to
prayer to what *he* sees to be best for us.
Of that we are not always good judges.
We never perceive it as clearly as our
Maker does, and in many things we
might be wholly mistaken. Certainly
we ought not to desire to be permitted
to ask anything which *God* would judge
not to be for our good. (3.) The expression must limit the petition to what it
will be *consistent* for God to bestow upon
us. We cannot expect that he will work
a miracle in answer to our prayers; we
cannot ask him to bestow blessings in
violation of any of the laws which he
has ordained, or in any other way than
that which he has appointed. It is
better that the particular blessing should
be withheld from us, than that the laws
which he has appointed should be disregarded. It is better that an idle man
should *not* have a harvest, though he
should pray for it, than that God should
violate the laws by which he has determined to bestow such favours as a reward
of industry, and work a special miracle
in answer to a lazy man's prayers. (4.)
The expression, 'according to his will,'
must limit the promise to what will be
for the good of the whole. God presides
over the universe: and though in him
there is an infinite fulness, and he regards the wants of every individual
throughout his immense empire, yet the
interests of the whole, as well as of the
individual, are to be consulted and re-

15 And if we know *a* that he hear us, whatsoever we ask, we know that we have the petitions that we desired of him.

16 If any man see his brother sin a sin *which is* not unto death,

he shall ask, and he shall give him life for them that sin not unto death. There is a sin unto death : *b* I do not say *c* that he shall pray for it.

a Pr.15.29; Jer.29.12,13.   *b* Mat.12,31,32.   *c* Jer.7.16.

garded. In a family, it is conceivable that a child might ask for some favour whose bestowment would interfere materially with the rights of others, or be inconsistent with the good of the whole, and in such a case a just father would of course withhold it. With these necessary limitations the range of the promise in prayer is ample ; and, with these limitations, it is true beyond a question that he does hear and answer prayer.

15. *And if we know that he hear us.* That is, if we are assured of this as a true doctrine, then, even though we may not *see* immediately that the prayer is answered, we may have the utmost confidence that it is not disregarded, and that it will be answered in the way best adapted to promote our good. The specific thing that we asked may not indeed be granted, (comp. Luke xxii. 42 ; 2 Cor. xii. 8, 9,) but the prayer will not be disregarded, and the thing which is most for our good will be bestowed upon us. The *argument* here is derived from the faithfulness of God ; from the assurance which we feel that when he has promised to hear us, there will be, sooner or later, a *real* answer to the prayer. ¶ *We know that we have the petitions,* &c. That is, evidently, we know that we *shall* have them, or that the prayer will be answered. It cannot mean that we already have the precise thing for which we prayed, or that will be a real answer to the prayer, for (*a*) the prayer may relate to something future, as protection on a journey, or a harvest, or restoration to health, or the safe return of a son from a voyage at sea, or the salvation of our souls—all of which are *future*, and which cannot be expected to be granted at once ; and (*b*) the answer to prayer is sometimes delayed, though ultimately granted. There may be reasons why the answer should be deferred, and the promise is not that it shall be immediate. The *delay* may arise from such causes as these : (1.)

To try our faith, and see whether the blessing is earnestly desired. (2.) Perhaps it could not be at once answered without a miracle. (3.) It might not be consistent with the Divine arrangements respecting others to grant it to us at once. (4.) Our own condition may not be such that it would be best to answer it at once. We may need further trial, further chastisement, before the affliction, for example, shall be removed ; and the answer to the prayer may be delayed for months or years. Yet, in the meantime, we may have the firmest assurance that the prayer *is* heard, and that it *will be* answered in the way and at the period when God shall see it to be best.

16. *If a man see his brother sin a sin,* &c. From the general assurance that God hears prayer, the apostle turns to a particular case in which it may be benevolently and effectually employed, in rescuing a brother from death. There has been great diversity of opinion in regard to the meaning of this passage, and the views of expositors of the New Testament are by no means settled as to its true sense. It does not comport with the design of these Notes to examine the opinions which have been held in detail. A bare reference, however, to some of them will show the difficulty of determining with certainty what the passage means, and the impropriety of any very great confidence in one's own judgment in the case. Among these opinions are the following. Some have supposed that the sin against the Holy Ghost is intended ; some that the phrase denotes any great and enormous sin, as murder, idolatry, adultery ; some that it denotes some sin that was punishable by death by the laws of Moses ; some that it denotes a sin that subjected the offender to excommunication from the synagogue or the church ; some that it refers to sins which brought fatal disease upon the offender, as in the case

of those who abused the Lord's Supper at Corinth, (see Notes on 1 Cor. xi. 30;) some that it refers to crimes committed against the laws, for which the offender was sentenced to death, meaning that when the charge alleged was false, and the condemnation unjust, they ought to pray for the one who was condemned to death, and that he would be spared; but that when the offence was one which had been really committed, and the offender deserved to die, they ought not to pray for him, or, in other words, that by 'the sin unto death,' offences against the civil law are referred to, which the magistrate had no power to pardon, and the punishment of which he could not commute; and by the 'sin not unto death,' offences are referred to which might be pardoned, and when the punishment might be commuted; some that it refers to sins *before* and *after* baptism, the former of which might be pardoned, but the latter of which might not be; and some, and perhaps this is the common opinion among the Roman Catholics, that it refers to sins that might or might not be pardoned *after* death, thus referring to the doctrine of purgatory. These various opinions may be seen stated more at length in Rosenmüller, Lücke, Pool, (*Synopsis*,) and Clarke, *in loc.* To go into an examination of all these opinions would require a volume by itself, and all that can be done here is to furnish what seems to me to be the fair exposition of the passage. The word *brother* may refer either to a member of the church, whether of the particular church to which one was attached or another, or it may be used in the larger sense which is common as denoting a fellow-man, a member of the great family of mankind. There is nothing in the word which necessarily limits it to one in the church; there is nothing in the connection, or in the reason assigned, why what is said should be limited to such an one. The *duty* here enjoined would be the same whether the person referred to was in the church or not; for it is our duty to pray for those who sin, and to seek the salvation of those whom we see to be going astray, and to be in danger of ruin, wherever they are, or whoever they may be. At the same time, the correct interpretation

of the passage does not depend on determining whether the word *brother* refers to one who is a professed Christian or not.

¶ *A sin* which is *not unto death.* The great question in the interpretation of the whole passage is, what is meant by the 'sin unto death.' The Greek (ἁμαρτία πρὸς θάνατον) would mean properly a sin which *tends* to death; which would *terminate* in death; of which death was the penalty, or would be the result, unless it were arrested; a sin which, if it had its own course, would terminate thus, as we should speak of a disease 'unto death.' Comp. Notes, John xi. 4. The word *death* is used in three significations in the New Testament, and as employed here might, so far as the *word* is concerned, be applied in any one of those senses. It is used to denote (*a*) literally the death of the body; (*b*) spiritual death, or death 'in trespasses and sin,' Eph. ii. 1; (*c*) the 'second death,' death in the world of woe and despair. If the sin here mentioned refers to *temporal* death, it means such a sin that temporal death *must* inevitably follow, either by the *disease* which it has produced, or by a judicial sentence where there was no hope of pardon or of a commutation of the punishment; if it refers to death in the future world, the second death, then it means such a sin as is unpardonable. That this last *is* the reference here seems to me to be probable, if not clear, from the following considerations: (1.) There *is* such a sin referred to in the New Testament, a sin for which there is forgiveness 'neither in this life nor the life to come.' See Notes, Matt. xii. 31, 32. Comp. Mark iii. 29. If there *is* such a sin, there is no impropriety in supposing that John would refer to it here. (2.) This is the *obvious* interpretation. It is that which would occur to the mass of the readers of the New Testament, and which it is presumed they do adopt; and this, in general, is one of the best means of ascertaining the sense of a passage in the Bible. (3.) The other significations attached to the word *death*, would be quite inappropriate here. (*a*) It cannot mean 'unto *spiritual death*,' that is, to a continuance in sin, for how could that be known? and if such a case occurred, why would it be improper to pray for it? Besides, the phrase 'a sin unto spiritual death,' or 'unto continuance in sin,' is one that is unmeaning. (b) It cannot be shown to refer to a disease that should be unto death, miraculously inflicted on account of sin, because, if such cases occurred, they were very rare, and even if a disease came upon a man miraculously in consequence of sin, it could not be certainly known whether it was, or was not, unto death. All who were visited in this way did not certainly die. Comp. 1 Cor. v. 4, 5, with 2 Cor. ii. 6, 7. See also 1 Cor. xi. 30. (c) It cannot be shown that it refers to the case of those who were condemned by the civil magistrate to death, and for whom there was no hope of reprieve or pardon, for it is not certain that there were such cases; and if there were, and the person condemned were innocent, there was every reason to pray that *God* would interpose and save them, even when there was no hope from man; and if they were guilty, and deserved to die, there was no reason why they should not pray that the sin might be forgiven, and that they might be prepared to die, unless it were a case where the sin was unpardonable. It seems probable, therefore, to me, that the reference here is to the sin against the Holy Ghost, and that John means here to illustrate the duty and the power of prayer, by showing that for *any sin short of that,* however aggravated, it was their duty to pray that a brother might be forgiven. Though it might not be easy to determine what *was* the unpardonable sin, and John does not say that those to whom he wrote could determine that with certainty, yet there were many sins which were manifestly *not* of that aggravated character, and for those sins it was proper to pray. There was clearly but *one* sin that was unpardonable — 'there is *a* sin unto death;' there might be many which were not of this description, and in relation to them there was ample scope for the exercise of the prayer of faith. The same thing is true now. It is not easy to define the unpardonable sin, and it is impossible for us to determine in any case with absolute certainty that a man

has committed it. But there are multitudes of sins which men commit, which on no proper interpretation of the passages respecting the sin which 'hath never forgiveness,' can come under the description of that sin, and for which it is proper, therefore, to pray that they may be pardoned. We know of cases enough where sin *may* be forgiven; and, without allowing the mind to be disturbed about the question respecting the unpardonable sin, it is our duty to bear such cases on our hearts before God, and to plead with him that our erring brethren may be saved. ¶ *He shall ask.* That is, he shall pray that the offender may be brought to true repentance, and may be saved. ¶ *And he shall give him life for them that sin not unto death.* That is, *God* shall give life, and he shall be saved from the eternal death to which he was exposed. This, it is said, would be given to 'him' who offers the prayer; that is, his prayer would be the means of saving the offending brother. What a motive is this to prayer! How faithful and constant should we be in pleading for our fellow-sinners, that we may be instrumental in saving their souls! What joy will await those in heaven who shall see there many who were rescued from ruin in answer to their prayers! Comp. Notes, James v. 15, 19, 20. ¶ *There is a sin unto death.* A sin which is of such a character that it throws the offender beyond the reach of mercy, and which is not to be pardoned. See Mark iii. 28, 29. The apostle does not here say what that sin is; nor how they might know what it is; nor even that in any case they could determine that it had been committed. He merely says that there *is* such a sin, and that he does not design that his remark about the efficacy of prayer should be understood as extending to that. ¶ *I do not say that he shall pray for it.* 'I do not intend that my remark shall be extended to *all* sin, or mean to affirm that all possible forms of guilt are the proper subjects of prayer, for I am aware that there is one sin which is an exception, and my remark is not to be applied to that.' He does not say that this sin was of common occurrence: or that they could know when it had been committed; or even that a case could ever occur in

17 All unrighteousness *a* is sin : and there *b* is a sin not unto death.

18 We know that whosoever is born of God sinneth not ; but he that is begotten of God keepeth himself, *c* and that wicked one toucheth him not.

a 1 Jn.3.4.   *b* Ro.5.20,21.   *c* Ja.1.27.

which they could determine that ; he merely says that in respect to that sin he did *not* say that prayer should be offered. It is indeed implied in a most delicate way that it would not be proper to pray for the forgiveness of such a sin, but he does not say that a case would ever happen in which they would *know* certainly that the sin had been committed. There were instances in the times of the prophets in which the sin of the people became so universal and so aggravated, that they were forbidden to pray for them. Isa. xiv. 11, ' Then said the Lord unto me, Pray not for this people for their good ;' xv. 1, ' Then said the Lord unto me, Though Moses and Samuel stood before me, yet my mind could not be toward this people; cast them out of my sight, and let them go forth.' Comp. Notes, Isa. i. 15. But these were cases in which the prophets were directly instructed by God not to pray for a people. We have no such instruction ; and it may be said now with truth, that as we can never be certain respecting any one that he has committed the unpardonable sin, there is no one for whom we may not with propriety pray. There may be those who are so far gone in sin that there may seem to be little, or almost no ground of hope. They may have cast off all the restraints of religion, of morality, of decency; they may disregard all the counsels of parents and friends ; they may be sceptical, sensual, profane ; they may be the companions of infidels and of mockers ; they may have forsaken the sanctuary, and learned to despise the sabbath ; they may have been professors of religion, and now may have renounced the faith of the gospel altogether, but still, while there is life it is our duty to pray for them, ' if peradventure God will give them repentance to the acknowledging of the truth,' 2 Tim. ii. 25. ' *All things* are possible with God ;' and he has reclaimed offenders more hardened, probably, than any that we have known, and has demonstrated that there is no form of depravity which he has not the power to subdue. Let us remember the cases of Manasseh, of Saul of Tarsus, of Augustine, of Bunyan, of Newton, of tens of thousands who have been reclaimed from the vilest forms of iniquity, and then let us never despair of the conversion of any, in answer to prayer, who may have gone astray, as long as they are in this world of probation and of hope. Let no parent despair who has an abandoned son ; let no wife cease to pray who has a dissipated husband. How many a prodigal son has come back to fill with happiness an aged parent's heart! How many a dissipated husband has been reformed to give joy again to the wife of his youth, and to make a paradise again of his miserable home !

17. *All unrighteousness is sin,* &c. This seems to be thrown in to guard what he had just said, and there is *one* great and enormous sin, a sin which could not be forgiven. But he says also that there are many other forms and degrees of sin, sin for which prayer may be made. Everything, he says, which is *unrighteous* — ἀδικία — everything which does not conform to the holy law of God, and which is not *right* in the view of that law, is to be regarded as sin ; but we are not to suppose that *all* sin of that kind is of such a character that it cannot possibly be forgiven. There are many who commit sin who we may hope will be recovered, and for them it is proper to pray. Deeply affected as we may be in view of the fact that there is a sin which can never be pardoned, and much as we may pity one who has been guilty of such a sin, yet we should not hastily conclude in any case that it has been committed, and should bear constantly in mind that while there is one such sin, there are multitudes that may be pardoned, and that for them it is our duty unceasingly to pray.

18. *We know that whosoever is born of God sinneth not.* Is not habitually and characteristically a sinner ; does not ultimately and finally sin and perish ; cannot, therefore, commit the unpar-

19 *And* we know that we are of God, and the whole world lieth in wickedness.

20 And we know that the Son of God is come, and hath given us an understanding, *a* that we may know him that is true: and we are in

a Lu.24.45.

donable sin. Though he may fall into sin, and grieve his brethren, yet we are never to cease to pray for a true Christian ; we are never to feel that he has committed the sin which has never forgiveness, and that he has thrown himself beyond the reach of our prayers. This passage, in its connection, is a full proof that a true Christian *will* never commit the unpardonable sin, and, therefore, is a proof that he will never fall from grace. Comp. Notes, Heb. vi. 4–8 ; x. 26. On the *meaning* of the assertion here made, that ' whosoever is born of God sinneth not,' see Notes on chap. iii. 6–9. ¶ *Keepeth himself.* It is not said that he does it by his own strength, but he will put forth his best efforts to keep himself from sin, and by Divine assistance he will be able to accomplish it. Comp. Notes on chap. iii. 3 ; Jude 21. ¶ *And that wicked one toucheth him not.* The great enemy of all good is repelled in his assaults, and he is kept from falling into his snares. The word *toucheth* (ἅπτεται) is used here in the sense of *harm* or *injure.*

19. And *we know that we are of God.* We who are Christians. The apostle supposed that true Christians might have so clear evidence on that subject as to leave no doubt on their own minds that they were the children of God. Comp. chap. iii. 14 ; 2 Tim. i. 12. ¶ *And the whole world.* The term *world* here evidently means not the *material* world, but the *people* that dwell on the earth, including all idolaters, and all sinners of every grade and kind. ¶ *Lieth in wickedness.* ' In the wicked one,' or under the power of the wicked one— ἐν τῷ πονηρῷ. It is true that the word πονηρῷ may be used here in the neuter gender, as our translators have rendered it, meaning ' in that which is evil,' or in ' wickedness ;' but it may be in the masculine gender, meaning ' the wicked one ;' and then the sense would be that the whole world is under his control or dominion. That this is the meaning of the apostle seems to be clear, because

(1) the corresponding phrase, (ver. 20,) ἐν τῷ ἀληθινῷ, ' in him that is true,' is evidently to be construed in the masculine, referring to God the Saviour, and meaning ' him that is true,' and not that we are ' in truth.' (2.) It makes better sense to say that the world lies under the control of the wicked one, than to say that it lies ' in wickedness.' (3.) This accords better with the other representations in the Bible, and the usuage of the word elsewhere. Comp. 1 John ii. 13, ' Ye have overcome the *wicked* one ;' ver. 14, ' ye have overcome the *wicked* one ;' iii. 12, ' who was of that *wicked* one.' See also Notes, 2 Cor. iv. 4, on the expression ' the god of this world ;' John xii. 31, where he is called ' the prince of this world ;' and Eph. ii. 2, where he is called ' the prince of the power of the air.' In all these passages it is supposed that Satan has control over the world, especially the heathen world. Comp. Eph. vi. 12 ; 1 Cor. x. 20. In regard to the *fact* that the heathen world was pervaded by wickedness, see Notes on Rom. i. 21–32. (4.) It may be added, that this interpretation is adopted by the most eminent critics and commentators. It is that of Calvin, Beza, Benson, Macknight, Bloomfield, Piscator, Lücke, &c. The word *lieth* here (κεῖται) means, properly, to lie ; to be laid ; to recline ; to be situated, &c. It seems here to refer to the *passive* and *torpid* state of a wicked world under the dominion of the prince of evil, as acquiescing in his reign; making no resistance ; not even struggling to be free. It *lies* thus as a beast that is subdued, a body that is dead, or anything that is wholly passive, quiet, and inert. There is no energy ; no effort to throw off the reign ; no resistance ; no struggling. The dominion is complete, and body and soul, individuals and nations, are entirely subject to his will. This striking expression will not unaptly now describe the condition of the heathen world, or of sinners in general. There would seem to be no government under which men are so little restive, and against which

him that is true, *even* in his Son | Jesus Christ. This " is the true
a Is.9.6. | God, and eternal life.

they have so little disposition to rebel, as that of Satan. Comp. 2 Tim. ii. 26. 20. *And we know that the Son of God is come.* We know this by the evidence that John had referred to in this epistle, chap. i. 1–4 ; v. 6–8. ¶ *And hath given us an understanding.* Not an ' understanding' considered as a faculty of the mind, for religion gives us no new faculties ; but he has so instructed us that we do understand the great truths referred to. Comp. Notes, Luke xxiv. 45. All the correct *knowledge* which we have of God and his government, is to be traced directly or indirectly to the great Prophet whom God has sent into the world, John i. 4, 18 ; viii. 12 ; ix. 5 ; Heb. i. 1–3 ; Matt. xi. 27. ¶ *That we may know him that is true.* That is, the true God. See Notes, John xvii. 3. ¶ *And we are in him that is true.* That is, we are united to him ; we belong to him ; we are his friends. This idea is often expressed in the Scriptures by being '*in* him.' It denotes a most intimate union, *as if* we were one with him—or were a *part* of him—as the branch is *in* the vine, John xv. 4, 6. The Greek construction is the same as that applied to ' the wicked one,' ver. 19, (ἐν τῷ ἀληθινῷ.) ¶ *This is the true God.** There has been much difference of opinion in regard to this important passage ; whether it refers to the Lord Jesus Christ, the immediate antecedent, or to a more remote antecedent—referring to God, as such. The question is of importance in its bearing on the doctrine of the divinity of the Saviour ; for if it refers to him, it furnishes an unequivocal declaration that he is Divine. The question is, whether John *meant* that it should be referred to him? Without going into an extended ex-

* Many mss. here insert the word *God*—' the true *God* '— τὸν ἀληθινὸν Θεὸν. This is also found in the Vulgate, Coptic, Æthiopic, and Arabic versions, and in the Complutensian edition of the New Testament. The reading, however, is not so well sustained as to be adopted by Griesbach, Tittman, or Hahn. That it *may* be a genuine reading is indeed possible, but the evidence is against it. Lücke supposes that it is genuine, and endeavours to account for the manner in which it was omitted in the mss.— *Commentary*, p. 349.
VOL. X.

amination of the passage, the following considerations seem to me to make it morally certain that by the phrase ' this is the true God,' &c., he did refer to the Lord Jesus Christ. (1.) The grammatical construction favours it. Christ is the immediate antecedent of the pronoun *this*—οὗτος. This would be regarded as the obvious and certain construction so far as the grammar is concerned, unless there were something in the thing affirmed which led us to seek some more remote and less obvious antecedent. No doubt would have been ever entertained on this point, if it had not been for the reluctance to admit that the Lord Jesus ·is the true God. If the assertion had been that ' *this* is the true Messiah ;' or that ' *this* is the Son of God ;' or that ' *this* is he who was born of the Virgin Mary,' there would have been no difficulty in the construction. I admit that this argument is not absolutely decisive; for cases do occur where a pronoun refers, not to the immediate antecedent, but to one more remote ; but cases of that kind depend on the ground of necessity, and can be applied only when it would be a clear violation of the sense of the author to refer it to the immediate antecedent. (2.) This construction seems to be demanded by the adjunct which John has assigned to the phrase ' the true God '—' eternal life.' This is an expression which John would be likely to apply to the Lord Jesus, considered as *life*, and *the source of life*, and not to God as such. ' How familiar is this language with John, as applied to Christ ! " In him (i. e. Christ) was life, and the life was the light of men—giving life to the world—the bread of life—my words are spirit and life—I am the way, and the truth, and the life. This life (Christ) was manifested, and we have *seen it*, and do testify to you, and declare the eternal life which was with the Father, and was manifested to us," 1 John i. 2.'—Prof. Stuart's Letters to Dr. Channing, p. 83. There is no instance in the writings of John, in which the appellation life, and *eternal* life is bestowed upon the Father, to designate him as the author of spiritual
z

21 Little children, keep your- selves from idols.^a Amen.

and eternal life ; and as this occurs so frequently in John's writings as applied to Christ, the laws of exegesis require that both the phrase 'the true God,' and 'eternal life,' should be applied to him. (3.) If it refers to God as such, or to the word 'true'—τὸν ἀληθινόν [Θεὸν] it would be mere tautology, or a mere truism. The rendering would then be, 'That we may know the *true* God, and we are in the *true* God : this *is* the true God, and eternal life.' Can we believe that an inspired man would affirm grave- ly, and with so much solemnity, and as if it were a truth of so much magni- tude, that the true God *is* the true God ? (4.) This interpretation accords with what we are sure John *would* affirm respecting the Lord Jesus Christ. Can there be any doubt that he who said, ' In the beginning was the Word, and the Word was with God, and the Word was God ;' that he who said, ' all things were made by him, and without him was not anything made that was made ;' that he who recorded the declaration of the Saviour, ' I and my Father are one,' and the declaration of Thomas, ' my Lord and my God,' would apply to him the appellation *the true God !* (5.) If John did *not* mean to affirm this, he has made use of an expression which was liable to be misunderstood, and which, as facts have shown, would be misconstrued by the great portion of those who might read what he had writ- ten ; and, moreover, an expression that would lead to the *very* sin against which he endeavours to guard in the next verse —the sin of substituting a creature in the place of God, and rendering to an- other the honour due to him. The lan- guage which he uses is just such as, according to its natural interpretation, would lead men to worship one as the true God who is *not* the true God, un- less the Lord Jesus be Divine. For these reasons, it seems to me that the fair interpretation of this passage de- mands that it should be understood as referring to the Lord Jesus Christ. If so, it is a direct assertion of his divinity, for there could be no higher proof of it than to affirm that he is the true God.

¶ *And eternal life.* Having 'life in himself,' (John v. 26,) and the source and fountain of life to the soul. No more frequent appellation, perhaps, is given to the Saviour by John, than that he is life, and the source of life. Comp. John i. 4 ; v. 26, 40 ; x. 10 ; vi. 33, 35, 48, 51, 53, 63 ; xi. 25 ; xiv. 6 ; xx. 31 ; 1 John i. 1, 2 ; v. 12.

21. *Little children.* This is a favour- ite mode of address with John, (see Notes on chap. ii. 1,) and it was proper to use it in giving his parting counsel ; em- bracing, in fact, all that he had to say —that they should keep themselves from idols, and suffer nothing to alienate their affections from the true God. His great object had been to lead them to the knowledge and love of God, and all his counsels would be practically followed, if, amidst the temptations of idolatry, and the allurements of sin, nothing were allowed to estrange their hearts from him. ¶ *Keep yourselves from idols.* From worshipping them ; from all that would imply communion with them or their devotees. Compare Notes, 1 Cor. x. 14. The word rendered *idols* here (εἰδώλων) means, properly, an image, spectre, shade—as of the dead ; then any image or figure which would represent anything, particularly anything invisi- ble ; and hence anything designed to represent God, and that was set up with a view to be acknowledged as repre- senting him, or to bring him, or his per- fections, more vividly before the mind. The word is applicable to idol-gods— heathen deities, 1 Cor. viii. 4, 7 ; x. 19 ; Rom. ii. 22 ; 2 Cor. vi. 16 ; 1 Thess. i. 9 ; but it would, also, be applicable to any *image* designed to represent the true God, and through or by which the true God was to be adored. The essential things in the word seem to be, (*a*,) an image or representation of the Deity, and (*b*) the making of that an object of adoration instead of the true God. Since one of these things would be likely to lead to the other, both are forbidden in the prohibitions of idolatry, Exod. xx. 4, 5. This would forbid all attempts to represent God by paintings or statuary ; all idol-worship, or worship of heathen

gods ; all images and pictures that would be substituted in the place of God as objects of devotion, or that might transfer the homage from God to the image ; and all giving of those affections to other beings or objects which are due to God. *Why* the apostle closed this epistle with this injunction he has not stated, and it may not be easy to determine It may have been for such reasons as these : (1.) Those to whom he wrote were surrounded by idolaters, and there was danger that they might fall into the prevailing sin, or in some way so act as to be understood to lend their sanction to idolatry. (2.) In a world full of alluring objects, there was danger then, as there is at all times, that the affections should be fixed on other objects than the supreme God, and that what is due to him should be withheld. It may be added, in the conclusion of the exposition of this epistle, that the same caution is as needful for us as it was for those to whom John wrote. We are not in danger, indeed, of bowing down to idols, or of engaging in the grosser forms of idol-worship. But we may be in no less danger than they to whom John wrote were, of substituting other things in our affections in the place of the true God, and of devoting to them the time and the affection which are due to him.   Our children it is possible to love with such an attachment as shall effectually exclude the true God from the heart. The world—its wealth, and pleasures, and honours—we may love with a degree of attachment such as

even an idolater would hardly shew to his idol-gods ; and all the time which he would take in performing his devotions in an idol-temple, we may devote with equal fervour to the service of the world. There is practical idolatry all over the world ; in nominally Christian lands as well as among the heathen ; in families that acknowledge no God but wealth and fashion ; in the hearts of multitudes of individuals who would scorn the thought of worshipping at a pagan altar ; and it is even to be found in the heart of many a one who professes to be acquainted with the true God, and to be an heir of heaven.   God should have the supreme place in our affections.   The love of everything else should be held in strict subordination to the love of him. He should reign in our hearts ; be acknowledged in our closets, our families, and in the place of public worship ; be submitted to at all times as having a right to command and control us ; be obeyed in all the expressions of his will, by his word, by his providence, and by his Spirit ; be so loved that we shall be willing to part without a murmur with the dearest object of affection when he takes it from us ; and so that, with joy and triumph, we shall welcome his messenger, *the angel of death*, when he shall come to summon us into his presence. To all who may read these illustrations of the epistle of the ' beloved disciple,' may God grant this inestimable blessing and honour.   AMEN.

INTRODUCTION

SECOND AND THIRD EPISTLES OF JOHN.

---

§ 1. *The authenticity of the second and third Epistles of John.*

THE authenticity of these two epistles was doubted by many in the early Christian church, and it was not before a considerable time had elapsed that their canonical authority was fully admitted. The first of the three epistles was always received as the undoubted production of the apostle John ; but, though not positively and absolutely rejected, there were many doubts entertained in regard to the authorship of the second and third. Their exceeding brevity, and the fact that they were addressed to individuals, and seemed not designed for general circulation, made them less frequently referred to by the early Christian writers, and renders it more difficult to establish their genuineness.

The *evidence* of their genuineness is of two kinds—external and internal. Though, from their brevity, the proof on these points must be less full and clear than it is in regard to the first epistle; yet it is such as to satisfy the mind, on the whole, that they are the production of the apostle John, and are entitled to a place in the canon of Scripture.

(1.) *External evidence.* The evidence of this kind, either for or against the authenticity of these epistles, is found in the following testimonies respecting them in the writings of the Fathers, and the following facts in regard to their admission into the canon.

(*a*) In the church and school at Alexandria they were both well known, and were received as a part of the sacred writings. Clement of Alexandria, and Alexander, bishop of Alexandria, quote them, or refer to them, as the writings of the apostle John.—Lardner's works, vi. 275; Lücke, p. 329. Origen, the successor of Clement, says, ' John left behind him an epistle of very few *stichoi;* perhaps also a second and third, though some do not consider these genuine. Both these together, however, contain only an hundred *stichoi.*' Dionysius of Alexandria shows that he was acquainted with all of them, but calls the two last φερόμεναι—writings alleged to be genuine. For the import of this word, as used by Dionysius, see Lücke's Com., pp. 330, 331.

(*b*) These epistles were known and received in the western churches in the second and third centuries. Of this fact, an important witness is found in Irenæus, who, on account of the place where he resided during his youth, and the school in which he was educated, deserves especial regard as a witness respecting the works of John.—*Hug.* He was born at Smyrna, and lived not long after the times of the apostles. He was a disciple of Polycarp, who was acquainted with the apostle John ; and having passed his early years in Asia Minor, must, in the circumstances in which he was placed, have been familiar with the writings of John, and have known well what writings were attributed to him. He quotes the second epistle, (ver. 11,) and with express reference to John as the author, under the name of ' John, the disciple of our Lord.' In another place, also, he refers to this epistle. After quoting from the first epistle, he continues, ' And

John, the disciple of Jesus, in the epistle before mentioned, commanded that they (the heretics) should be shunned, saying,' &c.   He then quotes, word for word, the seventh and eighth verses of the epistle.

(c) The African church, in the third century, regarded the second epistle, at least, as the production of John.   At a synod in Carthage, under Cyprian, Aurelius, the bishop of Chullabi, in giving his vote on the question of baptizing heretics, quotes the tenth verse of the second epistle as authority, saying, ' John, in his epistle, declares,' &c.

(d) There is some doubt in regard to the Syrian church, whether these epistles were at first received as genuine or not.   The manuscripts of the Peshito, or old Syriac version, at least since the sixth century, do not contain the epistle of Jude, the second epistle of Peter, or the second and third of John.   Yet Ephrem the Syrian, in the fourth century, quotes the epistle of Jude, the second epistle of Peter, and the second of John, as genuine and canonical.   As this father in the Syrian church was not acquainted with the Greek language, (*Lücke*,) it is clear that he must have read these epistles in a translation, and as would seem most probable in some Syriac version.   The probability would seem to be, as these epistles are not in the oldest Syriac version, that there was some doubt about their authenticity when that version was made, but that before the time of Ephrem they had come to be regarded as genuine, and were translated by some other persons.   Their use in the time of Ephrem would at least show that they were then regarded as genuine.   They may have been, indeed, at some period attached to the ancient version, but at a later period, as they did not originally belong to that version, they may have been separated from it.—*Lücke*, *in loc.*   At all events, it is clear that at an early period in the Syrian church they were regarded as genuine.

(e) Though there were doubts among many of the Fathers respecting the genuineness of these epistles, yet they were admitted in several councils of the church to be genuine.   In the eighty-fifth of the apostolic canons, (so called ;) in the sixtieth canon of the synod of Laodicea ; the council at Hippo, (A.D. 393,) and the third council of Carthage, (A.D. 397,) they were reckoned as undoubtedly pertaining to the inspired canon of Scripture.

(f) All doubts on the subject of the genuineness of these epistles were, however, subsequently removed in the view of Christian writers, and in the middle ages they were universally received as the writings of the apostle John.   Some of the Reformers again had doubts of their genuineness.   Erasmus quoted the sentiment of Jerome, that it was not the *apostle* John who wrote these epistles, but a *presbyter* of the same name ; and Calvin seems to have entertained some doubt of their genuineness, for he has omitted them in his commentaries ; but these doubts have also disappeared, and the conviction has again become general, and indeed almost universal, that they are to be ranked among the genuine writings of the apostle John.

It may be added here, that the doubts which have been entertained on the subject, and the investigations to which they have given rise, show the care which has been evinced in forming the canon of the New Testament, and demonstrate that the Christian world has not been *disposed* to receive books as of sacred authority without evidence of their genuineness.

(2.) There is strong *internal* evidence that they are genuine.   This is found in their style, sentiment, and manner.   It is true that one who was familiar with the writings of the apostle John *might* compose two short epistles like these, that should be mistaken for the real productions of the apostle.   There are, even in these brief epistles, not a few passages which seem to be a mere repetition of what John has elsewhere said.   But there are some things in regard to the internal evidence that they are the writings of the apostle John, and were not designedly forged, which deserve a more particular notice.   They are such as these :—

(a) As already said, the style, sentiment, and manner are such as are appropriate to John. There is nothing in the epistles which we might not suppose he would write ; there is much that accords with what he has written ; there is much in the style which would not be likely to be found in the writings of another man ; and there is nothing in the sentiments which would lead us to suppose that the manner of the apostle John had been *assumed*, for the purpose of palming upon the world productions which were not his   Resemblances between these epistles will strike every reader, and it is unnecessary to specify them.   The following passages, however, are so decidedly in the manner of John, that it may be presumed that they were either written by him, or by one who designed to copy from him : second epistle, vers. 5–7, 9 ; third epistle, vers. 11, 12.

(*b*) The fact that the *name* of the writer is not affixed to the epistles is much in the manner of John.   Paul, in every case except in the epistle to the Hebrews, affixed his name to his epistles ; Peter, James, and Jude did the same thing. John, however, has never done it in any of his writings, except the Apocalypse. He seems to have supposed that there was something about his style and manner which would commend his writings as genuine ; or that in some other way they would be so well understood to be his, that it was not necessary to specify it. Yet the omission of his name, or of something that would lay claim to his authority as an apostle, would not be likely to occur if these epistles were fabricated with a design of palming them upon the world as his.   The artifice would be too refined, and would be too likely to defeat itself, to be adopted by one who should form such a plan.

(*c*) The apparently severe and harsh remarks made in the epistle in regard to heretics, may be adverted to as an evidence that these epistles are the genuine writings of John the apostle.   Thus, in the second epistle, ver. 10, he says, ' If there come any unto you, and bring not this doctrine, receive him not into your house, neither bid him God speed.'   So in the third epistle, ver. 10 : ' If I come, I will remember his deeds which he doeth, prating against us with malicious words,' &c.   It has been made an objection to the genuineness of these epistles, that this is not in the spirit of the mild and amiable ' disciple whom Jesus loved ;' that it breathes a temper of uncharitableness and severity which could not have existed in him at any time, and especially when, as an old man, he is said to have preached nothing but ' love one another.'   But two circumstances will show that this, so far from being an objection, is rather a proof of their genuineness.   One is, that in fact these expressions accord with what we *know* to have been the character of John.   They are *not* inappropriate to one who was named by the Master himself, ' Boanerges—a son of thunder,' (Mark iii. 17;) or to one who was disposed to call down fire from heaven on the Samaritan who would not receive the Lord Jesus, (Luke ix. 54;) or to one who, when he saw another casting out devils in the name of Jesus, took upon himself the authority to forbid him, (Mark ix. 38.)   The truth is, that there was a remarkable mixture of *gentleness* and *severity* in the character of John ; and though the former was the most prominent, and may be supposed to have increased as he grew old, yet the other also often manifested itself.   There was that in the character of John, which, under some circumstances, and under other teaching than that of the Lord Jesus, *might* have been developed in the form of great exclusiveness, bigotry, and sternness—perhaps in the form of open persecution. Under the teaching of the Saviour, and through his example, his milder and better nature prevailed, and so decidedly acquired the ascendency, that we almost never think of the harsher traits of his character.   The other circumstance is, that it would never have occurred to one who should have attempted to forge an epistle in the name of John, to have *introduced* a passage of this kind.   The artifice would have been too little likely to have accomplished the end, to have occurred to the mind, or to have been adopted.   The public character of John was so amiable ; he was so uniformly spoken of as the ' disciple whom Jesus loved ;' gentleness and kindness seemed to be such pervading traits in his nature, that no one would have thought of introducing sentiments which *seemed* to be at variance with these traits, even though, on a close analysis, it could be made out that they were *not* contrary to his natural character.

(*d*) Perhaps, also, the appellation which the writer gives himself in these two epistles, (ὁ πρσσβύτερος—*the elder*,) may be regarded as some evidence that they are the writings of the apostle John ; that is, it is more probable that he would use this appellation than that any other writer would. It has, indeed, been made a ground of objection that the use of this term proves that they are *not* the productions of John. See Lücke, p. 340. But, as we have seen, John was not accustomed to prefix his own name to his writings ; and if these epistles were written by him when he was at Ephesus, nothing is more probable than that he should use this term. It can hardly be regarded as an appellation pertaining to *office*, for as there were many *elders* or *presbyters* in the church, (Acts xx. 17,) the use of the term ' *the* elder ' would not be sufficiently distinctive to designate the writer. It may be presumed, therefore, to have a particular respect to age ; and, under the circumstances supposed, it would apply to no one with so much propriety as to the apostle John—one who would be well known as *the* aged and venerable disciple of the Saviour. Compare, however, Lücke (pp. 340–343) on the use of this word.

§ 2. *Of the person to whom John addressed his second Epistle.*

This epistle purports to be addressed, as it is in our translation, to ' the elect lady '—ἐκλεκτῆ κυρία. There has been great diversity of opinion in regard to the person here referred to, and there are questions respecting it which it is impossible to determine with absolute certainty. The different opinions which have been entertained are the following : (*a*) Some have supposed that a Christian matron is referred to, a friend of John, whose name was either 'Εκλεκτή (*Eclecte*,) or Κυρία, (*Cyria*.) Œcumenius and Theophylact supposed that the proper name of the female referred to was *Eclecte ;* others have adopted the other opinion, that the name was *Cyria*. (*b*) Others among the ancients, and particularly Clement, supposed that the *church* was denoted by this name, under the delicate image of an elect lady ; either some particular church to whom the epistle was sent, or to the church at large. This opinion has been held by some of the modern writers also. (*c*) Others have supposed, as is implied in our common version, that it was addressed to some Christian matron, whose name is not mentioned, but who was well known to John, and perhaps to many others, for her piety, and her acts of kindness to Christians. The reason why her name was suppressed, it has been supposed, was that if it had been mentioned it might have exposed her to trouble in some way, perhaps to persecution. (*d*) Recently, Knauer (Studien und Kritik., 1833, Heft 2. s. 452, ff.) has endeavoured to show that it was addressed to the Virgin Mary, who is supposed then to have resided in Galilee. The improbability of this opinion is shown by Lücke, pp. 352, 353.

These questions are not very important to be determined, even if they could be with accuracy ; and at this period of time, and with the few data which we have for forming a correct judgment on the subject, it is not possible to settle them with entire certainty. The probable truth in regard to this point, and all which it seems now possible to ascertain with any degree of certainty, may be expressed in the following specifications :

(1.) The letter was addressed to an individual, and not to a church. If it had been to a particular church, it would have been specified, for this is the uniform mode in the New Testament. If it were addressed to the church at large, it is in the highest degree improbable that John should have departed from the style of address in his first epistle ; improbable in every way that he should have adopted another style so mystical and unusual in a plain prose composition. It is only in poetry, in prophecy, in compositions where figurative language abounds, that the church is represented as a female at all ; and it is wholly improbable that John, at the outset of a brief epistle, should have adopted this appellation. The fact that it was addressed to an individual female is further apparent from the mention of her children : vers. 1, 4, ' Unto the elect lady and *her children ;*' 'I found of *thy children* walking in truth.' This is not such language as one would use in addressing a church.

(2.) It is probable that the *name* of this lady was designed to be specified, and that it was *Cyria,* (Κυρία.) This, indeed, is not absolutely certain ; but the Greek will readily bear this, and it accords best with apostolic usage to suppose that the name of the person to whom the letter was addressed would be designated. This occurs in the third epistle of John, the epistles of Paul to Philemon, to Timothy, and to Titus, and, so far as appears, there is no reason why it should not have been done in the case before us. The Syriac and Arabic translators so understand it, for both have retained the name *Cyria.* It may do something to confirm this view, to remark that the name *Cyria* was not uncommon, in subsequent times, at least, among Christian females. See Corp. Inscript. Gruter, p. 1127, Num. xi. Φίνιτσος καὶ ἡ γυνὴ αὐτοῦ Κυρία. Comp. Lex. Hagiologic. Lips. 1719, p. 448, where two female martyrs of that name are mentioned. See also other instances referred to by Lücke, Com. p. 351. If these views are correct, then the true rendering of the passage would be, ' The presbyter unto the elect Cyria.'

(3.) Of this pious female, however, nothing more is known than what is mentioned in this epistle. From that we learn that John was warmly attached to her, (ver. 5 ;) that she was a mother, and that her children were pious, (vers. 1, 4 ;) and that she was of a hospitable character, and would be likely to entertain those who came professedly as religious teachers, vers. 10, 11. Where or when she lived, or when she died, we have no information whatever. At the time of writing this epistle, John had strong hopes that he would be permitted to come soon and see her, but whether he ever did so, we are not informed, ver. 12.

§. 3. *The canonical authority of the second and third Epistles of John.*

The canonical authority of these epistles depends on the following things :

(1.) On the evidence that they are the writings of the apostle John. In proportion as that evidence is clear, their canonical authority is of course established.

(2.) Though brief, and though addressed to individuals, they are admitted into the canon of Scripture with the same propriety as the epistles to Timothy, to Titus, and to Philemon, for those were addressed also to individuals.

(3.) Like those epistles, also, these contain things of general interest to the church. There is nothing in either that is inconsistent with what John has elsewhere written, or that conflicts with any other part of the New Testament; there is much in them that is in the manner of John, and that breathes his spirit; there is enough in them to tell us of the way of salvation.

Of the time when these epistles were written, and the place where, nothing is known, and conjecture would be useless, as there are no marks of time or place in either, and there is no historical statement that gives the information. It has been the common opinion that they were written at Ephesus, and when John was old. The appellation which he gives of himself, ' *the elder,*' accords with this supposition, though it does not make it absolutely certain

SECOND EPISTLE OF JOHN.

THE elder unto the elect lady and her children, whom I love in the truth; and not I only, but also all they that have known the truth;

ANALYSIS OF THE SECOND EPISTLE.

THE points embraced in this epistle are these : A salutation to the female to whom it is addressed, and an expression of warm attachment to her family, vers. 1–3. An expression of joy and gratitude that he had been permitted to learn that her children had embraced the truth, and were walking in it, ver. 4. An exhortation to live in the exercise of mutual love, in obedience to the great commandment of the Saviour, vers. 5, 6. The fact that many deceivers had gone out into the world, and an exhortation to be on their guard against their arts, vers. 7, 8. A test by which they might be known, and their true character ascertained, ver. 9. An exhortation to show them no countenance whatever; not to treat them in any such way, even in the rites of hospitality, as to give occasion to the charge that she was friendly to their doctrines, vers. 10, 11. A statement that, as he hoped to see her soon, he would not write more to her, ver. 12. And the salutation of the children of some one who is spoken of as her elect sister, ver. 13.

1. *The elder.* See the Intro., § 1, (2, *d.*) ¶ *Unto the elect lady.* The elect or chosen Cyria. See Intro., § 2. He addresses her as one chosen of God to salvation, in the use of a term often applied to Christians in the New Testament. ¶ *And her children.* The word here rendered *children* (τέκνα) would include in itself both sons and daughters, but as the apostle immediately uses a masculine pronoun, οὖς it would seem more probable that sons only were intended. At all events, the use of such a pronoun proves that some at least of her children were sons. Of their number and character we have no information, except that (Notes on ver. 4) a part of them were Christians. ¶ *Whom I love in the truth.* See Notes, 1 John iii. 18. The meaning here is, that he *truly* or *sincerely* loved them The introduction of the article *the* here, which is not in the original, (ἐν ἀληθίᾳ) somewhat obscures the sense, as if the meaning were that he loved them so far as they embraced the truth. The meaning however is, that he was sincerely attached to them. The word 'whom' here, (οὖς,) embraces both the mother and her children, though the pronoun is in the masculine gender, in accordance with the usage of the Greek language. No mention is made of her husband, and it may thence be inferred that she was a widow. Had he been living, though he might not have been a Christian, it is to be presumed that some allusion would have been made to him as well as to the children, especially as there is reason to believe that only a part of her children were pious. See Notes, ver. 4. ¶ *And not I only, but also all they that have known the truth.* That is, all those Christians who had had an opportunity of knowing them, were sincerely attached to them It would seem, from a subsequent part of the epistle, (ver. 10,) that this female was of a hospitable character, and was accustomed to entertain at her house the professed friends of religion, especially religious teachers, and it is probable that she was the more extensively known from this fact. The commendation of the apostle here shows that it is *possible* that a family shall be extensively known as one of order, peace, and

2 For the truth's sake, which dwelleth in us, and shall be with us for ever.

3 Grace be with you, mercy, *and* peace, from God the Father, and from the Lord Jesus Christ, the

Son of the Father, in truth and love.

4 I rejoiced greatly that I found of thy children walking in truth, as we have received a commandment from the Father.

---

religion, so that all who know it or hear of it shall regard it with interest, respect, and love.

2. *For the truth's sake.* They love this family *because* they love the truth, and see it so cordially embraced and so happily exemplified. They who love the gospel itself will rejoice in all the effects which it produces in society, on individuals, families, neighbourhoods, and their hearts will be drawn with warm affection to the places where its influence is most fully seen. ¶ *Which dwelleth in us.* In us who are Christians; that is, the truths of the gospel which we have embraced. Truth may be said to have taken up a permanent abode in the hearts of all who love religion. ¶ *And shall be with us for ever.* Its abode with us is not for a night or a day; not for a month or a year; not for the few years that make up mortal life; it is not a passing stranger that finds a lodging like the weary traveller for a night, and in the morning is gone to be seen no more; it has come to us to make our hearts its permanent home, and it is to be with us in all worlds, and while ceaseless ages shall roll away.

3. *Grace be unto you,* &c. See Notes Rom. i. 7. This salutation does not differ from those commonly employed by the sacred writers, except in the emphasis which is placed on the fact that the Lord Jesus Christ is 'the Son of the Father.' This is much in the style of John, in all of whose writings he dwells much on the fact that the Lord Jesus is the Son of God, and on the importance of recognising that fact in order to the possession of true religion. Comp. 1 John ii. 22, 23; iv. 15; v. 1, 2, 10–12, 20. ¶ *In truth and love.* This phrase is not to be connected with the expression 'the Son of the Father,' as if it meant that he was his Son ' in truth and love,' but is rather to be connected with the ' grace, mercy, and peace ' referred to, as a prayer that they

might be manifested to this family in promoting truth and love.

4. *I rejoiced greatly that I found,* &c. That I learned this fact respecting some of thy children. The apostle does not say *how* he had learned this. It may have been that he had become personally acquainted with them when they were away from their home, or that he had learned it from others. The word used (εὕρηκα) would apply to either method. Grotius supposed that some of the sons had come on business to Ephesus, and that John had become acquainted with them there. ¶ *Of thy children walking in truth.* That is, true Christians; living in accordance with the truth, for this constitutes the essence of religion. The expression used here, ' of thy children,' (ἐκ τῶν τέκνων,) means *some* of thy children; implying that he knew of a part of them who were true Christians. This is clear from the Greek construction, because (*a*) if he had meant to say that he had found them *all* to be of this description, the sentiment would have been directly expressed, ' *thy* children ;' but as it is, some word is necessary to be understood to complete the sense ; and (*b*) the same thing is demanded by the fact that the participle used (*walking—*περιπατοῦντας) is in the accusative case. If he had referred to them all, the participle would have been in the genitive, agreeing with the word *children,* (τῶν περιπατοῦντων.)—*Lücke.* Whether the apostle means to say that only a part of them had in fact embraced the gospel, or that he had only known that a part of them had done it, though the others might have done it without his knowledge, is not quite clear, though the former supposition appears to be the correct one, for if they had all become Christians it is to be presumed that he would have been informed of it. The probability seems to be that a part of her children only were truly pious, though there is no evidence that the

5 And now I beseech thee, lady, not as though I wrote a new commandment unto thee, but that which we had from the beginning, that we love *a* one another.

6 And this is love, *b* that we walk after his commandments. This is the commandment, That, as ye have

heard from the beginning, ye should walk in it.

7 For many *c* deceivers are entered into the world, who confess not that Jesus Christ is come in the flesh. This is a deceiver and an antichrist.

a 1 Jn.3.23.　　*b* Jn.14.15,21.　　*c* 1 Jn.4.1.

others were otherwise than correct in their moral conduct. If there had been improper conduct in any of her other children, John was too courteous, and too delicate in his feelings, to allude to so disagreeable a circumstance. But ' if that pious lady,' to use the language of Benson, ' had some wicked children, her lot was not peculiar. Her consolation was that she had some who were truly good. John commended those who were good, in order to excite them in the most agreeable manner to persevere.' ¶ *As we have received a commandment from the Father.* That is, as he has commanded us to live ; in accordance with the truth which he has revealed. The *Father*, in the Scripture, is everywhere represented as the source of law.

5. *And now I beseech thee, lady.* Dr, ' And now I entreat thee, *Cyria* ' (κυρία.) See Intro. § 2. If this was her proper name, there is no impropriety in supposing that he would address her in this familiar style. John was probably then a very old man ; the female to whom the epistle was addressed was doubtless much younger. ¶ *Not as though I wrote a new commandment unto thee.* John presumed that the command to love one another was understood as far as the gospel was known ; and he might well presume it, for true Christianity never prevails anywhere without prompting to the observance of this law. See Notes, 1 Thess. iv. 9. ¶ *But that which we had from the beginning.* From the time when the gospel was first made known to us. See Notes, 1 Jol n ii. 7 ; iii. 11. ¶ *That we love one another.* That is, that there be among the disciples of Christ mutual love ; or that in all circumstances and relations they should love one another, John xv. 12, 17. This general command, addressed to all the disciples of the Saviour, John doubtless

means to say was as applicable to him and to the pious female to whom he wrote as to any others, and ought to be exercised by them towards all true Christians ; and he exhorts her, as he did all Christians, to exercise it. It was a command on which, in his old age, he loved to dwell ; and he had little more to say to her than this, to exhort her to obey this injunction of the Saviour.

6. *And this is love, that we walk after his commandments.* This is the proper expression or evidence of love to God. See Notes, John xiv. 15, 21. ¶ *This is the commandment.* That is, this is his great and peculiar commandment ; the one by which his disciples are to be peculiarly characterized, and by which they are to be distinguished in the world. See Notes, John xiii. 34.

7. *For.* Οτι. This word *for* is not here to be regarded as connected with the previous verse, and as giving a reason why there should be the exercise of mutual love, but is rather to be understood as connected with the following verse, (8,) and as giving a reason for the caution there expressed : ' Because it is a truth that many deceivers have appeared, or since it has occurred that many such are abroad, look to yourselves lest you be betrayed and ruined.' The fact that there were many such deceivers was a good reason for being constantly on their guard, lest they should be so far drawn away as not to receive a full reward. ¶ *Many deceivers are entered into the world.* Are abroad in the world, or have appeared among men. Several MSS. read here, ' *have gone out* into the world,' (ἐξῆλθον,) instead of ' have entered into,' (εἰσῆλθον.) The common reading is the correct one, and the other was originated, probably, from the unusual form of the expression, ' have come into the world,' as if they had come from another abode. That, however, is not

8 Look *a* to yourselves, that we *b* lose not those things which we have [1] wrought, but that we receive a full reward.

a Mar.13.9.   *b* Phi.3.16; Re.3.11.

[1] Or, *gained.* Some copies read, *which ye have gained, but that ye.*

necessarily implied, the language being such as would be properly used to denote the idea that there were such deceivers in the world. ¶ *Who confess not that Jesus Christ is come in the flesh.* Who maintain that he assumed the *appearance* only of a man, and was not really incarnate. See Notes, 1 John iv. 2, 3. ¶ *This is a deceiver.* Every one who maintains this is to be regarded as a deceiver. ¶ *And an antichrist.* See Notes, 1 John ii. 18; iv. 3.

8. *Look to yourselves.* This seems to be addressed to the lady to whom he wrote, and to her children. The idea is, that they should be particularly on their guard, and that their first care should be to secure their own hearts, so that they should not be exposed to the dangerous attacks of error. When error abounds in the world, our first duty is not to attack it and make war upon it; it is to look to the citadel of our own souls, and see that all is well guarded there. When an enemy invades a land, the first thing will not be to go out against him, regardless of our own strength, or of the security of our own fortresses, but it will be to see that our forts are well manned, and that we are secure *there* from his assaults. If that is so, we may then go forth with confidence to meet him on the open field. In relation to an error that is in the world, the first thing for a Christian to do is to take care of his own heart. ¶ *That we lose not those things which we have wrought.* Marg., 'Or, *gained.* Some copies read, *which ye have gained, but that ye.*' The reading there referred to in the margin is found in several MSS. and also in the Vulgate, Syriac, and Æthiopic versions. It is not, however, adopted in the late critical editions of the New Testament, and the common reading is probably genuine. The sense is not materially varied, and the common reading is not unnatural. John was exhorting the family to whom this epistle was written to take good heed to themselves while so many artful errorists were around them, lest they should be drawn away from the truth, and lose a part of the full reward which they might hope to receive in heaven. In doing this, nothing was more natural than that he, as a Christian friend, should group himself with them, and speak of himself as having the same need of caution, and express the feeling that he ought to strive also to obtain the full reward, thus showing that he was not disposed to address an exhortation to them which he was not willing to regard as applicable to himself. The *truth* which is taught here is one of interest to all Christians—that it is possible for even genuine Christians, by suffering themselves to be led into error, or by failure in duty, to lose a part of the reward which they might have obtained. The crown which they will wear in heaven will be less bright than that which they might have worn, and the throne which they will occupy will be less elevated. The rewards of heaven will be in accordance with the services rendered to the Redeemer; and it would not be right that they who turn aside, or falter in their course, should have the same exalted honours which they might have received if they had devoted themselves to God with ever-increasing fidelity. It is painful to think how many there are who begin the Christian career with burning zeal, as if they would strike for the highest rewards in heaven, but who soon waver in their course, and fall into some paralysing error, until at last they receive, perhaps, not half the reward which they might have obtained. ¶ *But that we receive a full reward.* Such as will be granted to a life uniformly consistent and faithful; all that God has to bestow on his people when *most* faithful and true. But who can estimate the '*full* reward' of heaven, the unspeakable glory of those who make it the grand business of their lives to obtain all they can of its bliss. And who is there that does not feel that he *ought* to strive for a crown in which not one gem shall be wanting that *might* have sparkled there for ever?

9 Whosoever transgresseth, and abideth not in *a* the doctrine of Christ, hath not God. He that abideth in the doctrine of Christ, he hath both the Father and the Son.

10 If *b* there come any unto you, and bring not this doctrine, receive him not into *your* house, neither bid him God speed:

a Jn.15.6.   b Ga.1.8,9.

9. *Whosoever transgresseth, and abideth not in the doctrine of Christ, hath not God.* In the doctrine which Christ taught, or the true doctrine respecting him. The language is somewhat ambiguous, like the phrase ' the love of Christ,' which may mean either his love to us, or our love to him. Comp. John xv. 9. It is difficult to determine here which is the true sense—whether it means the doctrine or precepts which he taught, or the true doctrine respecting him. Macknight understands by it the doctrine *taught* by Christ and his apostles. It would seem most probable that this is the sense of the passage, but then it would include, of course, all that Christ taught respecting himself, as well as his other instructions. The essential idea is, that the truth must be held respecting the precepts, the character, and the work of the Saviour. Probably the immediate allusion here is to those to whom John so frequently referred as ' antichrist,' who denied that Jesus had come in the flesh, ver. 7. At the same time, however, he makes the remark general, that if any one did not hold the true doctrine respecting the Saviour, he had no real knowledge of God. See John i. 18; v. 23; xv. 23; xvii. 3; 1 John ii. 23. ¶ *Hath not God.* Has no true knowledge of God. The truth taught here is, that it is essential to piety to hold the true doctrine respecting Christ. ¶ *He that abideth in the doctrine of Christ.* In the true doctrine respecting Christ, or in the doctrine which he taught. ¶ *He hath both the Father and the Son.* There is such an intimate union between the Father and the Son, that he who has just views of the one has also of the other. Comp. Notes on John xiv. 7, 9, 10, 11, and 1 John ii. 23.

10. *If there come any unto you.* Any professed teacher of religion. There can be no doubt that she to whom this epistle was written was accustomed to entertain such teachers. ¶ *And bring not this*

doctrine. This doctrine which Christ taught, or the true doctrine respecting him and his religion. ¶ *Receive him not into* your *house.* This cannot mean that *no* acts of kindness, in any circumstances, were to be shown to such persons; but that there was to be nothing done which could be fairly construed as encouraging or countenancing them *as religious teachers.* The true rule would seem to be, in regard to such persons, that, so far as we have intercourse with them as neighbours, or strangers, we are to be honest, true, kind, and just, but we are to do *nothing* that will countenance them *as* religious teachers. We are not to attend on their instruction, (Prov. xix. 27;) we are not to receive them into our houses, or to entertain them as religious teachers; we are not to commend them to others, or to give them any reason to use our names or influence in propagating error. It would not be difficult to practise this rule, and yet to show to others all the kindness, and all the attention in circumstances of want, which religion demands. A man who is truly consistent is never suspected of countenancing error, even when he is distinguished for liberality, and is ready, like the good Samaritan, to pour in oil and wine in the wounds of *any* waylaid traveller. The command not to ' receive such an one into the house,' in such circumstances as those referred to by John, would be probably understood literally, as he doubtless designed that it should be. To do that, to meet such persons with a friendly greeting, would be construed as countenancing their doctrine, and as commending them to others; and hence it was forbidden that they should be entertained as such. This treatment would not be demanded where no such interpretation could be put on receiving a friend or relative who held different and even erroneous views, or in showing kindness to a stranger who differed from us, but it *would* apply to the receiving

11 For he that biddeth him God speed, is partaker *a* of his evil deeds.

12 Having many things to write unto you, I would not *write* with

paper and ink : but I trust to come unto you, and speak [1] face to face, that [2] our joy *b* may be full.

13 The children of thy elect sister greet thee. Amen.

and entertaining *a professed teacher of religion, as such;* and the rule is as applicable now as it was then. ¶ *Neither bid him God speed.* Καὶ χαίρειν αὐτῷ μὴ λέγετε —'and do not say to him, *hail,* or *joy.*' Do not wish him joy; do not hail, or salute him. The word used expresses the common form of salutation, as when we wish one health, success, prosperity, Matt. xxvi. 49 ; Acts xv. 23 ; xxiii. 26 ; James i. 1. It would be understood as expressing a wish for success in the enterprise in which they were embarked ; and though we should love all men, and desire their welfare, and sincerely seek their happiness, yet we can properly wish no one success in a career of sin and error.

11. *For he that biddeth him God speed, is partaker of his evil deeds.* Shows that he countenances and approves of the doctrine which is taught. Comp. Notes, 1 Tim. v. 22.

12. *Having many things to write unto you.* That I would wish to say. This language is such as would be used by one who was hurried, or who was in feeble health, or who hoped soon to see the person written to. In such a case only the points would be selected which were of most immediate and pressing importance, and the remainder would be reserved for a more free personal interview. ¶ *I would not* write *with paper.* The word *paper* here conveys an idea which is not strictly correct. *Paper,* as that term is now understood, was not invented until long after this period. The material designated by the word used by John (χάρτης) was the Egyptian papyrus, and the particular thing denoted was a leaf made out of that plant. The sheets were made of membranes of the plant closely pressed together. This plant was found also in Syria and Babylon, but it was produced in greater abundance in Egypt, and that was the plant which was commonly used. It was so comparatively cheap, that it in a great measure superseded the earlier

materials for writing—plates of lead, or stone, or the skins of animals. It is probable that the books of the New Testament were written on this species of paper. Comp. Hug, Intro. chap. iii., § 11. *And ink.* The ink which was commonly employed in writing was made of soot and water, with a mixture of some species of gum to give it consistency and durability.—*Lücke.* The instrument or *pen* was made of a reed. ¶ *But I trust to come unto you, and speak face to face.* Marg., as in Greek, *mouth to mouth.* The phrase is a common one, to denote conversation with any one, especially free and confidential conversation. Comp. Numb. xii. 8 ; Jer. xxxii. 4. ¶ *That our joy may be full.* Marg., *your.* The marginal reading has arisen from a variation in the Greek copies. The word *our* is best sustained, and accords best with the connection. John would be likely to express the hope that *he* would find pleasure from such an interview. See Notes, 1 John i. 4. Comp. Rom. i. 11, 12.

13. *The children of thy elect sister greet thee.* Of this ' elect sister ' nothing more is known. It would seem probable, from the fact that she is not mentioned as sending her salutations, that she was either dead, or that she was absent. John mentions her, however, as a Christian—as one of the elect or chosen of God.

REMARKS ON THIS EPISTLE.

In view of the exposition of this epistle we may make the following remarks :—

(1.) It is desirable for a family to have a character for piety so consistent and well understood that all who know it shall perceive it and love it, ver. 1. In the case of this lady and her household, it would seem that, as far as they were known, they were known as a well-ordered Christian household. Such a family John said he loved ; and he said that it was loved by all who had any knowledge of them. What is more lovely to the view than such a household? What is better fitted to make an impression on the world favourable to religion?

(2.) It is a matter of great rejoicing when *any* part of a family become truly religious, ver. 4. We should rejoice with our friends, and should render unfeigned thanks to God, if *any* of their children are converted, and walk in the truth. No greater blessing can descend on a family than the early conversion of children; and as angels rejoice over one sinner that is converted, we should rejoice when the children of our friends are brought to a knowledge of the truth, and devote themselves to God in early life.

(3.) It is our duty to be on our guard against the arts of the teachers of error, ver. 7. They abound in every age They are often learned, eloquent, and profound. They study and understand the arts of persuasion. They adapt their instructions to the capacity of those whom they would lead astray. They flatter their vanity; accommodate themselves to their peculiar views and tastes; court their society, and seek to share their friendship. They often appear to be eminently meek, and serious, and devout, and prayerful, for they know that no others can succeed who profess to inculcate the principles of religion. There are few arts more profound than that of leading men into error; few that are studied more, or with greater success. Every Christian, therefore, should be on his guard against such arts; and while he should on all subjects be open to conviction, and be ready to yield his own opinions when convinced that they are wrong, yet he should yield to *truth*, not to men; to *argument*, not to the influence of the *personal character* of the professed religious teacher.

(4.) We may see that it is *possible* for us to lose a portion of the reward which we *might* enjoy in heaven, ver. 8. The rewards of heaven will be apportioned to our character, and to our services in the cause of religion in this life, and they who 'sow sparingly shall reap also sparingly.' Christians often begin their course with great zeal, and

as if they were determined to reap the highest rewards of the heavenly world If they should persevere in the course which they have commenced, they would indeed shine as the stars in the firmament. But, alas! their zeal soon dies away. They relax their efforts, and lose their watchfulness. They engage in some pursuit that absorbs their time, and interferes with their habits of devotion. They connive at error and sin; begin to love the comforts of this life; seek the honours or the riches of this world; and though they may be saved at last, yet they lose half their reward. It should be a fixed purpose with all Christians, and especially with such as are just entering on the Christian life, to wear in heaven a crown as bright and studded with as many jewels *as can possibly be obtained.*

(5.) We may learn from this epistle how to regard and treat the teachers of error, ver. 10. *We are not to do anything that can be fairly construed as contenancing their doctrines.* This simple rule would guide us to a course that is right. We are to have minds open to conviction. We are to love the truth, and be ever ready to follow it. We are not to be prejudiced against anything. We are to treat all men with kindness; to be true, and just, and faithful in our intercourse with all; to be hospitable, and ever ready to do good to *all* who are needy, whatever their name, colour, rank, or opinions. We are not to cut the ties which bind us to our friends and kindred, though they embrace opinions which we deem erroneous or dangerous; but we are in no way to become the patrons of error, or to leave the impression that we are indifferent as to what is believed. The friends of truth and piety we should receive cordially to our dwellings, and should account ourselves honoured by their presence, (Ps. ci. 6, 7;) strangers we should not forget to entertain, for thereby we may entertain angels unawares, (Heb. xiii. 2;) but the open advocate of what we regard as dangerous error, we are *not* to receive in any such sense or way as to have our treatment of him fairly construed as patronising his errors, or commending him as a teacher to the favourable regards of our fellow-men. Neither by our influence, our names, our money, our personal friendship, are we to give him increased facilities for spreading pernicious error through the world. As men, as fellow-sufferers, as citizens, as neighbours, as the friends of temperance, of the prisoner, of the widow, the orphan, and the slave, and as the patrons of learning, we may be united in promoting objects dear to our hearts, but *as religious teachers* we are to show them no countenance, not so much as would be implied in the common form of salutation wishing them success. In all this there is no breach of charity, and no want of true love, for we are to love the truth more than we are the persons of men.

To the man himself we should be ever ready to do good. Him we should never injure in any way, in his person, property, or feelings. We should never attempt to deprive him of the right of cherishing his own opinions, and of spreading them in his own way, answerable, not to us, but to God. We should impose no pains or penalties on him for the opinions which he holds. But we should do nothing to give him increased power to propagate them, and should never place ourselves by any alliance of friendship, family, or business, in such a position that we shall not be perfectly free to maintain our own sentiments, and to oppose what we deem to be error, whoever may advocate it.

THE

THIRD EPISTLE OF JOHN

THE elder unto the well-beloved Gaius, whom I love [1] in the truth.

2 Beloved, I [2] wish above all things that thou mayest prosper

[1] Or, *truly.* [2] Or, *pray.*

and says that the same honourable testimony had been borne of him which had been of Gaius, ver. 12. VI. As in the second epistle, he says, in the close, that there were many things which he would be glad to say to him, but there were reasons why they should not be set down 'with ink and pen,' but he hoped soon to confer with him freely on those subjects face to face, and the epistle is closed by kind salutations, vers. 13, 14.

The *occasion* on which the epistle was written is no farther known than appears from the epistle itself. From this, the following facts are all that can now be ascertained: (1.) That Gaius was a Christian man, and evidently a member of the church, but of what church is unknown. (2.) That there were certain persons known to the writer of the epistle, and who either lived where he did, or who had been commended to him by others, who proposed to travel to the place where Gaius lived. Their particular *object* is not known, further than that it is said (ver. 7) that they 'went for his name's sake;' that is, in the cause of religion. It further appears that they had resolved not to be dependent on the heathen for their support, but wished the favour and friendship of the church—perhaps designing to preach to the heathen, and yet apprehending that if they desired their maintenance from them, it would be charged on them that they were mercenary in their ends. (3.) In these circumstances, and with this view, the author of this epistle wrote to the church, commending these brethren to their kind and fraternal regards. (4.)

and be in health, even as thy soul prospereth.

This recommendation, so far as appears, would have been successful, had it not been for one man, Diotrephes, who had so much influence, and who made such violent opposition, that the church refused to receive them, and they became dependent on private charity. The *ground* of the opposition of Diotrephes is not fully stated, but it seems to have arisen from two sources : (*a*) a desire to rule in the church ; and (*b*) a particular opposition to the writer of this epistle, and a denial of any obligation to recognise his instructions or commendations as binding. The idea seems to have been that the church was entirely independent, and might receive or reject any whom it pleased, though they were commended to them by an apostle. (5.) In these circumstances, Gaius, as an individual, and against the action of the church, received and hospitably entertained these strangers, and aided them in the prosecution of their work. In this office of hospitality another member of the church, Demetrius, also shared ; and to commend them for this work, particularly Gaius, at whose house probably they were entertained, is the design of this epistle. (6.) After having returned to the writer of this epistle, who had formerly commended them to the church, and having borne honourable testimony to the hospitality of Gaius, it would seem that they resolved to repeat their journey for the same purpose, and that the writer of the epistle commended them now to the renewed hospitality of Gaius. On this occasion, probably, they bore this epistle to him. See Notes on vers. 6, 7. Of Diotrephes nothing more is known than is here specified. Erasmus and Bede supposed that he was the author of a new sect ; but of this there is no evidence, and if he had been, it is probable that John would have cautioned Gaius against his influence. Many have supposed that he was a bishop or pastor in the church where he resided ; but there is no evidence of this, and as John wrote to '*the church*,' commending the strangers to *them*, this would seem to be hardly probable. Comp. Rev. ii. 1, 8, 12, 18; iii. 1, 7, 14. Others have sup-

posed that he was a deacon, and had charge of the funds of the church, and that he refused to furnish to these strangers the aid out of the public treasury which they needed, and that by so doing he hindered them in the prosecution of their object. But all this is mere conjecture, and it is now impossible to ascertain what office he held, if he held any. That he was a man of influence is apparent; that he was proud, ambitious, and desirous of ruling, is equally clear ; and that he prevailed on the church *not* to receive the strangers commended to them by the apostle is equally manifest. Of the rank and standing of Demetrius nothing more is known. Benson supposes that he was the bearer of this letter, and that he had gone with the brethren referred to to preach to the Gentiles. But it seems more probable that he was a member of the church to which Gaius belonged, and that he had concurred with him in rendering aid to the strangers who had been rejected by the influence of Diotrephes. If he had gone *with* these strangers, and had carried this letter, it would have been noticed, and it would have been in accordance with the apostolic custom, that he should have been commended to the favourable attentions of Gaius. In regard to the authenticity and the canonical authority of this epistle, see the Introduction at the beginning of the second epistle.

1. *The elder.* See Notes on the Second Epistle, ver. 1. ¶ *Unto the well-beloved Gaius.* Three persons of this name are elsewhere mentioned in the New Testament—Gaius, whom Paul in Rom. xvi. 23 calls ' his host,' and whom he says (1 Cor. i. 15) he baptized, residing at Corinth, (see Notes, Rom. xvi. 23;) Gaius of Macedonia, one of Paul's companions in travel, who was arrested by an excited mob at Ephesus, (Acts xix. 29;) and Gaius of Derbe, who went with Paul and Timothy into Asia, Acts xx. 4. Whether either of these persons is referred to here, cannot with certainty be determined. If it were any of them it was probably the last mentioned—Gaius of Derbe. There is no objection to the supposition that he was the one,

3 For I rejoiced greatly when the brethren came and testified of the truth that is in thee, even as thou walkest *a* in the truth.

a 2 Jn.4.

unless it be from the fact that this epistle was probably written many years after the transaction mentioned in Acts xx. 4, and the probability that Gaius might not have lived so long. The name was not an uncommon one, and it cannot be determined now who he was, or where he lived. Whether he had any office in the church is unknown, but he seems to have been a man of wealth and influence. The word translated ' well-beloved,' means simply *beloved*. It shows that he was a personal friend of the writer of this epistle. ¶ *Whom I love in the truth.* Marg., ' or *truly.*' See Notes on the Second Epistle, ver. 1.

2. *Beloved, I wish above all things.* Marg., *pray.* The word used here commonly means in the New Testament to pray; but it is also employed to express a strong and earnest desire for anything, Acts xxvii. 29; Rom. ix. 3; 2 Cor. xiii. 9. This is probably all that is implied here. The phrase rendered ' above all things '—περὶ πάντων—would be more correctly rendered here ' concerning, or in respect to all things ; ' and the idea is, that John wished earnestly that *in all respects* he might have the same kind of prosperity which his soul had. The common translation ' above all things ' would seem to mean that John valued health and outward prosperity more than he did anything else ; that he wished that more than his usefulness or salvation. This cannot be the meaning, and is not demanded by the proper interpretation of the original. See this shown by Lücke, *in loc.* The sense is, ' In every respect, I wish that it may go as well with you as it does with your soul ; that in your worldly prosperity, your comfort, and your bodily health, you may be as prosperous as you are in your religion.' This is the reverse of the wish which we are commonly constrained to express for our friends ; for such is usually the comparative want of prosperity and advancement in their spiritual interests, that it is an expression of benevolence to desire that they might prosper in that respect

as much as they do in others. ¶ *That thou mayest prosper. εὐοδοῦσθαι.* This word occurs in the New Testament only in the following places: Rom. i. 10, rendered *have a prosperous journey;* 1 Cor. xvi. 2, rendered *hath prospered ;* and in the passage before us. It means, properly, *to lead in a good way ; to prosper one's journey;* and then to make prosperous ; to give success to ; to be prospered. It would apply here to any plan or purpose entertained. It would include success in business, happiness in domestic relations, or prosperity in any of the engagements and transactions in which a Christian might lawfully engage. It shows that it is right to wish that our friends may have success in the works of their hands and their plans of life. ¶ *And be in health.* To enjoy bodily health. It is not necessary to suppose, in order to a correct interpretation of this, that Gaius was at that time suffering from bodily indisposition, though perhaps it is most natural to suppose that, as John makes the wish for his health so prominent. But it is common, in all circumstances, to wish for the health and prosperity of our friends ; and it is as proper as it is common, if we do not give that a degree of prominence above the welfare of the soul. ¶ *Even as. thy soul prospereth.* John had learned, it would seem, from the ' brethren ' who had come to him, (ver. 3,) that Gaius was living as became a Christian ; that he was advancing in the knowledge of the truth, and was exemplary in the duties of the Christian life; and he prays that in all other respects he might be prospered as much as he was in that. It is not *very* common that a man is more prospered in his spiritual interests than he is in his other interests, or that we can, in our wishes for the welfare of our friends, make the prosperity of the soul, and the practice and enjoyment of religion, the standard of our wishes in regard to other things. It argues a high state of piety when we can, as the expression of our highest desire for the welfare of our friends, express the hope that they may be in

4 I have no greater joy *a* than to hear that my children walk in truth.

5 Beloved, thou doest faithfully

b whatsoever thou doest to the brethren, and to strangers:

a Pr.23.24.   b 1 Pe.4.10.

all respects as much prospered as they are in their spiritual concerns.

3. *For I rejoiced greatly when the brethren came.* Who these were is not certainly known. They may have been members of the same church with Gaius, who, for some reason, had visited the writer of this epistle ; or they may have been the ' brethren ' who had gone from him with a letter of commendation to the church, (ver. 9,) and had been rejected by the church through the influence of Diotrephes, and who, after having been hospitably entertained by Gaius, had again returned to the writer of this epistle. In that case, they would of course bear honourable testimony to the kindness which they had received from Gaius, and to his Christian character. ¶ *And testified of the truth that is in thee.* That you adhere steadfastly to the truth, notwithstanding the fact that errors abound, and that there are many false teachers in the world. ¶ *Even as thou walkest in the truth.* Livest in accordance with the truth. The writer had made the same remark of the children of Cyria, to whom the second epistle was directed. See Notes on ver. 4 of that epistle.

4. *I have no greater joy than to hear that my children walk in truth.* That they adhere steadfastly to the truth, and that they live in accordance with it. This is such language as would be used by an aged apostle when speaking of those who had been converted by his instrumentality, and who looked up to him as a father ; and we may, therefore, infer that Gaius had been converted under the ministry of John, and that he was probably a much younger man than he was. John the aged apostle, says that he had no higher happiness than to learn, respecting those who regarded him as their spiritual father, that they were steadfast in their adherence to the doctrines of religion. The same thing may be said now (*a*) of all the ministers of the gospel, that their highest comfort is found in the fact that those to whom they minister, whether still under their

care or removed from them, persevere in a steadfast attachment to the true doctrines of religion, and live accordingly ; and (*b*) of all Christian parents respecting their own children. The highest joy that a Christian parent can have is to know that his children, whether at home or abroad, adhere to the truths of religion, and live in accordance with the requirements of the gospel of Christ. If a child wished to confer the highest possible happiness on his parents when with them, it would be by becoming a decided Christian ; if, when abroad, in foreign lands or his own, he wished to convey intelligence to them that would most thrill their hearts with joy, it would be to announce to them that he had given his heart to God. There is no joy in a family like that when children are converted ; there is no news that comes from abroad that diffuses so much happiness through the domestic circle as the intelligence that a child is truly converted to the Saviour. There is nothing that would give more peace to the dying pillow of the Christian parent, than to be able to leave the world with the assurance that his children would always walk in truth.

5. *Beloved, thou doest faithfully.* In the previous verses the writer had commended Gaius for his attachment to truth, and his general correctness in his Christian life. He now speaks more particularly of his acts of generous hospitality, and says that he had fully, in that respect, done his duty as a Christian. ¶ *Whatsoever thou doest.* In all your intercourse with them, and in all your conduct towards them. The particular thing which led to this remark was his hospitality ; but the testimony respecting his general conduct had been such as to justify this commendation. ¶ *To the brethren.* Probably to Christians who were well known to him—perhaps referring to Christians in his own church. ¶ *And to strangers.* Such as had gone to the church of which he was a member with a letter of commendation from John.

6 Which have borne witness of thy charity before the church: whom if thou bring forward *a* on their journey ¹ after a godly sort, thou shalt do well:

7 Because that for his name's sake they went forth, taking *b* nothing of the Gentiles.

8 We therefore ought to receive *c* such, that we might be fellowhelpers to the truth.

a Ac.15.3.   1 *worthy of God.*   *b* 1 Co.9.15,18.
   c Mat.10.40.

Compare Notes on Rom. xii. 13, and Heb. xiii. 2.

6. *Which have borne witness of thy charity before the church.* It would seem that they had returned to John, and borne honourable testimony to the love manifested to them by Gaius. Before *what* church they had borne this testimony is unknown. Perhaps it was the church in Ephesus. ¶ *Whom if thou bring forward on their journey.* οὖς προπέμψας. 'Whom bringing forward, or having brought forward.' The word refers to aid rendered them in their journey, in facilitating their travels, either by personally accompanying them, by furnishing them the means of prosecuting their journey, or by hospitably entertaining them. Probably Gaius aided them in every way in which it was practicable. It has been made a question whether this refers to the fact that he *had* thus aided them in some visit which they had made to the church where Gaius was, or to a visit which they purposed to make. The Greek would seem to favour the latter construction, and yet it would appear from the epistle, that the ' brethren and strangers' actually had been with him ; that they had been rejected by the church through the influence of Diotrephes, and had been thrown upon the hospitality of Gaius, and that they had returned, and had borne honourable testimony to his hospitality. These views can be reconciled by supposing, as Lücke does, that having been once on their travels, and having shared the hospitality of Gaius, they were purposing to visit that region again, and that John, praising him for his former hospitality, commends them again to him, stating the reason (vers. 9, 10) why he did not, in accordance with the usual custom, recommend them to the care of the church. They had now gone out (ver. 7) on the same errand on which they had formerly gone, and

they had now equal claims to the hospitality of the friends of religion. ¶ *After a godly sort.* Margin, as in Greek, *worthy of God.* The meaning is, As becomes those who serve God ; or as becomes those who are professors of his religion. ¶ *Thou shalt do well.* You will do that which religion requires in these circumstances.

7. *Because that for his name's sake.* The word '*his*' here refers to God ; and the idea is, that they had undertaken this journey not on their own account, but in the cause of religion. ¶ *They went forth.* Or, *they have gone forth*—ἐξῆλθον—referring to the journey which they had then undertaken ; not to the former one. ¶ *Taking nothing of the Gentiles.* The term *Gentile* embraced all who were not *Jews,* and it is evident that these persons went forth particularly to labour among the heathen. When they went, they resolved, it seems, to receive no part of their support from them, but to depend on the aid of their Christian brethren, and hence they were at first commended to the church of which Gaius and Diotrephes were members, and on this second excursion were commended particularly to Gaius. *Why* they resolved to take nothing of the Gentiles is not stated, but it was doubtless from prudential considerations, lest it should hinder their success among them, and expose them to the charge of being actuated by a mercenary spirit. There were circumstances in the early propagation of Christianity which made it proper, in order to avoid this reproach, to preach the gospel ' without charge,' though the doctrine is everywhere laid down in the Bible that it is the *duty* of those to whom it is preached to contribute to its maintenance, and that it is the *right* of those who preach to expect and receive a support. On this subject, see Notes on 1 Cor. ix., particularly vers. 15, 18.

9 I wrote unto the church: but Diotrephes, who loveth to have the pre-eminence *a* among them, receiveth us not.

a Mat.23.4-8; 1 Ti.6.3,4

8. *We therefore ought to receive such.* All of us ought hospitably to entertain and aid such persons. The work in which they are engaged is one of pure benevolence. They have no selfish aims and ends in it. They do not even look for the supplies of their wants among the people to whom they go to minister; and we ought, therefore, to aid them in their work, and to contribute to their support. The apostle doubtless meant to urge this duty particularly on Gaius; but in order to show that he recognised the obligation himself, he uses the term 'we,' and speaks of it as a duty binding on all Christians. ¶ *That we might be fellow-helpers to the truth.* All Christians cannot go forth to preach the gospel, but all may contribute something to the support of those who do; and in this case they would have a joint participation in the work of spreading the truth. The same reasoning which was applicable to that case, is also applicable now in regard to the duty of supporting those who go forth to preach the gospel to the destitute.

9. *I wrote unto the church.* That is, on the former occasion when they went forth. At that time, John naturally commended them to the kind attentions of the church, not doubting but that aid would be rendered them in prosecuting their benevolent work among the Gentiles. The epistle which was written on that occasion is now lost, and its contents cannot now be ascertained. It was, probably, however, a letter of mere commendation, perhaps stating the object which these brethren had in view, and soliciting the aid of the church. The Latin Vulgate renders this, *scripsissem forsan ecclesiæ,* ' I would have written,* perhaps, to the church, but Diotrephes,' &c. Macknight also renders this, ' I would have written,' supposing the sense to be, that John would have commended them to the whole church rather than to a private member, if he had not been aware of the influence and opposition of Diotrephes. The Syriac version also adopts the same rendering. Several manuscripts also,

of later date, introduced a particle, (*ἂν,*) by which the same rendering would be demanded in the Greek, though that reading is not sustained by good authority. Against this mode of rendering the passage, the reasons seem to me to be clear. (1.) As already remarked, the reading in the Greek which would require it is not sustained by good authority. (2.) The fair and obvious interpretation of the Greek word used by the apostle, (*ἔγραψα,*) without that particle, is, *I wrote*—implying that it had been already done. (3.) It is more probable that John had written to the church on some former occasion, and that his recommendation had been rejected by the influence of Diotrephes, than that he would be deterred by the apprehension that his recommendation *would be* rejected. It seems to me, therefore, that the fair interpretation of this passage is, that these brethren had gone forth on some former occasion, commended by John to the church, and had been rejected by the influence of Diotrephes, and that now he commends them to Gaius, by whom they had been formerly entertained, and asks him to renew his hospitality to them. ¶ *But Diotrephes, who loveth to have the pre-eminence among them, receiveth us not.* Does not admit our authority, or would not comply with any such recommendation. The idea is, that he rejected his interference in the matter, and was not disposed to acknowledge him in any way. Of Diotrephes, nothing more is known than is here specified. Compare the analysis of the epistle. Whether he were an officer in the church—a pastor, a ruling elder, a deacon, a vestry-man, a warden, or a private individual—we have no means of ascertaining. The presumption, from the phrase 'who *loveth* to have the pre-eminence,' would rather seem to be that he was an aspiring man, arrogating rights which he had not, and assuming authority to which he was not entitled by virtue of any office. Still he might have held an office, and might have arrogated authority, as many have done, beyond

10 Wherefore, if I come, I will remember his deeds which he doeth, prating ^a against us with malicious words: and not content therewith, neither doth he himself receive the brethren, and forbiddeth them that would, and casteth *them* out ^b of the church.

a Pr.10.8,10.　　　　b Is.66.5.

what properly belonged to it. The single word rendered 'who loveth to have the pre-eminence,' (φιλοπρωτεύων,) occurs nowhere else in the New Testament. It means simply, *who loves to be first*—meaning that he loved to be at the head of all things, to rule, to lord it over others. It is clearly supposed here, that the church would have complied with the request of the writer if it had not been for this man. What were the *alleged* grounds for the course which he constrained the church to take, we are not informed; the *real* ground, the apostle says, was his desire to rule. There may have been at the bottom of it some secret dislike of John, or some private grudge; but the *alleged* ground may have been, that the church was independent, and that it should reject all foreign interference; or that the church was unable to support those men; or that the work in which they were engaged was one of doubtful propriety. Whatever was the *cause*, the case furnishes an illustration of the bad influence of one ambitious and arrogant man in a church. It is often in the power of one such man to bring a whole church under his control, and effectually to embarrass all its movements, and to prevent all the good which it would otherwise accomplish. When it is said, 'but Diotrephes *receiveth* us not,' the reference is doubtless to John, and the meaning is, either that he did not acknowledge him as an apostle, or that he did not recognize his right to interfere in the affairs of the church, or that he did not regard his recommendation of these brethren. The first of these suppositions is hardly probable; but, though he may have admitted that he was an apostle, there were perhaps some reasons operating in this particular case why he prevailed on the church to reject those who had been thus commended to their hospitality.

10. *Wherefore, if I come.* He was evidently expecting soon to make a visit to Gaius, and to the church. ver. 14.

¶ *I will remember his deeds which he doeth.* That is, he would punish his arrogance and presumption; would take measures that he should be dealt with in a proper manner. There is no evidence whatever that this is said in a vindictive or revengeful spirit, or that the writer spoke of it merely as a personal matter. From anything that can be shown to the contrary, if it had been a private and personal affair merely, the matter might have been dropped, and never referred to again. But what had been done was public. It pertained to the authority of the apostle, the duty of the church, and the character of the brethren who had been commended to them. If the letter was written, as is supposed by the aged John, and his authority had been utterly rejected by the influence of this one man, then it was proper that that authority should be asserted. If it was the duty of the church to have received these men, who had been thus recommended to them, and it had been prevented from doing what it would otherwise have done, by the influence of one man, then it was proper that the influence of that man should be restrained, and that the church should see that he was not to control it. If the feelings and the character of these brethren had been injured by being rudely thrust out of the church, and held up as unworthy of public confidence, then it was proper that their character should be vindicated, and that the author of the wrong should be dealt with in a suitable manner. No one can show that this was not all that the apostle proposed to do, or that any feelings of private vindictiveness entered into his purpose to 'remember' what Diotrephes had done; and the existence of any such feelings should not be charged on the apostle without proof. There is no more reason to suppose this in his case than there was in the case of Paul, in administering discipline in the church of Corinth, (1 Cor. v. 3–5,) or than there is in any instance of administering dis-

11 Beloved, follow *a* not that which is evil, but that which is good. He *b* that doeth good is of God: but he that doeth evil hath not seen God.

a Ps.37.27.

12 Demetrius hath good report of all *men*, and of the truth itself: yea, and we *also* bear record; and ye know that our record is true.

b 1 Jn.3.6-9.

cipline now. ¶ *Prating against us.* The word *prate*, (φλυαρέω,) occurring nowhere else in the New Testament, means to ' overflow with talk,' (Gr. φλύω, Lat. *fluo*, flow;) to talk much without weight, or to little purpose; to be loquacious ; to trifle ; or, to use an expression common among us, and which accords well with the Greek, *to run on* in talk, without connection or sense. The word does not properly imply that there was malignity or ill-feeling in what was said, but that the talk was of an idle, foolish, and unprofitable character. As John here, however, specifies that there *was* a bad spirit in the manner in which Diotrephes expressed himself, the real thing which is implied in the use of the word here is, that there were *much* talk of that kind ; that he was addicted to this habit of *running on* against the apostle ; and that he was thus constantly undermining his influence, and injuring his character. ¶ *With malicious words.* Gr., ' *evil* words ;' words that were fitted to do injury. ¶ *And not content therewith.* Not satisfied with venting his private feelings in talk. Some persons seem to be satisfied with merely talking against others, and take no other measures to injure them; but Diotrephes was not. He himself rejected the brethren, and persuaded the church to do the same thing. Bad as evil talking is, and troublesome as a man may be who is always ' prating' about matters that do not go according to his mind, yet it would be comparatively well if things always ended with that, and if the loquacious and the dissatisfied never took measures openly to wrong others. ¶ *Neither doth he himself receive the brethren.* Does not himself treat them as Christian brethren, or with the hospitality which is due to them. He had not done it on the former visit, and John evidently supposed that the same thing would occur again. ¶ *And forbiddeth them that would.* From this it is clear that there were those in the church who were disposed to receive them in a proper

manner ; and from anything that appears, the church, as such, would have been inclined to do it, if it had not been for the influence of this one man. ¶ *And casteth* them *out of the church.* Comp. Luke vi. 22. It has been made a question whether the reference here is to the members of the church who were disposed to receive these brethren, or to the brethren themselves. Lücke, Macknight, and some others, suppose that it refers to those in the church who were willing to receive them, and whom Diotrephes had excommunicated on that account. Heumann, Carpzovius, Rosenmüller, Bloomfield, and others, suppose that it refers to these strangers, and that the meaning is, that Diotrephes would not receive them into the society of Christians, and thus compelled them to go to another place. That this latter is the correct interpretation seems to me to be evident, for it was of the treatment which they had received that the apostle was speaking.

11. *Beloved, follow not that which is evil, but that which is good.* There can be no doubt that in this exhortation the writer had Diotrephes particularly in his eye, and that he means to exhort Gaius not to imitate his example. He was a man of influence in the church, and though Gaius had shown that he was disposed to act in an independent manner, yet it was not improper to exhort him not to be influenced by the example of any one who did wrong. John wished to excite him to acts of liberal and generous hospitality. ¶ *He that doeth good is of God.* He shows that he resembles God, for God continually does good. See the sentiment explained in the Notes on 1 John iii. 7. ¶ *He that doeth evil hath not seen God.* See Notes, 1 John iii. 8–10

12. *Demetrius hath good report of all* men. Little is known of Demetrius. Lücke supposes that he resided near the place where the author of this epistle lived, and was connected with the church there, and was probably the bearer of

13 I had many things to write, but I will not with ink and pen write unto thee:

14 But I trust I shall shortly see thee, and we shall speak [1] face to face. Peace *be* to thee. *Our* friends salute thee. Greet the friends by name.

[1] *mouth to mouth.*

---

this epistle. It is impossible to determine with certainty on this point, but there is one circumstance which seems to make it probable that he was a member of the same church with Gaius, and had united with him in showing Christian hospitality to these strangers. It is the use of the phrase ' hath good report of all,' implying that some *testimony* was borne to his character beyond what the writer personally knew. It is possible, indeed, that the writer would have used this term respecting him if he lived in the same place with himself, as expressing the fact that he bore a good character, but it is a phrase which would be more appropriately used if we suppose that he was a member of the same church with Gaius, and that John means to say than an honourable testimony was borne of his character by all those brethren, and by all others as far as he knew. ¶ *And of the truth itself.* Not only by men, who might possibly be deceived in the estimate of character, but by *fact.* It was not merely a reputation founded on what *appeared* in his conduct, but in truth and reality. His deportment, his life, his deeds of benevolence, all concurred with the testimony which was borne by men to the excellency of his character. There is, perhaps, particular reference here to his kind and hospitable treatment of those brethren. ¶ *Yea, and we also bear record.* John himself had personally known him. He had evidently visited the place where he resided on some former occasion, and could now add his own testimony, which no one would call in question, to his excellent character. ¶ *And ye know that our record is true.* This is in the manner of John, who always spoke of himself as having such a character for truth that no one who knew him would call it in question. Every Christian *should* have such a character; every man *might* if he would. Comp. Notes, John xix. 35; xxi. 24.

13. *I had many things to write,* &c. This epistle closes, as the second does,

with a statement that he had many things to say, but that he preferred waiting till he should see him rather than put them on paper. Perhaps there were some things which he wished to say which he would not like to have exposed to the possibility of being seen by the public eye. ¶ *But I will not with ink and pen,* &c. Notes on the Second Epistle, ver. 12.

14. *But I trust I shall shortly see thee,* &c. Notes on the Second Epistle, ver. 12. ¶ Our *friends salute thee.* That is, your friends and mine. This would seem rather to refer to private friends of John and Gaius than to Christians as such. They had, doubtless, their warm personal friends in both places. ¶ *Greet the friends by name.* That is, each one individually. He remembered them as individuals, but did not deem it proper to specify them.

PRACTICAL REMARKS ON THE EPISTLE.

(1.) It is proper to desire for our friends all temporal good ; to wish their happiness in every respect, ver. 2. The welfare of the soul is indeed the great object, and the first desire in regard to a friend should be that his salvation may be secured ; but in connection with that we may properly wish them health of body, and success in their lawful undertakings. It is not common that in their spiritual interests they are so much more prosperous than they are in other respects, that we can make *that* the standard of our wishes in regard to them, but it sometimes does occur, as in the case of Gaius. In such cases we may indeed rejoice with a friend, and feel that all will be well with him. But in how few cases, even among professed Christians, can we with propriety make the prosperity of the soul the standard by which to measure the happiness which we desire for them in other respects ! Doddridge says, ' What a curse would this bring upon many to wish that they might prosper even as their souls prospered !' Of how much property would they at once be deprived; how embarrassed would be their affairs; how pale, and wan, and sickly would they be, if they should be in all respects as they are in their spiritual interests!

(2.) It is an unspeakable pleasure to a Christian to learn that his friends are living and acting as becomes sincere Christians; that they love what is true, and abound in the duties of hospitality, charity, and benevolence, vers. 3–6. When a friend learns this of a distant friend; when a pastor learns this of his people from whom he may be for a time separated; when those who have been instrumental in converting others learn this of their spiritual children; when a parent learns it of a son or daughter separated from him; when a teacher learns it of those who were formerly under his care, there is no joy that goes more directly to the heart than this— nothing that fills the soul with more true thankfulness and peace.

(3.) It is the duty and the privilege of those who love the cause of religion to go and preach the gospel to those who are destitute, expecting to receive nothing from them, and doing it as a work of pure benevolence, ver. 7. The missionary spirit existed early in the Christian church, and indeed may be regarded as the *prevailing* spirit in those times. It has always been the prevailing spirit when religion has flourished in the church. At such times there have been many who were willing to leave their own quiet homes, and the religious privileges connected with a well-organized church, and to break away from the ties which bind to country and kindred, and to go among a distant people to publish salvation. In this cause, and with this spirit, the apostles spent their lives. In this cause, the 'brethren' referred to by John went forth to labour. In this cause, thousands have laboured in former times, and to the fact that they were *willing* to do it is to be traced all the happy influence of religion in the world. Our own religious privileges now we owe to the fact that in former times there were those who were willing to 'go forth taking nothing of the Gentiles,' devoting themselves, without hope of reward or

fame, to the business of making known the name of the Saviour in what were then the dark places of the earth. The same principle is acted on now in Christian missions, and with the same propriety; and as *we* in Christian lands owe the blessings which we enjoy to the fact that in former times there were those who were willing thus to go forth, so it will be true that the richest blessings which are to descend on India, and Africa, and the islands of the sea, will be traced in future times to the fact that there are in *our* age those who are willing to follow the example of the apostles in going forth to do good to a dying world.

(4.) It is our duty to contribute to the support of those who thus go among the heathen, and to aid them in every way in which we can promote the object which they have in view. So John felt it to be the duty of the church in regard to those who went forth in his time; and so, when the church, under the influence of Diotrephes, had refused to do it, he commended Gaius for performing that duty, vers. 6, 8. Now, as then, from the nature of the case, missionaries to the heathen must go 'taking nothing' of those among whom they labour, and expecting that, for a long time at least, they will do nothing for their support. They go as strangers. They go to those who do not believe the truth of the gospel; who are attached to their own superstitions; who contribute largely to the support of their own temples, and altars, and priesthood; who are, as yet, incapable of appreciating the value of a purer religion; who have no desire for it, and who are disposed to reject it. In many cases, the heathen to whom the missionary goes are miserably poor, and it is only this religion, which as yet they are not disposed to receive, that can elevate them to habits of industry, and furnish them with the means of supporting religious teachers from abroad. Under these circumstances, no duty is more obvious than that of contributing to the support of those who go to such places as Christian missionaries. If the churches value the gospel enough to *send* their brethren among the heathen to propagate it, they should value it enough to minister to their wants when there; if they regard it as the duty of any of their number to leave their comfortable homes in a Christian land in order to preach to the heathen, they should feel that those who go make far greater sacrifices than those who contribute to their support. *They* give up all; *we* give only the small sum, not diminishing our own comforts, which is needful to sustain them.

(5.) For the same reason it is our duty to contribute to the support of missionaries in the destitute places of our own land, ver. 8. They often go among a people who are as destitute, and who will as little appreciate the gospel, and who are as much prejudiced against it, and who are as poor, as the heathen. They are as likely to be charged with being actuated by mercenary motives, if they ask for support, as missionaries among the heathen are. They often go among people as little able and disposed to build churches and school-houses as the heathen are. Nothing is more obvious, therefore, than that those who have the gospel, and who have learned to prize and value it in some measure as it should be, should contribute to the support of those who go to convey its blessings to others, until those to whom they go shall so learn to prize it as to be able and willing to maintain it. That, under a faithful ministry, and with the Divine blessing, will not be long; for the gospel *always*, when it secures a hold in a community, makes men feel that it confers infinitely more blessings than it takes away, and that, even in a pecuniary point of view, it contributes more by far than it takes. What community is more prospered, or is more rich in all that promotes the temporal welfare of man, than that where the gospel has the most decided influence?

(6.) We may see from this epistle that churches *ought* to be united in promoting the cause of religion, vers. 8, 9. They should regard it as a common cause in which one has as much concern as another, and where each should feel it a privilege to co-operate with his brethren. One church, in proportion to its ability, has as much interest in the spread of Christianity as another, and should feel that it has much responsi-

bility in doing it. Between different churches there should be that measure of confidence and love that they will deem it a privilege to aid each other in the common cause, and that one shall be ready to further the benevolent designs undertaken by another. In every Christian land, and among the people of every Christian denomination, missionaries of the gospel should find friends who will be willing to co-operate with them in advancing the common cause, and who, though they may bear a different name, and may speak a different language, should cheerfully lend their aid in spreading the common Christianity.

(7.) We may see, from this epistle, the evil of having *one* troublesome man in the church, ver. 10. Such a man, by his talents, his address, his superior learning, his wealth, or by his arrogance, pride, and self-confidence, may control a church, and effectually hinder its promoting the work of religion. The church referred to by the apostle would have done its duty well enough, if it had not been for one ambitious and worldly man. No one can properly estimate the evil which one such man can do, nor the calamity which comes upon a church when such a man places himself at its head. As a man of wealth, of talents, and of learning, may do great good, if his heart is right, so may a man similarly endowed do proportionate evil if his heart is wicked. Yet how often has the spirit which actuated Diotrephes prevailed in the church! There is nothing that confers so much *power* on men as the control in religious matters; and hence, in all ages, proud and ambitious men have sought dominion over the conscience, and have sought to bring the sentiments of men on religion to subjection to their will.

(8.) There may be circumstances where it is proper—where it is a duty—to receive those who have been cast out of the church, ver. 8. The decisions of a church, under some proud and ambitious partisan leader, are often eminently unjust and harsh. The most modest, humble, devoted, and zealous men, under a charge of heresy, or of some slight aberration from the formulas of doctrine, may be cast out as unworthy to be recognized as ministers of the gospel, or even as unworthy to have a place at the table of the Lord. Some of the best men on earth have been thus disowned by the church ; and it is no *certain* evidence against a man when he is denounced as a heretic, or disowned as a member, by those who bear the Christian name. If *we* are satisfied that a man is a Christian, we should receive him as such, however he may be regarded by others ; nor should we hesitate to help him forward in his Christian course, or in any way to assist him to do good.

(9.) Finally, let us learn from the examples commended in this brief epistle, to do good. Let us follow the example of Gaius—the hospitable Christian ; the large-hearted philanthropist; the friend of the stranger; the helper of those who were engaged in the cause of the Lord —a man who opened his heart and his house to welcome them when driven out and disowned by others. Let us imitate Demetrius, in obtaining a good report of those who know us ; in so living that, if the aged apostle John were still on earth, we might be worthy of his commendation, and more than all, of the approbation of that gracious Saviour before whom these good men have long since gone, and in whose presence we also must soon appear.

THE

GENERAL EPISTLE OF JUDE

INTRODUCTION.

§ 1. *The author of this Epistle.*

LITTLE is known of the author of this brief epistle. He styles himself (ver. 1) 'the servant of Jesus Christ, and brother of James;' but there has been some difference of opinion as to what *James* is meant. He does not call himself an *apostle*, but supposes that the terms which he uses would sufficiently identify him, and would be a sufficient reason for his addressing his brethren in the manner in which he does in this epistle. There were two of the name of *James* among the apostles, (Luke vi. 14, 15 ;) and it has been made a question of which of them he was the brother. There were also two of the name of Judas, or Jude ; but there is no difficulty in determining which of them was the author of this epistle, for the other had the surname of Iscariot, and was the traitor. In the catalogue of the apostles given by Matthew, (chap. x. 3,) the tenth place is given to an apostle who is there called 'Lebbeus,' whose surname was 'Thaddeus;' and as this name does not occur in the list given by Luke, (chap. vi. 15,) and as the tenth place in the catalogue is occupied by 'Simon, called Zelotes,' and as he afterwards mentions 'Judas the brother of James,' it is supposed that Lebbeus and Judas were the same persons. It was not uncommon for persons to have two or more names. Comp. Robinson's Harmony of the Gospels, § 40 ; Bacon's Lives of Apostles, p. 447 ; and Michaelis, iv., 365.

The title which he assumes, 'brother of James,' was evidently chosen because the James referred to was well-known, and because the fact that he was his brother would be a sufficient designation of himself, and of his right to address Christians in this manner. The name of the elder James, who was slain by Herod, (Acts xii. 2,) can hardly be supposed to be referred to, as he had been dead some time when this epistle is supposed to have been written ; and as that James was the brother of John, who was then living, it would have been much more natural for him to have mentioned that he was the brother of that beloved disciple. The other James—'James the Less,' or 'James the Just'—was still living ; was a prominent man in Jerusalem ; and was, besides, known as 'the brother of the Lord Jesus ;' and the fact of relationship to that James would sufficiently designate the writer. There can be little doubt, therefore, that this is the James here intended. In regard to his character and influence, see Intro. to the Epistle of James, § 1. If the author of this epistle was the brother of *that* James, it was sufficient to refer to that fact, without mentioning that he was an apostle, in order to give to his epistle authority, and to settle its canonical character.

Of Jude little is known. His name is found in the list of the apostles, but, besides that, it is but once mentioned in the Gospels. The only thing that is preserved of him in the Evangelists, is a question which he put to the Saviour, on the eve of his crucifixion. The Saviour had said, in his parting address to his disciples, 'He that hath my commandments, and keepeth them, he it is that loveth me ; and he that loveth me shall be loved of my Father ; and I will love him, and will manifest myself unto him.' In regard to the meaning of this remark, Judas is said to have asked the following question : ' Lord, how is it that thou wilt manifest thyself unto us, and not unto the world ?' John xiv. 21, 22. To this question the Saviour gave him a kind and satisfactory answer, and that is the last that is said of him in the Gospels.

Of his subsequent life we know little. In Acts xv. 22, he is mentioned as surnamed ' Barsabas,' and as being sent with Paul and Barnabas and Silas to Antioch. Paulinus says that he preached in Lybia, and that his body remained there. Jerome affirms, that after the ascension he was sent to Edessa, to king Abgarus ; and the modern Greeks say that he preached in that city, and throughout Mesopotamia, and in Judea, Samaria, Idumea, Syria, and principally in Armenia and Persia.—*Calmet's Dict.* Nothing certainly can be known in reference to the field of his labours, or to the place and circumstances of his death. On the question whether the Thaddeus who first preached the gospel in Syria was the same person as Jude, see Michaelis, Intro. iv., 367–371.

§ 2. *The authenticity of the Epistle.*

If this epistle was written by the apostle Jude, the brother of James and of our Lord, there can be no doubt of its canonical authority, and its claim to a place in the New Testament. It is true that he does not call himself an apostle, but simply mentions himself as ' a servant of Jesus Christ, and a brother of James.' By this appellation, however, he has practically made it known that he was one of the apostles, for all who had a catalogue of the apostles would know ' that Judas, the brother of James,' was one of them. At the same time, as the relation of James to our Lord was well understood, (Gal. i. 19,) his authority would be recognized as soon as he was known to be the author of the epistle. It may be asked, indeed, if he was an apostle, why he did not call himself such ; and why he did not seek to give authority and currency to his epistle, by adverting to the fact that he was the ' Lord's brother.' To the first of these questions, it may be replied, that to have called himself ' Judas, the apostle,' would not have designated him so certainly, as to call himself ' the brother of James ;' and besides, the naked title, ' Judas, the apostle,' was one which he might not choose to see applied to himself. After the act of the traitor, and the reproach which he had brought upon that name, it is probable that he would prefer to designate himself by some other appellation than one which had such associations connected with it. It may be added, also, that in several of his epistles Paul himself does not make use of the name of the apostle, Phil. i. 1 ; 1 Thess. i. 1 ; 2 Thess. i. 1 ; Philemon 1. To the second question, it may be replied, that *modesty* may have kept him from applying to himself the title, the ' Lord's brother.' Even James never uses it of himself ; and we only know that he sustained this relation from an incidental remark of the apostle Paul, Gal. i. 19. Great honour would be attached to that relationship, and it is possible that the reason why it was not referred to by James and Jude was an apprehension that it might produce jealousy, as if they claimed some special pre-eminence over their brethren.

For the evidence of the canonical authority of this epistle, the reader is referred to Lardner, vol. vi., pp. 304–313, and to Michaelis, Intro. vol. iv., p. 374, seq. Michaelis, chiefly on the internal evidence, supposes that it is not an inspired production. There were indeed, at first, doubts about its being inspired, as there were respecting the epistle of James, and the second epistle of Peter, but those doubts were ultimately removed, and it was received as a canonical epistle. Clemens of Alexandria cites the epistle under Jude's name, as the production of a prophetic mind. Origen calls it a production full of heavenly grace. Eusebius says that his predecessors were divided in opinion respecting it, and that it was not ranked among the universally acknowledged writings. It was not universally received among the Syrians, and is not found in the Peschito, the oldest Syriac version of the Scriptures. In the time of Jerome, however, it came to be ranked among the other sacred Scriptures as of Divine authority.—Hug, Intro., § 180.

The principal ground of doubt in regard to the canonical authority of the epistle, arose from the supposed fact that the author has quoted two apocryphal writings, vers. 9, 14. The consideration of this objection will be more appropriate in the Notes on those verses, for it obviously depends much on the true interpretation of these passages. I shall, therefore, reserve what I have to say on that point to the exposition of those verses. Those who are disposed to examine it at length, may consult Hug, Intro., § 183 ; Lardner, vi. 309–314, and Michaelis, Intro., iv., 378, seq.

§ 3. *The question when the Epistle was written, to whom, and its design.*

Nothing can be determined with entire certainty in regard to the persons to whom this epistle was written. Witsius supposed that it was addressed to Christians everywhere ; Hammond, that it was addressed to Jewish Christians alone, who were scattered abroad, and that its design was to secure them against the errors of the Gnostics ; Benson, that it was directed to Jewish believers, especially to those of the western dispersion ; Lardner, that it was written to all, without distinction, who had embraced the gospel. The principal argument for supposing that it was addressed to Jewish converts is, that the apostle refers mainly for proof to Hebrew writings, but this might be sufficiently accounted for by the fact that the writer himself was of Jewish origin.

The only way of determining anything on this point is from the epistle itself. The inscription is, ' To them that are sanctified by God the Father, and preserved in Jesus Christ, and called,' ver. 1. From this it would appear evident that he had no *particular* classes of Christians in his eye, whether of Jewish or Gentile origin, but that he designed the epistle for the general use of all who had em braced the Christian religion. The errors which he combats in the epistle were evidently wide-spread, and were of such a nature that it was proper to warn all Christians against them. They might, it is true, be more prevalent in some quarters than in others, but still they were so common that Christians every-where should be put on their guard against them.

The *design* for which Jude wrote the epistle he has himself stated, ver. 3. It was with reference to the ' common salvation '—the doctrines pertaining to salva-tion which were held by *all* Christians, and to show them the reasons for ' con-tending earnestly for the faith once delivered to the saints.' That faith was assailed. There were teachers of error abroad. They were insinuating and artful men—men who had crept in unawares, and who, while they professed to hold the Christian doctrine, were really undermining its faith, and spreading corruption through the church. The *purpose*, therefore, of the epistle is to put those to whom it was written on their guard against the corrupt teachings of these men, and to encourage them to stand up manfully for the great principles of Christian truth.

Who these errorists were, it is not easy now to determine. The leading charge against them, both by Jude and Peter, (2 Peter ii. 1,) is, that they denied our Lord, (ver. 4 ;) and yet it is said that they were numbered among Christians, and were found in their assemblies, 2 Peter ii. 13 ; Jude, ver. 12. By this denial, however, we are not to suppose that they literally and professedly denied that Jesus was the Christ, but that they held *doctrines* which amounted to a denial of him in fact. Comp. Notes, 2 Pet. ii. 1. For the general characteristics of these teachers, see Intro. to 2 Pet. § 4.

At this distance of time, and with our imperfect knowledge of the character-istics of the early erroneous sects in the church, it is difficult to determine precisely who they were. It has been a common opinion, that reference is had by Peter and Jude to the sect of the Nicolaitanes; and this opinion, Hug remarks, is ' neither improbable nor incompatible with the expressions of the two apostles, so far as we have any certain knowledge concerning this sect.' ' The statements of the ancients, in regard to their profligacy and their detestable course of life, are so consonant with each other and with the charges of the apostles, that the two epistles may be pertinently considered as referring to them.'—Intro., § 182.

It is not possible to ascertain with certainty the time when the epistle was written. There are no marks of time in it by which that can be known, nor is there any account among the early Christian writers which determines this. Benson supposes that it was written before the destruction of Jerusalem, a few weeks or months after the second epistle of Peter; Mill, that it was written about A.D. 90; Dodwell and Cave, that it was written *after* the destruction of Jerusalem, in the year 71 or 72; L'Enfant and Beausobre, that it was between the year 70 and 75; Witsius and Estius, that it was in the apostle's old age; Lardner, that it was about the year 65 or 66; Michaelis, that it was before the destruction of Jerusalem; and Macknight, that it was in the latter part of the apostolic age, and not long before the death of Jude. All this, it is manifest, is mostly con-ʲecture. There are only *two* things, it seems to me, in the epistle, which can be regarded as *any* indication of the time. One is the striking resemblance to the second epistle of Peter, referring clearly to the same kind of errors, and warning those whom he addressed against the arts of the same kind of teachers, thus showing that it was written at about the same time as that epistle; and the other is, that it seems to have been written *before* the destruction of Jerusalem, for, as Michaelis has well remarked, ' As the author has mentioned (vers. 5–8) several well-known instances of Divine justice in punishing sinners, he would probably, if Jerusalem had been already destroyed, not have neglected to add to his other examples this most remarkable instance of Divine vengeance, especially as Christ had himself foretold it.'—Intro. iv. 372. As there is reason to suppose that the second epistle of Peter was written about A.D. 64 or 65, we shall not, probably, err in supposing that this was written not far from that time.

§ IV. *The resemblance between this Epistle and the second chapter of the second Epistle of Peter.*

One of the most remarkable things respecting this epistle, is its resemblance to the second chapter of the second epistle of Peter—a similarity so striking as to make it quite certain that one of these writers had seen the epistle of the other, and copied from it; or rather, perhaps, adopted the language of the other as expressing his own views. It is evident, that substantially the same class of teachers is referred to by both; that they held the same errors, and were guilty of the same corrupt and dangerous practices; and that the two apostles, in describing them, made use of the same expressions, and employed the same arguments against them. They refer to the same facts in history, and to the same arguments from tradition; and if either of them quoted an apocryphal book, both have done it. On the resemblance, compare the following places:—Jude 8, with 2 Pet. ii. 10; Jude 10, with 2 Pet. ii. 12; Jude 16, with 2 Pet. ii. 18; Jude 4, with 2 Pet. i. 2, 3; Jude 7, with 2 Pet. ii. 6; Jude 9, with 2 Pet. ii. 11. The similarity between the two is so striking, both in the general structure of the argument and in the particular expressions, that it cannot have been accidental. It is not such a resemblance as would be likely to occur in two authors, if they had been writing in a wholly independent manner. In regard to this resemblance, there is but one of three ways in which it can be accounted for: either that the Holy Spirit inspired both of them to say the same thing, without the one having any knowledge of what the other said; or that they both copied from a common document, which is now lost; or that one copied from the other.

As to the first of these solutions, that the Holy Spirit inspired them both to say the same thing, it may be observed that no one can deny that this is *possible*, but is by no means probable. No other instance of the kind occurs in the Bible, and the supposition would not be in accordance with what seems to have been a law in inspiration, that the sacred writers were allowed to express themselves according to the bent of their own genius. See Notes, 1 Cor. xiv. 32.

As to the second of these suppositions, that they both copied from a common document, which is now lost, it may be observed, that this is wholly without evidence. That such a thing was *possible*, there can be no doubt, but the supposition should not be adopted without necessity. If there had been such an original inspired document, it would probably have been preserved ; or there would have been, in one or both of those who copied from it, some such allusion to it that it would have been possible to verify the supposition.

The remaining way of accounting for the resemblance, therefore, is to suppose that one of them had seen the epistle of the other, and adopted the same line of argument, and many of the same expressions. This will account for all the facts in the case, and can be supposed to be true without doing violence to any just view of their inspiration. A question still arises, however, whether Peter or Jude is the original writer from which the other has copied. This question it is impossible to determine with certainty, and it is of little importance. If the common opinion which is stated above be correct, that Peter wrote his epistle *first*, of course that determines the matter. But that is not absolutely certain, nor is there any method by which it can be determined. Hug adopts the other opinion, and supposes that Jude was the original writer. His reasons for this opinion are substantially these : (1.) That there is little probability that Jude, in so brief an epistle as his, consisting of only twenty-five verses, would have made use of foreign aid. (2.) That the style and phraseology of Jude is simple, unlaboured, and without ornament; while that of Peter is artificial, and wears the appearance of embellishment and amplification ; that the simple language of Jude seems to have been moulded by Peter into a more elegant form, and is embellished with participles, and even with rhetorical flourishes. (3.) That there is allusion in both epistles (2 Pet. ii. 11; Jude 9) to a controversy between angels and fallen spirits; but that it is so alluded to by Peter, that it would not be understood without the more full statement of Jude; and that Peter evidently supposed that the letter of Jude was in the hands of those to whom he wrote, and that thus the allusion would be at once understood. It could not be supposed that every reader would be acquainted with the fact alluded to by Peter; it was not stated in the sacred books of the Jews, and it seems probable that there must have been some book to which they had access, where the information was more full. Jude, however, as the original writer, stated it more at length, and having done this, a bare allusion to it by Peter was all that was necessary. Jude states the matter definitely, and expressly mentions the dispute of Michael with the devil about the body of Moses. But the language of Peter is so general and indefinite, that we could not know what he meant unless we had Jude in our possession. See Hug's Intro., § 176. It must be admitted that these considerations have much weight, though they are not absolutely conclusive. It should be added, that whichever supposition is adopted, the fact that one has expressed substantially the same sentiments as the other, and in nearly the same language, is no reason for rejecting either, any more than the coincidence between the Gospels is a reason for concluding that only one of them can be an inspired document. There might have been good reasons why the same warnings and counsels should have proceeded from two inspired men.

THE

GENERAL EPISTLE OF JUDE.

JUDE, [a] the servant of Jesus Christ, and brother of James, to them that are [b] sanctified by God

the Father, and preserved [c] in Jesus Christ, *and* called: [d]

a Lu.6.16. b Ac.20.32. c 1 Pe.1.5. d Ro.8.30.

ANALYSIS OF THE EPISTLE.

(1.) THE inscription and salutation, vers. 1, 2. (2.) A statement of the reasons why the epistle was written, vers. 3, 4. The author felt it to be necessary to write to them, because certain plausible errorists had crept in among them, and there was danger that their faith would be subverted. (3.) A reference to past facts, showing that men who embraced error, and who followed corrupt and licentious practices, would be punished, vers. 5–7. He refers particularly to the unbelieving Hebrews whom God had delivered out of Egypt; to the apostate angels ; and to the corrupt inhabitants of Sodom and Gomorrah. The object in this is to warn them from following the examples of those who would certainly lead them to destruction. (4.) He describes particularly the characteristics of these persons, agreeing substantially in the description with the statement of Peter, vers. 8–16. For these characteristics, comp. Intro. to 2 Peter, § 4. In general, they were corrupt, sensual, lewd, proud, arrogant, disorganizing, covetous, murmurers, complainers, wordy, windy, spots in their feasts of love. They had been and were professors of religion ; they were professed reformers; they made great pretensions to uncommon knowledge of religious things. In the course of this description, the apostle contrasts their spirit with that of the archangel Michael, (ver. 9,) and declares that it was with reference to such a class of men that Enoch long ago uttered a solemn prophecy, vers. 14, 15. (5.) He calls to their remembrance the fact that

it had been predicted that there would be such mockers in the last periods of the world ; and the faith of true Christians, therefore, was not to be shaken, but rather confirmed by the fact of their appearance, vers. 17–19. (6.) In view of these facts and dangers, the apostle addresses to them two exhortations : (a) to adhere steadfastly to the truths which they had embraced, vers. 20, 21; and (b) to endeavour to recall and save those who were led astray—carefully guarding themselves from the same contamination while they sought to save others, vers. 22, 23. (7.) The epistle closes with an appropriate ascription of praise to him who was able to keep them from falling, and to present them faultless before his throne, vers. 24, 25.

1. *Jude, the servant of Jesus Christ.* If the view taken in the Introduction to the epistle is correct, Jude sustained a near relation to the Lord Jesus, being, as James was, 'the Lord's brother,' Gal. i. 19. The reasons why he did not advert to this fact here, as an appellation which would serve to designate him, and as showing his authority to address others in the manner in which he proposed to do in this epistle, probably were, (1,) that the right to do this did not rest on his mere *relationship* to the Lord Jesus, but on the fact that he had called certain persons to be his apostles, and had authorized them to do it ; and, (2,) that a reference to this relationship, as a ground of authority, might have created jealousies among the apostles themselves. We may *learn* from the fact that Jude merely calls himself 'the *servant* of the Lord Jesus,' that is, a Christian, (a), that this is a distinction

2 Mercy unto you, and peace, and love, be multiplied.

3 Beloved, when I gave all diligence to write unto you of the common salvation, *a* it was needful for me to write unto you, and exhort *you* that ye should earnestly contend *b* for the faith which was once delivered unto the saints.

a Tit.1.4.   b Ga.2.5.

---

more to be desired than would be a mere natural relationship to the Saviour, and consequently (*b*) that it is a higher honour than *any* distinction arising from birth or family. Comp. Matt. xii. 46–50. ¶ *And brother of James.* See Intro., § 1. ¶ *To them that are sanctified by God the Father.* To those who are *holy*, or who are *saints.* Comp. Notes, Rom. i. 7 ; Phil. i. 1. Though this title is general, it can hardly be doubted that he had some *particular* saints in his view, to wit, those who were exposed to the dangers to which he refers in the epistle. See Intro., § 3. As the epistle was probably *sent* to Christians residing in a certain place, it was not necessary to designate them more particularly, though it was often done. The Syriac version adds here, ' To the *Gentiles* who are called, beloved of God the Father,' &c. ¶ *And preserved in Jesus Christ.* See Notes, 1 Pet. i. 5. The meaning is, that they owed their preservation wholly to him ; and if they were brought to everlasting life, it would be only by him. What the apostle here says of those to whom he wrote, is true of all Christians. They would all fall away and perish if it were not for the grace of God keeping them. ¶ And *called.* Called to be saints. See Notes, Rom. i. 7 ; Eph. iv. 1.

2. *Mercy unto you, and peace, and love, be multiplied.* This is not quite the form of salutation used by the other apostles, but it is one equally expressive of an earnest desire for their welfare. These things are mentioned as the choicest blessings which could be conferred on them : *mercy*—in the pardon of all their sins and acceptance with God ; *peace*—with God, with their fellow-men, in their own consciences, and in the prospect of death ; and *love*—to God, to the brethren, to all the world. What blessings are there which these do not include ?

3. *Beloved.* An expression of strong affection used by the apostles when addressing their brethren, Rom. i. 7; 1 Cor. iv. 14 ; x. 14; xv. 58; 2 Cor. vii. 1; xii. 19; Phil. ii. 12; iv. 1; and often elsewhere. ¶ *When I gave all diligence.* When I applied my mind earnestly ; implying that he had reflected on the subject, and thought particularly what it would be desirable to write to them. The state of mind referred to is that of one who was purposing to write a letter, and who thought over carefully what it would be proper to say. The mental process which led to writing the epistle seems to have been this : (*a*) For some reasons—mainly from his strong affection for them—he purposed to write to them. (*b*) The general subject on which he designed to write was, of course, something pertaining to the common salvation—for he and they were Christians. (*c*) On reflecting what particular thing pertaining to this common salvation it was best for him to write on, he felt that, in view of their peculiar dangers, it ought to be an exhortation to contend earnestly for the faith once delivered to them. Macknight renders this less correctly, ' Making all haste to write to you,' &c. But the idea is rather that he set himself diligently and earnestly to write to them of the great matter in which they had a common interest. ¶ *To write unto you of the common salvation.* The salvation *common* to Jews and Gentiles, and to all who bore the Christian name. The meaning is, that he did not think of writing on any subject pertaining to a particular class or party, but on some subject in which all who were Christians had a common interest. There are great matters of religion held in common by all Christians, and it is important for religious teachers to address their fellow Christians on those common topics. After all, they are more important than the things which we may hold as peculiar to our own party or sect, and should be more frequently dwelt upon. ¶ *It was needful*

4 For there are certain men crept in unawares, *a* who *b* were before of old ordained to this condemnation; ungodly men, turning *c* the grace of our God into lasciviousness, and denying the only Lord God, and our Lord Jesus Christ.

a 2 Pe.2.1.   *b* Ro.9.22.   *c* Ti.1.15,16.

for me to write to you. 'I reflected on the general subject, prompted by my affectionate regard to write to you of things pertaining to religion in general, and, on looking at the matter, I found there was a particular topic or aspect of the subject on which it was *necessary* to address you. I saw the danger in which you were from false teachers, and felt it not only necessary that I should write to you, but that I should make *this* the particular subject of my counsels.' ¶ *And exhort* you. 'That I should make my letter in fact an exhortation on a particular topic.' ¶ *That ye should earnestly contend.* Comp. Gal. ii. 5. The word here rendered *earnestly contend* — ἐπαγωνίζεσθαι — is one of those words used by the sacred writers which have allusion to the Grecian games. Comp. Notes, 1 Cor. ix. 24, seq. This word does not elsewhere occur in the New Testament. It means *to contend upon*—i. e. *for* or *about* anything ; and would be applicable to the earnest effort put forth in those games to obtain the prize. The reference here, of course, is only to contention by argument, by reasoning, by holding fast the principles of religion, and maintaining them against all opposers. It would not justify ' contention ' by arms, by violence, or by persecution ; for (*a*) that is contrary to the spirit of true religion, and to the requirements of the gospel elsewhere revealed ; (*b*) it is not demanded by the proper meaning of the word, all that that fairly implies being the effort to maintain truth by argument and by a steady life ; (*c*) it is not the most effectual way to keep up truth in the world to attempt to do it by force and arms. ¶ *For the faith.* The system of religion revealed in the gospel. It is called *faith*, because that is the cardinal virtue *in* the system, and because all depends on that. The rule here will require that we should contend in this manner for all *truth*. ¶ *Once delivered unto the saints.* The word here used (ἅπαξ) may mean either

once *for all*, in the sense that it was then complete, and would not be repeated ; or *formerly*, to wit, by the author of the system. Doddridge, Estius, and Beza, understand it in the former way ; Macknight and others in the latter ; Benson improperly supposes that it means *fully* or *perfectly*. Perhaps the more usual sense of the word would be, that it was done *once* in the sense that it is not to be done again, and therefore in the sense that it was then complete, and that nothing was to be added to it. There is indeed the idea that it was *formerly* done, but with this additional thought, that it was then complete. Compare, for this use of the Greek word rendered *once*, Heb. ix. 26 —28 ; x. 2 ; 1 Pet. iii. 18. The *delivering* of this faith to the saints here referred to is evidently that made by revelation, or the system of truth which *God* has made known in his word. Everything which He has revealed, we are to defend as true. We are to surrender no part of it whatever, for every part of that system is of value to mankind. By a careful study of the Bible we are to ascertain what that system *is*, and then in all places, at all times, in all circumstances, and at every sacrifice, we are to maintain it.

4. *For there are certain men crept in unawares.* The apostle now gives a *reason* for thus defending the truth, to wit, that there were artful and wicked men who had crept into the church, pretending to be religious teachers, but whose doctrines tended to sap the very foundations of truth. The apostle Peter, describing these same persons, says, ' who *privily* shall bring in damnable heresies.' See Notes, 2 Pet. ii. 1. Substantially the same idea is expressed here by saying that they ' had crept in *unawares ;*' that is, they had come in *by stealth ;* they had not come by a bold and open avowal of their real sentiments. They professed to teach the Christian religion, when in fact they denied some of its fundamental doc-

trines; they professed to be holy, when in fact they were living most scandalous lives. In all ages there have been men who were willing to do this for base purposes. ¶ *Who were before of old ordained to this condemnation.* That is, to the condemnation (*κρίμα*) which he proceeds to specify. The statements in the subsequent part of the epistle show that by the word used here he refers to the wrath that shall come upon the ungodly in the future world. See vers. 5–7, 15. The meaning clearly is, that the punishment which befell the unbelieving Israelites, (ver. 5;) the rebel angels, (ver. 6;) the inhabitants of Sodom, (ver. 7;) and of which Enoch prophesied, (ver. 15,) awaited those persons. The phrase *of old—πάλαι—* means *long ago,* implying that a considerable time had elapsed, though without determining how much. It is used in the New Testament only in the following places: Matt. xi. 21, 'they would have repented *long ago;*' Mark xv. 44, ' whether he had been *any while* dead;' Luke x. 13, ' they had *a great while ago* repented;' Heb. i. 1, ' spake *in time past* unto the fathers;' 2 Pet. i. 9, ' purged from his *old* sins;' and in the passage before us. So far as this word is concerned, the reference here may have been to *any* former remote period, whether in the time of the prophets, of Enoch, or in eternity. It does not *necessarily* imply that it was *eternal,* though it *might* apply to that, if the thing referred to was, from other sources, certainly known to have been from eternity. It may be doubted, however, whether, if the thing referred to had occurred from eternity, this would have been the word used to express it, (comp. Eph. i. 4;) and it is certain that it cannot be *proved* from the use of this word (*πάλαι*) that the ' ordination to condemnation ' was eternal. Whatever may be referred to by that ' ordaining to condemnation,' *this* word will not prove that it was an eternal ordination. All that is *fairly* implied in it will be met by the supposition that it occurred in *any* remote period, say in the time of the prophets. The word here rendered '*before ordained*'— *προγεγραμμένοι,* from *προγράφω*—occurs in the New Testament only here and in the following places : Rom. xv. 4, twice,

' Whatsoever things *were written aforetime, were written* for our learning;' Gal. iii. 1, ' Jesus Christ *hath been evidently set forth ;*' and Eph. iii. 3. ' As *I wrote afore* in few words.' Comp. Notes, Gal. iii. 1. In these places there is evidently no idea implied of *ordaining,* or *pre-ordaining,* in the sense in which those words are now commonly understood. To that word there is usually attached the idea of designating or appointing as by an arbitrary decree ; but no such meaning enters into the word here used. The Greek word properly means, *to write before ;* then *to have written before ;* and then, with reference to time future, *to post up beforehand in writing ; to announce by posting up on a written tablet,* as of some ordinance, law, or requirement ; as descriptive of what will be, or what should be. Comp. Rob. Lexicon. Burder (in Rosenmüller's Morgenland, *in loc.*) remarks that ' the names of those who were to be tried were usually posted up in a public place, as was also their sentence after their condemnation, and that this was denoted by the same Greek word which the apostle uses here. Elsner,' says he, ' remarks that the Greek authors use the word as applicable to those who, among the Romans, were said to be *proscribed;* that is, those whose names were posted up in a public place, whereby they were appointed to death, and in reference to whom a reward was offered to any one who would kill them.' The idea here clearly is that of some such designation beforehand as *would occur* if the persons had been publicly *posted* as appointed to death. Their *names,* indeed, were not mentioned, but there was such a description of them, or of their character, that it was clear who were meant. In regard to the question what the apostle *means* by such a designation or appointment beforehand, it is clear that he does not refer in this place to any arbitrary or eternal decree, but to such a designation as was made by the facts to which he immediately refers—that is, to the Divine prediction that there would be such persons, (vers. 14, 15, 18 ;) and to the consideration that in the case of the unbelieving Israelites, the rebel angels, and the inhabitants of

5 I will therefore put you in remembrance, though ye once knew this, how that the Lord, *a* having

a 1 Co.10.5-12.

Sodom, there was as clear a proof that such persons would be punished as if their names had been posted up. All these instances bore on just such cases as these, and in these facts they might read their sentence as clearly as if their names had been written on the face of the sky. This interpretation seems to me to embrace all that the words *fairly* imply, and all that the exigence of the case demands; and if this be correct, then two things follow: (1,) that this passage should not be adduced to prove that God has from all eternity, by an arbitrary decree, ordained a certain portion of the race to destruction, whatever may be true on that point; and, (2,) that *all* abandoned sinners now may see, in the facts which have occurred in the treatment of the wicked in past times, just as certain evidence of their destruction, if they do not repent, as if their names were written in letters of light, and if it were announced to the universe that they would be damned. ¶ *Ungodly men.* Men without piety or true religion, whatever may be their pretensions. ¶ *Turning the grace of our God into lasciviousness.* Abusing the doctrines of grace so as to give indulgence to corrupt and carnal propensities. That is, probably, they gave this form to their teaching, as Antinomians have often done, that by the gospel they were released from the obligations of the law, and might give indulgence to their sinful passions in order that grace might abound. Antinomianism began early in the world, and has always had a wide prevalence. The liability of the doctrines of grace to be thus abused was foreseen by Paul, and against such abuse he earnestly sought to guard the Christians of his time, Rom. vi. 1, seq. ¶ *And denying the only Lord God, and our Saviour Jesus Christ.* See Notes, 2 Pet. ii. 1. That is, the doctrines which they held were in fact a denial of the only true God, and of the Redeemer of men. It cannot be supposed that they openly and formally did this, for then they could

saved the people out of the land of Egypt, afterward destroyed *b* them that believed not.

b Nu.14.29,37; He.3.16-19.

have made no pretensions to the name Christian, or even to religion of any kind; but the meaning must be, that *in fact* the doctrines which they held amounted to a denial of the true God, and of the Saviour in his proper nature and work. Some have proposed to read this, 'denying the only Lord God, *even* (καὶ) our Lord Jesus Christ;' but the Greek does not demand this construction even if it would admit it, and it is most in accordance with Scripture usage to retain the common translation. It may be added, also, that the common translation expresses all that the exigence of the passage requires. Their doctrines and practice tended as really to the denial of the true God as they did to the denial of the Lord Jesus. Peter in his second epistle, (ch. ii. 1,) has adverted only to *one* aspect of their doctrine—that it denied the Saviour; Jude adds, if the common reading be correct, that it tended also to a denial of the true God. The word *God* (Θεὸν) is wanting in many manuscripts, and in the Vulgate and Coptic versions, and Mill, Hammond, and Bengel suppose it should be omitted. It is also wanting in the editions of Tittman, Griesbach, and Hahn. The amount of *authority* seems to be against it. The word rendered *Lord*, in the phrase 'Lord God,' is (Δεσπότης,) *despotes*, and means here *Sovereign*, or *Ruler*, but it is a word which may be appropriately applied to the Lord Jesus Christ. It is the same word which is used in the parallel passage in 2 Pet. ii. 1. See it explained in the Notes on that verse. If the word 'God' is to be omitted in this place, the passage would be wholly applicable, beyond question, to the Lord Jesus, and would mean, 'denying our only Sovereign and Lord, Jesus Christ.' It is perhaps impossible now to determine with certainty the true reading of the text; nor is it *very* material. Whichever of the readings is correct; whether the word (Θεὸν) *God* is to be retained or not, the sentiment expressed would be true, that their doctrines amounted to a

6 And the angels *a* which kept not their 1 first estate, but left their own habitation, he hath reserved in

a Jn.8.44.ˆ   1 *principality.*

everlasting chains, *b* under darkness, unto the judgment *c* of the great day.

b 2 Pe.2.4.   *c* Re.20.10.

practical denial of the only true God; and equally so that they were a denial of the only Sovereign and Lord of the true Christian.

5. *I will therefore put you in remembrance.* ' To show you what must be the doom of such men, I will call certain facts to your recollection, with which you are familiar, respecting the Divine treatment of the wicked in times past.' ¶ *Though ye once knew this.* That is, you were formerly made acquainted with these things, though they may not be now fresh in your recollection. On the different significations affixed to the word *once* in this place, see Bloomfield, *Crit. Digest, in loc.* The thing which seems to have been in the mind of the apostle was an intention to call to their recollection, as bearing on the case before him, facts with which they had formerly been familiar, and about which there was no doubt. It was the thing which we often endeavour to do in argument —to *remind* a person of some fact which he once knew very well, and which bears directly on the case. ¶ *How that the Lord, having saved the people out of the land of Egypt.* Comp. Notes, 1 Cor. x. 5–12. The bearing of this fact on the case, before the mind of Jude, seems to have been this—that, as those who had been delivered from Egypt were afterward destroyed for their unbelief, or as the mere fact of their being rescued did not prevent destruction from coming on them, so the fact that these persons *seemed* to be delivered from sin, and had become professed followers of God, would not prevent their being destroyed if they led wicked lives. It might rather be inferred from the example of the Israelites that they would be. ¶ *Afterward.* τὸ δεύτερον—*the second ;* that is, the second thing in order, or again. The expression is unusual in this sense, but the apostle seems to have fixed his mind on this event as a *second* great and important fact in regard to them. The *first* was that they were delivered ; the second, that they were destroyed. ¶ *Destroyed them that believed not.*

That is, *on account* of their unbelief. They were not permitted to enter the promised land, but were cut off in the wilderness. See the Notes on Heb. iii. 16–19.

6. *And the angels which kept not their first estate.* A second case denoting that the wicked would be punished. Comp. Notes, 2 Pet. ii. 4. The word rendered *estate* (ἀρχὴν) is, in the margin, *principality.* The word properly means, *beginning, commencement ;* and then that which surpasses others, which is *first,* &c., in point of rank and honour ; or pre-eminence, priority, precedence, princedom. Here it refers to the rank and dignity which the angels had in heaven. That rank or pre-eminence they did not keep, but fell from it. On the word used here, comp. Eph. i. 2; iii. 10; Col. ii. 10, as applied to angels; 1 Cor. xv. 24; Eph. vi. 12; Col. ii. 15, as applied to demons. ¶ *But left their own habitation.* To wit, according to the common interpretation, in heaven. The word rendered *habitation* (οἰκητήριον) occurs nowhere else in the New Testament. It means here that heaven was their native abode or dwelling-place. They left it by sin ; but the expression here would seem possibly to mean that they became *dissatisfied* with their abode, and voluntarily preferred to change it for another. If they did become thus dissatisfied, the cause is wholly unknown, and conjecture is useless. Some of the later Jews supposed that they relinquished heaven out of love for the daughters of men.—*Robinson.* ¶ *He hath reserved in everlasting chains.* See Notes, 2 Pet. ii. 4. Peter says, ' chains of darkness;' that is, the darkness encompasses them *as* chains. Jude says that those chains are ' everlasting,' (δεσμοῖς ἀϊδίοις.) Comp. Rom. i. 20, ' his *eternal* power and Godhead.' The word does not elsewhere occur. It is an appropriate word to denote that which is eternal ; and no one can doubt that if a Greek *wished* to express that idea, this would be a proper word to use. The sense is, that that deep darkness always

7 Even as Sodom *a* and Gomorrha, and the cities about them, in like manner giving themselves over to fornication, and going after [1] strange flesh, are set forth for an example, suffering the vengeance of eternal fire.

a Ge.19.24.   1 *other.*

endures; there is no intermission; no light; it will exist for ever. This passage in itself does not prove that the punishment of the rebel angels will be eternal, but merely that they are kept in a dark prison in which there is no light, and which is to exist for ever, with reference to the final trial. The punishment of the rebel angels *after* the judgment is represented as an everlasting fire, which has been prepared for them and their followers, Matt. xxv. 41. 7. *Even as Sodom and Gomorrha.* Notes, 2 Pet. ii. 6. ¶ *And the cities about them.* Admah and Zeboim, Gen. xiv. 2; Deut. xxix. 23; Hosea xi. 8. There may have been other towns, also, that perished at the same time, but these are particularly mentioned. They seem to have partaken of the same general characteristics, as neighbouring towns and cities generally do. ¶ *In like manner.* ' In a manner like to these,' (τὸν ὅμοιον τούτοις τρόπον.) The Greek word *these,* is in the plural number. There has been much diversity in interpreting this clause. Some refer it to the angels; as if it meant that the cities of Sodom and Gomorrah committed sin in a way similar to the angels; some suppose that it refers to the wicked teachers about whom Jude was discoursing, meaning that Sodom and Gomorrah committed the same kind of sins which they did; some that the meaning is, that ' the cities round about Sodom and Gomorrah' sinned in the same way as those cities; and some that they were punished in the same manner, and were set forth like them as an example. I see no evidence that it refers to the angels; and if it did, it would not prove, as some have supposed, that their sin was of the same kind as that of Sodom, since there might have been a resemblance in *some* respects, though not in all. I see no reason to believe, as Macknight holds, that it refers to *false teachers,* since that would be to suppose that the inhabitants of Sodom copied their example long *before* the example was set. It seems to me, therefore,

that the reference is to the cities round about Sodom; and that the sense is, that they committed iniquity in the same manner as the inhabitants of Sodom did, and were set forth in the same way as an example. ¶ *Going after strange flesh.* Marg., *other.* The reference seems to be to the peculiar sin which, from the name Sodom, has been called *sodomy.* Comp. Rom. i. 27. The meaning of the phrase *going after* is, that they were greatly addicted to this vice. The word *strange,* or *other,* refers to that which is contrary to nature. Doddridge, however, explains it, ' going after strange and detestable gratifications of their pampered and indulged flesh.' ¶ *Are set forth for an example.* They furnish a warning against all such conduct, and a demonstration that punishment shall come upon the ungodly. The condemnation of any sinner, or of any class of sinners, always furnishes such a warning. See Notes, 2 Pet. ii. 6. ¶ *Suffering the vengeance of eternal fire.* The word rendered *suffering* (ὑπέχουσαι) means, properly, *holding under*—as, for example, the hand; then to hold towards any one, as the ear—to give attention; then it is used as denoting to hold a discourse towards or with any one, or to hold satisfaction to any one, to make atonement; and then as *undergoing, paying,* or *suffering punishment,* when united, as it is here, with the word δίκην, (*punishment,* or *vengeance.*) See *Rob. Lex.* Here it expresses the idea of undergoing punishment. The word properly agrees in the construction with *cities,* (πόλεις,) referring to Sodom and Gomorrah, and the cities around them; but the things affirmed relate to the *inhabitants* of those cities. The word *vengeance* means punishment; that is, such vengeance as the Lord takes on the guilty; not vengeance for the gratification of private and personal feeling, but like that which a magistrate appoints for the maintenance of the laws; such as justice demands. The phrase ' eternal fire ' is one that is often used to denote future punishment—as ex-

8 Likewise also these *filthy* dreamers defile ᵃthe flesh, despise dominion, and speak evil of dignities.

9 Yet Michael ᵇthe archangel, when contending with the devil be

disputed about the body of Moses, ᶜ durst ᵈnot bring against him a railing accusation, but said, The Lord ᵉrebuke thee.

a 2 Pe.2.10,11.   *b* Da.12.1.   *c* De.34.6.
         d Ex.22.28.   *e* Ze.3.2.

pressing the severity and intensity of the suffering. See Notes, Matt. xxv. 41. As here used, it cannot mean that the fires which consumed Sodom and Gomorrah were literally eternal, or were kept always burning, for that was not true. The expression seems to denote, in this connection, two things : (1.) That the destruction of the cities of the plain, with their inhabitants, was as entire and perpetual *as if* the fires had been always burning—the consumption was absolute and enduring—the sinners were wholly cut off, and the cities for ever rendered desolate ; and (2) that, in its nature and duration, this was a striking emblem of the destruction which will come upon the ungodly. I do not see that the apostle here means to affirm that those particular sinners who dwelt in Sodom would be punished for ever, for his expressions do not directly affirm that, and his argument does not demand it ; but still the *image* in his mind, in the destruction of those cities, was clearly that of the utter desolation and ruin of which this was the emblem ; of the perpetual destruction of the wicked, like that of the cities of the plain. If this had not been the case, there was no reason why he should have used the word *eternal*—meaning here *perpetual* —since, if in his mind there was no image of future punishment, all that the argument would have demanded was the simple statement that they were cut off by fire. The passage, then, cannot be used to prove that the particular dwellers in Sodom will be punished for ever —whatever may be the truth on that point ; but that there *is* a place of eternal punishment, of which that was a striking emblem. The meaning is, that the case was one which furnished a demonstration of the fact that God will punish sin ; that this was an example of the punishment which God sometimes inflicts on sinners in this world, and a type of that eternal punishment which will be inflicted in the next.

8. *Likewise also.* In the same way do these persons defile the flesh, or resemble the inhabitants of Sodom ; that is, they practise the same kind of vices. What the apostle says is, that their character resembled that of the inhabitants of Sodom ; the example which he adduces of the punishment which wa₤ brought on those sinners, leaves it to be clearly inferred that the persons of whom he was speaking would be punished in a similar manner. ¶ *These* filthy *dreamers.* The word *filthy* has been supplied by our translators, but there is no good reason why it should have been introduced. The Greek word (ἐνυπνιάζω) means to dream ; and is applied to these persons as holding doctrines and opinions which sustained the same relation to truth which dreams do to good sense. Their doctrines were the fruits of mere imagination, foolish vagaries and fancies. The word occurs nowhere else in the New Testament, except in Acts ii. 17. where it is applied to visions in dreams, ¶ *Defile the flesh.* Pollute themselves; give indulgence to corrupt passions and appetites. See Notes, 2 Pet. ii. 10. ¶ *Despise dominion.* The same Greek word is used here which occurs in 2 Pet. ii. 10. See Notes on that verse. ¶ *And speak evil of dignities.* See Notes on 2 Pet. ii. 10.

9. *Yet Michael the archangel,* &c. This verse has given more perplexity to expositors than any other part of the epistle ; and in fact the difficulties in regard to it have been so great that some have been led to regard the epistle as spurious. The difficulty has arisen from these two circumstances : (1.) Ignorance of the origin of what is said here of Michael the archangel, nothing of this kind being found in the Old Testament ; and (2.) the improbability of the story itself, which looks like a mere Jewish fable. Peter in his second epistle, chap. ii. 2, made a *general* reference to angels as not bringing railing accusations against others before the

Lord: but Jude refers to a particular case—the case of Michael when contending about the body of Moses. The methods proposed of reconciling the passage with the proper ideas of inspiration have been various, though perhaps no one of them relieves it of all difficulty. It would be inconsistent with the design of these Notes to go into an extended examination of this passage. Those who wish to see a full investigation of it may consult Michaelis' Introduction to the New Testament, vol. iv. pp. 378–393; Lardner, vol. vi. p. 312, seq.; Hug, Intro. § 183; Benson, *in loc.;* Rosenmüller's Morgenland, iii. pp. 196, 197; and Wetstein, *in loc.* The principal methods of relieving the difficulty have been the following: I. Some have supposed that the reference is to the passage in Zechariah, chap. iii. 1, seq. 'And he showed me Joshua the high priest standing before the angel of the Lord, and Satan standing at his right hand to resist him. And the Lord said unto Satan, The Lord rebuke thee, O Satan,' &c. The opinion that Jude refers to this passage was held by Lardner. But the objections to this are very obvious: (1.) There is no similarity between the two, except the expression, 'the Lord rebuke thee.' (2.) The name Michael does not occur at all in the passage in Zechariah. (3.) There is no mention made of the ' body of Moses ' there, and no allusion to it whatever. (4.) There is no intimation that there was any such contention about his body. There is a mere mention that Satan resisted the angel of the Lord, as seen in the vision, but no intimation that the controversy had *any* reference to Moses in any way. (5.) The reason of the resistance which Satan offered to the angel in the vision as seen by Zechariah *is* stated. It was in regard to the consecration of Joshua to the office of high priest implying a return of prosperity to Jerusalem, and the restoration of the worship of God there in its purity; see Zech. iii. 2. To this Satan was of course opposed, and the vision represents him as resisting the angel in his purpose thus to set him apart to that office. These reasons seem to me to make it clear that Jude did not refer to the passage in Zechariah, nor is there any other place in the Old

Testament to which it can be supposed he had reference. II. Hug supposes that the reference here, as well as that in ver. 14, to the prophecy of Enoch, is derived from some apocryphal books existing in the time of Jude; and that though those books contained mere fables, the apostle appealed to them, not as conceding what was said to be true, but in order to refute and rebuke those against whom he wrote, out of books which they admitted to be of authority. Intro. § 183. Arguments and confutations, he says, drawn from the sacred Scriptures, would have been of no avail in reasoning with them, for these they evaded, (2 Pet. iii. 16,) and there were no surer means of influencing them than those writings which they themselves valued as the sources of their peculiar views. According to this, the apostle did not mean to vouch for the *truth* of the story, but merely to make use of it in argument. The objection to this is, that the apostle does in fact seem to refer to the contest between Michael and the devil as true. He speaks of it in the same way in which he would have done if he had spoken of the death of Moses, or of his smiting the rock, or of his leading the children of Israel across the Red Sea, or of any other fact in history. If he regarded it as a mere fable, though it would have been honest and consistent with all proper views of inspiration for him to have said to those against whom he argued, that on their own principles such and such things were true, yet it would not be honest to speak of it as a fact which *he* admitted to be true. Besides, it should be remembered that he is not arguing with *them,* in which case it might be admissible to reason in this way, but was making statements to others *about* them, and showing that they manifested a spirit entirely different from that which the angels evinced even when contending in a just cause against the prince of all evil. III. It has been supposed that the apostle quotes an apocryphal book existing in his time, containing this account, and that he means to admit that the account is true. Origen mentions such a book, called 'the Assumption of Moses,' (Αναληψις του Μωσεως,) as extant in his time, containing this very account of the contest between Michael and the devil about the body of Moses. That was a Jewish Greek book, and Origen supposed that this was the source of the account here. That book is now lost. There is still extant a book in Hebrew, called פטירת משה—'the Death of Moses,' which some have supposed to be the book referred to by Origen. *That* book contains many fabulous stories about the death of Moses, and is evidently the work of some Jew drawing wholly upon his imagination. An account of it may be seen in Michaelis, Intro. iv. p. 381, seq. There is no reason to suppose that this is the same book referred to by Origen under the name of ' the Assumption of Moses ;' and there is a moral certainty that an inspired writer could not have quoted it as of authority. Further, there can be no reasonable doubt that such a book as Origen refers to, under the title of ' the Assumption of Moses,' was extant in *his* time, but that does not prove by any means that it was extant in the time of Jude, or that he quoted it. There is, indeed, no positive proof that it was *not* extant in the time of Jude, but there is none that it was, and all the facts in the case will be met by the supposition that it was written afterwards, and that the tradition on the subject here referred to by Jude was incorporated into it. IV. The remaining supposition is, that Jude here refers to a prevalent *tradition* among the Jews, and that he has adopted it as containing an important truth, and one which bore on the subject under discussion. In support of this, it may be observed, (*a*) that it is well known that there were many traditions of this nature among the Jews. See Notes, Matt. xv. 2. (*b*) That though many of these traditions were puerile and false, yet there is no reason to doubt that some of them might have been founded in truth. (*c*) That an inspired writer might select those which were true, for the illustration of his subject, with as much propriety as he might select what was written ; since if what was thus handed down by tradition was *true*, it was as proper to use it as to use a fact made known in any other way. (*d*) That in fact such traditions *were* adopted by the inspired writers when they would

serve to illustrate a subject which they were discussing. Thus Paul refers to the tradition about Jannes and Jambres as true history. See Notes, 2 Tim. iii. 8. (*e*) If, therefore, what is here said was *true*, there was no impropriety in its being referred to by Jude as an illustration of his subject. The only material question then is, whether it is *true*. And who can prove that it is not? What evidence is there that it is not? How is it possible to demonstrate that it is not? There are many allusions in the Bible to angels ; there is express mention of such an angel as Michael, (Dan. xii. 1;) there is frequent mention of the devil ; and there are numerous affirmations that both bad and good angels are employed in important transactions on the earth. Who can prove that such spirits never meet, never come in conflict, never encounter each other in executing their purposes? Good men meet bad men, and why is it any more absurd to suppose that good angels may encounter bad ones? It should be remembered, further, that there is no need of supposing that the subject of the dispute was about burying the body of Moses ; or that Michael sought to bury it, and the devil endeavoured to prevent it— the one in order that it might not be worshipped by the Israelites, and the other that it might be. This indeed became incorporated into the tradition in the apocryphal books which were afterwards written ; but Jude says not one word of this, and is in no way responsible for it. All that he says is, that there was a contention or dispute (διακρινόμενος διελέγετο) respecting *his body*. But when it was, or what was the occasion, or how it was conducted, he does *not* state, and we have no right to ascribe to him sentiments ˉwhich he has not expressed. If ever such a controversy of any kind existed respecting that body, it is all that Jude affirms, and is all for which he should be held responsible. The sum of the matter, then, it seems to me is, that Jude has, as Paul did on another occasion, adopted a tradition which was prevalent in his time ; that there is nothing necessarily absurd or impossible in the fact affirmed by the tradition, and that no one can possibly demonstrate that it is not true.

10 But these speak evil of those things which they know not: but what they know naturally, as brute

beasts, in those things they corrupt themselves.

11 Woe unto them! for they have

¶ *The archangel.* The word *archangel* occurs only in one other place in the Scriptures. See Notes, 1 Thess. iv. 16. It means *ruling* or *chief* angel—the chief among the hosts of heaven. It is nowhere else applied to Michael, though his name is several times mentioned, Dan. x. 13, 21 ; xii. 1 ; Rev. xii. 7. ¶ *When contending.* This word (διακρινόμενος) refers here to a contention or strife with words—*a disputation.* Nothing farther is necessarily implied, for it is so used in this sense in the New Testament, Acts xi. 2, 12, (*Greek.*) ¶ *He disputed.* διελέγετο. *This* word also would denote merely a controversy or contention of words, Mark ix. 34 ; Acts xvii. 2, 17 ; xviii. 4, 19 ; xxiv. 12. ¶ *About the body of Moses.* The nature of this controversy is wholly unknown, and conjecture is useless. It is *not* said, however, that there was a strife which should get the body, or a contention about burying it, or any physical contention about it whatever. That there *may* have been, no one indeed can disprove ; but all that the apostle says would be met by a supposition that there was *any* debate of any kind respecting that body, in which Michael, though provoked by the opposition of the worst being in the universe, still restrained himself from any outbreaking of passion, and used only the language of mild but firm rebuke. ¶ *Durst not.* οὐκ ἐτόλμησε—' Did not dare.' It is not said that he did not dare to do it because he feared Satan ; but all that the word implies is met by supposing that he did not dare to do it because he feared the Lord, or because in any circumstances it would be wrong. ¶ *A railing accusation.* The Greek word is *blasphemy.* The meaning is, he did not indulge in the language of mere reproach : and it is implied here that such language would be wrong anywhere. If it would be right to bring a railing accusation against any one, it would be against the devil. ¶ *But said, The Lord rebuke thee.* The word here used (ἐπιτιμάω) means, properly, to put honour

upon ; and then to adjudge or confirm. Then it came to be used in the sense of commanding or *restraining*—as, e. g., the winds and waves, Matt. viii. 26 ; Mark iv. 39. Then it is used in the sense of *admonishing strongly ;* of enjoining upon one, *with the idea of censure,* Matt. xviii. 18 ; Mark i. 25 ; Luke iv. 35, 41. This is the idea here —the expression of a wish that *the Lord* would take the matter of the dispute to himself, and that he would properly restrain and control Satan, with the implied idea that his conduct was wrong. The *language* is the same as that recorded in Zech. iii. 2, as used by ' the angel ' respecting Satan. But, as before observed, there is no reason to suppose that the apostle referred to that. The fact, however, that the angel is said to have used the language on that occasion may be allowed to give confirmation to what is said here, since it shows that it is the language which angelic beings naturally employ.

10. *But these speak evil of those things which they know not.* These false and corrupt teachers employ reproachful language of those things which lie wholly beyond the reach of their vision. Notes, 2 Pet. ii. 12. ¶ *But what they know naturally.* As mere men ; as animals ; that is, in things pertaining to their physical nature, or in which they are on a level with the brute creation. The reference is to the natural instincts, the impulses of appetite, and passion, and sensual pleasure. The idea of the apostle seems to be, that their knowledge was confined to those things. They did not rise above them to the intelligent contemplation of those higher things, against which they used only the language of reproach. There are multitudes of such men in the world. Towards high and holy objects they use only the language of reproach. They do not understand them, but they can rail at them. Their knowledge is confined to the subjects of sensual indulgence, and all their intelligence in that respect is employed only to corrupt and destroy themselves. ¶ *As*

gone in the way of Cain, *a* and ran greedily after the error of Balaam *b* for reward, and perished in the gainsaying of Core. *c*

12 These are spots *d* in your feasts of charity, when they feast with you,

a Ge.4.5.   *b* Nu.22.7,21.   *c* Nu.16.1,&c.

feeding *e* themselves without fear: clouds *f* they are without water, carried *g* about of winds; trees whose fruit *h* withereth, without fruit, twice dead, *i* plucked *j* up by the roots;

d 2 Pe.2.13.   *e* Phi.3.19.   *f* Pr.25.14.   *g* Ep.4.14.
h Jn.15.4-6.   *i* He.6.4-6.   *j* Mat.15.13.

brute beasts. Animals without intelligence. Notes, 2 Pet. ii. 12. ¶ *In those things they corrupt themselves.* They live only for sensual indulgence, and sink deeper and deeper in sensual gratifications.

11. *Woe unto them!* See Matt. xi. 21. ¶ *For they have gone in the way of Cain.* Gen. iv. 5-12. That is, they have evinced disobedience and rebellion as he did ; they have shown that they are proud, corrupt, and wicked. The apostle does not specify the points in which they had imitated the example of Cain, but it was probably in such things as these—pride, haughtiness, the hatred of religion, restlessness under the restraints of virtue, envy that others were more favoured, and a spirit of hatred of the brethren (comp. 1 John iii. 15) which would lead to murder. ¶ *And ran greedily after the error of Balaam for reward.* The word rendered *ran greedily*—ἐξεχύθησαν, from ἐκχέω—means to pour out ; and then, when spoken of persons, that they are *poured out*, or that they *rush tumultuously* on an object, that is, that they give themselves up to anything. The idea here is, that all restraint was relaxed, and that they rushed on tumultuously to any course of life that promised gain. See Notes, 2 Pet. ii. 15. ¶ *And perished.* They perish, or they will perish. The result is so certain, that the apostle speaks of it as if it were already done. The thought seems to have lain in his mind in this manner : he thinks of them, as having the same character as Korah, and then at once thinks of them as destroyed in the same manner, or as if it were already done. They are *identified* with him in their character and doom. The word rendered *perish* (ἀπόλλυμι) is often used to denote future punishment, Matt. x. 28, 39 ; xviii. 14 ; Mark i. 24 ; Luke xiii. 3. 5 ; John iii. 15, 16 · x. 28 ; 2 Thess.

ii. 10 ; 2 Pet. iii. 9. ¶ *In the gainsaying of Core.* Of Korah, Numb. xvi. 1 -30. The word *gainsaying* here means properly contradiction, or speaking against ; then controversy, question, strife ; then contumely, reproach, or rebellion. The idea here seems to be, that they were guilty of insubordination ; of possessing a restless and dissatisfied spirit ; of a desire to rule, &c.

12. *These are spots.* See Notes, 2 Pet. ii. 13. The word used by Peter, however, is not exactly the same as that used here. Peter uses the word σπίλοι — *spiloi ;* Jude, σπιλάδες — *spilades.* The word used by Jude means, properly, *a rock* by or in the sea ; a cliff, &c. It may either be a rock *by* the sea, against which vessels may be wrecked, or a hidden rock *in* the sea, on which they may be stranded at an unexpected moment. See Hesychius and Pollux, as quoted by Wetstein, *in loc.* The idea here seems to be, not that they were *spots* and *blemishes* in their sacred feasts, but that they were like hidden rocks to the mariner. As those rocks were the cause of shipwreck, so these false teachers caused others to make shipwreck of their faith. They were as dangerous in the church as hidden rocks are in the ocean. ¶ *In your feasts of charity.* Your feasts of love. The reference is probably to the Lord's Supper, called a feast or festival of love, because (1,) it revealed the love of Christ to the world ; (2,) because it was the means of strengthening the mutual love of the disciples : a festival which love originated, and where love reigned. It has been supposed by many, that the reference here is to festivals which were subsequently called *Agapœ*, and which are now known as *love-feasts*—meaning a festival immediately *preceding* the celebration of the Lord's Supper. But there are strong objections to the supposition that there is reference here to such a

festival. (1.) There is no evidence, unless it be found in this passage, that such celebrations had the sanction of the apostles. They are nowhere else mentioned in the New Testament, or alluded to, unless it is in 1 Cor. xi. 17–34, an instance which is mentioned only to reprove it, and to show that such appendages to the Lord's Supper were wholly unauthorized by the original institution, and were liable to gross abuse. (2.) The supposition that they existed, and that they are referred to here, is not necessary in order to a proper explanation of this passage. All that it fairly means will be met by the supposition that the reference is to the Lord's Supper. *That* was in every sense a festival of love or charity. The words will appropriately apply to that, and there is no necessity of supposing anything else in order to meet their full signification. (3.) There can be no doubt that such a custom early existed in the Christian church, and extensively prevailed; but it can readily be accounted for without supposing that it had the sanction of the apostles, or that it existed in their time. (*a*) Festivals prevailed among the Jews, and it would not be unnatural to introduce them into the Christian church. (*b*) The custom prevailed among the heathen of having a 'feast upon a sacrifice,' or in connection with a sacrifice; and as the Lord's Supper commemorated the great sacrifice for sin, it was not unnatural, in imitation of the heathen, to append a feast or festival to that ordinance, either before or after its celebration. (*c*) This very passage in Jude, with perhaps some others in the New Testament, (comp. 1 Cor. xi. 25; Acts ii. 46; vi. 2,) might be so construed as to seem to lend countenance to the custom. For these reasons it seems clear to me that the passage before us does not refer to *love-feasts*; and, therefore, that they are not authorized in the New Testament. See, however, Coleman's Antiquities of the Christian church, chap. xvi., § 13. ¶ *When they feast with you.* Showing that they were professors of religion. Notes on 2 Pet. ii. 13. ¶ *Feeding themselves without fear.* That is, without any proper reverence or respect for the ordinance; attending on the Lord's Supper as if it

were an ordinary feast, and making it an occasion of riot and gluttony. See 1 Cor. xi. 20–22. ¶ *Clouds* they are, &c. Notes, 2 Pet. ii. 17. Comp. Eph. iv. 14. ¶ *Trees whose fruit withereth.* The idea here is substantially the same as that expressed by Peter, when he says that they were 'wells without water;' and by him and Jude, when they say that they are like clouds driven about by the winds, that shed down no refreshing rain upon the earth. Such wells and clouds only disappoint expectations. So a tree that should promise fruit, but whose fruit should always wither, would be useless. The word rendered *withereth* (φθινοπωρινὰ) occurs nowhere else in the New Testament. It means, properly, *autumnal;* and the expression here denotes *trees of autumn,* that is, trees stripped of leaves and verdure; trees on which there is no fruit. —*Robinson's Lex.* The sense, in the use of this word, therefore, is not exactly that which is expressed in our translation, that the fruit has *withered,* but rather that they are like the trees of autumn, which are stripped and bare So the Vulgate, *arbores autumnales.* The idea of their being without fruit is expressed in the next word. The *image* which seems to have been before the mind of Jude in this expression, is that of the naked trees of autumn as contrasted with the bloom of spring and the dense foliage of summer. ¶ *Without fruit.* That is, they produce no fruit. Either they are wholly barren, like the barren fig-tree, or the fruit which was set never ripens, but falls off. They are, therefore, useless as religious instructors—as much so as a tree is which produces no fruit. ¶ *Twice dead.* That is, either meaning that they are seen to be dead in two successive seasons, showing that there is no hope that they will revive and be valuable; or, using the word *twice* to denote emphasis, meaning that they are absolutely or altogether dead. Perhaps the idea is, that successive summers and winters have passed over them, and that no signs of life appear. ¶ *Plucked up by the roots.* The wind blows them down, or they are removed by the husbandman as only cumbering the ground. They are not cut down—leaving a

13 Raging waves *a* of the sea, foaming out their own shame; wandering *b* stars, to whom is reserved the blackness of darkness for ever.

a Is.57.20. *b* Re.8.10,11.

14 And Enoch also, the seventh from Adam, prophesied of these, saying, Behold, the Lord *c* cometh with ten thousand of his saints,

c Ze.14.5.

stump that might sprout again —but they are extirpated root and branch; that is, they are wholly worthless. There is a regular ascent in this climax. First, the apostle sees a tree apparently of autumn, stripped and leafless; then he sees it to be a tree that bears no fruit; then he sees it to be a tree over which successive winters and summers pass and no signs of life appear; then as wholly extirpated. So he says it is with these men. They produce no fruits of holiness; months and years show that there is no vitality in them; they are fit only to be extirpated and cast away. Alas! how many professors of religion are there, and how many religious teachers, who answer to this description!

13. *Raging waves of the sea.* Comp. 2 Pet. ii. 18. They are like the wild and restless waves of the ocean. The image here seems to be, that they were noisy and bold in their professions, and were as wild and ungovernable in their passions as the billows of the sea. ¶ *Foaming out their own shame.* The waves are lashed into foam, and break and dash on the shore. They seem to produce nothing *but* foam, and to proclaim their own shame, that after all their wild roaring and agitation they should effect no more. So with these noisy and vaunting teachers. What they impart is as unsubstantial and valueless as the foam of the ocean waves, and the result is in fact a proclamation of their own shame. Men with so loud professions *should* produce much more. ¶ *Wandering stars.* The word rendered *wandering* (πλανῆται) is that from which we have derived the word *planet.* It properly means one who wanders about; a wanderer; and was given by the ancients to planets because they seemed to wander about the heavens, now forward and now backward among the other stars, without any fixed law. —Pliny, Nat. Hist. ii. 6. Cicero, however, who saw that they were governed by certain established laws, says that the

name seemed to be given to them without reason.—De Nat. Deo. ii. 20. So far as the *words* used are concerned, the reference may be either to the planets, properly so called, or to comets, or to *ignes fatui,* or meteors. The proper idea is that of stars that have no regular motions, or that do not move in fixed and regular orbits. The laws of the planetary motions were not then understood, and their movements seemed to be irregular and capricious; and hence, if the reference is to them, they might be regarded as not an unapt illustration of these teachers. The sense seems to be, that the aid which we derive from the stars, as in navigation, is in the fact that they are regular in their places and movements, and thus the mariner can determine his position. If they had no regular places and movements, they would be useless to the seaman. So with false religious teachers. No dependence can be placed on them. It is not uncommon to compare a religious teacher to a star, Rev. i. 16; ii. 1. Comp. Rev. xxii. 16. ¶ *To whom is reserved the blackness of darkness for ever.* Not to the stars, but to the teachers. The language here is the same as in 2 Pet. ii. 17. See Notes on that verse.

14. *And Enoch also, the seventh from Adam.* The seventh in the direct line of descent from Adam. The line of descent is Adam, Seth, Enos, Cainan, Mahaleel, Jared, Enoch; see Gen. v. 3, seq. On the character of Enoch, see Notes on Heb. xi. 5. ¶ *Prophesied of these.* Uttered prophecies applicable to these men, or respecting just such men as these. It is not necessarily meant that he had these men specifically in his eye; but all that is fairly implied is, that his predictions were descriptive of them. There is no mention made in the writings of Moses of the fact that Enoch was a prophet; but nothing is more probable in itself, and there is no absurdity in supposing that a true prophecy, though unrecord-

15 To execute judgment upon all; *a* and to convince all that are ungodly among them of all their ungodly deeds which they have un-

godly committed, and of all their hard *speeches* *b* which ungodly sinners have spoken against him.

a Re.20.13.　　　　　*b* Ps.73.9.

ed, might be handed down by tradition. See Notes, 2 Tim. iii. 8 ; Jude 9. The source from which Jude derived this passage respecting the prophecy of Enoch is unknown. Amidst the multitude of traditions, however, handed down by the Jews from a remote antiquity, though many of them were false, and many of a trifling character, it is reasonable to presume that some of them were true and were of importance. No man can *prove* that the one before us is not of that character ; no one can show that an inspired writer might not be led to make the selection of a true prophecy from a mass of traditions ; and as the prophecy before us is one that would be every way worthy of a prophet, and worthy to be preserved, its quotation furnishes no argument against the inspiration of Jude. There is no clear evidence that he quoted it from any *book* extant in his time. There is, indeed, now an apocryphal writing called ' the Book of Enoch,' containing a prediction strongly resembling this, but there is no certain proof that it existed so early as the time of Jude, nor, if it did, is it absolutely certain that he quoted from it. Both Jude and the author of that book may have quoted a common tradition of their time, for there can be no doubt that the passage referred to was handed down by tradition. The passage as found in ' the Book of Enoch ' is in these words : ' Behold he comes with ten thousand of his saints, to execute judgment upon them, and destroy the wicked, and reprove all the carnal, for everything which the sinful and ungodly have done and committed against him,' chap. ii. Bib. Repository, vol. iv. p. 86. If the Book of Enoch was written after the time of Jude, it is natural to suppose that the prophecy referred to by him, and handed down by tradition, would be inserted in it. This book was discovered in an Æthiopic version, and was published with a translation by Dr. Laurence of Oxford, in 1821, and republished in 1832. A full account of it

and its contents may be seen in an article by Prof. Stuart in the Bib. Repository for January 1840, pp. 86–137. ¶ *The Lord cometh.* That is, the Lord will come. See Notes, 1 Cor. xvi. 22. It would seem from this to have been an early doctrine that the Lord would *descend* to the earth for judgment. ¶ *With ten thousand of his saints.* Or, *of his holy ones.* The word *saints* we now apply commonly to *redeemed* saints, or to Christians. The original word is, however, applicable to all who are *holy*, angels as well as men. The common representation in the Scriptures is, that he would come attended by the angels, (Matt. xxv. 31,) and there is doubtless allusion here to such beings. It is a common representation in the Old Testament also that God, when he manifests himself, is accompanied by great numbers of heavenly beings. See Psa. lxviii. 17 ; Deut. xxxiii. 2.

15. *To execute judgment upon all.* That is, he shall come to judge all the dwellers upon the earth, good and bad. ¶ *And to convince all.* The word *convince* we now use commonly in a somewhat limited sense, as meaning *to satisfy a man's own mind* either of the truth of some proposition, or of the fact that he has done wrong, as being in this latter sense synonymous with the word *convict.* This *conviction* is commonly produced by argument or truth, and is not necessarily followed by any sentence of disapprobation, or by any judicial condemnation. But this is clearly not the sense in which the word is used here. The purpose of the coming of the Lord will not be to *convince* men in that sense, though it is undoubtedly true that the wicked will see that their lives have been wrong ; but it will be to pronounce a sentence on them as the result of the evidence of their guilt. The Greek word which is here used occurs nowhere else in the New Testament. ¶ *All that are ungodly among them.* All that are not pious ; all that have no religion. ¶ *Of all their ungodly deeds, &c.* Of their

16 These are murmurers, complainers, walking after their own lusts; and their mouth speaketh great swelling *words*, having men's persons in admiration because of advantage.

17 But, beloved, remember ye the words which were spoken before of the apostles of our Lord Jesus Christ;

18 How that they told you *a* there

a 1 Ti.4.1.

wicked actions and words. This is the common doctrine of the Bible, that all the wicked actions and words of men will be called into judgment. In regard to this passage, thus quoted from an ancient prophecy, we may remark, (1.) that the *style* bears the marks of its being a quotation, or of its being preserved by Jude in the language in which it had been handed down by tradition. It is not the style of Jude. It is not so terse, pointed, energetic. (2.) It has every probable mark of its having been actually delivered by Enoch. The age in which he lived was corrupt. The world was ripening for the deluge. He was himself a good man, and, as would seem perhaps, almost the only good man of his generation. Nothing would be more natural than that he should be reproached by hard words and speeches, and nothing more natural than that he should have pointed the men of his own age to the future judgment. (3.) The doctrine of the final judgment, if this was uttered by Enoch, was an early doctrine in the world. It was held even in the first generations of the race. It was one of those great truths early communicated to man to restrain him from sin, and to lead him to prepare for the great events which are to occur on the earth. The same doctrine has been transmitted from age to age, and is now one of the most important and the most affecting that refers to the final destiny of men.

16. *These are murmurers.* The word here used does not elsewhere occur, though the word *murmur* is frequent, Matt. xx. 11; Luke v. 30; John vi. 41, 43, 61; vii. 32; 1 Cor. x. 10. Comp. John vii. 12; Acts vi. 1; Phil. ii. 14; 1 Pet. iv. 9. The sense is that of repining or complaining under the allotments of Providence, or finding fault with God's plans, and purposes, and doings. ¶ *Complainers.* Literally, finding fault with one's own lot (μεμψίμοιροι.) The word

VOL. X.

does not elsewhere occur in the New Testament; the *thing* often occurs in this world. Nothing is more common than for men to complain of their lot ; to think that it is hard; to compare theirs with that of others, and to blame God for not having made their circumstances different. The poor complain that they are not rich like others ; the sick that they are not well; the enslaved that they are not free; the bereaved that they are deprived of friends; the ugly that they are not beautiful; those in humble life that their lot was not cast among the great and the gay. The virtue that is opposed to this is *contentment*—a virtue of inestimable value. See Notes, Phil. iv. 11. ¶ *Walking after their own lusts.* Giving unlimited indulgence to their appetites and passions. See Notes, 2 Pet. iii. 3. ¶ *And their mouth speaketh great swelling words.* Notes on 2 Pet. ii. 18. ¶ *Having men's persons in admiration.* Showing great respect to certain persons, particularly the rich and the great. The idea is, that they were not *just* in the esteem which they had for others, or that they did not appreciate them according to their real worth, but paid special attention to one class in order to promote their selfish ends. ¶ *Because of advantage.* Because they hoped to derive some benefit to themselves.

17, 18. *But, beloved, remember ye,* &c. There is a striking similarity between these two verses and 2 Pet. iii. 1–3. It occurs in the same connection, following the description of the false and dangerous teachers against whom the apostle would guard them, and couched almost in the same words. See it explained in Notes on the similar passage in Peter. When Jude (ver. 17) entreats them to remember the words which were spoken by *the apostles*, it is not necessarily to be inferred that he was not himself an apostle, for he is speaking of what was past, and there might

2 C

should be mockers in the last time, who should walk after their own ungodly lusts.

19 These be they who separate *a* themselves, sensual, having not the Spirit.

20 But ye, beloved, building *b* up

a He.10.25.   *b* Col.2.7.   *c* Ep.6.18.
d Jn.15.2,10.   *e* Tit.2.13.

have been a special reason why he should refer to something that they would distinctly remember which had been spoken by the *other* apostles on this point. Or it might be that he meant also to include himself among them, and to speak of the apostles collectively, without particularly specifying himself. ¶ *Mockers.* The word rendered *mockers* here is the same which in the parallel place in 2 Pet. iii. 3 is rendered *scoffers.* Peter has stated more fully what was the particular subject on which they scoffed, and has shown that there was no occasion for it, 2 Pet. iii. 4, seq.

19. *These be they who separate themselves.* That is, from their brethren, and from the work of benevolence and truth. Comp. Rom. xvi. 17; Judg. v. 16, 23. ¶ *Sensual.* Under the influence of gross passions and appetites. ¶ *Having not the spirit.* The Holy Spirit, or the spirit of true religion.

20. *But ye, beloved, building up yourselves on your most holy faith.* Comp. Notes on ver. 3. On the word *building,* see Notes on 1 Cor. iii. 9, 10; Eph. ii. 20. It is said here that they were to ' build up *themselves;*' that is, they were to act as moral and responsible agents in this, or were to put forth their own proper exertions to do it. Dependent, as we are, and as all persons with correct views will feel themselves to be, yet it is proper to endeavour to do the work of religion as if we had ample power of ourselves. See Notes, Phil. ii. 12. The phrase ' most holy faith ' here refers to the system of religion which was founded on faith; and the meaning is, that they should seek to establish themselves most firmly in the belief of the doctrines, and in the practice of the duties of that system of religion. ¶ *Praying in the Holy Ghost.* See Notes. Eph. vi. 18.

yourselves on your most holy faith, praying *c* in the Holy Ghost,

21 Keep yourselves *d* in the love of God, looking *e* for the mercy of our Lord Jesus Christ unto eternal life.

22 And of some have compassion, making a difference :

21. *Keep yourselves in the love of God.* Still adverting to their own agency. On the duty here enjoined, see Notes on John xv. 9. The phrase ' the love of God ' *may* mean either God's love to us, or our love to him. The latter appears, however, to be the sense here, because it is not a subject which could be enjoined, that we should keep up *God's love to us.* That is a point over which we can have no control, except so far as it may be the result of our obedience ; but we *may* be commanded to love him, and to *keep* ourselves in that love. ¶ *Looking for the mercy of our Lord Jesus Christ.* Particularly when he shall come to receive his people to himself. See Notes, Tit. ii. 13 ; 2 Pet. iii. 12 ; 2 Tim. iv. 8.

22. *And of some have compassion.* This cannot be intended to teach that they were not to have compassion for all men, or to regard the salvation of all with solicitude, but that they were to have special and peculiar compassion for a certain class of persons, or were to approach them with feelings appropriate to their condition. The idea is, that the peculiar feeling to be manifest towards a certain class of persons in seeking their salvation was tender affection and kindness. They were to approach them in the gentlest manner, appealing to them by such words as *love* would prompt. Others were to be approached in a different manner, indicated by the phrase, ' save with fear.' The class here referred to, to whom *pity* (ἐλεεῖτε) was to be shown, and in whose conversion and salvation tender compassion was to be employed, appear to have been the timid, the gentle, the unwary; those who had not yet fallen into dangerous errors, but who might be exposed to them ; those, for there are such, who would be more likely to be influenced by kind words and a gentle manner

23 And others save with fear, pulling *a them* out of the fire; hating even the garment *b* spotted by the flesh.

24 Now unto him *c* that is able

to keep *d* you from falling, and to present *e you* faultless before the presence of his glory with exceeding joy,

a Ze.3.2-5.   b Re.3.4,18.   c Ro.16.25-27.
d 2 Ti.4.18.   e Col.1.22.

than by denunciation. The direction then amounts to this, that while we are to seek to save all, we are to adapt ourselves wisely to the character and circumstances of those whom we seek to save. See Notes, 1 Cor. ix. 19-22. ¶ *Making a difference.* Making a distinction between them, not in regard to your *desires* for their salvation, or your *efforts* to save them, but to the *manner* in which it is done. To be able to do this is one of the highest qualifications to be sought by one who endeavours to save souls, and is indispensable for a good minister of the gospel. The young, the tender, the delicate, the refined, need a different kind of treatment from the rough, the uncultivated, the hardened. This wisdom was shown by the Saviour in all his preaching; it was eminent in the preaching of Paul.

23. *And others.* Another class; those who were of such a character, or in such circumstances, that a more bold, earnest, and determined manner would be better adapted to them. ¶ *Save with fear.* That is, by appeals adapted to produce fear. The idea seems to be that the arguments on which they relied were to be drawn from the dangers of the persons referred to, or from the dread of future wrath. It is undoubtedly true, that while there is a class of persons who can be won to embrace religion by mild and gentle persuasion, there is another class who can be aroused only by the terrors of the law. Every method is to be employed, in its proper place, that we 'by all means may save some.' ¶ *Pulling* them *out of the fire.* As you would snatch persons out of the fire; or as you would seize on a person that was walking into a volcano. Then, a man would not use the mild and gentle language of persuasion, but by word and gesture show that he was deeply in earnest. ¶ *Hating even the garment spotted by the flesh.* The allusion here is not quite certain, though the idea

which the apostle meant to convey is not difficult to be understood. By 'the garment spotted by the flesh' there *may be* an allusion to a garment worn by one who had had the plague, or some offensive disease which might be communicated to others by touching even the clothing which they had worn. Or there may be an allusion to the ceremonial law of Moses, by which all those who came in contact with dead bodies were regarded as unclean, Lev. xxi. 11, Numb. vi. 6; ix. 6; xix. 11. Or there may be an allusion to the case mentioned in Lev. xv. 4, 10, 17; or perhaps to a case of leprosy. In all such instances, there would be the idea that the thing referred to by which the garment had been spotted was polluting, contagious, or loathsome, and that it was proper not even to touch such a garment, or to come in contact with it in any way. To something of this kind the apostle compares the sins of the persons here referred to. While the utmost effort was to be made to save them, they were in no way to partake of their sins; their conduct was to be regarded as loathsome and contagious; and those who attempted to save them were to take every precaution to preserve their own purity. There is much wisdom in this counsel. While we endeavour to save the *sinner*, we cannot too deeply loathe his *sins;* and in approaching some classes of sinners there is need of as much care to avoid being defiled by them, as there would be to escape the plague if we had any transaction with one who had it. Not a few have been deeply corrupted in their attempts to reform the polluted. There never could be, for example, too much circumspection and prayer for personal safety from pollution, in attempting to reform licentious and abandoned females.

24. *Now unto him that is able to keep you from falling.* This ascription to one who was able to keep them from falling is made in view of the facts ad-

404

JUDE.

[A. D. 66.

25 To *a* the only wise God our Saviour, *be* glory and majesty, dominion and power, both now and ever. Amen.

a 1 Tim.1.17.

verted to in the epistle—the dangers of being led away by the arts and the example of these teachers of error. Comp. ver. 3. On the ascription itself, comp. Notes on Rom. xvi. 25–27. The phrase 'to keep from falling' means here to preserve from falling into sin, from yielding to temptation, and dishonouring their religion. The word used (ἀπταιστους) occurs nowhere else in the New Testament. It means properly, *not stumbling* as of a horse; then *without falling into sin, blameless.* It is God only who, amidst the temptations of the world, can keep us from falling ; but, blessed be his name, he can do it, and if we trust in him he will. ¶ *And to present you faultless.* The word here rendered *faultless* is the same which is rendered *unblamable* in Col. i. 22. See the sentiment here expressed explained in the Notes on that passage. ¶ *Before the presence of his glory.* In his own glorious presence ; before himself encompassed with glory in heaven. The saints are to be presented there as redeemed and sanctified, and as made worthy by grace to dwell there for ever. ¶ *With exceeding joy.* With the abounding joy that they are redeemed ; that they are rescued from sorrow, sin, and death, and that heaven is to be their eternal home. Who now can form an adequate idea of the happiness of that hour ?
25. *To the only wise God.* See Notes, Rom. xvi. 27 ; 1 Tim. i. 17. ¶ *Our Saviour.* The word *Saviour* may be appropriately applied to God as such, because he is the great Author of salvation, though it is commonly applied to

the Lord Jesus Christ. That it *may* have been designed that it should be applied here to the Lord Jesus no one can certainly deny, nor can it be demonstrated that it was ; and in these circumstances, as all that is fairly implied in the language may be applied to God as such, it is most natural to give the phrase that interpretation. ¶ Be *glory and majesty.* Notes, 1 Tim. i. 17; Rom. xvi. 17. ¶ *Dominion and power,* &c. See Matt. vi. 13. It is common in the Scriptures to ascribe power, dominion, and glory to God, expressing the feeling that all that is great and good belongs to him, and the desire of the heart that he may reign in heaven and on earth. Comp. Rev. iv. 11; xix. 1. With the expression of such a desire it was not inappropriate that this epistle should be closed—and it is not inappropriate that this volume should be closed with the utterance of the same wish. In all our affections and aspirations, may God be supreme ; in all the sin and woe which prevail here below, may we look forward with strong desire to the time when his dominion shall be set up over all the earth ; in all our own sins and sorrows, be it ours to look onward to the time when in a purer and happier world his reign may be set up over our own souls, and when we may cast every crown at his feet and say, ' Thou art worthy, O Lord, to receive glory, and honour, and power: for thou hast created all things, and for thy pleasure they are and were created.—Alleluia; Salvation, and glory, and honour, and power, unto the Lord our God,' Rev. iv. 11 : xix. 1.